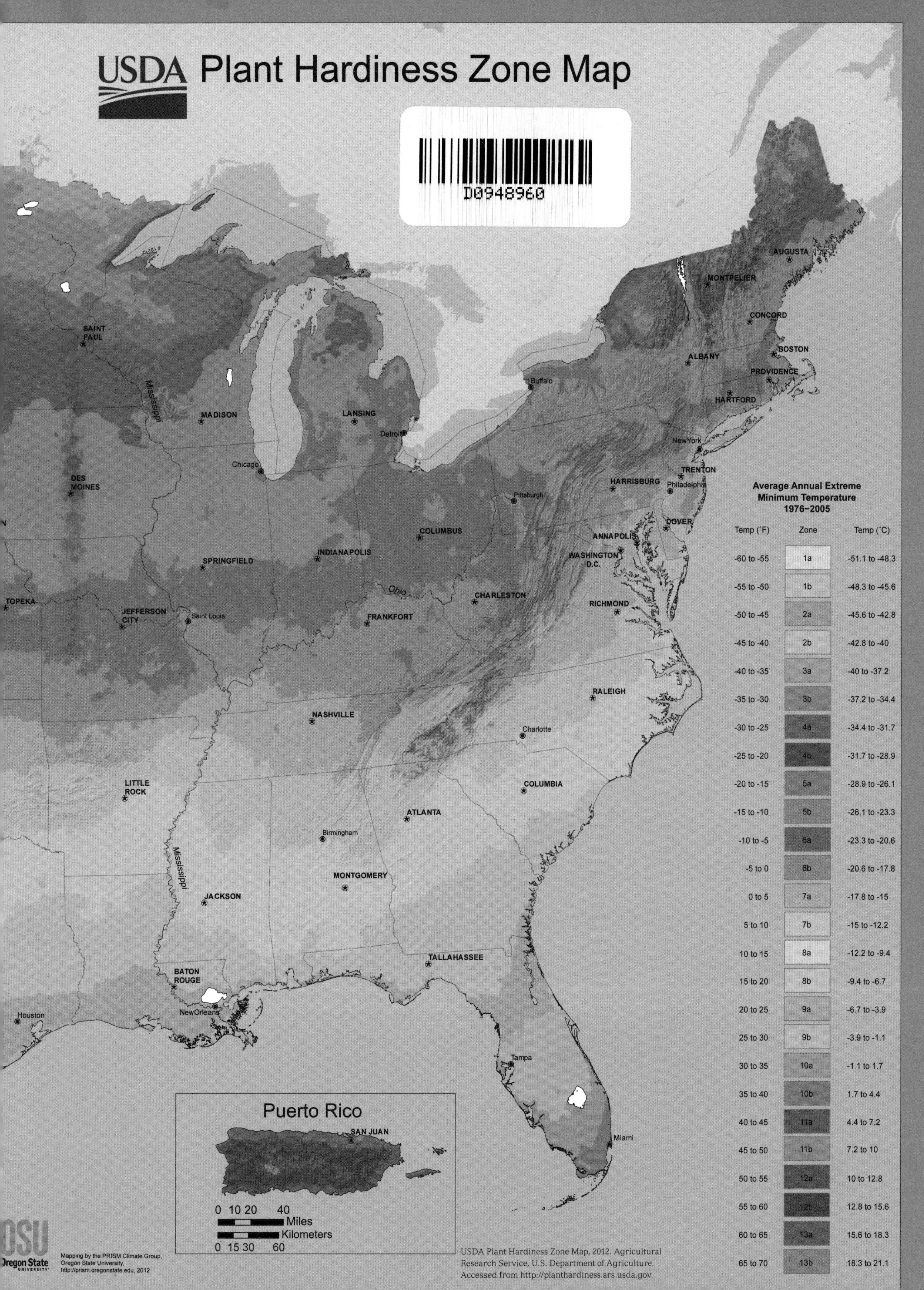
USDA Plant Hardiness Zone Map
SAINT PAUL
MADISON
LANSING
Detroit
Chicago
Mississippi
DES MOINES
Buffalo
AUGUSTA
MONTPELIER
CONCORD
BOSTON
ALBANY
PROVIDENCE
HARTFORD
NewYork
TRENTON
HARRISBURG
Philadelphia
Pittsburgh
DOVER
COLUMBUS
ANNAPOLIS
WASHINGTON D.C.
INDIANAPOLIS
SPRINGFIELD
Ohio
TOPEKA
JEFFERSON CITY
Saint Louis
FRANKFORT
CHARLESTON
RICHMOND
RALEIGH
NASHVILLE
Charlotte
LITTLE ROCK
COLUMBIA
ATLANTA
Birmingham
Mississippi
MONTGOMERY
JACKSON
TALLAHASSEE
BATON ROUGE
NewOrleans
Houston
Tampa
Miami
Puerto Rico
SAN JUAN
0 10 20 40
Miles
Kilometers
0 15 30 60
OSU
Oregon State UNIVERSITY
Mapping by the PRISM Climate Group, Oregon State University, http://prism.oregonstate.edu, 2012
USDA Plant Hardiness Zone Map, 2012. Agricultural Research Service, U.S. Department of Agriculture. Accessed from http://planthardiness.ars.usda.gov.
Average Annual Extreme Minimum Temperature 1976–2005
Temp (°F) Zone Temp (°C)
-60 to -55 1a -51.1 to -48.3
-55 to -50 1b -48.3 to -45.6
-50 to -45 2a -45.6 to -42.8
-45 to -40 2b -42.8 to -40
-40 to -35 3a -40 to -37.2
-35 to -30 3b -37.2 to -34.4
-30 to -25 4a -34.4 to -31.7
-25 to -20 4b -31.7 to -28.9
-20 to -15 5a -28.9 to -26.1
-15 to -10 5b -26.1 to -23.3
-10 to -5 6a -23.3 to -20.6
-5 to 0 6b -20.6 to -17.8
0 to 5 7a -17.8 to -15
5 to 10 7b -15 to -12.2
10 to 15 8a -12.2 to -9.4
15 to 20 8b -9.4 to -6.7
20 to 25 9a -6.7 to -3.9
25 to 30 9b -3.9 to -1.1
30 to 35 10a -1.1 to 1.7
35 to 40 10b 1.7 to 4.4
40 to 45 11a 4.4 to 7.2
45 to 50 11b 7.2 to 10
50 to 55 12a 10 to 12.8
55 to 60 12b 12.8 to 15.6
60 to 65 13a 15.6 to 18.3
65 to 70 13b 18.3 to 21.1

SMITHSONIAN

ENCYCLOPEDIA OF GARDEN PLANTS FOR EVERY LOCATION

Editor-in-Chief Zia Allaway
Senior Editors Chauney Dunford, Helen Fewster
Senior Art Editor Joanne Doran
Editors Jenny Hendy, Annelise Evans
Project Art Editors Vicky Read, Alison Shackleton
Senior Producer Alex Bell, Seyhan Esen
Pre-Production Producer Andy Hilliard
DK Images Romaine Werblow, Claire Bowers
Jacket Designer Nicola Powling
Managing Editor Penny Warren
Managing Art Editor Alison Donovan
Art Director Jane Bull
Publisher Mary Ling
Smithsonian Gardens Editor James Gagliardi

Smithsonian Enterprises
Product Development Manager Kealy Wilson
Licensing Manager Ellen Nanney
Director of Licensing Brigid Ferraro
Senior Vice President Carol LeBlanc

DK INDIA
Senior Editor Nidhilekha Mathur
Senior Art Editor Anchal Kaushal
Editors Divya Chandhok, Ekta Sharma
Art Editors Tarun Sharma, Vandna Sonkariya
DTP Designer Anurag Trivedi
Managing Editor Alicia Ingty
Managing Art Editor Navidita Thapa
Pre-Production Manager Sunil Sharma
Picture Researchers Nikhil Verma, Surya Sankash Sarangi

First published in 2014 in the United States in association with Smithsonian Gardens by Dorling Kindersley Limited, 4th Floor, 345 Hudson Street, New York, New York 10014

8 10 9 7 – 018 – 185918 – Sept/2014

A CIP catalog record for this book is available from the Library of Congress.

ISBN 978-1-4654-1439-7

To find out more about Smithsonian Gardens, visit www.gardens.si.edu

Printed and bound in China

A WORLD OF IDEAS:
SEE ALL THERE IS TO KNOW

www.dk.com

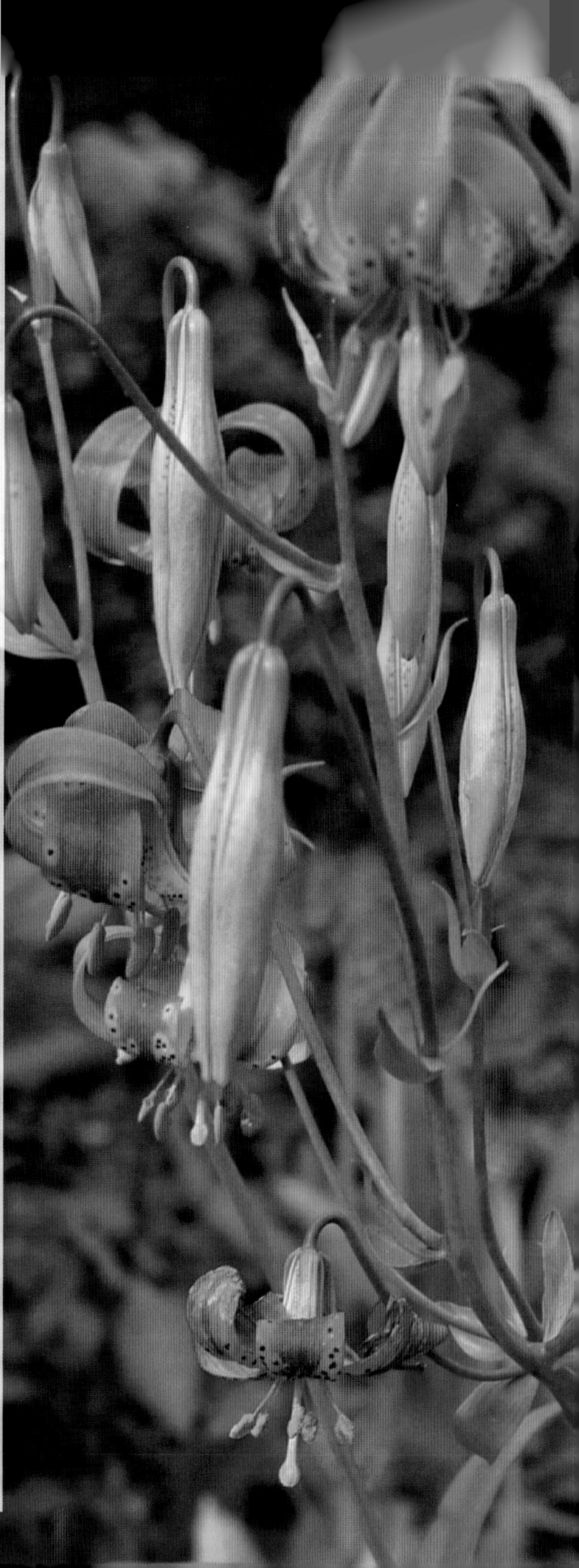

Image right: *Lilium superbum*, American Turkscap lily (see p.162)

SMITHSONIAN

ENCYCLOPEDIA OF GARDEN PLANTS FOR EVERY LOCATION

Contents

Foreword

Each year Smithsonian Gardens welcome over 30 million visitors to our lush gardens along the National Mall in Washington, D.C. These "living museums" have been created to complement the collections of the world's largest complex of museums, the Smithsonian Institution.

The talented staff of Smithsonian Gardens face challenges similar to those of any gardener. Overcoming these challenges to create a healthy and beautiful garden is part of what makes gardening so enjoyable and rewarding. With the release of *Encyclopedia of Garden Plants for Every Location*, Smithsonian Gardens is proud to extend our educational mission beyond our physical location, sharing our knowledge and passion for creating successful outdoor spaces.

It is our hope that this book will inspire you at home. As a comprehensive guide for gardeners of all levels, this book contains helpful information for planting in a wide array of garden conditions. Choosing the proper plant to suit your growing conditions will lead to a thriving and sustainable garden.

Every garden differs and part of their appeal is in the exploration. With such diverse conditions throughout North America, it is helpful to consult with your local extension office or trusted neighborhood garden center to make the best plant choices.

I speak for all my colleagues when I say that the publication of this volume is a proud moment in the history of Smithsonian Gardens. I would like to thank everyone who worked so thoroughly on this project, especially recognizing two members of the Smithsonian Gardens staff: horticulturist James Gagliardi, and collections and education manager Cynthia Brown. It is our hope that *Encyclopedia of Garden Plants for Every Location* becomes your new favorite garden plant reference book and motivates you to visit us someday at Smithsonian Gardens.

Barbara W. Faust

Barbara W. Faust
Director, Smithsonian Gardens

About this book

The core of this book is divided into two sections. The first, Plant Locations, recommends plants for different growing conditions. Part two, Plants for Special Effects, suggests plants suitable for different uses, including scent, and for various garden styles, such as Asian-style.

INTRODUCTION Gardening basics

PART ONE
Plant Locations

Gardens in Sun

Gardens in Shade

PART TWO
Plants for Special Effects

Plants for
Garden Styles

Plants for
Seasonal Interest

Plants for
Color and Scent

Plants for
Shape and Texture

Plants for
Garden Problems

Plant focus pages Found within the Plant Locations section, these features give detailed advice on many popular groups of garden plants, such as grasses and sedges.

Plant names Plants are listed by their Latin botanical names followed by a popular common name except in the herb and vegetable sections.

Key features The images focus on most important features of the plants and will not necessarily show its overall appearance and size.

Toxic plants Some plants are toxic or have irritating sap and should only be handled when wearing gloves.

Common names Some plants have more than one common name. Only the most widely used are given here.

Soil type This symbol shows the ideal soil type for the plant, although some plants will tolerate a range of growing conditions.

Sun or shade In the first section of the book, the ideal location for the plant is indicated by the sun or shade symbol located here.

CLIMBER LARGE

Gelsemium sempervirens
CAROLINA YELLOW JASMINE This evergreen twining climber has slim, lance-shaped dark green leaves. In summer, it produces clusters of trumpet-shaped bright yellow flowers. Grow against a sunny, sheltered wall or fence. All parts are toxic.
↕20ft (6m)
Z7–9 Ⓝ

Plant type and size These labels show what type the plant is, such as a tree, shrub, or perennial, and indicate its size. Use these for quick reference when choosing plants; the description provides detailed information.

Plant hardiness This shows the plant's ability to survive low temperatures. However, plants may die of other causes as well.

51

PLANTS FOR SANDY SOIL

PERENNIAL SMALL

Sedum spectabile
SHOWY STONECROP This sedum is a clump-forming perennial with succulent stems of fleshy gray-green leaves. From late summer to fall, it bears flat heads of pink flowers, followed by winter seedheads. Varieties include 'Brilliant' (above).
↔18in (45cm)
Z4–9

PERENNIAL MEDIUM

***Solidago* GOLDEN BABY**
GOLDENROD This perennial forms an upright clump of stems with narrow, pointed green leaves. From midsummer to early fall, it produces branching stems of small golden-yellow blooms. Deadhead to prolong the flowering display.
↕24in (60cm) ↔18ft (45cm)
Z4–8

PERENNIAL MEDIUM

Stipa tenuissima
MEXICAN FEATHER GRASS A deciduous perennial that forms a tuft of fine green leaves. From early summer, it produces panicles of silvery green flowers that turn beige as seeds form, giving the plant a hairlike appearance.
↕24in (60cm) ↔16in (40cm)
Z7–11 Ⓝ

SHRUB MEDIUM

Spiraea nipponica
SPIREA This is a spreading deciduous shrub with arching stems of narrow dark green leaves and dense clusters of white or pink flowers, which appear in early summer. Varieties include the white-flowered 'Snowmound' (above).
↕↔8ft (2.5m)
Z4–8

ANNUAL/BIENNIAL LARGE

Verbascum olympicum
OLYMPIC MULLEIN A semievergreen biennial or short-lived perennial with rosettes of gray felted leaves and tall branching stems of saucer-shaped, bright golden flowers, which appear from mid- to late summer. It may need staking.
↕6ft (2m) ↔3ft (1m)
Z5–9

SHRUB LARGE

Stachyurus praecox
STACHYURUS An open, spreading deciduous shrub with purplish red shoots and pale greenish yellow, bell-shaped flowers that appear from late winter to early spring, before the slim, tapering dark green leaves emerge. Can be trained on a wall.
↕12ft (4m) ↔10ft (3m)
pH Z6–8

PERENNIAL SMALL

Stokesia laevis
STOKES' ASTER An evergreen perennial with narrow midgreen leaves. It produces large, cornflowerlike, lavender- or purple-blue flowers on short stems from summer to mid-fall. Varieties include 'Purple Parasols' (above).
↕↔18in (45cm)
pH Z5–9 Ⓝ

PERENNIAL MEDIUM

Veronica austriaca* subsp. *teucrium
SAW-LEAVED SPEEDWELL This upright perennial has dark green, toothed-edged leaves and spikes of rich blue flowers in early summer. Deadhead to promote more flowers the following year.
↕↔24in (60cm)
Z4–8

BULB MEDIUM

Zephyranthes candida
RAIN LILY A tender bulb with narrow, erect grassy leaves. In summer, leafless stems carry white crocuslike flowers. Plants often burst into bloom following heavy rain. Add plenty of organic matter to the soil. Bulbs can be lifted for winter.
↕10in (25cm)
Z7–9

OTHER SUGGESTIONS

Perennials
Acanthus spinosus • *Achillea filipendulina* • *Anemone hupehensis* 'September Charm' • *Artemisia lactiflora* • *Baptisia australis* Ⓝ • *Campanula persicifolia* • *Cephalaria gigantea* • *Coreopsis verticillata* 'Grandiflora' Ⓝ • *Echinops ritro* • *Salvia lyrata* 'Purple Knockout' Ⓝ • *Salvia nemorosa* 'Caradonna' • *Symphyotrichum cordifolium* 'Avondale' Ⓝ • *Symphyotrichum ericoides* 'Monte Cassino' Ⓝ • *Verbascum* 'Caribbean Crush' • *Verbena stricta* Ⓝ

Shrubs
Cephalanthus occidentalis Ⓝ • *Morella cerifera* Ⓝ

Trees
Ginkgo biloba 'Princeton Sentry' • *Juniperus virginiana* 'Burkii' Ⓝ • *Quercus stellata* Ⓝ • *Washingtonia robusta* Ⓝ

Plant dimensions The sizes given are for typical plants in good growing conditions. Your plant may grow larger or smaller.

Other suggestions Use these lists for further recommendations of plants suitable for an location, soil type, or special effect.

KEY TO SYMBOLS

- ☼ Prefers sun
- Prefers partial shade
- Tolerates full shade
- Prefers well-drained soil
- Prefers moist soil
- Prefers wet soil
- ⓘ Toxic or irritant
- pH Needs acid soil

Z1–13 USDA plant hardiness zones
Based on the average annual minimum winter temperature, these zones indicate where a plant is most likely to thrive. A zone map is located at the front and back of the book.

Ⓝ **North American natives**
Plants with this symbol are indigenous to US, Canada, and/or Mexico.

SIZE CATEGORIES USED IN THIS BOOK

SMALL	MEDIUM	LARGE
	TREES	
UP TO 28FT (9M)	30–46FT (10–14M)	50FT (15M) AND ABOVE
	SHRUBS	
UP TO 4½FT (1.4M)	5–10FT (1.5–2.9M)	10FT (3M) AND ABOVE
	CLIMBERS	
UP TO 6FT (1.9M)	6–12FT (2–3.9M)	12FT (4M) AND ABOVE
	PERENNIALS; ANNUALS & BIENNIALS; WATER PLANTS	
UP TO 24IN (59CM)	24IN–3½FT (60CM–1.1M)	4FT (1.2M) AND ABOVE
	BULBS	
UP TO 5½IN (14CM)	6–24IN (15–60CM)	24IN (61CM) AND ABOVE

INTRODUCTION

GARDENS IN SUN

GARDENS IN SHADE

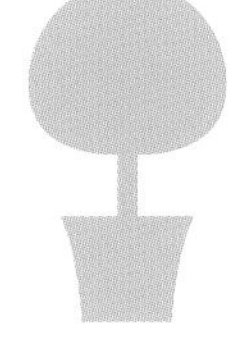
PLANTS FOR GARDEN STYLES

PLANTS FOR SEASONAL INTEREST

PLANTS FOR COLOR AND SCENT

PLANTS FOR SHAPE AND TEXTURE

PLANTS FOR GARDEN PROBLEMS

Identifying plant groups

Plants fall into various categories, defined by the length of their life cycle, size, shape, and habit, as well as physical structure. This guide explains how plants are grouped, and identifies how they will behave in your garden.

ANNUALS AND BIENNIALS

Plants that germinate, form stems and leaves, flower, set seeds, and die in one year are known as "annuals." Hardy annuals can withstand frost, while tender types require protection from the cold. Many bedding plants are annuals, and can either be sown from seed or bought as young plants. Confusingly, some bedding plants are actually perennials (*see below*), but are treated as annuals.

A biennial plant lives for two seasons, germinating, and forming stems and leaves during the first year, then, after overwintering, flowering, setting seed, and dying in the second.

Annuals This group of plants is ideal for short-lived seasonal color.

Biennials These produce flowers in their second year and then die.

True perennials These emerge and die back to the base each year.

Evergreen perennials This group gives year-round interest.

Woody perennials These retain a woody framework during winter.

Ferns Grown for their foliage, many are also evergreen perennials.

Grasses This is a large group of perennials and includes bamboo.

PERENNIALS

This group of plants lives for many years, emerging from underground roots in spring, then growing, flowering, and setting seeds, before dying back in fall. Most become dormant in winter, although some perennials are evergreen and retain their foliage year-round, while others die back to a woody base, rather than their roots. Some perennials are tender, only reemerging in spring if protected during winter or brought under cover, and are often treated as annuals for short-term color.

As well as conventional flowering plants, this group also includes deciduous and evergreen grasses, as well as ferns, which produce spores instead of flowers.

Aquatics Water lilies float on the surface but are rooted under water.

Marginals Many types of iris are ideal for pond-side positions.

MARGINALS AND WATER PLANTS

Plants that thrive in water fall into two main categories: marginals, which grow in shallow water, usually 3–6in (7–15cm) deep; and aquatic plants, which include water lilies, and generally grow at depths of between 12in (30cm) and 6ft (1.9m). Ideally, a natural pond will include a range of marginals and deep-water aquatics to create a balanced ecosystem, as well as a few "oxygenators." These are submerged, fast-growing plants that release oxygen into the pond, and compete for nutrients with pond weeds and algae, helping to keep the water clear. Hornwort and water crowfoot are examples of noninvasive oxygenators.

SHRUBS

These woody-stemmed plants produce a permanent network of branches that rise up from the ground or a central trunk to create a bushy form. They can be deciduous or evergreen, and provide a structural framework in many gardens. Shrubs are diverse in size, shape, and habit, from subshrubs like wormwood and lavender that have a woody base and tender new growth to treelike mock orange. Many shrubs give a long season of interest, bearing flowers, decorative fruits, and attractive fall foliage. Other shrubs can be made into features by pruning and training, such as boxwood, which is used in topiary.

Flowering Roses are highly popular summer-flowering shrubs.

Foliage and form Evergreen shrubs give texture and interest.

Bulbs Snowdrops are among the first bulbs to flower each year.

BULBS

This group includes all plants that form bulblike structures, such as corms, tubers, rhizomes, and true bulbs. Popular bulbous plants include spring tulips and daffodils, which are planted in fall, and summer-flowering dahlias, lilies, and gladioli, which are planted in spring.

Trees Highly varied, there are trees to suit all parts of the garden.

TREES

Providing the main architecture in the yard or garden, trees are also grown for their flowers, bark, and foliage. Whether deciduous or evergreen, they can form a spreading, rounded, conical, weeping, or columnar canopy of leafy branches from a central trunk, leading to trees of all shapes and sizes.

CLIMBERS

This group of woody-stemmed and perennial plants uses a variety of methods to climb over structures or through host plants. Twining climbers, such as clematis, use leaf stalks, tendrils, or stems to coil around a support, while the thorny stems of roses act as hooks to heave themselves up. Self-clinging climbers, including Virginia creeper and Boston ivy, attach themselves to supports with adhesive pads or aerial roots. Climbers can be evergreen or deciduous, fast or slow growing, and while perennial forms die back each year, many shrubby climbers develop a substantial and permanent structure.

Woody climbers These require a sturdy support to hold their stems.

Perennial climbers Dying back each year, these suit smaller plots.

Understanding soil and site

Plants have specific requirements and will thrive in the conditions they enjoy most, so taking time to assess your soil type and the amount of sunlight your garden receives will greatly improve your chances of success.

UNDERSTANDING SOILS

Assessing the soil in your garden is the first important step to help you choose the most suitable plants for your conditions. The structure and composition of soil determines how much water it can retain. This also affects its fertility because plants absorb nutrients held in a water solution. Most soils contain a proportion of sand and clay particles, but one type usually dominates. Sand-rich soils tend to be free-draining and have low fertility, due to soluble plants nutrients being washed away. However, they are also light and easy to dig. Clay soils are heavier and more difficult to cultivate, and although they hold water and nutrients well, they are also prone to waterlogging and cracking when dry. The ideal soil type is loam, which is comprised of roughly equal parts of sand and clay, and is both free-draining and water-retentive. To test your soil type, take samples from around your yard or garden and roll them between your fingers (*see below*).

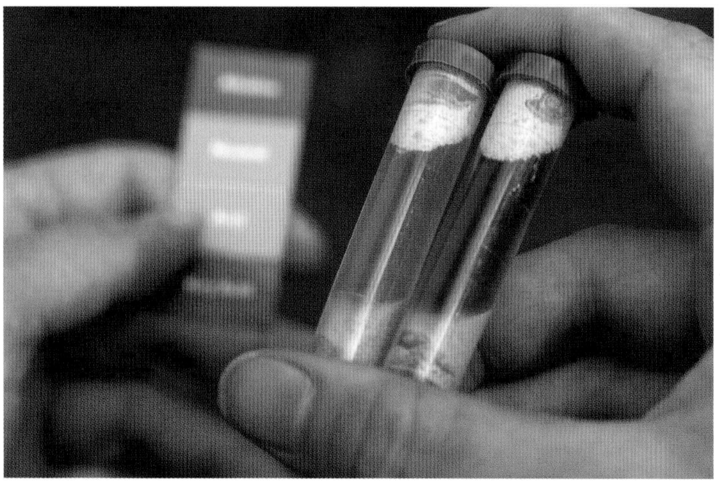

Acid or alkaline Soils range from acid to alkaline pH, which affects the plants you can grow. Most plants tolerate a range of pH levels but some are particular. Test your soil with an easy-to-use pH testing kit.

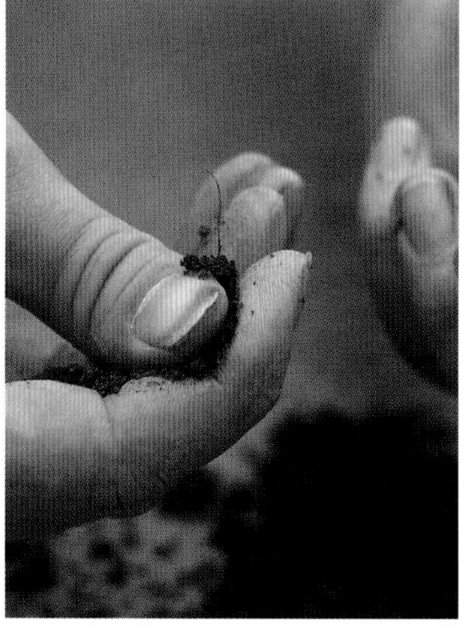

Sandy soil When rubbed between your fingers, sandy soil feels gritty, and can't easily be rolled into a ball.

Clay soil Soils rich in clay feel smooth and sticky, and can easily be molded into a ball or ribbon.

IMPROVING SOILS

Many soils benefit from the regular addition of organic matter, such as shredded leaves or garden compost. This improves soil structure, helping sandy soils retain water and nutrients, and improves drainage in clay soils. Dig organic matter into the top 12in (30cm) of soil, or use it as a mulch by applying a thick layer over the surface. For very heavy clay soils, grit can also be added to increase drainage.

Adding organic matter Turn organic matter into the soil with a shovel, pitchfork, or tiller.

Mulching Add a 2in (5cm) layer of well-rotted organic matter over the soil surface each year.

Adding grit Before planting, add small gravel particulates to very heavy clay soils to improve drainage.

WHICH WAY DOES YOUR YARD FACE?

When selecting plants, take time to assess the direction in which your yard faces and the amount of sunlight it receives every day. Understanding these aspects will help you make the right plant choices and also plan where to place trees and shrubs that may cast shade over your plot. With many plants suitable for areas in both sun and shade, there is a great choice for every situation.

SOUTH-FACING SITES

Sunny for most of the day in summer, south-facing sites provide optimal growing conditions for many flowering plants. However, soils dry out quickly here, and additional watering may be needed to support some species.

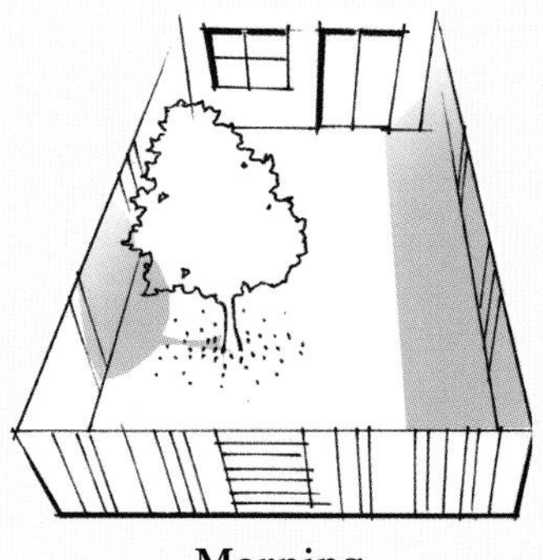

Morning

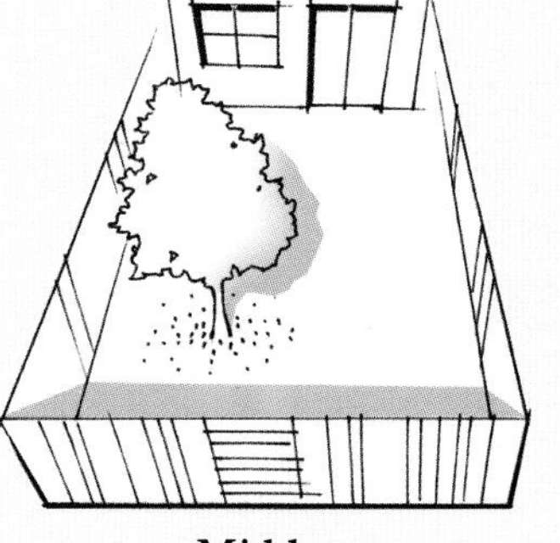

Midday

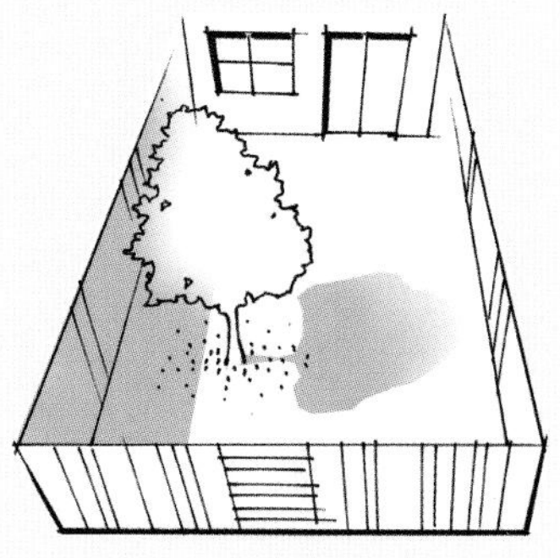

Evening

NORTH-FACING SITES

Many architectural foliage plants and a selection of flowers enjoy the shady, cool conditions of north-facing sites. When planting, position trees and large shrubs at the end of your plot to prevent them from casting even more shade.

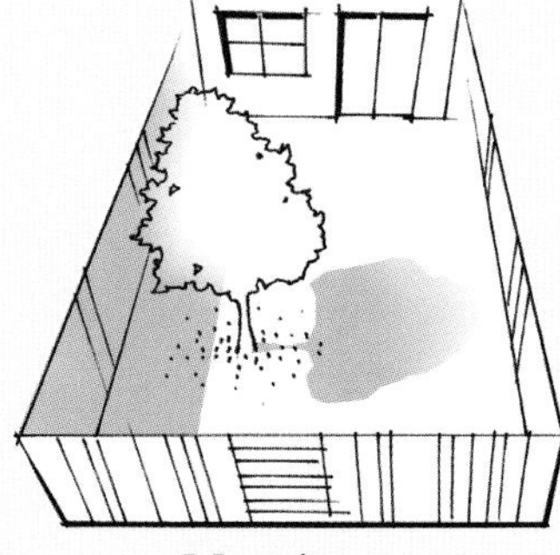

Morning

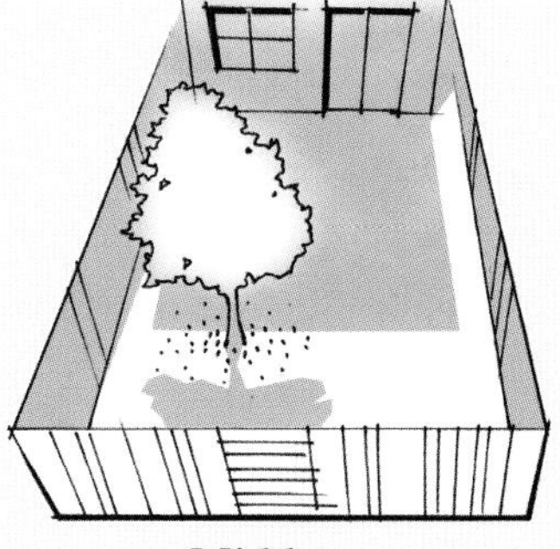

Midday

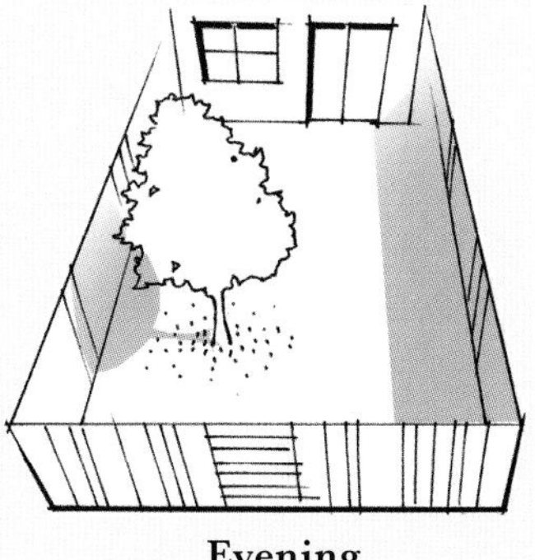

Evening

EAST-FACING SITES

These plots are sunny for many hours until midafternoon, and will support a large group of flowering and foliage plants that thrive in part or dappled shade. Grow sun-loving plants in areas of the yard that are bright for the longest periods.

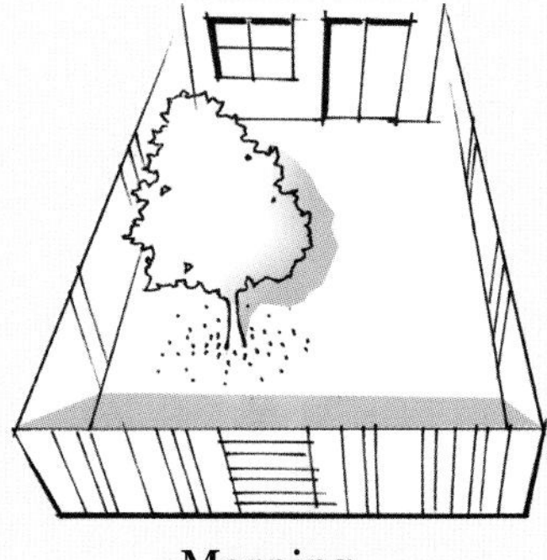

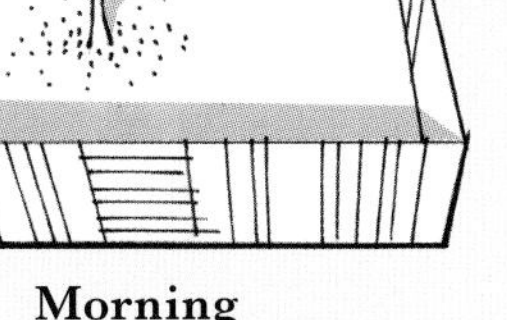

Morning

Midday

Evening

WEST-FACING SITES

Sunny from noon to evening in summer, west-facing yards provide ideal conditions for plants that are happy in full sun, or partial and dappled shade. Sun-loving plants should thrive in the brightest areas of a west-facing plot.

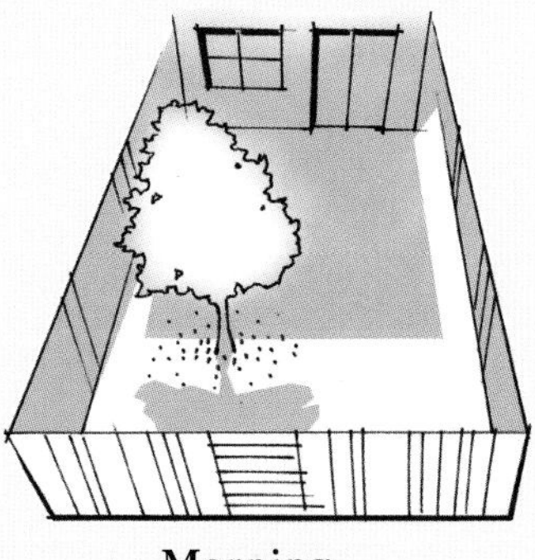

Morning

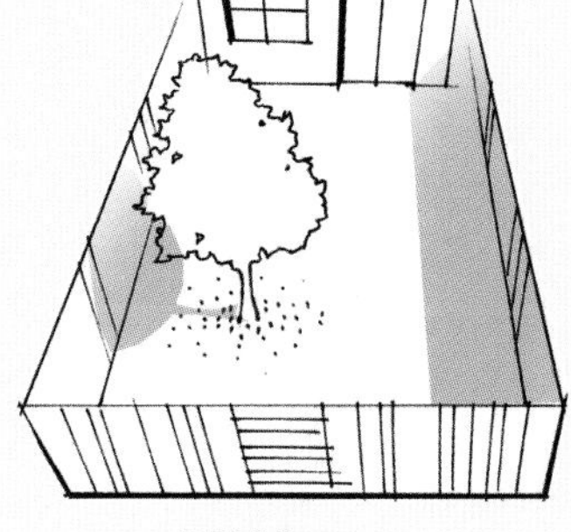

Midday

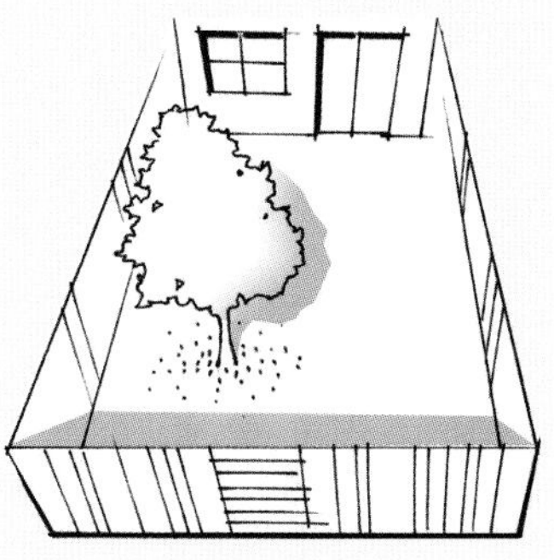

Evening

Planting styles

Your selection of plants and the way they are grouped convey the style or theme of a garden, be it formal, naturalistic, or traditional. Follow these guidelines to create your chosen design.

NATURAL SWATHES

Contemporary perennial, wildlife, and informal design styles reflect nature by replicating the way plants grow in the wild. Create beds in organic shapes with sweeping, curved edges, avoiding fussy, wiggly lines, and fill them with a restricted number of species, set out in bold flowing swathes. Designers also include smaller pockets of plants within these drifts to mimic the effects of self-seeding. Grasses and perennials, such as yarrow and feather grass (*see below*) are the mainstay of naturalistic schemes, with contrasting flower forms heightening interest.

Natural groups To create a naturalistic design, use a restricted palette of plants, set them out in organic-shaped swathes, and mix perennials and grasses with different shapes and forms to create exciting visual patterns.

Modern blocks Chic and sophisticated, modernist schemes are highly structured with plants grouped in blocks in geometric-shaped beds laid out in an asymmetric pattern. Clipped hedging is popular in these designs.

Formal symmetry Strict symmetrical and geometric beds are key to a formal design. Planting styles can be modern or traditional.

Traditional layers To achieve deep, layered schemes, create a bed that slopes slightly, and group plants in descending height order with periodic vertical interruptions.

MODERN vs. TRADITIONAL

Both formal and modernist planting schemes focus on visual effects, rather than attempting to mirror nature. Formal garden styles are rooted in the Classical architecture of Greece and Italy, and French Renaissance gardens, such as Versailles. The designs create elegant patterns with plants and present them in symmetrical beds. Parterres and knot gardens made from clipped boxwood and topiary shapes lend a sense of formality to schemes. More informal perennial plantings are also often included, but are confined to geometric beds to maintain the style. Designers who follow modernist principles adhere to the maxim that "less is more," and use a limited palette of plants set out in geometric beds, usually rectangles. Unlike formal garden designs, modernist schemes employ asymmetry, which creates a more dynamic effect. Upright grasses and hedges are often used, and perennials are limited to just one or two varieties to create uniform blocks of color and shape.

Traditional borders, as epitomized by Gertrude Jekyll, take elements from both formal and informal styles. While contemporary perennial schemes mix plants of different heights and forms on one plane, traditional schemes are often laid out in beds on a slight incline with the tallest plants at the back and shortest in front, allowing all to be seen clearly. However, plants are not designed in formal lines but grouped in interlocking diamond-shaped swathes that reflect natural landscapes and create a sense of movement.

USING PLANT TYPES TO CREATE A DESIGN

When creating a design, look at the structure and habit of the plants you have selected, as well as their flowers, and consider the role each will play in your scheme. Start by planning the position of permanent structural plants, such as trees and shrubs, which will form the main framework of your design and lend a sense of solidity. Then, add in seasonal plants to create a sequence of color and interest throughout the year, and midrange perennials to fill gaps between the structural elements. Focal plants with eye-catching shapes or colors, such as spiky irises or shrubs with dramatic leaves, provide highlights in a border, while those with spreading stems cover bare soil with a carpet of foliage and flowers.

Balancing shape and form This summer border shows how different plant forms can be used to create a harmonious display.

Focal points Spiky grasses and vertical perennials draw the eye and can be used to punctuate a border.

Midrange plants Use perennials and small shrubs to knit together seasonal flowers and larger plants.

Structural plants Create a permanent framework with well-placed evergreen and deciduous trees and shrubs.

Seasonal plants Sustain interest throughout the year by including a range of seasonal plants and flowers.

Ground cover Plants with spreading stems help to fill gaps in a border and can suppress weed growth too.

PLANTING YEAR

Gardens are like stage sets, with a change of scenery every few weeks helping to maintain the audience's interest. To put on this show, remember that while evergreens offer year-round color, they can't compete with the fleeting beauty of a tree in blossom or the unfurling petals of a rose in summer.

To create a garden that evolves month by month, you need to plan ahead. Punctuate boundaries and borders with trees and shrubs that produce different effects as the seasons turn, with flowers in spring and summer, followed by fiery foliage and berries in fall. Dress up these structural plants with climbers, such as clematis, that prolong their interest, and weave into your scheme a variety of early, mid-, and late-flowering perennials for a kaleidoscope of color. In fall, plant a range of spring bulbs in any gaps in your borders. These will provide a bright burst of flowers as winter fades.

Early to mid-spring Fall-planted bulbs, such as crocuses, grape hyacinths, and daffodils, together with early-flowering shrubs, including camellias, provide a blaze of color from early to mid-spring.

Late spring Bridge the gap between spring and summer with late-flowering tulips and alliums; clematis and shrubs, including New Jersey tea and lilacs; and perennials, such as bleeding heart and columbine.

Summer The choice of summer flowers is countless and includes every color, size, and shape imaginable. Place plants that perform early, such as roses, alongside late bloomers, like dahlias, to sustain the performance.

Fall As summer flowers start to fade, fall brings its own treasure trove of color and excitement. Flaming foliage is the main attraction, but also find a place for berried shrubs, grasses, and late flowers, such as asters.

Winter Choices dwindle as temperatures drop, but winter is still full of surprises. Flowers and bulbs, including snowdrops, brave the cold, and shrubs with evergreen leaves or bright stems, such as twig dogwood, also add color.

How to plant

Following tried and tested methods when planting will pay dividends, helping to get plants off to a good start, ensuring they thrive, and improving the long-term survival rate of permanent plants.

PREPARING THE SITE

The best times to plant are in the fall or spring, although container-grown plants can be planted at any time, unless the soil is frozen, waterlogged, or exceptionally dry. Borderline hardy plants are best planted in spring, which allows them to establish a mature root system before winter sets in.

A few weeks before you plan to plant, prepare your soil. Start by removing large stones and rubble, and then tackle the weeds. Dig out by hand perennial weeds, such as dandelions, docks, and bindweed, ensuring you remove the roots. Then hoe off the annual weeds. Leave the bed for a week or two and remove any new weeds that have appeared. If your soil needs improving, dig in composted organic matter and/or grit (*see p.12*).

SHRUBS AND PERENNIALS

Most container-grown shrubs and perennials are planted in the same way. About an hour before planting, give your plant a good soak, either with a watering can, or by placing it in a bucket of water, submerging the pot and waiting until bubbles no longer appear. Then lift it out and let it drain. Meanwhile, dig a hole twice as wide as the pot and a little deeper. Place the plant in the hole and check that it will be at the same depth when planted as it is in its pot. Add or remove soil accordingly, and fork over the bottom of the hole. Mix some slow-release granular fertilizer with the excavated soil, as directed on the package. Remove the plant from its pot, gently massage the root ball, and place it in position. Refill the hole, firming the soil with your hands to remove any air pockets, and water well.

Setting plants out Before planting, set your plants in position on the ground to check that you are happy with their arrangement, facing their best sides forward for an engaging display.

Planting Most plants are planted at the same depth as they were in their pots. After planting, firm the soil well with your hands to remove air pockets. Water well.

TREES AND LARGE SHRUBS

Use the following method to plant container-grown or balled and burlapped trees and large shrubs. Bare-root plants, available through fall and winter, are planted in the same way, but refill around the roots in stages to ensure that you eliminate all the air gaps. Do not add extra fertilizer or organic matter when planting, but prepare the soil well in advance.

Water your tree or shrub using the method described for perennials.

Remove the plant from its container or wrapping. Tease out the roots carefully and scrape away the top layer of soil if the plant is in a pot. Dig a planting hole of the same depth, and up to three times as wide as the root ball, and loosen the sides of the hole with a fork. Place the tree into the hole, ensuring that the area where the roots start to flare out is near the surface. Refill around the root ball, and firm the soil to remove air pockets. Water well.

Planting a tree Plant trees slightly above the soil surface, so the area where the roots flare out from the trunk is just visible. Place a stake over the pot to judge the right depth, and adjust the soil accordingly.

Providing support Trees gain strength by natural flexing and bending. When planted, additional support should not be installed on a tree unless conditions warrant, for example, very loose soil or in an area that receives high winds.

Aftercare After planting, apply a mulch, leaving a space of 4in (10cm) around the trunk. Water consistently for the first two years, and check and loosen tree ties regularly. Remove the tree stake after four years once established.

BULBS

Spring-flowering plants that grow from bulbs, such as daffodils and tulips, are planted in fall, while those that bloom in summer, including gladioli, are planted in spring. Most prefer free-draining soil, so if you have heavy clay, add sharp grit to the area where you plan to plant. Alternatively, bulbs requiring vernalization can be planted in frost-proof pots during fall.

Bulbs can be planted individually, but they look better and are easier to plant in a group. First, dig a wide hole to the appropriate depth. Most bulbs are planted at a depth of three times their height, except for tulips, which are planted at four times their height. For example, a 2in (5cm) daffodil bulb is planted at 6in (15cm), while a 2in (5cm) tulip bulb should be planted at 8in (20cm). Water well after planting.

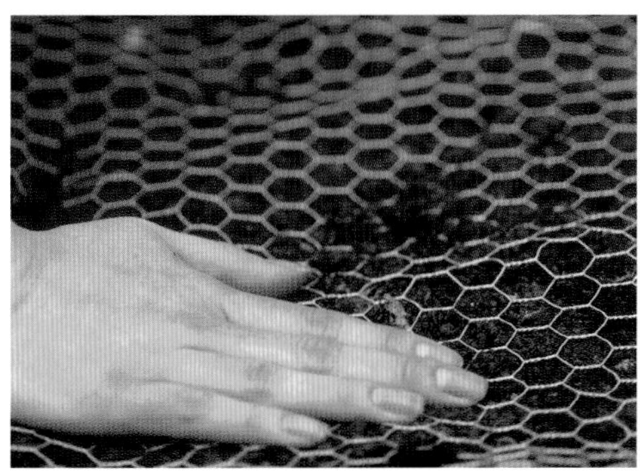

Planting dormant bulbs Plant bulbs with the pointed tip facing upward. To prevent animals from digging them up, cover the soil after planting with wire mesh. Secure the mesh with stakes.

Planting snowdrops Unlike other bulbs, snowdrops are best planted when in leaf, just after they have flowered in spring. This is known as planting "in the green."

CLIMBERS

When planting climbers, use stakes to guide the stems toward a permanent support, such as a fence. Prepare the soil and planting hole as for perennials (*see p.18*), at least 12in (30cm) from the support; dig a deeper hole for clematis, which should be planted with the root ball 3in (8cm) below the soil. Place the stakes in the hole before positioning the plant with its root ball angled slightly toward the supporting structure.

Providing initial support Dig a planting hole and insert three or four evenly spaced stakes into the base. Tie the top of the stakes to the wires to hold them in place.

Attaching horizontal wires Insert screw eyes 18in (45cm) apart along a fence, or use a drill and screw anchor to secure them into walls. Fix horizontal wires between the screw eyes.

Planting the climber Place the plant and backfill with soil and firm it to remove air pockets. Then, spread out the stems and tie them loosely to the stakes with soft twine.

Aftercare After planting, water well and add a mulch of organic matter or chipped bark to suppress weeds. Keep the mulch clear of the stems. Water regularly in the first year.

AQUATICS

Marginals and deep-water aquatics are planted using one simple method. Plant them in sterilized topsoil or heavy clay in pond baskets or planting bags. These hold the soil in place while allowing water to pass through, aerating the roots, and keeping the plants healthy.

Deep-water aquatics, such as water lilies, are best set on bricks on the bottom of the pond after planting to allow their leaves to float on the surface. Remove the bricks as the plant grows. Alternatively, deep-water plants can be suspended in the water using string and gradually lowered to the correct depth.

Set marginal plants on shelves in shallow water at the edge of the pond. Oxygenators, such as hornwort, do not require planting; simply place them in water at least 12in (30cm) deep, and they will spread out just beneath the surface.

Filling the pond basket First, line the bottom of the pond basket with clay or sterilized topsoil. Remove the plant from its original container and place it in the basket.

Planting the aquatic Fill around the plant with more compost and press gently in place. Apply a layer of pea gravel evenly over the surface to prevent the soil from floating out.

Aftercare Divide mature aquatics and marginals in spring. Remove plants from their baskets, cut up the root balls with a knife, and repot healthy sections. Topdress with grit or pea gravel.

CONTAINERS

When planting in containers, choose the ones large enough for your plants, and ensure they have drainage holes in the base. Bear in mind that, because they hold greater volumes of soil and water, large pots need watering less frequently than small ones. Also consider the material the container is made of. Choose frost-proof terra-cotta and lightweight materials, such as plastic or resin, for balconies and roof gardens.

Filling with soil Add an even layer of potting soil over the broken pots, selecting the correct type for your particular plant. Also add some slow-release fertilizer.

Ensuring good drainage Place pieces of broken terra-cotta pots or polystyrene to prevent the soil from falling through while keeping the holes clear for drainage.

Planting your selections Having first watered the plants, remove them from their pots and place them on the potting soil. Fill in around the plants and press gently.

Aftercare Leave a 2in (5cm) gap between the top of the soil and the rim of the pot to make watering easier. Water regularly, especially in summer. Topdress annually.

SEEDS

Growing annuals and vegetables from seeds is both rewarding and usually cheaper than buying mature plants. Growing perennial, trees, and shrubs by seeds can also be rewarding though often take more time and can require special efforts.

To sow indoors, fill a clean seed tray or pot with seed-starting mix, and press down gently. Water using a can fitted with a rose nozzle, then let drain. Sprinkle seeds thinly on the soil surface. Check the seed package for the required planting depth, and cover the seeds with sifted mix to that depth. Label the tray or pot, and cover with plastic. Place in a warm, lit area, such as a windowsill, and let the seeds germinate. Keep the soil moist, and remove the cover as soon as the seedlings emerge. Continue growing the seedlings indoors and transfer to larger pots as they grow. Acclimate them to the outdoors before planting them after the risk of frost has passed.

Using pots for large seeds Fill a small pot with potting soil, firm gently, and make holes to the depth indicated on the seed package.

Sowing the seeds Drop a seed into each hole, cover with potting soil, and water well. Cover with a clear plastic bag.

Growing the seedlings Once your seedlings have a few leaves, transfer them individually into modular trays or small pots.

Potting the seedlings Plant one seedling per module or pot, press them in gently, and water well. Continue to grow them under cover.

PLANT LOCATIONS

GARDENS IN SUN
GARDENS IN SHADE

Choosing plants for sun or shade

Some plants like it hot while others shy away from the sun, but whatever the conditions found in your plot, there's a wealth of beautiful plants to choose from to create a visual feast. The key is to match the plants to environmental conditions.

SUN-LOVING PLANTS

Dry dusty soil and blazing hot sun are challenging conditions for plant growth, and species unsuited to such sites will soon suffer. However, some of the most beautiful plants and flowers have adapted to thrive in these areas, including a whole host of colorful blooms, and sculptural shrubs and trees you can use even if your soil is sandy and your yard or garden faces south.

A plant's label will usually tell you the conditions it prefers, but you can often tell when plants are suited to hot, dry sites because many share key characteristics that help them survive. These include small leaves to reduce moisture loss, silvery foliage to reflect light, and hairs that store water droplets, protecting the surface from the sun and reducing evaporation. Succulents have fleshy stems and leaves that store water, while other sun-lovers have colorful flowers that shine in strong light, attracting pollinating insects. Use these visual clues, along with the plant labels, to identify plants best suited to your site.

Soaking up the rays These sun-loving specimens show the range of beautiful plants that can cope with strong light.

KEY CHARACTERISTICS OF SUN-LOVING PLANTS

Silver foliage Most plants with reflective silver leaves enjoy hot sites and shimmer in strong light.

Small leaves A reduced surface area helps foliage to minimize moisture loss during transpiration.

Furry foliage Hairy leaves trap moisture, helping to sustain plants during drought.

Fleshy stems and leaves Some plants from dry regions trap moisture in their leaves and stems.

SHADE-LOVING PLANTS

Cool woodland floors and other shady areas make perfect homes for a wide range of large-leaved architectural plants. Unlike sun-lovers, these shade-dwellers must mop up as much available light as possible and, as a consequence, their foliage is generally large and thin. The soil beneath trees may also be quite dry, so some plants also sport shiny leaves with a waxy outer surface to help conserve moisture. Pastel colors stand out in the gloom, which is why many shade-loving plants bear pale flowers that will catch the attention of pollinating insects. Other plants bloom in winter, making the most of the increased light levels that are available when any neighboring deciduous trees are not in leaf.

There are many degrees of shade, from deep shade, such as that experienced at the back of north-facing borders, to dappled and partial shade, where the sun may shine for a few hours of the day. Plant choices are restricted in areas of deep shade and the best option is to introduce as much light as possible. Prune overhead trees and shrubs, and consider removing any structures that cause shade. Moist shade suits more plants than dry shade, so try increasing soil moisture by improving it with organic matter, such as compost or shredded leaves, or create a plastic-lined bog garden.

To transform your gloomy garden into a cool calm oasis, combine foliage with different textures, sizes, and shapes, and include a range of seasonal flowers to highlight your scheme. As you will see, shade is a bonus, never a problem.

Cooling off in the shade Large dramatic leaves and delicate flowers can scorch under hot sun.

KEY CHARACTERISTICS OF SHADE-LOVING PLANTS

Large thin leaves Plants adapted to shade have large leaves that can absorb low light.

Glossy foliage Shiny foliage reflects the available light onto adjacent leaves and adds sparkle.

Winter flowers Some plants flower only in winter when deciduous trees are bare.

Evergreen foliage Permanent leaf cover enables many shade-lovers to grow all year.

Recipes for sunny sites

SUMMER FOCAL POINT FOR A PATIO

A dramatic flowering maple creates the central feature in this summer display, lending height and stature to the mix—you may need to support its stems with a discreet stake or two—while purple verbenas, white petunias, and the trailing silver licorice plant form a skirt around the edge. Plant this combination in all-purpose potting soil, incorporating a few slow-release fertilizer granules as you go along, and keep it well watered throughout summer. If the flowers start to flag toward the end of the season, apply a liquid fertilizer to perk them up.

Plant list
1 *Petunia* 'Trailing White'
2 *Verbena*—purple form
3 *Abutilon* 'Nabob'
4 *Helichrysum petiolare*

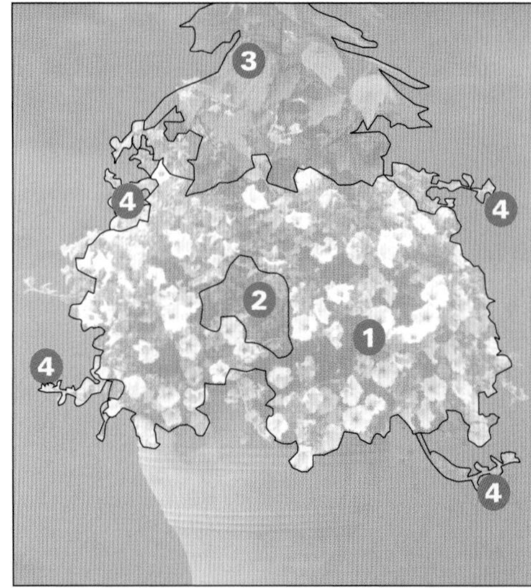

HERB FUSION

Herbs mix easily into a sunny mixed border on free-draining soil. Golden oregano makes a colorful edge, and bronze and green fennel make decorative feathery towers in midsummer, shading plants like Siberian bugloss that prefer cooler conditions (remember to snip off the fennel seeds frequently before they self-seed). Also try a bright yellow-flowered Scotch broom at the back of the bed to inject a splash of color in spring.

Plant list
1 *Origanum vulgare* 'Aureum'
2 *Brunnera macrophylla*
3 *Foeniculum vulgare* 'Purpureum'
4 *Foeniculum vulgare*
5 *Potentilla recta* 'Warrenii'

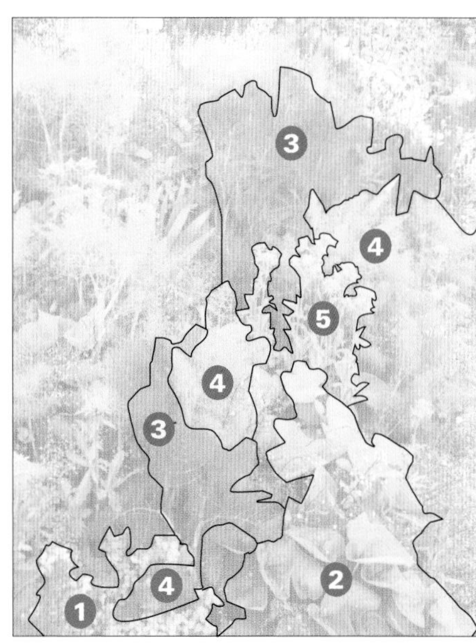

FIERY BORDER FOR SANDY SOIL

This confection of fiery shades will light up a sunny area of the garden throughout summer. Combine perennials, such as yarrow, sneezeweed, and red-hot poker in rich shades of gold and crimson, and tone them down with wispy Mexican feather grass, which thrives at the front of sunny borders. Tall decorative dahlias inject late-season color into the back of this display, while their dark foliage also provides a foil for the green leaves of other flowers. The fence, painted in a dark color, sharpens the effect of the hot hues.

Plant list

1 *Stipa tenuissima*
2 *Achillea* 'Terracotta'
3 *Helenium* varieties
4 *Kniphofia*—orange form
5 Decorative dahlia
6 *Geum*—orange form

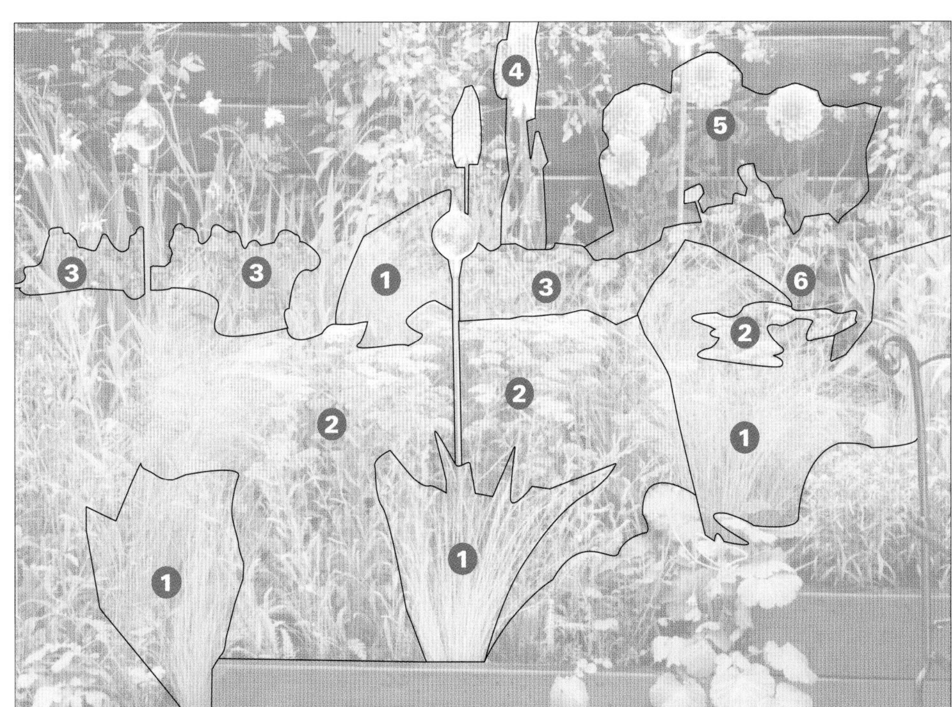

Recipes for sunny sites

PROFUSE POND PERIMETER

A small artificial pond creates a beautiful oasis, reflecting light into the garden and attracting a wide range of birds, small animals, and aquatic wildlife. Decorate the water surface with a small hardy water lily, and create a boggy area around your pond for a range of flowers and foliage plants. This pond edge features giant rhubarb, together with colorful astilbe, and gold-flowered leopard plant, which also sports beautiful leaves that hold the interest before the blooms appear. A variegated tatarian dogwood will provide structure throughout the year with its colorful winter stems and decorative leaves in summer. In smaller spaces, replace the giant rhubarb with a more manageable rodgersia.

Plant list

1 *Nymphaea pygmaea*
2 *Astilbe* x *arendsii*
3 *Ligularia dentata*
4 *Cornus alba* 'Elegantissima'
5 *Gunnera manicata*

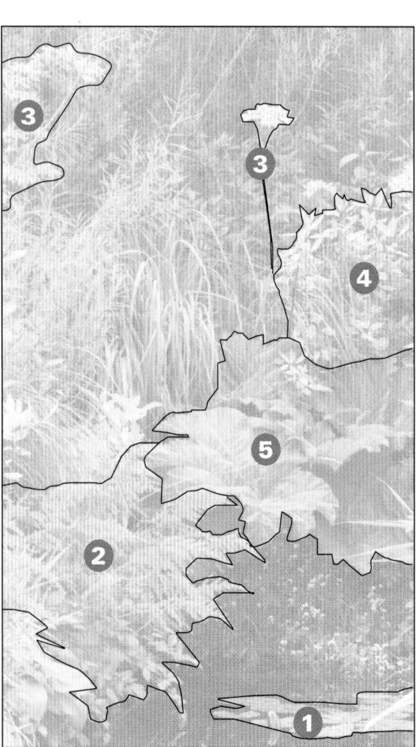

MONOCHROME BORDER FOR CLAY

The rose and perennials here will thrive in clay soils in a sunny site, though boxwood, cranesbill, and dark purple bugbane are equally happy in part shade. Prune the rose in late winter to keep it in check, and site it where you can enjoy its sweet fragrance.

Plant list

1 *Geranium sanguineum* 'Album'
2 *Rosa* WINCHESTER CATHEDRAL
3 *Actaea simplex* 'Brunette'
4 *Veronica spicata* 'Alba'
5 *Buxus sempervirens* 'Suffruticosa'

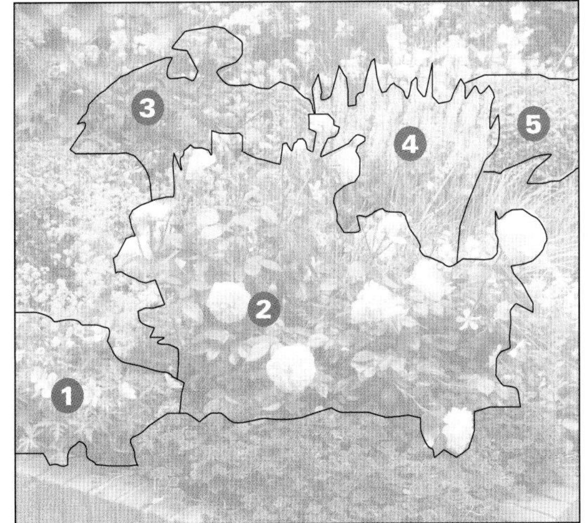

SUMMER SELECTION FOR A GRAVEL GARDEN

Gravel beds provide the free-draining conditions that salvias and spiky yellow-eyed grass enjoy, and they both flourish at the front of sunny beds and borders. A bronze sedge will also be happy in gravel and sun or part shade. Larkspur, however, need more moisture and an annual application of all-purpose granular fertilizer each spring, so leave them out if you cannot provide these conditions.

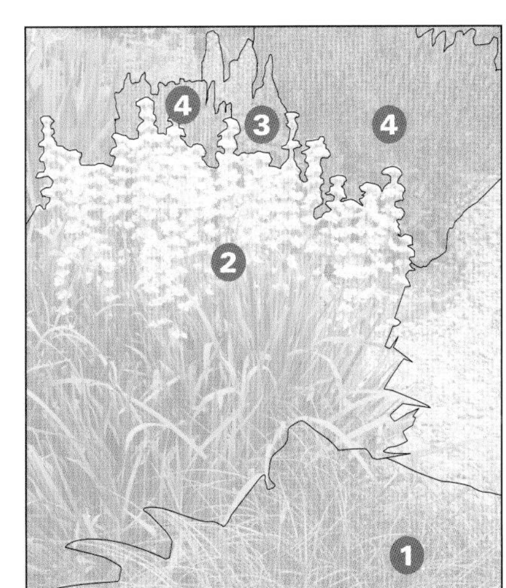

Plant list

1 *Carex comans*—bronze form
2 *Sisyrinchium striatum*
3 *Delphinium elatum*
4 *Salvia nemerosa*

Recipes for shady sites

LEAFY EDIBLES FOR PART SHADE

Lettuces tend to bolt quickly in bright sun, while thriving in a cool spot in part shade. Swiss chard will also adapt to some shade, and varieties with colorful stems make pretty partners for green and purple lettuces. Dot pot marigolds between your leafy crops for spots of orange or yellow to create a border that looks as good as it tastes. Guard against slugs, especially when the lettuces are young, and keep the border well-watered.

Plant list
1 Swiss chard
2 Pot marigold
3 Purple lettuce
4 Purple frilly-leaved lettuce ('Lollo Rossa')
5 Green lettuce ("cut and-come-again" variety)

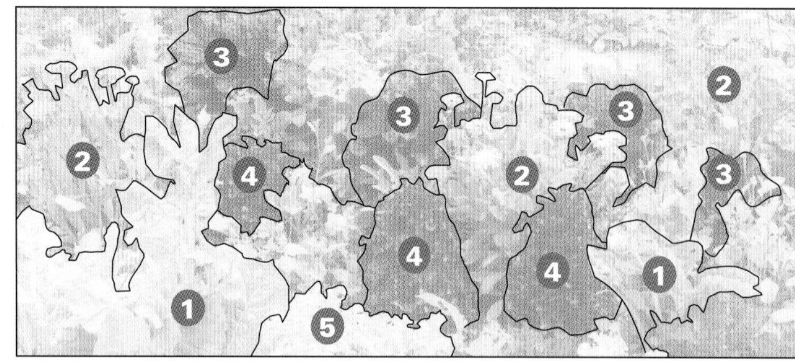

FOLIAGE TEXTURES FOR CLAY SOIL

This rich mix of foliage plants would be perfect for a shady site just beyond a tree canopy and needs few flowers to create a spectacular effect. Combine large-leaved hostas and pigsqueaks to smother the soil, and the majestic ostrich fern, for additional height and texture toward the back of the border. Flowers will appear from spring to summer, starting with the pigsqueaks and the acid-yellow blooms of the marsh euphorbia, and continuing with pale lilac hosta blooms as summer progresses, and tall stems of yellow leopard plant flowers, which appear later in the season. Take precautions against slug damage to ensure the hostas are not shredded.

Plant list
1 *Bergenia purpurascens*
2 *Hosta sieboldiana* var. *elegans*
3 *Polygonatum* x *hybridum*
4 *Euphorbia palustris*
5 *Ligularia dentata*
6 *Ligularia stenocephala*
7 *Matteuccia struthiopteris*
8 *Darmera peltata*

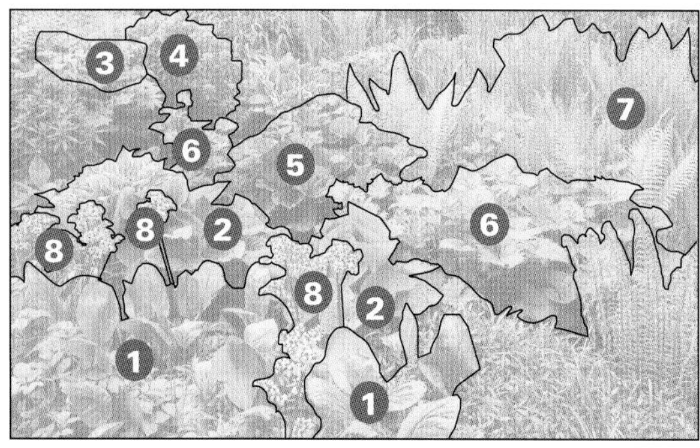

WOODLAND UNDERSTORY

This simple combination of ferns, purple astilbe, and the stark white stems of a Himalayan birch form an eye-catching display when the understory plants are repeated and set out in bold swathes. Ensure your soil is damp enough to please the astilbe, which prefers constant moisture. Adding a thick mulch of organic matter over clay soils in spring will help, or substitute them with Japanese anemone on free-draining sandy soils.

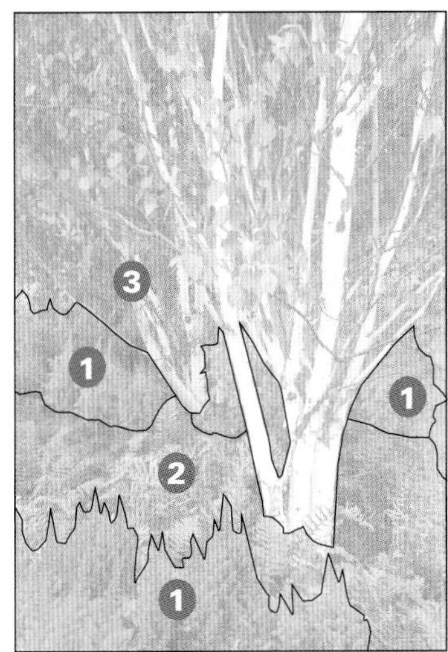

Plant list

1 *Astilbe* x *arendsii*
2 *Dryopteris affinis* 'Cristata'
3 *Betula utilis* var. *jacquemontii*

Recipes for shady sites

LEAFY WOODLAND CLEARING

The focus of this planting group is the purple-leaved European filbert, which will color up well in light dappled shade. Globeflower, spurge, and cranesbills are also best in part shade, but you can tuck the lady's mantle in a darker corner because it will grow almost anywhere. If you have space, squeeze in a few ferns, such as a shield fern or male fern, both of which tolerate deep shade. For a native alternative to the European filbert consider an eastern redbud. Select *Cercis canadensis* 'Forest Pansy' for its rich purple leaves or *C. canadensis* 'Hearts of Gold' for its bright chartreuse foliage. Pink pealike blooms that emerge in spring prior to the foliage are also a striking feature of this tree.

Plant list

1 *Alchemilla mollis*
2 *Euphorbia* species
3 *Trollius* x *cultorum*
4 *Corylus avellana* 'Fuscorubra'
5 *Geranium sylvaticum* 'Alba'

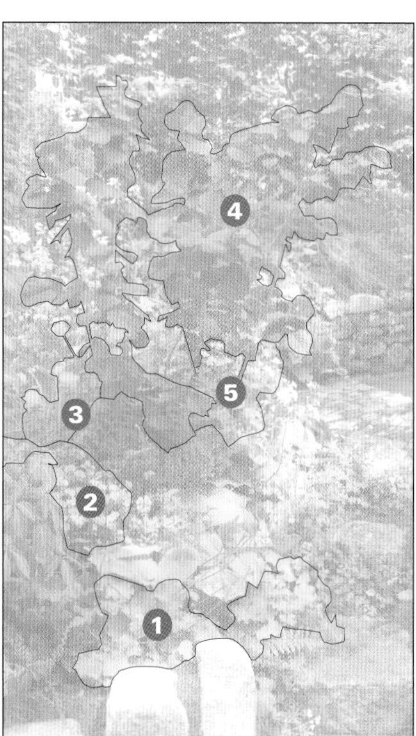

FOLIAGE BORDER FOR AN URBAN SPACE

This sophisticated combination will offer lasting color in a cool, shady urban garden. The fern and barrenwort are evergreen, creating permanent cushions of foliage, while the columbines form dainty late spring flowers in pastel shades of pink, blue, purple, and white. They tend to self-seed prolifically, so deadhead the blooms promptly to contain them. Tufted hair grass adds textural contrast to the mix and is one of the few grasses that performs best in shade.

Plant list

1 *Epimedium perralderianum*
2 *Polystichum* species
3 *Deschampsia cespitosa*
4 *Aquilegia vulgaris* (granny's bonnet)

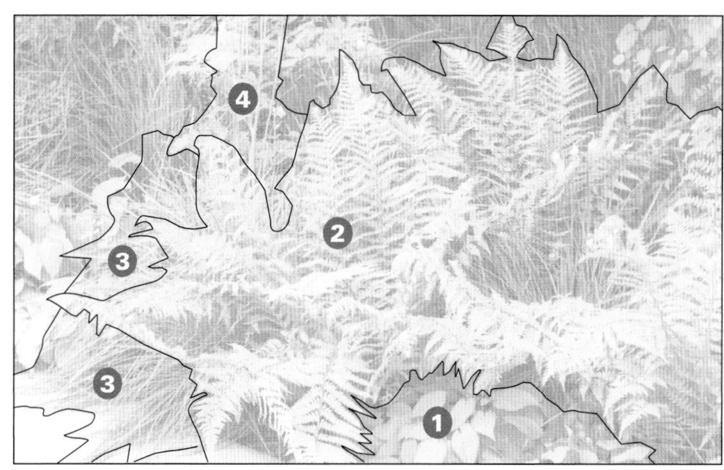

COLORFUL MIX FOR A CONTEMPORARY POT

While most summer bedding plants prefer full sun, a few tolerate part shade, and are particularly useful in urban gardens that are shaded by buildings. The best include fuchsias, trailing lobelia, mintleaf, and impatiens—opt for disease-resistant New Guinea types. Upright fuchsias make strong statement features for the center of a display, while trailing lobelia and mintleaf add a decorative frill. Squeeze the impatiens in between to add bright highlights.

Plant list

1 *Lobelia erinus*—trailing form
2 Tender fuchsia—bedding variety
3 *Impatiens*—white form
4 *Plectranthus madagascariensis* 'Variegated Mintleaf'

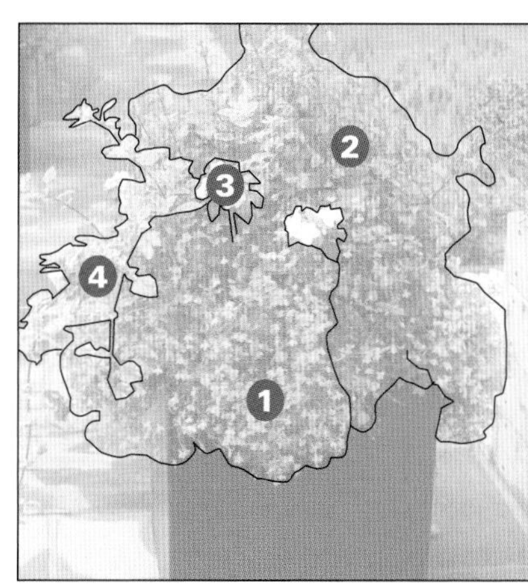

GARDENS in SUN

Sun-drenched gardens are perfect for a wealth of flowering plants, as well as those with sparkling silver foliage and richly colored leaves. Brightly lit patios are also an asset, providing ideal conditions for many spring bulbs, summer annuals, and edible plants, including soft fruits, Mediterranean vegetables, and tender green beans. And if you have a pond, indulge in a sumptuous water lily or two, and fringe your feature with marginals that will mirror their shapes and colors in the glassy surface.

Plants for clay soil

Moisture retentive and rich in nutrients, clay soils provide the perfect home for a whole host of garden plants, including roses, peonies, and clematis.

Cottage borders filled with black-eyed Susan, aster, columbine, and beebalm, or traditional shrub and perennial schemes will all thrive in clay soils in the sun. If you have modern designs in mind, you can opt for bamboo, canna, and Culver's root. Although clay soil can be a little difficult to manage, if treated the right way it can be extremely fertile. Clay is prone to waterlogging and cracking during dry spells, but these problems can be remedied by applying a mulch of organic material every year in spring. This will help to improve the structure of the clay and increase drainage.

PERENNIAL MEDIUM

Aconitum 'Stainless Steel'

MONKSHOOD A clump-forming perennial with deeply divided dark green leaves and dense upright spikes of unusual, silvery blue hooded flowers, which appear from mid- to late summer. All parts of the plant are poisonous.
↕3ft (1m) ↔24in (60cm)

💧 (!) Z4–8

ANNUAL/BIENNIAL LARGE

Amaranthus caudatus

LOVE-LIES-BLEEDING This is a tall, bushy annual with oval pale green leaves. From summer to fall, it produces long, pendulous, tassel-like red flowers, which are good for cutting and can be used for indoor displays.
↕4ft (1.2m) ↔18in (45cm)

💧

PERENNIAL MEDIUM

Amsonia tabernaemontana

WILLOW BLUE-STAR An upright perennial with slim tapering leaves that develop attractive tints before dropping in fall. It produces clusters of star-shaped blue flowers from late spring to summer. Grow in front of or in the center of a flowerbed.
↕↔3ft (1m)

💧 (!) Z3–9 (N)

PERENNIAL LARGE

Anemone hupehensis

CHINESE ANEMONE A perennial with dark green divided leaves. Tall upright stems of purple, red, pink, or white flowers with yellow eyes appear over many weeks from late summer to early fall. 'Hadspen Abundance' (above) has pale pink blooms.
↕4ft (1.2m) ↔18in (45cm)

💧 Z5–7 (N)

PERENNIAL MEDIUM

Aquilegia vulgaris var. *stellata*

COLUMBINE An upright perennial with round leaves and pompomlike flowers from late spring to early summer. Deadhead after flowering. 'Nora Barlow' (above) has greenish pink blooms with white tips.
↕30in (75cm) ↔20in (50cm)

💧 Z3–8

PERENNIAL LARGE

Aster novae-angliae

Renamed *Symphyotrichum novae-angilae* This New England aster has slim hairy leaves and, purple, pink, red, or white daisy-like flowers from late summer to fall. Best in neutral to alkaline soils; it has mildew resistance.
↕up to 5ft (1.5m) ↔24in (60cm)

💧 Z4–8 (N)

PERENNIAL MEDIUM

Astilbe 'Venus'

ASTILBE This perennial has divided foliage topped with feathery tapering plumes of tiny pale pink flowers in midsummer. The seedheads become dry and provide interest well into winter. Divide every 3–4 years. Needs moisture if planted in full sun.
↕↔3ft (1m)

💧 Z3–8

PERENNIAL MEDIUM

Astrantia major

MASTERWORT A clump-forming perennial, with divided midgreen leaves. It produces sprays of small greenish white, pink, or red flowers from midsummer to early fall. Deadhead regularly to prolong the display. Remove spent growth in fall.
↕24in (60cm) ↔18in (45cm)

💧 Z4–7

SHRUB LARGE

Berberis darwinii

DARWIN'S BARBERRY This vigorous, arching evergreen shrub has small, glossy dark green leaves. Numerous rounded, deep orange-yellow flowers appear from mid- to late spring, followed by bluish berries. Its vicious spines are good for security hedges.
↕↔10ft (3m)

💧 (!) Z7–9

PERENNIAL LARGE

Campanula lactiflora

MILKY BELLFLOWER An upright, branching perennial with narrowly oval green leaves and slender stems of nodding, bell-shaped blue, occasionally pink or white, blooms in midsummer. Needs reliably moist and fertile soil. Stake the stems on windy sites.

↕5ft (1.5m) ↔24in (60cm)

Z5–7

PERENNIAL LARGE

Canna 'Pretoria'

syn. *Canna* 'Striata' This upright perennial is grown for its green- and yellow-striped foliage and bright orange flowers, which appear from midsummer to early fall. Grow it in fertile soil, keep it well watered, and protect the rhizomes from frost.

↕5ft (1.5m) ↔20in (50cm)

Z8–11

TREE MEDIUM

Cercis canadensis

EASTERN REDBUD This spreading deciduous tree or shrub has heart-shaped dark green leaves that turn yellow in fall. Pale pink pealike flowers emerge from bare stems in mid-spring. *C. canadensis* var. *alba* (above) has white flowers.

↕↔30ft (10m)

Z4–9 (N)

SHRUB MEDIUM

Chaenomeles speciosa

FLOWERING QUINCE A bushy, vigorous deciduous shrub with thorny stems and oval dark green leaves. Red, white, or pink flowers are borne from early- to mid-spring, followed by fragrant yellow fruits.

↕8ft (2.5m) ↔15ft (5m)

Z4–8

PERENNIAL SMALL

Chrysanthemum 'Grandchild'

DECORATIVE GARDEN MUM This upright perennial has dark green lobed leaves and, from late summer to early fall, produces branching heads of bright mauve double flowers. It is good for cutting; deadhead regularly to prolong the flowering display.

↕18in (45cm) ↔16in (40cm)

(!) Z5–9

CLIMBER MEDIUM

Clematis JOSEPHINE

CLEMATIS This deciduous climber has green lance-shaped leaves. From summer to early fall, a succession of large double flowers appear; the pinkish purple petals are cream beneath, giving a layered effect. Best in rich soil; keep the roots shaded.

↕8ft (2.5m)

Z4–9

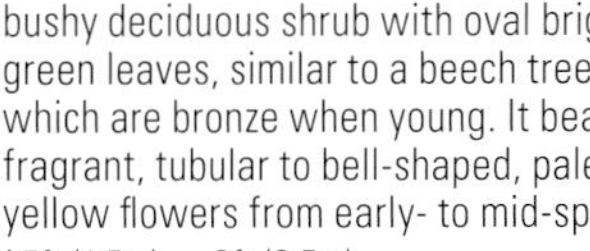

SHRUB MEDIUM

Corylopsis pauciflora

BUTTERCUP WINTER HAZEL A spreading bushy deciduous shrub with oval bright green leaves, similar to a beech tree's, which are bronze when young. It bears fragrant, tubular to bell-shaped, pale yellow flowers from early- to mid-spring.

↕5ft (1.5m) ↔8ft (2.5m)

pH Z6–8

SHRUB SMALL

Deutzia x *elegantissima* 'Rosealind'

ELEGANT DEUTZIA This rounded deciduous shrub has a flaky bark and dark green leaves. It bears clusters of sweet-smelling star- or cup-shaped flowers with a pink tinge from late spring to early summer.

↕4ft (1.2m) ↔5ft (1.5m)

Z6–8

PERENNIAL SMALL

Dodecatheon meadia

SHOOTING STAR This is a clump-forming perennial with pale green leaves. In spring, clusters of small purple flowers with reflexed petals appear, but it then becomes dormant in summer. *D. meadia* f. *album* (above) has white flowers.

↕8in (20cm) ↔6in (15cm)

Z4–8 (N)

SHRUB LARGE

Enkianthus campanulatus

REDVEIN ENKIANTHUS A large, spreading deciduous shrub with tufts of dull green leaves that turn bright red in fall. Small bell-shaped flowers in creamy yellow, veined pink to red, appear in late spring or early summer. It prefers acidic soil.

↕12ft (4m) ↔10ft (3m)

pH Z4–7

Plants for clay soil

PERENNIAL MEDIUM

Euphorbia griffithii 'Fireglow'

GRIFFITH'S SPURGE This upright bushy perennial has decorative lance-shaped midgreen leaves with pale red midribs. In early summer, it produces rounded clusters of small orange-red flowers. The sap is a skin irritant.

↕30in (75cm) ↔20in (50cm)

Z4–9

PERENNIAL LARGE

Filipendula rubra

QUEEN OF THE PRAIRIE An upright perennial with large aromatic leaves divided into jagged-edged green leaflets and, in midsummer, feathery plumes of soft rose-pink tiny flowers, which turn pale as they age. Use it at the back of a boggy site.

↕8ft (2.5m) ↔4ft (1.2m)

Z3–8 (N)

PERENNIAL MEDIUM

Filipendula ulmaria

MEADOWSWEET A deciduous perennial bog plant with leafy stems bearing midgreen divided foliage. Plumelike spikes of creamy white flowers form in midsummer. It self-seeds and is considered invasive in some areas.

↕3ft (1m) ↔24in (60cm)

Z3–9

SHRUB LARGE

Forsythia x *intermedia*

BORDER FORSYTHIA This vigorous, upright deciduous shrub has long stems covered with small, star-shaped yellow flowers from late winter to mid-spring, before the small bright green leaves appear. Varieties include 'Lynwood Variety' (above).

↕↔10ft (3m)

Z5–8

SHRUB SMALL

Fothergilla gardenii

DWARF FOTHERGILLA This is a bushy deciduous shrub with dark blue-green oval leaves that turn red, orange, and yellow in fall. Clusters of fragrant, white bottlebrush flowers appear from mid- to late spring. Best grown in fertile soil.

↕↔3ft (1m)

pH Z4–8 (N)

PERENNIAL SMALL

Geranium 'Ann Folkard'

CRANESBILL This spreading perennial forms mats of ivy-shaped, deeply cut bright yellowish green foliage. It produces an abundance of small rich magenta flowers with black centers and veins in midsummer. It may also bloom in fall.

↕20in (50cm) ↔3ft (1m)

Z5–9

PERENNIAL SMALL

Geum coccineum

AVENS This clump-forming perennial has irregularly lobed leaves, above which rise slender, branching hairy stems bearing single orange flowers with prominent yellow stamens in summer. Best in damp soils. 'Cooky' (above) is a popular variety.

↕↔12in (30cm)

Z5–7

PERENNIAL MEDIUM

Helenium 'Moerheim Beauty'

SNEEZEWEED A medium-sized upright perennial with dark green foliage below strong branching stems. Sprays of rich coppery red daisy-like flowers appear from mid- to late summer. It makes a valuable late season border plant.

↕3ft (1m) ↔24in (60cm)

(!) Z4–8

PERENNIAL MEDIUM

Helenium 'Wyndley'

SNEEZEWEED An upright perennial with branching stems bearing sprays of daisy-like orange-yellow flower heads for a long period, starting from late summer to fall. The foliage is dark green. It needs regular division in spring or fall.

↕32in (80cm) ↔20in (50cm)

(!) Z4–8

PERENNIAL LARGE

Helianthus 'Lemon Queen'

PERENNIAL SUNFLOWER This tall, vigorous, upright perennial has stout branched stems bearing coarse, lance-shaped dark green leaves and large, pale yellow daisy-like flowers from late summer to fall. Provide plant with plenty of space in back of border.

↕5ft (1.5m) ↔24in (60cm) or more

Z4–9 (N)

PERENNIAL MEDIUM

Heliopsis helianthoides

SMOOTH OXEYE This is an upright, medium-sized perennial with large lance-shaped leaves and rich yellow or orange daisy-like flowers, which appear from late summer to early fall. 'Summer Sun' (above) has large yellow flowers.

↕3ft (1m) ↔24in (60cm)

Z4–9 Ⓝ

SHRUB MEDIUM

Hydrangea arborescens

SMOOTH HYDRANGEA A rounded shrub with midgreen, tapered oval leaves. Domed, flattened clusters of long-lasting white blooms form in midusmmer; papery flower skeletons feature all winter. 'Annabelle' (above) has extra large flower heads.

↕↔5ft (1.5m)

(!) Z4–9 Ⓝ

PERENNIAL MEDIUM

Lysimachia punctata

WHORLED LOOSESTRIFE This is an upright, very vigorous, tall, clump-forming perennial, with midgreen leaves. In summer, it produces spikes of bright yellow flowers. It can become aggressive. Plant it in moist soils for the best results.

↕3ft (1m) ↔24in (60cm)

Z4–8

PERENNIAL MEDIUM

Leucanthemum x *superbum*

SHASTA DAISY This upright perennial has lance-shaped dark green leaves and large, daisy-like white flowers on long stems from midsummer to fall. Hidden staking helps keep the plant tidy. 'Wirral Pride' (above) is a double-flowered form.

↕3ft (1m) ↔24in (60cm)

Z5–9

TREE LARGE

Liquidambar styraciflua

SWEETGUM A conical to spreading deciduous tree with shoots that develop corky ridges. Its large, lobed, glossy dark green leaves turn brilliant orange, red, and purple in fall. Slender, compact cultivars are available.

↕80ft (25m) ↔40ft (12m)

pH Z5–9 Ⓝ

PERENNIAL LARGE

Monarda 'Prairie Night'

BEEBALM An upright clump-forming perennial with midgreen scented leaves. It produces tufted, two-lipped, tubular pinky violet blooms from mid- to late summer. Provide shade from hot sun; protect from wet winter soils.

↕4ft (1.2m) ↔24in (60cm)

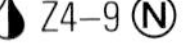

Z4–9 Ⓝ

BULB MEDIUM

Narcissus 'Scarlet Gem'

DAFFODIL A mid-spring-flowering dwarf daffodil that produces strap-shaped foliage and scented flowers with golden petals and deep red-orange cups. It increases to form clumps over time. Needs good drainage or the bulbs will rot.

↕14in (35cm)

(!) Z5–9

PERENNIAL MEDIUM

Paeonia mlokosewitschii

CAUCASIAN PEONY An erect, clump-forming perennial with pinkish leaf buds that unfurl as oval bluish green leaves, which then turn orange-brown in fall. Large, bowl-shaped lemon-yellow flowers appear from late spring to early summer.

↕↔30in (75cm)

Z5–8

PERENNIAL MEDIUM

Persicaria bistorta 'Superba'

BISTORT This vigorous, clump-forming perennial has large, oval, tapered green leaves, which spread to form a dense mat. From early summer to fall, spikes of soft pink flowers appear above the foliage.

↕30in (75cm) ↔24in (60cm)

(!) Z4–8

BAMBOO LARGE

Phyllostachys nigra

BLACK BAMBOO This is a large evergreen bamboo that produces clumps of grooved, greenish brown stems, or "culms," that turn black in their second season. The leaves are narrow and rustle in the wind. Protect it from cold, drying winds.

↕25ft (8m) ↔indefinite

Z7–11

PERENNIAL SMALL

Primula 'Wanda'

PRIMROSE This is a small evergreen or semievergreen perennial with lance-shaped to oval, bronze to dark green leaves. From winter to mid-spring, they produce loose clusters of dark wine-red flowers. Protect from heat.

↕4in (10cm) ↔6in (15cm)

Z3–9

PERENNIAL MEDIUM

Ranunculus aconitifolius

BACHELOR'S BUTTONS This upright, clump-forming perennial has deeply divided green leaves. Yellow-centered white flowers are produced on branched stems from late spring to summer. 'Flore Pleno' (above) has white double blooms.

↕30in (75cm) ↔20in (50cm)

Z5–9

PERENNIAL MEDIUM

Ratibida columnifera

MEXICAN HAT This perennial, grown as an annual, has pale green leaves and unusual summer flowers with reflexed yellow petals that surround a brown "cone." Deadhead often; it is drought-resistant. Best in mass, native meadow, or prairie planting.

↕32in (80cm) ↔12in (30cm)

Z4–9 Ⓝ

SHRUB LARGE

Rhododendron luteum

PONTIC AZALEA This is a large deciduous shrub with oblong- to lance-shaped leaves that develop orange and red tints in fall. In spring, it produces very fragrant, funnel-shaped, bright yellow flowers. Plant it in a cool spot.

↕↔12ft (4m)

pH Z7–9

SHRUB SMALL

Ribes sanguineum

FLOWERING CURRANT This spreading deciduous shrub has aromatic green leaves and pendent clusters of small pink or red spring flowers, followed by white-bloomed, blue-black fruits. 'Brocklebankii' (above) has pale green leaves; needs a cool spot.

↕↔4ft (1.2m)

Z6–8 Ⓝ

CLIMBER MEDIUM

Rosa CONSTANCE SPRY

ENGLISH SHRUB ROSE This rose bears grayish green leaves and numerous large, bowl-shaped, pure pink double flowers with a myrrh fragrance. The blooms appear in summer and last for about a month. Mulch annually with organic matter.

↕6ft (2m)

Z4–9

SHRUB SMALL

Rosa DOUBLE DELIGHT

HYBRID TEA ROSE This repeat-flowering hybrid tea rose has dark green foliage and, throughout summer and fall, it produces a succession of highly fragrant, fully double, creamy white flowers with dark red edges. Mulch annually with organic matter.

↕3ft (1m) ↔24in (60cm)

Z5–9

SHRUB SMALL

Rosa Knock Out Series

SHRUB ROSE A repeat-flowering modern shrub rose with disease-resistant dark green foliage. Flowers in shades of yellow, pink, and red are borne throughout summer and early fall, and have a light fragrance. Mulch annually with organic matter.

↕↔4ft (1.2m)

Z4–9

PERENNIAL MEDIUM

Rudbeckia fulgida var. *sullivantii* 'Goldsturm'

BLACK-EYED SUSAN This compact upright perennial has narrow, oval midgreen foliage and daisy-like, brown-centered golden blooms from late summer to fall. Leave faded flower heads for winter interest.

↕30in (75cm) ↔12in (30cm) or more

Z4–9 Ⓝ

PERENNIAL MEDIUM

Sanguisorba menziesii

BURNET A clump-forming upright perennial with attractive, feathery blue-gray foliage. The fluffy red bottlebrush flowers are held on tall stems and appear from early summer to early fall. The seedheads retain their color through winter.

↕30in (75cm) ↔24in (60cm)

Z4–8 Ⓝ

PERENNIAL LARGE

Thalictrum aquilegiifolium

MEADOW RUE An upright clump-forming perennial with divided blue-green leaves and slender branched stems topped with fluffy mauve-pink or white flowers from early- to midsummer. Grow in coastal or cold gardens in soil that does not dry out.

↕4ft (1.2m) ↔18in (45cm)

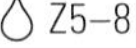

Z5–8

PERENNIAL LARGE

Rudbeckia laciniata

CUTLEAF CONEFLOWER This tall upright perennial has lance-shaped foliage and, from late summer to fall, daisy-like, single, green-centered yellow flowers. Leave faded flower heads for winter interest. Varieties include 'Autumn Sun' (above).

↕7ft (2.3m) ↔30in (75cm)

Z3–9 Ⓝ

PERENNIAL LARGE

Veronicastrum virginicum

CULVER'S ROOT A large upright perennial with tall stems of dark green lance-shaped leaves. From late summer to early fall, it produces spikes of small, star-shaped white, blue, or pink blooms. 'Album' (above) has white flowers.

↕4ft (1.2m) ↔18in (45cm)

Z4–8 Ⓝ

PERENNIAL LARGE

Sanguisorba canadensis

CANADIAN BURNET This is an upright, clump-forming perennial with divided midgreen leaves and bottlebrush white flower heads from summer to early fall. Plant in swaths for best effect in moist soil in cold, exposed gardens.

↕6ft (2m) ↔24in (60cm)

Z3–8 Ⓝ

PERENNIAL MEDIUM

Solidago GOLDEN BABY

GOLDENROD This is an upright clump-forming perennial with narrow, pointed green leaves. From midsummer to early fall, it produces flattened heads of small golden-yellow flowers. Deadhead to prolong the flowering display.

↕24in (60cm) ↔18in (45cm)

Z4–8

SHRUB MEDIUM

Viburnum acerifolium

MAPLELEAF VIBURNUM An upright deciduous shrub with bright green leaves that turn orange, red, and purple in fall. Decorative red fruits, which turn purple-black, follow creamy white flower heads in early summer. The berries are poisonous.

↕6ft (2m) ↔4ft (1.2m)

! Z4–8 Ⓝ

SHRUB LARGE

Syringa vulgaris

COMMON LILAC This vigorous deciduous shrub has midgreen heart-shaped foliage. In late spring, it bears large conical clusters of highly fragrant purple, pink, and white flowers. 'Paul Thirion' (above) has rose-pink blooms. Considered invasive in some areas.

↕↔22ft (7m)

Z3–7

OTHER SUGGESTIONS

Perennials

Bergenia cordifolia • *Camassia leichtlinii* Ⓝ • *Carex elata* 'Aurea' • *Carex oshimensis* 'Evergold' • *Helianthus salicifolius* Ⓝ • *Hemerocallis* 'Joan Senior' • *Perovskia atriplicifolia* • *Prunella vulgaris* Ⓝ • *Ratibida pinnata* Ⓝ • *Rudbeckia subtomentosa* 'Henry Eilers' Ⓝ • *Vernonia noveboracensis* Ⓝ

Shrubs

Abies concolor 'Compacta' Ⓝ • *Aesculus pavia* Ⓝ • *Arbutus unedo* • *Berberis x stenophylla* • *Calluna vulgaris* • *Cryptomeria japonica* 'Yoshino' • *Erica carnea* • *Hypericum* 'Hidcote' • *Ilex verticillata* Ⓝ • *Lindera benzoin* Ⓝ • *Rhus aromatica* Ⓝ • *Viburnum dentatum* Ⓝ

Trees

Crataegus laevigata 'Paul's Scarlet' • *Crataegus viridis* 'Winter King' Ⓝ • *Taxodium distichum* 'Cascade Falls' Ⓝ

Plant focus: roses

Reigning over the flower garden, roses are coveted for their exquisite blooms, tantalizing perfume, and long flowering season.

Roses have been grown for thousands of years and are celebrated for their beautiful, scented blooms and diverse habits. Ranging from ground-hugging shrubs to lofty climbers, they never fall out of fashion and suit almost every design style, including contemporary, formal, and cottage. The flowers comprise many different forms, spanning the single flowers of the species to spherical, fully double blooms with 40 petals or more. Most of them are also fragrant, and while some roses only flower once a year, modern bushes and shrubs often perform for many months from summer to fall, especially when deadheaded regularly. In addition, species and old garden roses produce large, brightly colored hips to decorate designs through fall and winter. Roses suffer from a number of diseases, most notably black spot, which causes the foliage to discolor and drop off. To prevent it, buy modern resistant forms or tough species that tend to not succumb to the disease.

USING ROSES

Shrub roses can be trained as standards; you can use them in pots to flank a doorway or as a centerpiece in formal designs. The elegant flowers of bush roses enhance the color and fragrance of mixed herbaceous borders in informal gardens, and climbing roses can be trained to create curtains of color.

Species roses make excellent hedges with their tough, disease-resistant foliage and early-summer flowers, followed by decorative hips. Their thorns also help to deter intruders.

Climbers trained on wires fixed to a pergola or series of arches provide a tunnel of flowers, foliage, and scent in a traditional garden design.

TYPES OF ROSE

Modern roses This group, developed after 1867, includes the hybrid tea, floribunda, grandiflora, miniature, and English roses.

Species roses These can be divided into four groups by their place of origin, either Europe, America, the Middle East, or Asia.

Old garden roses Sometimes called heritage roses, this group includes gallica, damask, alba, centifolia, and bourbon.

Shrub roses Many shrub roses result from crossing old and modern roses to develop more hardy and disease-resistant selections.

Patio and miniature roses Averaging 12in (30cm) tall miniature, roses are ideal for the front of the flower bed or as a container plant.

Climbing roses The thick rigid canes of climbing roses allow for a beautiful show of blossoms on a wall, trellis, or arbor.

Rambling roses An annual display of thick clusters of small flowers on long, slender, and flexible canes make this rose a favorite to many.

Groundcover roses Sometimes called landscape roses, these were developed to be easy to care for and useful for planting in mass.

Plants for sandy soil

Water and nutrients drain through sandy soils, but many plants live happily on such meager rations and may rot or flower poorly if given a richer diet.

Choose plants that tolerate drought and dislike wet roots in winter for this free-draining soil. Lavender, African lily, statice, and other plants from Mediterranean climates thrive in sandy conditions, as do most bulbs. Fashionable prairie plants, including stonecrop, yarrow, salvia, and coneflower, are also at home in sandy, sunny sites, while wildflower meadows will put on their best performance here. If you are looking for larger, more permanent plants, choose from the many shrubs and trees that like drier conditions, such as spiraea, ninebark, and juniper.

SHRUB MEDIUM

Abelia 'Edward Goucher'

ABELIA Deciduous or semievergreen, this arching shrub has oval, tapered green leaves that are bronze when young. From midsummer to fall, it produces masses of trumpet-shaped, pink, slightly fragrant blooms. Prune in spring.
↕5ft (1.5m) ↔6ft (2m)

Z6–9

PERENNIAL MEDIUM

Achillea 'Coronation Gold'

YARROW An upright perennial with fernlike gray-green foliage and flat heads of golden-yellow flowers in summer. The stems may need discreet support, ideally put into place in spring so the plants can grow up into them.
↕3ft (1m) ↔24in (60cm)

Z3–9

PERENNIAL SMALL

Achillea 'Paprika'

YARROW An upright semievergreen perennial with feathery, silvery green leaves. In summer, it produces flat heads of tiny scarlet flowers that fade with age. The dried flower heads can be left to provide winter interest.
↕↔18in (45cm)

Z3–8 Ⓝ

PERENNIAL MEDIUM

Agapanthus africanus

AFRICAN LILY An evergreen perennial with strap-shaped midgreen leaves and spherical heads of deep blue trumpet-shaped flowers, which appear from summer to early fall on tall sturdy stems. Protect from frost in winter.
↕3ft (1m) ↔20in (50cm)

Z8–10

PERENNIAL SMALL

Agastache aurantiaca

GIANT HYSSOP An upright perennial with gray-green scented leaves and, in summer, long-lasting spikes of small, orange, two-lipped tubular flowers. Popular varieties include 'Apricot Sprite' (above), with pale orange blooms.
↕20in (50cm) ↔3ft (1m)

Z6–10 Ⓝ

BULB MEDIUM

Allium cristophii

STARS OF PERSIA A summer-flowering bulb with narrow gray-green leaves that fade as the flowers appear. This short-stemmed allium then produces large balls of star-shaped violet flowers, followed by attractive seedheads.
↕16in (40cm)

(!) Z5–8

BULB MEDIUM

Alstroemeria ligtu hybrids

PERUVIAN LILY This summer-flowering tuber produces narrow twisted leaves and funnel-shaped flower heads in shades of pink, yellow, or orange, often spotted or streaked with contrasting colors. In cold areas, apply a deep mulch in winter.
↕24in (60cm)

(!) Z8–11

PERENNIAL MEDIUM

Anthemis tinctoria

GOLDEN MARGUERITE This is a clump-forming perennial with finely divided, aromatic leaves. It bears a mass of white or yellow daisy-like flowers on slim stems over a long period in summer. 'E.C. Buxton' (above) has lemon-yellow flowers.
↕↔3ft (1m)

Z3–8

SHRUB SMALL

Artemisia 'Powis Castle'

WORMWOOD This rounded evergreen, subshrub is grown for its finely divided, silver leaves. The small, yellow late-summer flowers are often removed to maintain the plant's foliage effect. May need protection in cold winters.
↕↔3ft (1m)

Z7–9

PERENNIAL LARGE

Asphodeline lutea

YELLOW ASPHODEL A tall, upright, clump-forming perennial that produces narrow, textured grassy leaves and dense spikes of star-shaped, bright yellow fragrant flowers in late spring. The blooms are followed by decorative seedpods.
↕4ft (1.2m) ↔3ft (1m)

Z6–9

SHRUB SMALL

Ballota pseudodictamnus

GRECIAN HOREHOUND This compact, low-growing evergreen subshrub is prized for its small, round gray-green leaves covered with white woolly hairs. Small pink flowers appear in early summer at the end of the leaf stems. Clip after flowering.

↕24in (60cm) ↔3ft (1m)

Z7–9

PERENNIAL MEDIUM

Baptisia australis

FALSE INDIGO This is a clump-forming perennial with gray-green divided foliage and spikes of small violet-blue flowers, which appear in summer. Decorative dark gray seedpods appear in fall. Provide it support in spring.

↕30in (75cm) ↔24in (60cm)

Z3–9 Ⓝ

PERENNIAL SMALL

Campanula carpatica

CARPATHIAN HAREBELL A low-growing, clump-forming perennial with round, open bell-shaped, violet-blue or white flowers, which appear over a mound of heart-shaped leaves in summer. 'White Clips' has pure white blooms.

↕4in (10cm) ↔12in (30cm)

Z4–7

PERENNIAL MEDIUM

Centranthus ruber

RED VALERIAN This upright perennial produces fleshy gray-green leaves and branching heads of small, star-shaped, deep reddish pink or white flowers from late spring to late summer. It thrives in poor soil and may self-seed widely.

↕3ft (1m) ↔24in (60cm) or more

Z5–8

SHRUB SMALL

Ceratostigma willmottianum

CHINESE PLUMBAGO A deciduous shrub with small green leaves that turn brilliant red in fall. Clusters of small sky-blue flowers appear from late summer to fall. It may die back in winter, reshooting in spring. Grow in well-drained soil.

↕3ft (1m) ↔5ft (1.5m)

Z6–8

SHRUB LARGE

Cercis chinensis

CHINESE REDBUD A large branching shrub or small tree with pealike pink flowers that appear on bare stems in late spring, before the foliage emerges. The large, decorative green foliage is heart shaped. Mulch with compost in spring.

↕20ft (6m) ↔15ft (5m)

Z6–9

TREE MEDIUM

Cercis siliquastrum

JUDAS TREE This bushy, spreading deciduous tree has attractive, green heart-shaped leaves. In mid-spring, before the leaves emerge, it produces bright pink pealike flowers on bare stems, followed by long purple pods in late summer.

↕↔30ft (10m)

Z6–9

SHRUB MEDIUM

Choisya ternata

MEXICAN ORANGE A rounded evergreen shrub with aromatic, glossy bright green leaves divided into three leaflets. Clusters of fragrant white blooms open from late spring to fall. Best in West Coast gardens. 'Aztec Pearl' has slender green leaves.

↕↔8ft (2.5m)

Z8–10 Ⓝ

SHRUB SMALL

Cistus x dansereaui

ROCK ROSE This small evergreen shrub has gray-green leaves and white, pink, or purple, bowl-shaped papery flowers in summer. 'Decumbens' (above) is low growing and compact, and produces white blooms with crimson blotches in the center.

↕24in (60cm) ↔3ft (1m)

Z8–10

ANNUAL/BIENNIAL LARGE

Cleome hassleriana

SPIDER FLOWER A tall, erect annual with spiny stems of divided, palm-shaped leaves. In summer, it produces rounded clusters of small spidery flowers, which have long stamens and a light fragrance, in shades of white, pink, and purple.

↕4ft (1.2m) ↔18in (45cm)

PERENNIAL SMALL

Coreopsis verticillata

THREADLEAF COREOPSIS A compact perennial with feathery, dark green foliage and daisy-like flowers, which appear in profusion over a long period in summer on wiry stems. Varieties include 'Moonbeam' (above) with lemon-yellow flowers.

↕20in (50cm) ↔18in (45cm)

Z3–9 Ⓝ

SHRUB LARGE

Cornus alba

TATARIAN DOGWOOD This upright deciduous shrub is grown for its winter display of bright scarlet young shoots and dark green foliage. Creamy white early summer flowers are followed by white fruits. 'Sibirica' (above) is a popular variety.

↕↔ 10ft (3m)

Z2–7

ANNUAL/BIENNIAL LARGE

Cosmos bipinnatus

COSMOS A tall, bushy, erect, half-hardy annual with feathery leaves and numerous large, daisy-like flowers in red, pink, or white, which appear from early summer to fall. Deadhead to encourage a long display of blooms.

↕ 4ft (1.2m) ↔ 18in (45cm)

PERENNIAL LARGE

Crambe cordifolia

COLEWORT This is a tall, robust perennial that produces a mound of large, crinkled lobed dark green foliage. In summer, branched stems supporting clouds of small, fragrant white flowers appear above the leaves.

↕ 6ft (2m) ↔ 4ft (1.2m)

Z5–9

BULB LARGE

Dahlia 'Café au Lait'

DECORATIVE DAHLIA This clump-forming tuber has toothed-edged dark green leaves. From midsummer to fall, it bears large, peach-flushed, cream-colored double flowers. Deadhead to encourage more blooms. Lift the tubers in winter.

↕ 3ft (1m)

Z9–11

SHRUB LARGE

Daphne bholua

PAPER DAPHNE An evergreen, occasionally deciduous, upright shrub with leathery dark green foliage and fragrant deep pink winter blooms. Performs best in West Coast gardens. 'Jacqueline Postill' (above) has purplish pink and white blooms.

↕ 10ft (3m) ↔ 5ft (1.5m)

Z7–9

PERENNIAL LARGE

Delphinium elatum

LARKSPUR This delphinium is an upright perennial with deeply cut green leaves. In midsummer, it produces tall spikes of bowl-shaped flowers in a wide range of colors, with many varieties to choose from. The stems require sturdy stakes.

↕ 6ft (2m) ↔ 3ft (1m)

Z3–7

PERENNIAL SMALL

Dianthus 'Dad's Favourite'

GARDEN PINK This dwarf evergreen perennial forms a mound of gray-green grasslike foliage. Throughout summer, it produces clove-scented, white semidouble flowers with maroon markings. Pink-flowered 'Bath's Pink' is a popular variety.

↕ 18in (45cm) ↔ 12in (30cm)

Z4–9

BULB LARGE

Dierama pulcherrimum

ANGEL'S FISHING ROD This is an upright, summer-flowering corm with narrow, strap-shaped evergreen leaves. In summer, it bears long arching stems, from which dangle deep pink funnel-shaped flowers. Enrich the soil with organic matter.

↕ 5ft (1.5m)

Z8–10

SHRUB LARGE

Dipelta floribunda

ROSY DIPELTA This is a vigorous, upright treelike deciduous shrub with peeling pale brown bark and pointed midgreen leaves. From late spring to early summer, it produces fragrant, pale pink blooms with yellow markings inside.

↕↔ 12ft (4m)

Z6–9

PERENNIAL LARGE

Echinacea purpurea

CONEFLOWER An erect, clump-forming perennial with slim, tapering green leaves. The daisy-like flowers have reflexed petals and a central brown disk. 'Kim's Knee High' (above) is a compact variety, with orange-centered, bright pink flowers.

↕ 5ft (1.5m) ↔ 18in (45cm)

Z3–8 Ⓝ

BULB LARGE

Eremurus stenophyllus

FOXTAIL LILY This is a tall, upright summer-flowering bulb that forms a clump of strap-shaped leaves. In summer, it bears torpedo-shaped heads of small yellow flowers on tall stems. May need staking in windy sites; apply fertilizer in spring.

↕3ft (1m)

Z6–9

PERENNIAL LARGE

Echinops bannaticus

GLOBE THISTLE An upright perennial with narrow, deeply cut leaves and pale to midblue, spiky, spherical flower heads, borne in late summer. The seedheads look good through winter. 'Taplow Blue' (above) has steely blue flowers.

↕5ft (1.5m) ↔30in (75cm)

Z4–9

PERENNIAL MEDIUM

Eryngium alpinum

ALPINE SEA HOLLY An upright perennial with heart-shaped, divided green leaves. In summer, it produces tall blue stems topped with cone-shaped purple flowers surrounded by spiny bracts. 'Superbum' (above) has dark blue blooms.

↕28in (70cm) ↔18in (45cm)

Z5–8

BULB MEDIUM

Eucomis bicolor

PINEAPPLE LILY A late summer-flowering bulb with wavy-edged leaves and spotted stems topped with clusters of greenish white flowers with purple-edged petals. With "hats" of leaflike bracts, the flowers resemble pineapples. Protect in winter.

↕20in (50cm)

Z8–10

SHRUB MEDIUM

Edgeworthia chrysantha

PAPER BUSH A rounded, open deciduous shrub with oval dark green leaves. From late winter to early spring, it produces rounded heads of fragrant, tubular yellow flowers, which are covered in silky white hairs. It needs a warm sheltered site.

↕↔5ft (1.5m)

Z8–10

SHRUB SMALL

Euphorbia characias subsp. *wulfenii*

MEDITERRANEAN SPURGE An evergreen subshrub with fingerlike, gray-green leaf clusters forming a frill around the stems, and heads of yellow-green spring flowers. Wear gloves to remove spent flower stems.

↕↔4ft (1.2m)

(!) Z7–10

SHRUB LARGE

Fatsia japonica

JAPANESE FATSIA An rounded, dense evergreen shrub with large, deeply lobed, hand-shaped dark green leaves. Dense clusters of tiny white flowers in mid-fall are followed by black fruits. Forms include 'Variegata' with white-edged leaves.

↕↔12ft (4m)

Z8–10

PERENNIAL SMALL

Geranium ROZANNE

CRANESBILL This sprawling deciduous perennial produces rounded, deeply divided midgreen leaves with marbled, pale green markings. For many weeks from summer to fall, it bears masses of shallow, cup-shaped blue flowers.

↕↔20in (50cm) or more

Z4–8

ANNUAL/BIENNIAL SMALL

Gypsophila elegans

ANNUAL BABY'S BREATH This fast-growing, erect, bushy annual has lance-shaped grayish green leaves. From summer to early fall, it bears clouds of tiny white flowers. 'Covent Garden' has pure white single flowers. Considered invasive in some areas.

↕24in (60cm) ↔12in (30cm) or more

SHRUB SMALL

Hebe 'Great Orme'

HEBE A rounded, open evergreen shrub with deep purple shoots and glossy dark green foliage. It bears slender spikes of pink, fading to white flowers, from midsummer to mid-fall. Trim in early spring to keep it compact. Best in West Coast gardens.

↕↔4ft (1.2m)

Z9–11

PERENNIAL MEDIUM

Helictotrichon sempervirens

BLUE OAT GRASS An evergreen perennial grass with stiff silvery blue leaves forming a large, airy mound and, in early summer, long arching stems of straw-colored flowers that are followed by long-lasting seedheads.

↕3ft (1m) ↔24in (60cm)

Z4–8

SHRUB LARGE

Juniperus scopulorum

ROCKY MOUNTAIN JUNIPER This conifer has a neat, narrow columnar habit, and does not require pruning. It has bright, steel-blue scalelike foliage and tolerates hot, dry sites. Plant it at the back of a border or as a "focal" plant.

↕50ft (15m) ↔20ft (6m)

Z3–7 Ⓝ

BULB LARGE

Lilium 'Red Hot'

ASIATIC LILY This large bulb produces long arching stems of slender green leaves topped with clusters of large, richly scented, white-edged rose-pink flowers during summer. The stems may need to be supported in exposed gardens.

↕3ft (1m)

Z5–8

PERENNIAL LARGE

Kniphofia uvaria

RED-HOT POKER An upright perennial with strap-shaped evergreen leaves, above which rise tall spikes of bicolored, cone-shaped flower heads in late summer. The small, tubular red and yellow flowers open from the base of the cluster.

↕4ft (1.2m) ↔24in (60cm)

Z5–9

PERENNIAL SMALL

Limonium sinuatum

STATICE A bushy perennial, grown as an annual, with lance-shaped, lobed deep green leaves and, from summer to early fall, clusters of tiny yellow, blue, or pink blooms that are ideal for drying. Varieties include the Fortress Series (above).

↕16in (40cm) ↔12in (30cm)

Z8–9

SHRUB LARGE

Hibiscus syriacus

ROSE OF SHARON A upright deciduous shrub with deep green lobed leaves. From late summer to mid-fall, it bears large blue, pink, or white saucer-shaped blooms. 'Red Heart' (above) has white flowers with pink center. Considered invasive in some areas.

↕10ft (3m) ↔6ft (2m)

Z5–9

SHRUB SMALL

Lavandula 'Willow Vale'

SPANISH LAVENDER A hybrid form of the traditional French lavender, this is an evergreen subshrub with narrow, aromatic gray-green foliage. From early- to midsummer, it produces purple flowers topped with wavy flower bracts.

↕↔28in (70cm)

Z8–9

SHRUB SMALL

Juniperus communis 'Compressa'

COMMON JUNIPER A slow-growing, dwarf evergreen coniferous shrub. It forms a slim, dense, tapering column of blue-gray foliage, and may need protection from cold winds in winter.

↕32in (80cm) ↔18in (45cm)

Z2–6 Ⓝ

BULB LARGE

Lilium 'Gran Paradiso'

ASIATIC LILY This bulb has upright stems with slender, red-flushed green leaves that are topped with heads of large, open, unscented deep orange flowers. It will gradually form a clump if left in the soil over winter. Stems may require support.

↕3ft (1m)

Z4–9

ANNUAL/BIENNIAL SMALL

Linaria maroccana

TOADFLAX A fast-growing, bushy annual with lance-shaped pale green leaves and tiny snap-dragon-like flowers in shades of red, pink, purple, yellow, or white during summer. Varieties include 'Fairy Bouquet' (above), which flowers in many colors.

↕8in (20cm) ↔6in (15cm)

PERENNIAL MEDIUM

Linum narbonense

SPANISH BLUE FLAX A clump-forming, short-lived perennial with lance-shaped grayish green leaves and clusters of saucer-shaped, pale to deep blue summer flowers. Trim after flowering to encourage further blooms. 'Heavenly Blue' is a popular choice.

↕24in (60cm) ↔12in (30cm)

Z5–9

PERENNIAL MEDIUM

Lupinus 'The Page'

LUPINE This short-lived perennial forms bushy clumps of dark green leaves divided into "fingers." In early summer, it produces tall stems of pink-red pealike blooms that may need to be supported in exposed sites.

↕3ft (1m) ↔30in (75cm)

(!) Z4–7

PERENNIAL MEDIUM

Lychnis coronaria

ROSE CAMPION An upright, clump-forming perennial, grown as a biennial, with oval, gray, slightly downy leaves. From mid- to late summer, small, bright pink flowers appear over a long period on branched gray stems. Deadhead to prevent self-seeding.

↕24in (60cm) ↔18in (45cm)

Z4–8

PERENNIAL LARGE

Melianthus major

HONEYBUSH Grown for its foliage, this perennial has blue-gray leaves divided into toothed-edged leaflets. Small, tubular brownish red flowers appear in late spring. Shelter from cold winds and provide a dry mulch in winter.

↕↔10m (3ft)

Z8–11

PERENNIAL SMALL

Oenothera speciosa

PINK EVENING PRIMROSE A short-lived, clump-forming perennial with fragrant, saucer-shaped, pure white summer flowers that age to pink, and spoon-shaped deeply cut leaves. The blooms open in the evening. Varieties include 'Rosea' (above).

↕↔ up to 12in (30cm)

Z4–8 (N)

SHRUB MEDIUM

Osmanthus delavayi

DELAVAY TEAOLIVE A rounded, bushy evergreen shrub with arching branches and glossy dark green leaves. From mid- to late spring, it forms a profusion of fragrant, tubular white flowers followed by blue-black fruits. Best in West Coast gardens.

↕6ft (2m) ↔12ft (4m) or more

Z7–9

PERENNIAL MEDIUM

Penstemon 'Sour Grapes'

BEARDTONGUE An upright semievergreen perennial with slender, lance-shaped green leaves. The tubular, bell-shaped purple-blue flowers are suffused with violet and white inside, and appear over many weeks from midsummer to fall.

↕24in (60cm) ↔18in (45cm)

Z7–10

SHRUB SMALL

Perovskia 'Blue Spire'

RUSSIAN SAGE This upright deciduous subshrub has aromatic silvery gray foliage. From late summer to fall, it bears upright branching spikes of tiny violet-blue flowers that last for several weeks. Taller plants may need support.

↕4ft (1.2m) ↔3ft (1m)

Z5–9

SHRUB MEDIUM

Philadelphus 'Belle Etoile'

MOCK ORANGE This arching deciduous shrub has small midgreen leaves and sweetly fragrant white flowers from late spring to early summer. Plant at the back of a border, or along a boundary wall or fence. The scent is strongest on sunny days.

↕6ft (1.8m) ↔8ft (2.5m)

Z5–8

PERENNIAL MEDIUM

Phlomis russeliana

STICKY JERUSALEM SAGE An evergreen perennial with large, rough-textured, heart-shaped leaves. In summer, it bears unusual hooded butter-yellow flowers set at intervals up the tall stout stems. The seedheads provide interest over winter.

↕3ft (1m) ↔24in (60cm) or more

Z4–9

SHRUB SMALL

Phygelius x *rectus*

CAPE FUCHSIA An upright semievergreen subshrub, which may die back in winter when young. It has lance-shaped green leaves and clusters of long tubular flowers in summer. 'African Queen' (above) has orange-red blooms.

↕3ft (1m) ↔4ft (1.2m)

Z8–9

SHRUB LARGE

Physocarpus opulifolius

NINEBARK A deciduous shrub with rounded lobed leaves. Compact, dome-shaped clusters of small white flowers appear in early summer, followed by reddish brown fruits. 'Diabolo' (above) sports deep purple foliage.

↕10ft (3m) ↔15ft (5m)

Z3–7 Ⓝ

SHRUB LARGE

Pittosporum tenuifolium

KOHUHU A columnar, later rounded, evergreen shrub or small tree with purple shoots and wavy-edged, oval, glossy midgreen leaves. In late spring, it bears tiny, honey-scented purple flowers. Best in West Coast gardens.

↕30ft (10m) ↔15ft (5m)

Z9–11

PERENNIAL SMALL

Potentilla 'Gibson's Scarlet'

CINQUEFOIL This clump-forming perennial has dark green leaves that resemble those of a strawberry plant. From early- to late summer, it produces saucer-shaped, bright scarlet flowers on branching stems. It also grows in part shade.

↕18in (45cm) ↔24in (60cm)

Z5–8

SHRUB MEDIUM

Prunus tenella

DWARF RUSSIAN ALMOND This is a medium-sized, bushy, upright deciduous shrub with narrowly oval, glossy green leaves. From mid- to late spring, the stems are clothed in bright pink saucer-shaped flowers.

↕↔5ft (1.5m)

(!) Z2–6

TREE LARGE

Quercus coccinea

SCARLET OAK This deciduous tree forms a rounded head of glossy, dark green lobed leaves. In fall, the foliage turns bright red, producing a bold display that can last for several weeks. Small acorns form at the same time. Best in large gardens.

↕70ft (20m) ↔50ft (15m)

Z4–9 Ⓝ

PERENNIAL LARGE

Romneya coulteri

TREE POPPY A vigorous, bushy, shrubby perennial with deeply divided gray-green leaves. It is grown for its large, fragrant, papery, golden-centered white flowers, which appear on stout stems in late summer. Mulch well with compost in fall.

↕↔6ft (2m)

Z8–10 Ⓝ

PERENNIAL MEDIUM

Rudbeckia hirta

BLACK-EYED SUSAN This is an upright, short-lived perennial, often grown as an annual, with midgreen leaves. From summer to fall, it produces daisy-like, golden or red flowers with brown centers. Varieties include 'Becky Mixed' (above).

↕up to 3ft (1m) ↔18in (45cm)

Z3–7 Ⓝ

PERENNIAL MEDIUM

Salvia x *sylvestris*

WOOD SAGE This is a compact perennial with small, dark green aromatic leaves. From early- to midsummer, 'May Night' (above) produces spikes of two-lipped, indigo-blue flowers over a long period. It is attractive to butterflies and bees.

↕32in (80cm) ↔12in (30cm)

Z4–9

SHRUB SMALL

Santolina chamaecyparissus

LAVENDER COTTON A rounded subshrub with soft, woolly, silvery white, finely divided foliage and short stems of yellow pompom flowers in summer. Trim after flowering. 'Lemon Queen' (above) has gray foliage and cream-colored blooms.

↕30in (75cm) ↔3ft (1m)

Z6–9

PERENNIAL MEDIUM

Scabiosa atropurpurea

PINCUSHION FLOWER This clump-forming perennial, grown as an annual, has lance-shaped gray-green leaves and masses of domed, lilac-purple summer flowers, adorned with creamy anthers that look like pins. Considered invasive in some areas.

↕3ft (1m) ↔12in (30cm)

Z9–11

PERENNIAL SMALL

Sedum spectabile

SHOWY STONECROP This sedum is a clump-forming perennial with succulent stems of fleshy gray-green leaves. From late summer to fall, it bears flat heads of pink flowers, followed by winter seedheads. Varieties include 'Brilliant' (above).

↕↔18in (45cm)

Z4–9

PERENNIAL MEDIUM

Solidago GOLDEN BABY

GOLDENROD This perennial forms an upright clump of stems with narrow, pointed green leaves. From midsummer to early fall, it produces branching stems of small golden-yellow blooms. Deadhead to prolong the flowering display.

↕24in (60cm) ↔18ft (45cm)

Z4–8

SHRUB MEDIUM

Spiraea nipponica

SPIREA This is a spreading deciduous shrub with arching stems of narrow dark green leaves and dense clusters of white or pink flowers, which appear in early summer. Varieties include the white-flowered 'Snowmound' (above).

↕↔8ft (2.5m)

Z4–8

ANNUAL/BIENNIAL LARGE

Verbascum olympicum

OLYMPIC MULLEIN A semievergreen biennial or short-lived perennial with rosettes of gray felted leaves and tall branching stems of saucer-shaped, bright golden flowers, which appear from mid- to late summer. It may need staking.

↕6ft (2m) ↔3ft (1m)

Z5–9

SHRUB LARGE

Stachyurus praecox

STACHYURUS An open, spreading deciduous shrub with purplish red shoots and pale greenish yellow, bell-shaped flowers that appear from late winter to early spring, before the slim, tapering dark green leaves emerge. Can be trained on a wall.

↕12ft (4m) ↔10ft (3m)

pH Z6–8

PERENNIAL MEDIUM

Veronica austriaca subsp. *teucrium*

SAW-LEAVED SPEEDWELL This upright perennial has dark green, toothed-edged leaves and spikes of rich blue flowers in early summer. Deadhead to promote more flowers the following year.

↕↔24in (60cm)

Z4–8

PERENNIAL MEDIUM

Stipa tenuissima

MEXICAN FEATHER GRASS A deciduous perennial that forms a tuft of fine green leaves. From early summer, it produces panicles of silvery green flowers that turn beige as seeds form, giving the plant a hairlike appearance.

↕24in (60cm) ↔16in (40cm)

Z7–11 Ⓝ

BULB MEDIUM

Zephyranthes candida

RAIN LILY A tender bulb with narrow, erect grassy leaves. In summer, leafless stems carry white crocuslike flowers. Plants often burst into bloom following heavy rain. Add plenty of organic matter to the soil. Bulbs can be lifted for winter.

↕10in (25cm)

Z7–9

PERENNIAL SMALL

Stokesia laevis

STOKES' ASTER An evergreen perennial with narrow midgreen leaves. It produces large, cornflowerlike, lavender- or purple-blue flowers on short stems from summer to mid-fall. Varieties include 'Purple Parasols' (above).

↕↔18in (45cm)

pH Z5–9 Ⓝ

OTHER SUGGESTIONS

Perennials

Acanthus spinosus • *Achillea filipendulina* • *Anemone hupehensis* 'September Charm' • *Artemisia lactiflora* • *Baptisia australis* Ⓝ • *Campanula persicifolia* • *Cephalaria gigantea* • *Coreopsis verticillata* 'Grandiflora' Ⓝ • *Echinops ritro* • *Salvia lyrata* 'Purple Knockout' Ⓝ • *Salvia nemorosa* 'Caradonna' • *Symphyotrichum cordifolium* 'Avondale' Ⓝ • *Symphyotrichum ericoides* 'Monte Cassino' Ⓝ • *Verbascum* 'Caribbean Crush' • *Verbena stricta* Ⓝ

Shrubs

Cephalanthus occidentalis Ⓝ • *Morella cerifera* Ⓝ

Trees

Ginkgo biloba 'Princeton Sentry' • *Juniperus virginiana* 'Burkii' Ⓝ • *Quercus stellata* Ⓝ • *Washingtonia robusta* Ⓝ

Plant focus: irises

Celebrated for their intricate and widely colored flowers, the iris family includes plants for borders, ponds, and pots.

IRISES COMPRISE A RANGE OF DIFFERENT SPECIES adapted to widely different conditions. They grow from rhizomes or bulbs and, while some thrive in shallow water, others require dry, well-drained soils. Irises that grow from rhizomes are divided into two main groups: bearded and beardless forms. Bearded types are ideal for sunny free-draining borders, with shorter species suitable for rock gardens, alpine beds, or troughs. Prone to rotting, their rhizomes must sit at or above soil level where they are exposed to full sun. Rhizomatic beardless irises have slimmer petals and most prefer well-drained borders in sun or partial shade. However, Louisiana and Laevigatae irises, which thrive in or near ponds, are also part of this group; some are invasive and should be restrained in pond baskets to prevent them from spreading. Bulbous irises include tall Dutch forms suitable for borders and cutting, colorful Juno irises, and tiny Reticulata types, ideal for planting in rock gardens and spring containers.

POPULAR IRIS FORMS

Bearded irises These early summer-flowering irises are characterized by tufted "beards" of soft hairs on the lower petals.

Beardless irises This group has slim hairless petals and includes water irises and Siberian forms that thrive in sun or part shade.

Water irises Beardless *I. laevigata*, *I. versicolor*, *I. ensata*, and the invasive flag iris, *I. pseudacorus*, grow well in shallow water and full sun.

Crested irises With a ridge on their lower petals, these early summer-flowering irises include *I. cristata* and *I. gracilipes*.

Dutch irises Grown from bulbs, these early summer-flowering forms have slim petals and grassy foliage; plant them in sun or part shade.

Reticulata irises These spring-flowering irises bear small, often scented, blooms on short stems, and are dormant from summer to winter.

USING IRISES

Irises flower from late winter to early summer and provide elegant forms and color in many parts of the garden. Plant the bulbs in fall and rhizome-forming plants in fall or spring.

Bold drifts of bearded irises create a naturalistic effect in a border teamed with late-flowering Oriental poppies.

Water irises make perfect pond-side plants. The white-striped foliage of *I. laevigata* 'Variegata' (*above*) prolongs the season of interest well after the summer flowers have faded.

Bearded irises add glamor to large containers filled with gritty free-draining soil and will flower every year if fed annually in spring.

Plants for pond perimeters

Plants that enjoy cool, damp soil at the water's edge are known as bog plants and include flowers such as iris, cardinal flower, and many forms of primrose.

Bog plants not only add interest to a garden, they also help develop and maintain habitats for the wildlife. If you have an artificial pond the water is contained, so the surrounding soil will be the same as elsewhere in the garden. However, you can replicate naturally occurring boggy conditions by digging out an area around your pond, lining it with pond liner punctured with a few drainage holes, and replacing the excavated soil, enriched with some organic material, on top of the liner. Remember to water the area well during dry spells.

PERENNIAL MEDIUM

Acorus calamus

SWEET FLAG This is an upright deciduous or semievergreen perennial marginal with grasslike green leaves and spikes of small, insignificant brown flowers in summer. Plant it in shallow water or in a bog garden.

↕3ft (1m) ↔24in (60cm)

Z4–10 Ⓝ

PERENNIAL LARGE

Aruncus dioicus

GOATSBEARD This form of goatsbeard is a tall, clump-forming perennial with large light green leaves divided into smaller leaflets. In midsummer, it produces arching stems that carry plumes of tiny, creamy white flowers.

↕6ft (2m) ↔ 4ft (1.2m)

Z3–7 Ⓝ

PERENNIAL MEDIUM

Acorus calamus 'Variegatus'

SWEET FLAG This upright deciduous or semievergreen perennial marginal produces swordlike cream-variegated leaves that are flushed rose-pink in spring. It forms a large clump that can be divided in spring.

↕30in (75cm) ↔24in (60cm)

Z4–10 Ⓝ

PERENNIAL SMALL

Acorus gramineus

GRASSY-LEAVED SWEET FLAG This is a compact semievergreen perennial marginal for bogs or ponds that produces grasslike dark green leaves. Popular varieties include 'Ogon' (above), which has attractively striped, creamy-yellow foliage.

↕10in (25cm) ↔ 6in (15cm)

Z5–9

PERENNIAL MEDIUM

Astilbe chinensis

ASTILBE This is a clump-forming perennial with deeply cut dark green leaves. In late summer, it produces upright plumes of tiny pink-white flowers. *A. chinensis* var. *pumila* has deep pink-red blooms. Keep it well watered.

↕24in (60cm) ↔ 8in (20cm)

Z4–8

PERENNIAL MEDIUM

Astilbe x *ardensii* 'Fanal'

ASTILBE This is a medium-sized, clump-forming perennial with deeply divided, fernlike dark green foliage. In midsummer, feathery dark pink flower heads appear on slim stems. Prefers rich soil; also grows well in shade.

↕24in (60cm) ↔18in (45cm)

Z3–8

BULB LARGE

Camassia leichtlinii

QUAMASH An upright deciduous bulb with long, narrow, erect lower leaves, and tall spikes of starry creamy white blooms from late spring to early summer. It flowers later than most camassias, extending its season. 'Semiplena' (above) has semidouble blooms.

↕5ft (1.5m)

Z5–9 Ⓝ

PERENNIAL LARGE

Canna 'Wyoming'

CANNA An erect perennial with decorative foliage and flowers. It produces large, oval purple-bronze leaves with darker purple veins, and gladiolus-like, pale orange flowers from midsummer to early fall. Lift the rhizomes in fall to overwinter.

↕6ft (1.8m) ↔20in (50cm)

Z8–11

PERENNIAL LARGE

Darmera peltata

UMBRELLA PLANT A spreading perennial grown for its large, round, deeply veined leaves that can become larger than dinner plates, and turn red in fall. In spring, it bears white or pale pink flower clusters on hairy stems, before the foliage appears.

↕4ft (1.2m) ↔24in (60cm)

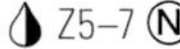 Z5–7 Ⓝ

PERENNIAL MEDIUM

Carex elata 'Aurea'

BOWLES' GOLDEN SEDGE An evergreen perennial sedge with arching golden-yellow leaves. Triangular stems bearing blackish brown flower spikes appear in summer. Plant at the edge of a bed or pond for a grassy effect.

↕28in (70cm) ↔18in (45cm)

Z5–9

PERENNIAL MEDIUM

Carex muskingumensis

PALM BRANCH SEDGE This sedge is a deciduous perennial with light green grassy foliage, which turns yellow before dying back. In spring, it produces small insignificant flowers, followed by attractive, brown seedheads. Cut back in fall.

↕↔30in (75cm)

Z4–8 Ⓝ

PERENNIAL MEDIUM

Carex pendula

PENDULOUS SEDGE An evergreen perennial sedge with long, green grassy leaves. In summer, greenish brown catkinlike flowers dangle from arching, triangular stems. Best in wildlife gardens or wild areas, where it will self-seed freely.

↕3ft (1m) ↔ up to 5ft (1.5m)

Z5–9

PERENNIAL LARGE

Eupatorium cannabinum

HEMP AGRIMONY This is a tall upright perennial with large divided leaves held on red stems. From late summer to early fall, it produces clusters of fluffy light pink or purple flowers, which are attractive to butterflies.

↕5ft (1.5m) ↔4ft (1.2m)

Z3–9

PERENNIAL LARGE

Eutrochium purpureum

JOE PYE WEED This is a stately, upright perennial with coarse oval leaves held on purplish green stems. From late summer to early fall, it produces fluffy pinkish purple flower heads on tall sturdy stems. Ideal for wildlife gardens.

↕7ft (2.2m) ↔3ft (1m)

Z4–9 Ⓝ

PERENNIAL LARGE

Filipendula purpurea

JAPANESE MEADOWSWEET This is a large, upright, clump-forming perennial with deeply divided green leaves. In late summer, it produces large clusters of tiny, rich reddish purple flowers, held on tall leafy stems.

↕4ft (1.2m) ↔24in (60cm)

 Z4–9

PERENNIAL LARGE

Filipendula rubra

QUEEN OF THE PRAIRIE An upright perennial with large aromatic leaves divided into jagged-edged green leaflets and, in midsummer, feathery plumes of tiny, soft rose-pink flowers, which pale as they age. Use it to spread through a boggy site.

↕up to 8ft (2.5m) ↔4ft (1.2m)

Z3–8 Ⓝ

PERENNIAL MEDIUM

Geum rivale

WATER AVENS This perennial forms neat rosettes of rounded green leaves. From late spring to summer, slender stems topped with nodding, bell-shaped pink or dark orange blooms appear. Plant it at the front of a bed; it may self-seed and spread slowly.

↕↔24in (60cm)

Z3–8

PERENNIAL SMALL

Houttuynia cordata 'Chameleon'

HOUTTUYNIA This vigorous deciduous perennial has aromatic, heart-shaped, yellow- and red-splashed green leaves and sprays of greenish white summer flowers. Contain to control invasive spread.

↕4in (10cm) ↔ indefinite

 Z5–10

PERENNIAL MEDIUM

Iris ensata

JAPANESE WATER IRIS This upright, clump-forming perennial has straplike, drooping green foliage and beardless yellow-blazed purple or red-purple flowers from early- to midsummer. 'Rose Queen' (above) has lilac-pink flowers.

↕3ft (1m) ↔ 24ft (60cm)

Z4–9

PERENNIAL MEDIUM

Iris sibirica

SIBERIAN IRIS A clump-forming perennial with upright, swordlike blue-green leaves and large beardless flowers in shades of blue, pink, white, and yellow from late spring to early summer. 'Butter and Sugar' (above) has yellow and white blooms.

↕3ft (1m) ↔ indefinite

(!) Z3–9

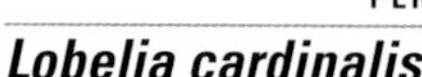

PERENNIAL MEDIUM

Lobelia cardinalis

CARDINAL FLOWER This upright deciduous perennial has narrow, lance-shaped glossy green leaves and striking scarlet spires of two-lipped summer flowers on tall stems. It is toxic; wear gloves when handling. It attracts butterflies and hummingbirds.

↕30in (75cm) ↔ 9in (23in)

(!) Z3–9 (N)

PERENNIAL MEDIUM

Iris versicolor

BLUE FLAG This upright, clump-forming perennial, with arching strap-shaped foliage and blue-purple flowers in early summer, can be grown in a bog or shallow water. Varieties include the purple-pink 'Kermensina' (above).

↕32in (80cm) ↔ indefinite

Z3–9 (N)

TREE MEDIUM

Liquidambar styraciflua

SWEET GUM A conical to spreading deciduous tree with large, lobed, glossy dark green leaves that turn brilliant orange, red, and purple in fall. 'Variegata' (above) has gold-splashed foliage. Site it some distance from the pond edge.

↕50ft (15m) ↔ 25ft (8m)

Z5–9 (N)

PERENNIAL MEDIUM

Lobelia siphilitica

BLUE CARDINAL FLOWER This is an upright perennial with narrow, lance-shaped light green leaves. From mid- to late summer, it produces tall spikes of long-lasting, tubular, two-lipped blue flowers. Plant it toward the back of a bed.

↕3ft (1m) ↔ 9in (23cm)

(!) Z4–8 (N)

PERENNIAL MEDIUM

Lysimachia clethroides

GOOSENECK LOOSESTRIFE This is a vigorous, clump-forming, spreading perennial with narrow, lance-shaped gray-green foliage. In late summer, it produces long, tapering flower heads comprising small white blooms.

↕↔3ft (1m)

Z3–8

PERENNIAL MEDIUM

Persicaria microcephala 'Red Dragon'

KNOTWEED This vigorous, spreading perennial has heart-shaped reddish green leaves with silver and bronze markings. Tiny white flowers appear in midsummer. Cut back spent flower stems in fall.

↕28in (70cm) ↔ 3ft (1m)

Z5–9

PERENNIAL LARGE

Physostegia virginiana var. *speciosa*

OBEDIENT PLANT An erect perennial with lance-shaped, toothed-edged green leaves and spikes of hooded, two-lipped rose-purple flowers in late summer. 'Variegata' (above) has white-edged leaves.

↕4ft (1.2m) ↔24in (60cm)

Z3–9 Ⓝ

PERENNIAL LARGE

Primula florindae

GIANT COWSLIP A clump-forming perennial with oval green leaves and clusters of fragrant, bell-shaped nodding flowers on slim stems in summer. Deadhead to prevent self-seeding and to encourage repeat flowering.

↕4ft (1.2m) ↔3ft (1m)

Z3–8

PERENNIAL SMALL

Primula japonica

JAPANESE PRIMROSE This deciduous perennial produces rosettes of oval, toothed-edged, pale green leaves. In early summer, clusters of tubular, deep red flowers appear on stout stems. 'Miller's Crimson' (above) has deep crimson flowers.

↕↔18in (45cm)

Z4–8

PERENNIAL MEDIUM

Primula vialii

ORCHID PRIMROSE This clump-forming perennial produces rosettes of oval green leaves. In late spring, tapering cones of small, tubular bluish purple and red flowers appear on slim stems above the leaves.

↕24in (60cm) ↔12in (30cm)

Z5–8

PERENNIAL LARGE

Salvia uliginosa

BOG SAGE This tall, upright, branching perennial has oblong to lance-shaped, deeply toothed, slightly sticky midgreen leaves. From late summer to fall, two-lipped blue flowers appear. The stems require staking; mulch well in fall.

↕6ft (2m) ↔3ft (1m)

Z6–10

PERENNIAL LARGE

Sanguisorba canadensis

CANADIAN BURNET This perennial has a clump-forming habit, and produces midgreen divided foliage that turns red in fall. From late summer to early fall, it produces upright spikes of bottlebrush-like white flowers on sturdy stems.

↕6ft (2m) ↔24in (60cm)

Z3–8 Ⓝ

TREE LARGE

Taxodium distichum

BALD CYPRESS This is a broadly conical deciduous conifer with feathery green foliage that turns yellow-brown in late fall before dropping. Small oval cones appear in summer. It is a large tree, best suited to large yards.

↕130ft (40m) ↔28ft (9m)

pH Z5–11 Ⓝ

PERENNIAL MEDIUM

Trollius x *cultorum*

GLOBEFLOWER An upright, clump-forming perennial with lobed, toothed-edged dark green leaves. From late spring to early summer, it produces buttercup-like, bowl-shaped semidouble flowers. 'Lemon Queen' (above) has pale yellow blooms.

↕24in (60cm) ↔18in (45cm)

Z3–7

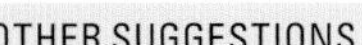

OTHER SUGGESTIONS

Perennials

Anagallis monellii • *Aruncus* 'Misty Lace' • *Asclepias incarnata* Ⓝ • *Cardamine concatenata* Ⓝ • *Carex testacea* • *Gunnera magellanica* • *Hibiscus coccineus* Ⓝ • *Hymenocallis caroliniana* Ⓝ • *Iris chrysographes* • *Iris virginica* Ⓝ • *Lobelia* 'Russian Princess' • *Primula beesiana* • *Primula* x *bulleesiana* • *Primula bulleyana* • *Ranunculus acris* 'Flore Pleno' • *Vernonia noveboracensis* Ⓝ

Shrubs

Cephalanthus occidentalis Ⓝ • *Ilex verticillata* 'Red Sprite' Ⓝ • *Salix integra* 'Hakuro-nishiki'

Trees

Halesia carolina Ⓝ • *Liquidambar styraciflua* 'Rotundiloba' Ⓝ

Plants for ponds

Reflections of colorful aquatic plants in pools of sparkling water create a magical scene in a yard or garden, large or small, in an open, sunny site.

You can plant a tiny, formal water feature in an urban garden, or a wildlife pond in a rambling plot, to create a textural backdrop. Use plants with different foliage forms, such as strap-leaved cattail alongside the spear-shaped leaves of arrowhead. Add a splash of color with bright yellow marsh marigold and scarlet monkey flower for hot schemes or cool-hued waterlily, iris, and calla lily for a pastel palette. Check plant labels for the correct planting depths. While some plants like their roots completely submerged, others are happier languishing in the shallows.

WATER PLANT MEDIUM

Alisma plantago-aquatica

WATER PLANTAIN A deciduous perennial marginal with large, oval bright green leaves held well above the water. It produces slim branching stems of small pale pink to white flowers in summer. May be aggressive. The leaves may irritate skin.

↕30in (75cm) ↔18in (45cm)

(!) Z5–8 (N)

PERENNIAL SMALL

Calla palustris

BOG ARUM A spreading deciduous or semievergreen, perennial marginal with heart-shaped, glossy dark green leaves. In late spring, it bears large, white petal-like "spathes," followed by red or orange berries in fall. All parts of the plant are poisonous.

↕10in (25cm) ↔12in (30cm)

(!) Z4–8 (N)

PERENNIAL SMALL

Caltha palustris

MARSH MARIGOLD This is a deciduous perennial marginal with rounded dark green leaves and clusters of cup-shaped bright golden-yellow flowers, which appear on upright stems above the foliage in spring. Also suitable for pond perimeters.

↕16in (40cm) ↔18in (45cm)

Z3–7 (N)

PERENNIAL SMALL

Caltha palustris 'Flore Pleno'

syn. *Caltha* 'Multiplex' This perennial has dark green rounded leaves and produces clusters of bright golden double flowers in spring. The form *C. palustris* var. *alba* is compact, with single white flowers. It is also suitable for pond perimeters.

↕↔10in (25cm)

Z3–7 (N)

WATER PLANT MEDIUM

Ceratophyllum demersum

HORNWORT This is a deep-water deciduous aquatic plant that helps to keep pond water clear and provides cover for wildlife. It produces slim spreading stems of feathery dark green foliage, and tiny white flowers in summer.

↔indefinite

Z6–9 (N)

PERENNIAL SMALL

Eriophorum angustifolium

COTTON GRASS This is a small, vigorous, spreading perennial marginal with grasslike green leaves. Downy white flowers that resemble cotton tufts appear on slim stems in summer. Contain in a pond basket to restrict its spread.

↕18in (45cm) ↔indefinite

pH Z5–9 (N)

PERENNIAL MEDIUM

Iris laevigata

JAPANESE WATER IRIS This is an upright, clump-forming perennial marginal with sword-shaped, smooth midgreen leaves. In early summer, it produces rich purple flowers with gold marks on the lower petals on tall slim stems.

↕3ft (1m) or more ↔indefinite

(!) Z4–9

PERENNIAL MEDIUM

Iris laevigata 'Variegata'

JAPANESE WATER IRIS This is an upright, clump-forming perennial marginal with sword-shaped white- and green-striped foliage. The purple-blue flowers, which appear in summer, sometimes bloom a second time in early fall.

↕3ft (1m) ↔20in (50cm)

(!) Z4–9

PERENNIAL MEDIUM

Iris versicolor

BLUE FLAG This is an upright, clump-forming perennial marginal with sword-shaped leaves. In early summer, it produces blue-purple flowers on branched stems. 'Whodunit' (above) bears purple-edged white flowers with purple veining.

↕32in (80cm) ↔indefinite

Z3–9 (N)

PERENNIAL SMALL

Juncus effusus f. *spiralis*

CORKSCREW RUSH An evergreen perennial marginal or bog plant with leafless tubular stems that twist and curl and are often prostrate. In summer, it produces small greenish brown flowers that seed easily; deadhead to keep in check.

↕12in (30cm) ↔24in (60cm)

Z6–9 (N)

WATER PLANT SMALL

Menyanthes trifoliata

BOG BEAN This perennial marginal has unusual upright green leaves divided into three leaflets held at the end of floating, spreading stems. Clusters of small fringed white flowers open from cerise buds in early spring.

↕9in (23cm) ↔indefinite

Z4–8 (N)

PERENNIAL MEDIUM

Mimulus cardinalis

SCARLET MONKEY FLOWER This is a spreading perennial marginal, often grown as an annual, with small, toothed, downy green leaves. Masses of two-lipped tomato-red flowers cover the plant from summer to early fall.

↕3ft (1m) ↔24in (60cm)

Z6–9 (N)

WATER PLANT LARGE

Nuphar lutea

YELLOW POND LILY This is a vigorous, spreading, deep-water aquatic perennial, with round, floating green leaves, similar to those of a water lily. In summer, buttercup-like flowers that smell like alcohol appear on stalks above the foliage.

↔5ft (1.5m)

Z3–9 (N)

WATER PLANT LARGE

Nymphaea 'Escarboucle'

HARDY WATERLILY A deep-water aquatic perennial with dark green, floating deciduous leaves. In summer, cup-shaped, deep crimson flowers with bright golden-yellow centers appear. It spreads and is best suited to larger ponds with calm water.

↔10ft (3m)

Z4–11

WATER PLANT SMALL

Nymphaea pygmaea 'Rubra'

HARDY WATERLILY This aquatic perennial has round, floating green leaves with red undersides and purple blotches. It bears rose-colored cup-shaped blooms from mid- to late summer, maturing to garnet-red. Ideal for smaller ponds; requires still water.

↔16in (40cm)

Z4–11 (N)

WATER PLANT SMALL

Orontium aquaticum

GOLDEN CLUB A deep-water deciduous aquatic perennial that helps to keep pond water clear. It produces blue-gray floating leaves and, in spring, pencil-like gold and white flower spikes. Restrict its spread by planting in a large pond basket.
↕18in (45cm) ↔30in (75cm)

Z6–10 Ⓝ

WATER PLANT SMALL

Persicaria amphibia

WATER SMARTWEED A vigorous perennial marginal with lance-shaped, dark green floating leaves. From midsummer to fall, it produces conical clusters of pink flowers on stout stems above the foliage, followed by glossy brown fruits.
↕12in (30cm) ↔6ft (2m)

Z3–9 Ⓝ

PERENNIAL MEDIUM

Pontederia cordata

PICKEREL WEED This is an upright perennial marginal with large, spear-shaped, glossy midgreen leaves. In late summer, dense spikes of blue flowers emerge on stout stems. Varieties include 'Alba' with white flowers.
↕30in (75cm) ↔18in (45cm)

Z3–11

PERENNIAL SMALL

Ranunculus aquatilis

WATER CROWFOOT This perennial marginal is one of the best flowering oxygenators, helping keep pond water clear. It bears mats of ivy-shaped, toothed leaves and yellow-centered, buttercup-like white floating flowers in summer.
↕½in (1cm) ↔indefinite

Z5–8

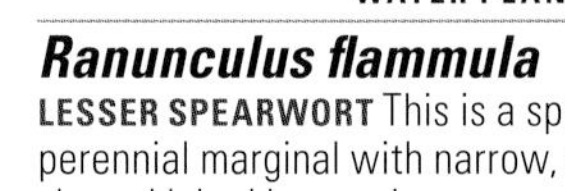

WATER PLANT MEDIUM

Ranunculus flammula

LESSER SPEARWORT This is a spreading perennial marginal with narrow, spear-shaped lobed leaves. In summer, it bears masses of buttercup-like, single yellow flowers on wiry stems. The plant is toxic, and the sap causes skin irritation.
↕28in (70cm) ↔30in (75cm)

(!) Z5–9

PERENNIAL LARGE

Sagittaria latifolia

BROADLEAF ARROWHEAD This large, vigorous perennial marginal is grown for its large, arrow-shaped green leaves. In summer, it produces small white flowers with yellow centers on leafless stems.
↕5ft (1.5m) ↔24in (60cm)

Z5–11 Ⓝ

PERENNIAL SMALL

Sagittaria sagittifolia

JAPANESE ARROWHEAD A perennial marginal, grown for its upright, arrow-shaped midgreen leaves. In summer, it produces clusters of three-petaled white flowers with dark purple centers. The cultivar 'Flore Pleno' is double-flowered.
↕18in (45cm) ↔12in (30cm)

Z5–9

PERENNIAL MEDIUM

Saururus cernuus

LIZARD'S TAIL This is a perennial marginal that produces clumps of heart-shaped midgreen leaves and long, slim stems of creamy white flowers in summer. Possibly aggressive, restrict its spread by planting in a large pond basket.
↕3ft (1m) ↔indefinite

Z5–10 Ⓝ

PERENNIAL LARGE

Schoenoplectus lacustris subsp. *tabernaemontani*

CLUB RUSH A tall, upright, spreading perennial aquatic sedge with leafless, grassy stems. Brown flower heads appear in summer. 'Zebrinus' (above) has creamy yellow leaves with horizontal stripes.

↕5ft (1.5m) ↔ indefinite

Z6–9 Ⓝ

PERENNIAL MEDIUM

Typha minima

DWARF CATTAIL This small cattail is a perennial marginal with grasslike midgreen leaves. It produces spikes of short, sausage-shaped blackish brown flower heads in late summer. Suitable for smaller ponds and patio water features.

↕24in (60cm) ↔ 12in (30cm)

Z3–11

PERENNIAL LARGE

Thalia dealbata

POWDERY ALLIGATOR FLAG This evergreen perennial marginal has large, oval gray-green leaves that are dusted with white powder. In summer, it bears long stems topped with small purple flowers.

↕5ft (1.5m) ↔ 24in (60cm)

Z6–11 Ⓝ

PERENNIAL LARGE

Typha angustifolia

NARROWLEAF CATTAIL A tall, vigorous, clump-forming perennial marginal with arching grasslike leaves. Sausage-shaped, dark brown flower heads appear in summer. The plant is aggressive; restrict its spread by planting in a large pond basket.

↕5ft (1.5m) ↔ indefinite

Z3–11 Ⓝ

PERENNIAL MEDIUM

Zantedeschia aethiopica

CALLA LILY This is a perennial marginal or bog plant with large, arrow-shaped dark green leaves. In summer, it produces white petal-like spathes, each with a yellow spike in the center. 'Crowborough' is a popular variety.

↕3ft (1m) ↔ 24in (60cm)

(!) Z8–10

PERENNIAL MEDIUM

Zantedeschia aethiopica 'Green Goddess'

CALLA LILY A semievergreen perennial marginal with large dark green leaves and green hoodlike "spathes" with splashes of white in the throat and yellow central spikes in summer. Suitable for bog gardens.

↕3ft (1m) ↔ 24in (60cm)

(!) Z8–10

PERENNIAL LARGE

Typha latifolia

BROADLEAF CATTAIL A large, vigorous perennial marginal with slender grasslike foliage. It bears sausage-shaped dark brown flower heads in summer. The plant is aggressive; best in large ponds, confine to a planting basket to prevent it spreading.

↕8ft (2.5m) ↔ 24in (60cm)

Z3–11 Ⓝ

OTHER SUGGESTIONS

Marginals

Acorus calamus Ⓝ • *Butomus umbellatus* Ⓝ • *Cabomba caroliniana* Ⓝ • *Canna* 'Endeavor' • *Cardamine pratensis* Ⓝ • *Carex muskingumensis* Ⓝ • *Carex stricta* Ⓝ • *Cyperus papyrus* 'King Tut' • *Eleocharis palustris* • *Equisetum hyemale* Ⓝ • *Hymenocallis caroliniana* Ⓝ • *Iris fulva* Ⓝ • *Iris versicolor* 'Mysterious Monique' Ⓝ • *Juncus* 'Blue Dart' • *Lysichiton americanus* Ⓝ • *Lysichiton camtschatcensis* • *Mentha aquatica* • *Menyanthes trifoliata* Ⓝ • *Mimulus guttatus* Ⓝ • *Mimulus ringens* Ⓝ • *Nelumbo lutea* Ⓝ • *Peltandra virginica* Ⓝ • *Ruellia brittoniana* 'Katie' Ⓝ • *Sagittaria graminea* Ⓝ • *Schoenoplectus validus* Ⓝ • *Scirpus atrovirens* Ⓝ • *Victoria* 'Longwood Hybrid'

Plant focus: water lilies

The most flamboyant of all aquatic plants, water lilies are prized for their large, colorful summer flowers and decorative foliage.

Water lilies, known botanically as *Nymphaea*, make beautiful features in ponds and pools, where their dramatic blooms and rounded leaves create waves of color throughout the summer months. As well as providing ornamental value, water lilies play a useful role in aquatic ecosystems, their large leaves helping to regulate the water temperature and shield resident flora and fauna from pests and predators. When choosing a water lily, check the plant label for its final spread to ensure it will suit the size and depth of your pond. Also note that the tropical blue and purple forms are not hardy in most gardens and can be treated as an annual or overwintered in a warm, frost-free environment, such as a conservatory. Most water lilies grow at depths of between 18in (45cm) and 4ft (1.2m), although dwarf hybrids will thrive in shallow water less than 12in (30cm) deep. All forms prefer full sun and still water and do not grow well in streams or too close to fountains or waterfalls.

WATER LILY FORMS

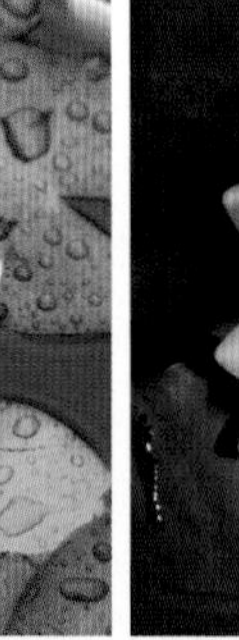

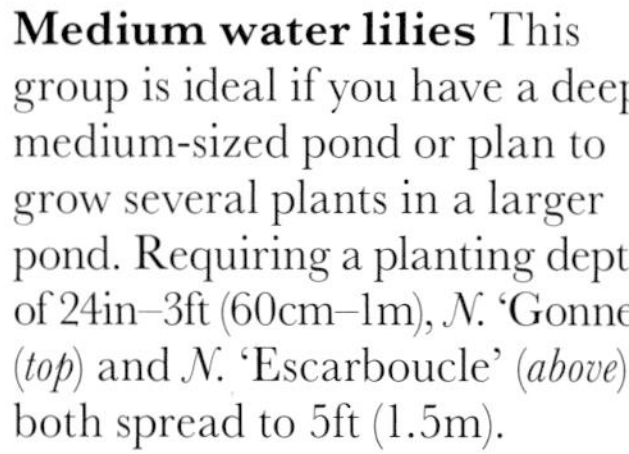

Small water lilies Best suited to smaller ponds and features, this group prefers shallow water and a planting depth of 12–18in (30–45cm). Varieties include the pink-red *N.* 'Ellisiana' (*top*) and the pale yellow *N.* 'Pygmaea Helvola' (*above*), which both spread to 3ft (1m).

Medium water lilies This group is ideal if you have a deeper, medium-sized pond or plan to grow several plants in a larger pond. Requiring a planting depth of 24in–3ft (60cm–1m), *N.* 'Gonnere' (*top*) and *N.* 'Escarboucle' (*above*) both spread to 5ft (1.5m).

Large water lilies Only suitable for large ponds and lakes, these water lilies require a planting depth of 3–6ft (1–2m) and spread to more than 6ft (1.8m) across. *N.* 'Attraction' (*top*) has white or pink blooms. *N. alba* (*above*) produces large, pure white summer flowers.

USING WATER LILIES

Although water lilies will tolerate light shade, they flower best in full sun. New plants may take a year or two to reach full flowering size and should be split every 4–5 years to maintain vigor.

Miniature ponds Small-sized pygmy water lily varieties are ideal for growing in watertight patio containers, such as a half-barrel fitted with pond liner.

Wildlife ponds The leaves of water lilies help protect pond wildlife by cooling the water during summer. They also help to reduce algal growth, which keeps the water clear, healthy, and well oxygenated.

Formal ponds One or two lilies grown as specimens in a raised pool add an elegant note to a formal garden design.

Plants for boundaries, hedges, and windbreaks

Plants make beautiful screens, carving up the space within a yard or a garden, or marking boundaries with foliage and flowers.

Choose from smooth, green walls made from clipped yew or boxwood to set off a formal scheme, or colorful, textured screens using abelia or forsythia for an informal design. Hedges that bear flowers include St. John's wort, lavender, and viburnum, which offer a long season of interest. If watching wildlife is your hobby, make a home for birds, animals, and insects with a medley of crabapple, rose, and hornbeam. Some shrubs can also provide protection, with their thorns helping to keep intruders at bay. So, if security is an issue, select the fiercely armored firethorn or a spiny holly.

SHRUB LARGE

Abelia x *grandiflora*

GLOSSY ABELIA This is an arching deciduous or semievergreen shrub with oval green leaves that are bronze when young. From midsummer to fall, it produces masses of trumpet-shaped, pink-tinged white blooms. Clip in spring.
↕10ft (3m) ↔12ft (4m)
Z6–9

SHRUB MEDIUM

Berberis julianae

WINTERGREEN BARBERRY An evergreen shrub with glossy, oval dark green leaves, spiny stems, and yellow late spring flowers followed by blue-black fruits. Trim lightly in summer after the blooms have faded. Use as a formidable anti-intruder hedge.
↕8ft (2.5m) ↔10ft (3m)
Z6–8

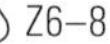

SHRUB LARGE

Berberis x *stenophylla*

HEDGE BARBERRY An arching, prickly evergreen shrub with narrow, spine-tipped dark green leaves, blue-gray beneath. Small yellow spring flowers are followed by small blue-black fruits. Trim lightly in summer after the flowers have faded.
↕10ft (3m) ↔15ft (5m)
Z6–9

SHRUB MEDIUM

Buxus sempervirens 'Elegantissima'

COMMON BOXWOOD This rounded, compact evergreen shrub has oval green leaves with white margins. It makes a dense, waist-high formal hedge; clip twice a year in early and late summer.
↕↔5ft (1.5m)
Z6–8

SHRUB SMALL

Buxus sempervirens 'Suffruticosa'

COMMON BOXWOOD This slow-growing, compact evergreen shrub has woody stems of small, oval green leaves. Ideal for topiary and for low, formal hedges or border edging. Clip twice a year in early and late summer.
↕3ft (1m) ↔5ft (1.5m)
Z6–8

TREE LARGE

Carpinus betulus

EUROPEAN HORNBEAM A deciduous tree with oval, veined dark green leaves that turn yellow and orange in fall; young stems retain the dried foliage in winter. Bears green catkins in late spring. Use for formal or wildlife hedging; prune in midsummer.
↕80ft (25m) ↔70ft (20m)
Z4–8

TREE SMALL

Cornus mas

CORNELIAN CHERRY This deciduous tree bears oval green leaves that turn purple in fall. From winter to early spring, small yellow flowers appear on bare shoots, followed by edible fruits. Use it as a screening plant; prune in early summer.
↕25ft (8m) ↔20ft (6m)
Z4–8

SHRUB LARGE

Corylus avellana

EUROPEAN FILBERT A large spreading shrub or small tree with rounded, deeply veined green leaves that turn yellow in fall. Yellow catkins in spring are followed by edible nuts in fall. Ideal for attracting wildlife; prune in late winter.
↕↔15ft (5m)
Z4–8

TREE LARGE

x *Cuprocyparis* 'Castlewellan'

LEYLAND CYPRSS This upright, vigorous conifer is slightly slower growing than the species. It bears bronze-tinged golden foliage. Makes an excellent hedge or windbreak in large yards or gardens. Cut annually in early fall to keep in check.
↕80ft (25m) ↔12ft (4m)
Z6–9

SHRUB LARGE

Elaeagnus x *ebbingei*

OLEASTER This vigorous evergreen shrub has broadly oval dark green leaves covered with a silvery dusting. Clip it in late summer. Colorful variegated forms, such as 'Gilt Edge', are also available, which form attractive informal screens.

↕↔ 15ft (5m)

Z7–9

SHRUB MEDIUM

Escallonia 'Apple Blossom'

ESCALLONIA A compact evergreen shrub with small, glossy, leathery dark green leaves. From early to midsummer, it bears a profusion of pink flowers on leafy stems. Clip hedges in late summer after flowering. Best in West Coast gardens.

↕↔ 8ft (2.5m)

Z8–9

TREE LARGE

Fagus sylvatica

EUROPEAN BEECH The oval, wavy-edged, textured green leaves of this large deciduous tree turn orange-brown in fall and persist through winter, if regularly pruned. Trim hedges in winter to keep them dense and compact.

↕ 80ft (25m) ↔ 50ft (15m)

Z4–7

SHRUB LARGE

Forsythia x *intermedia*

BORDER FORSYTHIA This deciduous shrub bears masses of pale yellow flowers from late winter to early spring, before the small green leaves appear. It makes a low screen when pruned in spring after flowering. 'Lynwood Variety' (above) is popular.

↕↔ 10ft (3m)

Z5–8

SHRUB MEDIUM

Fuchsia magellanica var. *molinae*

HARDY FUCHSIA An upright deciduous shrub with small, lance-shaped green leaves and pendent, pale pink flowers from summer to early fall on arching stems. Prune hedges in spring. Best in West Coast gardens.

↕↔ 6ft (2m)

Z7–9

SHRUB LARGE

Griselinia littoralis

NEW ZEALAND BROADLEAF A fast-growing evergreen shrub with leathery, midgreen oval leaves. Ideal for coastal areas; trim hedges lightly in summer with pruners to avoid damaging the leaves. A New Zealand native, it is best in West Coast gardens.

↕ 25ft (8m) ↔ 15ft (5m)

Z7–9

SHRUB SMALL

Hypericum 'Hidcote'

ST. JOHN'S WORT This is an evergreen or semievergreen shrub with oval dark green leaves. From midsummer to early fall, large golden-yellow flowers appear. Use it as an informal hedge; trim in spring with pruners.

↕ 4ft (1.2m) ↔ 5ft (1.5m)

Z6–9

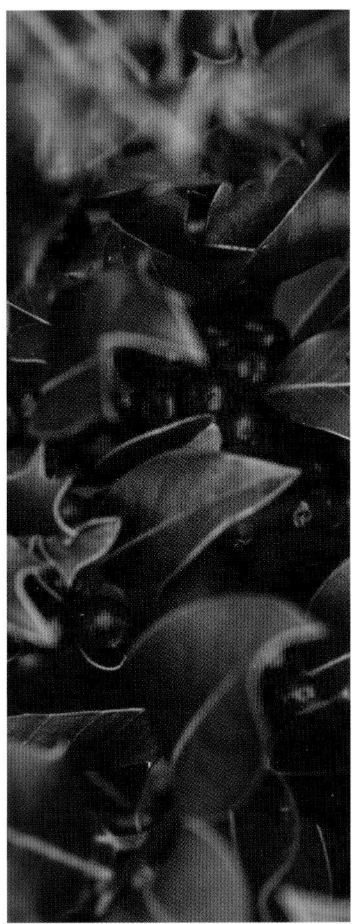

TREE LARGE

Ilex aquifolium

ENGLISH HOLLY A slow-growing evergreen tree with dark green glossy leaves. Armed with long pointed spines, it bears bright red berries in fall. Suitable for formal or wildlife hedges, and intruder-proof boundaries. Trim using pruners. Can be invasive.

↕ 70ft (20m) ↔ 20ft (6m)

(!) Z7–9

SHRUB SMALL

Lavandula angustifolia

ENGLISH LAVENDER A bushy evergreen subshrub with slim, aromatic silvery gray leaves. In summer, it bears spikes of small, fragrant violet-blue flowers. Creates a colorful low boundary. Trim in late winter to encourage strong, compact growth.

↕ 32in (80cm) ↔ 24in (60cm)

Z5–8

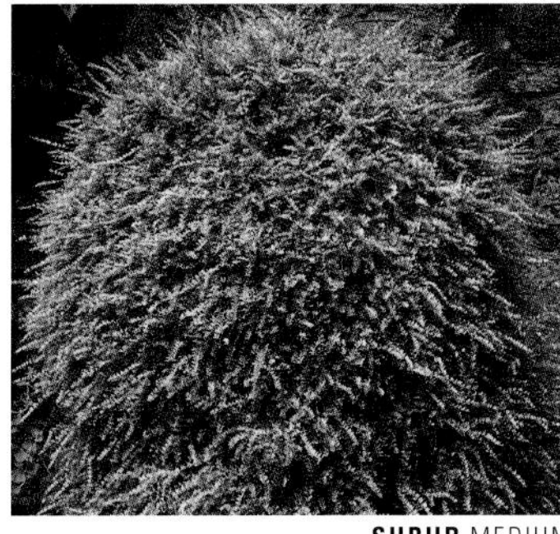

SHRUB MEDIUM

Lonicera nitida

BOXLEAF HONEYSUCKLE A bushy evergreen shrub with arching shoots covered with tiny dark green leaves. It is suitable for formal hedges; trim regularly between spring and fall. 'Baggesen's Gold' (above) has golden leaves.

↕ 6ft (2m) ↔ 10ft (3m)

(!) Z7–9

TREE LARGE

Magnolia grandiflora

SOUTHERN MAGNOLIA This dense evergreen tree has large glossy leaves and bears cup-shaped, fragrant white flowers in summer. Use it to create a tall informal boundary rather than clipped hedge. Trim lightly in spring using pruners.

↕60ft (18m) ↔50ft (15m)

Z7–9 Ⓝ

SHRUB LARGE

Malus sargentii

CRABAPPLE This spreading deciduous shrub has arching branches and white or pink mid-spring flowers followed by small red or yellow fruits, and vivid fall tints. Use to create an informal boundary with year-round interest. Prefers fertile soil.

↕12ft (4m) ↔15ft (5m)

Z4–8

SHRUB LARGE

Osmanthus x *burkwoodii*

OSMANTHUS This large, dense evergreen shrub bears glossy dark green foliage and a profusion of small, highly fragrant, white flowers from mid- to late spring. Use it as a tall formal or informal hedge; prune after flowering.

↕↔10ft (3m)

Z7–9

SHRUB LARGE

Photinia x *fraseri* 'Red Robin'

RED TIP A large, dense evergreen shrub with glossy dark reddish-green leaves, which are bright red when young. It makes a decorative, informal hedge or screen; trim with pruners in spring and again in summer.

↕↔15ft (5m)

Z7–9

BAMBOO LARGE

Phyllostachys viridiglaucescens

GREENWAX GOLDEN BAMBOO An evergreen bamboo with greenish brown canes that mature to yellow-green, and bright green linear leaves. Use as an informal screen; cut out dead, weak, and old canes in spring.

↕25ft (8m) ↔ indefinite

Z7–11

TREE LARGE

Pinus strobus

EASTERN WHITE PINE This is a conifer tree with gray-green foliage and cylindrical cones. The bark becomes fissured with age. Prune regularly and use as an informal boundary. It is only suitable for large yards or gardens.

↕120ft (35m) ↔25ft (8m)

Z3–8 Ⓝ

SHRUB LARGE

Prunus laurocerasus

CHERRY LAUREL A dense evergreen dense shrub with large, glossy dark green leaves and spikes of small white flowers in spring, followed by red fruits that turn black. Makes a dense informal hedge; prune in spring.

↕25ft (8m) ↔30ft (10m)

Z6–8

SHRUB LARGE

Prunus lusitanica

LAUREL This is a dense evergreen shrub with large glossy leaves. Slender spikes of small, fragrant white summer flowers are followed by purple fruits. Use as a formal hedge or informal boundary; prune in spring.

↕↔30ft (10m)

Z7–9

SHRUB LARGE

Pyracantha 'Mohave'

FIRETHORN An evergreen shrub with green leaves and spiny stems. Clusters of orange-red berries follow the white early summer blooms. Cut formal hedges in spring and late summer or leave to grow as a wildlife hedge. It is resistant to scab.

↕↔12ft (4m)

Z6–9

SHRUB MEDIUM

Ribes sanguineum

FLOWERING CURRANT This deciduous shrub has lobed ivy-shaped leaves and drooping clusters of crimson flowers in spring, followed by blue-black fruits with a white bloom. Use it as an informal hedge; prune in summer after fruiting.

↕6ft (2m) ↔8ft (2.5m)

Z6–8 Ⓝ

SHRUB MEDIUM

Rosa glauca

REDLEAF ROSE The arching red stems of this species rose bear grayish purple leaves and rose-pink single flowers in summer with pale centers, followed by red hips in fall. Use as an informal hedge; prune in late winter.

↕6ft (2m) ↔5ft (1.5m)

Z2–8

SHRUB MEDIUM

Symphoricarpos x *doorenbosii*

SNOWBERRY This dense, vigorous deciduous shrub has small, round dark green leaves and greenish white summer flowers, which are followed by round white fruits. Use it as an informal hedge; trim annually in early spring.

↕6ft (2m) ↔indefinite

 Z4–7

SHRUB LARGE

Syringa vulgaris

COMMON LILAC This upright, spreading deciduous shrub has glossy green leaves and blue, pink, or white scented flower spikes in summer. Use as an informal boundary; clip lightly after flowering. It has become invasive in many areas of the US.

↕↔22ft (7m)

Z3–7

TREE LARGE

Taxus baccata

ENGLISH YEW A bushy evergreen tree with needlelike dark green leaves and red berries in fall. It makes a superb hedge for boundaries or dividing up a garden. Clip in spring and summer; tolerates hard pruning, if necessary. All parts are highly toxic.

↕50ft (15m) ↔30ft (10m)

Z6–7

TREE SMALL

Taxus x *media*

YEW This evergreen conifer has flattened, needlelike dark green leaves and tiny white summer blooms, followed by red berries on female plants. It is faster growing than *T. baccata*; trim in spring and summer. All parts are toxic.

↕20ft (6m) ↔12ft (4m)

Z5–7

TREE LARGE

Thuja occidentalis

AMERICAN ARBORVITAE This evergreen conifer produces flat sprays of scalelike yellowish green leaves that are pale or grayish green beneath, and yellow-green cones that ripen to brown. It makes a dense formal hedge; trim in late winter.

↕50ft (15m) ↔15ft (5m)

Z2–7 Ⓝ

TREE LARGE

Thuja plicata

WESTERN RED CEDAR This is an evergreen conifer with scalelike, glossy dark green leaves, which give off a pineapple aroma when crushed. The green cones ripen to brown. Suitable as a formal hedge; trim it annually in late winter.

↕100ft (30m) ↔25ft (8m)

Z5–7 Ⓝ

TREE LARGE

Tilia cordata

LITTLELEAF LINDEN This deciduous tree has heart-shaped, glossy dark green leaves that turn yellow in fall. Small yellowish white flowers appear in summer. Ideal for pleaching or as a formal hedge; trim in summer.

↕100ft (30m) ↔40ft (12m)

Z3–7

TREE LARGE

Tsuga heterophylla

WESTERN HEMLOCK An evergreen conifer with drooping stems bearing needlelike, flattened dark green leaves that have silvery bands beneath. The green cones ripen to dark brown. Makes a tall, dense formal hedge; trim in early fall.

↕100ft (30m) ↔30ft (10m)

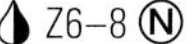

SHRUB LARGE

Viburnum farreri

FRAGRANT VIBURNUM This upright deciduous shrub has dark green foliage, bronze-tinted when young. From late fall to early spring, it bears fragrant white or pale pink blooms. Use as an informal screen; trim after flowering.

↕10ft (3m) ↔8ft (2.5m)

Z5–8

SHRUB LARGE

Viburnum tinus

LAURUSTINUS This is a bushy evergreen shrub with oval dark green leaves. Abundant flat heads of small white blooms open from pink buds during late winter and spring. Use as an informal screen; trim after flowering.

↕↔10ft (3m)

Z8–10

OTHER SUGGESTIONS

Shrubs

Aronia arbutifolia 'Brilliantissima' Ⓝ • *Buxus* CHICAGOLAND GREEN • *Cornus amomum* Ⓝ • *Corylus americana* Ⓝ • *Cotinus coggygria* GOLDEN SPIRIT • *Cotoneaster horizontalis* • *Fothergilla major* Ⓝ • *Ilex glabra* 'Shamrock' Ⓝ • *Itea virginica* Ⓝ • *Rosa pimpinellifolia* • *Rosa setigera* Ⓝ • *Viburnum lentago* Ⓝ • *Viburnum prunifolium* Ⓝ

Trees

Carpinus caroliniana Ⓝ • *Chamaecyparis lawsoniana* Ⓝ • *Fagus sylvatica* Atropurpurea Group • *Ilex opaca* 'Clarendon' Ⓝ • *Juniperus virginiana* 'Emerald Sentinel' Ⓝ • *Maclura pomifera* Ⓝ • *Prunus virginiana* 'Schubert' Ⓝ

Plants for beside hedges, walls, and fences

Plants grown beside walls and fences soften the hard surfaces with flowers and foliage, while hedges provide a leafy backdrop to colorful blooms.

The soil close to a man-made vertical surface may be in a rain shadow and will remain dry, even after a heavy downpour. Likewise, hedging plants soak up large volumes of water, drying out the soil next to them. Drought-tolerant plants that cope well in these conditions are the same as those that enjoy sandy soil, and include species, such as lamb's ears and juniper from rocky areas, and others, such as spurge and rosemary, from Mediterranean regions. A sunny, south-facing wall is the perfect location for many tender plants, providing the heat and shelter they need to survive outside all year in cooler climates.

PERENNIAL LARGE

Agastache foeniculum

ANISE HYSSOP This perennial has an upright habit and lance-shaped midgreen leaves that smell and taste like licorice. In late summer, it produces spikes of fluffy lavender-blue flowers, which are attractive to bees and butterflies.

↕4ft (1.2m) ↔12in (30cm)

Z4–9 (N)

PERENNIAL LARGE

Anemone x *hybrida*

JAPANESE ANEMONE This upright, branching perennial bears divided dark green leaves and white or pink flowers from late summer to early fall. It is useful for late season color. 'Queen Charlotte' (above) has pale pink flowers.

↕4ft (1.2m) ↔indefinite

Z4–8

PERENNIAL SMALL

Antennaria dioica 'Rubra'

PUSSYTOES A mat-forming semievergreen perennial with tiny, oval woolly leaves and small clusters of fluffy rose-pink flower heads from late spring to early summer. Ideal for planting along the bottom of hedges.

↕6in (15cm) ↔12in (30cm)

Z3–9 (N)

SHRUB LARGE

Argyrocytisus battandieri

PINEAPPLE BROOM A rounded deciduous shrub with gray-green leaves divided into leaflets and silky when they unfurl. Spikes of yellow pineapple-scented flowers appear in late summer. Prefers acidic soil and the protection of a south-facing screen.

↕↔12ft (4m)

pH (!) Z7–9

PERENNIAL LARGE

Artemisia ludoviciana

WESTERN MUGWORT A bushy perennial with aromatic, lance-shaped, toothed, silvery gray woolly leaves and slender plumes of tiny brownish yellow summer flowers. 'Silver Queen' has silver leaves. May spread aggressively in some areas.

↕4ft (1.2m) ↔24in (60cm)

Z4–9 (N)

PERENNIAL LARGE

Boltonia asteroides

FALSE ASTER This is a tall branching perennial with linear gray-green leaves and sprays of tiny, white daisy-like flowers, which appear starting in late summer. Reduce stems by one-third in spring to prevent them from flopping.

↕6ft (2m) ↔3ft (1m)

Z4–8 (N)

SHRUB LARGE

Buddleja alternifolia

FOUNTAIN BUTTERFLY BUSH This vigorous deciduous shrub produces arching stems bearing narrow gray-green leaves. Long clusters of fragrant lilac-purple flowers appear in early summer. The stems can be trained to form a small weeping tree.

↕↔12ft (4m)

Z6–9

BULB MEDIUM

Calochortus venustus

WHITE MARIPOSA This early summer-flowering bulb has gray-green grassy foliage and white, yellow, purple, or red cup-shaped flowers with a yellow-margined dark red blotch on each petal. Grow in dry soil beside a sunny wall.

↕24in (60cm)

Z6–10 (N)

PERENNIAL LARGE

Campanula latifolia

GIANT BELLFLOWER This tall, upright perennial has toothed midgreen foliage and clusters of tubular violet-purple blooms throughout summer. Varieties include 'Brantwood' (above). Best in alkaline soils. Needs partial shade in hot summers.

↕4ft (1.2m) ↔24in (60cm)

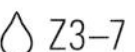 Z3–7

SHRUB MEDIUM

Carpenteria californica

TREE ANEMONE This bushy evergreen shrub has slim, glossy dark green leaves and fragrant yellow-centered white flowers appearing in early to midsummer. This California native is best suited to West Coast gardens.

↕6ft (2m) or more ↔6ft (2m)

Z8–9 Ⓝ

SHRUB MEDIUM

Ceanothus 'Dark Star'

CALIFORNIA LILAC A spreading evergreen shrub with oval dark green leaves. It produces round clusters of deep blue-purple flowers held on arching stems in late spring. Train the stems against a sunny fence or wall.

↕6ft (2m) ↔10ft (3m)

Z9–11 Ⓝ

SHRUB LARGE

Chaenomeles x *superba*

FLOWERING QUINCE This spiny deciduous shrub produces cup-shaped flowers in shades of red, pink, orange, and white in spring before the leaves appear. It also bears yellow edible fruits. 'Crimson and Gold' (above) has orange-red blooms.

↕3ft (1m) ↔6ft (2m)

Z5–8

PERENNIAL MEDIUM

Gaillardia x *grandiflora*

BLANKET FLOWER This bushy, short-lived perennial has slim green leaves and numerous large, daisy-like red flowers with yellow-tipped petals from midsummer to early fall. Deadhead regularly. Varieties include the dwarf form 'Kobold' (above).

↕3ft (1m) ↔18in (45cm)

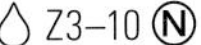 Z3–10 Ⓝ

PERENNIAL SMALL

Coreopsis grandiflora

TICKSEED A compact perennial, often grown as an annual, with serrated, green foliage. Masses of daisy-like, bright yellow, single or double flower heads appear throughout summer. 'Sunray' (above) has double flowers.

↕↔18in (45cm)

Z4–9 Ⓝ

SHRUB LARGE

Garrya elliptica

SILK-TASSEL BUSH This dense evergreen shrub has leathery, wavy-edged gray-green leaves. From midwinter to early spring, it is covered with gray-green catkins. Plant it against a wall or fence. This California native is best in West Coast gardens.

↕↔12ft (4m)

Z8–11 Ⓝ

SHRUB SMALL

Euphorbia characias subsp. *wulfenii*

MEDITERRANEAN SPURGE This upright evergreen subshrub has tall stems covered with slender gray-green leaves the first year, then large, vivid yellow-green flower spikes in spring. The sap is a skin irritant.

↕↔4ft (1.2m)

(!) Z7–10

PERENNIAL LARGE

Gaura lindheimeri

WAND FLOWER An upright, clump-forming perennial with lance-shaped green leaves and tall slim stems dotted with star-shaped white flowers, which appear from midsummer to early fall. The variety 'Siskiyou Pink' has pink flowers.

↕5ft (1.5m) ↔3ft (1m)

Z6–9 Ⓝ

SHRUB LARGE

Fremontodendron 'California Glory'

FLANNEL BUSH A vigorous evergreen or semievergreen treelike shrub with lobed, rounded dark green leaves. Saucer-shaped bright yellow blooms appear from late spring to mid-fall. Best in West Coast gardens.

↕20ft (6m) ↔12ft (4m)

(!) Z8–10 Ⓝ

PERENNIAL SMALL

Geranium macrorrhizum

BIGROOT GERANIUM This carpeting perennial has aromatic, rounded deeply lobed leaves and small magenta flowers in early summer. Cut back foliage in midsummer to restrict spreading. Needs partial shade in hot summers.

↕15in (38cm) ↔24in (60cm)

Z4–8

PERENNIAL MEDIUM

Iris 'Edith Wolford'

BEARDED IRIS This tall iris is an upright semievergreen perennial with sword-shaped gray-green foliage. The blooms appear in late spring and are pale yellow with blue-violet lower petals. Plant the rhizomes just above the soil surface.

↕3ft (1m) ↔24in (60cm)

Z3–9

PERENNIAL LARGE

Helianthus 'Lemon Queen'

PERENNIAL SUNFLOWER This vigorous, upright, rhizomatous perennial bears stout branched stems of rough, oval dark green leaves. It produces masses of large, daisy-like pale yellow flower heads with dark yellow centers from summer to fall.

↕5ft (1.5m) ↔24in (60cm) or more

Z4–9 Ⓝ

SHRUB LARGE

Hibiscus syriacus

ROSE OF SHARON This upright deciduous shrub has lobed dark green foliage and single blue, violet, or white flowers with dark centers from late summer to early fall. 'Blue Bird' (above) is a blue-flowered variety. Considered invasive in some areas.

↕10ft (3m) ↔6ft (2m)

Z5–9

PERENNIAL MEDIUM

Iris pallida 'Argentea Variegata'

DALMATION IRIS An upright semievergreen perennial with sword-shaped gray-green and white-striped foliage and pale blue-purple early summer flowers. Plant the rhizomes just above the soil surface.

↕4ft (1.2m) ↔ indefinite

(!) Z4–9

SHRUB LARGE

Juniperus scopulorum

ROCKY MOUNTAIN JUNIPER This is a narrow, upright conifer with a columnar habit. It produces bright steel-blue scalelike foliage and tolerates hot dry sites in front of walls or hedges. No pruning is required.

↕50ft (15m) ↔20ft (6m)

Z3–7 Ⓝ

SHRUB MEDIUM

Lupinus arboreus

TREE LUPINE This is a fast-growing, sprawling semievergreen shrub that, in early summer, bears short spikes of fragrant yellow flowers above hairy, feathery pale green leaves. Best in sandy soil; it can be short-lived.

↕↔6ft (2m)

(!) Z9–10 Ⓝ

TREE LARGE

Magnolia grandiflora

SOUTHERN MAGNOLIA A rounded evergreen tree with large, glossy dark green leaves and large, fragrant white flowers from midsummer to early fall. It prefers the shelter provided by south-facing walls. Prune in spring to keep it in check.

↕60ft (18m) ↔50ft (15m)

Z7–9 Ⓝ

TREE MEDIUM

Magnolia stellata

STAR MAGNOLIA A rounded deciduous tree with fragrant, star-shaped white flowers that open from silky buds in early spring, before the slim green leaves appear. Plant close to a south-facing wall to protect the blooms from frost.

↕↔30ft (10m)

Z4–8

BULB LARGE

Nectaroscordum siculum

MEDITERRANEAN BELLS An upright bulb with narrow, garlic-scented green leaves that fade when fountain-shaped clusters of pendent, bell-shaped cream and purple summer flowers appear on tall stems. Known for its shuttlecock-like seedheads.

↕4ft (1.2m)

Z6–10

PERENNIAL MEDIUM

Nepeta 'Six Hills Giant'

CATMINT This vigorous, clump-forming perennial bears narrow, oval, toothed, aromatic gray-green leaves. In summer, it becomes covered with spikes of tubular lavender-blue flowers. Cut back after flowers fade to keep the plant tidy.

↕3ft (1m) ↔4ft (1.2m)

Z3–8

SHRUB SMALL

Rosmarinus officinalis Prostratus Group

ROSEMARY This spreading evergreen subshrub has narrow aromatic foliage and small blue flower clusters from spring to early summer. It has a prostrate habit, ideal for a border edge. Suitable for culinary use.

↕6in (15cm) ↔5ft (1.5m)

Z8–11

PERENNIAL SMALL

Stachys byzantina

LAMB'S EARS This mat-forming perennial, evergreen in warm areas, has soft silvery gray foliage and spikes of small mauve-pink flowers in summer. Drought-tolerant, it makes an excellent ground-cover plant for the front of a south-facing flowerbed.

↕15in (38cm) ↔24in (60cm)

Z4–8

SHRUB MEDIUM

Ribes speciosum

FUCHSIA-FLOWERED GOOSEBERRY A bushy deciduous shrub with spiny stems of lobed, glossy green foliage. Pendent, tubular, fuchsialike red flowers appear in mid-spring, followed by red fruits. This California native is best suited to West Coast gardens.

↕↔6ft (2m)

Z8–10 Ⓝ

PERENNIAL MEDIUM

Rumex sanguineus

BLOODY DOCK A clump-forming perennial grown for its decorative, oval green leaves with distinctive red veins, which are edible when young. Spikes of small cream blooms appear in summer. Clip back after flowering to encourage new leaves.

↕3ft (1m) ↔12in (30cm)

Z6–8

BULB MEDIUM

Tigridia pavonia

TIGER FLOWER This tender bulb has sword-shaped, pleated green leaves and, in summer, unusual three-petaled flowers in red, pink, orange, yellow, and white with contrasting markings. The blooms often open just for a day.

↕18in (45cm)

Z8–10 Ⓝ

SHRUB MEDIUM

Rosmarinus officinalis

ROSEMARY An evergreen subshrub with aromatic, needlelike dark green foliage and small blue flowers that appear on top of leafy stems in spring. Varieties include 'Miss Jessopp's Upright', which has a slim erect habit.

↕↔5ft (1.5m)

Z8–10

SHRUB MEDIUM

Weigela florida 'Variegata'

WEIGELA This bushy deciduous shrub bears oval cream-edged green leaves and a profusion of funnel-shaped pink flowers from late spring to summer. An easy-going plant, it tolerates the dry soil close to a wall or fence.

↕↔9ft (2.5m)

Z5–8

TREE SMALL

Sophora SUN KING

KOWHAI This bushy evergreen tree produces long leafy stems comprised of small oval leaflets. From late winter to early spring, bell-shaped golden-yellow flowers appear in large clusters. Thrives in the shelter of a south-facing wall.

↕↔10ft (3m)

Z8–10

OTHER SUGGESTIONS

Annuals

Cosmos bipinnatus Sensation Series Ⓝ

Perennials

Abelmoschus moschatus • *Achillea millefolium* 'Paprika' Ⓝ • *Boltonia asteroides* 'Snowbank' Ⓝ • *Coreopsis* 'Jethro Tull' • *Echinops bannaticus* • *Echinops ritro* 'Veitch's Blue' • *Lychnis chalcedonica* • *Penstemon pinifolius* Ⓝ • *Phlomis russeliana* • *Schizachyrium scoparium* 'Prairie Blues' Ⓝ • *Verbena* 'Homestead Purple'

Bulbs

Agapanthus inapertus 'Graskop' • *Allium* 'Purple Sensation'

Shrubs

Camellia sasanqua • *Cotoneaster horizontalis*

Shrubs

Juniperus virginiana 'Blue Arrow' 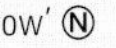

Plants for walls, fences, and vertical surfaces

Climbers and wall shrubs are perfect for decorating walls and fences, with flowers in all colors and interesting leaf textures and plant shapes.

To extend your flower display, grow climbers and wall shrubs that bloom at different times. Try teaming a rambling rose that peaks in early summer with a late-flowering clematis. Avoid partnering two clematis that require different pruning times because you risk cutting off the blooms of an early-flowering variety when pruning a later one to the ground in spring. While self-clinging climbers, such as Boston ivy, stick to surfaces with adhesive pads or roots, other climbers and wall shrubs, such as climbing rose and honeysuckle, need support. Use trellises or galvanized wires secured to a vertical surface or structure.

SHRUB MEDIUM

Abutilon megapotamicum

TRAILING ABUTILON An evergreen shrub with long flexible stems of slim, heart-shaped dark green leaves. It bears yellow and red, pendent bell-shaped flowers all summer. Train against a sunny wall in summer; protect against frost in winter.

↕↔ 6ft (2m)

💧 Z8–10

CLIMBER LARGE

Actinidia kolomikta

VARIEGATED KIWI VINE This woody-stemmed, vigorous, deciduous twining climber is grown for its oval green leaves, splashed with creamy white and pink markings on mature plants. Small, cup-shaped white flowers appear in summer.

↕ 12ft (4m)

💧 Z5–8

CLIMBER MEDIUM

Billardiera longiflora

CLIMBING BLUEBERRY A woody-stemmed, evergreen twining climber with narrow green leaves. Decorative purple-blue fruits in fall follow the small, bell-shaped green-yellow flowers. Grow it against a south-facing wall; protect in winter in cold areas.

↕ 6ft (2m)

💧 Z8–9

CLIMBER LARGE

Campsis x *tagliabuana*

TRUMPET VINE A vigorous, self-clinging deciduous climber with large leaves divided into oval leaflets. Trumpet-shaped orange flowers appear in summer followed by beanlike seedpods. Can be aggressive; prune in spring to keep it tidy.

↕ 40ft (12m)

💧 Z5–9

CLIMBER MEDIUM

Clematis alpina

ALPINE CLEMATIS This deciduous clematis has divided midgreen leaves and lantern-shaped blue, pink, or white flowers from early to late spring followed by fluffy silvery seedheads. It is ideal for exposed sites; keep the roots shaded.

↕ 10ft (3m)

💧 Z4–9

CLIMBER SMALL

Clematis ANGELIQUE

CLEMATIS A compact, mid- to late-season deciduous clematis with midgreen leaves. It produces numerous lilac-blue flowers for a long period from early summer to mid-fall. Use it to decorate a rose arch, pillar, or tripod.

↕ 4ft (1.2m)

💧 Z5–9

CLIMBER LARGE

Clematis armandii

EVERGREEN CLEMATIS A vigorous, early-flowering evergreen clematis with lance-shaped dark green foliage and scented, single white flowers in early spring. Grow it up a tree or wall in a sheltered, south- or southwest-facing site; shade the roots.

↕ 15ft (5m)

💧 Z7–9

CLIMBER LARGE

Clematis 'Bill MacKenzie'

CLEMATIS This vigorous, long-flowering deciduous clematis has dark green leaves. Yellow bell-shaped flowers with thick, almost waxy, petals from midsummer to late fall are followed by fluffy seedheads. Needs a large support; shade the roots.

↕22ft (7m)

Z5–9

CLIMBER SMALL

Clematis CHANTILLY

CLEMATIS A large-flowered clematis with midgreen leaves. From summer to fall, it produces scented, pale pink single flowers with a deeper pink central bar on each petal. Plant it against a wall, fence, or up a rose arch with the roots shaded.

↕4ft (1.2m)

Z4–9

CLIMBER MEDIUM

Clematis 'Doctor Ruppel'

CLEMATIS This early-flowering deciduous clematis has midgreen leaves and large, rich pink flowers with dark pink stripes in the center of each petal, which appear throughout summer. Grow it up an arch, fence, or wall, keeping the roots shaded.

↕8ft (2.5m)

Z4–9

CLIMBER MEDIUM

Clematis 'Duchess of Albany'

CLEMATIS This deciduous clematis has midgreen leaves and small, tulip-shaped, soft pink flowers with a deeper pink stripe inside each petal, from summer to early fall. Grow it on a fence, wall, or over an arch, keeping the roots shaded.

↕8ft (2.5m)

Z4–9

CLIMBER LARGE

Clematis 'Etoile Violette'

CLEMATIS A late-flowering deciduous clematis with midgreen leaves. It bears numerous flattish violet-purple flowers with cream stamens from midsummer to fall. Grow through a tree or up a fence, wall, or pergola. Keep the roots shaded.

↕15ft (5m)

Z4–9

CLIMBER LARGE

Clematis 'Fireworks'

CLEMATIS This deciduous clematis has midgreen leaves and, from late spring to early summer, large blue-mauve flowers with a central magenta stripe on each petal. Another flush of blooms appears in late summer. Keep the roots shaded.

↕12ft (4m)

Z4–9

CLIMBER LARGE

Clematis flammula

VIRGIN'S BOWER A vigorous clematis with dark green, divided deciduous foliage and masses of small, almond-scented, starry white flowers from summer to early fall followed by fluffy seedheads. Needs a large support; shade the roots.

↕15ft (5m)

Z4–9

CLIMBER SMALL

Clematis 'Fleuri'

CLEMATIS A compact deciduous clematis with midgreen leaves. From late spring to summer, it produces deep purple flowers with a red stripe down the center of each petal. Grow it up a rose pillar or tripod, with the roots in shade.

↕4ft (1.2m)

Z4–9

CLIMBER MEDIUM

Clematis florida var. *florida* 'Sieboldiana'

PASSION FLOWER CLEMATIS This deciduous or semievergreen clematis has midgreen foliage and creamy white flowers with a central boss of petal-like purple stamens. Train on a sunny, sheltered wall.

↕8ft (2.5m)

Z6–9

CLIMBER MEDIUM

Clematis 'Frances Rivis'

CLEMATIS An early-flowering deciduous, clematis with divided midgreen foliage. In spring, it produces nodding, bell-shaped violet-blue flowers with white centers. Makes a good specimen for a tripod, arch, wall, or fence. Keep the roots shaded.

↕10ft (3m)

Z4–9

CLIMBER LARGE

Clematis montana var. _grandiflora_

WHITE ANEMONE CLEMATIS A deciduous clematis with divided midgreen foliage and white flowers with yellow centers from late spring to early summer. Ideal for a tree, large wall, or pergola; shade the roots.
↕30ft (10m)

Z6–9

CLIMBER LARGE

Clematis 'Huldine'

CLEMATIS A vigorous, late-flowering deciduous clematis with midgreen divided foliage. From mid- to late summer, it forms a profusion of small white flowers, mauve beneath. Ideal for a pergola, arch, wall, or fence; keep the roots shaded.
↕12ft (4m)

Z4–9

CLIMBER LARGE

Clematis montana var. _rubens_ 'Tetrarose'

CLEMATIS A vigorous, early-flowering deciduous clematis with purple-green leaves and cream-centered pink flowers in late spring. Ideal for a tree, house wall, or large pergola; shade the roots.
↕30ft (10m)

Z6–9

CLIMBER MEDIUM

Clematis JOSEPHINE

CLEMATIS This deciduous climber has green, broadly lance-shaped leaves. From summer to early fall, a succession of large double flowers appears; the pinkish purple petals are cream beneath and produce a layered effect.
↕8ft (2.5m)

Z4–9

CLIMBER MEDIUM

Clematis 'Perle d'Azur'

CLEMATIS This late-flowering deciduous clematis has midgreen leaves. From midsummer to fall, it produces large azure-blue flowers with creamy green centers and pink-purple stripes on each petal. Plant the roots in shade.
↕10ft (3m)

Z4–9

CLIMBER LARGE

Clematis 'Purpurea Plena Elegans'

CLEMATIS This late-flowering deciduous clematis has pale green leaves and frilly, purple-pink double flowers with pale pink centers from midsummer to late fall. Grow on a wall or fence; shade the roots.
↕12ft (4m)

Z4–9

CLIMBER LARGE

Clematis rehderiana

NODDING VIRGIN'S BOWER This vigorous deciduous clematis has coarse green leaves. From midsummer to fall, it bears masses of fragrant, tubular, nodding yellow flowers. Grow through a tree, or on a large wall or pergola. Shade the roots.
↕22ft (7m)

Z6–9

CLIMBER LARGE

Clematis tangutica

GOLDEN CLEMATIS This vigorous, late-flowering clematis has midgreen leaves and lantern-shaped yellow flowers from summer to early fall. Fluffy silvery seedheads provide winter interest. Grow on a large wall or fence; shade the roots.
↕20ft (6m)

Z4–9

CLIMBER LARGE

Cobaea scandens

CUP-AND-SAUCER VINE This Mexican native, grown as an annual, is an evergreen perennial climber. It bears dark green foliage and, from midsummer to fall, scented cup-shaped, creamy green, aging to purple, blooms. Quickly covers a wall, arch, or tripod.
↕15ft (5m)

Z9–11 Ⓝ

CLIMBER LARGE

Distictis buccinatoria

MEXICAN BLOOD FLOWER This tender twining evergreen climber produces dark green leaves and trumpet-shaped crimson-red flowers in summer. It requires warm growing conditions and is best kept in a sunroom.

↕15ft (5m) or more

Z9–11 Ⓝ

SHRUB LARGE

Garrya elliptica

SILK-TASSEL BUSH This evergreen shrub has leathery, wavy gray-green leaves and, from midwinter to early spring, silvery gray catkins that tremble in the wind. Train it on wires against a wall. Prune when the catkins fade. Best in West Coast gardens.

↕↔12ft (4m)

Z8–11 Ⓝ

CLIMBER LARGE

Gelsemium sempervirens

CAROLINA YELLOW JASMINE This evergreen twining climber has slim, lance-shaped dark green leaves. In summer, it produces clusters of trumpet-shaped bright yellow flowers. Grow against a sunny, sheltered wall or fence. All parts are toxic.

↕20ft (6m)

(!) Z7–9 Ⓝ

CLIMBER LARGE

Humulus lupulus 'Aureus'

GOLDEN HOP A perennial twining climber, grown for its rough, toothed, lobed yellow-green foliage. In summer, it bears straw-colored pendent flower heads that resemble cones. Grow it over an arbor or on a large fence or wall.

↕20ft (6m)

Z4–8 Ⓝ

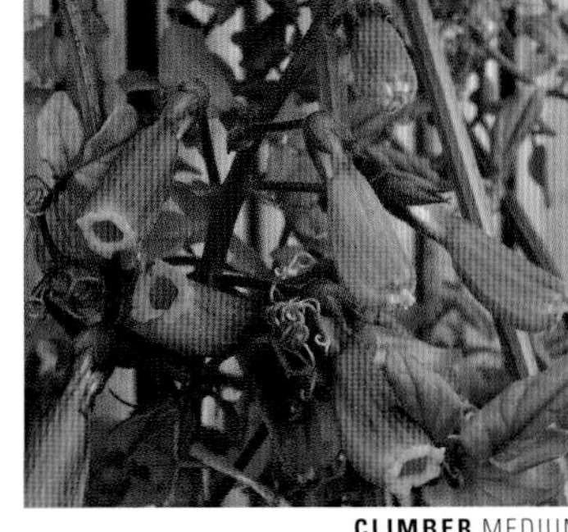

CLIMBER MEDIUM

Eccremocarpus scaber

CHILEAN GLORY FLOWER This evergreen perennial tendril climber, often grown as an annual, produces small green leaves and tubular orange-red flowers from summer to fall. Grow it in a sheltered spot on an arch, tripod, or fence.

↕10ft (3m)

Z9–11

CLIMBER MEDIUM

Ipomoea coccinea

RED MORNING GLORY A tender annual twining climber with heart-shaped midgreen leaves and small, fragrant, tubular scarlet flowers with yellow throats from late summer to fall. Ideal for a tripod, rose arch, or pillar.

↕10ft (3m)

(!) Ⓝ

CLIMBER MEDIUM

Ipomoea tricolor 'Heavenly Blue'

MORNING GLORY A fast-growing annual twining climber with heart-shaped leaves and, from summer to early fall, large, funnel-shaped, sky-blue morning flowers. Quickly covers a fence, wall, or rose arch.

↕10ft (3m)

(!) Z0

CLIMBER MEDIUM

Jasminum humile 'Revolutum'

ITALIAN JASMINE A shrubby evergreen climber with glossy bright green leaves divided into leaflets and clusters of small, fragrant, tubular yellow flowers from early spring to early summer.

↕8ft (2.5m)

Z7–9

CLIMBER LARGE

Jasminum officinale

COMMON JASMINE A woody-stemmed semievergreen or deciduous twining climber with green leaves divided into leaflets. From midsummer to fall, clusters of highly fragrant white flowers appear. Cut back in late winter.

↕40ft (12m)

Z8–10

CLIMBER LARGE

Lablab purpureus

HYACINTH BEAN This twining deciduous climber, often grown as an annual, has small dark green leaves and pink pealike summer flowers followed by decorative, long purple pods. Seedpods are toxic. Grow it on a fence, arch, or pillar.

↕20ft (6m)

Z9–11

CLIMBER LARGE

Lonicera x *brownii* 'Dropmore Scarlet'

SCARLET TRUMPET HONEYSUCKLE This twining semievergreen or deciduous climber has rounded blue-green leaves and tubular, unscented scarlet blooms from summer to early fall. Protect in winter.

↕12ft (4m)

Z4–8

CLIMBER LARGE

Lonicera x *heckrottii*

GOLDFLAME HONEYSUCKLE This twining deciduous or semievergreen, climber has oval dark green leaves, blue-green beneath. In summer, it produces fragrant pink flowers with orange throats, sometimes followed by red berries. Provide a large support.

↕15ft (5m)

Z6–9

CLIMBER LARGE

Lonicera periclymenum

WOODBINE This twining deciduous climber bears oval dark green leaves, whitish green below, and richly scented, tubular creamy white, yellow, or red flowers in summer. Use it to cover arbors, walls, fences, or trees. May be invasive in some areas.

↕22ft (7m)

Z5–9

CLIMBER LARGE

Lonicera x *tellmanniana*

TELLMANN'S HONEYSUCKLE A twining deciduous climber with blue-green leaves. Bright coppery orange, unscented flowers are carried in clusters from late spring to summer. Ideal for growing through a tree, or on a house wall or large fence.

↕15ft (5m)

Z7–9

CLIMBER MEDIUM

Mandevilla x *amoena* 'Alice du Pont'

MANDEVILLA A tender evergreen climber with dark green foliage and funnel-shaped pink flowers. Each bloom lasts several days. Grow it indoors in cold areas, or treat as an annual and train up a tripod or arch.

↕10ft (3m)

Z0

CLIMBER LARGE

Parthenocissus henryana

CHINESE VIRGINIA CREEPER This vigorous, self-clinging deciduous climber is grown for its palm-shaped dark green leaves with cream veining, which turns crimson in fall, when blue-black berries are also produced. Leaf color is best in light shade.

↕30ft (10m) or more

Z7–8

CLIMBER LARGE

Parthenocissus quinquefolia

VIRGINIA CREEPER This is a large, vigorous, self-clinging deciduous climber with rounded green leaves divided into oval toothed-edged leaflets. These turn bright red and orange in fall. Grow it against a large support.

↕50ft (15m) or more

Z4–9 Ⓝ

CLIMBER LARGE

Parthenocissus tricuspidata

BOSTON IVY This large, vigorous, woody-stemmed, deciduous tendril climber produces a spectacular, crimson leaf color in fall, and dull blue berries. Easily covers large expanses of wall. Considered invasive in some areas.

↕70ft (20m)

Z4–8

CLIMBER LARGE

Passiflora caerulea

BLUE PASSION FLOWER A semievergreen or evergreen tendril climber with glossy, lobed green leaves. From summer to fall, it bears white flowers with purple filaments, followed by egg-shaped orange fruits. Needs a large support. Protect from cold.
↕30ft (10m) or more

Z8–11

CLIMBER LARGE

Plumbago auriculata

CAPE LEADWORT A scrambling evergreen climber with small dark green leaves. Large clusters of sky-blue flowers appear from summer to early fall. Train on a trellis against a sunny, sheltered wall outside or under cover in regions with cold winters.
↕20ft (6m)

Z9–11

CLIMBER MEDIUM

Rhodochiton atrosanguineus

PURPLE BELL VINE An annual climber, native to Mexico, with heart-shaped midgreen leaves. From late spring to late fall, it bears dangling, umbrella-shaped flowers with pinky red "hats" and dark maroon lower tubes. Ideal for a tripod.
↕10ft (3m)

Z10–11 Ⓝ

CLIMBER LARGE

Rosa banksiae 'Lutea'

YELLOW BANKSIAN ROSE A vigorous, thornless climbing rose with small leaves. In late spring, it bears clusters of unscented, fully double, rosette-shaped yellow flowers in one flush. Needs a sunny, sheltered wall or fence; protect from drying winds.
↕30ft (10m)

Z8–9

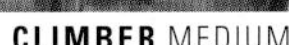

CLIMBER LARGE

Rosa 'Albertine'

CLIMBING ROSE This vigorous rambler rose has arching, thorny reddish stems and glossy dark green foliage. In summer, it produces clusters of scented, fully double salmon-pink flowers in a single flush. Grow it up a tree or on a large arbor.
↕15ft (5m)

Z5–9

CLIMBER MEDIUM

Rosa 'Aloha'

CLIMBING HYBRID TEA ROSE This climbing rose has disease-resistant, leathery dark green leaves. Fragrant, fully double rose- and salmon-pink flowers form in summer and again in fall. Train the stems over an arch or on a wall. Mulch annually in spring.
↕8ft (2.5m)

Z5–9

CLIMBER LARGE

Rosa 'Climbing Cécile Brünner'

POLYANTHA ROSE A vigorous climber with disease-resistant dark green leaves and, from summer to late fall, masses of fully double, sweetly-scented blush-pink blooms, fading to pearl. Ideal for an arbor or wall.
↕15ft (5m)

Z5–9

CLIMBER LARGE

Rosa 'Climbing Lady Hillingdon'

CLIMBING HYBRID TEA ROSE This vigorous rose has dark green foliage that is coppery mahogany when young. Fragrant apricot-yellow flowers are borne all summer. Train on a house wall or on an arbor.
↕15ft (5m)

Z6–9

CLIMBER MEDIUM

Rosa 'Compassion'

CLIMBING HYBRID TEA ROSE A climbing rose with disease-resistant, dark green glossy leaves. From summer to fall, it produces fragrant, double salmon-apricot flowers, which are tinted pink, on thorny stems. Grow it on a wall or an arbor.
↕10ft (3m)

Z5–9

CLIMBER MEDIUM

Rosa 'Dortmund'

KORDESII SHRUB ROSE This rose bears disease-resistant, glossy dark green foliage. Clusters of flat, single red flowers with white eyes and a slight scent are produced from summer to fall. Ideal for an arch or arbor. Mulch in spring.

↕10ft (3m)

Z5–9

CLIMBER MEDIUM

Rosa DUBLIN BAY

CLIMBING ROSE This rose produces disease-resistant, glossy dark green foliage and clusters of bright crimson double flowers in summer and again in fall. Grow it against a wall or on an arch or post. Mulch in spring.

↕7ft (2.2m)

Z5–9

CLIMBER LARGE

Rosa 'Félicité Perpétue'

RAMBLING HYBRID SEMPERVIRENS ROSE A vigorous rose with glossy green semievergreen leaves. Clusters of scented, fully double, blush pink to white flowers are produced in a single flush in summer. Grow it up a tree or large wall or over an arbor.

↕15ft (5m)

Z6–9

CLIMBER MEDIUM

Rosa LAURA FORD

CLIMBING MINIATURE ROSE This stiffly branching, climbing rose has small, dark, glossy, disease-resistant leaves. Sprays of scented, urn-shaped to flat, yellow double flowers appear in summer and again in fall. Grow it on arches or pillars.

↕7ft (2.2m)

Z5–9

CLIMBER LARGE

Rosa 'Mermaid'

HYBRID BRACTEATA ROSE This large rose bears glossy, green, disease-resistant foliage and flowers repeatedly from summer to fall producing single primrose-yellow blooms. The thorny stems can be used to deter intruders.

↕20ft (6m)

Z7–9

CLIMBER LARGE

Rosa 'New Dawn'

CLIMBING ROSE A climbing rose with disease-resistant, glossy dark green leaves and clusters of fragrant, pearl-pink double flowers from summer to fall. Ideal for sunny walls, fences, or arbors, it also tolerates north-facing sites. Mulch in spring.

↕15ft (5m)

Z5–9

CLIMBER LARGE

Rosa 'Rambling Rector'

RAMBLING ROSE A vigorous rose with disease-resistant, grayish green foliage. Clusters of scented, golden-centered, creamy white semidouble flowers form in one flush in summer. Grow it up a tree, large wall, or fence. Best for large gardens.

↕20ft (6m)

Z5–9

CLIMBER LARGE

Rosa 'Seagull'

RAMBLING ROSE A vigorous rose with disease-resistant, glossy light green leaves. In late spring, it bears clusters of fragrant, single, golden-centered white flowers in one flush. Grow it up a tree, large wall, or fence. Best for large gardens.

↕20ft (6m)

Z5–9

CLIMBER MEDIUM

Rosa SUMMER WINE

CLIMBING ROSE This climbing rose has disease-resistant, dark green leaves and small clusters of fragrant, flat-faced, semidouble coral-pink flowers from summer to fall. Ideal for a wall, fence, arch, or pillar. Mulch annually in spring.

↕10ft (3m)

Z5–9

CLIMBER LARGE

Schizophragma integrifolium

CHINESE HYDRANGEA VINE This is a large, self-clinging deciduous climber with heart-shaped green leaves. It produces clusters of tiny flowers with petal-like bracts resembling lacecap hydrangea blooms in summer.

↕40ft (12m)

Z5–9

CLIMBER MEDIUM

Thunbergia alata

BLACK-EYED SUSAN VINE This moderately fast-growing perennial twining climber, grown as an annual, has toothed, oval to heart-shaped leaves and rounded, flat, dark brown-centered orange or golden-yellow flowers from early summer to early fall.

↕10ft (3m)

Z10–11

CLIMBER MEDIUM

Tropaeolum speciosum

FLAME CREEPER A twining perennial climber with rounded blue-green leaves divided into oval leaflets. Scarlet flowers appear in summer, followed by spherical, bright blue fruits. Grow it through a tree with the roots shaded. Best in fertile soil.

↕10ft (3m)

Z8–11

CLIMBER LARGE

Vitis coignetiae

CRIMSON GLORY VINE A vigorous, deciduous tendril climber with large, heart-shaped textured leaves that turn red and purple in fall. Small black berries follow insignificant green summer flowers. Grow it on a large wall or an arbor.

↕50ft (15m)

Z5–9

CLIMBER LARGE

Solanum crispum 'Glasnevin'

CHILEAN POTATO TREE This is a large semievergreen scrambling climber with slim, oval green leaves and clusters of fragrant violet-blue flowers with yellow eyes from summer to fall. Grow it in a sheltered, sunny site.

↕20ft (6m)

(!) Z9–11

CLIMBER LARGE

Trachelospermum asiaticum

STAR JASMINE This is a large evergreen twining climber with small, glossy dark green leaves. Small, scented, star-shaped, buff-centered cream flowers that mature to yellow appear in summer. Grow it on a sunny, sheltered wall.

↕20ft (6m)

Z7–11

CLIMBER LARGE

Vitis vinifera 'Purpurea'

GRAPE VINE This deciduous tendril climber is grown for its lobed, maplelike purplish leaves that turn bright crimson in fall. Unpalatable purple berries follow the pale green summer blooms. Grow on a wall or an arbor. Considered invasive in some areas.

↕22ft (7m)

Z6–9

CLIMBER LARGE

Stauntonia hexaphylla

STAUNTONIA VINE A twining evergreen climber with rounded leaves divided into oval leaflets. Clusters of fragrant, violet-tinged white flowers appear in spring, followed by egg-shaped purple fruits on female plants. Grow it in a sheltered site.

↕30ft (10m)

Z9–10

CLIMBER LARGE

Trachelospermum jasminoides

STAR JASMINE A twining evergreen climber with glossy dark green leaves that turn bronze in winter. Clusters of fragrant starry white flowers appear in summer. Grow it on a sunny, sheltered wall.

↕28ft (9m)

Z8–10

OTHER SUGGESTIONS

Annual climbers

Ipomoea lobata Ⓝ • *Ipomoea quamoclit*

Perennial climbers

Aristolochia macrophylla Ⓝ • *Bignonia capreolata* 'Tangerine Beauty' Ⓝ • *Bougainvillea* 'Barbara Karst' • *Campsis radicans* 'Indian Summer' Ⓝ • *Celastrus scandens* Ⓝ • *Clematis* x *triternata* 'Rubromarginata' • *Codonopsis pilosula* • *Jasminum* x *stephanense* • *Lonicera flava* Ⓝ • *Lonicera sempervirens* 'Major Wheeler' Ⓝ • *Lonicera sempervirens* f. *sulphurea* 'John Clayton' Ⓝ • *Passiflora coccinea* • *Passiflora incarnata* Ⓝ • *Schisandra rubriflora* • *Solanum laxum* • *Wisteria frutescens* 'Amethyst Falls' Ⓝ • *Wisteria macrostachya* 'Blue Moon' Ⓝ

Plant focus: clematis

The vast range of flower forms and plant sizes make clematis invaluable additions to large or small gardens.

VALUED FOR THEIR VERSATILITY, clematis can be used to dress up arches and pergolas, scramble through trees, and cover walls and fences with climbing stems of colorful flowers. As well as beautiful blooms, many species also sport decorative seedheads and, with careful selection, clematis can decorate the garden almost year round. Clematis comprise a wide variety of species and cultivars. Many summer-flowering forms produce large showy blooms, while plants that perform in spring, late summer, and fall often bear smaller flowers. Most clematis, barring a few shrubby types, are hardy climbers and require support for their twining leaf stems to cling to. Use horizontal wires on walls and fences, or slim stakes to coax them onto trees and shrubs. To produce the best displays, clematis should be pruned annually, and the method you use depends on when they flower. Those that bloom in spring and early summer generally require a light trim, while later-flowering forms are cut back hard.

USING CLEMATIS

Cover walls and fences with the flowers and foliage of clematis by fixing horizontal wires or a trellis securely to the surface. Roses and clematis are a classic planting combination for arches and pergolas. Select plants that bloom at the same time for the most colorful display.

Compact clematis have been specially bred to grow in pots and are the best choice for patio displays. Plant them in a large container and provide a tripod to support their stems.

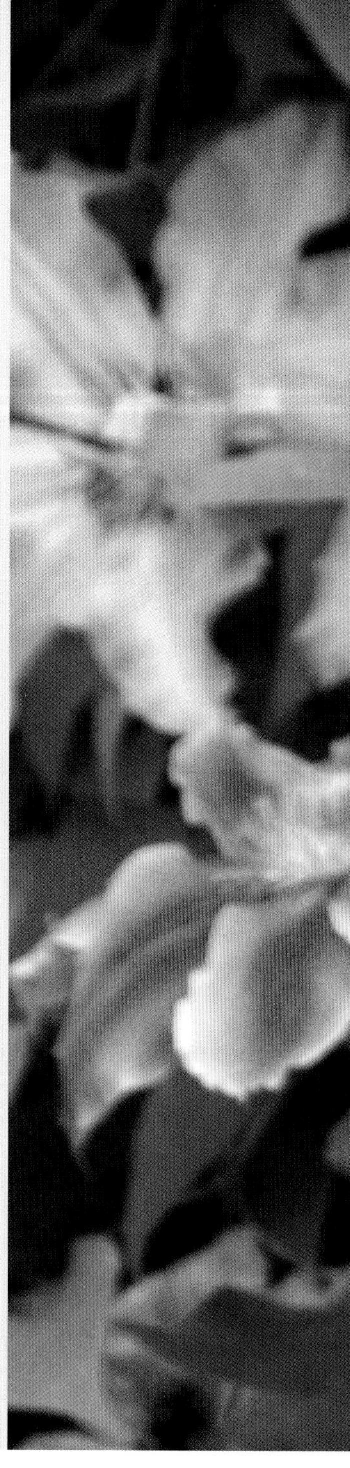

Large early summer-flowering clematis can be combined to decorate walls and fences with blooms, which form richly colored backdrops for beds and borders.

POPULAR CLEMATIS SPECIES

Evergreens The early spring-flowering *C. cirrhosa* and *C. armandii* have evergreen leaves and are not as hardy as deciduous types. Plant them in a sheltered site, away from cold winds.

Spring-flowering forms *C. macropetala* and *C. alpina* fall into this group, with their nodding, bell-shaped flowers, as do forms of the rambling *C. montana* with their star-shaped blooms.

Early-season large-flowered forms These include many popular forms that bear large single and double flowers in a wide range of colors from late spring to midsummer.

Late-summer large-flowered forms These bear large colorful flowers from midsummer to early fall on the current season's stems; prune them hard in spring.

Late-flowering species This group includes *C. tangutica* and *C. orientalis*, with their dainty nodding flowers, and the vigorous small-flowered *C. rehderiana* and *C. flammula* species.

Winter interest Many late-flowering clematis produce attractive fluffy seedheads that may persist into winter. These include *C. tangutica*, *C. orientalis*, *C. rehderiana*, and *C. flammula*.

Plants for cracks in walls and paving

Stone or old brick walls punctuated with small, spreading plants nestling in the cracks transform an ordinary landscaping feature into a focal point.

You can also soften the sharp outlines of paths and patios with colorful, low-growing plants squeezed between the slabs and bricks. Designs are most effective where the plants look as though they have self-seeded, and this is one option, using plants, such as sweet alyssum and Mexican fleabane. These grow easily from seed, given a little soil in which to germinate. Alternatively, remove the mortar between bricks or paving stones, or eliminate one altogether. Wrap the roots of your young plants or plugs in sticky, clay-rich soil and wedge them into the gap. Drizzle carefully with water until the plants have established.

BULB MEDIUM

Allium schoenoprasum

CHIVES A clump-forming, upright deciduous bulb with narrow, hollow, dark green edible leaves. In summer, it produces fluffy, pale purple pompon flower heads on slim stems. Ideal for paving cracks and tight spaces.

↕12in (30cm)

Z4–8

PERENNIAL SMALL

Arabis alpina subsp. *caucasica*

WALL ROCK CRESS A mat-forming evergreen perennial with small, hairy, gray-green leaves and, from early spring to early summer, masses of small white flowers. Grow it in wall or paving cracks.

↕↔6in (15cm)

Z4–7

PERENNIAL SMALL

Armeria maritima

THRIFT A clump-forming evergreen perennial with grasslike dark green leaves. Round heads of small white to pink flowers appear on slim stems in summer. Use it to fill gaps in paving; suitable for coastal areas.

↕4in (10cm) ↔6in (15cm)

Z4–8 Ⓝ

PERENNIAL SMALL

Aubrieta 'Argenteovariegata'

ROCK CRESS This trailing evergreen perennial forms mats of oval green leaves with cream edges. Small pinkish lavender flowers cover the plant throughout spring. Ideal for cracks in walls and paving. Cut back after flowering.

↕2in (5cm) ↔6in (15cm)

Z4–8

PERENNIAL SMALL

Aubrieta deltoidea

AUBRETIA This small, ground-hugging evergreen perennial forms spreading stems of rounded gray-green leaves and masses of pale mauve flowers in spring. 'Whitewell Gem' bears hundreds of violet-purple blooms.

↕2in (5cm) ↔24in (60cm)

Z4–8

PERENNIAL SMALL

Aurinia saxatilis

BASKET OF GOLD A clump-forming evergreen perennial with oval, hairy gray-green leaves. From spring to summer, it produces a mass of tiny chrome-yellow flowers on slim stems. Use it to brighten up walls and paving.

↕9in (23cm) ↔12in (30cm)

Z4–7

SHRUB SMALL

Calluna vulgaris

SCOTCH HEATHER A spreading evergreen shrub with upright stems covered with tiny bright green leaves and pink, white, or red blooms from midsummer to late fall. 'Spring Cream' (above) has white flowers and cream-colored new shoots in early summer.

↕24in (60cm) ↔30in (75cm)

pH Z4–6

PERENNIAL SMALL

Campanula carpatica

CARPATHIAN HAREBELL This clump-forming perennial produces a carpet of heart-shaped green leaves and open bell-shaped, violet-blue or white flowers throughout summer. Use it to fill gaps in walls and paving.

↕4in (10cm) ↔12in (30cm)

Z4–7

PERENNIAL SMALL

Campanula poscharskyana

SERBIAN BELLFLOWER This spreading perennial forms low mounds of round, serrated-edged midgreen leaves. Starry violet flowers appear on leafy stems from summer to early fall. Use it to cascade from walls or spread between paving.

↕6in (15cm) ↔ indefinite

Z3–8

PERENNIAL SMALL

Chamaemelum nobile

CHAMOMILE A mat-forming evergreen perennial with aromatic ferny foliage and white pompom flowers held on erect stems in summer. Use it to fill cracks in paving. 'Flore Pleno' (above) is a double-flowered variety.

↕12in (30cm) ↔ 18in (45cm)

Z5–9

SHRUB SMALL

Daboecia cantabrica

IRISH HEATH A spreading evergreen shrub with small, oval dark green leaves, silver-gray beneath. From early summer to fall, it bears urn-shaped, single or double white, purple, or mauve flowers. 'Bicolor' (above) has blooms in mixed colors.

↕18in (45cm) ↔ 24in (60cm)

pH Z6–8

PERENNIAL SMALL

Delosperma nubigenum

ICE PLANT A small, ground-hugging evergreen perennial that produces mats of succulent, triangular green leaves and daisy-like lemon-yellow flowers in summer. Plant it on top of a wall or gravel beside paving.

↕2in (5cm) ↔ 20in (50cm)

Z6–8

PERENNIAL SMALL

Dianthus alpinus

ALPINE PINK A small, mat-forming evergreen perennial with dark gray-green foliage and white, pink, or crimson flowers held on short stems in summer. 'Joan's Blood' (above) has deep crimson, dark-centered flowers.

↕3in (8cm) ↔ 4in (10cm)

Z3–8

PERENNIAL SMALL

Dryas octopetala

MOUNTAIN AVENS A mat-forming evergreen perennial with oval, leathery, dark green lobed leaves. Small, creamy white cup-shaped flowers appear from late spring to early summer, followed by feathery seedheads. Use in paving cracks.

↕2½in (6cm) ↔ indefinite

Z2–6 Ⓝ

SHRUB SMALL

Erica carnea

WINTER HEATH A small, spreading evergreen shrub, with needlelike dark green leaves. It produces tiny, tubular pink, red, or white flowers, which appear from early winter to late spring. Grow it in paving cracks.

↕12in (30cm) ↔ 18in (45cm) or more

pH Z5–7

PERENNIAL SMALL

Erigeron karvinskianus

MEXICAN FLEABANE This spreading perennial produces lance-shaped, hairy green leaves and, from summer to early fall, daisy-like flowers that open white, turn pink, and fade to purple. It makes a perfect addition to a wall or paving.

↕6in (15cm) ↔ indefinite

Z8–10 Ⓝ

PERENNIAL SMALL

Erinus alpinus

FAIRY FOXGLOVE A short-lived semievergreen perennial with soft midgreen foliage. From late spring to summer, small purple, pink, or white flowers appear on leafy stems. It will self-seed in the crevices in walls and paving.

↕↔3in (8cm)

Z4–7

PERENNIAL SMALL

Erodium manescavii

HERON'S BILL This small clump-forming perennial forms divided, ferny green leaves. Throughout summer, it produces loose clusters of magenta-purple flowers, and will self-seed freely in the cracks in walls and paving.

↕18in (45cm) ↔ 24in (60cm)

Z6–8

PERENNIAL SMALL

Festuca glauca

BLUE FESCUE An tuft-forming evergreen perennial grass with steel-blue foliage. The leaves are joined by short flower spikes in summer. It will self-seed in the cracks in paving. The cultivar 'Elijah Blue' has powder-blue foliage.

↕↔20in (50cm)

Z4–8

SHRUB SMALL

Helianthemum 'Wisley Pink'

ROCK ROSE This vigorous, spreading evergreen shrub produces small, slim gray-green leaves. Throughout summer, saucer-shaped, orange-centered pale pink flowers are held on lax stems. It looks beautiful trailing from a wall.

↕↔12in (30cm) or more

Z6–8

PERENNIAL SMALL

Gentiana septemfida

CRESTED GENTIAN This evergreen perennial forms trailing stems of small, oval dark green leaves and trumpet-shaped midblue flowers from summer to fall. Use it to trail from cracks in walls or spread out when planted in paving.

↕8in (20cm) ↔12in (30cm)

pH Z3–8

PERENNIAL SMALL

Geranium asphodeloides

CRANESBILL A spreading deciduous perennial with small, rounded, deeply dissected leaves and masses of starry white or light pink, magenta-veined flowers in early summer. Grow it between paving stones or flowing over walls.

↕↔12in (30cm)

Z6–9

PERENNIAL SMALL

Geranium sanguineum

BLOODY CRANESBILL This spreading perennial forms a neat mound of deeply dissected, dark green leaves. It flowers freely in summer, bearing an abundance of round, magenta-pink blooms. Grow it in paving cracks; water during dry spells.

↕10in (25cm) ↔12in (30cm) or more

Z4–8

SHRUB SMALL

Helichrysum italicum

CURRY PLANT A bushy evergreen subshrub grown for its narrow, curry-scented silvery gray leaves. Domed clusters of small, bright yellow flowers are produced on long, upright white shoots in summer. Grow it in cracks in paving.

↕24in (60cm) ↔3ft (1m)

Z7–10

SHRUB SMALL

Lavandula angustifolia 'Hidcote'

ENGLISH LAVENDER A bushy evergreen subshrub with aromatic, silver-gray leaves and dense spikes of fragrant deep purple flowers from mid- to late summer. Remove a paving stone and plant it in the gap.

↕24in (60cm) ↔30in (75cm)

Z5–8

ANNUAL/BIENNIAL SMALL

Limnanthes douglasii

POACHED-EGG FLOWER A spreading annual, easy to grow from seed, with feathery green foliage and cup-shaped, yellow-centered white flowers throughout summer. Sow seeds in the cracks in walls and paving. It may then self-seed.

↕6in (15cm) ↔4in (10cm)

PERENNIAL SMALL

Linaria alpina

ALPINE TOADFLAX A short-lived perennial, which produces trailing stems of lance-shaped, fleshy gray-green leaves and a succession of snap-dragon-like, orange-centered, purple-violet flowers in summer. Use it to decorate walls and paving.

↕6in (15cm) ↔6in (15cm)

Z4–9

SHRUB SMALL

Lithodora diffusa 'Heavenly Blue'

LITHODORA This evergreen subshrub forms a carpet of small, hairy green leaves on trailing stems. Funnel-shaped, deep blue flowers appear all summer. Grow in walls or paving cracks; trim stems after flowering.

↕12in (30cm) ↔18in (45cm)

pH Z8–11

ANNUAL/BIENNIAL SMALL

Lobularia maritima

SWEET ALYSSUM This easy-to-grow annual has lance-shaped green foliage and masses of round, fragrant, white or pink flower heads all summer. Sow seeds in wall and paving cracks. 'Easter Bonnet' (above) is popular. Considered invasive in some areas.

↕4in (10cm) ↔12in (30cm)

BULB MEDIUM

Muscari armeniacum

GRAPE HYACINTH This spring-flowering bulb produces grasslike green leaves and short spikes of small, fragrant, bell-shaped deep blue flowers held in cone-shaped clusters. Plant it in cracks in walls and paving, or in tight spaces.

↕8in (20cm)

Z4–8

PERENNIAL SMALL

Oenothera speciosa

PINK EVENING PRIMROSE This short-lived, clump-forming perennial bears fragrant, saucer-shaped, pure white summer flowers that age to pink above the spoon-shaped, deeply cut leaves. The blooms open in the evening. Varieties include 'Rosea' (above).

↕↔12in (30cm)

Z4–8 Ⓝ

PERENNIAL SMALL

Origanum vulgare 'Aureum'

GOLDEN OREGANO This clump-forming perennial forms a dense mat of aromatic, golden-yellow rounded leaves that turn pale yellow-green in midsummer. It also produces tiny mauve flowers in summer. Grow it in cracks in walls or paving.

↕3in (8cm) ↔ indefinite

Z4–8

PERENNIAL SMALL

Sedum 'Ruby Glow'

STONECROP This short, clump-forming deciduous perennial bears oval, fleshy purplish green leaves. In late summer, it produces loose heads of star-shaped, pink and ruby-red flowers on dark red stems. Plant it in cracks in paving.

↕8in (20cm) ↔16in (40cm)

Z5–9

PERENNIAL SMALL

Sempervivum tectorum

HENS AND CHICKS A mat-forming evergreen perennial, with rosettes of fleshy, blue-green leaves suffused with red-purple. Clusters of starry, reddish purple blooms form in summer. Plant in gaps in paving, but not where it will be stepped on.

↕6in (15cm) ↔8in (20cm)

Z4–8

PERENNIAL SMALL

Silene schafta

AUTUMN CATCHFLY This low-growing perennial has a spreading habit, forming mats of slender dark green leaves. From late summer to fall, it produces dainty, star-shaped magenta flowers. It will self-seed in cracks, but is easy to control.

↕10in (25cm) ↔12in (30cm)

Z4–8

SHRUB SMALL

Thymus serpyllum

MOTHER OF THYME This mat-forming evergreen subshrub forms trailing stems of hairy, aromatic, dark green leaves. It is covered with masses of tiny purple or pink flowers in summer. Plant in crevices in walls and paving. Ideal for culinary use.

↕10in (25cm) ↔18in (45cm)

Z4–8

PERENNIAL SMALL

Veronica prostrata

PROSTRATE SPEEDWELL A dense, mat-forming evergreen perennial with narrow, toothed green leaves and upright spikes of small, saucer-shaped, bright blue or lilac flowers in early summer. Use it in crevices in walls or paving.

↕12in (30cm) ↔ indefinite

Z5–8

OTHER SUGGESTIONS

Annuals

Iberis umbellata Fairy Series

Perennials

Arabis caucasica • *Arabis procurrens* • *Arenaria balearica* • *Arenaria montana* • *Aubretia* 'Doctor Mules' • *Calamintha nepeta* Ⓝ • *Callirhoe involucrata* Ⓝ • *Campanula garganica* 'Dickson's Gold' • *Cerastium tomentosum* • *Ceratostigma plumbaginoides* • *Delosperma* MESA VERDE • *Dianthus deltoides* • *Echeveria* 'Black Prince' • *Erodium* 'Natasha' • *Geranium cinereum* 'Ballerina' • *Iberis sempervirens* • *Mentha requienii* • *Phlox subulata* 'Scarlet Flame' Ⓝ • *Silene acaulis* • *Tradescantia pallida* 'Purpurea' Ⓝ

Shrubs

Cassiope 'Edinburgh' • *Cytisus* x *kewensis* • *Frankenia thymifolia* • *Lavandula angustifolia* 'Thumbelina Leigh'

Plants for patios, balconies, and windowsills

Decorative plants in pots will brighten up the smallest of spaces, while containers of different sizes help to create a dynamic effect.

The choice of container plants is extensive, from pretty annuals for baskets and windowboxes, to perennials to make up permanent displays, to shrubs for dramatic, sculptural statements. If the container is large enough and you are able to supply sufficient fertilizer and water, almost any plant will survive, but if time and space are limited, opt for those that will cope with some drought, such as tickseed, lavender, and mealycup sage. Shrubs, trees, and perennials are best housed in big pots that hold plenty of compost, which means they also hold more water and fertilizer; plant them in place because they will be very heavy when full.

SHRUB LARGE

Abutilon 'Nabob'

FLOWERING MAPLE An evergreen shrub with green maplelike foliage and bowl-shaped crimson summer flowers. In cooler areas, grow as annuals in soil-based potting mix. To overwinter, take tip cuttings in late summer or bring indoors in bright light.
↕↔10ft (3m)

Z9–10

TREE SMALL

Acer palmatum 'Bloodgood'

JAPANESE MAPLE A deciduous tree with reddish purple maplelike leaves that turn bright red in fall. Winged red fruits follow the small purple spring flowers. Grow in a large container of soil-based potting mix, shaded from full sun. Water well.
↕↔15ft (5m)

Z5–8

PERENNIAL LARGE

Agapanthus Headbourne hybrids

AFRICAN LILY This perennial has strap-shaped foliage and spherical clusters of blue funnel-shaped flowers from late summer to early fall. Grow in a sheltered site in soil-based potting mix with added grit.
↕4ft (1.2m) ↔24in (60cm)

Z6–9

PERENNIAL LARGE

Agave americana 'Variegata'

CENTURY PLANT This succulent has lance-shaped, pointed, cream-edged gray-green leaves. In hot summers, cream flowers may appear. Grow in a mix of potting soil and grit; move containerized plants indoors in areas with cold winters.
↕↔5ft (1.5m)

Z9–11 Ⓝ

PERENNIAL MEDIUM

Anthemis tinctoria

GOLDEN MARGUERITE This clump-forming perennial bears lacy aromatic leaves and daisy-like white or yellow flowers all summer. Plant in containers of soil-based potting mix. Varieties include the lemon-yellow-flowered 'E.C. Buxton' (above).
↕↔3ft (1m)

Z3–8

ANNUAL/BIENNIAL SMALL

Antirrhinum majus

SNAPDRAGON This small upright annual has lance-shaped green leaves and, from late spring to fall, it produces spikes of two-lipped flowers in pink, red, crimson, burgundy, white, and yellow. Grow it in groups in containers of potting soil.
↕↔18in (45cm)

ANNUAL/BIENNIAL MEDIUM

Arctotis fastuosa

CAPE DAISY This medium-sized upright annual produces lobed, silvery green leaves and masses of daisy-like, bright orange flowers with dark maroon and black eyes throughout summer. Plant it in groups in containers of potting soil.
↕24in (60cm) ↔12in (30cm)

SHRUB SMALL

Argyranthemum foeniculaceum

LANCE-LEAF MARGUERITE DAISY This evergreen subshrub, grown as an annual, has ferny gray-green foliage and yellow-centered white flowers all summer and early fall. Grow in containers of potting soil.
↕↔32in (80cm)

Z10–11

ANNUAL SMALL

Begonia Cocktail Series

WAX BEGONIA This small bushy annual produces rounded bronze-green leaves and flowers in shades of pink, red, or white from summer to fall. Use it to edge pots, windowboxes, and baskets; plant in all-purpose potting soil.

↕↔ 12in (30cm)

PERENNIAL SMALL

Begonia sutherlandii

SUTHERLAND'S BEGONIA This tuberous perennial forms trailing stems, lobed green leaves, and clusters of single orange flowers in summer. In late fall, leaves and stems die back prior to winter dormancy. Treat as an annual or lift and protect tubers.

↕ 32in (80cm) ↔ indefinite

Z8–10

PERENNIAL SMALL

Bellis perennis

ENGLISH DAISY A mound-forming perennial, often grown as an annual, with oval midgreen leaves and pompom-shaped pink, white, or red spring flowers. Plant it with spring bulbs in pots, baskets, and windowboxes in all-purpose potting soil.

↕↔ 8in (20cm)

Z4–8

ANNUAL/BIENNIAL SMALL

Brachyscome iberidifolia

SWAN RIVER DAISY This is a bushy annual with feathery green leaves and daisy-like blue, pink, purple, or white flowers that appear from summer to early fall. Perfect for baskets and containers; plant it in all-purpose potting soil.

↕ 10in (25cm) ↔ 18in (45cm)

SHRUB SMALL

Buxus sempervirens 'Suffruticosa'

COMMON BOXWOOD An evergreen shrub that forms a dense mass of oval bright green leaves. Plant it in a large container filled with soil-based potting mix, and clip to form decorative topiary shapes.

↕ 3ft (1m) ↔ 5ft (1.5m)

Z6–8

ANNUAL/BIENNIAL MEDIUM

Calendula officinalis

POT MARIGOLD This bushy annual bears lance-shaped, aromatic pale green leaves and, from spring to fall, daisy-like single or double flowers in yellow and orange. Grow it in windowboxes or containers in all-purpose potting soil.

↕↔ 24in (60cm)

PERENNIAL SMALL

Calibrachoa Million Bells Series

MILLION BELLS A semitrailing perennial, grown as an annual, with slender dark green leaves and, from summer to early fall, colorful trumpet-shaped blooms. Trail from windowboxes, containers, and baskets.

↕ 12in (30cm) ↔ 3ft (1m)

Z9–11

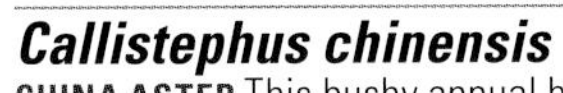

ANNUAL/BIENNIAL MEDIUM

Callistephus chinensis

CHINA ASTER This bushy annual has oval, lobed green leaves and, from late summer to fall, produces flowers in shades of pink, purple, white, and yellow. The Pom Pom Series (above) produces small rounded flowers.

↕ 24in (60cm) ↔ 18in (45cm)

PERENNIAL LARGE

Canna 'Pretoria'

syn. *Canna* 'Striata' This upright perennial is grown for its green- and yellow-striped foliage, and bright orange flowers, which appear from midsummer to early fall. Grow in soil-based potting mix; water well. In cool zones, dig and overwinter the rhizomes.

↕ 5ft (1.5m) ↔ 20in (50cm)

Z8–11

PERENNIAL SMALL

Carex comans

NEW ZEALAND HAIR SEDGE An evergreen perennial sedge with dense tufts of fine, grassy bronze-colored leaves. In summer, it also bears small brown flower spikes. Grow it in a container of soil-based potting mix. Remove dead growth in spring.

↕ 14in (35cm) ↔ 30in (75cm)

Z7–9

PERENNIAL MEDIUM

Carex 'Ice Dance'

SEDGE This evergreen perennial sedge has grassy green leaves with creamy white margins and small white flowers in spring. Plant it in containers and windowboxes in soil-based potting mix; keep well watered. May spread if planted in borders.

↕24in (60cm) ↔30in (75cm)

Z5–9

PERENNIAL SMALL

Carex testacea

ORANGE NEW ZEALAND SEDGE This evergreen perennial sedge produces mounds of olive-green to orange-brown grassy leaves and dark brown flower spikes in summer. It looks good in tall containers of soil-based potting mix.

↕18in (45cm) ↔24in (60cm)

Z7–9

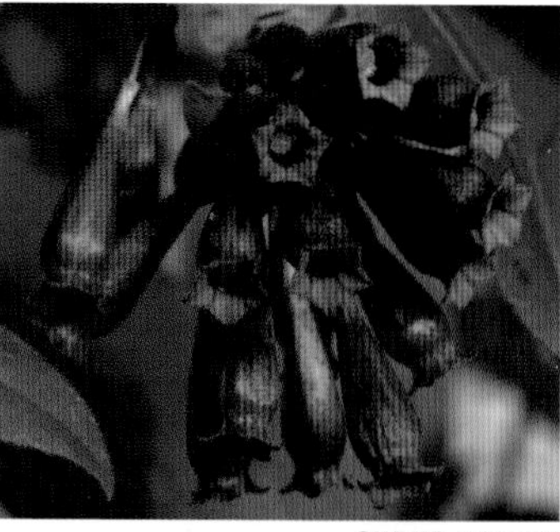

SHRUB MEDIUM

Cestrum elegans

PURPLE CESTRUM A tender evergreen shrub with large, spear-shaped, soft midgreen foliage and dense clusters of scented, tubular bright pink-red flowers during summer. Grow it in a large containers of soil-based potting mix; protect from frost.

↕↔10ft (3m)

Z8–11 Ⓝ

ANNUAL/BIENNIAL LARGE

Cleome hassleriana

SPIDER FLOWER A tall erect annual with spiny stems of divided palmlike leaves. In summer, it produces rounded heads of spidery flowers with long stamens, in shades of pink, white, and purple. 'Rose Queen' (above) has pink flowers.

↕5ft (1.5m) ↔18in (45cm)

SHRUB MEDIUM

Choisya ternata

MEXICAN ORANGE A rounded evergreen shrub with aromatic, glossy green leaves divided into three leaflets, and fragrant white blooms from late spring to fall. SUNDANCE (above) has golden foliage. Suitable for West Coast gardens.

↕↔ up to 8ft (2.5m)

Z8–10 Ⓝ

TREE SMALL

Cordyline australis Purpurea Group

CABBAGE PALM This small evergreen tree bears a fountain of spiky purple foliage. Use as a specimen plant in a tall or large container of soil-based potting mix for taproot; keep indoors during winter.

↕up to 10ft (3m) ↔3ft (1m)

Z10–11

ANNUAL/BIENNIAL MEDIUM

Coreopsis tinctoria

TICKSEED This erect annual produces finely divided, ferny green leaves. Daisy-like lemon-yellow flowers appear on wiry stems throughout summer. Grow it in groups in a large container of soil-based potting mix.

↕24in (60cm) ↔12in (30cm)

CLIMBER SMALL

Clematis SHIMMER

CLEMATIS A compact, long-flowering deciduous climber with midgreen leaves and large, deep lilac summer-long blooms that fade to midblue and have a paler central bar. Plant in a container of soil-based potting mix, with a tripod support.

↕6ft (1.8m)

Z4–9

ANNUAL/BIENNIAL LARGE

Cosmos bipinnatus

COSMOS A compact annual, easy to grow from seed, it has feathery green foliage and large daisy-like flowers in shades of pink, red, and white from summer to early fall. Plant it in groups in containers of potting mix. Deadhead regularly.

↕up to 4ft (1.2m) ↔18in (45cm)

PERENNIAL LARGE

Ensete ventricosum

ABYSSINIAN BANANA This palmlike evergreen perennial has large paddle-shaped leaves with cream midribs and red undersides. Plant in a large container of soil-based potting mix and grit. In cooler areas, move indoors for winter; protect from frost.

↕↔ 10ft (3m) in a pot

Z10–11

SHRUB SMALL

Felicia amelloides

BLUE DAISY Grown as an annual, this subshrub has small dark green foliage and a mass of yellow-eyed blue flowers from summer to fall. It forms a bushy clump. Grow in windowboxes, baskets, and containers in potting soil. Deadhead often.

↕↔ 10in (25cm)

10–11

BULB MEDIUM

Dahlia 'Gallery Art Deco'

DECORATIVE DAHLIA A dwarf perennial with lobed dark green leaves and from midsummer to fall pale orange, burgundy-edged double flowers. Grow in containers of potting soil. Dies back in fall. Protect tubers from frost, lift them in cooler areas.

↕ 18in (45cm)

Z9–11

SHRUB SMALL

Fuchsia 'Mrs Popple'

FUCHSIA This upright deciduous shrub bears small dark green leaves and red and purple flowers in summer. It makes a statement in a large container of soil-based potting mix. Best grown only in warmer areas.

↕↔ 3½ft (1.1m)

Z9–11

BULB MEDIUM

Eucomis bicolor

PINEAPPLE LILY A late-summer flowering bulb with wavy-edged leaves and spotted stems, topped with clusters of greenish white flowers and purple-edged petals. With "hats" of leaflike bracts, the flowers resemble pineapples. Protect from frost.

↕ 20in (50cm)

Z8–10

ANNUAL/BIENNIAL MEDIUM

Dianthus barbatus

SWEET WILLIAM An upright biennial with lance-shaped green leaves and domed heads of sweetly-scented pink, red, or burgundy flowers, which appear in early summer. Grow it in groups in containers of potting soil.

↕ 28in (70cm) ↔ 12in (30cm)

Z3–9

SHRUB LARGE

Fatsia japonica

JAPANESE FATSIA An evergreen shrub, with large, hand-shaped, glossy dark green leaves and small, spherical white flower heads in fall, followed by black fruits. Ideal for winter interest. Plant in large containers of soil-based potting mix.

↕↔ 12ft (4m)

Z8–10

SHRUB SMALL

Fuchsia 'Thalia'

FUCHSIA A small, upright deciduous shrub with dark green leaves that are maroon beneath. Clusters of pendent, tubular red flowers appear from summer to early fall. Plant it in a large container of soil-based potting mix.

↕↔ 24in (60cm)

Z9–11

PERENNIAL SMALL

Gazania Talent Series

TREASURE FLOWER A dwarf perennial, grown as an annual, with narrow, gray-felted leaves and daisy-like yellow, orange, pink, or maroon summer flowers. Plant in containers or windowboxes in potting soil. Varieties include 'Talent Yellow' (above).
↕↔10in (25cm)

Z8–10

PERENNIAL SMALL

Gerbera hybrids

TRANSVAAL DAISY A perennial, grown as an annual, with oval, lobed green leaves and tall stems of daisy-like black-eyed flowers, which appear from summer to fall in nearly every color. Plant in containers of potting soil; protect from frost.
↕↔16in (40cm)

Z8–11

SHRUB SMALL

Hebe 'Red Edge'

HEBE A small evergreen shrub that bears oval blue-green leaves with red margins and clusters of pale mauve to white flowers in summer. Plant it in a container of soil-based potting mix, and place in a sheltered site. Trim after flowering to keep compact.
↕18in (45cm) ↔24in (60cm)

Z9–10

ANNUAL/BIENNIAL MEDIUM

Helianthus debilis

SUNFLOWER This erect annual produces slim midgreen leaves and large, chocolate-centered creamy white summer flowers. Grow it in groups in a large container of potting soil in a sheltered site. Stake the tall flower stems.
↕4ft (1.2m) ↔24in (60cm)

SHRUB SMALL

Helichrysum italicum

CURRY PLANT A bushy evergreen subshrub grown for its slender, curry-scented silvery gray leaves. It bears domed clusters of small bright yellow flowers on long upright shoots in summer. Grow it in containers of soil-based potting mix and grit.
↕24in (60cm) ↔3ft (1m)

Z7–10

PERENNIAL SMALL

Heuchera 'Amber Waves'

CORAL BELLS An evergreen perennial with lobed, ruffled orange-yellow leaves that are pale burgundy underneath and sprays of small, bell-shaped pink summer flowers. Plant in soil-based potting mix. Use it to edge pots, windowboxes, and baskets.
↕12in (30cm) ↔20in (50cm)

Z4–9

PERENNIAL SMALL

Ipomoea batatas 'Blackie'

SWEET POTATO VINE This trailing evergreen perennial, often grown as an annual, produces lobed, ivy-shaped, almost black, leaves. A beautiful edging plant for tropical-style arrangements, grow it in a tall container of potting soil.
↕10in (25cm) ↔24in (60cm)

Z9–11

ANNUAL/BIENNIAL SMALL

Ismelia carinata

PAINTED DAISY This is a small, erect branching annual with feathery gray-green leaves. From summer to fall, it produces daisy-like, brown-eyed flowers in shades of red, yellow, white, or purple.
↕24in (60cm) ↔12in (30cm)

PERENNIAL SMALL

Isotoma axillaris

LAURENTIA This mound-forming perennial, grown as an annual, has feathery green foliage and masses of star-shaped lilac or blue flowers from summer to early fall. Grow it with other annuals in containers of potting soil.
↕↔12in (30cm)

Z10–11

CLIMBER MEDIUM

Lathyrus odoratus

SWEET PEA This annual climber produces oval green leaves and scented white, pink, purple, and red summer flowers. 'Knee High' (above) is a dwarf form suitable for hanging baskets or pots with a tripod support. Grows best in cool environment.
↕10ft (3m)

TREE MEDIUM

Laurus nobilis

BAY LAUREL This conical evergreen shrub is grown for its leathery, glossy, aromatic dark green leaves that can be used for cooking. Plant it in a large container of soil-based potting mix; clip it to form topiary shapes. Prune regularly to restrict its size.
↕40ft (12m) ↔30ft (10m)

Z8–10

SHRUB SMALL

Lavandula stoechas

SPANISH LAVENDER This evergreen subshrub has aromatic gray-green foliage. From late spring to summer, it bears blue, white, or mauve scented flowers with upright "ears." 'Kew Red' (above) has deep pink flowers. Plant in soil-based potting mix.
↕↔18in (45cm)

Z8–9

BULB LARGE

Lilium Golden Splendor Group

YELLOW TRUMPET LILY This perennial has slim green leaves and tall stems. In summer, scented, trumpet-shaped golden flowers appear. Plant in soil-based potting mix with added grit; stake the stems.
↕6ft (2m)

Z5–8

PERENNIAL SMALL

Lobelia erinus

TRAILING LOBELIA A perennial, grown as an annual, with tiny green leaves. Masses of small white, blue, or mauve blooms appear in summer. Use it to edge windowboxes, pots, or baskets, and plant in potting soil. 'Snowball' (above) has white flowers.
↕9in (23cm) ↔6in (15cm)

Z10–11

PERENNIAL SMALL

Lotus berthelotii

CORAL GEM This trailing perennial, grown as an annual, has feathery silver-green foliage and clusters of summer flowers with pointed petals that resemble birds' beaks. Grow it in containers, baskets, or windowboxes in potting soil.
↕8in (20cm) ↔indefinite

Z10–12

SHRUB SMALL

Mahonia aquifolium

OREGON GRAPEHOLLY This spreading evergreen shrub has glossy, spiny dark green leaves and clusters of yellow flowers in spring followed by black berries. Ideal for year-round color; plant it in a large container of soil-based potting mix.
↕↔3ft (1m)

Z5–8 Ⓝ

PERENNIAL SMALL

Matthiola incana

STOCK This is a small tender perennial, grown as an annual, that produces oval green leaves. Throughout summer, it bears spikes of clove-scented flowers in shades of pink, purple, and white. Plant it in containers of potting soil.
↕↔10in (25cm)

Z6–9

BULB MEDIUM

Muscari latifolium

GRAPE HYACINTH A dwarf bulb with gray-green strap-shaped leaves and tiny, bell-shaped two-tone spring flowers, dark blue at the base and pale blue on top. Plant the bulbs in fall in containers of soil-based potting mix with added grit.
↕10in (25cm)

Z4–8

BULB MEDIUM

Narcissus 'Canaliculatus'

DAFFODIL This dwarf bulb produces linear green leaves and slim stems bearing clusters of small, fragrant spring flowers with reflexed white petals and yellow cups. Plant in frostproof containers during fall.
↕9in (23cm)

(!) Z6–10

BULB MEDIUM

Narcissus 'Fortune'

DAFFODIL An upright bulb that produces linear green leaves. From early- to mid-spring, single flowers with lemon-yellow petals and orange cups appear. Plant the bulbs in fall in containers of soil-based potting mix with added grit.

↕16in (40cm)

Z3–7

ANNUAL SMALL

Nemesia caerulea

NEMESIA A compact, mat-forming annual with narrow dark green leaves and fragrant blue-mauve flowers from summer to early fall. Use it to edge containers, windowboxes, and hanging baskets; plant in all-purpose potting soil.

↕↔12in (30cm)

Z9–10

ANNUAL SMALL

Nemesia 'KLM'

NEMESIA This mat-forming compact annual has narrow green leaves and bears small blue and white flowers throughout summer. Useful for edging containers, windowboxes, and baskets; plant in all-purpose potting soil.

↕12in (30cm) ↔6in (16cm)

ANNUAL/BIENNIAL SMALL

Nemophila menziesii

BABY BLUE-EYES An easy-to-grow spreading annual with serrated gray-green leaves. Small, saucer-shaped blue flowers with white centers appear in summer. Grow it in pots, windowboxes, and baskets in all-purpose potting soil.

↕8in (20cm) ↔6in (15cm)

PERENNIAL MEDIUM

Nicotiana alata

FLOWERING TOBACCO An upright perennial, grown as an annual, with oval midgreen leaves. Clusters of trumpet-shaped white, pink, or green flowers, which are fragrant at night, appear from summer to early fall. Plant it in containers of potting soil.

↕30in (75cm) ↔12in (30cm)

Z10–11

PERENNIAL MEDIUM

Osteospermum hybrids

AFRICAN DAISY An clump-forming evergreen perennial, grown as an annual, with narrow gray-green leaves and pink, white, and yellow daisy-like flowers from summer to early fall. Plant in containers filled with all-purpose potting soil.

↕24in (60cm) ↔12in (30cm)

Z10–11

PERENNIAL SMALL

Pelargonium 'Lord Bute'

REGAL GERANIUM An upright herbaceous, evergreen perennial, often grown as an annual. It has rounded hairy leaves and produces deep purple-red ruffled flowers throughout summer. Plant in all-purpose potting soil in containers and windowboxes.

↕18in (45cm) ↔12in (30cm)

Z10–11

PERENNIAL SMALL

Pelargonium Mini Cascade Series

IVY GERANIUM An evergreen perennial, grown as an annual, with ivy-shaped, glossy green foliage. Red or lilac blooms appear from summer to fall. Ideal for a hanging basket, pot, or windowbox.

↕↔18in (45cm)

Z10–11

PERENNIAL SMALL

Pelargonium Multibloom Series

ZONAL GERANIUM These erect, bushy evergreen perennials, grown as annuals, have rounded leaves and white, red, pink, and purple flowers from summer to fall. Grow in containers or baskets in potting soil.

↕↔12in (30cm)

Z10–11

PERENNIAL SMALL

Petunia Prism Series

PETUNIA A spreading perennial, grown as an annual, with dark green leaves and large, trumpet-shaped yellow flowers from summer to early fall. Grow in baskets, containers, and windowboxes in potting soil. 'Prism Sunshine' (above) is popular.

↕14in (35cm) ↔20in (50cm)

Z10–11

PERENNIAL MEDIUM

Phormium 'Bronze Baby'

NEW ZEALAND FLAX An upright evergreen perennial, grown for its fountain of arching, sword-shaped purple-bronze leaves. Use it to make a statement in a large container of soil-based potting mix. Overwinter indoors in cooler areas.

↕↔24in (60cm)

Z9–11

SHRUB SMALL

Picea abies 'Ohlendorffii'

NORWAY SPRUCE A slow-growing, bushy conifer with tightly packed green needles. It develops a rounded shape as it matures. Considered invasive in some areas. Plant in large containers of soil-based potting mix for evergreen interest; water well.

↕↔3ft (1m)

Z3–7

SHRUB MEDIUM

Pieris japonica

LILY OF THE VALLEY BUSH An evergreen shrub with leathery green leaves, bright red when young, and clusters of white, red, or pink urn-shaped spring flowers. Grow in a pot of acidic plant soil. 'Flamingo' (above) has dark red buds that open to a deep pink.

↕up to 6ft (2m) in a pot ↔5ft (1.5m)

pH Z5–8

SHRUB SMALL

Pinus mugo 'Mops'

MUGO PINE This compact evergreen conifer forms a neat mound of dense, needlelike dark green leaves, providing year-round interest. Plant it in a large container of soil-based potting mix, underplanted with small bulbs.

↕3ft (1m) ↔6ft (2m)

Z2–7

PERENNIAL MEDIUM

Rehmannia elata

CHINESE FOXGLOVE An erect perennial, with slim, toothed-edged green leaves and foxglovelike, yellow-throated rose-purple flowers in summer. Plant it in a sheltered site in cooler areas in a large container of soil-based potting mix. Protect from frost.

↕3ft (1m) ↔18in (45cm)

Z9–10

PERENNIAL SMALL

Rhodanthemum hosmariense

MORROCAN DAISY A small, shrubby evergreen perennial with silvery green leaves and white daisy-like flowers from late spring to early fall. Grow it in soil-based potting mix, with added grit, in a sheltered area. Deadhead regularly.

↕6in (15cm) or more ↔12in (30cm)

Z8–11

CLIMBER MEDIUM

Rhodochiton atrosanguineus

PURPLE BELL VINE This deciduous, native Mexican perennial climber, grown as an annual, has heart-shaped midgreen foliage and dangling umbrella-shaped blooms with pinky red hats and dark maroon tubes from late spring to late fall.

↕10ft (3m)

Z10–11 Ⓝ

SHRUB MEDIUM

Rhododendron yakushimanum

YAKUSHIMA RHODODENDRON A dome-shaped evergreen shrub with dark green leaves, silvery when young, and funnel-shaped pink late spring flowers. Grow in acidic potting soil, shaded from full sun.

↕↔6ft (2m)

pH (!) Z5–8

SHRUB MEDIUM

Rosa GERTRUDE JEKYLL

ENGLISH SHRUB ROSE An upright shrub rose, it has disease-resistant grayish green leaves. It produces highly fragrant, rose-pink fully double flowers that bloom throughout summer. Grow it in a large container or tub of soil-based potting mix.

↕6ft (2m) ↔4ft (1.2m)

Z5–9

PERENNIAL MEDIUM

Salvia farinacea

MEALYCUP SAGE An upright perennial, often grown as an annual, with lance-shaped green foliage and spikes of small purple-blue flowers from midsummer to fall. Grow it in mixed displays in containers of potting soil; deadhead regularly.

↕24in (60cm) ↔12in (30cm)

Z8–11 Ⓝ

PERENNIAL SMALL

Salvia splendens

SCARLET SAGE This upright perennial, grown as an annual, has spear-shaped dark green leaves. Spikes of tubular bright scarlet, pink, or white flowers appear through summer. Plant in windowboxes, containers, and baskets in potting soil.

↕10in (25cm) ↔14in (35cm)

Z11

ANNUAL/BIENNIAL SMALL

Salvia viridis

ANNUAL CLARY An upright annual with gray-green leaves, it bears small tubular flowers in summer, concealed beneath leaflike bracts, in shades of white, pink, and purple. The stems can be cut and dried; the dry bracts retain their color well.

↕18in (45cm) ↔8in (20cm)

ANNUAL/BIENNIAL SMALL

Sanvitalia procumbens

CREEPING ZINNIA This spreading native Mexican annual has slim, oval green leaves. A profusion of small, daisy-like yellow flowers with black centers appear in summer. Grow in windowboxes, baskets, and containers of potting soil.

↕6in (15cm) ↔12in (30cm)

PERENNIAL SMALL

Scaevola aemula

FAIRY FAN-FLOWER An evergreen perennial, grown as an annual, with toothed green leaves on trailing stems and fan-shaped blue, lilac, or white flowers in summer. Ideal for windowboxes and baskets; plant it in potting soil.

↕↔20in (50cm)

Z11–12

PERENNIAL SMALL

Solenostemon 'Black Prince'

COLEUS This bushy perennial is grown as an annual. It produces spear-shaped, dark purple foliage with a bright pink midrib. Plant it with brightly colored flowering annuals in containers, baskets, and windowboxes of potting mix.

↕↔20in (50cm)

Z11–12

PERENNIAL SMALL

Solenostemon scutellarioides

COLEUS A bushy perennial, grown as an annual, with spear-shaped foliage in a variety of colors including pink, red, green, and yellow. Plant it in containers, baskets, and windowboxes in potting soil.

↕18in (45cm) ↔12in (30cm) or more

Z11–12

ANNUAL/BIENNIAL SMALL

Tagetes patula

FRENCH MARIGOLD This native Mexican annual has deeply divided, aromatic green leaves and yellow, orange, red, or mahogany single or double flowers from summer to early fall. Plant in containers of all-purpose potting soil. Deadhead regularly.

↕↔12in (30cm)

PERENNIAL SMALL

Tanacetum parthenium 'Aureum'

GOLDEN FEVERFEW This bushy perennial, grown as an annual, has deeply cut, golden, aromatic foliage and daisy-like white flowers from summer to early fall. Grow in containers or windowboxes in potting soil.

↕↔18in (45cm)

Z5–8

SHRUB SMALL

Teucrium chamaedrys

WALL GERMANDER A bushy evergreen subshrub, it has oval, aromatic dark green leaves. From late summer to early fall, spikes of purple-pink flowers appear. Grow it in soil-based potting mix with added grit.

↕24in (60cm) ↔12in (30cm)

Z5–9

SHRUB SMALL

Thymus vulgaris

THYME This ground-cover subshrub has tiny, round, aromatic green leaves and, in summer, produces a mass of pink flowers. Combine it with other herbs in shallow containers of potting soil with added grit. Attractive to bees.

↕12in (30cm) ↔16in (40cm)

Z4–9

BULB MEDIUM

Tulipa 'Ballerina'

TULIP This late-spring, lily-flowered tulip produces gray-green leaves and single, goblet-shaped orange flowers with an orange-red central section on the petals. Plant the bulbs in groups in frostproof pots during fall.

↕24in (60cm)

(!) Z3–8

BULB MEDIUM

Tulipa 'Cape Cod'

TULIP This is a mid- to late spring-flowering bulb with gray-green leaves that have maroon mottling and single, bowl-shaped yellow flowers with a red strip on the petals. Plant the bulbs in groups in frostproof pots during fall.

↕18in (45cm)

(!) Z3–8

BULB MEDIUM

Tulipa 'Purissima'

TULIP This is an early- to mid-spring-flowering bulb with purple-marked gray-green leaves and single, bowl-shaped creamy white flowers. Plant the bulbs in groups in frostproof containers during fall.

↕16in (40cm)

(!) Z3–8

ANNUAL/BIENNIAL SMALL

Tropaeolum majus

NASTURTIUM A bushy annual with round green leaves and trumpet-shaped red, yellow, or orange flowers from summer to fall. Grow in tall containers, baskets or windowboxes in potting soil. Alaska Series (above) has cream-splashed foliage.

↕12in (30cm) ↔18in (45cm)

PERENNIAL SMALL

Verbena 'Peaches and Cream'

VERBENA This perennial, grown as an annual, has small, narrow, toothed leaves. It bears clusters of pink, pale peach, and cream blooms throughout summer and fall, if deadheaded regularly. Grow it in containers and baskets.

↕↔20in (50cm)

Z9–10

PERENNIAL SMALL

Viola x *wittrockiana*

PANSY A perennial, grown as an annual, with lobed green leaves and large ruffled flowers in shades of red, purple, yellow, and white from early spring to summer. Plant it in groups in containers, baskets, and windowboxes in potting soil.

↕9in (23cm) ↔12in (30cm)

Z4–8

ANNUAL/BIENNIAL SMALL

Zinnia 'Thumbelina Mix'

ZINNIA A dwarf bushy annual with oval dark green leaves. From summer to early fall, it bears semidouble flowers in shades of red, yellow, maroon, and pink. Grow it in mixed containers, baskets, and windowboxes in potting soil.

↕6in (15cm) ↔8in (21cm)

OTHER SUGGESTIONS

Annuals

Begonia 'Illumination Rose' • *Leonotis leonurus* • *Tagetes patula* (N)

Perennials

Eustoma grandiflorum (N) • *Oenothera macrocarpa* (N) • *Oxalis tetraphylla* 'Iron Cross' (N) • *Rudbeckia hirta* 'Indian Summer' (N) • *Sporobolus heterolepis* (N) • *Symphyotrichum oblongifolium* 'Raydon's Favorite' (N)

Bulbs

Crocus chrysanthus 'Blue Pearl' • *Lilium* 'Connecticut King'

Shrubs and climbers

Cornus stolonifera 'Baileyi' (N) • *Corylus avellana* 'Contorta' • *Cuphea llavea* 'Tiny Mice' (N) • *Hypericum calycinum* 'Briggadoon' • *Juniperus scopulorum* 'Wichita Blue' (N) • *Physocarpus opulifolius* 'Dart's Gold' (N) • *Picea abies* 'Nidiformis'

Plant focus: dahlias

Bold and beautiful, dahlias decorate the garden from summer to early fall with vividly colored and varied flowers.

Comprising ten different flower forms, and with plant sizes ranging from compact to towering giants, dahlias can be used in a wide variety of garden situations. Use ball, pompom, and rounded decorative dahlias to create spherical accents in a border of plant spires, such as mullein and salvias, and try spiky cactus forms to add drama and texture to a scheme. Single and collarette dahlias complement naturalistic designs, such as prairie-style borders, and many single varieties attract bees and other beneficial insects. Diminutive bedding dahlias are perfect for patio containers, while taller varieties suit large pots, but their bloom-laden stems may need staking. Dahlias are easy to grow from tubers or young plants bought in spring. Set them outside in a sunny position in free-draining soil after all risk of frost has passed. Also guard them against slugs, which can decimate plants. Bring tubers inside over winter or, in mild areas, cover them with a thick mulch.

USING DAHLIAS

Short-stemmed dahlias are perfect for patio planters and bedding schemes and give a long display if deadheaded regularly. Taller varieties are best suited to borders, where they can be given additional support. Dahlias with long stems are ideal to use as cut flowers and can be picked regularly from midsummer.

Dwarf dahlias that don't fit any of the eight main groups are often sold as bedding plants for pots and baskets. Overwinter the tubers or discard them at the end of the season.

Dahlias such as 'Bishop of Llandaff' (*right*) and 'Yellow Hammer' have dark foliage, providing a dramatic contrast to brightly flowered plants.

TYPES OF DAHLIA

Decorative The fully double ruffled flowers are composed of broad petals that may have gently twisted or curved edges.

Anemone The fully double flowers comprise one or more rings of flattened petals overlaid with shorter tubular petals.

Water lily The fully double blooms are comprised of flat or slightly curved petals and resemble those of water lilies.

Collarette The flowers are formed of oval petals with an inner ruffled "collar" made up of smaller petals surrounding a central disk.

Single The flowers have a daisy-like appearance, with a central disk surrounded by oval petals. They are attractive to bees.

Ball The fully double spherical flowers, sometimes flattened on top, are formed of small, densely packed tubular petals.

Pompom These are miniature forms of ball dahlia, but are more spherical, with fully double tubular petals.

Cactus The fully double blooms are formed of narrow pointed petals that can be straight or curved inward, giving a shaggy effect.

Plants for productive patios

The beauty of a sunny patio is that you can combine flowers with ornamental crops to produce delicious displays that taste as good as they look.

Many crops are happy to live in pots, especially tropical types, such as chili peppers, tomatoes, and eggplants, which need a sheltered, hot spot for their fruits to ripen. Dwarf and miniature fruit trees can also thrive here, given large containers and plenty of water; consider installing an automatic watering system to ensure a constant supply. Fruits in pots also benefit from regular feeding. Pots provide the perfect habitat for leafy salads, too—container cultivation makes it easier to protect their leaves against marauding pests—while potatoes, beans, and peas will thrive in big tubs.

BULB MEDIUM

Onion

Allium cepa This onion crop can be planted as sets or seed during spring, and harvested from mid- to late summer. Lift and dry the bulbs once the tops bend over. Plant in large pots and growing bags in a sunny position.
↕24in (60cm)

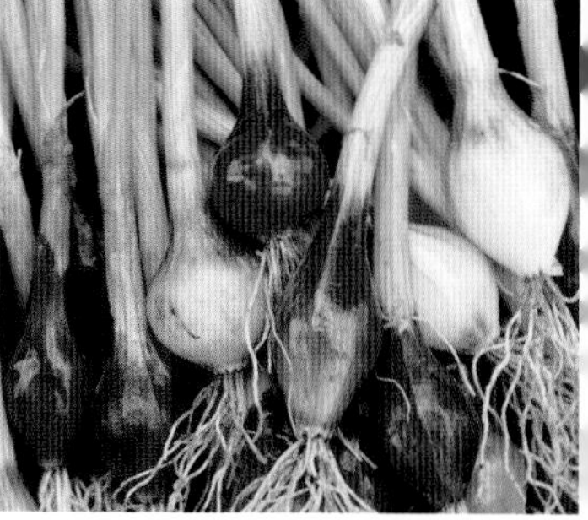

BULB MEDIUM

Spring onion

Allium cepa This small onion is sown from seed from spring to fall, and is ready to harvest in 6–8 weeks. It is ideal for containers and windowboxes placed in a sunny position. White- and red-stemmed varieties (above) are available.
↕10in (25cm) when harvested

BULB MEDIUM

Chives

Allium schoenoprasum A perennial bulb with hollow, grassy dark green mild onion-flavored leaves, which can be used in salads and other dishes. It bears pale purple or pink pompom flowers in summer. Suitable for containers and windowboxes.
↕12in (30cm)

Z4–8

SHRUB LARGE

Lemon verbena

Aloysia triphylla This shrub has spear-shaped leaves that smell and taste of lemon, and can be used to make tea or to flavor sweet dishes. In summer, it bears spikes of small white flowers. Grow it in a large container; protect from hard frosts.
↕↔10ft (3m)

Z8–11

ANNUAL/BIENNIAL LARGE

Chinese spinach

Amaranthus tricolor This upright plant is raised from seed and grown for its leaves, which can be used in salads or left to flower and harvested for its edible seeds, which are used as grain. Add this colorful plant to decorative displays.
↕4½ft (1.4m) ↔18in (45cm)

ANNUAL/BIENNIAL MEDIUM

Celeriac

Apium graveolens Sown from seed in spring, this crop bears large swollen roots, with a nutty, celery-like flavor. Harvest in fall or in summer as baby roots. Best in large pots. In zones 7 and higher, plant it in summer for a fall, winter, or spring crop.
↕3ft (1m) ↔18in (45cm)

ANNUAL/BIENNIAL SMALL

Beet

Beta vulgaris Sown from seed in spring and summer, this sweet-tasting earthy root can be harvested as soon as it reaches a good size. It has attractive stems and leaves, and looks good in decorative container displays.
↕9in (23cm) ↔18in (45cm)

ANNUAL/BIENNIAL SMALL

Swiss chard

Beta vulgaris Grown from seed in spring, this crop produces large glossy green leaves, which can be used raw in salads or steamed, and fleshy stems that are best cooked. Harvest plants lightly throughout summer, and water regularly.
↕↔18in (45cm)

ANNUAL/BIENNIAL SMALL

Mustard greens

Brassica juncea This crop is grown for its peppery-tasting leaves. Sow seeds in spring and summer, and harvest the plant young as "cut-and-come-again" leaves, or let mature. Grow in windowboxes and pots; water well. Considered invasive in some areas.
↕↔12in (30cm)

ANNUAL/BIENNIAL SMALL

Kohlrabi

Brassica oleracea* var. *gongylodes This crop is grown for its nutty-tasting swollen stems that mature in as little as six weeks. Sow seeds in repeated batches in growing bags and containers in early spring or fall, and harvest when large enough.
↕↔18in (45cm)

PERENNIAL MEDIUM

Cayenne chili

Capsicum annuum This annual or short-lived perennial produces long, tapering fiery fruits that are packed with seeds. The fruits ripen from green and yellow to red. It is ideal for windowboxes and pots in full sun. Harvest regularly for the best crop.

↕3ft (1m) ↔12in (30cm)

💧 Z9–11

PERENNIAL MEDIUM

Jalapeño chili

Capsicum annuum Producing short, pointed, fleshy-skinned fruits, this annual or short-lived perennial ripens from green to red. It is ideal for containers, pots, and windowboxes in full sun. Harvest regularly for the best crop.

↕3ft (1m) ↔12in (30cm)

💧 Z9–11

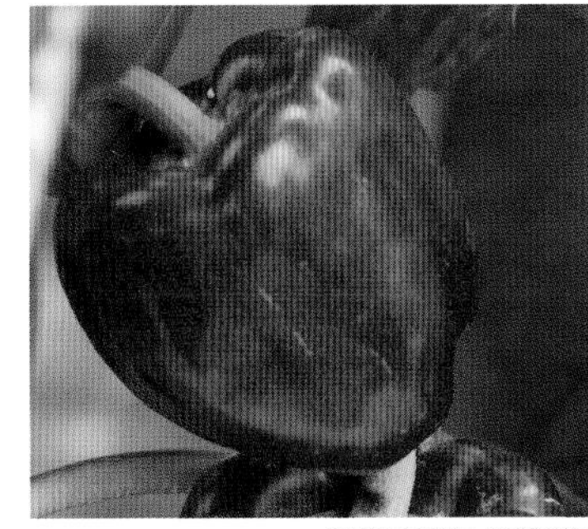

PERENNIAL MEDIUM

Sweet pepper

Capsicum annuum This annual or short-lived perennial produces large, yellow, red, orange, and black fleshy summer fruits with a sweet mild flavor. Plant in large containers in full sun. Water and feed regularly; tall varieties may need staking.

↕3ft (1m) ↔18in (45cm)

💧 Z9–11

PERENNIAL MEDIUM

Aji chili

Capsicum baccatum With a mild fruity flavor, this annual or short-lived perennial ripens through various colors in summer, although it can be picked at any stage once large enough. Grow in full sun in large pots. Water regularly; stake tall plants.

↕3ft (1m) ↔18in (45cm)

💧 Z9–11

PERENNIAL MEDIUM

Scotch bonnet chili

Capsicum chinense An annual or short-lived perennial, this extremely hot chili pepper bears flattened, rounded green, yellow, and red summer fruits. Best in warmer areas with long summers. Plant it in containers in full sun. Water regularly.

↕↔3ft (1m)

💧 Z9–11

TREE SMALL

Lemon

Citrus* x *limon This evergreen tree has glossy green leaves. In spring, it produces fragrant white blooms followed by fruits, which take up to a year to ripen. Feed the plant well while in flower and fruit. Move it indoor in areas with cold winters.

↕10ft (3m) ↔6ft (2m)

💧 pH Z9–11

ANNUAL/BIENNIAL SMALL

Cilantro

Coriandrum sativum A quick-growing annual herb with rounded, green aromatic leaves. Grown from seed, the whole plant can be used in cooking. Grow in containers and windowboxes. Best in cool areas and well watered.

↕20in (50cm) ↔8in (20cm)

💧

ANNUAL/BIENNIAL MEDIUM

Zucchini

Cucurbita pepo This plant produces a mound of leaves below which the bright yellow flowers and green fruits develop in summer. Harvest the fruits while young and tender. Ideal for growing bags and pots; water and feed the plant well.

↕↔24in (60cm)

💧

ANNUAL/BIENNIAL MEDIUM

Summer squash

Cucurbita pepo This vigorous plant blooms and fruits in summer, bearing squashes in a range of colors and shapes. Suitable for large pots, train plants vertically or leave to trail. Feed and water regularly; harvest squashes when they are small and tender.

↕↔3ft (1m)

💧

ANNUAL/BIENNIAL MEDIUM

Long carrot

Daucus carota Sow seeds for this type of carrot throughout spring and summer. It can be harvested young and tender a few weeks after sowing or left longer to produce larger roots. Best planted in deep containers; water well.

↕24in (60cm) ↔10in (25cm)

💧

ANNUAL/BIENNIAL SMALL

Short carrot

Daucus carota This type of carrot bears short, round sweet-tasting roots. Sow seeds directly in windowboxes and containers in spring and summer, and harvest once large enough, then re-sow new batches. Water regularly.

↕12in (30cm) ↔6in (15cm)

💧

TREE SMALL

Fig

Ficus carica This tree has lobed glossy foliage and pear-shaped summer fruits. In cooler areas, select hardier cultivars like 'Brown Turkey' and 'Chicago Hardy'; protect in winter. Grow in soil-based potting mix. Considered invasive in some areas.

↕10ft (3m) ↔12ft (4m)

Z6–9

PERENNIAL LARGE

Fennel

Foeniculum vulgare This tall upright perennial has ferny aromatic leaves that taste and smell of anise. Edible seeds follow the clusters of tiny yellow summer flowers. Plant in a large pot; use it as a foil for other plants. Considered invasive in some areas.

↕6ft (1.8m) ↔18in (45cm)

Z4–9

PERENNIAL SMALL

Everbearing strawberry

Fragaria* x *ananassa This perennial has mildly flavored summer fruits and a second smaller crop into fall. Plant in windowboxes, pots, or growing bags; water and feed well. Everbearing cultivars bear continuous crop throughout the growing season.

↕12in (30cm) ↔indefinite

Z4–8

PERENNIAL SMALL

Junebearing strawberry

Fragaria* x *ananassa This variety of strawberry gives a single crop of fruits, which have a rich sweet flavor, from early- to midsummer. Ideal for containers that can be moved from view after cropping. Water and feed regularly.

↕12in (30cm) ↔20in (50cm)

Z4–8

PERENNIAL SMALL

Alpine strawberry

Fragaria vesca This strawberry plant has a compact habit. Throughout summer, it bears tiny bright red fruits, which have a intense sweet flavor. It is ideal for containers and windowboxes. Water and feed regularly.

↕12in (30cm) ↔indefinite

Z5–9 Ⓝ

ANNUAL/BIENNIAL SMALL

Lettuce

Lactuca sativa Sown or planted in spring and summer, this small leafy crop can be picked young as "cut-and-come-again" leaves or left to mature into full heads. Many colors and leaf textures are available; water the plants regularly.

↕↔12in (30cm)

TREE MEDIUM

Bay laurel

Laurus nobilis This evergreen tree produces dark green aromatic leaves that can be clipped into stunning shapes to create topiary. Grow it in a sheltered area. Use the leaves to flavor stews and casseroles.

↕40ft (12m) ↔30ft (10m)

Z8–10

TREE SMALL

Cooking apple

Malus domestica This small tree bears large fruits from summer to fall. Choose trees grafted onto dwarfing rootstocks to limit their size. Plant in a large container of soil-based potting mix; feed and water regularly from spring to summer.

↕25ft (8m) ↔6ft (2m) in a pot

Z4–8

TREE SMALL

Dessert apple

Malus domestica This tree bears fruits from late summer to fall. Choose trees grafted onto dwarfing rootstocks. Plant in a large container of soil-based potting mix; feed and water regularly. You may need a pollenizer variety.

↕20ft (6m) ↔6ft (2m) in a pot

Z4–8

PERENNIAL SMALL

Lemon balm

Melissa officinalis This herb has toothed and textured green leaves that emit a rich lemon scent when crushed. 'Aurea' (above) has bright gold-marked leaves. It is considered invasive in some areas.

↕↔18in (45cm)

Z4–9

PERENNIAL MEDIUM

Sweet basil

Ocimum basilicum A bushy annual or short-lived perennial with fragrant, bright green leaves and pink summer flower spikes. Add the leaves to salads or other dishes. Grow it in pots; water and feed well, and harvest regularly.

↕24in (60cm) ↔12in (30cm)

Z9–11

PERENNIAL MEDIUM

Purple basil

Ocimum basilicum* var. *purpurascens A bushy annual or short-lived perennial with aromatic purple leaves, which can be used in savoury dishes and salads. 'Dark Opal' (above) has pink-purple flowers in summer. Water and feed well, and pick regularly.

↕24in (60cm) ↔12in (30cm)

Z9–11

CLIMBER LARGE

Borlotti bean

Phaseolus vulgaris This climbing crop is grown for its beans, which are borne in long green pods, often flushed red. Harvest the beans while young and tender to eat fresh, or leave to mature fully for drying. Provide support; water and feed well.

↕6ft (1.8m)

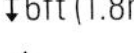

ANNUAL/BIENNIAL MEDIUM

Snow pea

Pisum sativum This form of pea is sown or planted in spring or early summer. From late spring to fall, it bears flattened crisp pods, which are eaten whole. Grow in large containers, water regularly and harvest often for the best crop.

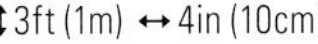
↕3ft (1m) ↔4in (10cm)

PERENNIAL SMALL

Oregano

***Origanum* 'Kent Beauty'** A spreading perennial herb with trailing stems of small oval aromatic leaves and unusual pale pink summer blooms. It is grown for ornament; plant *O. vulgare* for culinary purposes. Ideal for baskets and windowboxes.

↕8in (20cm) ↔12in (30cm)

Z6–9

CLIMBER LARGE

French bean

Phaseolus vulgaris This climber bears long, rounded green or purple pods all summer. For the best crop, harvest before the seeds swell. Dwarf and tall varieties are available. Grow in large pots, provide support, and water and feed well.

↕6ft (1.8m)

ANNUAL/BIENNIAL MEDIUM

Sugar snap pea

Pisum sativum Sown from seed in spring or early summer, this climbing plant produces crisp pods from late spring to fall. Pick regularly, before the seeds inside are fully formed, and eat whole. Ideal for large pots; water regularly.

↕24in (60cm) ↔20in (50cm)

ANNUAL/BIENNIAL MEDIUM

Parsley

Petroselinum crispum This clump-forming biennial, best grown as an annual, has divided, green aromatic leaves, which are used as an edible garnish and to flavor various dishes. Grow in pots and windowboxes; water well in summer.

↕32in (80cm) ↔24in (60cm)

Z5–9

PERENNIAL SMALL

Tomatillo

Physalis ixocarpa This tender perennial produces large green leaves, yellow flowers, and tangy-tasting fruits that are concealed within papery cases from mid- to late summer. Ideal for large pots, it needs full sun and a long summer to crop well.

↕18in (45cm) ↔24in (60cm)

Z9–11Ⓝ

TREE SMALL

Sour cherry

Prunus cerasus This tree bears white or pink flowers in spring, followed by sharp-tasting red fruits in summer. Choose self-fertile varieties on dwarfing rootstocks. Plant in large containers of soil-based potting mix. Water and feed regularly.

↕↔12ft (4m)

Z4–8

CLIMBER SMALL

Runner bean

Phaseolus coccineus Suitable for large containers, this climbing bean bears long flattened green pods throughout summer. For the best crop, harvest pods regularly, before the beans inside are fully formed. It needs tall supports; water and feed well.

↕6ft (1.8m)

ANNUAL/BIENNIAL MEDIUM

Garden pea

Pisum sativum This form of pea is grown for traditional podded peas that appear from late spring to fall. Climbing or dwarf varieties are available. Plant or sow in large containers from spring to early summer. Water well and pick regularly.

↕28in (70cm) ↔20in (50cm)

TREE SMALL

Sweet cherry

Prunus cerasus This tree bears white or pink blossom in spring, followed by sweet-tasting fruits from summer to late fall. Select a self-fertile variety on a dwarfing rootstock. Plant in a large container of soil-based potting mix; water and feed well.

↕↔12ft (4m)

Z4–8

TREE SMALL

Peach

Prunus persica This crop produces large juicy fruits, which ripen from midsummer to early fall. Choose a compact modern variety for the best harvest. Plant in soil-based potting mix; water and feed well, and protect from frost in spring.

↕↔ 6ft (2m) in a pot

Z5–8

ANNUAL/BIENNIAL SMALL

Summer radish

Raphanus sativus Sown from spring to early fall, this crop forms succulent peppery roots in just five weeks. Pull the roots once large enough, then re-sow a new batch. Ideal for windowboxes and pots. Considered invasive in some areas.

↕↔ 8in (20cm)

SHRUB MEDIUM

Black currant

Ribes nigrum An upright branching shrub that flowers in spring, leading to strings of sharp-tasting black berries. Plant it in a large container of soil-based potting mix. Mulch with compost in spring and water regularly throughout summer.

↕↔ 5ft (1.5m)

Z3–8

SHRUB MEDIUM

Red currant

Ribes rubrum This branching shrub blooms in spring and bears trailing strings of sharp-tasting bright red fruits in summer. Plant in a large container of soil-based potting mix. Mulch in spring; water regularly in summer. Considered invasive in some areas.

↕↔ 5ft (1.5m)

Z3–8

SHRUB MEDIUM

White currant

Ribes rubrum This upright, branching spring-flowering shrub forms strings of sharp-tasting, almost transparent, white berries in summer. Plant in soil-based potting mix. Mulch in spring; water well in summer. Considered invasive in some areas.

↕↔ 5ft (1.5m)

Z3–8

SHRUB MEDIUM

Culinary gooseberry

Ribes uva-crispa This branching, often thorny, shrub produces large crops of round sharp-tasting berries in summer that are best cooked before eating. Plant in a container of soil-based potting mix; water regularly and mulch in spring.

↕↔ 5ft (1.5m)

Z5–9

SHRUB MEDIUM

Dessert gooseberry

Ribes uva-crispa This often thorny, branching shrub flowers in spring. It bears round, red or green sweet-tasting fruits in summer, which can be eaten raw or cooked. Plant in a container of soil-based potting mix and water well. Mulch in spring.

↕↔ 5ft (1.5m)

Z5–9

SHRUB MEDIUM

Rosemary

Rosmarinus officinalis A tall bushy evergreen subshrub with aromatic, dark green needlelike leaves and purplish blue blooms from spring to summer. Use the leaves to flavor meat dishes. Grow in a large pot of soil-based potting mix.

↕↔ 5ft (1.5m)

Z8–10

CLIMBER MEDIUM

Thornless blackberry

Rubus fruticosus This climbing shrub has dissected leaves and thornless stems. From late summer to fall, it bears clusters of large glossy black berries. Plant in a large container of soil-based potting mix; provide support for the stems.

↕ 8ft (2.5m)

Z3–8

PERENNIAL MEDIUM

Common sorrel

Rumex acetosa This upright perennial has oval, aromatic green leaves that are patterned with red veins in some forms. Pick the young tangy leaves throughout summer to add to salads, or cook them like spinach to make soups and purées.

↕↔ 24in (60cm)

Z3–7

SHRUB SMALL

Sage

Salvia officinalis This shrubby evergreen subshrub has textured, aromatic gray-green leaves that are used in cooking. It bears spikes of lilac-pink flowers in summer. Plant in soil-based potting mix; it can also be used in winter displays.

↕ 32in (80cm) ↔ 3ft (1m)

Z5–9

SHRUB SMALL

Purple sage

***Salvia officinalis* 'Purpurascens'** This shrubby evergreen subshrub, suitable as an annual, has oval, aromatic purple leaves that fade with age. The lilac-pink summer flower spikes can be removed to promote leaf growth. Use the leaves in cooking.

↕ 32in (80cm) ↔ 3ft (1m)

Z5–9

PERENNIAL MEDIUM

Lavender cotton

Santolina chamaecyparissus This evergreen perennial, suitable as an annual, has aromatic foliage that can be dried for potpourri or used as a moth repellant. The yellow pompom summer blooms last many weeks. Plant in soil-based potting mix.
↕30in (75cm) ↔3ft (1m)

Z6–9

PERENNIAL LARGE

Eggplant

Solanum melongena An upright, branching short-lived perennial, often grown as an annual, with downy green leaves and glossy purple, pink, white, or stripped fruits from late summer to early fall. Best in areas with long summers.
↕4ft (1.2m) ↔20in (50cm)

Z9–11

SHRUB SMALL

Thyme

Thymus vulgaris A low-growing subshrub with tiny, aromatic gray-green leaves that spread to form a low carpet. It bears a mass of purple to white flowers in summer. Ideal for windowboxes, containers, and baskets; it can also be used for winter interest.
↕12in (30cm) ↔16in (40cm)

Z4–9

ANNUAL/BIENNIAL SMALL

Summer savoury

Satureja hortensis This upright annual has slender bronze-green leaves, which can be used to flavor salads or meat and fish dishes. It bears small tubular pale pink blooms in late summer. Grow it among other plants in patio containers.
↕10in (25cm) ↔12in (30cm)

BULB LARGE

Potato

Solanum tuberosum Plant these potatoes in spring in large pots, barrels, and raised garden beds, and allow to grow until fall to produce full-sized tubers. There are many varieties to choose from, with either red, white, yellow, or purple skins.
↕3ft (1m)

SHRUB MEDIUM

Blueberry

Vaccinium corymbosum This deciduous shrub bears white flowers in spring followed by clusters of sweet-tasting blue-black berries that ripen in late summer and fall. Plant in pots of acidic soil mix; water and feed well.
↕↔ up to 5ft (1.5m)

pH Z3–7 N

ANNUAL/BIENNIAL SMALL

Bush tomato

Solanum lycopersicum An annual that is perennial in tropics, this tomato plant has a bushy habit. Ideal for growing outdoors in pots and growing bags. Varieties with fruits in a range of flavors, colors, and shapes are available. Harvest regularly.
↕↔18in (45cm)

ANNUAL/BIENNIAL LARGE

Corn

Zea mays This upright annual crop is grown for its large sweet-tasting "cobs" that mature in late summer. It can be grown in clusters in large containers to help pollinate the flowers. Provide support for stems and harvest regularly.
↕6ft (2m) ↔24in (60cm)

ANNUAL/BIENNIAL MEDIUM

Tumbling tomato

Solanum lycopersicum This annual perennial in tropics, has a trailing habit. Ideal for hanging baskets and raised containers. Many varieties are available, and all produce small fruits. Water and feed well in summer; harvest regularly.
↕24in (60cm) ↔18in (45cm)

BULB LARGE

Fingerling potato

Solanum tuberosum The tubers of this type of potato are small and thin-skinned. Plant them in spring in large pots or barrels, and turn the potatoes out when large enough to harvest in summer. There are many varieties to grow.
↕3ft (1m)

OTHER SUGGESTIONS

Fruit trees

Apple 'Ashmead's Kernel' • Apple 'Egremont Russet' • Apple 'Grimes Golden' • Apple 'Royal Gala'• Lemon 'Meyer Improved' • Pear 'Doyenné du Comice' • Pear 'Williams' Bon Chrétien'

Soft fruits

Blackberry 'Triple Crown' • Blackcurrant 'Ben Sarek' • Blueberry 'Northland' • Blueberry 'Spartan' • Redcurrant 'Red Lake' • Strawberry 'Allstar'

Vegetables

Beet 'Red Ace' • Carrot 'Chantenay Red Cored' • Chili 'Numex Twilight' • Eggplant 'Rosa Bianca' • French bean 'Purple Queen' • Potato 'Red Norland' • Potato 'Yukon Gold' • Runner bean 'Painted Lady' • Spring onion 'White Lisbon' • Sweet pepper 'Sweet Banana' • Tomato 'Sungold' • Tomato 'Tigerella' • Zucchini 'Eight Ball'

Plant focus: tomatoes

Delicious and versatile, tomatoes are an ideal crop for small spaces, producing bumper yields on relatively compact plants.

Bearing beautiful fruits that are both tasty and decorative, tomatoes come in a wide variety of shapes and sizes. Choose from tiny cherries, medium-sized fruits, or large beefsteaks, and look for reliable disease-resistant forms that guarantee a good crop. Tomatoes are divided into two main groups: determinate which bloom and set fruit all at once and indeterminate which grow, blooms, and sets fruit until frost. Both groups should be grown in full sun in well-drained, fertile soil. For earlier fruit, start plants indoors and move them outside when soil temperatures rise above 60°F (15.5°C). Dwarf bushes and patio plants can be grown in smaller pots or hanging baskets. Indeterminate tomato varieties require long stakes, as they grow tie in the main stem to the stake, pinch out any sides hoots that form, and remove the top shoot when the stem has reached about 5ft (1.5m) in height. Water the plants regularly in summer and use a nutrient rich feed once the fruits begin to show.

FORMS OF TOMATO

Determinate tomatoes These fruit on spreading sideshoots that are allowed to grow. Insert several stakes or a cage to support the stems.

Indeterminate tomatoes Fruits are produced on a single, tall upright stem that requires support. There are many varieties to grow.

Colored fruits Although most varieties produce red fruits, tomatoes range in color from yellow to blackish red when ripe.

Patio crops Many compact bush varieties are ideal for patio containers and require no pinching out or staking. The fruits are small.

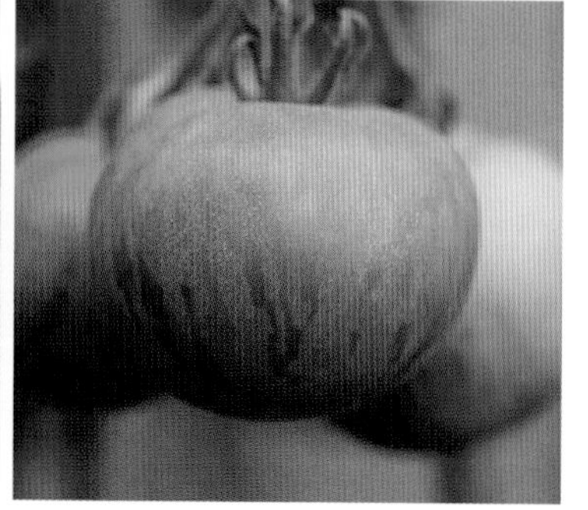

Heirloom tomatoes Many older varieties have distinctive fruits that vary from modern cultivars in size, shape, color, and flavor.

USING TOMATOES

Tomatoes are easy to grow and need less frequent watering if grown directly in the ground or in a raised bed—the volume of soil retains more water and nutrients than potting soil in a container.

Many tomatoes grow happily on sunny patios and make decorative displays when matched with other sun-lovers.

Containers for tomatoes can produce a successful crop if they are large, mulched, watered often, and fertilized to provide important nutrients.

Compact dwarf bushes, such as the trailing, cherry-fruited Tumbler types, are perfect for large hanging baskets in sheltered sites.

Plants for herb gardens

Culinary and medicinal herbs have been grown for centuries and many modern herb gardens still reflect medieval and Renaissance designs.

You can opt for a traditional style and dedicate small, rectangular beds to individual plants, or try combining herbs with ornamentals in a mixed bed. Low-growing herbs, such as thyme, also make a great edging for a border. Many compact herbs are suitable for containers, but restrict rampant growers, such as mint and lemon balm, to a pot of their own. Shrubby herbs, including rosemary and sage, will develop into substantial plants and are best grown in the ground in the long term and pruned each spring before bud break to encourage new growth.

BULB MEDIUM

Chives

Allium schoenoprasum This spring-flowering perennial bulb has hollow, dark green grassy leaves and pale purple or pink pompom flowers. Use the mild onion-flavored leaves in salads and other dishes and flowers for vinegars.

↕12in (30cm)

Z4–8

SHRUB LARGE

Lemon verbena

Aloysia triphylla This spreading shrub has lance-shaped leaves that smell and taste of lemon. Spikes of small white flowers appear in summer. Infuse the leaves in water to make a soothing tea, and use them to flavor sweet dishes.

↕↔10ft (3m)

Z8–11

ANNUAL/BIENNIAL LARGE

Dill

Anethum graveolens A tall upright annual with aromatic, fernlike gray-green leaves and rounded clusters of gold-green summer flowers followed by edible seeds. Use the leaves to flavor fish and poultry dishes; readily reseeds in gardens.

↕4ft (1.2m) ↔24in (60cm)

ANNUAL/BIENNIAL LARGE

Angelica

Angelica archangelica A tall biennial that produces decorative, deeply cut green leaves and domed heads of tiny green flowers in summer. The leaves are used for tea infusions, and tender young stems can be candied. It self-seeds freely.

↕6ft (2m) ↔3ft (1m)

ANNUAL/BIENNIAL SMALL

Chervil

Anthriscus cerefolium A biennial member of the parsley family, it has anise-flavoured fernlike green foliage and flat clusters of tiny white flowers in summer. Use the leaves in salads and other dishes.

↕20in (50cm) ↔10in (24cm)

PERENNIAL LARGE

French tarragon

***Artemisia dracunculus* 'Sativa'** An upright perennial with aromatic, linear green leaves on wiry stems. Grow in a sheltered area or in a container; it can be short-lived. Use its peppery leaves in salads or to flavor chicken and egg dishes.

↕up to 3ft (1m) ↔12in (30cm)

Z3–7 Ⓝ

ANNUAL/BIENNIAL MEDIUM

Borage

Borago officinalis An upright annual with cucumber-flavored aromatic, oval green leaves that are added to salads or summer drinks. The small, star-shaped, blue edible flowers in summer can be used as garnish. Leave spent blooms to allow self-seeding.

↕3ft (1m) ↔12in (30cm)

ANNUAL/BIENNIAL MEDIUM

Pot marigold

Calendula officinalis This annual has aromatic green leaves. From spring to fall, daisy-like flowers in shades of yellow and orange appear. The young leaves can be added to salads, and the flowers used as a garnish.

↕↔24in (60cm)

PERENNIAL SMALL

Chamomile

Chamaemelum nobile A mat-forming evergreen perennial with aromatic finely divided leaves and white daisy-like flowers from late spring to summer. Infuse the flowers in boiling water to make a soothing tea.

↕4in (10cm) ↔18in (45cm)

Z5–9

PERENNIAL LARGE

Chicory

Cichorium intybus A wild form of salad vegetable, this is an upright perennial with tiny green foliage and blue summer blooms. Use its leaves and flowers in salads, and the ground roots to make a coffee substitute. Considered invasive in some areas.

↕4ft (12m) ↔18in (45cm)

Z4–8

ANNUAL/BIENNIAL SMALL

Cilantro

Coriandrum sativum A small annual herb, easily grown from seed, with rounded, green aromatic leaves. The leaves, stems, and seeds are all commonly used in cooking. Keep it well watered to prevent bolting.

↕20in (50cm) ↔8in (20cm)

BULB SMALL

Saffron crocus

Crocus sativus This fall-flowering perennial bulb has saucer-shaped, purple dark-veined flowers with bright red stigmas that yield saffron. The flowers appear just before the grasslike leaves emerge. Plant the bulbs in late summer.

↕2in (5cm)

Z6–8

PERENNIAL LARGE

Fennel

Foeniculum vulgare This tall upright perennial bears aromatic fernlike leaves that taste of anise, and clusters of tiny yellow flowers followed by edible seeds. Add the seeds to salads and other dishes. Considered invasive in some areas.

↕6ft (1.8m) ↔18in (45cm)

Z4–9

PERENNIAL MEDIUM

Hyssop

Hyssopus officinalis This upright perennial has aromatic leaves that smell and taste of anise, and spikes of fluffy lavender-blue summer flowers, attractive to bees and butterflies. Use the leaves to make tea and to flavor various dishes.

↕24in (60cm) ↔3ft (1m)

Z4–9

TREE MEDIUM

Bay laurel

Laurus nobilis An evergreen tree with aromatic dark green leaves that can be clipped into shapes to create topiary. Grow it in a sheltered site, and use the leaves to flavor stews and casseroles.

↕up to 40ft (12m) ↔up to 30ft (10m)

Z8–10

SHRUB SMALL

English lavender

Lavandula angustifolia A bushy evergreen subshrub with aromatic, slim silvery gray leaves. In summer, it produces spikes of small, fragrant violet-blue flowers. May also be used in cooking; use the flowers in potpourri.

↕32in (80cm) ↔24in (60cm)

Z5–8

PERENNIAL LARGE

Lovage

Levisticum officinale A tall upright perennial with celery-flavored divided leaves and flat heads of tiny yellow flowers in summer. The leaves and stems can be used to flavor dishes such as soups and stews.

↕4ft (1.2m) ↔3ft (1m)

Z4–7

PERENNIAL SMALL

Spearmint

Mentha spicata A spreading perennial with aromatic, textured green foliage and pink summer flowers. Infuse the leaves to make tea or use to flavor savoury dishes. Grow in a pot to stop the roots from spreading. Considered invasive in most areas.

↕20in (50cm) ↔indefinite

Z4–7

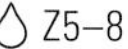

PERENNIAL MEDIUM

Bee balm

Monarda didyma A tall clump-forming perennial with aromatic, lance-shaped green leaves and hooded red, pink, white, or lilac summer flowers. Infuse the leaves in drinks or teas for a refreshing herbal drink.

↕3ft (1m) ↔18in (45cm)

Z4–9 Ⓝ

PERENNIAL MEDIUM

Sweet cicely

Myrrhis odorata This medium-sized perennial produces aromatic, fernlike midgreen foliage. Fragrant creamy white flowers appear in early summer. The leaves have an anise flavor and are commonly used in cooking.

↕3ft (1m) ↔24in (60cm)

Z4–8

PERENNIAL MEDIUM

Sweet basil

Ocimum basilicum A bushy annual or short-lived perennial with aromatic, lance-shaped bright green leaves. Fragrant pink flowers appear in summer. Use the leaves in cooking. Grow it in pots; protect from frost.

↕24in (60cm) ↔12in (30cm)

Z9–11

PERENNIAL MEDIUM

Cinnamon basil

***Ocimum basilicum* 'Cinnamon'** This bushy annual or short-lived perennial has aromatic, lance-shaped green leaves with a cinnamon-basil taste and purple summer flowers. Use the leaves to flavor hot drinks and salads. Plant in pots; protect from frost.

↕24in (60cm) ↔12in (30cm)

Z9–11

PERENNIAL MEDIUM

Thai basil

***Ocimum basilicum* 'Siam Queen'** A bushy annual or short-lived perennial with red stems and pink-white summer flowers. Its green leaves have a licorice scent and basil taste. Use them in curried foods and other dishes. Plant it in pots; protect from frost.

↕24in (60cm) ↔12in (30cm)

Z9–11

PERENNIAL MEDIUM

Purple basil

Ocimum basilicum* var. *purpurascens A bushy annual or short-lived perennial with aromatic, lance-shaped purple leaves, used in dishes and salads. 'Dark Opal' (above) has pink-purple summer flowers. Grow in pots; protect from frost.

↕24in (60cm) ↔12in (30cm)

Z9–11

PERENNIAL SMALL

Oregano

***Origanum* 'Kent Beauty'** This spreading perennial produces trailing stems clothed in small, oval aromatic leaves. Pale pink flowers appear in summer. The leaves can be used as an infusion to make tea or in various dishes and salads.

↕8in (20cm) ↔12in (30cm)

Z6–9

ANNUAL/BIENNIAL MEDIUM

Parsley

Petroselinum crispum This clump-forming biennial, best grown as an annual, produces aromatic, deeply divided green leaves that are used to flavor a wide range of dishes and make a decorative edible garnish.

↕32in (80cm) ↔24in (60cm)

Z5–9

SHRUB MEDIUM

Rosemary

Rosmarinus officinalis This tall bushy evergreen shrub has aromatic, dark green needlelike leaves. Small purplish blue to white flowers appear from spring to summer. Use the leaves to flavor meat dishes.

↕↔5ft (1.5m)

Z8–10

PERENNIAL MEDIUM

Common sorrel

Rumex acetosa An upright perennial with oval, aromatic green leaves that are patterned with red veins in some forms. Pick the young tangy leaves throughout summer to add to salads, or cook them like spinach to make soups and purées.

↕↔24in (60cm)

Z3–7

SHRUB SMALL

Variegated sage

***Salvia officinalis* 'Tricolor'** This evergreen subshrub, also grown as an annual, has aromatic, cream- and pink-edged gray-green foliage and lilac-pink summer blooms. Infuse the leaves to make a soothing tea, or use to flavor meat dishes.

↕32in (80cm) ↔3ft (1m)

Z5–9

PERENNIAL LARGE

Common comfrey

Symphytum officinale A tall upright perennial with large, coarse green leaves. In late spring and summer, it bears pink, purple, or white flowers. Steep the nutrient-rich leaves in water to make organic fertilizer or compost to improve soil.

↕3ft (1m) ↔30in (75cm)

Z4–9

SHRUB SMALL

Lavender cotton

Santolina chamaecyparissus A mound-forming evergreen subshrub that can be grown as an annual, with aromatic, finely cut silvery gray foliage and pompomlike, yellow summer flowers. Use the leaves in potpourri or to repel moths.

↕30in (75cm) ↔3ft (1m)

Z6–9

SHRUB SMALL

Lemon thyme

Thymus x citriodorus A bushy evergreen shrub with small, oval lemon-scented foliage and pale lavender-pink flowers in summer. The citrus-flavored leaves are used in fish dishes. 'Variegata' has cream-edged leaves.

↕12in (30cm) ↔10in (25cm)

Z5–9

SHRUB SMALL

Sage

Salvia officinalis This evergreen subshrub, which can be grown as an annual, produces oval, aromatic gray-green foliage and spikes of lilac-pink flowers in summer. The leaves are used to flavor meat dishes and to make stuffing.

↕↔32in (80cm)

Z5–9

SHRUB SMALL

Thyme

Thymus vulgaris A low-growing evergreen subshrub with small, oval, aromatic gray-green leaves and purple to white flowers in early summer. Use the leaves to flavor stews and soups. Trim annually to encourage growth.

↕12in (30cm) ↔16in (40cm)

Z4–9

SHRUB SMALL

Purple sage

***Salvia officinalis* 'Purpurascens'** An evergreen subshrub, also grown as an annual, with oval, aromatic purple leaves that are red-purple when young. Lilac-pink flowers appear in summer. Use the leaves to flavor meat dishes and to make stuffing.

↕↔12in (30cm)

Z5–9

ANNUAL/BIENNIAL SMALL

Summer savoury

Satureja hortensis This upright annual produces slim, linear bronze-green leaves and small, tubular rose-white flowers in late summer. Use the leaves meat and fish dishes or to add flavor to salads.

↕10in (25cm) ↔12in (30cm)

OTHER SUGGESTIONS

Annuals and biennials

White borage (*Borago officinalis* 'Alba') • Golden mustard (*Brassica juncea* 'Golden Streaks') • Caraway (*Carum carvi*) • Lime basil (*Ocimum americanum* 'Lime')

Perennials

Anise hyssop (*Agastache foeniculum*) Ⓝ • Korean mint (*Agastache rugosa*) • Sea kale (*Crambe maritima*) • Coneflower (*Echinacea angustifolia*) Ⓝ • Giant fennel (*Ferula communis*) • Wild strawberry (*Fragaria vesca*) • Lemon balm (*Melissa officinalis*) • Salad burnet (*Sanguisorba minor*)

Bulbs

Welsh onion (*Allium fistulosum*) • Garlic chives (*Allium tuberosum*)

Climbers

Common hop (*Humulus lupulus*) Ⓝ

Plants for gravel gardens

Gravel adds a decorative finish to designs, and is particularly suitable for gardens with sandy soil and drought-tolerant plants.

Take inspiration from the designs of celebrated English plantswoman Beth Chatto, who transformed a dry and dusty parking lot into a world-famous garden using plants that need no watering and take care of themselves once established. To recreate this on a smaller scale, combine plants with different forms and textures, such as spiky blue oat grass, flat-topped yarrow, and daisy-flowered golden marguerites. Tough annuals, including California poppies, will self-seed in the gravel, creating a naturalistic effect, while bulbs, such as ornamental onions, tulips, and spider lilies, add seasonal highlights from spring to fall.

PERENNIAL MEDIUM

Achillea 'Coronation Gold'

YARROW This upright perennial has fernlike gray-green leaves and, in summer, bears flattened heads of golden-yellow flowers that are highly attractive to bees. Can be short-lived; has tall but study stems.

↕3ft (1m) ↔24in (60cm)

Z3–9

PERENNIAL MEDIUM

Achillea 'Summerwine'

YARROW This upright perennial has feathery dark green leaves. In summer, it produces flat heads of white-eyed crimson flowers that fade to pink. Plant it toward the front of a border; it may require staking.

↕↔32in (80cm)

Z3–9

PERENNIAL MEDIUM

Aeonium 'Zwartkop'

PURPLE CREST AEONIUM This tender evergreen perennial is grown for its rosettes of fleshy, glossy dark purple-black leaves produced on branching stems. Protect it from frost during winter by bringing it under cover.

↕24in (60cm) ↔3ft (1m)

Z9–11

PERENNIAL MEDIUM

Agastache 'Black Adder'

HYSSOP An upright perennial with lance-shaped bright green leaves and spikes of fluffy violet-purple flowers, which appear from late summer to mid-fall. Plant in a sheltered spot with grasses and round-headed flowers, such as dahlias.

↕24in (60cm) ↔18in (45cm)

Z6–9

PERENNIAL SMALL

Agave parryi

CENTURY PLANT A succulent evergreen perennial with large rosette of spiky gray-green to blue-green leaves. Protect from freezing temperatures during winter by covering or bringing it under cover. Use it as a statement plant in a gravel bed.

↕20in (50cm) ↔3ft (1m)

Z7–11 Ⓝ

BULB LARGE

Allium cernuum

NODDING ONION This upright perennial bulb produces strap-shaped gray-green leaves that fade before the tall stems holding clusters of pendent purplish pink flowers appear in summer. Plant the bulbs in bold groups in fall.

↕28in (70cm)

Z3–9 Ⓝ

BULB LARGE

Allium 'Purple Sensation'

FLOWERING ONION An upright perennial bulb with strap-shaped gray-green foliage, which fades as sturdy stems of deep violet spherical flower heads appear in early summer. Plant the bulbs in fall between other plants that will hide its dying leaves.

↕32in (80cm)

Z3–8

PERENNIAL SMALL

Anaphalis triplinervis

PEARLY EVERLASTING This is a low-growing, clump-forming perennial that produces lance-shaped pale gray-green leaves and clusters of small white flowers in summer. It is useful as a cut or dried flower.

↕20in (50cm) ↔24in (60cm)

Z3–8

PERENNIAL SMALL

Androsace carnea

ROCK JASMINE A mound-forming, dwarf evergreen perennial with linear green leaves and rounded clusters of yellow-eyed pink flowers, which appear in late spring. Use it between paving stones set into a gravel path.

↕↔2in (5cm)

Z4–7

PERENNIAL MEDIUM

Anemanthele lessoniana

PHEASANT'S TAIL GRASS A clump-forming semievergreen grass with arching green leaves tinged with red and orange in summer and fall. Sprays of red-brown flowers appear in late summer. It self-seeds prolifically; weed out unwanted seedlings.

↕3ft (1m)

Z8–10

PERENNIAL MEDIUM

Anthemis tinctoria

GOLDEN MARGUERITE A clump-forming perennial that produces finely dissected green leaves and an abundance of white or yellow daisy-like flowers on branching stems throughout summer. 'E.C. Buxton' (above) is a popular variety.

↕↔3ft (1m)

Z3–8

PERENNIAL MEDIUM

Aquilegia canadensis

COLUMBINE This upright perennial produces fernlike green leaves and, from mid-spring to summer, red flowers with yellow centers that hang gracefully from wiry stems. 'Zulu Prince' (above) has creamy yellow flowers.

↕24in (60cm) ↔12in (30cm)

Z3–8 (N)

PERENNIAL LARGE

Calamagrostis x *acutiflora*

FEATHER REED GRASS This perennial grass produces a clump of arching green leaves, above which appear stems of upright architectural summer flower heads, which can be left in place for fall interest. 'Overdam' (above) has variegated leaves.

↕↔4ft (1.2m)

Z5–9

ANNUAL/BIENNIAL MEDIUM

Arctotis fastuosa

CAPE DAISY An upright annual with lobed silvery green leaves and masses of bright orange daisy-like flowers with dark maroon and black eyes throughout summer. Plant it in groups in containers of all-purpose potting soil.

↕24in (60cm) ↔12in (30cm)

Z11

ANNUAL/BIENNIAL MEDIUM

Argemone mexicana

DEVIL'S FIG An upright annual with prickly, deeply divided dark green leaves and saucer-shaped, pale lemon-yellow flowers from late summer to fall. Sow seeds in spring directly into the gravel; it will self-seed readily in following years.

↕24in (60cm) ↔12in (30cm)

(!) Z0 (N)

PERENNIAL MEDIUM

Asclepias tuberosa

BUTTERFLY WEED An upright perennial, with lance-shaped green leaves. From late summer to early fall, it bears clusters of small bright orange-red flowers, which are magnets for bees and butterflies, followed by decorative seedpods.

↕30in (75cm) ↔18in (45cm)

(!) Z4–9 (N)

PERENNIAL LARGE

Calamagrostis brachytricha

KOREAN FEATHER REED GRASS A clump-forming deciduous grass with arching gray-green leaves and upright, feather-shaped, tall pink-tinted silver summer flower heads, followed by straw-colored seedheads that persist through winter.

↕4½ft (1.4m) ↔20in (50cm)

Z4–9

SHRUB LARGE

Ceanothus 'Concha'

CALIFORNIA LILAC An evergreen shrub with small, oval dark green leaves. In late spring, rounded clusters of red-purple buds open to reveal dark blue flowers. Plant close to a fence or wall; prune lightly after flowering. Best in West Coast gardens.

↕↔10ft (3m)

Z9–10 (N)

PERENNIAL MEDIUM

Centranthus ruber

RED VALERIAN A perennial that forms a clump of fleshy leaves. From late spring to fall, it bears heads of small, star-shaped, deep reddish pink or white flowers. Thrives in poor soil and self-seeds readily; stems may need staking.

↕3ft (1m) ↔24in (60cm) or more

💧 Z5–8

ANNUAL/BIENNIAL MEDIUM

Cerinthe major

HONEYWORT An upright annual with erect stems that bear oval gray-green leaves topped with tubular purple and yellow summer flowers. Stems may need some support; the plant may self-seed in gravel. 'Purpurascens' (above) is a popular variety.

↕24in (60cm) ↔12in (30cm)

💧

BULB MEDIUM

Chionodoxa forbesii

GLORY OF THE SNOW This perennial bulb produces linear midgreen foliage. In early spring, star-shaped blue flowers with white centers appear on slender stems. Plant the bulbs in groups in fall.

↕↔6in (15cm)

💧 Z3–8

SHRUB SMALL

Cistus x *lenis* 'Graysword Pink'

ROCK ROSE An evergreen shrub with oval gray-green leaves and saucer-shaped pale pink flowers, each lasting a day and appearing in succession throughout summer. Best in West Coast gardens.

↕24in (60cm) ↔3ft (1m)

💧 Z8–10

TREE SMALL

Cordyline australis

CABBAGE PALM This evergreen tree forms a fountain of sword-shaped green leaves. Protect young specimens from frost. Other colorful variegated forms are available. Grow in a large pot to accommodate taproot and overwinter in a sunny spot indoors.

↕10ft (3m) ↔3ft (1m)

💧 Z10–11

PERENNIAL MEDIUM

Coreopsis grandiflora

TICKSEED This bushy, short-lived self-seeding perennial has lance-shaped green leaves and golden-yellow single or double blooms throughout summer. Sow seeds in early spring, or set out young plants in spring in bold groups.

↕30in (75cm) ↔24in (60cm)

💧 Z4–9 Ⓝ

PERENNIAL SMALL

Coreopsis 'Mango Punch'

TICKSEED A bushy perennial, grown as an annual, with feathery green foliage and masses of saucer-shaped orange-yellow flowers that bloom throughout summer. Use it to edge a path or at the front of a bed.

↕18in (45cm) ↔12in (30cm)

💧 Z9–10

PERENNIAL MEDIUM

Crocosmia x *crocosmiiflora*

MONTBRETIA An upright perennial with arching, sword-shaped green leaves and small trumpet-shaped flowers from summer to fall. 'Star of the East' (above) has pure orange flowers. Considered invasive in some coastal areas of the US.

↕28in (70cm) ↔3in (8cm)

💧 Z6–9

BULB SMALL

Crocus chrysanthus

CROCUS This dwarf perennial bulb produces grassy green foliage and fragrant, bowl-shaped yellow early spring flowers with purple stripes on the outer petals. Plant the bulbs in fall in bold groups.

↕3in (7cm)

💧 Z3–8

PERENNIAL LARGE

Cynara cardunculus

CARDOON A tall upright perennial, which can be grown as an annual, with spiny silver-gray foliage and, from summer to fall, large, thistlelike purple blooms. Plant at the back of a gravel bed; provide support in exposed sites. Invasive in West Coast regions.

↕6ft (2m) ↔3ft (1m)

💧 Z7–9

BULB MEDIUM

Dahlia 'HS First Love'

SINGLE DAHLIA An upright perennial tuber, often sold as an annual, with divided dark maroon-green foliage and, from summer to early fall, contrasting bright peach flowers with a red-ringed eye. Plant it in groups at the front of a bed. Lift to overwinter.
↕24in (60cm)

Z8–11

BULB MEDIUM

Dahlia 'Roxy'

SINGLE DAHLIA An upright perennial tuber, with divided, dark purple-green leaves and magenta-pink flowers with yellow-edged centers from summer to fall. Pot up tubers indoors in spring, or plant directly outside after the threat of frosts. Lift to overwinter.
↕18in (45cm)

Z8–11

PERENNIAL SMALL

Dianthus 'Dad's Favourite'

GARDEN PINK A low-growing evergreen perennial that forms a neat mound of grassy grey-green foliage. During summer, it bears fragrant, white semidouble flowers with maroon markings. Deadhead regularly to prolong the display.
↕up to 18in (45cm) ↔12in (30cm)

Z4–9

PERENNIAL LARGE

Echinacea purpurea

CONEFLOWER An upright, clump-forming perennial, with narrow, tapering green leaves. From mid- to late summer, it bears simple daisy-like flowers with brown, prickly centers. Best planted in drifts. 'Kim's Knee High' (above) is a compact variety.
↕5ft (1.5m) ↔18in (45cm)

Z3–8 Ⓝ

PERENNIAL SMALL

Erigeron glaucus

BEACH ASTER A compact, clump-forming perennial with slim, spoon-shaped green leaves and daisy-like yellow-centered mauve-pink flowers from late spring to midsummer. Use to edge a path or at the front of a bed. Ideal for coastal areas.
↕12in (30cm) ↔18in (45cm)

Z5–8 Ⓝ

PERENNIAL LARGE

Eryngium giganteum

SEA HOLLY An upright, short-lived perennial with marbled, heart-shaped gray-green foliage and tall stems that are topped with conelike, silvery gray summer flowers surrounded by spiny bracts. It self-seeds freely in gravel.
↕3ft (1m) ↔12in (30cm)

Z4–8

PERENNIAL LARGE

Gaura lindheimeri

WAND FLOWER This large upright perennial produces spoon-shaped, green leaves and pink-tinged buds that open to reveal small white flowers from midsummer to fall. 'Karalee White' (above) is a popular modern variety.
↕5ft (1.5m) ↔3ft (1m)

Z5–9 Ⓝ

PERENNIAL MEDIUM

Erysimum 'Bowles's Mauve'

PERENNIAL WALLFLOWER This is an evergreen perennial bearing narrow dark gray-green foliage and small mauve flower spikes from early spring to late fall. Deadhead regularly to prolong the display. Can be short-lived.
↕24in (60cm) ↔16in (40cm)

 Z6–10

ANNUAL/BIENNIAL SMALL

Eschscholzia californica

CALIFORNIA POPPY A bushy clump-forming annual with feathery blue-green leaves and a profusion of small, bowl-shaped orange, red, and yellow flowers in summer. Sow seeds in beds in spring; it may self-seed after its first season.
↕12in (30cm) ↔6in (15cm)

Ⓝ

PERENNIAL MEDIUM

Gentiana asclepiadea

WILLOW GENTIAN This clump-forming perennial produces arching stems of lance-shaped midgreen leaves and trumpet-shaped dark- to light blue flower clusters from late summer to early fall. Plant in acidic soil in the middle of a bed.

↕3ft (1m) ↔24in (60cm)

pH Z6–9

BULB LARGE

Gladiolus callianthus

ABYSSINIAN GLADIOLUS An upright perennial bulb with arching, grassy green leaves and fragrant, hooded maroon-centered white flowers in summer. Plant the bulbs in groups in spring. Protect from frost by lifting in fall after flowering.

↕3ft (1m)

Z8–10

SHRUB SMALL

***Hebe ochracea* 'James Stirling'**

HEBE A dwarf, dome-forming evergreen shrub with yellow-green scalelike foliage, resembling a conifer. In late spring, it bears small white flowers. Best planted at the front of a bed. Trim after flowering.

↕18in (45cm) ↔24in (60cm)

Z8–10

PERENNIAL SMALL

***Helianthemum* 'Fire Dragon'**

ROCK ROSE This spreading evergreen perennial has trailing stems of soft, gray-green leaves and yellow-eyed orange-red flowers in summer. Use it as ground cover at the front of a bed. Deadhead regularly to prolong display.

↕12in (30cm) ↔18in (45cm)

Z6–8

PERENNIAL MEDIUM

Helictotrichon sempervirens

BLUE OAT GRASS This is an evergreen grass with upright blue-grey leaves and straw-colored flower heads held on long arching stems in summer. Use it as a focal plant with perennials that have rounded foliage.

↕3ft (1m) ↔24in (60cm)

Z4–8

PERENNIAL MEDIUM

***Hemerocallis* 'Golden Chimes'**

DAYLILY This is a tall semievergreen perennial with arching, grasslike green leaves and trumpet-shaped golden-yellow flowers that appear in succession in summer and each last a day. Plant toward the back of a bed.

↕3½ft (1.1m) ↔24in (60cm)

Z3–10

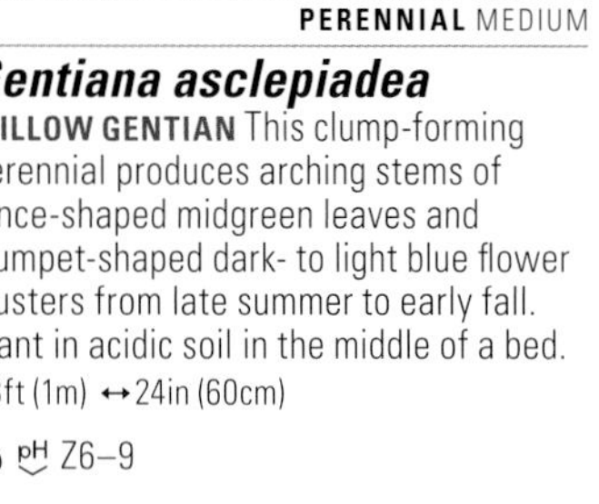

PERENNIAL MEDIUM

Hordeum jubatum

FOXTAIL BARLEY A short-lived perennial grass with green leaves and silvery pink, feathery flower plumes in summer. Sow seeds directly in the gravel in spring, and combine with brightly colored plants, such as dahlias. It may self-seed.

↕24in (60cm) ↔12in (30cm)

Z4–8 Ⓝ

PERENNIAL MEDIUM

***Iris* 'Harriette Halloway'**

BEARDED IRIS An upright, rhizome-forming perennial with gray-green swordlike leaves. From early- to midsummer, it bears large, scented, yellow-centered, pale blue bearded flowers. Plant the rhizomes just above the soil surface.

↕28in (70cm) ↔12in (30cm)

Z3–9

BULB MEDIUM

Iris reticulata

RETICULATED IRIS This perennial bulb bears grassy green leaves and small, blue early spring flowers with yellow and white marks on the lower petals. In fall, plant the bulbs in pots or at the front of a bed where they can be easily seen.

↕6in (15cm)

Z5–8

SHRUB SMALL

Juniperus horizontalis

CREEPING JUNIPER A prostrate evergreen conifer with scalelike blue-green foliage that will spread to provide ground cover. Use it as a foil for colorful bulbs and perennials. Varieties include 'Bar Harbor', with purple-tinted winter foliage.

↕20in (50cm) ↔indefinite

Z3–9 Ⓝ

PERENNIAL MEDIUM

Knautia macedonica

KNAUTIA This upright perennial has lobed, green basal leaves. In summer, it produces a succession of button-shaped crimson flowers on wiry stems. Easily grown from seed. 'Melton Pastels' (above) has pink and crimson flowers.

↕30in (75cm) ↔24in (60cm)

Z5–9

PERENNIAL MEDIUM

Kniphofia triangularis

RED HOT POKER This upright perennial produces grassy green foliage and clusters of contrasting bright orange-red tubular flowers in late summer or early fall. Plant it in groups with blue- or purple-flowered plants.

↕3ft (1m) ↔18in (45cm)

Z5–9

PERENNIAL LARGE

Lychnis chalcedonica

JERUSALEM CROSS This erect perennial has green basal leaves and tall stems topped with domed clusters of bright scarlet flowers in summer. Allow it to self-seed to create naturalistic groups. The stems require staking.

↕4ft (1.2m) ↔18in (45cm)

Z3–8

SHRUB SMALL

Lavandula pinnata

FERNLEAF LAVENDER This compact subshrub, sometimes sold as an annual, has fernlike silver-green foliage. From summer to early fall, it produces triangular clusters of scented violet-blue flowers. Grow it in a sheltered spot.

↕↔3ft (1m)

Z9–10

SHRUB SMALL

Leucophyta brownii

CUSHION BUSH A rounded evergreen shrub, often grown as an annual, with silver stems bearing scalelike, aromatic silver-gray leaves and creamy yellow buttonlike flowers in summer. Grow it alongside colorful annuals.

↕30in (75cm) ↔3ft (1m)

Z9–10

PERENNIAL SMALL

Lewisia cotyledon

SISKIYOU LEWISIA A clump-forming evergreen perennial with rosettes of lobed dark green foliage and funnel-shaped flowers in shades of pink, yellow, and orange that appear from late spring to summer. Grow it at the front of a bed.

↕12in (30cm) ↔6in (15cm)

pH Z6–8 Ⓝ

BULB MEDIUM

Narcissus 'Cheerfulness'

DAFFODIL This perennial bulb bears blue-green straplike leaves. In mid-spring, small clusters of long-lasting, small, sweetly scented, white and yellow fully double blooms appear. Excellent as a cut flower.

↕16in (40cm)

! Z3–9

BULB MEDIUM

Nerine bowdenii

SPIDER LILY This upright perennial bulb bears strap-like green leaves and, in fall, clusters of spidery pale pink flowers on long slim stems. Use it for late-season color, and plant the bulbs in groups in spring.

↕24in (60cm)

! Z8–10

PERENNIAL SMALL

Oenothera speciosa

PINK EVENING PRIMROSE This compact perennial has small, divided green leaves and a spreading habit. From late spring to early summer, it bears fragrant, cup-shaped, white flowers that age to pink. Plant it at the front of a gravel bed.

↕12in (30cm) ↔12in (30cm)

Z4–8 Ⓝ

PERENNIAL SMALL

Ophiopogon planiscapus 'Nigrescens'

MONDO GRASS A clump-forming perennial with shiny black grasslike leaves. In summer, clusters of purple-pink flowers appear, followed by black berries. Plant it in groups at the front of a bed.

↕9in (23cm) ↔12in (30cm)

Z6–10

PERENNIAL MEDIUM

Osteospermum hybrids

AFRICAN DAISY An herbaceous evergreen perennial, grown as an annual, with slim midgreen leaves and showy pink, yellow, and white daisy-like summer blooms, with bluish purple centers. Adds interest to the front of a gravel bed.

↕24in (60cm) ↔12in (30cm)

Z10–11

BULB MEDIUM

Puschkinia scilloides

STRIPED SQUILL This perennial bulb has strap-shaped green leaves and clusters of dark blue-striped bluish white spring flowers. Grow it with other spring bulbs, such as *Muscari* and species tulips, at the front of a bed.

↕6in (15cm)

Z4–8

PERENNIAL LARGE

Phormium tenax

NEW ZEALAND FLAX This large, clump-forming evergreen perennial produces arching, sword-shaped gray-green leaves and, during hot summers, dark red flowers on top of tall stems. Grow it as a focal plant.

↕10ft (3m) ↔6ft (2m)

Z9–11

PERENNIAL MEDIUM

Potentilla thurberi 'Monarch's Velvet'

CINQUEFOIL A spreading perennial with strawberry-like, hairy green leaves and abundant, small, saucer-shaped, dark velvety red summer flowers. Combine with spiky plants, such as hyssop.

↕30in (75cm) ↔24in (60cm)

Z4–8 Ⓝ

BULB MEDIUM

Roscoea cautleyoides

ROSCOEA This compact perennial produces narrow dark green leaves and short spikes of yellow, purple, or white orchidlike flowers in summer. Plant it in groups toward the front of a gravel bed in a sheltered site.

↕10in (25cm)

Z6–9

PERENNIAL SMALL

Scabiosa lucida

GLOSSY SCABIOUS A clump-forming, low-growing perennial with lance-shaped silver-gray leaves and a profusion of button-shaped lilac-pink summer flowers. Deadhead regularly to prolong the display. This plant can be short-lived.

↕8in (20cm) ↔6in (15cm)

Z5–9

PERENNIAL MEDIUM

Schizostylis coccinea

CRIMSON FLAG An upright perennial with sword-shaped light green leaves and red, pink, or white starry flowers from late summer to late fall. Protect against winter frost; plant in large groups. 'Sunrise' (above) has salmon-pink flowers.

↕24in (60cm) ↔12in (30cm)

Z7–9

PERENNIAL SMALL

Sedum erythrostictum 'Frosty Morn'

STONECROP This clump-forming perennial forms a mound of fleshy gray-green leaves, marked with bold white edges and pale pink flower heads in late summer. A useful plant for a long season of interest.

↕12in (30cm) ↔18in (45cm)

Z4–9

PERENNIAL MEDIUM

Sedum telephium Atropurpureum Group

STONECROP A clump-forming perennial, with dark purple stems, fleshy leaves, and domed, pinkish white flower clusters from late summer to fall. Combine with green-leaved perennials at the front of beds.
↕24in (60cm) ↔12in (30cm)

Z4-9

PERENNIAL SMALL

Sempervivum arachnoideum

COBWEB HOUSELEEK A low-growing evergreen perennial with rosettes of fleshy green leaves covered with fine, cobweblike white hairs and reddish pink flowers in summer. Grow it at the front of a gravel bed.
↕5in (12cm) ↔4in (10cm) or more

Z5–8

PERENNIAL SMALL

Silene schafta

AUTUMN CATCHFLY A spreading perennial, it has narrow dark green leaves and, from late summer to late fall, it produces simple, starlike, rose-magenta flowers. Plant it at the front of a gravel bed where it can spread.
↕10in (25cm) ↔12in (30cm)

Z4–8

PERENNIAL MEDIUM

Stipa tenuissima

MEXICAN FEATHER GRASS A deciduous perennial grass with fine green leaves and silvery green flower heads in early summer that turn beige as seeds form. Weave this wispy grass through colorful perennials to create a naturalistic effect.
↕24in (60cm) ↔16in (40cm)

Z7–11 Ⓝ

PERENNIAL MEDIUM

Sisyrinchium striatum

YELLOW-EYED GRASS This upright evergreen perennial produces sword-shaped gray-green leaves and spikes of small pale yellow flowers all summer. Combine it with bearded iris and plant it in drifts in a bed, or use it to line a walkway.
↕24in (60cm) ↔12in (30cm)

Z7–8

PERENNIAL SMALL

Stachys byzantina

LAMB'S EARS This small perennial, evergreen in warm areas, produces downy, silvery gray foliage and spikes of small mauve-pink flowers in summer. Grow it at the front of a sunny bed, or use it to line a gravel path.
↕15in (38cm) ↔24in (60cm)

Z4–8

BULB MEDIUM

Tulipa clusiana var. *chrysantha*

LADY TULIP This medium-sized perennial bulb has linear gray-green leaves. In spring, it produces vase-shaped yellow flowers with a red flash on the outer petals. Plant the bulbs in groups in fall.
↕12in (30cm)

(!) Z3–8

PERENNIAL LARGE

Verbena bonariensis

PURPLETOP VERVAIN This upright perennial has lance-shaped dark green leaves and clusters of scented purple flowers from midsummer to fall. Its slim stems create a see-through veil in gravel beds. Self-seeds freely. Considered invasive in some areas.
↕5ft (1.5m) ↔24in (60cm)

Z7–11

OTHER SUGGESTIONS

Annuals

Gomphrena 'Strawberry Fields'

Perennials

Aquilegia caerulea Ⓝ • *Delosperma* 'Fire Spinner' • *Echinacea angustifolia* Ⓝ • *Erigeron pulchellus* Ⓝ • *Kniphofia* 'Nancy's Red' • *Phlomis tuberosa* • *Sedum* 'Ruby Glow' • *Sisyrinchium angustifolium* Ⓝ • *Solidago sphacelata* 'Golden Fleece' • *Vernonia lettermannii* 'Iron Butterfly' Ⓝ

Bulbs

Allium acuminatum Ⓝ • *Allium sphaerocephalon* • *Gladiolus* 'Atom' • *Ornithogalum magnum*

Shrubs

Ceanothus americanus Ⓝ • *Hypericum kalmianum* Ⓝ

Plant focus: sedums

Fleshy-stemmed sedums make beautiful rock, roof, and container garden plants, while taller species are perfect for borders.

SEDUMS ARE TOUGH, DROUGHT-RESISTANT SUCCULENTS that have a range of uses in the garden. Taller forms are perfect for gravel gardens or sunny borders, while hardy low-growing species suit life up on the roof, forming a dense insulating carpet of foliage that can tolerate sun, wind, and subzero temperatures. Mat-forming sedums can also be used in rock gardens, cracks in walls and paving, or in troughs filled with gritty compost. The fleshy foliage, variegated or purple in some cultivars, is highly decorative, as are the heads of star-shaped flowers, which appear from midsummer to fall. Forms of *S. spectabile* and other large named cultivars are also valued for their ornamental seedheads, which persist through winter. Sedums thrive in full sun, although some will tolerate light shade, and are happiest in free-draining sandy soil—the stems will rot in wet conditions. Divide the larger forms every few years to stop the stems from flopping, leaving an unsightly gap in the center of the clump.

USING SEDUMS

Try the tallest forms of sedum in beds and borders. The dark, fleshy foliage of *S. telephium* cultivars creates an exciting contrast with variegated and green linear-leaved plants in a border, while the flat-topped flowers of *S.* AUTUMN JOY, add color to late-season displays and are followed by graphic seedheads.

The leafy *S. reflexum* and the tender, white-flowered *S. sedoides* make perfect partners for other succulents in a container.

Sedums are practical plants for roofs, requiring the thinnest layer of soil, little fertilizer, and no irrigation once established.

POPULAR SEDUM SPECIES

Sedum acre Golden moss is an evergreen perennial that forms a dense mat of fleshy green or variegated foliage and star-shaped yellow flowers in summer or fall.

Sedum spathulifolium A low-growing evergreen perennial; most of its cultivars have silver or purple foliage and contrasting yellow summer flowers. It is effective in pots.

Sedum reflexum (syn. *S. rupestre*) This low-growing plant has spreading stems of blue-gray needlelike foliage that resembles conifer leaves, and yellow summer flowers.

Sedum kamtschaticum A reliable roof plant producing mounds of semievergreen foliage that turns pinkish red in fall. It bears yellow flowers in late summer.

Sedum spectabile This perennial features stout stems of fleshy leaves and flat heads of small pink, red, or white flowers from late summer, followed by decorative seedheads.

Sedum telephium This species has knee-high stems of deciduous green leaves, dark purple in some forms, teamed with flat heads of pinkish purple or white flowers from late summer.

Plants for rock gardens

Rock gardens have undergone a renaissance in recent years as gardeners rediscover the beauty of the diminutive sun-lovers they accommodate.

Rock and alpine plants are easy to care for, requiring very little annual maintenance once established. Create your rock garden in a sunny site, ideally on a naturally occurring slope. Excellent drainage is a must for all of these plants, so add plenty of grit to wet clay soils. Also include flowers for every season, starting in spring with bulbs, such as daffodils and tulips, together with perennial aubretia and rock cress. Continue the show with summer-flowering garden pink and rock rose, and end the year with heath and autumn crocus.

PERENNIAL SMALL

Anemone sylvestris

SNOWDROP WINDFLOWER A dwarf perennial with divided midgreen leaves. Fragrant white flowers with yellow centers appear from spring to early summer. Plant in moist spot at the bottom of slope and protect from midday sun.
↕↔ 12in (30cm)
Z3–8

PERENNIAL SMALL

Arabis alpina subsp. *caucasica*

WALL ROCK CRESS A mat-forming evergreen perennial with small, hairy gray-green leaves. It forms a carpet of white flowers from early spring to early summer. 'Variegata' (above) has white-edged leaves.
↕↔ 6in (15cm)
Z4–7

PERENNIAL SMALL

Arenaria tetraquetra

SPANISH SANDWORT A cushion-forming evergreen perennial with tiny gray-green leaves. Stemless, star-shaped white flowers appear in late spring. It makes a great partner for dwarf spring bulbs, such as grape hyacinth and daffodils.
↕ 1in (2.5cm) ↔ 6in (15cm) or more
Z3–5

PERENNIAL SMALL

Armeria maritima

THRIFT A clump-forming evergreen perennial that forms rounded tufts of grassy green leaves. Round heads of small white to pink flowers appear on slim stems in summer. Suitable as a "dot" plant in a rock garden and in alpine planters.
↕ 4in (10cm) ↔ 6in (15cm)
Z4–8 Ⓝ

PERENNIAL SMALL

Asperula arcadiensis

ARCADIAN WOODRUFF A cushion-forming perennial with tiny, hairy gray leaves. Numerous pale pink flowers appear in early summer. Add well-rotted compost to the soil in the planting area to improve moisture retention in summer.
↕ 3in (8cm) ↔ 12in (30cm)
Z5–7

PERENNIAL SMALL

Aubrieta deltoidea

AUBRETIA An evergreen perennial with spreading stems of rounded gray-green leaves. In spring, it becomes covered with tiny blooms in shades of white, pink, red, and purple. Plant it at the edge of a bed where it will slowly spread.
↕ 2in (5cm) ↔ 24in (60cm)
Z4–8

PERENNIAL SMALL

Calamintha nepeta

LESSER CALAMINT This is an upright dwarf perennial that produces soft, aromatic, dark green basal leaves. From late summer to early fall, it bears spikes of tiny lilac-pink flowers that are attractive to bees.
↕ 18in (45cm) ↔ 30in (75cm)
Z5–9

SHRUB SMALL

Calluna vulgaris

SCOTCH HEATHER A bushy, low-growing evergreen shrub with linear gray-, yellow-, or bright green leaves and bell-shaped flowers in shades of pink, white, and purple from midsummer to late fall. Plant it in acidic soil.
↕ 24in (60cm) ↔ 18in (45cm)
pH Z4–6

PERENNIAL SMALL

Campanula carpatica

CARPATHIAN HAREBELL This clump-forming perennial forms a dense mat of green leaves and open bell-shaped, violet-blue or white flowers throughout summer. Plant it in rock gardens or trail over the edge of alpine planters.
↕4in (10cm) ↔12in (30cm)

Z4–7

PERENNIAL SMALL

Ceratostigma plumbaginoides

PLUMBAGO A low-growing, bushy perennial bearing small, oval green leaves that turn red in fall and clusters of blue single flower on branched, reddish green stems from late summer to fall.
↕18in (45cm) ↔8in (20cm)

Z5–9

BULB MEDIUM

Colchicum autumnale

MEADOW SAFFRON This fall-flowering perennial bulb has strap-shaped leaves that appear after, or at the same time as, the small, vase-shaped lavender-pink flowers. Plant it where it is easily visible and not lost among other plants.
↕6in (15cm)

Z4–8

BULB SMALL

Crocus 'Snow Bunting'

CROCUS This perennial corm has grassy dark green leaves marked with white lines. In early spring, fragrant white flowers with mustard-yellow centers and a faint purple blush on the outer petal appear. Plant the corms in groups in fall.
↕3in (7cm)

pH Z3–8

BULB MEDIUM

Crocus speciosus

AUTUMN CROCUS This perennial corm produces grassy, silver-striped green leaves, which appear in late fall, just after the vase-shaped lilac-blue flowers with darker veins form. Plant the corms in late summer in groups between rocks.
↕6in (15cm)

Z3–8

PERENNIAL SMALL

Dianthus 'Doris'

GARDEN PINK This mound-forming evergreen perennial has linear gray-green leaves and numerous fragrant pale pink semidouble flowers, each with a salmon-red ring in the center, which appear throughout summer. Deadhead regularly.
↕10in (25cm) ↔10in (25cm)

Z3–8

PERENNIAL SMALL

Diascia barberae

TWINSPUR A mat-forming semievergreen perennial, sometimes sold as an annual, with narrow, oval green leaves and bell-shaped flowers in a wide range of colors from summer to fall. 'Blackthorn Apricot' (above) has apricot-pink flowers.
↕10in (25cm) ↔20in (50cm)

Z8–9

PERENNIAL SMALL

Dodecatheon meadia

EASTERN SHOOTING STAR This summer-dormant, rosette-forming perennial has green basal leaves and magenta-pink spring flowers with reflexed petals. Plant where it will not overshadow mat-forming plants. Add organic matter to soil before planting.
↕12in (30cm) ↔6in (15cm)

Z4–8 Ⓝ

PERENNIAL SMALL

Dryas octopetala

MOUNTAIN AVENS A prostrate evergreen perennial that forms mats of oval, lobed, leathery dark green leaves. From late spring to early summer, it produces cup-shaped, creamy white flowers, followed by attractive, feathery seeds.
↕2½in (6cm) ↔indefinite

Z2–6 Ⓝ

SHRUB SMALL

Erica x *darleyensis*

DARLEY HEATH A mound-forming dwarf evergreen shrub with linear cream-tipped dark green foliage and urn-shaped white or pink flowers from late winter to early spring. 'White Glow' (above) is compact with masses of white flowers.
↕10in (25cm) ↔20in (50cm)

Z6–8

PERENNIAL SMALL

Erinus alpinus

FAIRY FOXGLOVE A short-lived, rosette-forming semievergreen perennial with soft midgreen foliage. From late spring to summer, it produces short upright stems of purple, pink, or white flowers. It self-seeds and spreads, so deadhead after flowering.
↕↔3in (8cm)

Z4–7

PERENNIAL SMALL

Erodium x *kolbianum* 'Natasha'

HERON'S BILL This is a mat-forming evergreen perennial with deeply cut silver-green leaves. From spring to summer, it has white flowers with dark purple blotches and veining. Plant at the front of a rock garden.
↕4in (10cm) ↔12in (30cm)

Z7

PERENNIAL SMALL

Euphorbia myrsinites

MYRTLE SPURGE This prostrate evergreen perennial bears woody stems clothed with small, pointed, fleshy gray leaves and bright yellow-green flower clusters in spring. Let it sprawl across rocky surfaces. Remove spent flowers wearing gloves.
↕3in (8cm) ↔8in (20cm)

Z5–9

SHRUB SMALL

Euryops acraeus

BUSH DAISY A dome-shaped evergreen shrub that produces clusters of linear silvery blue leaves on short stems and daisy-like bright yellow flowers from late spring to early summer. It makes a good partner for purple-flowered aubretia.
↕↔12in (30cm)

Z8–11

PERENNIAL SMALL

Gentiana sino-ornata

CHINESE GENTIAN This is a mound-forming perennial with needlelike green leaves. Funnel-shaped deep blue flowers, with white stripes within appear in fall. Plant at the front of a rock garden in acidic soil. Best in moist but well-drained soil.
↕2in (5cm) ↔12in (30cm)

Z4–7

PERENNIAL SMALL

Geranium cinereum

CRANESBILL A spreading perennial with round, deeply lobed gray-green leaves. A succession of cup-shaped pink or mauve flowers with deep purple centers and veins appear from late spring to summer. 'Ballerina' (above) is a popular variety.
↕4in (10cm) ↔12in (30cm)

Z5–9

PERENNIAL SMALL

Gypsophila repens

CREEPING BABY'S BREATH This spreading semievergreen perennial produces mats of narrow bluish green leaves, above which tiny, round pale pink flowers, which age to deep pink, appear over a long period from midsummer. Trim back after flowering.
↕8in (20cm) ↔12in (30cm) or more

Z4–8

SHRUB SMALL

Hebe cupressoides 'Boughton Dome'

HEBE A slow-growing, dome-shaped evergreen shrub with scalelike gray-green leaves. Paler young leaves give a two-toned look in summer. Blooms rarely, but is a good backdrop to colorful alpines and bulbs.
↕12in (30cm) ↔24in (60cm)

Z8–9

PERENNIAL SMALL

Helianthemum 'Fire Dragon'

ROCK ROSE This is a small evergreen perennial that produces trailing stems of soft gray-green leaves and bright red flowers with contrasting yellow eyes in summer. The cultivar 'Henfield Brilliant' bears vivid orange blooms.
↕12in (30cm) ↔18in (45cm)

Z6–8

ANNUAL/BIENNIAL SMALL

Iberis umbellata

CANDYTUFT This upright, bushy annual has lance-shaped midgreen leaves and domed heads of tiny flowers in shades of pink, red, purple, or white from spring to summer. Use it to fill gaps between permanent plantings.

↕↔ 8in (20cm)

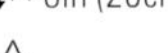

BULB MEDIUM

Ipheion uniflorum

SPRING STARFLOWER This bulb has narrow, grasslike pale green leaves and fragrant, star-shaped white, violet, or pale blue flowers from late winter to spring. 'Froyle Mill' (above) has pale mauve flowers. Protect with mulch in cold areas.

↕ 6in (15cm)

Z5–9

BULB MEDIUM

Iris reticulata

RETICULATED IRIS This perennial bulb has upright, grasslike green foliage and bears small blue flowers with yellow and white markings during early spring. Plant the bulbs in fall in small clumps where the plants will be seen easily.

↕ 6in (15cm)

Z5–8

BULB SMALL

Iris unguicularis

ALGERIAN IRIS A dwarf perennial bulb with grasslike green leaves. In late winter, violet, lavender-blue, or purple flowers, with white and yellow markings on the lower petals, appear. *I. unguicularis* subsp. *cretensis* (above) has rich blue flowers.

↕ 10cm (4in)

 Z7–9

PERENNIAL SMALL

Leontopodium alpinum

EDELWEISS A compact perennial with linear, woolly gray-green leaves and small silvery white, starry flowers in late spring or early summer. Plant it in groups with low-growing spreading perennials, such as wood sorrel.

↕↔ 8in (20cm)

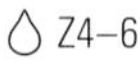 Z4–6

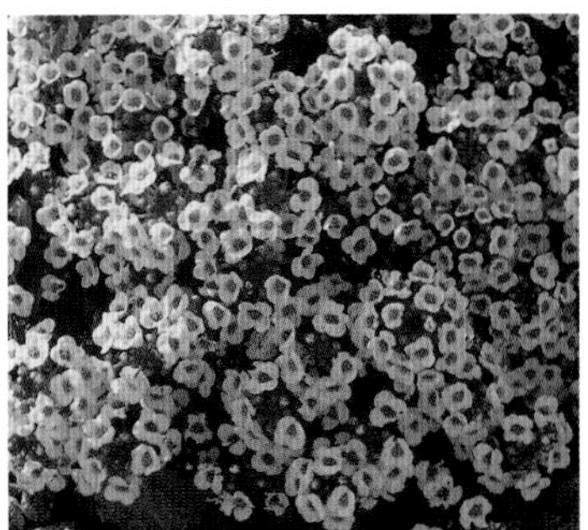

PERENNIAL SMALL

Lobularia maritima

SWEET ALYSSUM This ground-hugging perennial, grown as an annual, has narrow midgreen leaves and fragrant white blooms from summer to early fall. 'Snow Crystals' (above) is ideal for gaps between rocks. Considered invasive in some areas.

↕ 10in (25cm) ↔ 14in (35cm)

Z10–11

BULB MEDIUM

Narcissus bulbocodium

HOOP PETTICOAT DAFFODIL A perennial bulb with grasslike dark green leaves and unusual, funnel-shaped golden-yellow flowers surrounded by slim petals. Plant the bulbs in fall; ensure the soil is moist in winter and spring.

↕ 6in (15cm)

 Z5–9

BULB MEDIUM

Narcissus 'Pipit'

JONQUILLA DAFFODIL This perennial bulb bears narrow, cylindrical green leaves. It produces fragrant lemon-yellow flowers with creamy white cups in mid-spring. Plant the bulbs in groups in fall.

↕ 10in (25cm)

Z4–8

PERENNIAL SMALL

Oenothera fruticosa 'Fireworks'

SUNDROPS An upright perennial with lance-shaped bronze-green leaves on purple-tinted stems and, from summer to early fall, evening-fragrant cup-shaped flowers. Plant at the back of a rock garden.

↕↔ 15in (38cm)

Z4–8 Ⓝ

PERENNIAL SMALL

Oxalis adenophylla

CHILEAN WOOD SORREL This low-growing perennial forms a mat of small, distinctive, umbrella-like gray-green leaves. In spring, it bears rounded purplish pink flowers with darker purple eyes. Don't allow it to be swamped by neighboring plants.

↕2in (5cm) ↔4in (10cm)

Z6–9

PERENNIAL MEDIUM

Parahebe perfoliata

DIGGER'S SPEEDWELL A woody evergreen perennial with willowy stems, oval blue-green leaves and branching sprays of small blue flowers in late summer. Plant at the back of a rock garden or in a gravel bed. Cut back each spring.

↕24in (60cm) ↔18in (45cm)

pH Z9–11

PERENNIAL SMALL

Phlox subulata

CREEPING PHLOX A spreading evergreen perennial with trailing stems of needlelike green foliage. In summer, it is covered with pink, white, or mauve flowers, forming a mound of color. 'Emerald Pink' (above) has soft pink flowers.

↕6in (15cm) ↔20in (50cm)

Z3–9 Ⓝ

SHRUB SMALL

Picea pungens 'Montgomery'

COLORADO SPRUCE This is a compact, slow-growing evergreen conifer that makes a mound of needlelike gray-blue leaves. Ideal for imparting year-round color to the garden, it can be used as a foil for flowering plants and bulbs.

↕↔24in (60cm)

pH Z2–7 Ⓝ

SHRUB SMALL

Pinus mugo 'Ophir'

MUGO PINE A slow-growing, rounded, dwarf evergreen conifer with needlelike, golden-yellow foliage and small cones on mature plants. Use it for year-round color, and as a foil for flowering plants and dwarf spring bulbs.

↕↔24in (60cm)

Z3–7

PERENNIAL SMALL

Pulsatilla vulgaris

PASQUE FLOWER This clump-forming perennial produces feathery, light green leaves, silky when young. In spring, it bears nodding, cup-shaped flowers in shades of purple, red, pink, or white, followed by silky seedheads.

↕↔9in (23cm)

(!) Z5–8

PERENNIAL SMALL

Rhodanthemum hosmariense

MORROCAN DAISY An evergreen perennial, it forms a dense carpet of finely cut, silvery green leaves. White, daisy-like flowers appear on short stems from late spring to early fall. Deadhead after flowering. Grow in a sheltered location.

↕6in (15cm) or more ↔12in (30cm)

Z8–11

PERENNIAL SMALL

Saxifraga Southside Seedling Group

SAXIFRAGE A rosette-forming evergreen perennial with large pale green leaves that die back after flowering. In late spring and early summer, it bears clusters of open cup-shaped, red-centered white flowers.

↕12in (30cm) ↔8in (20cm)

Z4–6

BULB MEDIUM

Scilla siberica

SIBERIAN SQUILL This perennial bulb has strap-shaped midgreen leaves and nodding, bell-shaped blue flowers in spring. Plant the bulbs in groups in fall, together with other dwarf, spring-flowering bulbs, such as miniature daffodils.

↕8in (20cm) ↔2in (5cm)

Z4–8

PERENNIAL SMALL

Scutellaria baicalensis

SKULLCAP An upright perennial with small, hairy midgreen leaves and spikes of hooded purple and white flowers in late summer, followed by bronze-purple seedpods. The blooms are attractive to bees.

↕↔12in (30cm)

Z5–8

PERENNIAL SMALL

Sedum acre

GOLDEN MOSS This mat-forming evergreen perennial produces tiny, triangular yellow-green leaves with white tips and clusters of star-shaped yellow-green flowers in summer. Good companion for spring bulbs.

↕2in (5cm) ↔indefinite

(!) Z3–8

PERENNIAL SMALL

Sedum 'Vera Jameson'

STONECROP A spreading perennial with purple stems and fleshy, oval blue-green leaves that turn purple over time. From late summer to early fall, it produces rounded clusters of star-shaped rose-pink flowers.

↕12in (30cm) ↔18in (45cm)

Z3–9

PERENNIAL SMALL

Sempervivum giuseppii

HENS AND CHICKS This ground-hugging evergreen perennial produces rosettes of spiky green leaves with purple-pointed tips. In summer, clusters of star-shaped, deep pink or red flowers appear on upright stems.

↕in flower 4in (10cm) ↔4in (10cm)

Z7–9

PERENNIAL SMALL

Sempervivum tectorum

HENS AND CHICKS A mat-forming evergreen perennial with fleshy rosettes of blue-green leaves, often suffused red-purple, and short stems of star-shaped reddish purple flowers in summer. Plant at the front of a bed, away from spreading plants.

↕6in (15cm) ↔8in (20cm)

Z4–8

PERENNIAL SMALL

Stokesia laevis

STOKES' ASTER An evergreen perennial with slender green leaves and large, cornflower-like purple-blue flowers from summer to mid-fall. Use it to give height to a rock garden. 'Purple Parasols' (above) has violet-purple blooms.

↕↔18in (45cm)

pH Z5–9 (N)

BULB SMALL

Tulipa biflora

MINIATURE TULIP This dwarf perennial bulb has gray-green leaves. In mid-spring, it bears yellow-centered white flowers that are flushed greenish pink on the outside. Plant the bulbs in late fall in groups or drifts for the best effect.

↕4in (10cm) ↔5in (13cm)

(!) Z5–8

BULB MEDIUM

Tulipa 'Madame Lefèber'

TULIP This perennial bulb has oval, tapered gray-green leaves and large, bright red bowl-shaped flowers that appear from early- to mid-spring. Plant the bulbs in groups in late fall together with other spring-flowering plants.

↕16in (40cm)

(!) Z3–8

OTHER SUGGESTIONS

Annuals

Omphalodes linifolia

Perennials

Anthyllis vulneraria • *Arabis alpina* • *Arenaria alfacarensis* • *Asperula suberosa* • *Cerastium tomentosum* • *Fragaria* 'Lipstick' • *Phlox* x *procumbens* 'Variegata' • *Ruellia humilis* (N) • *Saxifraga paniculata* • *Scutellaria incana* (N) • *Silene acaulis* (N) • *Sisyrinchium angustifolium* 'Lucerne' (N) • *Pennisetum alopecuroides* 'Little Bunny'

Bulbs

Narcissus 'Hawera' • *Narcissus* 'Ice Wings' • *Tulipa* 'Little Beauty' • *Tulipa bakeri* 'Lilac Wonder' • *Tulipa sylvestris*

Shrubs

Juniperus squamata • *Pinus heldreichii* 'Smidtii'

Plants for urban gardens

Sheltered by a blockade of tall buildings, city gardens are warmer year-round than more rural plots, broadening your choice of plants.

Plants, such as Peruvian lily, that often suffer in winter sail through unscathed in snug city enclaves. Pollution, rubble-filled soils, and lack of privacy are the main problems for urban gardeners, but all of these can be overcome by digging out the debris and by planting strategically. Line the boundaries with well-behaved shrubs, such as ninebark and lilac, to shield your space from prying eyes, and fill flowerbeds with tough, colorful plants, or create an elegant monotone scheme. In tiny plots, restrict your palette to just a few species to produce a more cohesive design.

SHRUB LARGE

Abutilon hybrids

FLOWERING MAPLE These upright deciduous shrubs have narrow, lobed, gray-green felted foliage. From late spring to early summer, they bear flowers in many soft tones. Grow near a south-facing wall. Suitable as annuals in colder climates.

↕12ft (4m) ↔8ft (2.5m)

💧 Z9–10

PERENNIAL LARGE

Acanthus mollis

COMMON BEAR'S BREECHES An upright perennial with large, deeply lobed dark green foliage and tall sturdy spikes of hooded white and pale purple flowers from mid- to late summer. The decorative leaves extend the season of interest.

↕4ft (1.2m) ↔24in (60cm)

💧 Z7–11

TREE LARGE

Acer rubrum 'October Glory'

RED MAPLE The glossy dark green leaves of this deciduous spreading tree turn deep red in fall, particularly on neutral to acidic soil. In spring, the bare branches are covered with tiny red flower clusters. Best in open areas as shallow roots can crack sidewalks.

↕70ft (20m) ↔30ft (10m)

💧 pH Z3–9 Ⓝ

PERENNIAL MEDIUM

Alstroemeria ligtu hybrids

PERUVIAN LILY An upright rhizome-forming perennial with lance-shaped gray-green leaves and funnel-shaped flowers in a range of showy colors that appear in summer and are ideal for cutting. Plant it in groups in a sheltered spot; mulch in winter.

↕24in (60cm)

💧 ⓘ Z8–11

TREE SMALL

Amelanchier laevis

ALLEGHENY SERVICEBERRY A small, upright deciduous tree with purple-tinted young leaves that mature to dark green, then turn orange-red in fall. The white flowers in spring are followed by round edible berries in summer.

↕↔25ft (8m)

💧 pH Z4–8 Ⓝ

SHRUB LARGE

Amelanchier lamarckii

JUNEBERRY This small, upright deciduous tree or large shrub has bronze-tinted young leaves that are dark green when mature, and orange and red in fall. White flowers in spring are followed by red to purple berries that are loved by birds.

↕15ft (5m) ↔20ft (6m)

💧 pH Z4–8 Ⓝ

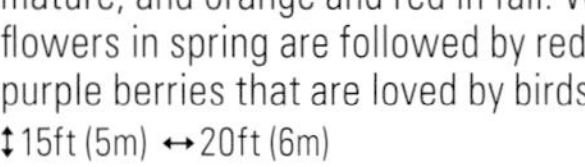

PERENNIAL MEDIUM

Artemisia ludoviciana 'Silver Queen'

WESTERN MUGWORT An upright perennial with slim, toothed-edged silver-gray leaves. Small yellow flower plumes may form in summer; cut to maintain the foliage effect. May spread aggressively.

↕↔30in (75cm)

💧 Z4–9 Ⓝ

SHRUB LARGE

Buddleja globosa

ORANGE BALL TREE This semievergreen shrub produces lance-shaped dark green leaves and globe-shaped, scented, bright orange flower heads in early summer. A reliable background plant for a border, it will also thrive beside a fence.

↕↔15ft (5m)

💧 Z7–9

SHRUB LARGE

Callistemon citrinus 'Splendens'

CRIMSON BOTTLEBRUSH An upright evergreen shrub with arching stems, lance-shaped, glossy green leaves and, in summer, spikes of bottlebrush crimson flower heads. Grow against a wall; protect from frost.

↕↔ 10ft (3m)

Z9–11

TREE LARGE

Catalpa bignonioides

INDIAN BEAN TREE A spreading deciduous tree with broad, oval pale green leaves and white spring flowers, and then beanlike seedpods. Cut back the branches hard in late winter to keep compact. Pollard to encourage larger leaves. Can be weedy.

↕↔ up to 50ft (15m)

Z5–9 (N)

SHRUB MEDIUM

Ceanothus x *delileanus* 'Gloire de Versailles'

CALIFORNIA LILAC This vigorous, bushy deciduous shrub has oval midgreen leaves and powdery blue branching flower heads from midsummer to early fall. Deadhead regularly. Best in West Coast gardens.

↕↔ 5ft (1.5m)

Z7–10 (N)

SHRUB MEDIUM

Ceanothus thyrsiflorus 'Born Again'

BLUE BLOSSOM An evergreen shrub with oval dark green and greenish yellow variegated leaves and, from late spring to early summer, fluffy blue oval flower heads. Grow in shelter. Best in West Coast gardens.

↕↔ 8ft (2.5m)

Z7–10 (N)

SHRUB LARGE

Ceanothus thyrsiflorus var. *repens*

CREEPING BLUE BLOSSOM Cascade this low, spreading evergreen shrub with oval green leaves and light blue rounded late spring to early summer flower clusters over a raised bed or wall in West Coast gardens.

↕↔ 20ft (6m)

Z7–10 (N)

SHRUB LARGE

Chionanthus virginicus

FRINGE TREE This vase-shaped deciduous shrub or small tree has peeling bark and oval green leaves, white beneath, and scented, spidery white summer to late spring blooms. Good for year-round interest in a small garden; needs long summers to flower well.

↕↔ 10ft (3m)

Z4–9 (N)

PERENNIAL LARGE

Crambe cordifolia

COLEWORT This robust perennial forms a mound of large, crinkled lobed leaves. In summer, it produces a cloud of small, fragrant white flowers in branching sprays. It needs space to be seen at its best.

↕ 6ft (2m) ↔ 4ft (1.2m)

Z5–9

SHRUB SMALL

Cryptomeria japonica 'Globosa Nana'

JAPANESE CEDAR A dome-shaped evergreen dwarf conifer with scaly green leaves. Makes a great specimen for winter interest in a border or large container, or as a green foil for colorful blooms.

↕↔ 3ft (1m)

Z6–9

TREE LARGE

Davidia involucrata

DOVE TREE This deciduous tree produces oval green leaves and small reddish brown spring flowers surrounded by petal-like creamy white bracts. Best in larger gardens; use it as a specimen in a lawn or border.

↕ 50ft (15m) ↔ 30ft (10m)

Z6–8

PERENNIAL SMALL

Delosperma nubigenum

ICE PLANT An evergreen perennial with trailing stems of small, succulent pale green leaves. In summer, it produces bright lemon-yellow daisy-like flowers that attract butterflies. An excellent specimen for trailing over raised edges.

↕ 2in (5cm) ↔ 20in (50cm)

Z6–8

SHRUB LARGE

Elaeagnus x *ebbingei*

OLEASTER This vigorous evergreen shrub has oval, tapered dark green leaves dusted with gray flecks. It makes a good screen or windbreak; clip in late summer. Variegated varieties include 'Gilt Edge', which has yellow-splashed leaves.

↕↔15ft (5m)

Z7–9

BAMBOO LARGE

Fargesia murielae

UMBRELLA BAMBOO This large, clump-forming bamboo produces arching yellow-green canes and lance-shaped bright green leaves. Use it as screen to divide a garden or as an accent plant in a border or gravel bed.

↕12ft (4m) ↔ indefinite

Z5–9

ANNUAL/BIENNIAL SMALL

Gazania Kiss Series

TREASURE FLOWER A dwarf perennial, grown as an annual, with oval dark green leaves. From summer to fall, it bears daisy-like flowers in shades of gold, bronze, pink, and white with contrasting eyes. Grow it in shallow containers of potting mix.

↕12in (30cm) ↔10in (25cm)

Z8–10

PERENNIAL SMALL

Geranium himalayense 'Plenum'

CRANESBILL A clump-forming, low-growing perennial, with lobed silver-green foliage that turns red in fall and double, blue-purple summer flowers with darker veins. Use to line a path or as ground cover.

↕10in (25cm) ↔24in (60cm)

Z4–7

PERENNIAL SMALL

Geranium sanguineum 'Album'

BLOODY CRANESBILL This clump-forming, spreading perennial has deeply cut dark green leaves, which turn red in fall. White flowers appear in early summer. Use to line a path or as ground cover.

↕12in (30cm) ↔16in (40cm)

Z3–8

PERENNIAL SMALL

Gerbera hybrids

TRANSVAAL DAISY This upright divided perennial, often grown as an annual, bears oval, lobed, green basal leaves and daisy-like flowers in nearly every color from summer to fall. Plant it in a large container or use to add color to a bed.

↕↔16in (40cm)

Z8–11

PERENNIAL MEDIUM

Geranium pratense

MEADOW CRANESBILL This clump-forming perennial has hairy stems and divided, lobed midgreen leaves, bronze in fall, and saucer-shaped, violet-blue, veined summer flowers. 'Mrs Kendall Clark' (above) has pearl-gray, pale-pink flushed flowers.

↕↔24in (60cm)

Z4–8

PERENNIAL SMALL

Geum 'Borisii'

AVENS This clump-forming perennial produces round, divided midgreen leaves and slender stems topped with saucer-shaped, bright orange-red flowers from late spring to early summer. Plant it in groups at the front of a bed.

↕20in (50cm) ↔12in (30cm)

Z3–7

TREE LARGE

Ginkgo biloba

MAIDENHAIR TREE A conical deciduous tree, with fan-shaped, pale green leaves that turn yellow in fall. Female plants produce yellow fruits in fall; male plants are preferred in cities to avoid fruit drop. Use it as a specimen or street tree.

↕100ft (30m) ↔25ft (8m)

Z4–9

TREE MEDIUM

Gleditsia triacanthos 'Sunburst'

HONEYLOCUST A deciduous tree with large golden-yellow leaves divided into leaflets, which turn green in summer and yellow in fall. With its long season of interest, it looks pretty in a small garden.

↕40ft (12m) ↔30ft (10m)

Z3–8 Ⓝ

PERENNIAL LARGE

Lupinus 'The Chatelaine'

LUPINE An upright perennial with round leaves divided into lance-shaped leaflets. Tall spikes of dark pink and white flowers appear in early summer adding color to the middle of a flower bed. It may need staking. The seeds are toxic.

↕4ft (1.2m) ↔18in (45cm)

(!) Z4–8

SHRUB SMALL

Hypericum calycinum

AARON'S BEARD A dwarf semi- or fully evergreen shrub with dark green leaves. From midsummer to mid-fall, it bears large, open bright yellow flowers with a tuft of fluffy stamens in the center. It can be used for ground cover.

↕24in (60cm) ↔indefinite

Z5–9

TREE SMALL

Magnolia x *soulangeana*

SAUCER MAGNOLIA A spreading deciduous tree with oval dark green leaves and goblet-shaped white, pink, or purple flowers from mid- to late spring. Use it as a feature in a lawn or flower bed; protect flower buds from late frosts.

↕↔20ft (6m)

pH Z5–9

PERENNIAL MEDIUM

Leucanthemum x *superbum*

SHASTA DAISY This upright perennial has lance-shaped dark green leaves and daisy-like white flowers with golden-yellow eyes in summer. Grow in groups in the middle of borders. 'Beauté Nivelloise' (above) has spidery flowers.

↕up to 3ft (1m) ↔24in (60cm)

Z5–9

TREE SMALL

Malus domestica

syn. ***Malus pumila*** A compact tree when grafted onto a dwarfing rootstock. It bears oval green leaves, pale pink or white flowers in spring, and edible fruits in fall. Choose from the many varieties available; provide a sheltered site.

↕↔25ft (8m)

Z4–8

TREE MEDIUM

Malus floribunda

JAPANESE FLOWERING CRABAPPLE This deciduous tree has a round head of oval green leaves. In spring, crimson buds open to reveal pale pink flowers followed, in fall, by edible red and yellow fruits ideal for making jelly. May be invasive.

↕↔30ft (10m)

Z4–8

PERENNIAL MEDIUM

Malva moschata

MUSK MALLOW An upright perennial with heart-shaped basal leaves and ferny leaves on the upper stems. Saucer-shaped pale pink flowers appear from summer to early fall. Its long flowering period is useful in a small city garden.

↕3ft (1m) ↔24in (60cm)

Z3–8

TREE MEDIUM

Morus nigra

BLACK MULBERRY This tree has a rounded canopy of heart-shaped green leaves and blackberry-like edible fruits in fall. Grow it in a lawn, away from patios, as the fruits will stain paving. Prune from late fall to midwinter to avoid weeping wounds.

↕40ft (12m) ↔50ft (15m)

Z5–9

PERENNIAL MEDIUM

Papaver orientale

ORIENTAL POPPY An upright perennial with divided midgreen leaves. From early summer, it bears large saucer-shaped blooms with dark eyes. Plant it in groups at the front of a flower bed. 'Karine' (above) has salmon-pink flowers.

↕↔ 3ft (1m)

Z3–8

SHRUB SMALL

Philadelphus 'Belle Etoile'

MOCK ORANGE An arching deciduous shrub with small midgreen leaves. From late spring to early summer, it bears highly fragrant white flowers, each with a pale purple mark at the base. Plant it near seating to enjoy the fragrance.

↕ 4ft (1.2m) ↔ 8ft (2.5m)

Z5–8

BAMBOO LARGE

Phyllostachys aureosulcata f. *aureocaulis*

GOLDEN GROOVE BAMBOO A tall, upright, clump-forming bamboo with yellow canes and lance-shaped midgreen leaves. Good as a boundary screen; best in fertile soil. Use root barriers to confine it in small areas.

↕ 20ft (6m) ↔ indefinite

Z5–10

SHRUB LARGE

Physocarpus opulifolius

NINEBARK This is a fast-growing deciduous shrub with lobed green leaves and, in early summer, it produces clusters of small white blooms. Many cultivars with purple to yellow foliage are also available.

↕ 10ft (3m) ↔ 15ft (1.5m)

Z3–7 Ⓝ

BAMBOO SMALL

Pleioblastus variegatus

DWARF WHITE-STRIPE BAMBOO This compact evergreen bamboo has pale green canes and broad, creamy white striped green leaves. Plant it in a large container or a bed, or use it to line a path. It performs best in fertile soil.

↕ 32in (80cm) ↔ indefinite

Z6–11

PERENNIAL SMALL

Potentilla 'Gibson's Scarlet'

CINQUEFOIL A small clump-forming perennial with lobed soft green leaves and sprays of small black-eyed bright scarlet flowers in summer. Use it to brighten up the front of a bed. Avoid hot dry sites.

↕ 18in (45cm) ↔ 24in (60cm)

Z5–8

TREE SMALL

Prunus dulcis

COMMON ALMOND This small deciduous tree bears bowl-shaped, single or double pink flowers in spring before the lance-shaped, green leaves appear. Plant it in a border or as a specimen in a lawn. Edible nuts form in fall following a warm summer.

↕↔ 25ft (8m)

Z7–9

TREE MEDIUM

Prunus 'Kanzan'

JAPANESE FLOWERING CHERRY This vase-shaped deciduous tree produces pink double spring flowers before the oval bronze leaves appear. The foliage turns green in summer and orange in fall. Plant it as a specimen in a lawn or flower bed.

↕↔ 30ft (10m)

Ⓘ Z5–8

TREE LARGE

Quercus palustris

PIN OAK This pyramid-shaped deciduous tree has oval, deeply lobed green leaves that turn bright red in fall. It bears flowers in spring, followed by small-sized acorns. It is best grown as a street tree in most areas due to its large size.

↕ 70ft (20m) ↔ 40ft (12m)

Z4–8 Ⓝ

SHRUB LARGE

Rhus typhina 'Dissecta'

STAGHORN SUMAC A small deciduous tree or large spreading shrub with velvety stems, bright green dissected leaves that turn yellow and red in fall, and large maroon, bud-shaped fruit clusters on female plants. Leave ample space for suckers to naturalize.

↕↔10ft (3m)

Z3–8 Ⓝ

SHRUB MEDIUM

Rosa FOURTH OF JULY

CLIMBING ROSE This floribunda-type rose has dark green glossy leaves. From summer to fall, it produces cupped, semidouble, red-splashed cream flowers, with a light fruity perfume. It is a disease-resistant variety.

↕5ft (1.5m) ↔3½ft (1.1m)

Z5–9

SHRUB SMALL

Rosa RHAPSODY IN BLUE

SHRUB ROSE This modern shrub rose produces disease-resistant green leaves and clusters of scented, purple semidouble flowers that fade to slate blue from summer to early fall. Plant it in a flower bed or large container.

↕4ft (1.2m) ↔3ft (1m)

Z5–9

SHRUB SMALL

Santolina pinnata

LAVENDER COTTON This bushy evergreen subshrub has slender, finely toothed silver foliage and a profusion of pompomlike, pale lemon-yellow summer flowers. *S. pinnata* subsp. *neapolitana* has gray-green foliage and bright yellow flowers.

↕30in (75cm) ↔3ft (1m)

Z9–11

PERENNIAL MEDIUM

Solidago GOLDEN BABY

GOLDENROD An upright, clump-forming perennial, it has slender, pointed green leaves. From mid- to late summer, it produces branching heads of golden-yellow blooms. Deadhead to prolong the display; plants may need staking.

↕24in (60cm) ↔18in (45cm)

Z4–8

SHRUB LARGE

Syringa vulgaris

COMMON LILAC This vigorous, deciduous shrub has heart-shaped midgreen foliage and large rounded clusters of fragrant late spring flowers in shades of purple, pink, and white. Use compact varieties in smaller plots. May be invasive in some areas.

↕↔22ft (7m)

Z3–7

TREE LARGE

Tilia cordata

LITTLELEAF LINDEN This deciduous tree has heart-shaped, glossy dark green leaves that turn yellow in fall. Small yellowish white flowers appear in summer. Good as a "shade" or street tree. Keep compact by pleaching, or grow it as a formal hedge.

↕100ft (30m) ↔40ft (12m)

 Z3–7

PERENNIAL SMALL

Veronica spicata

SPIKE SPEEDWELL This upright clump-forming perennial has lance-shaped toothed green leaves and bright blue summer flower spikes. Grow in groups at the front of a flower bed with other summer-flowering perennials. 'Red Fox' (above) has deep pink flowers.

↕↔22in (50cm)

Z3–8

OTHER SUGGESTIONS

Perennials

Andropogon gerardii Ⓝ • *Delosperma cooperi* • *Echinacea purpurea* Ⓝ • *Liatris spicata* Ⓝ • *Macleaya cordata* • *Muhlenbergia capillaris* Ⓝ • *Penstemon* 'Garnet' • *Salvia microphylla* Ⓝ • *Solidago rugosa* 'Fireworks' Ⓝ

Shrubs

Arctostaphylos uva-ursi 'Massachusetts' Ⓝ • *Callistemon rigidus* • *Genista lydia* • *Myrica pensylvanica* Ⓝ • *Rhus aromatica* 'Gro-Low' Ⓝ • *Sambucus canadensis* Ⓝ • *Yucca filamentosa* 'Bright Edge' Ⓝ

Trees

Chionanthus retusus • *Gymnocladus dioica* Ⓝ • *Quercus alba* Ⓝ • *Robinia pseudoacacia* 'Bessoniana' Ⓝ • *Sabal palmetto* Ⓝ

Plant focus: grasses and sedges

Elegant and versatile, the slender foliage and airy flowers of grasses and sedges contrast beautifully with broad-leaved plants.

Ornamental grasses and sedges comprise a range of shapes and sizes, from tall and slender to short and squat, and form the key ingredient of many garden styles. Those with slim leaves and delicate flower heads, such as reed grass, blend perfectly into naturalistic schemes, while the spikes of blue fescue are ideal for container displays. Sedges, including those in the *Acorus* family, make elegant features in the boggy ground beside natural water features. Although sedges and grasses look similar, they are adapted to different environments. With a few exceptions, grasses are deciduous and prefer sun and free-draining soils, while the majority of sedges are evergreen and happy in sun or shade and moist soils. Grasses also tend to have more dramatic flower- and seedheads adding to their decorative value. Both grasses and sedges help to heighten the beauty of winter landscapes: the leaves of deciduous species tend to remain intact throughout the season, providing useful structure in herbaceous borders.

POPULAR GRASS AND SEDGE SPECIES

Acorus Sweet flags are moisture-loving evergreen sedges and thrive in shade. They include striped and golden-leaved forms.

Calamagrostis Deciduous feather reed grasses produce low clumps of leaves teamed with tall stems of feathery summer flowers.

Carex This group of evergreen and deciduous sedges includes moisture-lovers, shade-tolerant varieties, and bronze forms that prefer drier soils.

Panicum The most popular form is *P. virgatum*, a deciduous perennial grass with blue, red, or purple-tinted foliage.

Pennisetum Long, bristlelike flower heads and mounds of slender leaves are features of this deciduous grass; some forms are tender.

Stipa Often used interchangeably with *Nassella*, many of these grasses feature feathery inflorescence from early summer to autumn.

USING GRASSES AND SEDGES

Grasses are used in prairie-style schemes for their summer foliage and flowers and winter structure. Use sedges for year-round color and interest at the front of a bed.

Short compact grasses, including the vivid Japanese forest grass, create graphic displays in pots. Evergreen sedges are ideal for winter displays.

Tall slim-leaved grasses, such as feather reed grass, make bold accents in mixed herbaceous borders, while their transparency allows welcome glimpses of the plants behind.

Bronze forms of *Carex* and airy Mexican feather grass provide contrasting textures and colors to flower displays in both modern and traditional garden designs.

Plants for roof and terrace gardens

Bright and breezy, roof gardens demand windproof plants that are happy basking in full sun and thrive in pots or well-drained soil.

Most roofs and terraces are container gardens. However, weight restrictions often apply, so opt for lighter pots made from galvanized metal and man-made materials, or try wooden raised beds and troughs for a rustic design. Also, consider investing in an automatic watering system because the sun and wind quickly dry out the soil, especially in the height of summer. Despite these limitations, roof terraces offer plenty of range. Shrubs and small trees provide height, structure, and shade, while roses, perennials, and annuals lend themselves to romantic schemes, and flax and grasses complement modern designs.

PERENNIAL SMALL

Agastache aurantiaca

GIANT HYSSOP This upright perennial has gray-green scented leaves. From mid- to late summer, it bears long-lasting spikes of small tubular flowers. 'Apricot Sprite' (above) has pale orange blooms. Plant it in groups in a bed or container.

↕20in (50cm) ↔3ft (1m)

Z6–10 Ⓝ

PERENNIAL MEDIUM

Anthemis tinctoria

GOLDEN MARGUERITE This clump-forming, low-growing perennial forms a mat of finely cut green leaves. In summer, it becomes speckled with a mass of daisy-like white or yellow flowers held on slender stems. 'E.C. Buxton' (above) has lemon-yellow flowers.

↕↔3ft (1m)

Z3–8

PERENNIAL SMALL

Armeria maritima

THRIFT This is a small mound-forming perennial with grasslike green leaves. In summer, it becomes dotted with heads of small, round white or pink flowers. Suitable for small pots, raised beds, or on exposed green roofs.

↕4in (10cm) ↔6in (15cm)

Z4–8 Ⓝ

SHRUB SMALL

Artemisia 'Powis Castle'

WORMWOOD A clump-forming semievergreen subshrub with fernlike silvery gray leaves that make an excellent foil for other plants. Yellow pompom flowers may appear in summer, but are best removed to retain its silvery foliage effect.

↕↔3ft (1m)

Z7–9

SHRUB SMALL

Buxus sempervirens 'Suffruticosa'

COMMON BOXWOOD A compact, slow-growing evergreen shrub with woody stems of small oval green leaves; clip into architectural shapes and topiary. Grow in a pot, or use as a low hedge or bed edging.

↕3ft (1m) ↔5ft (1.5m)

(!) Z6–8

PERENNIAL LARGE

Calamagrostis x *acutiflora*

FEATHER REED GRASS A clump-forming deciduous grass with long, arching green leaves. Tall bronze flower heads, borne in summer, fade to buff. The seedheads give winter interest. Use as a screen or backdrop; cut back in early spring.

↕6ft (1.8m) ↔4ft (1.2m)

Z5–9

TREE SMALL

Carpinus betulus

EUROPEAN HORNBEAM This deciduous tree produces oval, prominently veined dark green leaves that turn yellow and orange in fall; young stems retain the dried foliage in winter. Cut it into a hedge on a roof terrace.

↕15ft (5m) as a hedge ↔70ft (20m)

Z4–8

SHRUB SMALL

Chamaecyparis obtusa 'Rigid Dwarf'

HINOKI CYPRESS This compact, dwarf evergreen conifer makes a cone of dark green leaves. Use it as a foil for drought-tolerant plants on a roof terrace or plant in a large container of soil-based potting mix.

↕4ft (1.2m) ↔24in (60cm)

Z4–8

PERENNIAL LARGE

Crocosmia masoniorum

MONTBRETIA A clump-forming perennial with arching, sword-shaped dark green leaves pleated lengthways. Orange-red flowers appear in late summer and last for several weeks. Plant in large containers in prime positions in a roof garden.

↕5ft (1.5m) ↔18in (45cm)

 Z6–9

PERENNIAL SMALL

Hakonechloa macra 'Aureola'

JAPANESE FOREST GRASS A small, slow-growing deciduous grass with purple stems, green-striped yellow leaves and reddish brown flower spikes from early fall to winter. Protect from midday sun and water well.

↕16in (40cm) ↔24in (60cm)

Z5–9

SHRUB SMALL

Chamaecyparis pisifera 'Plumosa Compressa'

SAWARA CYPRESS This irregularly-shaped, slow-growing evergreen conifer bears light sulfur-yellow foliage, yellow-green in winter. Plant with small shrubs and bulbs in a container of soil-based potting mix.

↕↔4ft (1.2m)

Z4–8

PERENNIAL SMALL

Erigeron karvinskianus

MEXICAN FLEABANE This spreading low-growing perennial produces lance-shaped, hairy green leaves and daisy-like summer flowers that open white, turn pink, and fade to purple. Use it to cascade over pots and ledges.

↕6in (15cm) ↔indefinite

Z8–10 (N)

SHRUB SMALL

Juniperus procumbens

DWARF JAPANESE JUNIPER This low-growing, mat-forming evergreen conifer produces dense prickly leaves that provide good ground cover. Use it to create year-round color at the edge of a planter or raised bed.

↕8in (20cm) ↔30in (75cm)

Z4–9

CLIMBER MEDIUM

Clematis macropetala

DOWNY CLEMATIS A compact climber with midgreen leaves divided into leaflets. From late spring to early summer, it is covered with mauve-blue semidouble flowers, followed by fluffy seedheads. Grow in a pot or through a shrub; shade the roots.

↕10ft (3m)

Z4–8

SHRUB SMALL

Lavandula stoechas subsp. *pedunculata*

SPANISH LAVENDER An evergreen subshrub with aromatic gray-green foliage and violet, scented flowers with purple-pink "ears" from late spring to summer. In northern areas, protect in winter or treat as an annual.

↕↔32in (80cm)

Z8–9

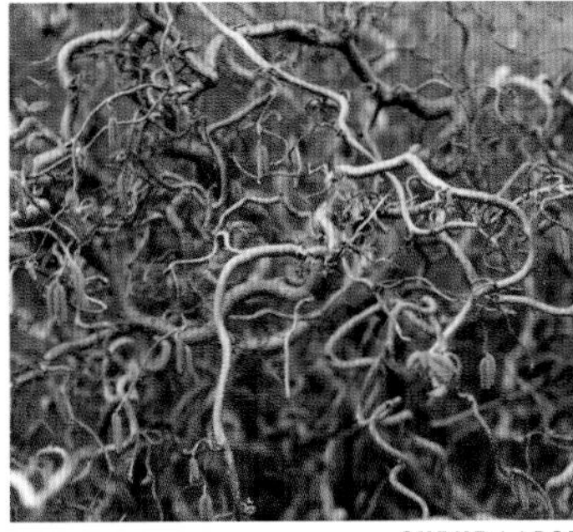

SHRUB LARGE

Corylus avellana 'Contorta'

HARRY LAUDER'S WALKING STICK A bushy shrub or small tree with midgreen foliage, it is grown for its distinctive contorted stems. In late winter, pale yellow catkins form on bare stems. Use as a winter focal point. Considered invasive in some areas.

↕↔10ft (3m)

Z4–8

SHRUB MEDIUM

Fuchsia magellanica var. *molinae*

HARDY FUCHSIA An upright deciduous shrub with lance-shaped green leaves and pendent pale pink flowers from summer to early fall. Plant in a container of soil-based potting mix. Best in West Coast gardens.

↕↔6ft (2m)

Z7–9

BULB MEDIUM

Narcissus 'Ice Follies'

DAFFODIL This is a perennial bulb with sword-shaped green leaves. In mid-spring, creamy white single flowers with yellow cups that fade to near white appear. Plant groups of bulbs into frostproof pots during fall.

↕16in (40cm)

(!) Z3–8

PERENNIAL MEDIUM

Osteospermum hybrids

AFRICAN DAISY An herbaceous evergreen perennial, grown as an annual, with slim midgreen leaves and pink, yellow, and white daisy-like summer blooms with bluish purple centers. Plant in a container of potting mix or along the edge of a path.

↕24in (60cm) ↔12in (30cm)

💧 Z10–11

PERENNIAL SMALL

Pelargonium 'Lady Plymouth'

SCENTED GERANIUM A small, tender spreading perennial, often grown as an annual, with eucalyptus-scented, lobed, silver-margined green leaves and lavender-pink summer flowers. Grow in pots or raised beds.

↕16in (40cm) ↔8in (20cm)

💧 (!) Z10–11

SHRUB SMALL

Perovskia 'Blue Spire'

RUSSIAN SAGE This upright deciduous subshrub produces white stems of small, aromatic gray-green leaves and branched spikes of blue-purple flowers from late summer to fall. Plant it in a mixed bed or in containers of soil-based potting mix.

↕4ft (1.2m) ↔3ft (1m)

💧 Z5–9

PERENNIAL MEDIUM

Phormium 'Bronze Baby'

NEW ZEALAND FLAX An upright evergreen perennial with a fountainlike mound of arching, sword-shaped purple-bronze leaves. Makes a statement in a container of soil-based potting mix or in a gravel bed. Overwinter indoors in colder areas.

↕↔24in (60cm)

💧 Z9–11

SHRUB SMALL

Pinus mugo 'Mops'

MUGO PINE This small, compact evergreen conifer produces a mound of needlelike dark green leaves. Combine it with spring bulbs or other small shrubs in a large container of soil-based potting mix.

↕3ft (1m) ↔6ft (2m)

💧 Z2–7

SHRUB SMALL

Rosa Flower Carpet Series

GROUNDCOVER ROSE These spreading roses form a dense mound of glossy, green disease-resistant leaves. Semidouble cupped flowers in pink, red, yellow, peach, and white are freely produced from summer to fall. Plant them in large containers.

↕↔24in (60cm)

💧 Z5–10

SHRUB SMALL

Rosa ICEBERG

FLORIBUNDA ROSE This bush rose produces glossy green leaves and sprays of pink-tinted buds that open to reveal cupped, white fully double flowers from summer to early fall. Grow it along the boundary of a roof garden.

↕30in (75cm) ↔26in (65cm) or more

💧 Z5–9

SHRUB SMALL

Rosa KENT

GROUNDCOVER ROSE A spreading rose with disease-resistant, glossy midgreen leaves and clusters of flat white semidouble flowers from summer to fall. Allow it to trail over the edge of a large container filled with soil-based potting mix.

↕32in (80cm) ↔3ft (1m)

💧 Z5–9

SHRUB SMALL

Rosa SUNSET CELEBRATION

HYBRID TEA ROSE This bushy rose has disease-resistant midgreen leaves. In summer and fall, it has scented, coral-pink fully double pointed flowers that mature to rose-pink. Plant it in a large container of soil-based potting mix or a bed.

↕3ft (1m) ↔32in (80cm)

💧 Z7–10

SHRUB MEDIUM

Rosmarinus officinalis

ROSEMARY This evergreen shrub produces aromatic, needlelike dark green foliage and small blue flowers in spring. Grow it in a raised bed with other culinary herbs or in a container filled with soil-based potting mix.

↕↔5ft (1.5m)

💧 Z8–10

PERENNIAL SMALL

Salvia greggii Navajo Series

AUTUMN SAGE This woody perennial has oval midgreen leaves with clusters of small red, purple, pink, or white flowers from late summer to fall. Plant it in groups in containers, raised beds, or beds. Protect from hard frosts.

↕↔ 20in (50cm)

Z7–9 Ⓝ

PERENNIAL SMALL

Sempervivum arachnoideum

COBWEB HOUSELEEK This low-growing evergreen perennial forms small rosettes of fleshy green leaves covered with fine white webbing and branching heads of reddish pink flowers in summer; it is suitable for green roofs.

↕ 5in (12cm) ↔ 4in (10cm) or more

Z5–8

SHRUB SMALL

Santolina chamaecyparissus

COTTON LAVENDER A mound-forming evergreen subshrub with finely cut, aromatic silvery gray leaves and yellow pompomlike summer flowers. Use it in a raised bed, or to edge a bed or path. Trim it back after flowering to keep it neat.

↕ 30in (75cm) ↔ 3ft (1m)

Z6–9

SHRUB LARGE

Sambucus racemosa 'Plumosa Aurea'

EUROPEAN RED ELDER An upright deciduous shrub with bronze leaflets that mature to golden-yellow in early summer. Scarlet fruits follow star-shaped yellow spring flowers. Grow in large pots in some shade.

↕↔ 10ft (3m)

Z3–7

PERENNIAL MEDIUM

Sedum AUTUMN JOY

STONECROP This clump-forming perennial has oval, fleshy gray-green leaves and small, star-shaped, brick-red flattened flower heads in late summer, followed by brown seedheads that persist through winter. Plant it in a bed or raised bed.

↕ 24in (60cm) ↔ 20in (50cm)

Z3–10

PERENNIAL MEDIUM

Tanacetum coccineum

PYRETHRUM An upright perennial with feathery dark green leaves and daisy-like, yellow-centered pink or red flowers in early summer. Plant it in groups in pots, raised beds, or beds. Deadhead to encourage more blooms. This plant can be short-lived.

↕ 24in (60cm) ↔ 18in (45cm) or more

Z5–9

PERENNIAL SMALL

Sedum rupestre

REFLEXED STONECROP A low-growing evergreen perennial that forms mats of trailing stems bearing narrow fleshy leaves. Tiny bright yellow flowers appear in summer. Use it to trail over raised beds, in shallow containers, or on green roofs.

↕ 8in (20cm) ↔ indefinite

(!) Z5–9

OTHER SUGGESTIONS

Perennials

Andropogon gerardii 'Pawnee' Ⓝ • *Coreopsis verticillata* 'Moonbeam' Ⓝ • *Diascia barberae* • *Erigeron* 'Darkest of All' • *Eryngium alpinum* 'Blue Star' • *Festuca glauca* 'Elijah Blue' Ⓝ • *Oenothera fremontii* 'Lemon Silver' Ⓝ • *Opuntia macrorhiza* Ⓝ • *Pennisetum alopecuroides* 'Hameln' • *Sedum rupestre* 'Angelina' • *Sempervivum ciliosum* • *Yucca filamentosa* 'Color Guard' Ⓝ

Bulbs

Allium christophii • *Narcissus* 'Cheerfulness'

Shrubs and Climbers

Bougainvillea 'Texas Dawn' • *Cordyline australis* • *Potentilla fruticosa* 'Abbotswood' Ⓝ • *Pyracantha* 'Teton' • *Rhus typhina* 'Dissecta' Ⓝ

Plants for exposed sites

Select resilient plants for gardens where temperatures dip well below freezing in winter or are buffeted by strong winds or coastal spray.

Trees and shrubs from mountainous regions are ideal for frosty and exposed sites, their names often giving clues to their antecedents—*Alchemilla alpina* and *Geranium himalayense*, for example. Many hardy perennials avoid the worst of the winter weather by disappearing beneath the surface and lying dormant until spring, while hardy evergreens fight the cold with an antifreeze solution of sugars and amino acids within their cells. Choose a selection of plants, such as snowdrops, that flower in winter to brighten up this bleak time of the year, and use evergreens for permanent structure and color.

TREE LARGE

Abies concolor

WHITE FIR This evergreen conifer tree is grown for its silver foliage and Christmas-tree shape. Plant it as a lawn specimen or part of a mixed, windbreak screen in large yards. Pruning may spoil the shape.

↕100ft (30m) ↔25ft (8m)

Z3–7 (N)

TREE LARGE

Acer negundo

BOXELDER This tree has a rounded head and reddish brown lobed leaves that turn midgreen in summer and have striking fall color. 'Flamingo' (above) has white and pink variegated leaves. Pollard to keep it compact.

↕50ft (15m) ↔30ft (10m)

Z3–8

TREE LARGE

Acer saccharinum

SILVER MAPLE A large, lobed, round-headed tree, with dark green foliage that develops a fiery color in fall, particularly in colder regions. Use it as a specimen; plant in a sheltered site to avoid wind damage: it is prone to breakage in heavy storms.

↕70ft (20m) ↔40ft (12m)

Z3–9 (N)

PERENNIAL SMALL

Alchemilla alpina

ALPINE LADY'S MANTLE This mat-forming perennial has rounded, dark green divided leaves with a silver hairy reverse and frothy greenish yellow summer flowers. Hardy and wind-resistant, plant it in a rock garden or wild corner. Avoid hot dry areas.

↕6in (15cm) ↔24in (60cm) or more

Z3–7

PERENNIAL MEDIUM

Aquilegia vulgaris

COLUMBINE A ferny green-leaved perennial with wiry upright stems of bell-shaped blue, pink, purple, or white flowers in late spring and early summer. Grow in informal and cottage borders in cold sites; weed out unwanted seedlings.

↕24in (60cm) ↔20in (50cm)

Z3–8

SHRUB SMALL

Arctostaphylos uva-ursi

BEARBERRY A creeping evergreen shrub with glossy, oval green leaves, silver below. The small, pink or white urn-shaped blooms appear from spring to early summer, followed by red berries. Cascade this mountain plant over walls or rock gardens.

↕4in (10cm) ↔20in (50cm)

pH Z2–6 (N)

PERENNIAL SMALL

Armeria maritima

THRIFT A hummock-forming evergreen with grasslike leaves and stiff stems bearing pompom-shaped pink flowers from late spring to summer. This hardy plant is salt- and wind-tolerant, ideal for alpine troughs, rock gardens, and raised beds.

↕4in (10cm) ↔6in (15cm)

Z4–8 (N)

PERENNIAL SMALL

Aster alpinus

ALPINE ASTER A clump-forming perennial with midgreen, narrow lance-shaped leaves. It bears large, daisy-like violet-blue late summer blooms with a yellow central disk. Plant this wind-proof alpine on banks and in gravel gardens and raised beds.

↕6in (15cm) ↔18in (45cm)

Z4–8

TREE LARGE

Betula papyrifera

PAPER BIRCH A tall, sparsely branched, narrowly conical tree with white peeling bark, pale orange beneath. The oval dark green leaves turn yellow in fall, and yellow catkins appear in spring. Use multistemmed forms as focal points.

↕70ft (20m) ↔30ft (10m)

Z2–7 Ⓝ

SHRUB LARGE

Berberis darwinii

DARWIN'S BARBERRY This evergreen shrub has small, glossy, prickly dark green leaves and, in spring, hanging clusters of dark orange flowers followed by blue-black berries. It makes intruder-proof windbreaks in informal or coastal gardens.

↕↔10ft (3m)

(!) Z7–9

PERENNIAL SMALL

Bergenia cordifolia

PIGSQUEAK This clump-forming evergreen perennial has leathery, midgreen rounded leaves and in early spring, red stems bearing clusters of deep pink bells appear. Use as weed-suppressing ground cover. Performs best in moist soil.

↕↔20in (50cm)

Z3–8

TREE LARGE

Betula pendula

EUROPEAN WHITE BIRCH A white-barked deciduous tree with sparse upright branches and slender cascading stems. Catkins appear in spring followed by diamond-shaped leaves, which turn yellow in fall. It suits exposed wild gardens.

↕80ft (25m) or more ↔30ft (10m)

Z2–7

PERENNIAL MEDIUM

Briza media

COMMON QUAKING GRASS This perennial makes a tuft of grassy blue-green leaves. From late spring to midsummer, upright stems bear green heart-shaped flower heads that turn straw-colored. Plant at the front of a cottage or wildlife bed.

↕24in (60cm) ↔4in (10cm)

Z4–11

SHRUB SMALL

Calluna vulgaris 'Silver Knight'

SCOTCH HEATHER A low-growing evergreen shrub with upright branches covered with scalelike gray leaves that tinge purple in winter, and lavender late-summer flower spikes. Ideal for ground cover or bed edging.

↕12in (30cm) ↔16in (40cm)

(!) Z4–7

TREE LARGE

Carpinus betulus

EUROPEAN HORNBEAM A deciduous tree with oval, toothed dark green leaves, yellow in fall, with a pleated appearance and hoplike fruits in late summer. 'Fastigiata' (above) is compact and narrowly upright when young; becoming flame-shaped.

↕up to 80ft (25m) ↔70ft (20m)

Z4–8

PERENNIAL MEDIUM

Centaurea dealbata

PERSIAN CORNFLOWER A clump-forming perennial with gray-green cut leaves. From early- to midsummer, it bears white-eyed pink flowers with fringed petals. Robust on poor soil, this drought-resistant flower suits windy coastal sites; may need staking.

↕3ft (1m) ↔24in (60cm)

Z3–8

TREE MEDIUM

Chamaecyparis pisifera 'Filifera Aurea'

SAWARA CYPRESS This slow-growing, broadly conical evergreen conifer makes a mound of weeping branches that carry golden-yellow scalelike leaves. Use as a specimen in cold or coastal areas.

↕40ft (12m) ↔15ft (5m)

Z4–8

SHRUB LARGE

Chionanthus virginicus

FRINGE TREE This rounded shrub or small spreading tree has oval dark green leaves and, in early summer, pendent, long-petaled, fragrant white flowers followed by blue-black fruits. It is cold-tolerant, but needs shelter from strong winds.

↕↔ 10ft (3m)

Z4–9 Ⓝ

PERENNIAL SMALL

Coreopsis 'Rum Punch'

TICKSEED This bushy perennial, often grown as an annual, has narrow divided leaves and slender stems topped with daisy-like flowers in early summer. It is drought-tolerant and ideal for windy flower borders. Deadhead it regularly.

↕ 18in (45cm) ↔ 24in (60cm)

Z9–10 Ⓝ

SHRUB LARGE

Cotinus 'Grace'

SMOKE TREE This large, bushy deciduous shrub has rounded, rich purple-tinged red leaves, becoming flame-red in fall. Misty purplish flower plumes appear in summer. Grow it for foliage contrast in a mixed border in a windy coastal plot.

↕ 20ft (6m) ↔ 15ft (5m)

Z5–8

TREE SMALL

Crataegus crus-galli

COCKSPUR HAWTHORN A small deciduous tree, var. *inermis* has thornless branches and glossy dark green leaves that turn bright red in fall. It flowers briefly in late spring, and bears red berries attractive to birds. Suitable for windy or cold sites.

↕ 25ft (8m) ↔ 30ft (10m)

Z4–7 Ⓝ

SHRUB LARGE

Cornus alba

TATARIAN DOGWOOD An upright deciduous shrub with red young stems and dark green leaves that develop bold fall tints. White berries follow the flat white flower heads in late spring. 'Sibirica Variegata' (above) has bold white-edged leaves.

↕↔ 10ft (3m)

Z2–7

SHRUB LARGE

Corylus avellana

EUROPEAN FILBERT A spreading shrub or small tree, this wind-tolerant plant has rounded deep green leaves that turn yellow in fall. In early spring, yellow catkins form and may be followed by filberts. Grow in a wild or informal garden, or as a hedge.

↕↔ 15ft (5m)

Z4–8

PERENNIAL MEDIUM

Crocosmia 'Lucifer'

MONTBRETIA A clump-forming perennial with slender, sword-shaped green foliage. It produces branched stems with sprays of bold red, tubular late summer blooms that last several weeks. Wind-tolerant, it is ideal for mild coastal gardens.

↕ 3ft (1m) ↔ 10in (25cm)

Z6–9

SHRUB SMALL

Cytisus x *praecox*

SCOTCH BROOM A bushy deciduous shrub with narrow, sparsely branched green stems bearing small leaves. From mid- to late spring, it produces a profusion of pale creamy yellow pealike blooms. 'Allgold' has dark yellow flowers.

↕ 4ft (1.2m) ↔ 5ft (1.5m)

(!) Z6–9

PERENNIAL LARGE

Delphinium elatum

LARKSPUR A bushy perennial with deeply-cut dark green leaves and tall spires of blue, pink, cream, or white flowers in summer, depending on the variety. Plant at the back of borders and support the stems. Most varieties are ideal for cold sites.

↕ 5ft (1.5m) ↔ 24in (60cm)

(!) Z3–8

PERENNIAL SMALL

Dianthus deltoides 'Flashing Light'

MAIDEN PINK A cold-tolerant, mat-forming evergreen perennial with narrow green leaves and cerise-red summer blooms. A good front-of-border plant for seaside, cottage and rock gardens, or gravel areas.

↕8in (20cm) ↔12in (30cm)

Z3–9

PERENNIAL MEDIUM

Dictamnus albus var. *purpureus*

DITTANY A bushy perennial with glossy, lemon-scented divided leaves and butterflylike, pinky purple early-summer blooms on purple stems. Good for cold sites; prefers rich soil.

↕3ft (1m) ↔24in (60cm)

(!) Z3–9

PERENNIAL LARGE

Echium pininana

TREE ECHIUM This biennial or short-lived perennial has lance-shaped green leaf rosettes, tall spires of small blue blooms, and pointed leafy bracts from mid- to late summer. Ideal for windy coastal areas; protect in winter in frosty sites.

↕12ft (4m) ↔3ft (1m)

Z9–10

PERENNIAL SMALL

Eryngium maritimum

SEA HOLLY This upright perennial has prickly blue-green basal leaves with white veins. From early summer to early fall, it produces metallic blue thimblelike blooms, each with a collar of spiny leaflike bracts. Add it to a seaside garden.

↕20in (50cm) ↔18in (45cm)

Z5–9

SHRUB LARGE

Euonymus hamiltonianus

HAMILTON'S SPINDLE TREE This large deciduous shrub has lance-shaped green leaves with fiery fall tints. Small summer flowers lead to pendulous pink fruits that split to reveal orange seeds. Cold-tolerant; prefers shelter from wind.

↕↔25ft (8m)

(!) Z5–8

TREE LARGE

Fagus sylvatica

EUROPEAN BEECH This large tree has a broad spreading crown and produces oval leaves that are light green in spring, darkening in summer, and turning coppery in fall. Grow this plant as a hedge in cold areas.

↕80ft (25m) ↔50ft (15m)

Z4–7

BAMBOO LARGE

Fargesia nitidia

CHINESE FOUNTAIN BAMBOO A clump-forming evergreen bamboo with slender, arching purple-tinged stems clothed in narrow green leaves. This cold-tolerant bamboo makes a dense hedge or windbreak in fertile, moisture-retentive soil.

↕15ft (5m) ↔5ft (1.5m) or more

Z5–9

PERENNIAL MEDIUM

Gaillardia x *grandiflora*

BLANKET FLOWER A bushy short-lived perennial with lance-shaped or lobed gray-green leaves and a succession of daisy-like flowers from midsummer to fall, if deadheaded. 'Kobold' (above) has yellow-tipped red petals. Very cold tolerant.

↕3ft (1m) ↔18in (45cm)

Z3–10 (N)

BULB MEDIUM

Galanthus nivalis 'Flore Pleno'

SNOWDROP This dwarf cold-tolerant perennial bulb has grassy gray-green leaves. The fragrant, late-winter white double blooms have green-tipped inner petals. Grow under deciduous shrubs or on grassy banks and rock gardens.

↕6in (15cm)

(!) Z3–8

SHRUB SMALL

Genista pilosa

SILKYLEAF WOADWAXEN A wind-tolerant, spreading deciduous shrub with narrow oval leaves, silky-haired beneath. Bright yellow flowers appear in profusion from late spring to early summer. 'Vancouver Gold' is a prostrate form.

↕↔12in (30cm)

Z5–7

PERENNIAL SMALL

Geranium himalayense 'Plenum'

CRANESBILL A mat-forming perennial, with rounded, lobed green leaves and bowl-shaped, violet-blue double flowers in summer with a white eye and dark veining. Very hardy, use it as ground cover.
↕10in (25cm) ↔24in (60cm)

Z4–7

SHRUB LARGE

Griselinia littoralis

NEW ZEALAND BROADLEAF An evergreen shrub with oval, waxy-textured apple-green leaves. Inconspicuous flowers on female plants, if fertilized, lead to purple fall fruits. Makes a dense hedge or screen in windy, seaside plots. Best in West Coast gardens.
↕25ft (8m) ↔15ft (5m)

Z7–9

SHRUB LARGE

Hippophae rhamnoides

SEA BUCKTHORN This is a deciduous, bushy, arching shrub for windy coastal sites with narrow silvery leaves. In mid-spring, it bears tiny yellow flowers, which are followed in fall by bright orange berries on female plants. Prefers poor soil.
↕↔20ft (6m)

Z4–7

TREE SMALL

Juniperus communis

COMMON JUNIPER This cold-tolerant, evergreen conifer's habit varies from prostrate to upright and bushy. It has needlelike gray-green leaves and blue-tinged black berries. 'Hibernica' is a columnar form.
↕25ft (8m) ↔12ft (4m)

Z2–6 Ⓝ

SHRUB SMALL

Juniperus rigida

NEEDLE JUNIPER This prostrate evergreen conifer has needlelike gray-green leaves and black fruits with a blue bloom. Tolerant of salt-laden air and drought, use it in low maintenance gardens. 'Pendula' has primary leader with secondary weeping branches.
↕12in (30cm) ↔indefinite

Z6–9

SHRUB LARGE

Juniperus squamata

SINGLESEED JUNIPER This evergreen conifer for cold sites varies in habit from prostrate to bushy or upright. It has sharp, scalelike, dark gray-green to blue-green leaves with black fruits. 'Blue Carpet' (above) has blue-gray foliage.
↕12ft (30cm) ↔10ft (3m)

Z4–8

PERENNIAL LARGE

Lavatera maritima

TREE MALLOW This is a shrublike semievergreen perennial with rounded, lobed, gray-green felted leaves. From late summer, it produces saucer-shaped, pale pinky lilac blooms, with darker veins. Grow it in windy seaside gravel gardens or beds.
↕5ft (1.5m) ↔3ft (1m)

Z6–8

PERENNIAL LARGE

Liatris spicata

GAYFEATHER This upright, cold- and salt-tolerant perennial produces clumps of linear leaves and, from late summer to early fall, pokerlike spikes of fluffy, pinky purple or white flowers. 'Kobold' (above) has vivid purple-pink blooms.
↕5ft (1.5m) ↔18in (45cm)

Z4–9 Ⓝ

PERENNIAL MEDIUM

Limonium platyphyllum

SEA LAVENDER This perennial forms a basal rosette of oval, wavy-edged green foliage. In late summer, airy, branched heads bear tiny lavender blue to violet flowers. Salt- and cold-tolerant; grow it in coastal gravel gardens or rock gardens.
↕24in (60cm) ↔18in (45cm)

Z3–9

PERENNIAL SMALL

Linum perenne

PERENNIAL FLAX A clump-forming perennial with wiry stems, narrow, lance-shaped leaves tinged blue-gray, and, from early- to midsummer, sky-blue flower clusters that close late afternoon. Cold-, heat-, and wind-tolerant; allow to self-seed.

↕12in (30cm) ↔6in (15cm)

Z5–9

SHRUB MEDIUM

Lupinus arboreus

LUPINE A bushy semievergreen shrub with divided, gray-green silky-haired leaves and spires of fragrant, pealike pale yellow blooms in late spring and summer. Wind-tolerant; it will naturalize in grass or gravel in mild coastal gardens.

↕↔6ft (2m)

(!) Z9–10 (N)

PERENNIAL MEDIUM

Lupinus 'The Page'

LUPINE This short-lived bushy perennial forms clumps of divided dark green leaves with slender "fingers." Tall stems of pink-red pealike blooms appear in early summer. It is very cold-tolerant, but needs plenty of moisture in spring.

↕3ft (1m) ↔30in (75cm)

(!) Z4–7

PERENNIAL MEDIUM

Lysimachia clethroides

GOOSENECK LOOSESTRIFE This upright clump-forming perennial has lance-shaped midgreen leaves and arching, tapered gray-white flower clusters from mid- to late summer. Very cold-hardy, grow it in semi-wild areas or toward the back of beds.

↕↔3ft (1m)

Z3–8

PERENNIAL LARGE

Molinia caerulea

PURPLE MOOR GRASS This grass forms a clump of narrow, midgreen arching leaves that are richly colored in fall. Through summer and fall, slender stems bear airy purple flower heads. Ideal for coastal gardens; plant in mass. Cut back in spring.

↕5ft (1.5m) ↔16in (40cm)

Z5–9

ANNUAL/BIENNIAL SMALL

Malcolmia maritima

VIRGINIAN STOCK A low-growing annual with slender branched stems of small, narrow green leaves. From spring to fall, masses of fragrant pink, white, red, or purple, blooms appear. Salt- and wind-tolerant, use to front flowerbeds.

↕8in (20cm) ↔3in (8cm)

PERENNIAL MEDIUM

Malva moschata

MUSK MALLOW A bushy perennial, with woody stems deeply lobed dark green leaves and saucer-shaped pale pink blooms from summer to fall. Ideal for exposed sites. White-flowered *M. moschata* f.*alba* is a popular form.

↕3ft (1m) ↔24in (60cm)

Z3–8

SHRUB LARGE

Olearia macrodonta

ARORANGI An upright evergreen shrub with glossy dark green leaves, silver felted beneath, similar to holly. Masses of small, fragrant white daisy-like flowers appear in summer. Use it as a windbreak or hedge in coastal gardens.

↕20ft (6m) ↔15ft (5m)

Z9–10

PERENNIAL MEDIUM

Paeonia officinalis

PEONY This bushy perennial has divided dark green leaves and bowl-shaped flowers with pink, red, or white petals from early- to midsummer. 'Rubra Plena' (above) is a red double form. Cold-tolerant, but needs shelter from strong winds.

↕↔30in (75cm)

(!) Z3–8

SHRUB LARGE

Philadelphus 'Virginal'

MOCK ORANGE This large upright shrub has oval dark green leaves and highly fragrant, double white flowers from early- to midsummer. Very hardy and wind-resistant, this shrub creates shelter in exposed gardens at the back of a bed.

↕10ft (3m) ↔8ft (2.5m)

Z5–8

TREE LARGE

Picea breweriana

BREWER'S SPRUCE This cone-shaped evergreen conifer has drooping stems covered with dark gray-green needles. Female cones are red-brown. Thrives with some shade and shelter from wind; makes a striking lawn specimen.

↕50ft (15m) ↔12ft (4m)

pH Z5–6 Ⓝ

TREE LARGE

Picea pungens 'Koster'

COLORADO SPRUCE An evergreen conifer with stiff, silvery blue needlelike foliage and gray scaly bark. Upright cones form toward the ends of the branches on mature plants. Ideal for a cold garden, in neutral to acidic soil. Good in all but wet soils.

↕50ft (15m) ↔15ft (5m)

pH Z2–7 Ⓝ

TREE MEDIUM

Pseudotsuga menziesii var. *glauca*

BLUE DOUGLAS FIR This evergreen conifer, with dark green needles, makes a columnar tree, topped by a spreading crown. Younger plants are compact and conical. Ideal for exposed sites.

↕↔30ft (10m)

Z4–6 Ⓝ

TREE LARGE

Quercus robur f. *fastigiata*

ENGLISH OAK This deciduous tree has a flame-shaped profile with lobed green leaves and fall acorns. Slow-growing and cold-tolerant, use it as a lawn specimen in larger gardens. Considered invasive in some Northeast and Northwest areas in US.

↕↔50ft (15m)

Z5–8

TREE LARGE

Pinus nigra

AUSTRIAN PINE When mature, this is a large domed-headed evergreen tree with long, dark green needles and yellow-brown cones. It can be planted as a windbreak, and will tolerate coastal sites. It is best grown on larger plots.

↕100ft (30m) ↔25ft (8m)

Z4–7

SHRUB SMALL

Potentilla fruticosa

CINQUEFOIL This cold- and wind-tolerant shrub has divided dark to gray-green leaves. Small yellow, white, pink, orange, and red flowers open from summer to fall. Varieties include the yellow-flowered 'Goldfinger' (above).

↕3ft (1m) ↔5ft (1.5m)

Z2–7 Ⓝ

SHRUB SMALL

Rosmarinus officinalis

ROSEMARY An wind-tolerant, aromatic evergreen, subshrub with dark green needlelike leaves and small blue, pink, or white blooms from spring to early summer. Prostratus Group (above) will cascade over walls.

↕6in (15cm) ↔5ft (1.5m)

Z8–11

PERENNIAL LARGE

Rudbeckia laciniata

CUTLEAF CONEFLOWER This upright, very hardy perennial has dark green leaves and tall stems topped with daisy-like yellow flowers with a greenish yellow central cone from midsummer to fall. 'Gold Drop' (above) has double flowers.

↕6ft (2m) ↔30in (75cm)

Z3–9 Ⓝ

SHRUB SMALL

Senecio cineraria

DUSTY MILLER This bushy evergreen subshrub, usually grown an annual, is good for mild windy coasts. It has deeply lobed silver leaves and daisy-like yellow flower heads, which are best removed in summer.

↕↔12in (30cm)

Z8–11

TREE LARGE

Thuja occidentalis

AMERICAN ARBORVITAE A slow-growing, cold-tolerant conifer with orange-brown bark and flat sprays of scalelike green leaves grayish green beneath smelling of apples when crushed. Ovoid cones are yellow-green, ripening to brown.

↕50ft (15m) ↔15ft (5m)

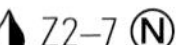

Z2–7 Ⓝ

TREE LARGE

Taxus baccata

ENGLISH YEW This bushy evergreen conifer, variable in habit, has dark green needles and small yellow spring flowers followed by red berries. Use it as formal hedging in cold regions; it can be pruned hard if necessary. All parts are toxic.

↕50ft (15m) ↔30ft (10m)

Ⓘ Z6–7

PERENNIAL MEDIUM

Veronica austriaca subsp. *teucrium*

SAW-LEAVED SPEEDWELL This mound-forming perennial has oval gray-green leaves and blue summer flower spikes. The deep blue 'Crater Lake Blue' (above) is both hardy and salt-tolerant.

↕↔24in (60cm)

Z4–8

PERENNIAL LARGE

Sanguisorba canadensis

CANADIAN BURNET This is an upright clump-forming perennial with divided green leaves and white bottlebrush flower heads from summer to early fall. For best effect, plant in swaths in soil that does not dry out.

↕6ft (2m) ↔24in (60cm)

Z3–8 Ⓝ

TREE SMALL

Taxus x *media* 'Hicksii'

YEW This is an evergreen conifer with flattened, dark green needlelike leaves. In summer, it produces tiny white blooms followed by red berries on female plants. Faster growing than *T. baccata*; all parts of the plant are poisonous.

↕20ft (6m) ↔12ft (4m)

Ⓘ Z5–7

PERENNIAL SMALL

Viola tricolor

JOHNNY JUMP UP An annual or short-lived perennial with oval, serrated green leaves and, from spring to fall, a succession of purple, yellow, and white petal blooms streaked with purple. A hardy self-seeder, it provides color during the colder months.

↕6in (15cm) ↔6in (15cm) or more

Z3–9

PERENNIAL LARGE

Thalictrum aquilegiifolium

MEADOW RUE This upright perennial forms clumps of divided blue-green leaves and slender branched stems topped, from early- to midsummer, with fluffy pale mauve-pink or white flowers. Grow in cold or coastal gardens in soil that does not dry out.

↕4ft (1.2m) ↔18in (45cm)

Z5–8

OTHER SUGGESTIONS

Perennials

Achillea millefolium Ⓝ • *Asclepias incarnata* 'Ice Ballet' Ⓝ • *Cardamine pratensis* Ⓝ • *Maianthemum racemosum* Ⓝ • *Potentilla* 'Melton Fire' • *Solidago caesia* Ⓝ

Shrubs

Comptonia peregrina Ⓝ • *Cornus amomum* Ⓝ • *Juniperus conferta* • *Juniperus virginiana* 'Grey Owl' Ⓝ • *Prunus maritima* Ⓝ • *Rosa virginiana* Ⓝ • *Vaccinium macrocarpon* Ⓝ • *Viburnum sargentii* 'Onondaga'

Trees

Acer saccharum 'Green Mountain' Ⓝ • *Nyssa sylvatica* Ⓝ • *Pinus palustris* Ⓝ • *Sabal palmetto* Ⓝ • *Zanthoxylum americanum* Ⓝ

GARDENS in SHADE

Spring ephemerals and large-leaved plants that thrive in shade can transform a gloomy garden into a lush oasis. Few plants tolerate permanent deep shade, but many flourish in partial or dappled shade, where brighter spells boost growth and encourage blossoms. Foliage plants, such as ferns and hostas, are the stars of shady schemes, but if you are looking for brightly colored flowers, opt for rhododendrons, camellias, daffodils, and cranesbills. These will sing out against the darkness, acting as beacons of color.

Plants for clay soil

Cool, shady borders on heavy clay soils may seem unpromising, but they can provide the fertile conditions that many plants enjoy.

Clay-rich soils offer a rich supply of nutrients and moisture for most of the year. There is plenty of choice for gardeners with lively color schemes in mind because dazzling maple, pink turtlehead, blue aster, and camellia of all hues will be happy in partial shade. Lighten up darker areas with the bright blooms of spiderwort and pigsqueak, or choose a more subdued palette of hellebore, anemone, and leafy hosta, which will also tolerate deep shade. To add an element of surprise to a design, spice up your beds with sweetly scented deutzia or sweet box.

TREE LARGE

Acer davidii

SNAKEBARK MAPLE This multistemmed, deciduous tree has white-streaked green bark and dark purple shoots. The oval, tapered green leaves turn red in fall. Hanging clusters of yellow flowers appear in spring. Grow in a sheltered site.

↕↔ 50ft (15m)

Z5–7

SHRUB MEDIUM

Acer palmatum var. *dissectum*

JAPANESE MAPLE This slow-growing shrub has a domed to cascading habit and produces deep purple lobed leaves with finely divided tapering "fingers." The foliage also sports rich fall color. Plant it in a sheltered site.

↕ 5ft (1.5m) ↔ 3ft (1m)

Z6–8

PERENNIAL MEDIUM

Aconitum 'Bressingham Spire'

MONKSHOOD This clump-forming perennial produces glossy, green, rounded, and deeply divided leaves. Erect spires of violet-purple flowers appear from midsummer to early fall. May need staking. Toxic if ingested.

↕ 3ft (1m) ↔ 20in (50cm)

(!) Z3–7

PERENNIAL LARGE

Aconitum napellus

MONKSHOOD An upright perennial with deeply divided dark green foliage and tall spires of indigo-blue blooms that appear from mid- to late summer and need staking. Plants tolerate poor drainage. Toxic if ingested.

↕ 5ft (1.5m) ↔ 12in (30cm)

(!) Z3–8

PERENNIAL LARGE

Actaea racemosa

BLACK COHOSH This upright perennial has deeply divided leaves, above which appear bottlebrush-like spikes of white flowers in midsummer. The dried brown seedheads are also attractive. Water well during dry spells.

↕ 5ft (1.5m) ↔ 24in (60cm)

Z3–8 (N)

PERENNIAL SMALL

Actaea rubra

RED BANEBERRY A clump-forming perennial with leaves divided into lobed and toothed leaflets and oval, fluffy white flower heads from mid-spring to early summer followed by shiny red, poisonous berries. Water well in dry spells.

↕ 20in (50cm) ↔ 12in (30cm)

(!) Z3–8 (N)

PERENNIAL LARGE

Actaea simplex 'Brunette'

BUGBANE An upright perennial with dark purple divided foliage. From early- to mid-fall, narrow, arching bottlebrush flowers appear on slender stems. The tiny off-white blooms are tinged purple. Plant in drifts; water well during dry spells.

↕ 4ft (1.2m) ↔ 24in (60cm)

Z4–8

PERENNIAL SMALL

Ajuga reptans 'Atropurpurea'

BUGLEWEED An evergreen ground-cover perennial, it spreads freely by runners. It has small rosettes of glossy, deep bronze-purple leaves and short spikes of blue spring blooms, which attract bumblebees. Considered invasive in some areas.

↕ 6in (15cm) ↔ 3ft (1m)

Z3–9

PERENNIAL MEDIUM

Anemanthele lessoniana

PHEASANT'S TAIL GRASS This mound-forming semievergreen grass has narrow, arching leaves and purple-tinged flowers from midsummer to early fall. Summer foliage is a green-tinged orange, but the whole plant turns orange-brown in winter.

↕↔ 3ft (1m)

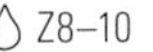 Z8–10

PERENNIAL LARGE

Anemone hupehensis

CHINESE ANEMONE An upright perennial with dark green divided leaves. Large, simple pink or white flowers with yellow eyes open over a long period from mid- to late summer. 'Hadspen Abundance' (above) has dark pink blooms.

↕ 4ft (1.2m) ↔ 18in (45cm)

Z5–7 Ⓝ

PERENNIAL MEDIUM

Anemone rivularis

WINDFLOWER A clump-forming perennial, with hairy, dark green three-lobed leaves. It flowers in late spring and early summer, occasionally in fall. The slender branched stems carry 10–20 white blooms, often with a blue reverse.

↕ 24in (60cm) ↔ 12in (30cm)

Z6–8

PERENNIAL SMALL

Aruncus aethusifolius

GOATSBEARD A compact, clump-forming, ground-cover perennial with deeply cut, fernlike midgreen leaves that turn yellow in fall. Sprays of tiny creamy white blooms appear from early- to midsummer. Water well during dry spells.

↕↔ 16in (40cm)

 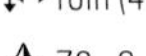 Z3–9

PERENNIAL LARGE

Aruncus dioicus

GOATSBEARD An upright bushy perennial with long, midgreen divided leaves. It flowers between early- and midsummer. In the showier male plants, feathery creamy white plumes appear above the foliage. Water well during dry spells.

↕ 6ft (2m) ↔ 4ft (1.2m)

Z3–7 Ⓝ

PERENNIAL MEDIUM

Aquilegia canadensis

COLUMBINE A mound-forming perennial with ferny foliage. Slender upright flower stems bear nodding bell-shaped blooms, which are colored red and pale yellow, between mid-spring and midsummer. Plants spread via self-seeding.

↕ 24in (60cm) ↔ 12in (30cm)

Z3–8 Ⓝ

PERENNIAL SMALL

Asarum caudatum

WILD GINGER A ground-covering evergreen perennial, it smells like ginger when the green heart-shaped leaves are crushed. Purple hidden blooms with three tapering petals appear from mid- to late spring. It needs rich acid soil, and tolerates full shade.

↕ 3in (8cm) ↔ 10in (25cm) or more

pH Z7–9 Ⓝ

PERENNIAL LARGE

Aster cordifolius

Preferred name *Symphyotrichum cordifolium* Blue wood aster is a large upright bushy perennial with small, oval, dark green toothed leaves. It bears sprays of small, pale blue daisy-like flowers on arching stems from late summer to fall.

↕ 4ft (1.2m) ↔ 3ft (1m)

Z3–8 Ⓝ

SHRUB LARGE

Berberis x *stenophylla*

HEDGE BARBERRY An evergreen shrub with a rounded habit, spiny stems, and small, leathery, dark green lance-shaped leaves. The light orange-yellow late spring flowers open from red-tinged buds and are followed by small blue-black berries.

↕10ft (3m) ↔15ft (5m)

Z6–9

PERENNIAL SMALL

Astilbe x *arendsii*

ASTILBE This clump-forming, ferny-leaved perennial produces frothy plumes of white, pink, lilac, or red flowers between early and late summer. Brown seedheads feature in winter. 'Fanal' has red flowers and dark foliage.

↕18in (45cm) ↔12in (30cm)

Z4–8

PERENNIAL MEDIUM

Astrantia major

MASTERWORT This clump-forming perennial has midgreen divided leaves and sprays of greenish white, pink, or red blooms from early- to midsummer. 'Sunningdale Variegated' (above) has cream-splashed leaves. Deadhead often.

↕3ft (1m) ↔18in (45cm)

Z4–7

PERENNIAL MEDIUM

Bergenia 'Ballawley'

PIGSQUEAK An clump-forming evergreen perennial, with glossy, rounded midgreen leaves that turn bronze-purple in winter. Bell-shaped crimson flower clusters appear on reddish stems from mid- to late spring. Shelter from wind; cut untidy foliage.

↕↔24in (60cm)

Z6–9

PERENNIAL SMALL

Bergenia cordifolia

PIGSQUEAK A spreading to clump-forming evergreen perennial with large, rounded, leathery deep green leaves that develop purple tints in winter. White or pink flowers appear in early spring. Best planted in moist soil.

↕↔20in (50cm)

Z3–8

PERENNIAL SMALL

Bergenia SILVERLIGHT

PIGSQUEAK A clump-forming evergreen perennial with leathery rounded leaves. Red-tinged stems carry clusters of white bell-shaped spring blooms that sometimes develop pink tinges. Flowers have contrasting deep red bud cases.

↕18in (45cm) ↔20in (50cm)

Z3–8

PERENNIAL MEDIUM

Blechnum spicant

DEER FERN This evergreen fern has a tufted habit and divided, stiff leathery leaves with narrow leaflets and forms low, arching hummocks. The upright spore-bearing fronds resemble fish bones. Trim old foliage in spring. Tolerates full shade.

↕30in (75cm) ↔18in (45cm)

pH Z5–8 Ⓝ

PERENNIAL SMALL

Brunnera macrophylla

SIBERIAN BUGLOSS This spreading, clump-forming ground-cover perennial has heart-shaped green leaves. Airy sprays of light blue spring flowers, similar to forget-me-nots, appear above the foliage. 'Dawson's White' (above) has variegated leaves.

↕18in (45cm) ↔24in (60cm)

Z3–8

SHRUB LARGE

Camellia japonica

JAPANESE CAMELLIA An upright evergreen shrub with glossy, rounded dark green leaves. It bears single or double flowers in white, pink, and red in spring. 'Blood of China' (above) has semidouble red flowers. Grow in a sheltered site.

↕10ft (3m) ↔6ft (2m)

pH Z7–9

SHRUB LARGE

Camellia x *williamsii*

CAMELLIA The williamsii cultivars are evergreen shrubs with leathery, glossy oval leaves and single or double, white to deep pink spring flowers. 'Donation' (above) is upright, with rose-pink semidouble blooms. All forms tolerate full shade.

↕15ft (5m) ↔8ft (2.5m)

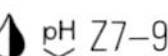 Z7–9

BULB LARGE

Cardiocrinum giganteum

GIANT LILY An upright bulbous perennial with heart-shaped green leaves. Trumpet-shaped white flowers with purple throats top sturdy stems in summer. Large seedpods follow the blooms. Plant in a sheltered site and rich soil.

↕10ft (3m)

Z7–9

PERENNIAL MEDIUM

Chelone obliqua

TURTLEHEAD A bushy, erect perennial with broadly lance-shaped, dark green, heavily-veined, and toothed leaves. Short but showy spikes of purple-pink blooms appear from late summer to early fall. Tolerates boggy ground.

↕3ft (1m) ↔20in (50cm)

Z3–9 Ⓝ

TREE SMALL

Cornus Jersey Star Series

DOGWOOD This spreading deciduous tree has oval, pointed, glossy green leaves with great fall color. From late spring to early summer, it features large blooms, which are followed by showy fruit. Resistant to anthracnose and powdery mildew.

↕↔25ft (8m)

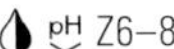 Z6–8

PERENNIAL SMALL

Corydalis flexuosa

BLUE CORYDALIS A clump-forming perennial with finely cut blue-green foliage, tinged purple. From spring to early summer, blue tubular flowers appear on wiry stems; the foliage dies back later in summer. 'Blue Panda' is compact and free-flowering.

↕12in (30cm) ↔8in (20cm)

Z6–8

PERENNIAL MEDIUM

Crocosmia 'Lucifer'

MONTBRETIA This clump-forming perennial has narrow, sword-shaped midgreen foliage. Sprays of vivid red, flared tubular blooms appear over many weeks in late summer. Best in light shade; deadhead to prevent self-seeding. Can be weedy.

↕3ft (1m) ↔10in (25cm)

Z6–9

SHRUB SMALL

Cryptomeria japonica 'Globosa Nana'

JAPANESE CEDAR This dwarf evergreen conifer has a dense, bushy rounded habit and green foliage. Scalelike leaves closely overlap on the short, arching, cordlike branchlets. Plant in light shade only.

↕↔3ft (1m)

Z6–9

SHRUB SMALL

Deutzia x *elegantissima* 'Rosealind'

ELEGANT DEUTZIA A rounded deciduous shrub with green leaves and, in most cases, flaking bark. Clusters of star- or cup-shaped, fragrant pink-flushed white blooms appear from late spring to early summer.

↕4ft (1.2m) ↔5ft (1.5m)

Z6–8

PERENNIAL SMALL

Dicentra cucullaria

DUTCHMAN'S BREECHES A clump-forming perennial with ferny blue-green leaves. Unusual twin-spurred yellow-tipped white flowers appear on arching stems in early spring. Shelter young growth from frost damage. Leaves die back in summer.

↕6in (15cm) ↔12in (30cm)

Ⓘ Z3–8 Ⓝ

SHRUB SMALL

Gaultheria mucronata

CHILEAN PERNETTYA This low, suckering evergreen shrub has small, dark green prickle-tipped leaves and tiny, white, bell-shaped late-spring flowers. Female forms bear white berries in fall, if a male variety is grown nearby. Best in West Coast gardens.

↕↔ 4ft (1.2m)

Z7–9

SHRUB MEDIUM

Enkianthus cernuus f. *rubens*

ENKIANTHUS This bushy deciduous shrub produces dense, oval, bright green purple-tinged foliage, which turns purple-red in fall. In late spring, hanging bunches of dark red, fringed bell-shaped flowers appear.

↕↔ 8ft (2.5m)

Z5–7

PERENNIAL MEDIUM

Euphorbia griffithii 'Fireglow'

GRIFFITH'S SPURGE A spreading perennial with dense strands of red upright stems bearing narrow, oblong, copper-tinged dark green leaves that intensify in color in fall. Domed clusters of orange-red flowers appear in early summer. Best in fertile soil.

↕ 30in (75cm) ↔ 3ft (1m)

Z4–9

PERENNIAL MEDIUM

Geranium sylvaticum

WOOD CRANESBILL A perennial that produces clumps of lobed midgreen leaves and round blue-purple flowers with white centers from late spring to early summer. Grow it in groups on moist soil at the front of a flower bed.

↕ 30in (75cm) ↔ 24in (60cm)

Z3–8

PERENNIAL LARGE

Gillenia trifoliata

syn. ***Porteranthus trifoliate*** A spreading perennial with erect, sparsely-branched reddish stems bearing three-lobed, dark green, prominently veined leaves. From late spring to late summer, airy sprays of starry white flowers open from red buds.

↕ 4ft (1.2m) ↔ 24in (60cm)

Z4-8

PERENNIAL SMALL

Glaucidium palmatum

JAPANESE WOOD POPPY A clump-forming perennial with maplelike, lobed, light green cut leaves. Pale pinky lilac, saucer-shaped blooms appear from late spring to early summer. Grow in a sheltered spot in moist fertile soil. It tolerates full shade.

↕↔ 20in (50cm)

Z5–9

PERENNIAL SMALL

Hacquetia epipactis

HACQUETIA This clump-forming perennial has glossy, round, deeply lobed leaves. Tiny yellow flowers surrounded by greenish yellow petal-like bracts appear from late winter to early spring. Ensure that it isn't overwhelmed by neighboring plants.

↕ 2½in (6cm) ↔ 9in (23cm)

Z5–7

SHRUB LARGE

Hamamelis mollis

CHINESE WITCH HAZEL A spreading shrub with dark green leaves that turn yellow in fall. Fragrant, yellow spidery blooms sprout from bare branches in late winter. Plant where its scent can be enjoyed. Some varieties have orange flowers.

↕↔ 12ft (4m) or more

Z5–8

PERENNIAL SMALL

Helleborus x *ericsmithii*

HELLEBORE A clump-forming semievergreen perennial with toothed, silver-veined green leaves and pink-tinged or white saucer-shaped blooms with green-striped petals on reddish green stems in midwinter. Trim old leaves in late winter.

↕15in (38cm) ↔18in (45cm)

 Z5–9

PERENNIAL MEDIUM

Helleborus x *hybridus*

LENTEN ROSE This clump-forming semievergreen perennial has green lobed leaves and bears single or double, plain or speckled white, green, yellow, pink, purple, or red blooms between midwinter and mid-spring. Remove old leaves in late winter.

↕↔24in (60cm)

Z5–9

PERENNIAL SMALL

Helleborus niger

CHRISTMAS ROSE This semievergreen perennial forms clumps of lobed dark green leaves and white, aging to pinkish, saucer-shaped blooms with yellow stamens from midwinter to early spring. Tolerates heavy clay mixed with organic matter.

↕↔12in (30cm)

 Z3–8

PERENNIAL SMALL

Hepatica nobilis

LIVERLEAF This slow-growing semievergreen perennial forms a neat dome of rounded, lobed, fleshy green leaves. In early spring, it bears cup-shaped blooms in shades of violet or purple. Plant it at the front of a shady bed.

↕3in (8cm) ↔5in (12cm)

Z5–8

PERENNIAL SMALL

Hosta 'Fire and Ice'

PLAINTAIN LILY A clump-forming perennial with mounds of heart-shaped, ribbed dark green foliage with a bold white splash in the center of each leaf. Tall spires of lilac blooms appear in summer; cut them back after flowering. Protect from slugs.

↕16in (40cm) ↔indefinite

Z3–8

SHRUB MEDIUM

Hydrangea arborescens

SMOOTH HYDRANGEA A large rounded shrub with green tapered leaves. In midsummer, it bears flattened clusters of white flowers, which persist to provide interest in winter. 'Annabelle' (above) has extra large flower heads.

↕↔5ft (1.5m)

Z4–9 Ⓝ

SHRUB MEDIUM

Hydrangea macrophylla

LACECAP HYDRANGEA A rounded shrub with large, oval light green leaves. Tiny blue flowers and larger pale blue to pink, petal-like florets form lace-cap flower heads from midsummer to early fall. The dried flowers provide winter interest.

↕6ft (2m) ↔8ft (2.5m)

Z6–9

SHRUB LARGE

Hydrangea paniculata

PANICLE HYDRANGEA An upright shrub with pointed, glossy mid- to dark green leaves, often deeply veined. In late summer, cone-shaped white or pink flower heads develop. 'Phantom' has extra large white blooms. Considered invasive in some areas.

↕↔10ft (3m)

Z3–8

SHRUB MEDIUM

Hydrangea quercifolia

OAKLEAF HYDRANGEA This mound-forming shrub has lobed midgreen leaves with striking red and purple fall color. From midsummer to fall, it bears cone-shaped cream flower heads that turn a pink-tinged-white. Prefers neutral to acidic soil.

↕6ft (2m) ↔8ft (2.5m)

pH Z5–9 Ⓝ

PERENNIAL MEDIUM

Inula hookeri

HOOKER INULA This clump-forming perennial has upright stems with soft hairs that bear abundant lance-shaped, deeply veined midgreen leaves and yellow daisy-like blooms with long narrow petals from late summer to fall. Water during dry spells.

↕30in (75cm) ↔18in (45cm)

Z5–8

PERENNIAL SMALL

Jeffersonia dubia

CHINESE TWINLEAF A woodland perennial with lobed, kidney-shaped or rounded blue-green leaves, initially tinged purple. From late spring to early summer, cup-shaped lavender-blue blooms appear above the emerging leaves. Tolerates full shade.

↕6in (15cm) ↔9in (23cm)

pH Z5–8

BULB MEDIUM

Leucojum aestivum

SUMMER SNOWFLAKE This perennial bulb makes an upright clump of strap-shaped, narrow glossy leaves. In spring, leafless stems bear small clusters of bell-shaped, drooping white blooms with green tips. 'Gravetye Giant' (above) is popular.

↕24in (60cm) ↔3in (8cm)

Z3–9

SHRUB MEDIUM

Leucothoe fontanesiana 'Rainbow'

DROOPING LEUCOTHOE This mound-forming evergreen shrub has arching red-tinged branches with glossy lance-shaped leaves mottled and streaked with cream, pink, and maroon, and cream spring-flower clusters.

↕up to 5ft (1.5m) ↔6ft (2m)

pH (!) Z5–8 Ⓝ

PERENNIAL MEDIUM

Lysimachia punctata

WHORLED LOOSESTRIFE This vigorous, tall, upright perennial with midgreen leaves spreads rapidly to form large clumps. In summer, it produces spikes of bright yellow flowers. Best suited to larger plots; it can be aggressively invasive.

↕3ft (1m) ↔24in (60cm)

Z4–8

TREE SMALL

Magnolia x *soulangeana*

SAUCER MAGNOLIA A small upright tree with a bushy habit and oval dark green leaves. From mid- to late spring, as the leaves unfurl, goblet-shaped pink to violet-purple or white blooms appear. 'Rustica Rubra' (above) has purple-red blooms.

↕↔20ft (6m)

pH Z5–9

PERENNIAL MEDIUM

Maianthemum racemosum

FALSE SPIKENARD This is a medium-sized arching perennial with oval light green leaves that turn yellow in fall. Feathery sprays of white flowers appear from late spring to early summer, followed by fleshy red fruits.

↕3ft (1m) ↔24in (60cm)

pH Z3–8 Ⓝ

PERENNIAL MEDIUM

Onoclea sensibilis

SENSITIVE FERN This ground-covering creeping deciduous fern has deeply lobed, toothed light green fronds. Stiff brown fronds stand erect in late summer, lasting into winter. Requires neutral to acid soil. Water if dry in summer; can be invasive.

↕24in (60cm) ↔3ft (1m)

pH Z4–9 Ⓝ

PERENNIAL SMALL

Phlox divaricata subsp. *laphamii*

LAPHAM'S PHLOX This creeping semievergreen perennial bears narrow, lance-shaped midgreen leaves on purplish upright stems. From mid- to late spring, small lavender-blue blooms appear.
↕12in (30cm) ↔8in (20cm)

Z4–8 Ⓝ

TREE LARGE

Picea pungens 'Koster'

COLORADO SPRUCE An evergreen conifer with stiff, needlelike silvery blue foliage. Upright cones form toward the ends of the branches. It requires neutral to acidic soil, shelter, and prefers only light shade. Adaptable to any soil but wet soil.
↕50ft (15m) ↔15ft (5m)

pH Z2–7 Ⓝ

SHRUB SMALL

Sarcococca confusa

SWEET BOX This bushy evergreen shrub has glossy, oval to lance-shaped dark green leaves. Tiny, sweetly fragrant white winter blooms are followed by shiny black fruits. Plant where the scent can be enjoyed. Tolerates deep shade.
↕↔3ft (1m)

Z6–9

SHRUB LARGE

Pieris japonica

LILY OF THE VALLEY BUSH This compact evergreen shrub has glossy, oval dark green leaves, often brightly colored at first. Small, creamy white flask-shaped blooms hang in tassels in spring. 'Mountain Fire' has red young leaves.
↕12ft (4m) ↔10ft (3m)

pH (!) Z5–8

PERENNIAL MEDIUM

Tradescantia Andersoniana Group

SPIDERWORT This clump-forming perennial has long, narrow arching leaves and pink, blue, purple or white triangular flower clusters. 'Concord Grape' (above) has violet-purple blooms and bluish green leaves.
↕↔24in (60cm)

Z4–9 Ⓝ

PERENNIAL MEDIUM

Polemonium caeruleum

JACOB'S LADDER A clump-forming perennial with leaves divided into lance-shaped, narrow green leaflets. Clusters of white or lavender-blue bell-shaped blooms appear in early summer. Requires part- to full shade. Self-seeds under optimal conditions.
↕↔24in (60cm)

Z4–8

SHRUB MEDIUM

Skimmia japonica

JAPANESE SKIMMIA An compact evergreen shrub with glossy, oval to lance-shaped green leaves. Males have red or green, cone-shaped bud clusters through winter, opening to white spring flowers. Females produce red berries. Best in West Coast gardens.
↕↔5ft (1.5m)

(!) Z6–8

PERENNIAL MEDIUM

Tricyrtis formosana

TOAD LILY This slow-spreading, upright, clump-forming perennial has lance-shaped midgreen leaves. It bears upturned clusters of intricately shaped, purple-spotted white blooms in fall. Mulch annually with compost. It tolerates full shade.
↕3ft (1m) ↔18in (45cm)

Z5–9

OTHER SUGGESTIONS

Perennials

Anemone canadensis Ⓝ • *Aquilegia flabellate* f. *alba* var. *pumila* • *Asarum europaeum* • *Bergenia* 'Bressingham White' • *Carex elata* 'Aurea' • *Disporum sessile* 'Variegatum' • *Dodecatheon meadia* Ⓝ • *Euphorbia* 'Excalibur' • *Matteuccia struthiopteris* Ⓝ • *Tradescantia virginiana* Ⓝ

Shrubs

Aucuba japonica 'Mr. Goldstrike' • *Calycanthus floridus* Ⓝ • *Corylopsis glabrescens* • *Staphylea trifolia* Ⓝ • *Viburnum davidii* • *Viburnun dentatum* BLUE MUFFIN Ⓝ

Trees

Carpinus caroliniana Ⓝ • *Sassafras albidum* Ⓝ

Plant focus: hostas

Invaluable in cool shady sites, the dramatic, sculptural leaves of hostas add color and texture to many areas of the garden.

THEIR DRAMATIC FOLIAGE and love of cool damp conditions make hostas popular plants for shady sites. Plant them as ground cover at the edge of tree canopies, include them in a bog garden beside a pond, or use colorful forms to create architectural container displays. Most hostas are knee-high, although taller and dwarf forms are also available, and they are grown for their dramatic blue, golden, or green leaves, which can be a solid color or variegated. The foliage is joined in summer by tall spires of lilylike, often fragrant, flowers. Although fairly undemanding and tolerant of periods of drought, all hostas suffer to some degree from slug and snail damage, with thin-leaved forms being the worst affected. To prevent shredded foliage, protect plants by covering tender new growth with grit and sand, or surround mature plants with copper rings. Also, look for slug-resistant cultivars, such as 'Krossa Regal', 'Great Expectations', 'Halcyon', and 'Big Daddy'.

POPULAR HOSTA FORMS

Large-leaved hostas With leaves growing up to 16in (40cm) long, popular choices include 'Sagae' and 'Sum and Substance'.

Dwarf forms Less than 18in (45cm) in height, dwarf hostas include *H. venusta*, *H.* 'Dorset Blue', 'Hadspen Heron', and 'Pilgrim'.

Variegated forms Large or small, these colorful and variable plants feature white or golden margins, or pale or darker central markings.

Golden-leaved forms Requiring some sunlight, the golden-leaved forms include a range of plant sizes and foliage shapes. Popular forms include 'Yellow River', 'Yellow Splash', 'Piedmont Gold', 'Golden Prayers', 'Gold Drop', 'Fortunei Aureomarginata', and 'Fortunei Albopicta'.

Blue-leaved forms Grown for its blue, textured foliage, this group ranges from the large-leaved 'Blue Angel' to the dainty 'Blue Moon'.

USING HOSTAS

Dense, overlapping hosta leaves make useful ground cover. These plants thrive in shade, with bright variegated forms adding a splash of color. They are ideal for planting at the edge of woodland or beneath larger shrubs.

Pots of hostas of contrasting sizes, leaf colors, and shapes add a cool elegant note to a shady patio display.

Bright variegated hostas, such as 'Patriot', combine well with astilbes, ferns, and lady's mantle in shady beds and borders in a cottage garden.

Hostas thrive beside ponds and streams and, although shade-lovers, they will tolerate more sun where the soil is reliably damp in summer.

Plants for sandy soil

Free-draining sandy sites are generally more suited to sun-lovers, but there are a good number of plants that will cope with dry shade.

Most plants prefer dappled shade or sun for part of the day, but you can try experimenting with cranesbill, barrenwort, and lady's mantle in darker areas. Also consider painting walls and fences white or cream to reflect light into your garden to broaden your scope, and trim off the lower branches of shrubs and trees to allow more sun to filter through. Choose from a selection of shrubs such as viburnum, witch hazel, and mock orange for background structure, and seasonal bulbs and perennials to inject some color into your garden.

PERENNIAL SMALL

Alchemilla mollis

LADY'S MANTLE This perennial forms spreading clumps of rounded, pale green velvety leaves with crinkled edges. It produces small sprays of tiny, acid greenish yellow flowers in midsummer. Use it as ground cover or bed edging.

↕↔20in (50cm)

Z4–7

BULB LARGE

Allium stipitatum

ORNAMENTAL ONION This upright perennial bulb produces strap-shaped gray-green leaves that wither as tall sturdy stems topped with spherical white flower heads appear in late spring. 'Violet Beauty' has violet-pink flower heads.

↕4½ft (1.4m)

Z4–9

TREE MEDIUM

Amelanchier arborea

DOWNY SERVICEBERRY This is a small deciduous tree with a dense oval habit and copper-red young leaves that mature to green and then turn vivid red in fall. It also produces masses of white flowers in spring that lead to attractive red berries.

↕30ft (10m) ↔40ft (12m)

Z4–9 Ⓝ

TREE SMALL

Amelanchier canadensis

SHADBLOW SERVICEBERRY This dense upright tree or large deciduous shrub has oval white-haired leaves that age to dark green and turn orange-red in fall. Edible sweet and juicy summer fruits follow the starry white mid- to late spring flowers.

↕20ft (6m) ↔10ft (3m)

Z3–7 Ⓝ

TREE SMALL

Amelanchier laevis

ALLEGHENY SERVICEBERRY A spreading deciduous tree or large shrub with oval bronze leaves that turn dark green in summer, then red and orange in fall. It produces sprays of white flowers in spring, followed by round, juicy red fruits.

↕↔25ft (8m)

pH Z4–8 Ⓝ

SHRUB LARGE

Amelanchier lamarckii

JUNEBERRY This spreading deciduous tree's or large shrub's bronze new leaves and airy sprays of starry white flowers open together from mid- to late spring. The mature foliage is dark green, but becomes brilliant red and orange in fall.

↕25ft (8m) ↔20ft (6m)

pH Z4–8 Ⓝ

PERENNIAL MEDIUM

Anaphalis margaritacea

PEARLY EVERLASTING A bushy perennial with lance-shaped, gray-green or white-edged silvery gray leaves felted on the undersides. In late summer, papery, pearl-like white flower clusters form in profusion on erect stems. Plant in light shade.

↕30in (75cm) ↔24in (60cm)

Z3–8 Ⓝ

PERENNIAL SMALL

Anemone nemorosa

WOOD ANEMONE A vigorous carpeting perennial with deeply divided midgreen leaves. From spring to early summer, masses of starry white flowers appear. Varieties include 'Vestal', which has double flowers with buttonlike centers.

↕6in (15cm) ↔12in (30cm)

(!) Z4–8

PERENNIAL MEDIUM

Aquilegia vulgaris

COLUMBINE A clump-forming, upright perennial with gray-green leaves divided into rounded leaflets. Pink, crimson, blue, purple, and white bell-shaped flowers appear in late spring. 'William Guiness' (above) has maroon and white flowers.

↕3ft (1m) ↔20in (50cm)

Z3–8

SHRUB LARGE

Aronia x prunifolia

PURPLE CHOKEBERRY This is an upright deciduous shrub with oval dark green leaves that turn bright red in fall. White spring flowers are followed by edible red or purple-black berries that are packed with antioxidants.

↕10ft (3m) ↔8ft (2.5m)

Z4–8 Ⓝ

PERENNIAL SMALL

Bergenia cordifolia

PIGSQUEAK This is a clump-forming evergreen perennial with large, rounded, leathery green leaves that are tinted purple in winter and spikes of cup-shaped bright pink flowers in spring. Tolerant to a wide range of soils.

↕↔20in (50cm)

 Z3–8

SHRUB LARGE

Buddleja alternifolia

FOUNTAIN BUTTERFLY BUSH An arching deciduous shrub with slender stems and narrow gray-green leaves. Clusters of fragrant lilac-purple blooms clothe the pendent branches in early summer. It can be trained as a small weeping tree.

↕↔12ft (4m)

Z6–9

PERENNIAL MEDIUM

Campanula persicifolia

PEACH-LEAVED BELLFLOWER This upright perennial forms rosettes of narrow, lance-shaped bright green leaves and nodding, papery, bell-shaped white or blue summer flowers. 'Chettle Charm' (above) has large white flowers with violet-blue tinted edges.

↕24in (60cm) ↔12in (30cm)

Z3–7

SHRUB LARGE

Corylus avellana

EUROPEAN FILBERT This large shrub or small tree has a spreading habit, and bears rounded green leaves that turn yellow in fall. In spring, it produces dangling yellow catkins, which may be followed by edible nuts in fall. Plant it to encourage wildlife.

↕↔15ft (5m)

Z4–8

PERENNIAL MEDIUM

Dictamnus albus

DITTANY An upright, clump-forming perennial with divided, glossy light green leaves. From late spring to early summer, it produces fragrant white or pink flowers followed by ornamental, star-shaped seedheads in fall.

↕3ft (1m) ↔24in (60cm)

Z3–8

PERENNIAL LARGE

Crocosmia x *crocosmiiflora*

MONTBRETIA This perennial corm forms clumps of upright, sword-shaped, pleated midgreen leaves. Branched stems bear large, trumpet-shaped yellow, orange, or red flowers from mid- to late summer. Considered invasive in some areas.

↕↔4ft (1.2m)

Z6–9

PERENNIAL SMALL

Epimedium x *rubrum*

RED BARRENWORT A carpeting perennial with abundant, heart-shaped midgreen leaves that flush brownish red in spring and fall, and last into winter. Clusters of cup-shaped crimson flowers with yellow spurs appear in spring on wiry stems.

↕12in (30cm) ↔8in (20cm)

Z5–8

PERENNIAL LARGE

Deschampsia cespitosa

TUFTED HAIR GRASS A tuft-forming deciduous perennial that bears clouds of tiny golden-yellow flowers on long stems in summer. Both the seedheads and foliage turn golden-yellow in fall. Varieties include 'Goldtau' (above).

↕up to 6ft (2m) ↔20in (50cm)

Z4–9 Ⓝ

PERENNIAL SMALL

Epimedium x *warleyense*

BARRENWORT This carpeting evergreen perennial has heart-shaped light green leaves that are tinged purple-red in spring and fall. Cup-shaped coppery orange flower clusters appear on wiry stems in spring. It makes a good ground-cover plant.

↕↔12in (30cm)

Z5–8

PERENNIAL SMALL

Dicentra formosa

WESTERN BLEEDING HEART A spreading perennial with fernlike gray-green leaves. From late spring to early summer, slender arching stems bearing nodding, heart-shaped pink or dusky red flowers appear. Plant in groups in beds or cottage gardens.

↕18in (45cm) ↔12in (30cm)

Z4–8

PERENNIAL MEDIUM

Erysimum 'Bowles's Mauve'

PERENNIAL WALLFLOWER This evergreen perennial has narrowly oval gray-green leaves. From late winter to summer, spikes of small mauve flowers open from dark purple buds. Deadhead regularly to prolong the flowering display.

↕24in (60cm) ↔16in (40cm)

Z6–10

SHRUB MEDIUM

Escallonia 'Apple Blossom'

ESCALLONIA A compact evergreen shrub with small, leathery, glossy dark green leaves. From early- to midsummer, it bears a profusion of pink flowers. It makes a beautiful flowering hedge or back-of-bed shrub. Best in West Coast gardens.

↕↔ 8ft (2.5m)

Z8–9

PERENNIAL MEDIUM

Euphorbia amygdaloides var. *robbiae*

WOOD SPURGE A spreading evergreen perennial with rosettes of oblong, leathery, shiny dark green leaves and, in spring, rounded heads of small lime-green flowers and bracts. May be aggressive.

↕↔ 24in (60cm)

Z6–9

SHRUB MEDIUM

Exochorda x *macrantha*

PEARLBUSH This medium-sized deciduous shrub forms a dense mound of arching stems covered with dark green foliage, which turns yellow and orange in fall. A profusion of white flowers appears from late spring to early summer.

↕ 6ft (2m) ↔ 10ft (3m)

Z5–8

SHRUB LARGE

Forsythia x *intermedia*

BORDER FORSYTHIA This vigorous, upright deciduous shrub bears long stems covered with small, star-shaped yellow flowers from late winter to mid-spring before the green leaves appear. 'Lynwood Variety' (above) has larger bright yellow blooms.

↕↔ 10ft (3m)

Z5–8

SHRUB MEDIUM

Fuchsia magellanica

FUCHSIA An upright deciduous shrub with oval to tapering midgreen leaves. Throughout summer, it produces an abundance of small, pendent, tubular red and purple flowers followed by black fruits. Use it in a wildlife border.

↕↔ 6ft (2m)

Z6–9

SHRUB SMALL

Gaultheria mucronata

CHILEAN PERNETTYA A bushy evergreen shrub with prickly, glossy dark green leaves and tiny white flowers from late spring to early summer. Only female plants bear sprays of showy long-lasting berries. Best in West Coast gardens.

↕↔ 4ft (1.2m)

pH Z7–9

SHRUB SMALL

Gaultheria procumbens

WINTERGREEN An evergreen shrub with oval, aromatic leathery leaves that flush red in winter and small, bell-shaped pink-flushed white flowers in summer, followed by red berries. Best in cooler areas. 'Very Berry' (above) has bright scarlet berries.

↕ 6in (15cm) ↔ indefinite

pH Z3–8 N

PERENNIAL SMALL

Geranium 'Ann Folkard'

CRANESBILL A spreading perennial with swaths of deeply dissected, lobed yellowish green leaves that mature to green. In midsummer and sometimes in fall, it bears saucer-shaped magenta flowers with black centers and veins.

↕ 20in (50cm) ↔ 3ft (1m)

Z5–9

PERENNIAL SMALL

Geranium macrorrhizum

BIGROOT GERANIUM A carpeting perennial has soft, rounded, divided aromatic leaves with bright fall hues and magenta early summer flowers. Makes decorative ground cover next to hedges and walls. Plant in partial shade in hot summer areas.

↕ 15in (38cm) ↔ 24in (60cm)

Z4–8

PERENNIAL SMALL

Geranium x *oxonianum*

CRANESBILL A clump-forming perennial with toothed, divided green leaves. Pink, rounded dark-veined flowers with notched petals appear from late spring to midsummer. 'Wargrave Pink' (above) has pale salmon-pink blooms.

↕ 18in (45cm) ↔ 24in (60cm)

Z4–8

PERENNIAL MEDIUM

Geranium pratense

MEADOW CRANESBILL A clump-forming perennial with deeply lobed and divided green leaves that develop fall tints. In summer, saucer-shaped violet-blue flowers with attractive veins appear. 'Mrs Kendall Clark' (above) is a popular variety.

↕↔ 24in (60cm)

Z4–8

PERENNIAL SMALL

Geranium wallichianum

CRANESBILL A perennial with toothed, divided, white-marbled midgreen leaves. Veined, lilac or pink-purple saucer-shaped flowers appear from midsummer to fall. 'Buxton's Variety' (above) has white-centered light violet-blue flowers.

↕ 18in (45cm) ↔ 3ft (1m)

Z5–8

SHRUB LARGE

Hamamelis x *intermedia*

WITCH HAZEL A vase-shaped shrub with broadly oval leaves that turn yellow in fall. Lightly scented spidery flowers appear on bare stems from early- to midwinter. Varieties include 'Jelena' (above) with large coppery orange flowers.

↕↔12ft (4m)

Z5–8

PERENNIAL MEDIUM

Helleborus argutifolius

CORSICAN HELLEBORE This clump-forming evergreen perennial has leathery, divided, spiny-edged dark green leaves. Clusters of nodding, bowl-shaped pale green flowers appear from late winter to spring. Grow it in a lightly shaded bed.

↕24in (60cm) ↔18in (45cm)

Z6–9

SHRUB SMALL

Hypericum 'Hidcote'

ST. JOHN'S WORT This tough evergreen or semievergreen shrub forms a dense bush of narrowly oval dark green leaves. Masses of saucer-shaped golden-yellow flowers appear from midsummer to early fall. Site it midbed in part shade.

↕4ft (1.2m) ↔5ft (1.5m)

Z6–9

PERENNIAL MEDIUM

Iris foetidissima

STINKING IRIS This evergreen rhizome-forming perennial has strap-shaped, glossy green leaves and, from early- to midsummer, yellow-tinged, dull purple or yellow flowers. Grown for its scarlet berrylike winter fruits. Does not remain evergreen in colder areas.

↕3ft (1m) ↔indefinite

Z6–9

PERENNIAL MEDIUM

Lamprocapnos spectabilis

BLEEDING HEART This perennial has fernlike midgreen foliage. From late spring to early summer, heart-shaped rose-red and white flowers hang from wiry arching stems. Plant in small groups in a cottage garden or informal bed.

↕↔3ft (1m)

Z3–9

PERENNIAL SMALL

Lathyrus vernus

SPRING VETCH This clump-forming perennial has soft, pointed dark green leaves and small, sweet pealike, purple and blue, red-veined spring flowers. Best at the front of a bed. Easy to grow from seed. Can be grown in cooler areas in zones 8–9.

↕↔12in (30cm)

Z5–7

PERENNIAL MEDIUM

Leucanthemum x *superbum*

SHASTA DAISY A clump-forming perennial with slightly toothed dark green leaves and white yellow-centered daisy-like flowers on tall stems from early summer to fall. 'Wirral Pride' (above) has double flowers. Plant in a lightly shaded area.

↕3ft (1m) ↔24in (60cm)

Z5–9

BULB LARGE

Lilium henryi

TRUMPET LILY This is an upright perennial bulb with scattered, narrow lance-shaped leaves. In late summer, it produces nodding, turks-cap black-spotted orange flowers in dramatic sprays. It prefers acidic soil.

↕3ft (1m)

pH Z5–8

BULB LARGE

Lilium lancifolium

TIGER LILY This upright perennial bulb has long, narrow lance-shaped leaves and, from summer to early fall, nodding, turks-cap, purple-spotted pink- to red-orange flowers. 'Splendens' (above) has larger, black-spotted red-orange blooms.

↕5ft (1.5m)

pH Z3–8

BULB LARGE

Lilium longiflorum

EASTER LILY An upright perennial bulb with long, shiny lance-shaped leaves. In summer, this classic lily produces sprays of fragrant, large, outward-facing, funnel-shaped pure white flowers with petals that curve back slightly. Excellent for cutting.

↕3ft (1m)

Z7–9

BULB LARGE

Lilium nepalense

HIMALAYAN LILY An upright or arching perennial bulb with lance-shaped scattered leaves. Its summer blooms are large, nodding, greenish white or greenish yellow trumpets with dark reddish purple throats and reflexed petals.

↕3ft (1m)

pH Z7–8

BULB LARGE

Lilium pardalinum

LEOPARD LILY This is an upright perennial bulb with long narrow leaves. In summer, it produces nodding, turks-cap crimson flowers with orange markings and maroon spots on tall stems. The blooms are often scented.

↕5ft (1.5m)

Z5–8 Ⓝ

BULB LARGE

Lilium speciosum

SPECIES LILY This upright perennial bulb has broad lance-shaped leaves. Sprays of large, scented, pale pink or white turks-cap flowers that are splashed deeper pink appear from late summer to early fall. *L. speciosum* var. *rubrum* is popular.

↕4ft (1.2m)

pH Z5–8

BULB LARGE

Lilium superbum

TURKSCAP LILY An upright perennial bulb with mottled stems bearing lance-shaped, green leaves. From late summer to early fall, it produces nodding, turks-cap, orange blooms, with maroon spots and green stars in the throats.

↕6ft (2m)

pH Z4–8 Ⓝ

PERENNIAL SMALL

Liriope muscari

LILYTURF This spreading evergreen perennial forms dense clumps of grasslike, glossy dark green leaves. In fall, upright, lavender- or purple-blue, thickly clustered flower spikes appear, followed by black berries. Considered invasive in some areas.

↕12in (30cm) ↔18in (45cm)

pH Z6–10

PERENNIAL SMALL

Luzula sylvatica 'Aurea'

GREATER WOODRUSH This clump-forming evergreen perennial has glossy grasslike leaves that become yellow-green in winter and spring, and green in summer. Tiny brown flowers appear from late spring to early summer. It tolerates deep shade.

↕16in (40cm) ↔18in (45cm)

Z4–9

PERENNIAL MEDIUM

Lysimachia clethroides

GOOSENECK LOOSESTRIFE This vigorous, clump-forming, spreading perennial has narrow pointed leaves. Nodding spikes of small, white flowers become upright as they open in late summer. The tall stems may need support. Can be agressive in gardens.

↕↔3ft (1m)

Z3–8

PERENNIAL MEDIUM

Lysimachia punctata

WHORLED LOOSESTRIFE Vigorous and large, this upright, clump-forming perennial has oval midgreen leaves, and produces spikes of small bright yellow flowers over a long period in summer. It can be aggressive. 'Alexander' (above) has variegated foliage.

↕3ft (1m) ↔24in (60cm)

Z4–8

SHRUB MEDIUM

Mahonia x *media*

MAHONIA An upright evergreen shrub with large leaves formed of dark green hollylike leaflets. Long, slender spikes of small, scented lemon-yellow flowers appear from late fall through winter. 'Charity' (above) has upright, then spreading spikes.

↕6ft (1.8m) ↔12ft (4m)

Z7–9

SHRUB MEDIUM

Paeonia lutea var. *ludlowii*

TIBETAN PEONY This medium-sized, upright deciduous shrub produces deeply lobed dark green leaves, blue-green beneath. Nodding, cup-shaped yellow flowers appear in late spring. Plant it at the rear of a bed.

↕↔8ft (2.5m)

Z6–9

CLIMBER LARGE

Parthenocissus quinquefolia

VIRGINIA CREEPER This large, woody deciduous climber has divided, toothed, dull green leaves that blaze crimson in fall, when blue-black berries also appear. Grow this plant up a large fence or wall at the rear of a bed.

↕50ft (15m) or more

Z4–9 Ⓝ

PERENNIAL MEDIUM

Persicaria bistorta 'Superba'

BISTORT This dense clump-forming, vigorous perennial produces oval, tapering green leaves. Spikes of soft pink blooms appear from early- to late summer. Deadhead it regularly to encourage repeat-flowering.

↕30in (75cm) ↔24in (60cm)

Z4–8

SHRUB MEDIUM

Philadelphus 'Belle Etoile'

MOCK ORANGE This deciduous shrub produces slightly arching stems of oval leaves and very fragrant, white single flowers with maroon centers in early summer. Grow it toward the rear of a bed in part shade.

↕6ft (1.8m) ↔4ft (1.2m)

Z5–8

SHRUB LARGE

Pittosporum tobira

JAPANESE PITTOSPORUM This dense evergreen shrub has a neat, bushy-headed shape and leathery dark green leaves. In late spring, it produces clusters of very sweetly scented, small, starry white flowers that age to creamy yellow.

↕30ft (10m) ↔10ft (3m)

Z8–10

SHRUB MEDIUM

Ribes sanguineum

FLOWERING CURRANT This spreading deciduous shrub has lobed aromatic leaves and small pink, red, or white bell-shaped flower clusters in spring, followed by white-coated black fruits. 'Pulborough Scarlet' (above) has deep crimson blooms.

↕6ft (2m) ↔8ft (2.5m)

Z6–8 Ⓝ

SHRUB LARGE

Sambucus nigra BLACK LACE

BLACK ELDER A rounded deciduous shrub with fernlike, almost black foliage and, from late spring to early summer, scented, pale pink flower heads followed by blackish red fall berries. May die back in colder areas.

↕↔20ft (6m)

Z5–7

PERENNIAL MEDIUM

Tradescantia Andersoniana Group

SPIDERWORT This clump-forming perennial has lance-shaped arching leaves and, from early summer to fall, flowers in shades of white, red, blue, purple, or pink. 'Concord Grape' (above) has bright purple blooms.

↕↔24in (60cm)

Z4–9 Ⓝ

SHRUB MEDIUM

Vaccinium corymbosum

HIGHBUSH BLUEBERRY This soft fruit, deciduous bush has an upright, slightly arching habit. The foliage reddens in fall. Small white or pinkish flowers from late spring to early summer are followed by sweet, blue-black edible berries.

↕↔ up to 5ft (1.5m)

pH Z3–7 Ⓝ

PERENNIAL LARGE

Veronicastrum virginicum

CULVER'S ROOT An upright perennial with narrow, lance-shaped dark green leaves, punctuated in late summer by slender spikes of small, starry purple-blue, pink, or white flowers held on long stems. It is suitable for light shade only.

↕6ft (2m) ↔18in (45cm)

Z3–8 Ⓝ

SHRUB MEDIUM

Viburnum davidii

DAVID VIBURNUM This domed evergreen shrub has leathery, deeply veined dark green leaves. Clusters of small white flowers appear above the foliage in late spring. For decorative metallic blue berries on females, grow plants of both sexes.

↕↔5ft (1.5m)

Z7–9

SHRUB LARGE

Viburnum rhytidophyllum

LEATHERLEAF VIBURNUM This large evergreen shrub has long, broad, veined, corrugated dark green leaves. Large, dense domed heads of small creamy white flowers appear in spring, followed by oval red fruits, which ripen to black.

↕15ft (5m) ↔12ft (4m)

Z5–8

OTHER SUGGESTIONS

Perennials

Acanthus mollis • *Bergenia* 'Overture' • *Centaurea montana* • *Coreopsis lanceolata* Ⓝ • *Dicentra eximia* Ⓝ • *Eurybia divaricata* Ⓝ • *Persicaria affinis* 'Superba' • *Silene virginica* Ⓝ

Bulbs

Allium 'Purple Sensation'

Climbers

Actinidia arguta • *Campsis radicans* Ⓝ • *Celastrus scandens* Ⓝ

Shrubs and trees

Aronia arbutifolia 'Brilliantissima' Ⓝ • *Chaenomeles* x *superba* 'Texas Scarlet' • *Cornus alternifolia* GOLDEN SHADOWS Ⓝ • *Corylus avellana* 'Contorta' • *Jasminum nudiflorum* • *Myrica pensylvanica* Ⓝ • *Pinus strobus* Ⓝ • *Prunus maritima* Ⓝ

Plants for pond perimeters

Shady areas close to ponds are perfect for some of the most dramatic plants, the cool moist environment provides ideal growing conditions.

Combine big-leaved beauties such as meadowsweet, leopard plant, rhubarb, and rodgersia to produce lush tropical-style displays and add splashes of color with bright yellow or orange globeflower and monkey flower, together with striking pink and purple astilbe, turtlehead, and joe pye weed. Alternatively, opt for a cool fernery around your pond, with the bold varying textures of ostrich fern, sensitive fern, and royal ferns. Spring flowering primrose complement ferns beautifully—choose a range of candelabra and drumstick forms for their elegant shapes and compelling colors.

PERENNIAL SMALL

Ajuga reptans

BUGLEWEED This tough, fast-spreading evergreen perennial has rosettes of glossy dark green leaves and, from late spring to early summer, short dark blue flower spikes. Considered invasive in some areas. 'Atropurpurea' (above) has purple leaves.

↕6in (15cm) ↔3ft (1m)

Z3–9

PERENNIAL SMALL

Arisaema triphyllum

JACK-IN-THE-PULPIT An upright perennial with a few large leaves divided into broad lance-shaped leaflets. It has striking, hooded, goblet-shaped green or purple summer blooms formed by fleshy bracts. Bright red berries follow the flowers.

↕20in (50cm) ↔18in (45cm)

pH ! Z4–9 N

PERENNIAL MEDIUM

Astilbe 'Venus'

ASTILBE A leafy perennial with divided leaves and feathery tapering plumes of tiny pale pink flowers on tall stems in midsummer. The dry flower heads provide interest into winter. Best in fertile soil. Needs moisture if exposed to sun or heat.

↕↔3ft (1m)

Z3–8

PERENNIAL SMALL

Aruncus aethusifolius

GOATSBEARD A clump-forming, compact ground-cover perennial with deeply dissected, fernlike green foliage that turns yellow in fall before dropping. In early summer, it produces sprays of tiny creamy white flowers above the leaves.

↕↔16in (40cm)

Z3–9

PERENNIAL SMALL

Astilbe x *arendsii*

ASTILBE This clump-forming, ferny-leaved perennial produces frothy plumes of white, pink, lilac, or red flowers between early and late summer, depending on the cultivar. The seedheads feature in winter. 'Fanal' has red flowers and dark foliage.

↕18in (45cm) ↔12in (30cm)

Z4–8

PERENNIAL MEDIUM

Astilbe chinensis

ASTILBE This perennial forms loose clumps of toothed, deeply cut dark green leaves. In late summer, soft plumes of tiny pinkish white flowers appear on tall stems. *A. chinensis* var. *pumila* is shorter with fluffy raspberry-red spikes.

↕24in (60cm) ↔8in (20cm)

Z4–8

PERENNIAL MEDIUM

Carex elata 'Aurea'

BOWLES' GOLDEN SEDGE An evergreen perennial that forms tufts of long, gently arching, narrow golden-yellow leaves. Thin, grasslike blackish brown flower spikes form in summer. Plant in masses to brighten a shady area.

↕20in (50cm) ↔18in (45cm)

Z5–9

PERENNIAL MEDIUM

Chelone obliqua

TURTLEHEAD This upright perennial has toothed, lance-shaped green leaves. From late summer to fall, spikes of two-lipped dark pink or purple flowers form. Pinch out stem tips in spring for bushier growth. Add compost for optimum growth.

↕3ft (1m) ↔20in (50cm)

pH Z3–9 N

SHRUB LARGE

Cornus amomum

SILKY DOGWOOD This deciduous shrub has purplish winter shoots and lance-shaped dark green leaves that turn red and orange in fall. Purple-blue fruits follow late spring creamy white flower heads. Some plants have bright red stems for winter display.

↕10ft (3m) ↔12ft (4m)

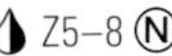 Z5–8 Ⓝ

PERENNIAL LARGE

Darmera peltata

UMBRELLA PLANT This large spreading perennial forms clumps of round dinner-plate-sized leaves on long stalks that burnish red in fall. Flat clusters of white or pale pink flowers appear on hairy stems in spring before the foliage.

↕4ft (1.2m) ↔24in (60cm)

Z5–7 Ⓝ

PERENNIAL LARGE

Eutrochium purpureum

JOE PYE WEED A stately upright perennial with oval green leaves held on purplish green stems. From late summer to fall, it produces tall stems of fluffy pinkish purple flowers. It is a perfect back-of-bed plant for a large bog garden.

↕7ft (2.2m) ↔3ft (1m)

Z4–9 Ⓝ

PERENNIAL LARGE

Filipendula purpurea

JAPANESE MEADOWSWEET This upright clump-forming perennial has toothed, divided green leaves and large airy sprays of tiny reddish purple flowers atop tall branching stems in late summer. Plant it at the rear of a pond perimeter.

↕4ft (1.2m) ↔24in (60cm)

Z4–9

PERENNIAL LARGE

Filipendula rubra

QUEEN OF THE PRAIRIE This upright perennial has large aromatic leaves. In midsummer, it produces branching stems of feathery pink plumes that fade as they age. Use it to spread through a boggy site.

↕up to 8ft (2.5m) ↔4ft (1.2m)

Z3–8 Ⓝ

PERENNIAL MEDIUM

Filipendula ulmaria

MEADOWSWEET This leafy perennial has divided blue-green leaves that turn brilliant red in fall. Upright stems bear lacy clusters of tiny, fragrant white summer flowers. 'Aurea' (above) has golden-yellow spring foliage. Considered invasive in some areas.

↕3in (1m) ↔24in (60cm)

Z4–9

PERENNIAL MEDIUM

Geum rivale

WATER AVENS This medium-sized perennial forms neat rosettes of scalloped green leaves above which rise slim stems bearing nodding, bell-shaped pink to dark orange flowers from late spring to summer.

↕↔24in (60cm)

Z3–8

PERENNIAL MEDIUM

Hosta sieboldiana

PLANTAIN LILY This clump-forming perennial has large, broad blue- and gray-green leaves with a puckered texture and bell-shaped, lilac-gray early-summer-flower spikes. *H. sieboldiana* var. *elegans* has larger bluer leaves and pale lilac flowers.

↕3ft (1m) ↔4ft (1.2m)

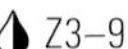 Z3–9

PERENNIAL MEDIUM

Iris ensata

JAPANESE WATER IRIS An upright clump-forming perennial with sword-shaped gray-green leaves. It bears beardless flowers in purple, pink, and white from early- to midsummer. 'Katy Mendez' has purple-blue flowers with yellow blotches.

↕3ft (1m) ↔24in (60cm)

 Z4–9

PERENNIAL MEDIUM

Kirengeshoma palmata

YELLOW WAX BELLS An upright perennial with reddish stems and large, rounded, lobed, serrated-edged bright green leaves above which clusters of narrow, bell-shaped creamy yellow flowers appear on strong stems from late summer to fall.

↕3ft (1m) ↔24in (60cm)

pH Z5–8

PERENNIAL LARGE

Ligularia dentata

LEOPARD PLANT An upright, clump-forming perennial with large, leathery, heart-shaped rich green leaves. From midsummer to early fall, it bears large, orange-yellow daisy-like flowers. 'Desdemona' (above) has brownish green leaves.

↕4ft (1.2m) ↔24in (60cm)

Z4–8

PERENNIAL MEDIUM

Lysimachia ephemerum

WILLOW-LEAVED LOOSESTRIFE A clump-forming perennial with willowlike, rough gray-green leaves. Light green seedheads follow the tapering spikes of starry grayish white summer flowers. Mulch in winter. It is more contained than other forms.

↕3ft (1m) ↔12in (30cm)

Z7–9

PERENNIAL MEDIUM

Lysimachia punctata

WHORLED LOOSESTRIFE A vigorous clump-forming perennial with soft haired midgreen leaves and, in summer, tall spikes of bright yellow flowers nestling between the leaves. The flowers are good for cutting and attract butterflies; it can be aggressive.

↕3ft (1m) ↔24in (60cm)

Z4–8

PERENNIAL LARGE

Ligularia stenocephala

LEOPARD PLANT This clump-forming perennial has large, toothed green leaves and, in summer, slender, daisy-like yellow flower spikes on dark brown tall stems. 'The Rocket' (above) has ragged-edged foliage and black stems.

↕6ft (1.8m) ↔3ft (1m)

Z4–8

SHRUB LARGE

Lindera benzoin

SPICEBUSH This deciduous shrub has dark green leaves, yellow in fall, and aromatic when crushed. Showy clusters of tiny, fragrant greenish yellow flowers form in spring. For small scarlet berries on females, grow plants of both sexes.

↕↔10ft (3m)

pH Z4–9 Ⓝ

TREE MEDIUM

Magnolia virginiana

SWEETBAY MAGNOLIA This conical semievergreen or deciduous shrub or tree has glossy dark green leaves, bluish white beneath, and vanilla-scented, creamy white cup-shaped flowers from early summer to early fall. Grow at the back of a boggy bed.

↕30ft (10m) ↔20ft (6m)

Z5–9 Ⓝ

PERENNIAL MEDIUM

Matteuccia struthiopteris

OSTRICH FERN This deciduous fern has lance-shaped, deeply divided green fronds that sprout from a central crown, producing a "shuttlecock" effect. Some fronds dry and last into winter; cut back all growth in spring.

↕3ft (1m) ↔18in (45cm)

Z2–8 Ⓝ

PERENNIAL SMALL

Mimulus guttatus

MONKEY FLOWER A mat-forming perennial with toothed leaves. Clusters of yellow snap-dragon-like flowers that are spotted reddish brown on the lower petals are borne in succession over summer and early fall. Grow as an annual in northern areas.

↕12in (30cm) ↔24in (60cm)

Z6–9 Ⓝ

PERENNIAL MEDIUM

Onoclea sensibilis

SENSITIVE FERN This creeping deciduous fern covers the ground with deeply lobed, toothed-edged light green fronds. Stiff, brown fertile fronds stand erect in late summer, lasting into winter. Plants prefer moist soil in dappled shade.

↕24in (60cm) ↔3ft (1m)

pH Z4–9 Ⓝ

PERENNIAL LARGE

Osmunda regalis

ROYAL FERN This large deciduous fern forms upright clumps of elegant, deeply divided bright green fronds, pinkish when young and red-brown in fall. Mature plants bear tassel-like spikes of rust-brown spores at the ends of taller fronds.

↕6ft (2m) ↔3ft (1m)

Z3–10 Ⓝ

PERENNIAL SMALL

Primula japonica

JAPANESE PRIMROSE A deciduous perennial with rosettes of toothed, green basal leaves and tubular deep red, white, pink, or crimson early summer blooms. 'Postford White' (above) has white flowers. Plant in groups around a part-shaded pond.

↕↔18in (45cm)

Z4–8

PERENNIAL MEDIUM

Primula pulverulenta

CANDELABRA PRIMROSE This upright perennial bears rosettes of large, oblong green leaves and upright white-coated stems studded with clusters of reddish purple flowers in early summer. Grow it in groups around a part-shaded pool.

↕3ft (1m) ↔24in (60cm)

Z4–8

PERENNIAL SMALL

Primula veris

COWSLIP This evergreen or semievergreen perennial forms rosettes of oval to lance-shaped, toothed leaves and tight clusters of fragrant, nodding, tubular butter-yellow flowers on stout stems in spring. Try it in boggy meadows by pools.

↕↔10in (25cm)

Z3–8

PERENNIAL LARGE

Rheum palmatum

CHINESE RHUBARB This upright perennial has huge, jaggedly lobed dark green leaves, purple-red beneath. In early summer, sturdy stems bear large plumes of fluffy cream to red flowers. Allow plenty of space for large foliage.

↕↔6ft (2m)

(!) Z4–7

PERENNIAL LARGE

Rodgersia pinnata

RODGERSIA A clump-forming perennial with large, corrugated, divided dark green leaves and conical spires of small pink, red, or yellow-white summer blooms. 'Superba' (above) has bronze-tinged emerald leaves and bright pink flowers.

↕4ft (1.2m) ↔30in (75cm)

Z4–7

PERENNIAL MEDIUM

Saururus cernuus

LIZARD'S TAIL This perennial marginal water or bog plant has clumps of heart-shaped green leaves and slender nodding spires of tiny cream flowers in summer. It can become aggressive, so divide it regularly if growing in a bog garden.

↕3ft (1m) ↔indefinite

Z5–10 (N)

TREE LARGE

Taxodium distichum

BALD CYPRESS This conical deciduous conifer has slender fresh green leaves that turn rich orange-brown in fall. It has green female and red male cones. Plant it in boggy soil in a large garden at some distance from open water.

↕130ft (40m) ↔28ft (9m)

pH Z5–11 (N)

PERENNIAL LARGE

Thalictrum delavayi

YUNNAN MEADOW RUE A clump-forming perennial with fernlike midgreen leaves. From late summer to fall, it produces large billowing panicles of tiny lavender blooms. 'Hewitt's Double' (above) has dainty double flowers.

↕5ft (1.5m) ↔24in (60cm) or more

Z4–7

PERENNIAL MEDIUM

Tradescantia Andersoniana Group

SPIDERWORT This tufted clump-forming perennial has erect branching stems and arching, narrow, lance-shaped midgreen leaves. 'Concord Grape' (above) has purple flowers. Grow in part shade around a pond.

↕↔24in (60cm)

Z4–9 (N)

PERENNIAL MEDIUM

Trollius chinensis

GLOBEFLOWER This clump-forming perennial has lobed, toothed green leaves and bowl-shaped golden-orange flowers with upright central stamens in summer. It tolerates light shade and looks best planted in groups around a pond edge.

↕3ft (1m) ↔18in (45cm)

Z4–8

PERENNIAL MEDIUM

Trollius x *cultorum*

GLOBEFLOWER This clump-forming perennial has deeply divided, fernlike green foliage and cup-shaped, orange-yellow double flowers from mid-spring to early summer. Use it to brighten up the banks of a pond or stream.

↕30in (75cm) ↔18in (45cm)

Z4–7

OTHER SUGGESTIONS

Annuals

Mimulus Magic Series

Perennials

Actaea matsumurae 'White Pearl' • *Aruncus dioicus* (N) • *Astilbe chinensis* var. *taquetii* 'Superba' • *Chelone lyonii* 'Hot Lips' (N) • *Chrysogonum virginianum* (N) • *Eupatorium cannabinum* • *Eupatorium rugosum* 'Chocolate' (N) • *Eutrochium maculatum* (N) • *Gunnera manicata* • *Hosta* 'Frances Williams' • *Gunnera manicata* • *Gunnera tinctoria* • *Helianthus divaricatus* (N) • *Hosta* 'Frances Williams' • *Ligularia* 'Britt Marie Crawford' • *Ligularia przewalskii* • *Primula alpicola* • *Primula beesiana* • *Primula denticulata* • *Rheum* 'Ace of Hearts' • *Rodgersia sambucifolia* • *Salvia uliginosa* • *Trollius europaeus*

Plants for ponds

The list of plants for shady pools is considerably shorter than the list for ponds in sun. Most water plants need some light to put on the best show.

Unless you have a natural pond in deep shade, choose the brightest site available for a water feature, or your options will be limited to the spring-flowering skunk cabbage, which, although beautiful, acquired its common name for a good reason. However, in partly shaded ponds, your choice of iris, marsh marigold, calla lily, and other marginals will create a dynamic display of colorful reflections from spring until fall. The few evergreens for ponds include water figwort and horsetail; keep the latter's roots confined to a pond basket.

PERENNIAL MEDIUM

Acorus calamus

SWEET FLAG This upright perennial can be either deciduous or semievergreen. It is grown largely for its clumps of grasslike green leaves. In summer, it produces insignificant brown flowers. It is tolerant of light shade.

↕↔ 24in (60cm)

Z4–10 Ⓝ

PERENNIAL SMALL

Calla palustris

BOG ARUM A spreading deciduous or semievergreen marginal perennial with heart-shaped glossy leaves and large, vase-shaped white bracts, each surrounding a fleshy spike of minute flowers followed by red or orange berries.

↕ 10in (25cm) ↔ 12in (30cm)

(!) Z4–8 Ⓝ

PERENNIAL SMALL

Cardamine pratensis

LADY'S SMOCK This small perennial marginal or bog plant produces divided leaves. It bears clusters of pinkish mauve flowers in late spring. Grow this plant in very shallow water or a bog garden in shade.

↕ 18in (45cm) ↔ 12in (30cm)

Z4–8 Ⓝ

PERENNIAL SMALL

Caltha palustris

MARSH MARIGOLD This perennial marginal produces rounded, heart-shaped green leaves and golden-yellow single or double flowers on lax stems in early spring. It tolerates light shade with some sun during the day. It will self-seed and spread.

↕ 16in (40cm) ↔ 18in (45cm)

Z3–7 Ⓝ

PERENNIAL SMALL

Caltha palustris 'Flore Pleno'

syn. *Caltha palustris* 'Multiplex' This small perennial bears the same dark green leaves as the species. Clusters of bright golden double flowers appear in spring. It is also suitable for pond perimeters.

↕↔ 10in (25cm)

Z3–7 Ⓝ

PERENNIAL MEDIUM

Cyperus involucratus

UMBRELLA PLANT An evergreen perennial marginal sedge treated as an annual. Its tall, upright slender stems end in a whorl of horizontal grassy bracts. Airy sprays of tiny yellowish green flowers arise from the "umbrellas" in summer. Protect from frost.

↕ 3ft (1m) ↔ 12in (30cm)

Z9–11

PERENNIAL SMALL

Houttuynia cordata

HOUTTUYNIA This vigorous spreading perennial has heart-shaped, orange-scented blue-green leaves. Yellow-centered white blooms form in late spring. Restrict its roots in a pond basket. 'Chameleon' (above) has yellow- and red-splashed foliage.

↕ 12in (30cm) ↔ indefinite

Z5–10

PERENNIAL MEDIUM

Iris ensata

JAPANESE WATER IRIS This upright perennial has sword-shaped gray-green leaves. From early- to midsummer, it produces flowers in shades of purple, pink, and white, depending on the variety. Plant it in shallow water.

↕ 3ft (1m) ↔ 24in (60cm)

(!) Z4–9

PERENNIAL MEDIUM

Lysichiton americanus

YELLOW SKUNK CABBAGE This vigorous perennial marginal produces large green leaves followed by bright yellow bracts in spring. Avoid planting it near streams as it spreads rapidly, or too close to seating as it has a rancid odor.

↕30in (75cm) ↔4ft (1.2m)

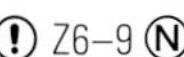

(!) Z6–9 (N)

PERENNIAL MEDIUM

Lysichiton camtschatcensis

ASIAN SKUNK CABBAGE This clump-forming perennial marginal has large bright green leaves and white spring flowers, which comprise petal-like bracts around spikes of tiny flowers. Its scent may be unpleasant.

↕30in (75cm) ↔24in (60cm)

(!) Z5–9

PERENNIAL MEDIUM

Peltandra virginica

GREEN ARROW ARUM This perennial marginal is grown for its bold, arrow-shaped, glossy dark green leaves formed on long stalks. In late summer, it produces minute flowers inside upright bracts that look like green chili peppers.

↕3ft (1m) ↔24in (60cm)

Z5–9 (N)

PERENNIAL MEDIUM

Pontederia cordata

PICKEREL WEED This upright perennial produces large, spear-shaped, glossy green leaves. In summer, it produces sturdy spikes of blue flowers. Remove the spent growth in fall. The variety 'Alba' has white flowers.

↕30in (75cm) ↔18in (45cm)

Z3–11

WATER PLANT SMALL

Persicaria amphibia

WATER SMARTWEED A vigorous perennial aquatic with lance-shaped, dark green floating leaves. From midsummer to fall, it produces clusters of pink flowers on upright stems above the foliage, followed by glossy brown fruits.

↕12in (30cm) ↔6ft (2m)

Z3–9 (N)

PERENNIAL MEDIUM

Petasites japonicus var. *giganteus*

GIANT JAPANESE BUTTERBUR A spreading perennial with large round leaves, edible stems, and lime-green spring-flower spikes. Can be invasive. 'Variegatus' (above) has cream-splashed green leaves.

↕3½ft (1.1m) ↔5ft (1.5m)

Z5–9

PERENNIAL MEDIUM

Saururus cernuus

LIZARD'S TAIL A perennial marginal with spreading clumps of heart-shaped leaves and soft tapering spires of tiny creamy white flowers in summer. Confine it in a basket in small ponds and water features as it can be aggressive.

↕3ft (1m) ↔indefinite

Z5–10 (N)

PERENNIAL MEDIUM

Scrophularia auriculata

WATER FIGWORT This is a tall, clump-forming evergreen perennial marginal with oval, rough-textured, cream-edged dark green leaves. In summer, it produces small brown flowers, which are attractive to bees.

↕3ft (1m) ↔12in (30cm) or more

Z5–9

PERENNIAL MEDIUM

Zantedeschia aethiopica

CALLA LILY This is a perennial marginal or bog plant with large, arrow-shaped dark green leaves. In summer, it produces white petal-like spathes, each with a yellow spike in the center. Overwinter plants indoor in colder areas.

↕↔3ft (1m)

Z8–10

OTHER SUGGESTIONS

Water plants

Aponogeton distachyos • *Azolla filiculoides* (N) • *Nuphar lutea* (N) • *Nymphoides indica*

Perennial marginals

Acorus calamus 'Variegatus' (N) • *Acorus gramineus* 'Minimus Aureus' • *Acorus gramineus* 'Ogon' • *Carex elata* 'Aurea' • *Carex nigra* 'Variegata' • *Carex muskingumensis* 'Oehme' (N) • *Carex riparia* 'Variegata' • *Ceratopteris pteridoides* • *Cyperus alternifolius* • *Cyperus papyrus* KING TUT • *Dionaea muscipula* (N) • *Eleocharis dulcis* • *Equisetum arvense* (N) • *Equisetum hyemale* (N) • *Houttuynia cordata* 'Variegata' • *Hymenocallis caroliniana* (N) • *Juncus ensifolius* (N) • *Ludwigia alternifolia* (N) • *Mentha aquatica* • *Oenanthe javanica* 'Flamingo' • *Sagittaria graminea* 'Crushed Ice' (N) • *Scirpus atrovirens* (N) • *Zantedeschia* PICASSO

Plants for boundaries, hedges, and windbreaks

Hedging and wall plants are both decorative and useful, helping to create shelter, mark boundaries, and divide up large gardens.

Conifers make excellent hedges, but most prefer a sunny site. Evergreens to consider for shady areas include firethorn, boxwood, and laurel. Oakleaf hydrangea, mountain laurel, and forsythia can provide texture and add colorful blooms to a dark spot in the garden. However, all these plants need sun for part of the day to put on a good show. For areas in dense shade, opt for a holly or Japanese laurel to create your hedge. If you are using large shrubs, clip them to size and shape; smaller shrubs can be used as edging or low hedges.

SHRUB MEDIUM

Aucuba japonica

JAPANESE LAUREL A rounded evergreen shrub with oval, glossy green leaves. Small purple spring flowers are followed by red berries on female plants, if a male plant is grown close by. Many varieties with yellow spotted leaves are available.

↕↔ 6ft (2m)

💧 (!) Z7–10

SHRUB LARGE

Buxus sempervirens

COMMON BOXWOOD An evergreen shrub with small, oval, glossy green foliage and tiny yellowish spring flowers. A classic hedging and topiary plant, clip in late spring or early summer to allow time for the new growth to mature to avoid frost damage.

↕↔ 15ft (5m)

💧 Z6–8

TREE LARGE

Carpinus betulus

EUROPEAN HORNBEAM This deciduous tree has oval, corrugated dark green leaves that turn yellow and orange in fall. Green catkins in spring precede clusters of winged nuts. A formal or informal hedging plant, trim it in late summer and midwinter.

↕ 80ft (25m) ↔ 70ft (20m)

💧 Z4–8

SHRUB LARGE

Elaeagnus x *ebbingei*

OLEASTER This vigorous evergreen shrub has oval dark green leaves that are dusted with gray flecks. It produces small, scented white flowers in fall. Plant it as a screen or windbreak. It tolerates light shade only; trim in late summer.

↕↔ 15ft (5m)

💧 Z7–9

SHRUB LARGE

Fatsia japonica

JAPANESE FATSIA An evergreen shrub with large, palm-shaped, glossy dark green leaves. Round white flower heads in fall are followed by black fruits. Use as an informal screen; prune in spring, if required. Can be grown as a houseplant in cooler areas.

↕↔ 12ft (4m)

💧 Z8–10

SHRUB LARGE

Forsythia x *intermedia*

BORDER FORSYTHIA A vigorous deciduous shrub with long stems of golden-yellow early spring flowers before the small green foliage appears. Grow as an informal hedge; prune after flowering. 'Lynwood Variety' (above) has larger golden blooms.

↕↔ 10ft (3m)

💧 Z5–8

SHRUB MEDIUM

Hydrangea quercifolia

SNOW QUEEN

OAKLEAF HYDRANGEA A deciduous shrub with large, lobed green leaves that turn purple and red in fall. Its white conical late summer flower heads form, turning pink as they age. Use as a screen; clip it in spring.

↕ 6ft (2m) ↔ 8ft (2.5m)

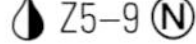

💧 Z5–9 (N)

TREE LARGE

Ilex aquifolium

ENGLISH HOLLY An evergreen shrub or tree with wavy-edged, spiny dark green leaves and scarlet berries on pollinated female plants. Thornless and variegated forms are also available. Trim with pruners in late summer. Considered invasive.

↕ up to 70ft (20m) ↔ 20ft (6m)

💧 (!) Z7–9

SHRUB LARGE

Kalmia latifolia

MOUNTAIN LAUREL A dense evergreen shrub with glossy dark green foliage. In early summer, large clusters of pale pink flowers open from darker pink, attractively crimped buds. Grow it as a flowering screen, and prune lightly after flowering.

↕↔ 10ft (3m)

💧 pH (!) Z4–9 (N)

SHRUB MEDIUM

Lonicera nitida

BOXLEAF HONEYSUCKLE A popular formal or informal hedging plant, this evergreen shrub has arching shoots and small dark green leaves. Varieties include 'Baggesen's Gold' with greenish yellow leaves. Cut it few times a year between spring and fall.

↕6ft (2m) ↔10ft (3m)

Z7–9

SHRUB SMALL

Lonicera pileata

PRIVET HONEYSUCKLE A dense, spreading evergreen shrub grown mainly for its narrow, glossy dark green leaves. Purple berries follow the small, tubular cream flowers in late spring. It is easy to train into a low hedge; trim in late spring.

↕24in (60cm) ↔8ft (2.5m)

Z5–9

SHRUB LARGE

Osmanthus heterophyllus

FALSE HOLLY A dense, rounded evergreen shrub with hollylike, prickly dark green foliage and tiny, fragrant white flowers in fall. 'Aureomarginatus' (above) has gold-edged leaves. Use as a low screen in a sheltered warm garden; trim in late spring.

↕↔15ft (5m)

Z7–9

BAMBOO LARGE

Phyllostachys nigra

BLACK BAMBOO This clump-forming evergreen bamboo has grooved greenish brown stems, which turn black when mature, and long narrow leaves. Grow it as a screen in part shade; cut out dead and old canes in spring.

↕25ft (8m) ↔indefinite

Z7–11

SHRUB LARGE

Prunus laurocerasus

CHERRY LAUREL A dense evergreen shrub with large, oval, glossy green leaves. From mid- to late spring, upright spikes of small, white single flowers appear, followed by cherry-red, later black fruits. Prune hedges hard in spring.

↕25ft (8m) ↔30ft (10m)

Z6–8

SHRUB LARGE

Prunus lusitanica

LAUREL This dense evergreen shrub has reddish purple shoots and glossy dark green foliage. Fragrant, slender, frothy white flower spikes appear in early summer, followed by deep purple fruits. Prune hedges in late spring.

↕↔30ft (10m)

Z7–9

SHRUB LARGE

Pyracantha 'Mohave'

FIRETHORN This dense evergreen shrub has small green leaves and very spiny stems. Orange-red berries follow the clusters of small white summer blooms. Use it to deter intruders; prune in spring. It is resistant to scab.

↕↔12ft (4m)

Z6–9

SHRUB MEDIUM

Ribes odoratum

BUFFALO CURRANT This deciduous shrub has lobed bright green leaves that flush red and purple in fall. Clusters of spicily scented, starry golden flowers appear in spring; purple berries follow. Grow it as an informal screen; trim after flowering.

↕↔6ft (2m)

Z4–8 Ⓝ

SHRUB MEDIUM

Symphoricarpos x *doorenbosii*

SNOWBERRY This vigorous deciduous shrub forms a dense barrier of twiggy stems and small green leaves. It produces small white blooms in summer, followed by round white fruits in fall. Use it for informal and wildlife hedges; trim in spring.

↕6ft (2m) ↔indefinite

Z4–7

TREE LARGE

Taxus baccata

ENGLISH YEW This bushy evergreen tree produces dark green needlelike leaves and red berries in fall. It makes a superb hedge for boundaries, and is useful for dividing up a garden. Clip it in spring and summer. All parts are highly toxic.

↕50ft (15m) ↔30ft (10m)

Z6–7

SHRUB LARGE

Viburnum prunifolium

BLACKHAW VIBURNUM A round-headed deciduous shrub with elliptical, toothed, shiny dark green leaves that turn reddish purple in fall. White flowers in late spring are followed by edible pink fruits that ripen to bluish black. Trim after flowering.

↕15ft (5m) ↔12ft (4m)

Z3–9 Ⓝ

OTHER SUGGESTIONS

Bamboo

Phyllostachys aureosulcata f. *aureocaulis*

Shrubs

• *Aucuba japonica* 'Salicifolia' • *Berberis julianae* • *Berberis stenophylla* • *Buxus microphylla* • *Cephalotaxus harringtonia* 'Duke Gardens' • *Corylus americana* Ⓝ • *Dirca palustris* Ⓝ • *Illicium floridanum* Ⓝ • *Morella cerifera* Ⓝ • *Prunus caroliniana* Ⓝ • *Rhododendron catawbiense* Ⓝ • *Rhododendron* 'English Roseum' • *Rhododendron mucronulatum* 'Cornell Pink' • *Sambucus canadensis* Ⓝ • *Sambucus nigra* BLACK BEAUTY • *Sarcococca ruscifolia* • *Symphoricarpos orbiculatus* Ⓝ • *Viburnum lentago* Ⓝ

Shrubs

Ilex opaca Ⓝ • *Ptelea trifoliata* Ⓝ • *Tsuga canadensis* Ⓝ

Plants for beside hedges, walls, and fences

Areas shaded by vertical structures or hedges do not make natural homes for many plants, but a few tolerate the dark and drought.

Apart from plants that can naturally survive in such areas, you can increase your choices by offering some additional moisture, either by improving the structure of the soil with annual applications of well-rotted compost or by installing a an irrigation system to increase soil water levels. Deep shade is also a limitation, although barrenwort, deadnettle, and some ferns will cope. To cover a wall or fence, consider a shrub, such as flowering quince, and others that will climb when confronted with a vertical surface.

PERENNIAL LARGE

Acanthus mollis

COMMON BEAR'S BREECHES This upright semievergreen perennial has long, deeply cut, bright green basal leaves. Tall spikes of funnel-shaped white flowers nestle between dusky purple bracts in summer. Tolerates dry soil and partial shade.

↕4ft (1.2m) ↔24in (60cm)

Z7–11

PERENNIAL LARGE

Aconitum carmichaelii

MONKSHOOD An upright perennial with deeply divided midgreen leaves and tall spikes of hooded lavender-blue flowers in fall. Use it to inject late-season color at the back of a bed or along a boundary. 'Arendsii' (above) has rich blue flowers.

↕5ft (1.5m) ↔12in (30cm)

Z3–8

PERENNIAL SMALL

Arum italicum

ITALIAN ARUM A low-growing perennial with arrow-shaped green leaves, which may disappear in extreme cold or heat; a second flush may occur in spring. Considered invasive in some areas. 'Marmoratum' (above) has attractively veined leaves.

↕10in (25cm) ↔12in (30cm)

Z5–9

PERENNIAL SMALL

Centaurea montana

PERENNIAL CORNFLOWER This perennial has oval, tapering green leaves that are hairy beneath. In early summer, it bears thistlelike flowers in shades of purple, blue, white, or pink. A cottage garden favorite, leave it to spread beside a wall or hedge.

↕20in (50cm) ↔24in (60cm)

 Z3–8

SHRUB MEDIUM

Chaenomeles x superba

FLOWERING QUINCE A deciduous shrub with spiny branches and narrow, oval, glossy green leaves. In late spring, it bears clusters of cup-shaped flowers in shades of white, pink, orange, or red, depending on the variety. Train it on a wall or fence.

↕5ft (1.5m) ↔6ft (2m)

Z5–9

SHRUB LARGE

Crinodendron hookerianum

LANTERN TREE An architectural evergreen shrub with stiff branches and narrow, lance-shaped dark green leaves. From late spring to early summer, lanternlike red flowers appear. Train against a sheltered wall. Best in West Coast gardens.

↕20ft (6m) ↔15ft (5m)

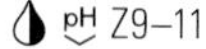 Z9–11

PERENNIAL MEDIUM

Dryopteris dilatata

BROAD BUCKLER FERN This deciduous or semievergreen fern forms a rosette of arching fronds with triangular to oval serrated segments and dark brown stems. It tolerates the dry soil next to hedges, if watered well in the first season.

↕3ft (1m) ↔18in (45cm)

 Z5–8

PERENNIAL SMALL

Epimedium perralderianum

BARRENWORT A semievergreen perennial with large, toothed, glossy, heart-shaped dark green leaves. Airy spikes of small, bright yellow pendent flowers form on wiry stalks in spring before new foliage appears. An effective ground cover in deep shade.

↕12in (30cm) ↔18in (45cm)

 Z5–8

PERENNIAL MEDIUM

Lamium galeobdolon

YELLOW ARCHANGEL A vigorous, mat-forming evergreen perennial with creeping stems of oval, silver-marked dark green leaves and spikes of brown-spotted yellow summer flowers. 'Hermann's Pride' (above) is a less aggressive spreader in gardens.

↕24in (60cm) ↔indefinite

Z4–8

PERENNIAL SMALL

Lamium maculatum

SPOTTED DEADNETTLE A mat-forming semievergreen perennial with variegated midgreen foliage and hooded flower spikes from late spring to summer. 'White Nancy' (above) bears white flowers above silver leaves. Considered invasive in some areas.

↕6in (15cm) ↔3ft (1m)

Z4–8

PERENNIAL LARGE

Macleaya microcarpa

PLUME POPPY An upright perennial with large, deeply lobed gray-green leaves, white beneath. In summer, sprays of tiny buff-pink flowers form on tall stems above the foliage. Grow it near the rear of a bed in light shade only.

↕8ft (2.5m) ↔4ft (1.2m)

Z4–9

BULB MEDIUM

Narcissus 'Actaea'

DAFFODIL This late-spring-flowering perennial bulb bears narrow, strap-shaped gray-green leaves and white flowers with shallow, red-rimmed yellow cups. Plant the bulbs in groups close to a partly shaded wall, fence, or hedge in fall.

↕16in (40cm)

(!) Z3–8

SHRUB MEDIUM

Paeonia delavayi

TREE PEONY This is an upright deciduous shrub with deeply lobed dark green leaves that are blue-green beneath. It produces nodding, cup-shaped dark red flowers in late spring. Plant it next to a wall or fence.

↕↔6ft (2m)

Z4–8

PERENNIAL SMALL

Pulmonaria officinalis

LUNGWORT This semievergreen perennial bears oval, pointed green leaves with white spots and clusters of funnel-shaped pink, blue, or white flowers in spring. It is shade- and drought-tolerant. 'Sissinghurst White' (above) has white flowers.

↕12in (30cm) ↔24in (60cm)

Z4–8

PERENNIAL SMALL

Saxifraga 'Aureopunctata'

LONDON PRIDE A low-growing perennial that forms rosettes of mid- to dark green- and yellow-variegated leaves. From late spring to early summer, masses of star-shaped, tiny pink flowers appear. Grow it at the front of a bed.

↕12in (30cm) ↔indefinite

Z6–7

PERENNIAL MEDIUM

Tolmiea menziesii

PIGGYBACK PLANT This semievergreen perennial has textured, ivy-shaped green leaves and spikes of nodding, tubular greenish yellow flowers in spring. 'Taff's Gold' (above) has cream and green variegated foliage.

↕24in (60cm) ↔6ft (2m)

Z6–9 (N)

PERENNIAL MEDIUM

Tricyrtis formosana

TOAD LILY This upright perennial produces dark green leaves with purplish green spots. Star-shaped, purple-spotted cream flowers appear from late summer to early fall. Grow it in the shelter of a wall in full or part shade.

↕32in (80cm) ↔18in (45cm)

Z6–9

PERENNIAL MEDIUM

Uvularia grandiflora

BELLWORT This clump-forming perennial has lance-shaped leaves and clusters of long, bell-shaped, yellow mid- to late spring flowers with slightly twisted petals that hang from slender stems. It is useful for deep shade beside walls and hedges.

↕24in (60cm) ↔12in (30cm)

Z4–9 (N)

SHRUB MEDIUM

Viburnum acerifolium

MAPLELEAF VIBURNUM This upright deciduous shrub has corrugated, jagged-edged green leaves that turn orange, red, and purple in fall. Clusters of small creamy white early summer flowers are followed by berries that ripen to purple-black.

↕6ft (2m) ↔4ft (1.2m)

Z4–8 (N)

SHRUB LARGE

Viburnum x *bodnantense*

BODNANT VIBURNUM An upright deciduous shrub with bronze leaves that turn dark green. From late fall to early spring, clusters of sweetly scented pink to white-pink flowers appear on bare branches. 'Dawn' (above) has dark pink buds and pink flowers.

↕10ft (3m) ↔6ft (2m)

(!) Z5–8

OTHER SUGGESTIONS

Perennials

Anemone canadensis (N) • *Asarum canadense* (N) • *Asarum splendens* 'Quicksilver' • *Bletilla striata* • *Disporum flavens* • *Dryopteris erythrosora* • *Epimedium grandiflorum* • *Geranium* 'Johnson's Blue' • *Geranium phaeum* 'Variegatum' • *Geranium* ROZANNE • *Meehania cordata* (N)

Bulbs

Allium 'Purple Sensation' • *Caladium* 'Carolyn Whorton' • *Narcissus* 'February Gold' • *Narcissus* 'Jetfire' • *Nectaroscordum siculum*

Shrubs

Chaenomeles x *superba* 'Crimson and Gold' • *Euphorbia amygdaloides* var. *robbiae* • *Forsythia* x *intermedia* • *Lindera benzoin* (N) • *Viburnum lentago* (N)

Plants for walls, fences, and vertical surfaces

Plants that scramble up vertical surfaces are chiefly useful in small gardens where they bolster color and interest while taking up little ground space.

Many climbers and shrubs prefer their roots shaded, while their stems clamber or are trained toward the sun. Clematis are a perfect example, and most are happy if their top growth can bathe in sunlight for a few hours each day in summer. Some clematis, including 'Niobe', bloom on north-facing walls, while others like 'Nelly Moser' prefer shade as the sun can bleach out their subtle flower colors. Deep shade is not a problem for natural forest dwellers, such as Virginia creeper and Boston ivy, while those used to life on the edge of a woodland, like hydrangea and honeysuckle need sunshine for part of the day.

CLIMBER MEDIUM

Clematis alpina
ALPINE CLEMATIS A deciduous climber with divided midgreen leaves. From early- to late spring, it bears lantern-shaped blue, pink, or white flowers, depending on the variety, followed by fluffy silvery seedheads. Keep the roots shaded.
↕10ft (3m)
Z4–9

CLIMBER LARGE

***Clematis* 'Bill MacKenzie'**
CLEMATIS A deciduous climber with dark green leaves and bell-shaped, waxy yellow flowers that appear from midsummer to late fall. The blooms are followed by fluffy seedheads. Requires a large support. Cut back in late winter or early spring.
↕22ft (7m)
Z5–9

CLIMBER MEDIUM

Clematis cirrhosa
EARLY VIRGIN'S-BOWER This evergreen climber has jagged-edged green leaves. From late winter to early spring, it produces small, bell-shaped cream flowers that are spotted red inside. Provide a sturdy support and a sheltered site; shade the roots.
↕10ft (3m)
Z7–11

CLIMBER LARGE

Clematis montana
HIMALAYAN CLEMATIS A deciduous climber with divided midgreen foliage. From late spring to early summer, it bears numerous scented white blooms with yellow centers. Provide a large support, such as a tree, large wall, or pergola.
↕40ft (12m)
Z6–9

CLIMBER MEDIUM

***Clematis* 'Nelly Moser'**
CLEMATIS This medium-sized deciduous climber has dark green leaves. In early summer, it produces large rose-mauve blooms, with a carmine stripe on each petal, followed by globular seedheads. Trim lightly after flowering if needed.
↕10ft (3m)
Z4–9

CLIMBER MEDIUM

***Clematis* 'Niobe'**
CLEMATIS This is a deciduous climber with dark green leaves. Throughout summer, it produces masses of velvety, deep red single flowers that have contrasting yellow anthers. Trim lightly after flowering if needed.
↕10ft (3m)
Z4–9

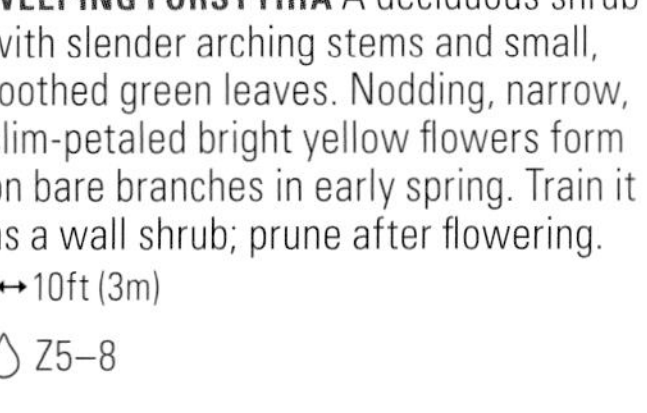

SHRUB LARGE

Forsythia suspensa

WEEPING FORSYTHIA A deciduous shrub with slender arching stems and small, toothed green leaves. Nodding, narrow, slim-petaled bright yellow flowers form on bare branches in early spring. Train it as a wall shrub; prune after flowering.

↕↔10ft (3m)

Z5–8

CLIMBER LARGE

Holboellia coriacea

SAUSAGE VINE This evergreen climber has dark green leaves divided into three leaflets. Sausage-shaped purple seedpods follow the clusters of fragrant pale purple male and greenish white female spring flowers. Provide shelter in colder areas.

↕15ft (5m)

Z9–11

CLIMBER MEDIUM

Clematis 'White Swan'

CLEMATIS This large deciduous clematis produces divided green foliage and nodding, open bell-shaped white flowers from late spring to early summer. Grow it on wires or through a large shrub. Prune after flowering.

↕10ft (3m)

Z4–9

CLIMBER LARGE

Hydrangea anomala subsp. *petiolaris*

CLIMBING HYDRANGEA A self-clinging deciduous climber with woody stems and rounded dark green leaves. In summer, it bears flattened white flower heads. Grow against a support, such as a fence or wall.

↕50ft (15m)

Z4–8

SHRUB LARGE

Itea virginica

VIRGINIA SWEETSPIRE This spreading shrub has arching stems that bear oval, spiny dark green leaves. From midsummer to early fall, it produces decorative greenish white racemes. Grow dense suckering colonies against wall.

↕10ft (3m) ↔5ft (1.5m)

pH Z5–9 Ⓝ

CLIMBER MEDIUM

Jasminum humile

ITALIAN JASMINE An evergreen shrub with glossy green leaves divided into leaflets and fragrant, tubular yellow flower clusters from early spring to early summer. Grow in a sheltered site. 'Revolutum' (above) is hardier than the species.

↕8ft (2.5m)

Z7–9

CLIMBER MEDIUM

Lathyrus odoratus

SWEET PEA Moderately fast-growing annual tendril climber, it has oval midgreen leaves with tendrils. From summer to early fall, scented flowers in shades of pink, blue, purple, or white appear. Dwarf non-climbing cultivars are also available.

↕10ft (3m)

CLIMBER LARGE

Lonicera x *brownii*

SCARLET TRUMPET HONEYSUCKLE This twining semievergreen or deciduous climber has rounded blue-green leaves. 'Dropmore Scarlet' (above) has unscented, tubular scarlet blooms from summer to early fall. Provide a large support.

↕12ft (4m)

💧 (!) Z4–8

CLIMBER LARGE

Lonicera periclymenum

WOODBINE A twining climber with dark green leaves. Red berries follow fragrant white to yellow summer flowers. Prune it in early spring. 'Serotina' (above) has creamy white flowers, streaked dark red-purple. Considered invasive in some areas.

↕22ft (7m)

💧 (!) Z5–9

CLIMBER LARGE

Lonicera x *tellmanniana*

TELLMANN'S HONEYSUCKLE A woody-stemmed twining deciduous climber with oval leaves; the upper leaves are joined and resemble saucers. Yellowish orange flowers are carried in clusters at the ends of shoots from late spring to summer.

↕15ft (5m)

💧 (!) Z7–9

CLIMBER LARGE

Parthenocissus henryana

CHINESE VIRGINIA CREEPER A vigorous self-clinging deciduous climber with palm-shaped, cream-veined dark green leaves. In fall, the foliage turns fiery crimson when blue-black berries also form. Ideal for a house wall; prefers partial shade.

↕30ft (10m) or more

💧 Z7–8

CLIMBER LARGE

Parthenocissus quinquefolia

VIRGINIA CREEPER This is a vigorous self-clinging deciduous climber grown for its rounded, divided green leaves that turn vibrant red and orange in fall. Provide it with a large support, such as a house wall or boundary fence.

↕50ft (15m) or more

💧 Z4–9 (N)

CLIMBER LARGE

Parthenocissus tricuspidata

BOSTON IVY A self-clinging deciduous climber with large, lobed green leaves that turn spectacular shades of crimson in fall. Use it to cover large expanses of a wall or boundary fence. Provide sturdy support. Considered invasive in some areas.

↕70ft (20m)

💧 Z4–8

CLIMBER LARGE

Rosa 'Albéric Barbier'

RAMBLING ROSE This vigorous semievergreen rambler rose has disease-resistant bright green leaves. Clusters of slightly fragrant, creamy white double blooms are produced in one flush and last several weeks during summer.

↕15ft (5m)

💧 Z5–9

CLIMBER MEDIUM

Rosa CONSTANCE SPRY

ENGLISH SHRUB ROSE This rose has grayish green leaves and numerous large, bowl-shaped, pink double flowers, with a rich myrrhlike scent, which appear for about a month during summer. Add a mulch of organic matter each spring.

↕6ft (2m)

💧 Z4–9

CLIMBER LARGE

Schizophragma integrifolium

CHINESE HYDRANGEA VINE This large self-clinging deciduous climber has heart-shaped or oval green leaves and clusters of tiny blooms with petal-like bracts in summer. Grow it against a large support.

↕40ft (12m)

Z5–9

CLIMBER LARGE

Solanum crispum

CHILEAN POTATO TREE A scrambling semievergreen climber with oval green leaves and fragrant, yellow-eyed violet-blue flower clusters from summer to fall. Grow in a warm lightly shaded spot. 'Glasnevin' (above) has purple-blue flowers.

↕20ft (6m)

(!) Z9–11

CLIMBER LARGE

Rosa 'Mermaid'

HYBRID BRACTEATA ROSE A slow-growing climbing rose with disease-resistant, glossy green foliage. Flowering repeatedly from summer to fall, it bears flat, primrose-yellow single blooms. The stems have large hooked thorns; plant it to deter intruders.

↕20ft (6m)

Z7–9

CLIMBER LARGE

Rosa 'New Dawn'

CLIMBING ROSE This climbing rose has disease-resistant, glossy green foliage and flowers repeatedly from summer to fall, producing clusters of fragrant, pale pink double flowers. Deadhead regularly to prolong the display.

↕15ft (5m)

Z5–9

SHRUB LARGE

Stachyurus praecox

STACHYURUS A deciduous shrub with purplish red shoots and bell-shaped, pale greenish yellow blooms that hang from bare stems from late winter to early spring. The slim dark green leaves appear soon after. Train against a wall or fence.

↕12ft (4m) ↔10ft (3m)

pH Z6–8

CLIMBER LARGE

Trachelospermum jasminoides

STAR JASMINE This twining evergreen climber has clusters of sweetly fragrant white flowers in summer. Its glossy dark green leaves turn bronze in fall and winter, and it is ideal for partly shaded walls.

↕28ft (9m)

Z8–10

CLIMBER MEDIUM

Tropaeolum speciosum

FLAME CREEPER A perennial climber with twining stems and rounded blue-green leaves divided into oval leaflets. In summer, it bears scarlet flowers followed by spherical bright blue fruits. Best in fertile soil; it tolerates light shade only.

↕10ft (3m)

pH Z8–11

OTHER SUGGESTIONS

Climbers

Aristolochia macrophylla (N) • *Aristolochia tomentosa* (N) • *Berchemia scandens* (N) • *Celastrus scandens* (N) • *Clematis macropetala* • *Clematis macropetala* 'Blue Bird' • *Clematis montana* 'Freda' • *Clematis tangutica* • *Decumaria Barbara* (N) • *Fallopia baldschuanica* • *Ficus pumila* • *Hedera colchica* 'Sulphur Heart' • *Holboellia angustifolia* • *Lonicera flava* (N) • *Lonicera* x *italica* HARLEQUIN • *Lonicera sempervirens* (N) • *Menispermum canadense* (N) • *Schizophragma hydrangeoides* 'Moonlight' • *Wisteria frutescens* (N)

Plants for cracks in walls and paving

Dull walls and paved patios in shady yards can be transformed into decorative features with leafy ferns or small flowering plants between the cracks.

While some plants such as small ferns may seed themselves in dry stone walls, creeping campanulas will grow in the most inhospitable of places, their stems of small blue flowers enlivening structures in deep shade. Shady paving offers a good home for a range of pretty saxifrages, and the golden-yellow flowers of fleabane are perfect for lightening paving or walls in gloomy gardens. For year-round color in shaded walls and patios, opt for evergreen bugleweed, the Hart's tongue fern, and creeping phlox.

PERENNIAL SMALL

Alchemilla alpina

ALPINE LADY'S MANTLE A mound-forming perennial with lobed, white-edged green leaves, silky-haired beneath, and greenish yellow summer-flower spikes. Grow in cracks in walls and paving with moisture. Cut back untidy foliage and blooms.

↕6in (15cm) ↔24in (60cm) or more

Z3–7

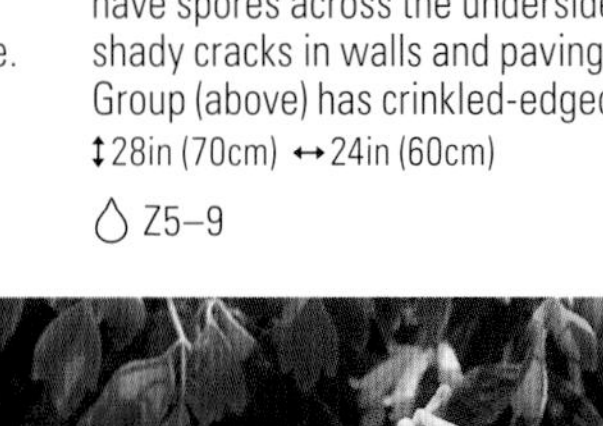

PERENNIAL MEDIUM

Asplenium scolopendrium

HART'S TONGUE FERN This evergreen fern has an upright rosette of tongue-shaped, long, leathery bright green fronds that have spores across the undersides. Plant in shady cracks in walls and paving. Crispum Group (above) has crinkled-edged leaves.

↕28in (70cm) ↔24in (60cm)

Z5–9

PERENNIAL SMALL

Athyrium niponicum var. *pictum*

JAPANESE PAINTED FERN This deciduous fern has deeply divided, purple- and silver-tinted gray-green leaves. Plant it in damp shaded paving or walls. Thrives in deep shade.

↕12in (30cm) ↔indefinite

Z4–8

PERENNIAL SMALL

Ajuga reptans 'Atropurpurea'

BUGLEWEED This mat-forming evergreen perennial has creeping stems of bronze-purple leaves and short spikes of small deep blue blooms from late spring to early summer. Plant in a shady paving or cracks in a wall. Considered invasive in some areas.

↕6in (15cm) ↔3ft (1m)

Z3–9

PERENNIAL SMALL

Campanula poscharskyana

SERBIAN BELLFLOWER This spreading perennial forms low mounds of round, serrated-edged midgreen leaves. Starry violet flowers appear on leafy stems from summer to early fall. Use it to cascade from walls or spread between paving.

↕6in (15cm) ↔indefinite

Z3–8

PERENNIAL SMALL

Corydalis lutea

YELLOW CORYDALIS This evergreen perennial forms a mound of delicate, ferny gray-green leaves. Slender yellow flowers with spurred petals appear from late spring to summer. Sprinkle the seeds in paving and on top of stone walls.

↕↔12in (30cm)

Z5–7

PERENNIAL SMALL

Erigeron aureus

FLEABANE A clump-forming perennial with small, spoon-shaped, hairy gray-green leaves and large, golden-yellow daisy-like blooms in summer. Plant it in cracks in walls and paving; tolerates light shade only. 'Canary Bird' (above) has pale blooms.

↕4in (10cm) ↔6in (15cm)

Z5–8 Ⓝ

PERENNIAL SMALL

Geranium asphodeloides

CRANESBILL A spreading deciduous perennial with small, deeply cut rounded leaves and masses of starry, magenta-veined white or light pink flowers in early summer. Grow it between paving stones or in cracks in walls in part shade.

↕↔12in (30cm)

Z6–9

PERENNIAL SMALL

Phlox subulata

CREEPING PHLOX This evergreen perennial has narrow, pointed green leaves. From late spring to early summer, it bears numerous starry flowers in shades of purple, red, pink, lilac, or white, depending on the variety. It is ideal for cracks in walls in dappled shade.

↕6in (15cm) ↔20in (50cm)

Z3–8 Ⓝ

PERENNIAL SMALL

Geranium dalmaticum

DALMATIAN GERANIUM An evergreen, except in severe winters, mat-forming perennial with aromatic, dissected, glossy dark green leaves and round shell-pink flowers in summer. It grows taller in shade and is good for paving cracks.

↕4in (10cm) or more ↔8in (20cm)

Z5–7

PERENNIAL SMALL

Geranium sanguineum

BLOODY CRANESBILL This hummock-forming spreading perennial has deeply dissected dark green foliage and abundant round magenta-pink summer flowers. Use it to fill gaps in paving or walls; deadhead regularly to prolong flowering.

↕10in (25cm) ↔12in (30cm) or more

Z4–8

PERENNIAL SMALL

Mentha requienii

CORSICAN MINT This mat-forming semievergreen perennial has diminutive rounded apple-green leaves that emit a peppermint scent when crushed. Tiny lavender-purple flowers appear in summer. Grow it in full or part shade in paving.

↕½in (1cm) ↔indefinite

Z6–9

PERENNIAL SMALL

Saxifraga fortunei

SAXIFRAGE This semievergreen perennial forms rosettes of rounded, frilly green leaves that are red beneath. In fall, it produces airy sprays of tiny, starry white flowers. Grow it in cracks in paving in part or deep shade.

↕↔12in (30cm)

Z7–9

PERENNIAL SMALL

Saxifraga Southside Seedling Group

SAXIFRAGE This evergreen perennial has pale green leafy rosettes, which die back after flowering, and open, cup-shaped, red-banded white blooms from late spring to early summer. Plant on wall tops or paving.

↕12in (30cm) ↔8in (20cm)

Z4–6

PERENNIAL SMALL

Silene schafta

AUTUMN CATCHFLY A spreading perennial with narrow, lance-shaped green leaves. From late summer to late fall, it bears small upright sprays of starry rose-magenta flowers with notched petals. Grow in walls or paving.

↕10in (25cm) ↔12in (30cm)

Z4–8

PERENNIAL SMALL

Viola odorata

SWEET VIOLET This small, spreading semievergreen perennial forms loose mats of heart-shaped toothed-edged leaves and flat-faced, fragrant violet or white flowers from late winter to early spring. Leave it to spread through paving cracks in part shade.

↕8in (20cm) ↔12in (30cm)

Z6–8

PERENNIAL SMALL

Viola sororia

BLUE VIOLET This small perennial has rounded dark green leaves and dainty blue flowers in summer. 'Freckles' (above) has white flowers marked with violet-purple speckles. Like most violas, it self-seeds in cracks in pavings and walls.

↕5in (12cm) ↔6in (15cm)

Z3–9 Ⓝ

OTHER SUGGESTIONS

Perennials

Aquilegia alpina • *Anemone sylvestris* • *Asplenium trichomanes* Ⓝ • *Campanula carpatica* • *Campanula garganica* • *Chrysogonum virginianum* Ⓝ • *Dodecatheon meadia* f. *album* Ⓝ • *Galium odoratum* • *Geranium cinereum* 'Ballerina' • *Herniaria glabra* • *Leptinella squalida* 'Platt's Black' • *Oxalis enneaphylla* • *Penstemon hirsutus* 'Pygmaeus' Ⓝ *Phlox* 'Chattahoochee' • *Sanguinaria canadensis* 'Multiplex' Ⓝ • *Woodsia obtusa* Ⓝ

Bulbs

Narcissus bulbocodium • *Narcissus* 'Pipit' • *Scilla siberica*

Shrubs

Juniperus squamata 'Blue Star'

Plants for patios, balconies, and windowsills

While most colorful bedding plants require sun to bloom, shady patio and balcony displays can also be stunning displays of blooms and foliage.

Many annuals will flower in light shade, but if your area is darker, choose fuchsia, impatiens, and wishbone flower for summerlong displays. For fall and winter troughs on windowsills, include some young shrubs, such as skimmia and wintergreen, which produce pretty buds and berries and can be planted in pots of their own when they outgrow their first home; shrubs can be kept small by clipping. In fall, squeeze daffodil and grape hyacinth bulbs between the shrubs for a burst of color in early spring. If you have space, add a few large shrubs in bold containers to lend permanent structure to your design.

PERENNIAL SMALL

Begonia Olympia Series

WAX BEGONIA This is an evergreen perennial, often sold as annual summer bedding. It produces glossy green leaves and small white, pink, or red flowers with golden eyes. Plant it in containers and baskets of all-purpose potting soil.

↕↔ 10in (25cm)

Z10–11

PERENNIAL SMALL

Bellis perennis

ENGLISH DAISY This evergreen perennial bears rosettes of spoon-shaped dark green leaves and white daisies in late spring. Tasso Series (above) has pink, white, or red, pompomlike flowers. Plant in containers, baskets, and windowboxes in potting mix.

↕↔ 8in (20cm)

Z4–8

ANNUAL/BIENNIAL MEDIUM

Calendula officinalis

POT MARIGOLD A bushy annual with lance-shaped, pale green aromatic leaves and daisy-like single or double flowers in shades of yellow and orange from spring to fall. Sow seeds directly in containers of all-purpose potting soil.

↕↔ 24in (60cm)

SHRUB LARGE

Camellia x *williamsii*

CAMELLIA This evergreen shrub has oval, pointed, glossy bright green leaves and, in spring, large clusters of pink or white blooms. Varieties include 'Donation' (above) with pink semidouble flowers. Plant it in large pots of acidic soil mix.

↕ 15ft (5m) ↔ 8ft (2.5m)

pH Z7–9

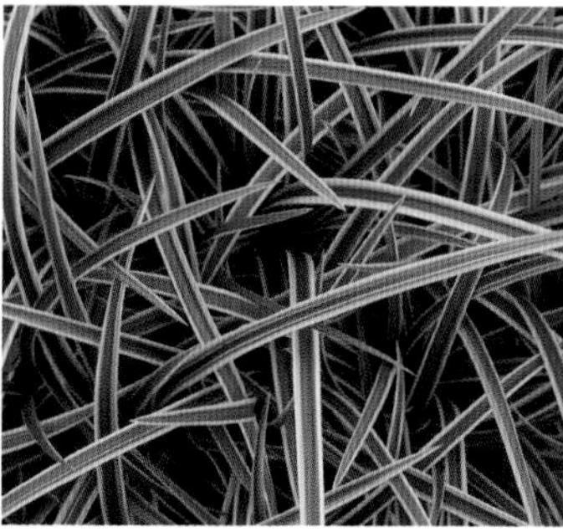

PERENNIAL MEDIUM

Carex 'Ice Dance'

SEDGE An evergreen perennial sedge, featuring mounds of grassy green leaves, with creamy white margins and small white spring flowers. Plant it in containers and windowboxes in soil-based potting mix; water well.

↕ 24in (60cm) ↔ 30in (75cm)

Z5–9

PERENNIAL SMALL

Carex oshimensis

JAPANESE SEDGE This evergreen perennial has glossy, arching, cream-striped dark green leaves and insignificant flower spikes in summer. Yellow-striped 'Evergold' (above) gives bright winter interest in containers and windowboxes in soil-based potting mix.

↕↔ 8in (20cm)

Z5–9

PERENNIAL SMALL

Carex siderosticha

BROAD-LEAVED SEDGE A deciduous or semievergreen perennial with arching, grassy green leaves and small, brown spring-flower spikes. Plant in containers or baskets of soil-based potting mix. 'Variegata' (above) has cream-edged foliage.

↕ 12in (30cm) ↔ 16in (40cm)

Z5–9

SHRUB MEDIUM

Clethra alnifolia

SUMMERSWEET This deciduous shrub has oval, serrated midgreen leaves. From late summer to early fall, it produces spikes of fragrant, bell-shaped white flowers. Plant it in a large pot of acidic soil mix in full or part shade.

↕↔ 8ft (2.5m)

Z3–9 Ⓝ

BULB SMALL

Cyclamen coum

HARDY CYCLAMEN A dwarf perennial bulb with rounded, silver-marbled dark green leaves and deep pink blooms with a purple blotch at the base of each petal in late winter. Goes dormant in summer heat. Plant in soil-based potting mix with added grit.

↕ 4in (10cm)

(!) Z5–9

BULB SMALL

Cyclamen hederifolium

IVY-LEAVED CYCLAMEN A dwarf perennial with silvery-green patterned leaves that appear just after the fall flowers. The pink petals are darker at the mouth. Ideal for containers filled with gritty soil-based potting mix. Becomes dormant in summer.

↕4in (10cm) ↔6in (15cm)

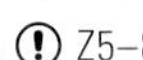 Z5–8

PERENNIAL SMALL

Dichondra argentea

SILVER PONYFOOT An evergreen perennial, 'Silver Falls' (above) is sold as bedding plant. With its cascading silver stems of round, shiny silvery green foliage, it is ideal for a windowbox or basket. Tolerates light shade only; plant in all-purpose potting soil.

↕20in (50cm) ↔indefinite

Z10–12

SHRUB SMALL

Fuchsia 'Genii'

FUCHSIA A bushy deciduous shrub with oval, pointed gold-green foliage. It bears pendent, cerise and purple single or double flowers from summer to fall. Plant it in a container of all-purpose potting soil. Shelter from cold drying winds.

↕↔30in (75cm)

Z8–10

SHRUB SMALL

Fuchsia 'Tom Thumb'

FUCHSIA This dwarf deciduous shrub produces oval dark green leaves. From summer to fall, numerous pendent, bell-shaped red and mauve-blue flowers appear. Grow it in windowboxes, containers, and baskets in soil-based potting mix.

↕↔20in (50cm)

Z9–11

BULB MEDIUM

Galanthus nivalis

SNOWDROP A perennial bulb with grasslike green foliage and nodding white flowers that appear in late winter. Plant it with other early-flowering bulbs and violas in containers or windowboxes filled with soil-based potting mix.

↕6in (15cm)

Z3–8

SHRUB SMALL

Gaultheria procumbens

WINTERGREEN A dwarf evergreen shrub with oval leathery leaves that are tinged red in winter. Scarlet berries follow small, pink-flushed white summer flowers. Plant in a winter basket or windowbox in acidic soil mix. Best in cooler areas and moist soil.

↕6in (15cm) ↔indefinite

pH Z3–8 Ⓝ

PERENNIAL LARGE

Gaura lindheimeri

WAND FLOWER An upright perennial with small, lance-shaped green leaves and tall slim stems dotted with starry, butterfly-shaped, pink-budded white flowers that appear all summer. Grow it in large containers of soil-based potting mix.

↕5ft (1.5m) ↔3ft (1m)

Z5–9 Ⓝ

SHRUB SMALL

Heliotropium arborescens

HELIOTROPE A bushy evergreen shrub, grown as an annual, with oval, crinkled dark green leaves and clusters of fragrant purple or white flowers throughout summer. Plant it in containers of all-purpose potting soil near seating or paths.

↕↔18in (45cm)

Z10–11

PERENNIAL SMALL

Heuchera 'Plum Pudding'

CORAL BELLS An evergreen perennial with rounded, lobed and veined maroon-purple leaves. It bears slim stems of small white flowers in summer. Grow it as a foil for colorful flowers in windowboxes and containers filled with soil-based potting mix.

↕20in (50cm) ↔12in (30cm)

Z4–9 Ⓝ

PERENNIAL SMALL

x *Heucherella* 'Tapestry'

FOAMY BELLS This evergreen or semievergreen perennial has deeply lobed green foliage with purple centers and veins and sprays of small pink flowers in early summer. Plant it in windowboxes or pots in a sheltered spot. Remove spent blooms.

↕↔12in (30cm)

Z4–9

CLIMBER MEDIUM

Lathyrus odoratus

SWEET PEA This annual climbs by tendrils. It has divided midgreen leaves and scented pink, blue, purple, or white flowers from summer to early fall. Plant it in large containers of potting mix using a tripod support. Deadhead regularly.

↕ up to 10ft (3m)

BULB MEDIUM

Narcissus 'Jack Snipe'

DAFFODIL This early- to mid-spring-flowering dwarf perennial bulb has narrow dark green leaves and creamy white flowers with short yellow cups. Plant in groups in containers and windowboxes filled with all-purpose potting soil.

↕ 9in (23cm)

Z4–9

PERENNIAL SMALL

Impatiens New Guinea Group

NEW GUINEA IMPATIENS This shrubby perennial, grown as an annual, has glossy, lance-shaped green leaves and vibrant pink, red, lavender, and white flowers that appear in summer. It is suitable for containers filled with all-purpose potting soil.

↕ 14in (35cm) ↔ 12in (30cm)

Z10–12

PERENNIAL SMALL

Lobelia erinus

TRAILING LOBELIA A tender perennial, grown as an annual, with branching stems of green leaves and numerous tiny blue, pink, or white flowers from summer to fall. Trailing and bushy varieties are available. Grow in potting mix; water daily in summer.

↕ 8in (20cm) ↔ 6in (15cm)

Z10–11

BULB MEDIUM

Narcissus 'Tete-a-tete'

DAFFODIL This spring-flowering perennial bulb has strap-shaped leaves. It is a dwarf early-flowering form bearing bright golden-yellow blooms. Plant it in containers, windowboxes, and baskets filled with all-purpose potting soil.

↕ up to 12in (30cm)

Z4–9

BULB MEDIUM

Muscari armeniacum

GRAPE HYACINTH A spring-flowering perennial bulb with narrow grassy leaves and short spikes of small, fragrant, bell-shaped blue flowers held in cone-shaped clusters. Combine with other spring bulbs in containers of gritty soil-based potting mix.

↕ 8in (20cm)

Z4–8

ANNUAL/BIENNIAL SMALL

Nemophila maculata

FIVE-SPOT A fast-growing spreading annual with lobed leaves. It bears small, bowl-shaped white flowers with purple petal tips throughout summer, provided it is watered well. Grow it in potting mix as edging in mixed containers. May self-sow.

↕↔ 12in (30cm)

PERENNIAL SMALL

Impatiens walleriana

BUSY LIZZIE This evergreen perennial, grown as an annual, has oval green leaves and a proliferation of rounded blooms in shades of red, pink, purple, violet, orange, or white from spring to fall. Plant it in containers of potting soil.

↕↔ up to 12in (30cm)

Z10–11

BULB MEDIUM

Narcissus 'Hawera'

DAFFODIL This perennial bulb has upright, straplike green foliage and is grown for its small, nodding yellow flowers held on upright stems in mid-spring. Best in light shade only; plant it in containers, baskets, and windowboxes.

↕ 6in (15cm)

Z4–9

PERENNIAL SMALL

Nicotiana Domino Series

FLOWERING TOBACCO These short-lived perennials, grown as annuals, have sticky midgreen leaves and heads of long, tubular white summer flowers. Plant in large pots and support the stems; plant where the evening fragrance can be enjoyed.

↕ 18in (45cm) ↔ 16in (40cm)

Z10–11

PERENNIAL LARGE

Nicotiana sylvestris

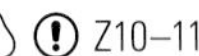

FLOWERING TOBACCO This tall perennial, grown as an annual, has long, sticky midgreen leaves. Heads of long, tubular white flowers appear in summer. Plant it in large containers of potting soil, where you can enjoy its evening fragrance.
↕5ft (1.5m) ↔30in (75cm)

💧 (!) Z10–11

PERENNIAL SMALL

Ophiopogon planiscapus 'Nigrescens'

MONDO GRASS An clump-forming evergreen perennial with leathery, grasslike black leaves. Black berries follow the bell-shaped, white or mauve summer blooms. Plant in containers of soil-based potting mix.
↕9in (23cm) ↔12in (30cm)

💧 Z6–10

PERENNIAL SMALL

Petunia Surfinia Series

PETUNIA This group of trailing petunias has green foliage and numerous trumpet-shaped pink, purple, red, white, and yellow flowers. Grown as annuals, these perennials can be used to trail from windowboxes and baskets of potting soil. Plant in light shade.
↕16in (40cm) ↔3ft (1m)

💧 Z10–11

SHRUB MEDIUM

Rhododendron yakushimanum

YAKUSHIMA RHODODENDRON A medium-sized compact evergreen shrub with leathery green leaves that are felted beneath and bell-shaped, pink-budded white flowers in spring. Grow it in acidic soil mix; water in dry periods.
↕↔ up to 6ft (2m)

💧 pH (!) Z5–8

ANNUAL/BIENNIAL SMALL

Phlox drummondii

ANNUAL PHLOX A bushy annual with neat green leaves and clusters of small pink, red, purple, blue, and white flowers, which appear throughout summer. Use it to edge a container display, and grow it in containers of potting soil.
↕18in (45cm) ↔10in (25cm)

💧 (N)

SHRUB MEDIUM

Skimmia japonica

JAPANESE SKIMMIA This evergreen shrub has oval mid- to dark green leaves. Red berries on females (above) follow the white spring-flower clusters. Plant in soil-based potting mix. Performs best in West Coast gardens.
↕↔ up to 5ft (1.5m) in a pot

💧 (!) Z6–8

SHRUB LARGE

Physocarpus opulifolius

NINEBARK A deciduous shrub with lobed green, yellow, or purple-red leaves. Brown fruits follow the domed clusters of pale pink summer blooms. Grow it in a large container of soil-based potting mix; prune after flowering.
↕up to 10ft (3m) ↔15ft (1.5m)

💧 Z3–7 (N)

ANNUAL/BIENNIAL SMALL

Torenia fournieri

WISHBONE FLOWER A bushy annual with serrated light green leaves and, from summer to early fall, flared blooms with pale lilac and blue-purple petals and white and yellow throats. Plant in a shaded windowbox in all-purpose potting soil.
↕12in (30cm) ↔8in (20cm)

💧

PERENNIAL SMALL

Primula Crescendo Series

POLYANTHUS PRIMROSE This perennial, grown as an annual, has rosettes of corrugated dark green leaves. From winter to spring, it bears clusters of yellow-eyed flowers in many colors. Plant it in containers of potting mix.
↕↔8in (20cm)

💧 Z5–7

OTHER SUGGESTIONS

Perennials

Ipomoea batatas 'Blackie' • *Oxalis* Charmed Series • *Primula vulgaris* 'Miss Indigo' • *Solenostemon scutellariodes* • *Sutera* SNOWSTORM GIANT SNOWFLAKE • *Teucrium chamaedrys*

Bulbs

Caladium 'Rosebud' • *Cyclamen persicum* • *Galanthus elwesii*

Shrubs, trees, and climbers

Acer palmatum 'Bloodgood' • *Buxus sempervirens* 'Suffruticosa' • *Choisya ternata* SUNDANCE (N) • *Fatsia japonica* • *Fuchsia* 'Mrs Popple' • *Hebe* 'Red Edge' • *Hydrangea* Endless Summer Series • *Itea virginica* 'Merlot' (N) • *Rhododendron impeditum* • *Vaccinium angustifolium* (N)

Plant focus: begonias

Sporting colorful flowers and patterned leaves, begonias are ideal plants for shady summer container and bedding displays.

MOST BEGONIAS ARE TENDER PERENNIALS, grown in shady summer gardens. The rex and rhizomatous forms, with their colorful, intricately patterned foliage, create dramatic displays in pots. The trailing pendula group offers both foliage and flower interest, and makes excellent hanging basket plants, while the taller, upright cane-forming hybrids and large-flowered tuberous types are perfect for larger summer containers. The compact Semperflorens begonias, often sold as bedding, produce a frill of colorful flowers around beds and borders. Most begonias thrive in warm, sheltered, shady gardens; where temperatures dip below 50°F (10°C) for long periods in summer, grow plants in a sunroom or indoors. Many dislike wet soil, so avoid overwatering them. Apply a balanced fertilizer weekly when plants are in full growth. Water evergreens sparingly in winter and store the dormant tubers of deciduous plants in a cool, dry, frost-free place—repot in late spring and plant outside when the risk of frost has passed.

USING BEGONIAS

In cool areas, begonias are best grown on an outdoor windowsill where the heat of the building provides additional warmth and encourages the plants to bloom. Trailing begonias are suitable for hanging baskets and tall pots, but give them a sheltered position to prevent damage to the brittle leaves and stems. Keep plants well watered during summer.

Semperflorens begonias tolerate some sun and can be used as decorative edging plants or as the ingredients for a traditional bedding scheme.

Rex-cultorum begonias, with their large ornamental leaves, offer a textural contrast to colorful foliage plants, such as coleus, in a contemporary patio container display.

POPULAR BEGONIA SPECIES

Rex-cultorum begonias These perennials, mostly evergreens, have colorful foliage, which is often arranged on plants in a spiral pattern. Small inconspicuous flowers appear in spring.

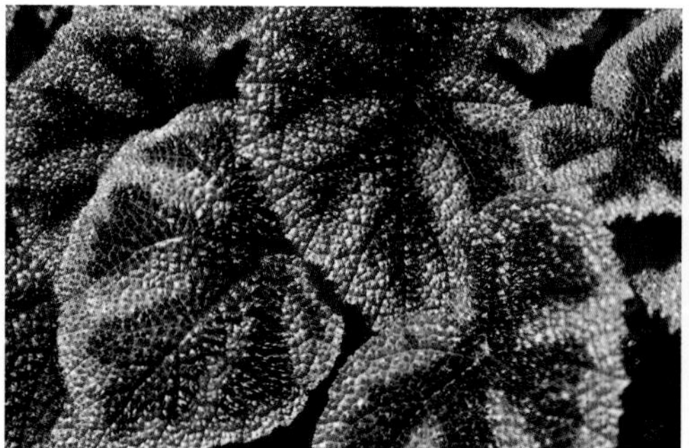

Rhizomatous begonias These are grown for their decorative, mostly evergreen leaves, which are often arranged in spirals, have unusual textures, and feature colorful markings.

Semperflorens begonias These compact, bushy evergreen perennials, often grown as annuals, have rounded, bronze or green leaves and small single or double summer flowers.

Tuberous begonias Either upright and bushy or trailing and pendulous, these perennials offer tear-shaped foliage and bright summer flowers from winter-dormant tubers.

Shrublike begonias Often grown as houseplants, these evergreens have ornamental leaves and small flowers from spring to summer. They can be grown outside in summer in warm areas.

Cane-stemmed begonias Tough, bamboo-like stems bear silver-spotted or splashed leaves, some finely cut or with wavy margins, and showy pink or white summer flowers.

Plants for productive patios

You'll struggle to create a productive patio in deep shade, but partial shade affords the cool growing conditions preferred by a number of leafy crops.

Lettuce, Swiss chard, arugula, herbs such as mint and parsley, and other leafy crops thrive in light shade. Fruit crops that ripen in light or dappled shade include blackberries, alpine strawberries, currants, and some apple varieties, so although the choice is not extensive, there are still plenty of options for a healthy harvest. Plant fruit trees and shrubs in large tubs of soil-based potting mix and replace the top layer with fresh potting mix with added all-purpose granular fertilizer each spring. Apart from peas and beans, which need big containers, vegetables and herbs will be happy in medium-sized containers of potting mix.

BULB MEDIUM

Chives

Allium schoenoprasum This herb forms a clump of upright, slender green leaves that have a mild onionlike flavor. Its fluffy pale pink pompom summer flowers can also be cropped. Plant it in windowboxes and containers of potting mix.

↕30cm (12in)

Z4–8

ANNUAL/BIENNIAL MEDIUM

Celeriac

Apium graveolens This crop is grown for its swollen roots that have a mild nutty celerylike flavor. Sow seeds in spring, and harvest baby roots in summer or mature crops in fall. In zones 7 and higher, plant in summer for a fall, winter, or spring crop.

↕3ft (1m) ↔18in (45cm)

ANNUAL/BIENNIAL SMALL

Land cress

Barbarea verna A low-growing annual, this alternative to watercress has pepper-flavored leaves. Sow seeds in windowboxes and pots in spring and summer; harvest the leaves and stems when large enough. Re-sow regularly; water and feed well.

↕↔12in (30cm)

ANNUAL/BIENNIAL SMALL

Swiss chard

Beta vulgaris This crop is grown for its leaves, which can be eaten raw or steamed, and its fleshy stems that are best cooked. Sow seeds in spring and harvest in summer. Ideal for containers and windowboxes; water regularly.

↕↔18in (45cm)

ANNUAL/BIENNIAL SMALL

Mustard greens

Brassica juncea Grown for its peppery leaves, which can be repeat-harvested when young or left to mature. Sow seeds in spring and summer. Grow in containers and windowboxes in light shade. Water well. Considered invasive in many areas.

↕↔12in (30cm)

ANNUAL/BIENNIAL SMALL

Kale

***Brassica oleracea* Acephala Group** This upright leafy crop is planted in summer and can be harvested from fall to winter. When grown in containers, it is best picked as individual leaves when required. Water well and stake if required.

↕↔18in (45cm)

ANNUAL/BIENNIAL SMALL

Mizuna

Brassica rapa* subsp. *nipposinica* var. *laciniata Sown from seed from spring to summer, this leaf crop has a peppery flavor. Harvest after a few weeks as a "cut-and-come-again" salad or cut whole plants at the base. Considered invasive in many areas.

↕↔6in (15cm)

PERENNIAL SMALL

Chicory

Cichorium intybus This green-leaved chicory has rounded heads of crisp bitter-tasting leaves. Planted in early summer, it can be harvested until spring, if protected. Grow in containers of potting mix; water well. Considered invasive in most areas.

↕↔12in (30cm) when harvested

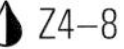 Z4–8

PERENNIAL SMALL

Radicchio

Cichorium intybus This red-leaved chicory forms rounded heads of crisp bitter-tasting leaves. Planted in early summer, it can be harvested until spring, if protected. Grow it in containers of potting mix; water well. Considered invasive in some areas.

↕↔12in (30cm) when harvested

Z4–8

ANNUAL/BIENNIAL SMALL

Cilantro

Coriandrum sativum This quick-growing annual herb has rounded, green aromatic leaves. The leaves, stems, and seeds can be used in cooking. Grown from seed, it is ideal for containers and windowboxes in light shade; water well to prevent bolting.

↕20in (50cm) ↔8in (20cm)

ANNUAL/BIENNIAL SMALL

Arugula

Eruca sativa This annual forms a rosette of long lobed leaves, which have a peppery flavor. Sow it directly in containers and windowboxes in spring and summer, and cut the leaves as required, leaving the base to regrow. Water well.

↕↔8in (20cm) when harvested

PERENNIAL LARGE

Fennel

Foeniculum vulgare This upright perennial bears aromatic fernlike leaves that taste of aniseed. Edible seeds follow the clusters of tiny yellow flowers. Grow it in large containers of soil-based potting mix in light shade. Considered invasive in some areas.

↕6ft (1.8m) ↔18in (45cm)

Z4–9

ANNUAL/BIENNIAL SMALL

Florence fennel

Foeniculum vulgare* var. *azoricum This crop is grown for its swollen, aniseed-flavored leaf stems that form a "bulb" at the base of the plant. Sow seeds in summer, harvest young if large enough, or leave to reach full-size. Can be invasive.

↕↔12in (30cm)

PERENNIAL SMALL

Alpine strawberries

Fragaria vesca Forming a low mound of toothed-edged leaves, this type of strawberry is ideal for containers. It bears small richly flavored fruits from early- to late summer. Water and feed plants regularly; best in light shade only.

↕12in (30cm) ↔indefinite

Z5–9 Ⓝ

ANNUAL/BIENNIAL SMALL

Lettuce

Lactuca sativa Suitable for cropping young as "cut-and-come-again" leaves or left to mature into full heads, lettuce comes in many colors and textures. Sow or plant in spring, and keep plants well watered. Best in light shade only.

↕↔12in (30cm)

TREE SMALL

Cooking apple

Malus domestica This tree bears fruits from late summer to fall. Buy plants on dwarfing rootstocks to restrict their size. Plant in a large container of soil-based potting mix; feed and water regularly from spring to summer. Best in light shade.

↕↔up to 8m (25ft)

Z4–8

TREE SMALL

Dessert apple

Malus domestica Many varieties are available, but choose one grafted onto a dwarfing rootstock to restrict its size. Ideal for large containers of soil-based potting mix; plant in light shade only. You may also need a pollenizer variety.

↕up to 20ft (6m) ↔up to 4m (12ft)

Z4–8

PERENNIAL MEDIUM

Lemon balm

Melissa officinalis This herb has toothed, textured green leaves that release a rich lemon scent when brushed. Remove the blooms in summer to encourage leaf growth. Grow in pots and windowboxes on its own. Considered invasive in some areas.

↕3ft (1m) ↔18in (45cm)

Z4–9

PERENNIAL SMALL

Peppermint

Mentha* x *piperita A spreading perennial with spikes of pink-purple summer blooms and textured green aromatic leaves used to flavor dishes or as an infusion to make tea. Plant in containers of soil-based potting mix. Considered invasive in many areas.

↕20in (50cm) ↔3ft (1m)

Z4–8

PERENNIAL SMALL

Spearmint

Mentha spicata This perennial has green, textured aromatic foliage and short spikes of pink summer blooms. Infuse the leaves to make tea or use to flavor dishes. Plant in a pot to prevent the roots from spreading. Considered invasive in most areas.

↕20in (50cm) ↔indefinite

Z4–7

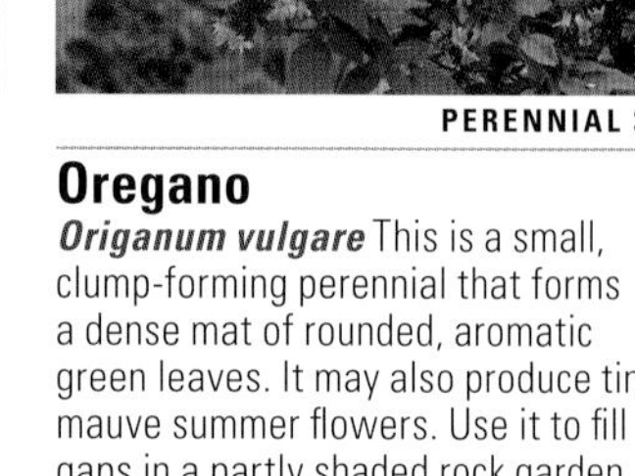

PERENNIAL SMALL

Oregano

Origanum vulgare This is a small, clump-forming perennial that forms a dense mat of rounded, aromatic green leaves. It may also produce tiny, mauve summer flowers. Use it to fill gaps in a partly shaded rock garden.

↕↔18in (45cm)

Z4–8

ANNUAL/BIENNIAL MEDIUM

Parsley

Petroselinum crispum This clump-forming biennial, best grown as an annual, has deeply divided, aromatic green leaves, which are commonly used for decorative edible garnishes and to flavor a wide range of dishes.

↕32in (80cm) ↔24in (60cm)

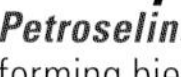

Z5–9

CLIMBER SMALL

Runner bean

Phaseolus coccineus This climbing bean bears long flattened green pods all summer. Harvest regularly, before the seeds swell, for the best crop. Provide tall supports, and water and feed well. Ideal for large containers in light shade.

↕6ft (1.8m)

ANNUAL/BIENNIAL MEDIUM

Garden pea

Pisum sativum These traditional podded peas crop from late spring to autumn when sown in spring or early summer. Plant in large containers in light shade and water well. Dwarf and climbing varieties are available; harvest regularly.

↕28in (70cm) ↔20in (50cm)

ANNUAL/BIENNIAL MEDIUM

Snow pea

Pisum sativum These peas are grown for their crisp flattened pods, which are produced from late spring to fall, and are eaten whole. Sow or plant in large containers in spring or early summer. Water well and pick regularly.

↕3ft (1m) ↔4in (10cm)

ANNUAL/BIENNIAL MEDIUM

Sugar snap pea

Pisum sativum This short climbing plant bears crisp pods from late spring to fall, if sown in spring or early summer. The pea pods are eaten whole. Best planted in large containers in light shade; keep well watered and pick regularly.

↕24in (60cm) ↔20in (50cm)

TREE SMALL

Sour cherry

Prunus cerasus This small tree has white or pink flowers in spring, followed by sharp-tasting red berries in summer. Select self-fertile varieties on dwarfing rootstocks. Best in light shade in large containers of soil-based potting mix; water and feed well.

↕↔12ft (4m)

Z4–8

SHRUB MEDIUM

Black currant

Ribes nigrum This upright branching shrub flowers in spring, and bears strings of glossy black sharp-tasting fruits in summer. Grow it in a large container of soil-based potting mix in light shade. Mulch in spring; water well in summer.

↕↔5ft (1.5m)

Z3–8

ANNUAL/BIENNIAL SMALL

Summer radish

Raphanus sativus This type of radish is grown for its crisp, rounded peppery roots. Sow seeds in windowboxes and pots from spring to early fall. Pull the roots once large enough, after five weeks, then re-sow. Ideal for light shade; water well. Can be invasive.

↕↔8in (20cm)

PERENNIAL LARGE

Rhubarb

Rheum* x *hybridum A vigorous perennial with large, glossy green leaves, it is grown for its sharp-tasting stems, which are eaten cooked. Plant in a large container of soil-based potting mix; water and feed well. Harvest stems from spring to midsummer.

↕↔6ft (2m)

Z3–8

SHRUB MEDIUM

Red currant

Ribes rubrum A branching, spring-flowering shrub with strings of sharp-tasting glossy red fruits. Plant in a large container of soil-based potting mix. Mulch in spring; water well during summer. Considered invasive in some Northeast and Northwest areas.

↕↔5ft (1.5m)

Z3–8

CLIMBER MEDIUM

Blackberry

Rubus fruticosus This vigorous climbing shrub flowers in spring, and bears clusters of sweet black berries in summer. It is best trained against a support; plant in a large container of soil-based potting mix. Be careful of its sharp thorns.

↕8ft (2.5m)

Z3–8

CLIMBER MEDIUM

Thornless blackberry

Rubus fruticosus This climbing shrub has dissected leaves and thornless stems and, from late summer to fall, clusters of large black berries. Plant in a large container of soil-based potting mix in light shade; provide support for its stems.

↕8ft (2.5m)

Z3-8

PERENNIAL SMALL

Sweet violets

Viola odorata A semievergreen perennial with heart-shaped leaves and, from late winter to early spring, fragrant, flat-faced violet flowers, which can be added to salads or crystallized to decorate cakes and desserts. 'Alba' (above) has white flowers.

↕8in (20cm) ↔12in (30cm)

Z6–8

OTHER SUGGESTIONS

Fruit trees

Apple 'Ashmead's Kernel' • Apple 'Royal Gala'

Soft fruits

Blackberry 'Triple Crown' • Redcurrant 'Rovada'

Herbs

Angelica • Garlic chives • Moroccan mint

Vegetables

Chop suey greens • Kale 'Nero di Toscana' • Kale 'Redbor' • Lambs lettuce • Lettuce 'Little Gem' • Lettuce 'Red Salad Bowl' • Lettuce 'Winter Density' • Mustard 'Giant Red' • Pea 'Green Arrow' • Pea 'Lincoln' • Radish 'Cherry Belle' • Radish 'Easter Egg' • Runner bean 'Painted Lady' • Spinach 'Tyee' • Spring onion 'White Lisbon' • Swiss chard 'Bright Lights' • Wild arugula

Plant focus: leafy greens

Easy to grow and delicious when fresh, lettuces and other salad leaves are the perfect crop for small gardens and patios.

Despite their high price in the grocery stores, lettuces and other leafy greens are easy to grow from seed, economical, and taste twice as nice when picked fresh. They are pretty plants and can be used in combination with edible flowers, such as nasturtiums and violas in container displays. To grow leafy greens, sow seeds in trays under cover in early spring and, once a good root system has developed and the plants have been acclimated to the outdoors, plant them in moist but free-draining soil in sun or part shade. Sow additional seeds directly outside starting in late spring to extend the harvest period. Keep the plants well watered and protected from slugs. Where space allows, grow head-forming lettuce and harvest when mature. For smaller plots, grow arugula, mustard greens, and loose-leaf lettuce varieties as a "cut-and-come again crop," cutting the leaves about ¾in (2cm) from the soil when plants are 4in (10cm) in height. When well watered, the plants will regrow to give you repeated summer crops.

USING LEAFY GREENS

Grow greens in raised beds, which are close at hand and make picking easy, with edible flowers and herbs. Incorporate varieties with colored or frilly leaves into bedding schemes as foliage plants, or use to edge beds. Crops can also be grown in individual pots on a windowsill.

Loose-leaved greens can be harvested as "microgreens," grown in pots and trays. Where space is limited, plant them in a green-wall growing system.

Swiss chard grows best in light shade where it is less prone to bolting. Cut individual leaves when young and tender, leaving the base to regrow.

TYPES OF LEAFY GREEN

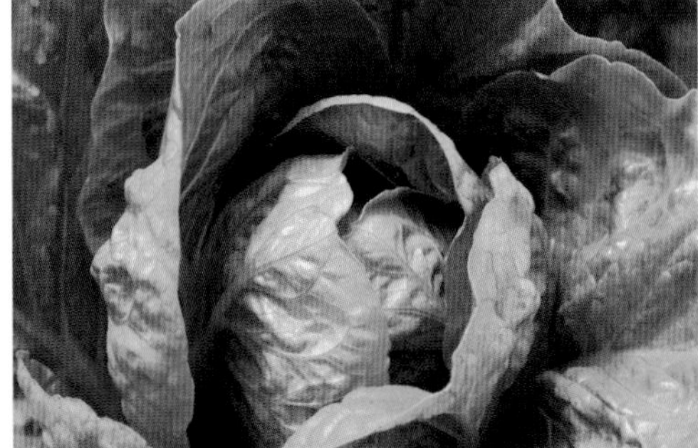

Romaine lettuces Also known as cos lettuces, they produce a tall head of crisp leaves with a rib down the center of each leaf. Leave plants to form a head before harvesting.

Butterhead lettuces Also known as Boston or Bibb lettuce, these produce tender leaves with the sweetest at the center forming a loose heart. Provide them with enough space to mature fully.

Loose-leaf lettuces This group produces loose green or red leaves without a central heart and includes oak- and frilly-leaved forms, such as 'Lollo Rossa' (*above*).

Head lettuces Known as iceberg lettuces, these plants develop a solid heart of firm, rounded, densely packed pale leaves. These are the traditional summer lettuces.

Arugula Short plants produce dark green oval or divided leaves with a peppery flavor and edible flowers. Grow it as a "cut-and-come-again" crop or as "microgreens." Sow seeds regularly.

Mustard greens These hardy plants develop loose leaves, often red-tinged, with a peppery flavor that intensifies as the plants mature. Harvest the leaves individually when required.

Plants for woodland gardens

Cool, shady forests are home to a range of elegant shrubs, climbers, bulbs, and perennials—visit native woodlands for inspiration.

Use seasonal variations to the best effect in your woodland garden. Spring is the highlight of the year, when bulbs and flowers come into bloom, making the most of the light before the tree canopies darken the woodland floor. As summer approaches, use foliage plants such as ferns to provide interest and grow foxglove and other flowers in the partial shade at the edge of the tree line. For a fall display, choose maples, whose red and orange foliage burns brightly, and berried plants for added color. Winter stems make an impact when foliage has fallen, creating a graphic picture as temperatures tumble.

PERENNIAL MEDIUM

Actaea pachypoda

WHITE BANEBERRY This clump-forming perennial has divided bright green leaves. Spikes of fluffy white midsummer flowers are followed by oval, black-tipped white berries on stiff bright red stalks. Plant it in moist soil just beyond tree canopies.
↕3ft (1m) ↔20in (50cm)

Z3–8 Ⓝ

PERENNIAL SMALL

Adonis amurensis

AMUR ADONIS A clump-forming perennial with ferny midgreen leaves. In early spring, just as the foliage unfolds, golden-yellow, cup-shaped single blooms with many small petals appear. Grow it in part or full shade in soil that does not dry out.
↕↔12in (30cm)

Z4–7

SHRUB LARGE

Aesculus parviflora

BOTTLEBRUSH BUCKEYE This suckering deciduous shrub has palm-shaped bronze leaves, which age to dark green and turn yellow in fall, and spires of fluffy white flowers from mid- to late summer. Plant it in gaps between trees.
↕10ft (3m) ↔15ft (5m)

Z4–8 Ⓝ

BULB MEDIUM

Allium moly

GOLDEN GARLIC This is a clump-forming perennial bulb with narrow, lance-shaped gray-green leaves. In summer, domed heads of star-shaped golden-yellow blooms appear. It is an ideal plant for naturalizing in deciduous woodland.
↕14in (35cm)

Z3–9

BULB MEDIUM

Anemone blanda 'Violet Star'

GRECIAN WINDFLOWER A tuber-forming, spreading perennial bulb with dark green divided leaves and daisy-like, amethyst-violet flowers with white centers in early spring. Plant the tubers in fall. Keep the plant well watered.
↕6in (15cm)

Z5–8

BULB SMALL

Anemone blanda 'White Splendour'

GRECIAN WINDFLOWER This tuber-forming perennial bulb forms carpets of divided leaves. Daisy-like white flowers appear in early spring. Plant the tubers in groups in fall.
↕4in (10cm)

Z5–8

PERENNIAL SMALL

Anemone nemorosa

WOOD ANEMONE This vigorous carpeting perennial has deeply cut midgreen leaves and, from spring to early summer, daisy-like flowers with a central tuft of yellow stamens. Suitable for naturalizing, it is available in many colors and flower forms.
↕6in (15cm) ↔12in (30cm)

Z4–8

PERENNIAL SMALL

Anemone sylvestris

SNOWDROP WINDFLOWER This carpeting perennial has divided midgreen leaves and, from spring to early summer, white bowl-shaped flowers with yellow centers. With its spreading roots, it may become aggressive; suitable for wild gardens.
↕↔12in (30cm)

Z3–8

PERENNIAL SMALL

Anemonella thalictroides

RUE ANEMONE This tuberous-rooted perennial has delicate, dark blue-green leaves divided into rounded leaflets and, from spring to early summer, cup-shaped white or pink blooms. It thrives in dappled shade; plant in mass under trees.

↕4in (10cm) ↔1½in (4cm) or more

Z4–7 Ⓝ

BULB MEDIUM

Arisaema triphyllum

JACK-IN-THE-PULPIT This perennial bulb has triangular-shaped leaves divided into three leaflets. Green or purple- and white-striped, hooded summer spathes surround a central column of tiny blooms. Bright red berries follow. Plant the tubers in late winter.

↕20in (50cm)

pH (!) Z4–9 Ⓝ

PERENNIAL SMALL

Arisarum proboscideum

MOUSE PLANT A clump-forming perennial with arrow-shaped leaves. In spring, it bears strange maroon blooms with a white base that consists of a "hood", drawn out into a mouselike tail. The hood conceals the tiny flowers. Dies back after flowering.

↕6in (15cm) ↔12in (30cm)

Z7–9

PERENNIAL SMALL

Blechnum penna-marina

ALPINE WATER FERN A fast-growing, carpeting evergreen fern with narrow, ladderlike dark green fronds that are attractively tinged red when young. Grow it in consistently moist soil between tree canopies in part or deep shade.

↕12in (30cm) ↔18in (45cm)

 Z8–10

PERENNIAL SMALL

Asarum caudatum

WILD GINGER This evergreen perennial forms clumps of glossy, heart-shaped dark green leaves. Unusual hidden, pitcher-shaped reddish to purple-brown flowers with tail-like lobes appear in early summer. It thrives in deep shade beneath trees.

↕3in (8cm) ↔10in (25cm) or more

pH Z7–9 Ⓝ

PERENNIAL MEDIUM

Asplenium scolopendrium

HART'S TONGUE FERN This evergreen fern has rosettes of long, slender, crimp-edged green leaves. It makes a beautiful addition to understory plantings beneath deciduous trees. Tolerates deep shade. Crispum Group (above) has crinkle-edged leaves.

↕28in (70cm) ↔24in (60cm)

Z5–9

PERENNIAL SMALL

Asplenium trichomanes

MAIDEN-HAIR SPLEENWORT A compact evergreen fern that produces rosettes of dark-stemmed fronds divided into rounded segments. It provides a textural carpet beneath deciduous trees, and is tolerant of deep shade.

↕6in (15cm) ↔12in (30cm)

Z3–8 Ⓝ

PERENNIAL SMALL

Brunnera macrophylla

SIBERIAN BUGLOSS This ground cover perennial has oval leaves speckled or edged with silvery white and blue spring flowers. 'Dawson's White' (above) has heart-shaped, creamy-white-edged leaves. Grow beneath trees in a sheltered site.

↕18in (45cm) ↔24in (60cm)

Z3–8

SHRUB LARGE

Callicarpa bodinieri var. *giraldii*

BEAUTYBERRY This shrub has lance-shaped leaves and pink summer blooms. 'Profusion' (above) has purple-tinged leaves, rosy pink in fall, and violet berries. Plant in groups for more berries. Grow in shelter in cool areas.

↕10ft (3m) ↔8ft (2.5m)

 Z5–8

SHRUB LARGE

Camellia x *williamsii*

CAMELLIA A bushy evergreen shrub with glossy, oval dark green leaves. It bears showy single or double blooms in shades of pink or white from early- to mid-spring. The upright 'Donation' (above) has pink flowers with golden stamens.

↕15ft (5m) ↔8ft (2.5m)

pH Z7–9

PERENNIAL MEDIUM

Carex grayi

GRAY'S SEDGE This evergreen perennial has tufts of narrow, grassy bright green leaves. In summer, its upright stems are topped with clusters of green flowers that are followed by star-shaped greenish brown fruits. Plant on the edge of a woodland.

↕24in (60cm) ↔8in (20cm)

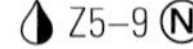

Z5–9 Ⓝ

PERENNIAL MEDIUM

Carex buchananii

LEATHERLEAF SEDGE This evergreen perennial has narrow, grasslike upward, then arching, copper-colored leaves, red toward the base. Triangular stems bear brown flower clusters in summer. Grow in groups on the edge of a woodland garden.

↕24in (60cm) ↔8in (20cm)

Z6–9

PERENNIAL MEDIUM

Chelone glabra

TURTLEHEAD This medium-sized upright perennial produces oval midgreen leaves. From late summer to early fall, unusual, two-lipped white flowers appear. It is best planted just beyond the tree canopies.

↕up to 3ft (1m) ↔18in (45cm)

pH Z3–8 Ⓝ

BULB MEDIUM

Chionodoxa forbesii

GLORY OF THE SNOW This perennial bulb bears grasslike foliage and small, purple-blue flowers with white centers in early spring. Plant the bulbs in large groups in fall in soil that will not dry out in summer.

↕6in (15cm)

Z3–8

SHRUB MEDIUM

Clethra alnifolia

SUMMERSWEET This bushy shrub has oval, serrated midgreen leaves that turn yellow in fall. In late summer, slender spires of small, fragrant, bell-shaped white blooms form. It is a good choice for damp soil, just beyond the tree canopies.

↕↔8ft (2.5m)

Z3–9 Ⓝ

SHRUB LARGE

Cornus mas

CORNELIAN CHERRY This spreading, open shrub has oval dark green leaves that turn reddish purple in fall. Rounded clusters of yellow star-shaped blooms form on bare stems in late winter, followed by edible red fruits. Suitable for light shade only.

↕↔15ft (5m)

Z4–8

PERENNIAL SMALL

Corydalis flexuosa

BLUE CORYDALIS An upright perennial with gray-blue-tinged ferny leaves. From late spring to summer, sprays of tubular blue flowers with white throats form. It dies back completely in summer. Plant it in dappled shade beneath deciduous trees.

↕12in (30cm) ↔8in (20cm)

Z6–8

SHRUB MEDIUM

Corylopsis pauciflora

BUTTERCUP WINTER HAZEL This bushy spreading shrub has oval, serrated bright green leaves, bronze- or red-tinged when young. In spring, short clusters of bell-shaped, fragrant pale yellow blooms hang from bare stems. Plant it in dappled shade.

↕5ft (1.5m) ↔8ft (2.5m)

pH Z6–8

BULB SMALL

Cyclamen coum

HARDY CYCLAMEN This perennial bulb has rounded leaves, often marked with silver marbling, and pink flowers that bloom from late winter to early spring. Plant the bulbs in bold groups beneath trees in fall. It becomes dormant in summer heat.

↕4in (10cm)

(!) Z5–9

BULB SMALL

Cyclamen hederifolium

IVY-LEAVED CYCLAMEN This perennial bulb has variable, ivy-shaped dark green leaves, usually overlaid with silvery green marbling. It bears pink or white flowers in fall, before or with the foliage. Tolerates dry shade beneath trees. Goes dormant in summer.

↕4in (10cm)

(!) Z5–8

PERENNIAL LARGE

Dicksonia antarctica

AUSTRALIAN TREE FERN A treelike evergreen, fern with a stout, brown fibrous "trunk" and a palmlike crown of arching, much divided fronds. Grow it in a sheltered spot in large containers, and overwinter the plant indoors.

↕20ft (6m) or more ↔12ft (4m)

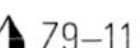

Z9–11

PERENNIAL LARGE

Digitalis ferruginea

RUSTY FOXGLOVE This perennial has a basal rosette of oval dark green leaves. In midsummer, long, slender, upright spikes of funnel-shaped, orange-brown and white blooms appear. Plant in groups in partial shade beneath trees.

↕4ft (1.2m) ↔12in (30cm)

Z4–9

PERENNIAL MEDIUM

Digitalis grandiflora

LARGE YELLOW FOXGLOVE This clump-forming evergreen perennial has a basal rosette of oval dark green leaves and spires of tubular, downward-pointing creamy yellow blooms in summer. Plant it beneath trees in part shade; it can be short-lived.

↕3ft (1m) ↔18in (45cm)

Z3–8

PERENNIAL SMALL

Dodecatheon dentatum

WHITE SHOOTING STAR This clump-forming perennial makes rosettes of oval midgreen leaves and, in late spring, slim stems of nodding white flowers with swept-back petals. Grow it between tree canopies in a woodland in rich soil.

↕↔8in (20cm)

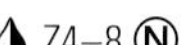

Z4–8 (N)

PERENNIAL MEDIUM

Dryopteris affinis

GOLDEN MALE FERN A virtually evergreen perennial, it makes a "shuttlecock" of lance-shaped divided fronds, which are pale green as they unfurl in spring, contrasting with the scaly golden-brown midribs. Grow beneath tree canopies; tolerates drought.

↕↔3ft (1m)

Z5–8

PERENNIAL SMALL

Dryopteris erythrosora

JAPANESE SHIELD FERN A clump-forming semievergreen fern with broadly triangular, arching divided fronds, copper-red when young and aging to pinkish green or bronze tinged, and then bright green. Tolerates dry shade, but water well in first year.

↕16in (40cm) ↔12in (30cm)

Z5–9

PERENNIAL LARGE

Dryopteris filix-mas

MALE FERN This deciduous or semievergreen fern forms "shuttlecocks" of arching, upright midgreen fronds that arise from crowns of large, upright brown-scaled rhizomes. It thrives in deep shade beneath deciduous trees.

↕4ft (1.2m) ↔3ft (1m)

Z4–8 Ⓝ

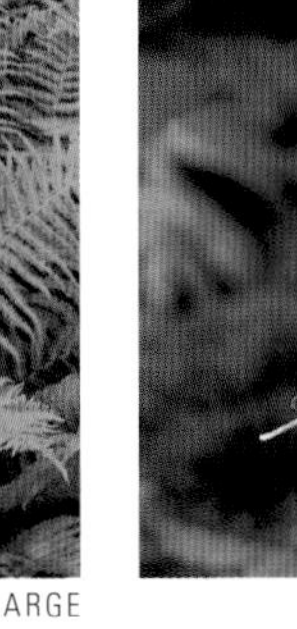

PERENNIAL SMALL

Epimedium grandiflorum

BISHOP'S HAT A clump-forming perennial, with heart-shaped green leaves, bronze-tinged when young. In spring, nodding white, yellow, pink, or purple flowers appear. 'Lilafee' (above) has purple blooms and is sometimes sold as 'Lilac Fairy.'

↕10in (25cm) ↔12in (30cm)

Z5–8

PERENNIAL SMALL

Erythronium dens-canis

DOG'S-TOOTH VIOLET This tuberous-rooted perennial has paired, oval, maroon-mottled basal leaves. In spring, single stems bear nodding mauve-pink flowers with swept-back petals and red-brown and yellow shading at the base. Plant it between trees.

↕10in (25cm) ↔4in (10cm)

Z3–9

BULB LARGE

Fritillaria pallidiflora

SIBERIAN FRITILLARY An upright perennial bulb with lance-shaped blue-green leaves and nodding, bell-shaped greenish yellow flowers in early summer. Plant the bulbs at four times their own depth in fall just beyond the tree canopies.

↕28in (70cm)

Z4–9

BULB MEDIUM

Galanthus nivalis

SNOWDROP This perennial bulb produces clumps of grasslike gray-green leaves. In late winter, it bears nodding, white single flowers with green-tipped inner petals. Plant it in groups in deciduous woodland and allow to naturalize.

↕6in (15cm)

Z3–8

PERENNIAL SMALL

Galium odoratum

SWEET WOODRUFF A spreading perennial with emerald-green foliage formed of rounded clusters of lance-shaped leaves. From late spring to midsummer, it produces a froth of tiny, starry, white blooms. Use it as ground cover beneath trees.

↕6in (15cm) ↔12in (30cm) or more

Z4–8

PERENNIAL MEDIUM

Geranium phaeum

MOURNING WIDOW This erect, clump-forming perennial has rounded, deeply cut midgreen leaves. From late spring to early summer, dusky purple, lilac, or white flowers appear. It thrives in dappled shade under trees.

↕30in (75cm) ↔18in (45cm)

Z4–8

PERENNIAL MEDIUM

Geranium sylvaticum

WOOD CRANESBILL This bushy perennial has lobed, deeply cut midgreen leaves and, from late spring to early summer, pink, blue, white, or purple, saucer-shaped blooms. 'Album' (above) has white flowers. It thrives in dappled shade.

↕30in (75cm) ↔24in (60cm)

Z4–8

PERENNIAL SMALL

Hacquetia epipactis

HACQUETIA This clump-forming perennial has lobed green leaves that unfurl after the appearance of late winter to early spring flowers, which are yellow-green and surrounded by notched, apple-green, petal-like bracts. Plant in dappled shade.

↕2½in (6cm) ↔9in (23cm)

pH Z5–7

PERENNIAL MEDIUM

Helleborus foetidus

STINKING HELLEBORE A bushy evergreen perennial with palm-shaped glossy leaves divided into narrow leaflets and nodding, pale green, red-margined cup-shaped blooms from late winter to early spring. Grow in dappled shade.

↕↔24in (60cm)

 Z6–9

BULB MEDIUM

Hyacinthoides non-scripta

ENGLISH BLUEBELL A vigorous perennial bulb with narrow, strap-shaped, glossy dark green leaves. In spring, midblue or, occasionally, white, bell-shaped fragrant flowers hang from arching stems. Grow it in large swaths beneath deciduous trees.

↕16in (40cm)

Z5–7

PERENNIAL MEDIUM

Kirengeshoma palmata

YELLOW WAX BELLS This upright perennial has rounded, slightly hairy, lobed bright green leaves on purple-red stems. From late summer to fall, small clusters of narrow, funnel-shaped, pendulous creamy yellow flowers appear. Grow it in moist soil.

↕3ft (1m) ↔24in (60cm)

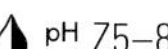 Z5–8

PERENNIAL MEDIUM

Helleborus orientalis

LENTEN ROSE This evergreen woodland perennial has leathery dark green leaves divided into slim leaflets and saucer-shaped white or greenish cream flowers, which age to dark pink from midwinter to spring. Deadhead to prevent self-seeding.

↕24in (60cm) ↔18in (45cm)

Z4–9

BULB MEDIUM

Leucojum aestivum

SUMMER SNOWFLAKE This perennial bulb makes an upright clump of narrow, strap-shaped, glossy dark green leaves. Small clusters of green-tipped white, drooping bell-shaped blooms form in spring. 'Gravetye Giant' (above) is popular.

↕24in (60cm)

Z3–9

PERENNIAL SMALL

Hosta 'Revolution'

PLANTAIN LILY A clump-forming perennial with dark green leaves that have irregular creamy white central markings and green speckles. Spikes of lavender flowers appear briefly in summer. Grow it in dappled shade to add bright highlights to beds.

↕20in (50cm) ↔3½ft (1.1m)

Z3–9

PERENNIAL SMALL

Hylomecon japonica

WOOD POPPY This vigorous, spreading perennial has dark green soft leaves divided into toothed leaflets. From late spring to summer, cup-shaped, bright yellow, poppylike single flowers appear. Plant it in a large woodland garden.

↕12in (30cm) ↔8in (20cm)

Z6–8

BULB LARGE

Lilium martagon

TURKSCAP LILY This clump-forming perennial bulb has lance-shaped leaves on erect stems and nodding, dark-spotted, pink or purple summer flowers with swept-back petals and protruding stamens. Grow on the edge of a woodland garden.

↕up to 6ft (2m)

Z3–8

SHRUB LARGE

Kalmia latifolia

MOUNTAIN LAUREL A bushy evergreen shrub with oval, glossy green leaves and, from late spring to early summer, clusters of cup-shaped pink flowers that open from attractively crimped buds. Grow it in dappled shade between tree canopies.

↕↔10ft (3m)

pH Z4–9 Ⓝ

BULB LARGE

Lilium nepalense

HIMALAYAN LILY This upright perennial bulb has lance-shaped green leaves and trumpet-shaped, scented greenish cream flowers with chocolate-red throats. Plant it in part shade in deep fertile soil, just beyond the tree canopies.

↕3ft (1m)

pH Z7–8

Plants for woodland gardens

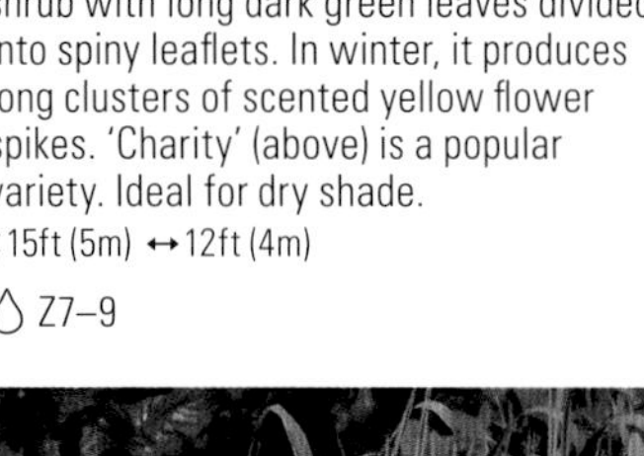

SHRUB LARGE

Mahonia x *media*

MAHONIA An architectural evergreen shrub with long dark green leaves divided into spiny leaflets. In winter, it produces long clusters of scented yellow flower spikes. 'Charity' (above) is a popular variety. Ideal for dry shade.

↕15ft (5m) ↔12ft (4m)

Z7–9

PERENNIAL MEDIUM

Maianthemum racemosum

FALSE SPIKENARD An upright perennial, with oval, prominently veined green leaves. It bears scented, fluffy cream plumes from mid- to late spring, followed by red berries. Shelter from wind. Best planted in mass in larger gardens.

↕3ft (1m) ↔24in (60cm)

pH Z3–8 Ⓝ

PERENNIAL MEDIUM

Matteuccia struthiopteris

OSTRICH FERN This large, shuttlecock-shaped deciduous fern produces long pale green fronds divided into toothed-edged segments. It is ideal for growing in the damp soil just beyond tree canopies in a woodland setting.

↕3ft (1m) ↔18in (45cm)

Z2–8 Ⓝ

PERENNIAL LARGE

Meconopsis betonicifolia

BLUE POPPY A short-lived, rosette-forming perennial with serrated bluish green leaves and saucer-shaped, pure blue early summer blooms. Can be difficult to grow. Best in dappled shade in the cool moist gardens of the Pacific Northwest.

↕4ft (1.2m) ↔18in (45cm)

pH Z7–8

PERENNIAL MEDIUM

Milium effusum 'Aureum'

GOLDEN MILLET GRASS A semievergreen perennial, also sold as annual foliage, with narrow, arching golden-yellow leaves and airy sprays of yellow summer flower heads. Allow it to self-seed and form carpets in dappled shade just beyond tree canopies.

↕24in (60cm) ↔12in (30cm)

Z5–8 Ⓝ

BULB MEDIUM

Narcissus 'February Gold'

DAFFODIL This perennial bulb has narrow midgreen leaves and, from late winter to early spring, golden-yellow blooms with swept-back petals and long trumpets. Plant the bulbs in groups in fall, and allow it to naturalize beneath deciduous trees.

↕12in (30cm)

(!) Z3–9

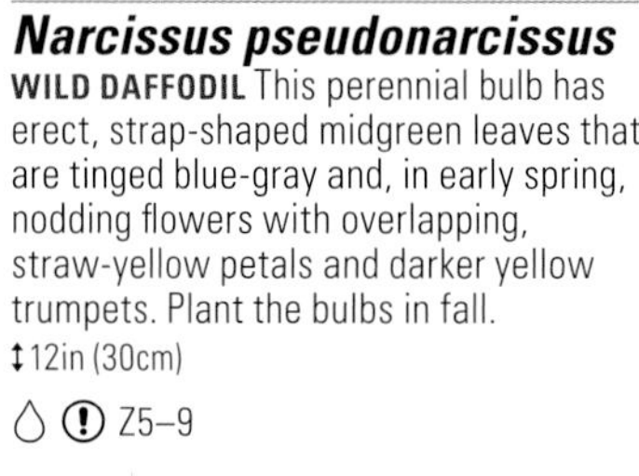

BULB MEDIUM

Narcissus pseudonarcissus

WILD DAFFODIL This perennial bulb has erect, strap-shaped midgreen leaves that are tinged blue-gray and, in early spring, nodding flowers with overlapping, straw-yellow petals and darker yellow trumpets. Plant the bulbs in fall.

↕12in (30cm)

(!) Z5–9

PERENNIAL SMALL

Omphalodes cappadocica

NAVELWORT This is a clump-forming perennial with deeply veined, oval to heart-shaped midgreen leaves. In early spring, it forms airy heads of white-eyed sky-blue blooms. 'Cherry Ingram' (above) is a more compact, deep blue form.

↕12in (30cm) ↔24in (60cm)

Z6–8

SHRUB LARGE

Osmanthus x *burkwoodii*

OSMANTHUS An dense evergreen shrub with glossy dark green foliage and a profusion of small, highly fragrant white flowers from mid- to late spring. Use it as a tall formal or informal hedge; prune the plant after flowering.

↕↔10ft (3m)

Z7–9

PERENNIAL SMALL

Pachysandra procumbens

ALLEGHENY SPURGE This clump-forming evergreen perennial has rounded, lobed dark green leaves. Spikes of fragrant, white bottlebrush-like flowers are borne in spring as new leaves develop. Use it as ground cover in deep shade beneath trees.

↕10in (25cm) ↔24in (60cm)

pH Z5–9 Ⓝ

PERENNIAL MEDIUM

Polemonium caeruleum

JACOB'S LADDER This clump-forming perennial has finely divided fernlike leaves. Loose clusters of small, cup-shaped lavender-blue blooms with orange-yellow stamens open in early summer. Plant it in dappled shade beneath deciduous trees.

↕↔24in (60cm)

Z4–8

PERENNIAL MEDIUM

Persicaria bistorta

BISTORT This vigorous, clump-forming perennial has large, prominently veined green leaves and dense spikes of small pale pink flowers from summer to early fall. Use it sparingly as it spreads rapidly. 'Superba' (above) is a popular variety.

↕30in (75cm) ↔24in (60cm)

Z4–8

PERENNIAL LARGE

Polygonatum x *hybridum*

SOLOMON'S SEAL An arching leafy perennial with oval green leaves. In early summer, it bears clusters of small, tubular green-tipped white flowers that hang from the stems. It thrives in full shade beneath trees. Often misapplied as *P. multiflorum*.

↕up to 4ft (1.2m) ↔3ft (1m)

Z3–8

SHRUB MEDIUM

Pieris 'Flaming Silver'

LILY OF THE VALLEY BUSH This upright evergreen shrub produces leathery, lance-shaped bright red young leaves that age to green with white margins. In spring, branching clusters of bell-shaped creamy white flowers appear.

↕5ft (1.5m) ↔3ft (1m)

pH Z5–9

PERENNIAL MEDIUM

Polygonatum odoratum

FRAGRANT SOLOMON'S SEAL This arching perennial has oval to lance-shaped midgreen leaves. From late spring to early summer, it bears fragrant, hanging, tubular to bell-shaped, green-tipped white flowers. Thrives in deep shade beneath trees.

↕24in (60cm) ↔12in (30cm)

PERENNIAL SMALL

Podophyllum versipelle

CHINESE MAYAPPLE This unusual perennial produces large, umbrella-shaped bright green leaves, under which crimson flowers form in summer. It makes an eye-catching addition to a shady bed. 'Spotty Dotty' (above) has red-spotted foliage.

↕18in (45cm) ↔24in (60cm)

Z6–9

PERENNIAL MEDIUM

Polystichum polyblepharum

JAPANESE TASSEL FERN This evergreen fern forms "shuttlecocks" of spreading, lance-shaped, divided green fronds that are covered with golden hairs when they unfurl. The oval frond segments have spiny-toothed margins. Prefers full shade.

↕32in (80cm) ↔3ft (1m)

Z6–8

PERENNIAL LARGE

Polystichum setiferum

SOFT SHIELD FERN This clump-forming fern produces large, lance-shaped midgreen fronds divided into segments. The leafstalks feature orange-brown scales. Grow it beneath trees in partial or deep shade to produce a naturalistic effect.

↕4ft (1.2m) ↔3ft (1m)

Z6–9

PERENNIAL MEDIUM

Primula beesiana

CANDELABRA PRIMROSE This is a rosette-forming deciduous or semievergreen perennial, with toothed, midgreen leaves. In summer, it produces whorls of tubular, yellow-eyed reddish pink flowers that are carried on upright stems.

↕24in (60cm) ↔12in (30cm)

Z5–8

PERENNIAL SMALL

Primula japonica

JAPANESE PRIMROSE This perennial has basal rosettes of oval, wrinkled pale green leaves. Clusters of white, pink, red, or crimson flowers are held on upright stems in late spring. Varieties include the white-flowered 'Postford White' (above).

↕↔ 18in (45cm)

 Z4–8

PERENNIAL SMALL

Primula vulgaris

ENGLISH PRIMROSE This perennial forms basal rosettes of oval pale green leaves. It produces scented primrose-yellow flowers in early spring. Plant it with woodland spring bulbs in dappled shade beneath deciduous trees.

↕ 8in (20cm) ↔ 14in (35cm)

 Z4–8

SHRUB SMALL

Rhododendron 'Yaku Prince'

RHODODENDRON This rounded evergreen shrub has olive-green leaves with orange-brown hairs on the undersides. Large clusters of orange-red-spotted pink flowers appear from late spring to early summer. Plant in acidic soil in a woodland bed.

↕↔ 3ft (1m)

Z5–9

PERENNIAL SMALL

Pulmonaria officinalis

LUNGWORT This ground-cover perennial has oval, pointed green leaves, with silvery spots. In spring, it bears funnel-shaped, blue and purple or pink and white blooms. Varieties include the white 'Sissinghurst White' (above). Tolerates deep shade.

↕ 12in (30cm) ↔ 24in (60cm)

 Z4–8

PERENNIAL SMALL

Sanguinaria canadensis

BLOODROOT This is a small clump-forming perennial with scalloped, kidney-shaped blue-gray leaves and cup-shaped, white single flowers in spring. Varieties include 'Multiplex' (above), which has double blooms. Plant in dappled shade.

↕ 6in (15cm) ↔ 12in (30cm)

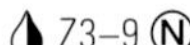 Z3–9

SHRUB SMALL

Sarcococca confusa

SWEET BOX A bushy evergreen shrub with glossy, lance-shaped dark green leaves. In winter, it bears clusters of tiny, sweetly fragrant white blooms followed by shiny black fruits. It tolerates full shade and the dry soil beneath trees.

↕↔ 3ft (1m)

Z6–9

PERENNIAL SMALL

Saxifraga fortunei

SAXIFRAGE A clump-forming semievergreen perennial with rounded, jaggedly lobed, fleshy brownish green leaves, red beneath. Airy heads of small, white-tinged pink starry flowers open in late summer. Use it as ground cover beneath trees.

↕↔ 12in (30cm)

Z7–9

PERENNIAL MEDIUM

Tellima grandiflora

FRINGE CUPS A clump-forming semievergreen perennial with serrated, heart-shaped, green-tinted purple leaves and, from late spring to midsummer, spikes of small, bell-shaped, fringed cream blooms. Allow it to naturalize in dappled shade.
↕↔24in (60cm)

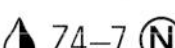
Z4–7 Ⓝ

PERENNIAL MEDIUM

Silene dioica

RED CAMPION This clump-forming semievergreen perennial has oval, dark green basal leaves. From late spring to midsummer, it bears clusters of small pink flowers. Use it to provide color in the dappled shade beneath tree canopies.
↕32in (80cm) ↔18in (45cm)

Z6–9

TREE MEDIUM

Styrax obassia

FRAGRANT SNOWBELL A spreading tree with rounded dark green leaves, blue-gray beneath, that turn yellow in fall. Long pendent clusters of fragrant, bell-shaped white flowers appear in early summer. Use it to create a woodland setting.
↕40ft (12m) ↔22ft (7m)

Z5–8

PERENNIAL SMALL

Tiarella wherryi

FOAMFLOWER This spreading evergreen perennial has lobed, pale green leaves with veins that turn bronze-red in winter. Spikes of fluffy white flowers appear from late spring to early summer. It makes excellent ground cover in deep shade.
↕8in (20cm) ↔12in (30cm) or more

Z3–7 Ⓝ

PERENNIAL SMALL

Thalictrum kiusianum

DWARF MEADOW RUE This mat-forming perennial has small, fernlike, dark blue-green leaves. In early summer, it produces loose clusters of fluffy, pale purple-pink flowers with prominent stamens. Plant in part shade in soil that does not dry out.
↕3in (8cm) ↔6in (15cm)

Z4–8

PERENNIAL MEDIUM

Tricyrtis formosana

TOAD LILY An upright, clump-forming, slow-spreading perennial with lance-shaped midgreen leaves and upturned clusters of intricately-shaped, purple-spotted white fall blooms. Fall frost may kill the flowers. Mulch annually with compost.
↕3ft (1m) ↔18in (45cm)

Z5–9

PERENNIAL SMALL

Trillium chloropetalum

GIANT WAKEROBIN This clump-forming perennial has gray- or maroon-marbled dark green leaves that form in groups of three. The large purplish pink to white flowers stand erect just above the leaves in spring. Thrives in partial shade.
↕↔18in (45cm)

Z6–9 Ⓝ

PERENNIAL MEDIUM

Uvularia grandiflora

BELLWORT This clump-forming perennial has arching stems clothed in bright green lance-shaped leaves. Clusters of long, bell-shaped yellow flowers with twisted petals appear from mid- to late spring. Thrives in deep shade beneath trees.
↕24in (60cm) ↔12in (30cm)

Z4–9 Ⓝ

OTHER SUGGESTIONS

Perennials

• *Asarum canadense* Ⓝ • *Athyrium filix-femina* Ⓝ • *Dicentra cucullaria* Ⓝ • *Mertensia virginica* Ⓝ • *Phlox divaricate* Ⓝ • *Prosartes smithii* Ⓝ • *Spigelia marilandica* Ⓝ

Bulbs

Allium ursinum • *Chionodoxa luciliae* 'Violet Beauty' • *Fritillaria camschatcensis* Ⓝ • *Hyacinthoides hispanica*

Shrubs

Callicarpa americana Ⓝ • *Camellia* x *williamsii* 'Mary Christian' • *Fothergilla gardenii* Ⓝ • *Hydrangea quercifolia* 'Alice' Ⓝ • *Pieris* 'Forest Flame' • *Rhododendron calendulaceum* Ⓝ • *Styrax americanus* Ⓝ

Plant focus: azaleas and rhododendrons

Big and bold or small and dainty, azaleas and rhododendrons offer a great choice of blooms in spring and early summer.

AZALEAS AND RHODODENDRONS ARE PART OF THE RHODODENDRON FAMILY but, confusingly, while all azaleas are rhododendrons, not all rhododendrons are azaleas. Azaleas can be deciduous or evergreen, while rhododendrons are strictly evergreen and they also have slightly different flowers. However, both groups produce abundant, often scented, blooms in spring and early summer, and make excellent specimens for beds, borders, and containers. The larger rhododendrons are also useful as a hedge. Some species can be finicky growers, so choose those in this book or ask a specialist nursery for advice on the best plants for your garden. All require acidic soil, so test your soil before planting, and if you have alkaline conditions, grow compact or dwarf forms in pots of acidic planting mix. Happiest in moist soil and dappled or partial shade, trim plants lightly to keep them in shape in early summer, after flowering.

USING AZALEAS AND RHODODENDRONS

Large, shrubby rhododendrons make beautiful flowering evergreen screens. Trim them to shape in midsummer after flowering. Compact or dwarf rhododendrons are perfect for large containers or barrels, but they must be planted in acid soil or acidic planting mix. Water container-grown plants regularly, especially during summer.

The compact *R. yakushimanum* hybrids are invaluable for shady borders, producing masses of medium-sized flowers in late spring. There is a large range of colorful varieties to choose from.

Ideal for woodlands, azaleas and rhododendrons thrive in the cool dappled shade cast by neighboring trees. Plant them in groups for the best display.

TYPES OF AZALEA AND RHODODENDRON

Compact rhododendrons Forming mounds less than 3ft (1m) tall, this useful group consists of *R. yakushimanum* and *R. williamsianum* hybrids, which flower in late spring.

Shrub rhododendrons Most rhododendrons are rounded shrubs reaching hip- to head-height. Their colorful, often fragrant, flowers appear from mid-spring to early summer.

Evergreen hybrid azaleas Growing 3ft (1m) tall, this group includes dwarf and cascading varieties. The mostly unscented flowers, appear from mid-spring to early summer.

Deciduous hybrid azaleas These reach up to 5ft (1.5m) in height and include Ghent and Exbury hybrids. The flowers, often scented, appear from mid-spring to early summer.

Dwarf rhododendrons These tough, alpine evergreen shrubs flower mainly in mid-spring and most grow to just 20in (50cm) in height. They are ideal for rock gardens and containers.

Plants for rock gardens

Rock features are normally associated with sunny sites, but a surprising number of alpines and low-growing plants will thrive in some shade.

Most alpine plants require a few hours of sun each day and may not flower if left to languish in deep shade, so site your rock garden carefully. You can maintain year-round color and interest with a succession of seasonal displays, starting in spring with a range of bulbs and progressing into early summer with early-flowering perennials, such as fawn lily, columbine, and bleeding heart. Midsummer highlights include sweet woodruff and lady's mantle. The striking red berries of wintergreen pops against leathery foliage, while other evergreens like juniper and hebe provide additional color and interest in the winter months.

PERENNIAL SMALL

Adiantum aleuticum

WESTERN MAIDENHAIR FERN A compact deciduous or semievergreen fern with pale green fronds divided into oblong segments. Ideal for rock gardens with rich soil. The dwarf form 'Subpumilum' has black stalks and fronds with overlapping segments.
↕↔ 18in (45cm)

Z3–8 Ⓝ

PERENNIAL SMALL

Alchemilla alpina

ALPINE LADY'S MANTLE This mound-forming perennial has lobed, white-edged green leaves that are silky-haired beneath. Spikes of tiny greenish yellow flowers with larger green outer petals appear in summer. Trim untidy foliage. Avoid dry soils.
↕ 6in (15cm) ↔ 24in (60cm) or more

Z3–7

BULB MEDIUM

Allium schoenoprasum

CHIVES A clump-forming, upright perennial bulb with narrow, hollow, dark green edible leaves. In spring, it produces fluffy, pale purple pompomlike flower heads. It is ideal for rock gardens; plant in dappled shade.
↕ 12in (30cm)

Z4–8

PERENNIAL SMALL

Anemone blanda

GRECIAN WINDFLOWER This perennial corm produces divided leaves and blue, pink, or white in early spring. Varieties include 'Violet Star' (above), which has amethyst-violet flowers. Plant the tubers in fall where they will receive some sun.
↕↔ 6in (15cm)

(!) Z5–8

PERENNIAL SMALL

Anemone nemorosa

WOOD ANEMONE This dwarf perennial has deeply cut midgreen leaves. From spring to early summer, a profusion of yellow-eyed white daisy-like flowers appears. Plant it in groups at the front of a partly shaded rock garden.
↕ 6in (15cm) ↔ 12in (30cm)

(!) Z4–8

PERENNIAL SMALL

Anemone sylvestris

SNOWDROP WINDFLOWER This dwarf perennial has divided midgreen leaves. From spring to early summer, it produces fragrant, bowl-shaped white flowers with yellow centers. It prefers neutral to alkaline soil; can be aggressive.
↕↔ 12in (30cm)

(!) Z3–8

PERENNIAL SMALL

Anemonella thalictroides

RUE ANEMONE A dwarf perennial with dark blue-green leaves divided into rounded leaflets. From spring to early summer, it produces cup-shaped white or pink blooms. Grow it at the front of a rock garden in a sheltered spot.
↕ 4in (10cm) ↔ 1½in (4cm) or more

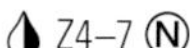

Z4–7 Ⓝ

PERENNIAL SMALL

Aquilegia fragrans

FRAGRANT COLUMBINE This upright perennial has finely cut bluish green leaves and nodding, bell-shaped, fragrant creamy white flowers with bluish- or pinkish white outer sepals in summer. Deadhead spent blooms to prevent excessive self-seeding.
↕ 16in (40cm) ↔ 8in (20cm)

Z5–8

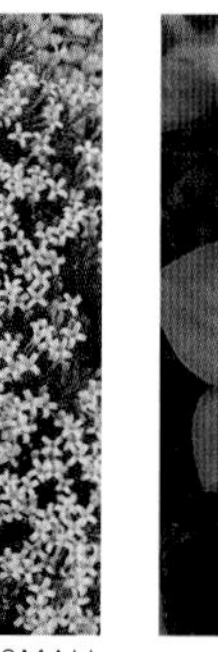

PERENNIAL SMALL

Asperula arcadiensis

ARCADIAN WOODRUFF This clump-forming perennial makes a mound of loose stems with tiny, hairy gray leaves. It bears tiny, pale pink tubular flowers in early summer. Dislikes wet winter soils and is best planted in gritty, free-draining soil.
↕ 3in (8cm) ↔ 12in (30cm)

Z5–7

PERENNIAL SMALL

Campanula raineri

RAINER'S HAREBELL A ground cover perennial with oval, toothed-edged gray-green leaves. Pale lavender bell-shaped, flowers appear in summer. Allow it to spread over the rocks in areas where it will receive some sun during the day.
↕ 3in (8cm) ↔ 8in (20cm)

Z5–7

BULB MEDIUM

Chionodoxa forbesii

GLORY OF THE SNOW An early-spring-flowering perennial bulb with linear midgreen foliage and star-shaped blue flowers with white eyes. Ideal for rock gardens with sharp drainage. Grow in light shade. Plant the bulbs in groups in fall.
↕6in (15cm)

Z3–8

BULB SMALL

Crocus banaticus

BYZANTINE CROCUS This fall-flowering perennial corm produces pale violet cup-shaped flowers before the narrow basal leaves appear in spring. Plant it in groups where it will receive some sun during the day.
↕4in (10cm)

Z3–8

PERENNIAL SMALL

Dicentra formosa

WESTERN BLEEDING HEART This spreading perennial forms finely divided gray-green leaves and clusters of pendent, heart-shaped pink flowers from late spring to early summer. Varieties include 'Bacchanal' (above) with deep crimson blooms.
↕18in (45cm) ↔12in (30cm)

Z3–9 Ⓝ

PERENNIAL SMALL

Dodecatheon hendersonii

SAILOR CAPS This clump-forming perennial has a rosette of oval green leaves, above which deep pink flowers with reflexed petals appear in late spring. It prefers rich soil; all growth dies down in summer. Keep the soil moist during the growing season.
↕12in (30cm) ↔10in (25cm)

Z5–7 Ⓝ

PERENNIAL SMALL

Epimedium x *versicolor*

BISHOP'S HAT This clump-forming evergreen perennial has heart-shaped green leaves, copper-red when young, and sprays of small pink and yellow spring flowers. Tolerates full shade. 'Sulphureum' (above) has primrose-yellow blooms.
↕↔12in (30cm)

Z5–9

BULB SMALL

Eranthis hyemalis

WINTER ACONITE This clump-forming tuber produces stalkless, cup-shaped yellow flowers with leaflike ruffs from late winter to early spring. The leaves are lobed and green. Grow it in pockets between rocks, and combine with spring bulbs.
↕4in (10cm)

(!) Z4–7

BULB MEDIUM

Erythronium californicum

FAWN LILY This clump-forming perennial bulb has mottled dark green leaves and creamy white flowers with reflexed petals in spring. 'White Beauty' (above) has creamy white flowers with red-brown throats. Plant the bulbs in fall.
↕14in (35cm)

Z3–9 Ⓝ

BULB MEDIUM

Galanthus nivalis

SNOWDROP This dwarf perennial bulb has grassy gray-green leaves that disappear in summer. From late winter to early spring, 'Flore Pleno' (above) has green-tinged white, fragrant double blooms. Plant it in soil that does not dry out in summer.
↕6in (15cm)

(!) Z3–8

BULB MEDIUM

Galanthus 'Sam Arnott'

SNOWDROP This dwarf perennial bulb produces grasslike gray-green leaves and, in late winter, small, nodding white flowers with green marks on the inner segments. Plant it in groups in soil that does not dry out in summer.
↕6in (15cm)

Z4–8

PERENNIAL SMALL

Galium odoratum

SWEET WOODRUFF This spreading perennial has small, palm-shaped, dark green leaves and small, starry, divided white flowers in summer. Can be used in large, partly shaded rock gardens where it will spread freely between the rocks.
↕6in (15cm) ↔12in (30cm) or more

Z4–8

SHRUB SMALL

Gaultheria procumbens

WINTERGREEN This dwarf evergreen shrub has oval, leathery dark green leaves, tinged red in winter. Scarlet berries follow the pink-flushed white summer blooms. Grow it for winter color in part or deep shade. Needs moist soil and does best in cooler areas.
↕6in (15cm) ↔ indefinite

pH (!) Z3–8 Ⓝ

PERENNIAL SMALL

Gentiana verna

SPRING GENTIAN This small evergreen perennial produces rosettes of oval dark green leaves and tubular bright blue flowers with white throats in early spring. Grow this plant in some sun; provide shade in summer.

↕↔ 2in (5cm)

pH Z4–7

PERENNIAL SMALL

Geranium cinereum

CRANESBILL A spreading perennial with round, deeply lobed gray-green leaves. Cup-shaped pink or mauve flowers with deep purple centers and veins appear from late spring to summer. 'Ballerina' (above) has pale pink blooms.

↕ 4in (10cm) ↔ 12in (30cm)

Z5–9

SHRUB SMALL

Hebe ochracea 'James Stirling'

HEBE A dense, dome-shaped dwarf shrub with bright yellow-green scalelike foliage. In late spring, small white flowers appear. Use it to provide structure in a rock garden and combine with low-growing perennials.

↕ 18in (45cm) ↔ 24in (60cm)

Z8–10

PERENNIAL SMALL

Helleborus purpurascens

HELLEBORE A clump-forming perennial with dark green leaves divided into lance-shaped leaflets and cup-shaped, nodding purple blooms flushed pink-purple or light green inside and with cream stamens in spring. Cut untidy foliage in fall or late winter.

↕↔ 12in (30cm)

(!) Z4–8

PERENNIAL SMALL

Hepatica nobilis

LIVERLEAF A clump-forming semievergreen perennial with silky-haired leaves featuring three rounded lobes. In early spring, it produces rounded violet or purple blooms with white stamens. Grow it in soil that does not dry out in summer.

↕ 3in (8cm) ↔ 5in (12cm)

Z5–8

SHRUB SMALL

Juniperus procumbens

DWARF JAPANESE JUNIPER This compact, mat-forming evergreen conifer produces dense prickly leaves that provide good ground cover. It bears small, round brown or black fruits. Plant it in a rock garden in dappled or light shade.

↕ 8in (20cm) ↔ 30in (75cm)

Z4–9

PERENNIAL SMALL

Lewisia cotyledon

SISKIYOU LEWISIA This clump-forming evergreen perennial has rosettes of dark green foliage. From late spring to summer, funnel-shaped flowers in shades of pink, yellow, or orange appear. Grow it in light shade in free-draining soil.

↕ 12in (30cm) ↔ 6in (15cm)

Z6–8 (N)

BULB MEDIUM

Muscari armeniacum

GRAPE HYACINTH This spring-flowering bulb produces grasslike green leaves and short spikes of small, fragrant, bell-shaped deep blue flowers held in cone-shaped clusters. Plant it in cracks between rocks.

↕ 8in (20cm)

Z4–8

BULB MEDIUM

Narcissus 'Jumblie'

DAFFODIL This bulb has strap-shaped leaves and golden single flowers with orange-yellow cups in early spring. Other dwarf daffodils come in shades of orange or white, sometimes bicolored. Plant the bulbs in groups in fall.

↕ 8in (20cm)

(!) Z4–9

BULB MEDIUM

Narcissus 'Tete-a-tete'

DAFFODIL A spring bulb with strap-shaped leaves and up to three yellow blooms per stem. Other dwarf varieties of daffodils come in shades of orange or white, sometimes bicolored. Plant the bulbs in groups in fall throughout a rock garden.

↕ 12in (30cm)

(!) Z4–9

PERENNIAL SMALL

Origanum vulgare

OREGANO This is a small clump-forming perennial that forms a dense mat of aromatic, rounded green leaves. It may also bear tiny mauve flowers in summer. Use it to fill gaps in a partly shaded rock garden.

↕↔ up to 18in (45cm)

Z4–8

PERENNIAL SMALL

Oxalis adenophylla

CHILEAN WOOD SORREL A mat-forming perennial with rounded gray-green leaves divided into narrow wavy leaflets. In spring, rounded purplish pink flowers with darker purple eyes form. Use it to spread over the rocks in a shady rock garden.

↕2in (5cm) ↔4in (10cm)

Z6–9

PERENNIAL SMALL

Phlox stolonifera

CREEPING PHLOX A low-growing evergreen perennial with oval pale green leaves and saucer-shaped purple blooms in early summer. 'Bruce's White' (above) has white blooms. It is ideal for a shaded rock garden; cut back after flowering.

↕6in (15cm) ↔12in (30cm)

pH Z4–8 (N)

PERENNIAL SMALL

Primula marginata

ALPINE PRIMROSE This semi- or fully evergreen perennial has rosettes of oblong, toothed midgreen leaves. Grow with spring bulbs at the front of a rock garden. Lavender-blue spring flowers top upright stems on 'Kesselring's Variety' (above).

↕6in (15cm) ↔12in (30cm)

Z4–8

BULB MEDIUM

Puschkinia scilloides

STRIPED SQUILL This perennial bulb produces strap-shaped green leaves and, in spring, clusters of bell-shaped white flowers. Grow it with other spring bulbs, such as grape hyacinths and species tulips dappled shade.

↕6in (15cm)

Z4–8

PERENNIAL SMALL

Sedum kamtschaticum

STONECROP A spreading semievergreen perennial with fleshy, oval cream-edged leaves and clusters of orange-flushed yellow flowers in early fall. 'Variegatum' (above) has pink-tinted midgreen leaves. Established plants are drought tolerant.

↕3in (8cm) ↔8in (20cm)

(!) Z3–8

BULB MEDIUM

Roscoea cautleyoides

ROSCOEA A compact, summer-flowering tuberous perennial bulb, which produces linear dark green leaves and short spikes of orchidlike yellow, purple, or white flowers. Plant it in groups in a sheltered site in dappled shade.

↕10in (25cm)

pH Z6–9

PERENNIAL SMALL

Silene alpestris

ALPINE CAMPION This evergreen perennial has narrow, lance-shaped midgreen leaves and small, rounded, fringed white, occasionally pink-flushed, flowers from late spring to early summer. Grow it in light dappled shade in gritty soil.

↕6in (15cm) ↔8in (20cm)

Z4–7

PERENNIAL SMALL

Viola cornuta

HORNED VIOLET This small, spreading evergreen perennial produces oval toothed-edged leaves and flat-faced purplish blue, occasionally white, flowers from spring to late summer. Plant it in groups in a rock garden.

↕8in (20cm) ↔8in (20cm) or more

Z6–9

BULB SMALL

Scilla mischtschenkoana

SQUILL An early-spring-flowering perennial bulb with strap-shaped basal leaves. Cup-shaped pale blue flowers with darker blue veins appear from late winter to early spring. Plant the bulbs in groups in fall throughout a rock garden.

↕4in (10cm)

(!) Z4–7

OTHER SUGGESTIONS

Perennials

Adiantum pedatum (N) • *Alchemilla erythropoda* • *Aquilegia flabellate* var. *pumila* f. *alba* • *Campanula carpatica* • *Campanula garganica* 'Dickson's Gold' • *Campanula poscharskyana* • *Carex pensylvanica* (N) • *Claytonia virginica* (N) • *Dodecatheon pulchellum* (N) • *Gentiana acaulis* • *Helleborus odorus* • *Hosta* 'Blue Mouse Ears' • *Oxalis enneaphylla* • *Packera aurea* (N) • *Saxifraga fortunei* • *Silene caroliniana* subsp. *wherryi* 'Short and Sweet' (N)

Bulbs

Chionodoxa sardensis • *Scilla bifolia*

Shrubs

Juniperus horizontalis 'Mother Lode' (N) • *Mitchella repens* (N)

Plants for urban gardens

Urban gardens are generally warmer than their surrounding areas and provide suitable growing conditions for a wide range of plants.

Even though most urban gardens are small, they can be made to look larger by disguising their boundaries with leafy trees and shrubs, such as ninebark, magnolia, and viburnum. Always remember that the soil next to walls and fences will be sheltered from the rain and therefore dry, so plant at least 12in (30cm) away from vertical surfaces where roots will find more moisture. You can create year-round color with evergreens and add a selection of deciduous plants for their seasonal flowers, fruit, and fall foliage.

TREE SMALL

Amelanchier canadensis

SHADBLOW SERVICEBERRY An upright, dense deciduous shrub with oval white-haired leaves that age to dark green and turn orange-red in fall. It bears starry white flowers from mid- to late spring and edible maroon, sweet and juicy fruits in summer.

↕20ft (6m) ↔10ft (3m)

pH Z3–7 Ⓝ

PERENNIAL LARGE

Anemone x *hybrida*

JAPANESE ANEMONE This is an upright perennial with divided, dark green basal leaves. From late summer to early fall, it produces large, pink or white single or double flowers. 'Queen Charlotte' (above) is a popular pink double variety.

↕4ft (1.2m) ↔indefinite

Z4–8

PERENNIAL MEDIUM

Aquilegia vulgaris Vervaeneana Group

WOODSIDE SERIES COLUMBINE This upright perennial has rounded, divided, orange- and gold-splashed olive-green leaves. In spring, two-tone flowers in white, red, pink, or blue appear. Deadhead to prevent self-seeding.

↕3ft (1m) ↔18in (45cm)

Z3–8

PERENNIAL MEDIUM

Aspidistra elatior

CAST-IRON PLANT An evergreen perennial with upright, narrow, glossy dark green leaves. Cream to purple summer flowers may appear near soil level. 'Variegata' (above) has cream-striped leaves. Ideal for summer borders or pots in deep shade.

↕24in (60cm) ↔18in (45cm)

Z7–10

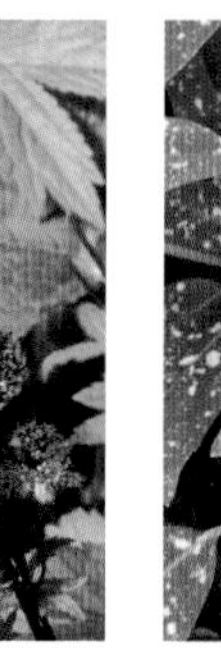

PERENNIAL MEDIUM

Astrantia major

MASTERWORT A clump-forming perennial with divided midgreen leaves. From midsummer to early fall, it produces sprays of small green and white, pink or red flowers. 'Hadspen Blood' (above) produces dark red flowers.

↕3ft (1m) ↔18in (45cm)

Z4–7

SHRUB MEDIUM

Aucuba japonica

JAPANESE LAUREL This bushy evergreen shrub has glossy dark green leaves. Small purplish flowers in mid-spring are followed by red berries on female plants. 'Crotonifolia' (above) has yellow-spotted foliage. Trim it annually in spring.

↕↔6ft (2m)

! Z7–10

PERENNIAL SMALL

Brunnera macrophylla

SIBERIAN BUGLOSS This ground-cover perennial has large heart-shaped leaves that form a low carpet and delicate sprays of small bright blue spring flowers. Shelter it from drying winds. 'Dawson's White' (above) has cream-variegated foliage.

↕18in (45cm) ↔24in (60cm)

Z3–8

SHRUB LARGE

Buxus sempervirens

COMMON BOXWOOD This evergreen shrub has oval, glossy dark green leaves. It tolerates close clipping and makes a dense low hedge or screen in a city garden. Disinfect pruning tools regularly to prevent the spread of fungal diseases.

↕↔15ft (5m)

Z6–8

SHRUB LARGE

Camellia japonica

JAPANESE CAMELLIA A bushy evergreen shrub with glossy, ovate, leathery dark green leaves. Plants are covered with single or double, white to deep pink flowers for a month or longer in spring. It tolerates full shade.

↕10ft (3m) ↔6ft (2m)

pH Z7–9

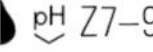

SHRUB LARGE

Camellia x *williamsii*

CAMELLIA The williamsii camellias are evergreen shrubs with glossy dark green leaves and white to deep pink single or double flowers in spring. Varieties include 'Anticipation', with crimson double blooms. It tolerates full shade.

↕15ft (5m) ↔8ft (2.5m)

pH Z7–9

PERENNIAL MEDIUM

Carex comans

NEW ZEALAND HAIR SEDGE This clump-forming perennial has arching, grasslike blue-green leaves that curl at the ends and resemble hair. Grow in a container or gravel bed. The bronze-leaved form 'Frosted Curls' (above) needs some sun for the best color.

↕24in (60cm) ↔18in (45cm)

Z7–9

PERENNIAL SMALL

Chiastophyllum oppositifolium

LAMB'S TAIL An evergreen perennial with large, oval, scalloped midgreen leaves and arching stems of small, bell-shaped bright yellow flowers from spring to summer. Plant it in part shade.

↕8in (20cm) ↔6in (15cm)

Z6–9

SHRUB LARGE

Daphne bholua

PAPER DAPHNE An evergreen shrub with oval, leathery dark green leaves. In late winter, clusters of sweetly fragrant pink and white flowers appear, followed by black berries. Grow it in a border to provide winter scent. Best in West Coast gardens.

↕10ft (3m) ↔5ft (1.5m)

(!) Z7–9

PERENNIAL LARGE

Deschampsia cespitosa

TUFTED HAIR GRASS This tuft-forming deciduous perennial bears clouds of tiny golden-yellow summer flowers on long stems. Both the seedheads and the linear, sharp-edged green leaves turn golden in fall. 'Goldtau' (above) is a popular form.

↕up to 6ft (2m) ↔20in (50cm)

Z4–9 (N)

PERENNIAL SMALL

Deschampsia flexuosa

WAVY HAIR GRASS This evergreen grass produces tufts of bluish green leaves and silvery bronze or purple flower heads held on long slim stems in summer. 'Aurea' (above) has bright yellow-green leaves and bronze flower heads.

↕up to 20in (50cm) ↔12in (30cm)

Z4–8 (N)

SHRUB SMALL

Deutzia gracilis

SLENDER DEUTZIA A compact deciduous shrub with lance-shaped green leaves. In early summer, it bears star-shaped white or pink, sometimes fragrant, flowers. 'Nikko' (above) has white blooms and purple-tinted leaves in fall. Grow it in a mixed bed.

↕↔3ft (1m)

Z5–8

PERENNIAL SMALL

Dicentra 'Stuart Boothman'

BLEEDING HEART A compact perennial with finely cut, fernlike gray-green leaves. From late spring to summer, it produces arching stems of pendent, heart-shaped carmine-pink flowers. Plant it with later-flowering plants in front of a bed.

↕12in (30cm) ↔16in (40cm)

(!) Z3–9

PERENNIAL MEDIUM

Digitalis parviflora

FOXGLOVE This deciduous perennial has glossy, dark green basal leaves and, in early summer, tall spikes of orange-brown flowers, each with a purple lip. Grow it in groups in dappled shade. All parts of the plant are toxic.

↕24in (60cm) ↔12in (30cm)

(!) Z4–9

PERENNIAL MEDIUM

Dryopteris affinis

GOLDEN MALE FERN This evergreen or semievergreen fern produces a "shuttlecock" of tall, lance-shaped, divided pale green fronds, which mature to dark green with scaly golden-brown midribs. Grow it beneath trees and shrubs.

↕↔3ft (1m)

Z5–8

PERENNIAL LARGE

Ensete ventricosum

ABYSSINIAN BANANA With its large paddle-shaped leaves, textured cream midribs, and red undersides, this evergreen perennial has a palmlike appearance. Grow it in a large container of soil-based potting mix and grit; overwinter indoors.

↕6ft (2m) ↔3ft (1m)

Z10–11

PERENNIAL SMALL

Epimedium x *youngianum* 'Niveum'

YOUNG'S BARRENWORT A ground-cover perennial with heart-shaped, serrated bronze-tinted leaves that turn green in late spring, when small, cup-shaped white blooms appear. Grow under trees.
↕↔12in (30cm)

Z4–8

BAMBOO LARGE

Fargesia murielae

UMBRELLA BAMBOO This clump-forming bamboo has arching yellow-green canes and lance-shaped bright green leaves. It is ideal to grow as a screen to add privacy or create an enclosure in busy urban environments. Best in fertile soil.
↕12ft (4m) ↔indefinite

Z5–9

SHRUB MEDIUM

x *Fatshedera lizei*

TREE IVY This is an upright evergreen shrub, often trained as a climber, with deeply lobed, glossy dark green leaves. In fall, it produces sprays of small, white flowers. Train it up a pillar or against a wall or fence.
↕6ft (2m) ↔10ft (3m)

Z8–11

SHRUB LARGE

Fatsia japonica

JAPANESE FATSIA This rounded, dense evergreen shrub has stout shoots and very large, deeply lobed, glossy dark green leaves. Spherical clusters of tiny white mid-fall flowers are followed by black fruits. Can be grown as a house plant in cooler areas.
↕↔12ft (4m)

Z8–10

PERENNIAL MEDIUM

Geranium phaeum

MOURNING WIDOW An upright, clump-forming perennial with lobed green leaves. From late spring to early summer, rounded maroon or white flowers with curved-back petals appear on lax stems. Drought- and shade-tolerant; grow beside a wall or fence.
↕30in (75cm) ↔18in (45cm)

Z4–8

PERENNIAL SMALL

Hakonechloa macra 'Aureola'

JAPANESE FOREST GRASS This slow-growing deciduous grass has purple stems and green-striped yellow leaves, aging to reddish brown. From early fall to winter, it bears reddish brown flower spikes. Use it to brighten a partly shaded bed or path.
↕16in (40cm) ↔24in (60cm)

Z5–9

SHRUB SMALL

Hebe topiaria

HEBE This compact, rounded evergreen shrub has dense stems bearing small gray-green leaves ideal for clipping into shapes. Clusters of small white flowers appear in summer. Use it to edge a bed, or for a small topiary. Best grown in West Coast gardens.
↕24in (60cm) ↔3ft (1m)

Z8–10

PERENNIAL MEDIUM

Helleborus foetidus

STINKING HELLEBORE This upright evergreen perennial has palmlike dark green leaves. From late winter to early spring, clusters of cup-shaped, red-margined pale green flowers with an unpleasant odor appear. Plant it away from seating.
↕↔24in (60cm)

(!) Z6–9

PERENNIAL MEDIUM

Helleborus x *hybridus*

LENTEN ROSE A semievergreen perennial with dark green leaves divided into lance-shaped toothed leaflets. Nodding saucer-shaped flowers in shades of white, pink, yellow, green, and purple appear from midwinter to spring.
↕↔24in (60cm)

Z5–9

PERENNIAL SMALL

Heuchera 'Plum Pudding'

CORAL BELLS This compact evergreen or semievergreen perennial is grown for its rounded, lobed maroon leaves. Tiny white flowers appear on wiry stems in summer. Trim off spent blooms to keep the plant tidy.
↕20in (50cm) ↔12in (30cm)

Z4–9 (N)

PERENNIAL MEDIUM

Hosta 'Honeybells'

PLANTAIN LILY A clump-forming perennial, grown for its large pale green leaves that are blunt at the tips and have wavy margins. In late summer, it bears short-lived, fragrant pale lilac flowers, which should be removed as soon as they fade.
↕24in (60cm) ↔4ft (1.2m)

Z3–8

BULB MEDIUM

Hyacinthus orientalis

HYACINTH A late-spring-flowering bulb with linear bright green leaves and spikes of highly scented bell-shaped flowers in a wide range of colors, including white, yellow, pink, red, and orange. Plant the bulbs in fall at the front of a bed or in pots.

↕12in (30cm)

Z4–8

SHRUB MEDIUM

Hydrangea macrophylla

BIGLEAF HYDRANGEA A deciduous shrub with broadly oval dark green leaves, which turn yellow in fall, and flat clusters of mauve-pink or blue summer flowers. Grow as a specimen, or at the rear of a bed. Blue forms (above) need acidic soil.

↕6ft (2m) ↔8ft (2.5m)

Z6–9

SHRUB SMALL

Hypericum calycinum

AARON'S BEARD This dwarf semi- or fully evergreen shrub has dark green leaves and, from midsummer to mid-fall, large, open, bright yellow flowers with a tuft of fluffy stamens in the center. Tolerates partial shade. Ideal for ground cover.

↕24in (60cm) ↔indefinite

Z5–9

SHRUB MEDIUM

Leucothoe fontanesiana

DROOPING LEUCOTHOE An arching evergreen shrub with toothed, leathery, dark green leaves and bell-shaped white flowers in spring. 'Rainbow' (above) has reddish green stems and mottled leaves. It tolerates deep shade and needs acidic soil.

↕up to 5ft (1.5m) ↔6ft (2m)

pH Z5–8 N

SHRUB LARGE

Itea virginica

VIRGINIA SWEETSPIRE This spreading shrub has arching stems that bear oval, spiny dark green leaves. From midsummer to early fall, it produces decorative greenish white racemes. Attractive red foliage in fall may persist into winter.

↕10ft (3m) ↔5ft (1.5m)

pH Z5–9 N

SHRUB SMALL

Juniperus squamata

SINGLESEED JUNIPER This dense, rounded evergreen conifer produces a low mound of slender, bright blue-gray foliage and makes a good foil for pastel- and hot-colored flowers in a city garden. It is suitable for large containers of soil-based potting mix.

↕16in (40cm) ↔3ft (1m)

Z4–8

PERENNIAL SMALL

Liriope muscari

LILYTURF A spreading evergreen perennial with grasslike, glossy dark green leaves and tiny lavender or purple-blue fall flower spikes. Use it to edge a shady border or as ground cover beneath shrubs. Considered invasive in some areas of the Southeast US.

↕12in (30cm) ↔18in (45cm)

pH Z6–10

TREE SMALL

Magnolia x *soulangeana*

SAUCER MAGNOLIA A spreading deciduous tree with oval, dark green leaves and, from mid- to late spring, pink, white, or purple goblet-shaped flowers. Use it as a feature in a lawn or mixed bed; protect flower buds from late frosts.

↕↔20ft (6m)

pH Z5–9

BULB MEDIUM

Narcissus 'Jack Snipe'

DAFFODIL This early- to mid-spring-flowering perennial bulb has narrow dark green leaves and creamy white flowers with short bright yellow cups. Plant the bulbs in groups in fall at the front of a bed or in containers.

↕9in (23cm)

Z4–9

BULB MEDIUM

Narcissus jonquilla

JONQUIL A mid-spring-flowering perennial bulb with narrow dark green leaves and clusters of richly fragrant yellow flowers with shallow, dark golden-yellow cups. Plant the bulbs in groups in fall at the front of a bed or in pots.

↕12in (30cm)

Z4–9

PERENNIAL MEDIUM

Onoclea sensibilis

SENSITIVE FERN A creeping deciduous fern with handsome arching, almost triangular, divided, fresh pale green fronds, often suffused pinkish brown in spring. In fall, fronds turn an attractive yellowish brown color.

↕24in (60cm) ↔3ft (1m)

pH Z4–9 (N)

PERENNIAL SMALL

Ophiopogon planiscapus 'Nigrescens'

MONDO GRASS This clump-forming evergreen perennial has narrow grasslike leaves and small, bell-shaped white or mauve summer flowers followed by black berries. Plant it to edge beds.

↕9in (23cm) ↔12in (30cm)

Z6–10

SHRUB LARGE

Osmanthus heterophyllus

FALSE HOLLY This evergreen shrub has hollylike, glossy bright green leaves and, in fall, tiny, fragrant white flowers. Grow it as a screen or in a border; protect it from hard frosts. 'Aureomarginatus' (above) has gold-edged leaves.

↕↔15ft (5m)

Z7–9

PERENNIAL SMALL

Pachysandra procumbens

ALLEGHENY SPURGE A clump-forming evergreen perennial with rounded, lobed dark green leaves and spikes of small, white mint-scented flowers in spring. Tolerates full shade; grow it as ground cover beneath trees and shrubs.

↕10in (25cm) ↔24in (60cm)

pH Z5–9 (N)

PERENNIAL MEDIUM

Paeonia lactiflora 'Sarah Bernhardt'

PEONY This clump-forming perennial has divided leaves and large, fragrant double flowers with ruffled rose-pink petals, fading to silvery blush white at the margins. Grow in a mixed bed in fertile soil; feed well.

↕↔3ft (1m)

(!) Z3–8

SHRUB MEDIUM

Paeonia suffruticosa

TREE PEONY This is an upright deciduous shrub with deeply lobed dark green leaves. In late spring, bowl-shaped, sometimes scented, pink, white, red, or purple flowers appear. Grow it next to a wall or fence in fertile soil.

↕↔7ft (2.2m)

(!) Z5–8

SHRUB MEDIUM

Physocarpus opulifolius

NINEBARK A deciduous shrub with peeling bark and lobed midgreen leaves. It bears domed white flower clusters in late spring, followed by red-brown fruits. Use at the rear of a bed or to mask a fence. 'Dart's Gold' (above) has yellow young foliage.

↕6ft (2m) ↔8ft (2.5m)

pH Z3–7 (N)

PERENNIAL MEDIUM

Physostegia virginiana

OBEDIENT PLANT This compact, erect perennial has toothed midgreen leaves. From late summer to early fall, it bears spikes of tubular white, pink, or purple flowers that can be placed in position. 'Vivid' (above) has purple flowers.

↕↔24in (60cm)

Z3–9 (N)

PERENNIAL SMALL

Pulmonaria saccharata

BETHLEHEM SAGE This clump-forming semievergreen perennial has bristly, white-spotted blue-green leaves and clusters of blue-purple funnel-shaped spring flowers. Use as ground cover beneath trees or shrubs, or to edge a flowerbed.

↕12in (30cm) ↔24in (60cm)

Z3–8

PERENNIAL MEDIUM

Salvia nemorosa

SAGE A compact perennial with lance-shaped, wrinkled midgreen leaves and spikes of pink, white, or purple flowers from summer to early fall. Plant it in light shade. 'East Friesland' (above) has violet-blue flowers with pink bracts.

↕up to 30in (75cm) ↔24in (60cm)

Z4–8

SHRUB SMALL

Salvia officinalis

SAGE This evergreen or semievergreen subshrub has aromatic gray-green or pale green leaves and, tubular purple-blue summer flowers. 'Aurea' (above) has yellow-variegated leaves. Use to edge a bed or as ground cover. Can be treated as an annual.

↕32in (80cm) ↔3ft (1m)

Z5–8

SHRUB SMALL

Sarcococca confusa

SWEET BOX A bushy evergreen shrub with glossy, lance-shaped, dark green leaves. In winter, clusters of white, tiny, sweetly fragrant blooms appear, followed by shiny black fruits. Plant it next to a path in part or deep shade.

↕↔3ft (1m)

Z6–9

SHRUB MEDIUM

Sarcococca hookeriana var. *digyna*

SWEET BOX A bushy evergreen shrub with glossy, lance-shaped dark green leaves. Clusters of tiny, white fragrant winter blooms are followed by shiny black fruits. Plant it next to a path to enjoy the scent.

↕5ft (1.5m) ↔6ft (2m)

Z6–9

SHRUB LARGE

Skimmia japonica

JAPANESE SKIMMIA This evergreen shrub has glossy green leaves and clusters of tiny, pink-budded white spring flowers. Females (above) bear bright red berries when grown near a male plant. Grow in moist, well-drained soil. Best in West Coast gardens.

↕↔20ft (6m)

(!) Z6–8

PERENNIAL MEDIUM

Spigelia marilandica

INDIAN PINK This is a medium-sized upright perennial with oval, undivided, paired green leaves. In early summer, it produces clusters of tubular red flowers with star-shaped yellow tips. Plant it in part shade.

↕24in (60cm) ↔18in (45cm)

Z5–9 (N)

TREE MEDIUM

Taxus baccata 'Fastigiata'

IRISH YEW This upright, slender evergreen conifer is better suited to small gardens than the species. It has needlelike dark green leaves. Female plants bear red berries. It makes a neat focal point, and tolerates deep shade. All parts are toxic.

↕up to 30ft (10m) ↔12ft (4m)

(!) Z6–7

TREE SMALL

Trachycarpus fortunei

WINDMILL PALM This evergreen palm has an unbranched stem and head of large, deeply divided, fanlike midgreen leaves. Sprays of fragrant creamy yellow flowers appear in early summer. Plant it in a sheltered area, away from drying winds.

↕up to 6ft (2m) ↔8ft (2.5m)

Z8–10

SHRUB MEDIUM

Viburnum davidii

DAVID VIBURNUM This dome-shaped evergreen shrub has deeply veined foliage and small white late-spring-flower clusters. Female plants produce decorative metallic blue fruits, if both sexes are grown. Use as ground cover, or grow under trees.

↕↔5ft (1.5m)

(!) Z7–9

SHRUB LARGE

Viburnum farreri

FRAGRANT VIBURNUM This deciduous, upright shrub has dark green foliage, bronze when young. In late fall and during mild periods in winter and early spring, clusters of fragrant white or pale pink blooms form, followed by red, blue, or black berries.

↕10ft (3m) ↔8ft (2.5m)

(!) Z5–8

OTHER SUGGESTIONS

Perennials

Carex appalachica (N) • *Begonia* Illumination Series • *Bergenia purpurascens* • *Dennstaedtia punctilobula* (N) • *Epimedium* x *versicolor* 'Sulphureum' • *Eurybia divaricata* (N)

Shrubs and climbers

Acer palmatum 'Atropurpureum' • *Buddleja davidii* • *Daphne laureola* subsp. *philippi* • *Daphne pontica* • *Euonymus japonicus* 'Microphyllus Albovariegatus' • *Hebe rakaiensis* • *Juniperus chinensis* 'Pyramidalis' • *Juniperus squamata* 'Blue Star' • *Lapageria rosea* • *Lonicera nitida* • *Physocarpus* 'Diabolo' • *Salix* 'Hakuro Nishiki' • *Skimmia* x *confusa*

Trees

Acer palmatum 'Atropurpureum' • *Carpinus caroliniana* (N)

Plant focus: ferns

Perfect for shady gardens, ferns form carpets of textured foliage that provide a decorative foil for woodland flowers.

RANGING FROM TINY CREEPING PLANTS, such as the Himalayan maidenhair fern, to the tall, stately royal fern, which reaches up to 6ft (2m) in height, this group of sun-shy woodland plants offers the gardener many exciting design opportunities. Ferns are grown primarily for their textured foliage, which provides a lacy backdrop to spring bulbs and other shade-tolerant blooms. For continuous color and interest throughout the year, mix evergreen ferns, such as Christmas fern, with deciduous ferns, which produce coiled shoots as their leaves unfurl in spring and turn rusty brown in fall. Although most ferns prefer damp soil, a few, such as the *Polypodium* family and male fern, do well in drier conditions and are invaluable for providing understory planting beneath trees and large shrubs.

Ferns create a luscious green blanket in cool shady areas where few others plants will thrive.

USING FERNS

Ferns look delicate, with their fine lacy foliage, but most are very cold tolerant and have many uses. They are also highly varied, offering solid or finely divided, glossy or matte green leaves, some decorated with purple or silver variegation. They look most effective planted together in shady borders, but many also make good specimen plants in containers, such as soft shield fern, with its elegant arching fronds.

Shade-loving astilbes and coral bells provide the perfect planting partners for lady fern and other ferns in a mixed border where the soil is moist.

Ferns of different sizes and shapes, such as hart's tongue fern and male fern, make excellent subjects for a textural foliage container.

TYPES OF FERNS

Adiantum Forms include *A. aleuticum* (*above*), with fingerlike deciduous fronds; *A. pedatum* with black-stalked segmented fronds; and evergreen *A. venustrum*.

Asplenium The hart's tongue fern, *A. scolopendrium* (*above*), bears rosettes of long, glossy evergreen fronds. The foliage of *A. trichomanes* is divided into oblong segments.

Athyrium The lady fern, *A. filix-femina* (*above*), has deciduous fronds made up of long segments. The deciduous Japanese painted fern, *A. niponicum*, is very attractive.

Blechnum Deer fern, *B. spicant* (*above*), has narrow, dark green, divided evergreen fronds. *B. penna-marina* is shorter and bears reddish young fronds that mature to green.

Dryopteris Most species of buckler fern produce large deciduous fronds, crested in some forms, arranged like an elegant shuttlecock.

Matteuccia The large-sized ostrich or shuttlecock fern, *M. struthiopteris* (*above*), bears large, pale green deciduous fronds divided into fingerlike segments.

Ferns often naturalize in cracks in shady walls, softening the edges and adding interest.

Osmunda The royal fern, *O. regalis*, has very tall deciduous fronds divided into long segments, with rust-colored spore-bearing segments at the tips of some segments.

Polypodium This genus includes many hardy evergreen ferns; including the low-growing *P. vulgare* (*above*), with triangular-shaped dark-green fronds.

Polystichum Most holly or shield ferns are hardy with large, dark green, triangular evergreen fronds, divided into feathery segments, with shuttlecock-like crowns.

Plants for exposed sites

Grow spring bulbs, summer-flowering perennials, deciduous trees and shrubs for fall foliage, and frostproof evergreens to dress winter schemes.

Many ferns are unfazed by freezing temperatures and add a textural backdrop to colorful bulbs and perennials such as Siberian squill, iris, and columbine, while fragrant plants lend a sensory note to planting schemes; grapeholly, Solomon's seal, and spring-flowering daffodils will all help to perfume your plot. Large shrubs and trees can help shelter an exposed garden, but plant them on the north side to ensure that they don't cast even more shade. Also use tough hedging plants, such as hawthorn and yew, to create a warmer seating area; a shoulder-high screen will help protect a patio.

PERENNIAL SMALL

Adiantum aleuticum

WESTERN MAIDENHAIR FERN A deciduous or semievergreen fern with black-stalked midgreen fronds divided into oblong segments. New fronds may be tinged pink. It is tolerant of low temperatures, but avoid planting in deep shade.

↕↔18in (45cm)

Z3–8 Ⓝ

PERENNIAL SMALL

Alchemilla mollis

LADY'S MANTLE This clump-forming perennial has rounded pale green leaves with crinkled edges. In summer, small sprays of tiny, bright greenish yellow flowers appear. Ideal as a ground-cover plant; trim back untidy leaves.

↕↔20in (50cm)

Z4–7

PERENNIAL MEDIUM

Aquilegia vulgaris

COLUMBINE This upright perennial has green leaves divided into rounded lobed leaflets. From late spring to early summer, it bears pendent single or double flowers in shades of purple and blue to pink and white. Deadhead after flowering.

↕3ft (1m) ↔20in (50cm)

Z3–8

PERENNIAL MEDIUM

Astilbe x *ardensii* 'Fanal'

ASTILBE A clump-forming perennial with attractive, deeply divided, fernlike dark green foliage. In summer, it produces dense spikes of feathery dark pink flowers on slim dark stems. Plant it in moist, fertile soil in partial shade.

↕24in (60cm) ↔18in (45cm)

pH Z3–8

PERENNIAL LARGE

Athyrium filix-femina

LADY FERN This deciduous fern produces arching, lance-shaped pale green fronds divided into narrow segments with toothed-edged margins. It thrives in deep shade in moist, acidic soil, but avoid planting in windy sites.

↕4ft (1.2m) ↔3ft (1m)

pH Z4–9 Ⓝ

TREE LARGE

Betula utilis var. *jacquemontii*

HIMALAYAN BIRCH This vase-shaped deciduous tree is grown for its stunning white bark. Its diamond-shaped leaves turn yellow in fall. Use it as a specimen or to make a small copse.

↕60ft (18m) ↔30ft (10m)

Z4–7

PERENNIAL MEDIUM

Blechnum spicant

DEER FERN This evergreen fern has narrow, lance-shaped dark green fronds divided into linear segments. Good in deep shade in cold and exposed gardens where the soil is reliably moist year round. Remove old foliage in spring.

↕30in (75cm) ↔18in (45cm)

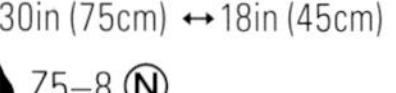

Z5–8 Ⓝ

SHRUB SMALL

Calluna vulgaris

SCOTCH HEATHER A bushy, low-growing evergreen shrub with tiny gray, yellow, or bright green leaves and bell-shaped single or double flowers in shades of pink, white, and purple from midsummer to late fall. Survives cold weather if protected.

↕12in (30cm) ↔14in (35cm)

pH Z4–6

TREE SMALL

Crataegus crus-gali

COCKSPUR HAWTHORN A small deciduous tree, var. *inermis* has thornless branches and glossy dark green leaves that turn bright red in fall. It flowers for a short period in late spring, and bears red berries, attractive to birds. Suitable for windy or cold sites.

↕25ft (8m) ↔30ft (10m)

Z4–7 Ⓝ

PERENNIAL MEDIUM

Crocosmia x *crocosmiiflora*

MONTBRETIA An upright perennial with arching, sword-shaped green leaves and, from summer to early fall, clusters of small trumpet-like blooms. 'Star of the East' (above) has apricot-yellow flowers. Considered invasive in some coastal areas.

↕28in (70cm) ↔3in (8cm)

Z6–9

PERENNIAL LARGE

Digitalis ferruginea

RUSTY FOXGLOVE An upright perennial with basal rosettes of oval, rough dark green leaves. Long slender spikes of funnel-shaped orange-brown and white flowers appear in midsummer. An excellent border plant for cold and exposed gardens.

↕4ft (1.2m) ↔12in (30cm)

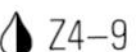

PERENNIAL MEDIUM

Dryopteris wallichiana

WALLICH'S WOOD FERN A clump-forming deciduous fern with a "shuttlecock" of lance-shaped, divided, bright yellow-green fronds, aging to dark green, and brownish black scaly stems. Best in fertile soil; it tolerates deep shade and dry conditions.

↕3ft (1m) ↔30in (75cm)

Z5–7

BULB LARGE

Fritillaria pallidiflora

SIBERAIN FRITILLARY A perennial bulb with lance-shaped blue-green leaves that die back after flowering. It bears nodding, bell-shaped greenish yellow flowers that are checkered brownish red within in early summer. Plant the bulbs in groups in fall.

↕28in (70cm)

Z4–9

PERENNIAL SMALL

Helleborus niger

CHRISTMAS ROSE This clump-forming evergreen perennial has divided, leathery dark green leaves and, from winter to early spring, cup-shaped, nodding, white or pink-flushed flowers with green "eyes." 'Potter's Wheel' (above) has pure white blooms.

↕↔12in (30cm)

Z3–8

TREE SMALL

Juniperus scopulorum

ROCKY MOUNTAIN JUNIPER A cold-tolerant pyramidal conifer with sharply pointed scalelike leaves and small cones. 'Skyrocket' (above) has a narrow columnar habit and blue-gray foliage; ideal for a small garden in light shade.

↕20ft (6m) ↔30in (75cm)

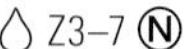

PERENNIAL MEDIUM

Hosta 'Krossa Regal'

PLANTAIN LILY This clump-forming, vase-shaped perennial has arching, deeply ribbed grayish blue leaves. In summer, it produces spikes of short-lived lilac flowers. Suitable for cold sites; shelter it from drying winds, and protect from slugs.

↕28in (70cm) ↔30in (75cm)

Z3–8 Ⓝ

SHRUB LARGE

Kalmia latifolia

MOUNTAIN LAUREL A bushy evergreen shrub with oval, glossy green leaves. From late spring to early summer, large clusters of pink cup-shaped flowers appear from crimped buds. Prune lightly after flowering to keep it neat.

↕↔10ft (3m)

pH Z4–9 Ⓝ

PERENNIAL MEDIUM

Iris sibirica

SIBERIAN IRIS A rhizome-forming perennial with upright, swordlike blue-green leaves and large, beardless pink, blue, white, or yellow flowers from late spring to early summer. 'Butter and Sugar' (above) has yellow and white blooms.

↕3ft (1m) ↔indefinite

Z3–9

PERENNIAL MEDIUM

Lamprocapnos spectabilis 'Alba'

BLEEDING HEART A clump-forming perennial with fernlike foliage. From late spring to early summer, it produces pendent, white heart-shaped blooms; dies back after flowering.

↕30in (75cm) ↔24in (60cm)

Z3–9

SHRUB SMALL

Juniperus x *pfitzeriana*

JUNIPER This flat-topped, shrubby evergreen conifer has scalelike, gray-green leaves and dark, fading to pale purple, cones. 'Pfitzeriana Aurea' (above) has golden foliage, which turns yellow-green in winter. Best in dappled shade.

↕3ft (1m) ↔6ft (2m)

Z4–9

SHRUB SMALL

Mahonia aquifolium

OREGON GRAPEHOLLY A spreading evergreen shrub with spiny, glossy dark green leaves that turn bronze in cold weather. In spring, it bears clusters of scented yellow flowers followed by black berries. It is ideal for all-year color.

↕3ft (1m) ↔5ft (1.5m)

Z5–8 Ⓝ

PERENNIAL MEDIUM

Maianthemum racemosum

FALSE SPIKENARD This upright perennial has prominently veined, oval green leaves. From mid- to late spring, it bears scented, fluffy cream plumes, which are sometimes followed by red berries. Ideal for cold sites; shelter it from strong, drying winds.

↕3ft (1m) ↔24in (60cm)

pH Z3–8 (N)

PERENNIAL MEDIUM

Mertensia virginica

VIRGINIA BLUEBELLS This is a compact perennial with soft blue-green leaves and clusters of nodding, funnel-shaped blue flowers in spring. The plant dies down in summer. It tolerates low temperatures, but only light shade.

↕24in (60cm) ↔18in (45cm)

Z3–8 (N)

BULB MEDIUM

Narcissus bulbocodium

HOOP PETTICOAT DAFFODIL A dwarf perennial bulb, with grasslike dark green leaves and unusual funnel-shaped golden-yellow flowers surrounded by slim petals. Plant the bulbs in fall in soil that is reliably moist in winter and spring.

↕6in (15cm)

(!) Z5–9

PERENNIAL LARGE

Persicaria amplexicaulis

RED BISTORT This clump-forming perennial has oval green leaves and slender spikes of bell-shaped white or pink flowers from summer to early fall. Varieties include 'Firetail' (above) with bright red blooms. It is ideal for cold or coastal gardens.

↕↔4ft (1.2m)

(!) Z4–8

PERENNIAL MEDIUM

Polygonatum odoratum

FRAGRANT SOLOMON'S SEAL An arching perennial with oval to lance-shaped midgreen leaves and fragrant, tubular, green-tipped white flowers in late spring. Grow it in full or part shade in cold gardens, sheltered from drying winds.

↕24in (60cm) ↔12in (30cm)

Z3–8

PERENNIAL MEDIUM

Polystichum acrostichoides

CHRISTMAS FERN An evergreen perennial with slender, lance-shaped dark green fronds divided into segments. It will produce clumps over time, and is tolerant of cold, shady sites, including deep shade. It thrives in most soils.

↕24in (60cm) ↔18in (45cm)

Z3–9 (N)

PERENNIAL MEDIUM

Polystichum munitum

GIANT HOLLY FERN This evergreen "shuttlecock" perennial produces large, erect, leathery, triangular-shaped dark green fronds consisting of small spiny-margined segments. Tolerant of deep shade and cold sites, where the soil is moist.

↕3ft (1m) ↔4ft (1.2m)

pH Z3–8 (N)

SHRUB SMALL

Potentilla fruticosa

CINQUEFOIL A deciduous shrub with small dark green leaves divided into narrow leaflets and saucer-shaped flowers in shades of yellow, red, pink, orange, or white from late spring to early fall, depending on the cultivar. Grow in partial shade.

↕3ft (1m) ↔5ft (1.5m)

Z2–7 (N)

PERENNIAL SMALL

Primula vulgaris

ENGLISH PRIMROSE This small-sized perennial forms basal rosettes of oval pale green leaves. In early spring, it produces clusters of often scented primrose-yellow flowers. It lives happily in cold gardens in dappled shade.

↕8in (20cm) ↔14in (35cm)

Z4–8

PERENNIAL SMALL

Sagina subulata

HEATH PEARLWORT This mat-forming perennial has small, pointed green leaves and tiny white summer flowers. 'Aurea' (above) has yellow-green foliage. Grow it as ground cover or a lawn alternative in moist, acidic soil, at a site shaded at noon.

↕4in (10cm) ↔12in (30cm)

pH Z4–7

PERENNIAL SMALL

Saxifraga fortunei

SAXIFRAGE A deciduous or semievergreen perennial with lobed midgreen leaves, red-purple beneath. Upright red stems supporting pendent clusters of white flowers appear in late summer or fall. Ideal for a cold, shaded garden.

↕↔ 12in (30cm)

Z7–9

BULB MEDIUM

Scilla siberica

SIBERIAN SQUILL This is a dwarf perennial bulb with grasslike midgreen leaves and nodding, bell-shaped blue flowers in spring. Plant the bulbs in groups in fall. If left undisturbed, plants will slowly naturalize.

↕ 8in (20cm)

Z4–8 (N)

TREE LARGE

Taxus baccata

ENGLISH YEW This bushy evergreen conifer has dark green needles and small yellow spring flowers that are followed by red berries. Use it as formal hedging, or a windbreak in cold regions, or to attract wildlife. All parts are toxic.

↕ 50ft (15m) ↔ 30ft (10m)

(!) Z6–7

PERENNIAL SMALL

Tiarella wherryi

FOAM FLOWER A clump-forming compact perennial with deeply lobed, maroon-tinted green leaves. From late spring to early summer, clusters of tiny, frothy white or pink flower heads appear. It makes a good edging plant in deep shade.

↕ 8in (20cm) ↔ 6in (15cm)

Z3–7 (N)

SHRUB LARGE

Tsuga canadensis

CANADIAN HEMLOCK An evergreen conifer with needlelike blue-green leaves, white beneath, held on pendent stems, and brown cones. 'Pendula' (above) is a slow-growing, mound-forming spreading shrub. Woolly adelgid is a problem in East Coast regions.

↕ 80ft (25m) ↔ 30ft (10m)

Z3–7 (N)

SHRUB SMALL

Vaccinium vitis-idaea Koralle Group

LINGONBERRY A spreading evergreen shrub with glossy dark green leaves. From late spring to early summer, bell-shaped, nodding white or pink flowers appear, followed by edible red berries.

↕ 10in (25cm) ↔ indefinite

pH Z2–6

SHRUB LARGE

Viburnum plicatum f. *tomentosum*

DOUBLEFILE VIBURNUM A wide-spreading deciduous shrub with tiered branches that carry prominently veined dark green leaves, which turn purple in fall. In late spring, it produces white flower heads.

↕ 10ft (3m) ↔ 12ft (4m)

(!) Z5–8

SHRUB LARGE

Viburnum tinus

LAURUSTINUS A large-sized, bushy evergreen shrub with oval, lobed dark green leaves. From late winter to spring, it produces flattened clusters of small white flowers followed by metallic blue berries.

↕↔ 10ft (3m)

(!) Z8–10

PERENNIAL SMALL

Viola cornuta

HORNED VIOLET This small, spreading evergreen perennial has oval toothed leaves and, from spring to late summer, flat-faced purplish blue, occasionally white, flowers. Grow it in a wind-blown garden or bed; ideal for ground cover.

↕ 8in (20cm) ↔ 8in (20cm) or more

Z6–9

SHRUB MEDIUM

Weigela florida

WEIGELA An arching deciduous shrub with oval, toothed midgreen leaves. From late spring to early summer, it produces dark pink flowers, pale pink to white inside. Good for cold sites. 'Java Red' has bronze-green foliage.

↕↔ 8ft (2.5m)

Z5–8

OTHER SUGGESTIONS

Perennials

Amsonia tabernaemontana (N) • *Chelone lyonii* 'Hot Lips' (N) • *Gentiana septemfida* • *Geranium pyrenaicum* 'Bill Wallis' • *Osmunda regalis* (N) • *Polemonium reptans* 'Stairway to Heaven' (N) • *Tiarella cordifolia* (N)

Bulbs

Chionodoxa luciliae • *Galanthus nivalis* 'Flore Pleno' • *Leucojum vernum*

Shrubs

Physocarpus opulifolius (N) • *Rhododendron yakushimanum* • *Ribes alpinum* • *Sambucus racemosa* • *Viburnum trilobum* 'Wentworth' (N)

Trees

Betula nigra HERITAGE (N) • *Juniperus communis* (N)

PLANTS for SPECIAL EFFECTS

PLANTS FOR
GARDEN STYLES
PLANTS FOR
SEASONAL INTEREST
PLANTS FOR
COLOR AND SCENT
PLANTS FOR
SHAPE AND TEXTURE
PLANTS FOR
GARDEN PROBLEMS

Choosing plants for special effects

When planning a design, choose plants for their color, texture, shape, and scent, and introduce seasonal changes by using species that add interest at various times. Add evergreens and plants with a bold structure for year-round appeal.

PLANNING YOUR SCHEME

The first section of this book helps you to pinpoint plants that thrive in the particular conditions of your site, while this second section focuses on sense and style by providing you with a selection of plants that can be used to create a particular design or achieve a specific effect. For example, you may be looking for ideas to create a Asian-style garden, or plants that will draw a range of birds and insects to a wildlife border. Also look at pp.14–17, which explain how to group plants to achieve certain effects, such as a formal or contemporary design.

Once you have chosen a style, you should think about introducing seasonal interest to keep the color going and attract attention throughout the year. This is particularly important in small plots, where the whole space is on view at all times. When selecting seasonal plants, try to combine those that flower or fruit consecutively to avoid peaks and troughs—the description of each plant featured tells you whether it is an early-, mid-, or late-season performer. Also, combine your blooming plants with leafy species and evergreens for long-lasting appeal.

GARDEN STYLES

Creating a style To produce a chosen garden style, select an appropriate palette of plants. The Asian-style garden above uses architectural plants in muted colors to offset the bold features.

Using plants Combine plants within a style so that they contrast or complement each other. Here yellow foxtail lilies contrast with the adjacent purple dianthus (*left*).

SEASONAL INTEREST

Seasonal highlights To capture the essence of a season, use plants that celebrate that time of year, such as spring bulbs or trees with fiery fall leaves, like the Japanese maple above.

Retaining interest The flowers of many plants, such as sea holly (*left*) and hydrangeas, dry in place, and last into winter, providing interest for more than one season.

APPEALING TO THE SENSES

Plants with scented leaves and flowers are prized because they introduce a sensory quality that can lift the spirits at all times of the year. The perfume from a mahonia or witch hazel in the depths of winter is tempting enough to venture outside for, while the scent of honeysuckle is reason enough to spend summer evenings relaxing next to it. You will find a wealth of fragrant plants of all types outlined on pp.340–345.

You can also add a designer element to your garden by using plants that have different shapes, foliage color, and textures. Such plants also provide a permanent decorative framework for the more transitory elements.

The final section of the book focuses on problem areas, such as sun-baked sites, slopes, and waterlogged areas, as well as recommends plants to choose for gardens where pests are a nuisance. This section also offers low-maintenance solutions for large areas by offering a selection of weed-suppressing ground cover plants.

COLOR AND SCENT

Sensory pleasure Plants that produce colorful or sweetly scented flowers or leaves, such as lavender (*above*), form a key element of the sensory experience you can enjoy in your garden.

Choice plants Some plants, such as peonies (*left*), have exquisite, but short-lived blooms. Position them with other plants that provide longer-lasting color.

SHAPE AND TEXTURE

Enduring appeal Plants with bold stem and leaf structures and textures, such as the silvery mulleins above, will sustain interest over a longer period than plants with transient flower forms.

Creating shapes Many plants are ideal for training, shaping, or using as topiary (*left*), allowing you to create enduring dramatic and artistic effects in your garden.

PROBLEM SOLVING

Plant allies Ground-cover plants, such as lungwort (*above*) and leafy cranesbills, are perfect for suppressing unwanted weeds in shady areas.

Recipes for garden styles

TRADITIONAL COTTAGE BORDER

This medley of classic cottage garden favorites in pastel hues provides the perfect setting for a romantic border in sun. The tall larkspur provide height and structure behind a blend of roses and masterworts. Other plants to consider if you have space include lupine, both tall and spreading forms of bellflowers, and cranesbills. Add herbs and vegetables to the design to enhance the classic cottage feel. Feeding annually in spring with an all-purpose granular fertilizer and a mulch of well-rotted organic matter, such as shredded leaves.

Plant list
1 *Astrantia major*
2 *Rosa*—pink shrub variety
3 *Delphinium elatum*

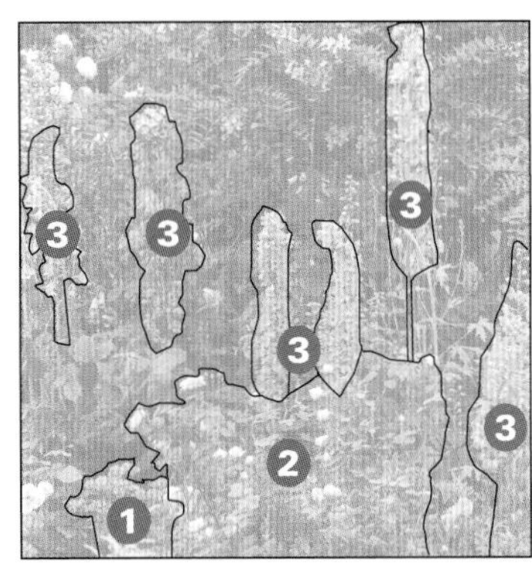

CHIC MODERNIST DESIGN

The trick to producing an elegant modernist scheme is to keep your planting designs simple, selecting varieties for their structural qualities, and minimizing color choices. In this scheme, white summer-flowering alliums provide accents above crisply clipped boxwood balls, while ferns and Mexican feather grass offer textural contrasts. All of these plants like free-draining conditions, except for the ferns, which require more moisture.

Plant list
1 *Stipa tenuissima*
2 *Allium*—white form
3 *Buxus sempervirens*
4 *Asplenium scolopendrium*

PERENNIAL BORDER FOR A SMALL SPACE

Combine naturalistic swathes of just a few plant species to create a small-scale prairie. Here, flat-topped yarrow is teamed with spires of purple salvias and allium globes to give an exciting contrast of flower shapes and textures. Leafy grasses provide a cool and long-lasting foil for the flowers. To extend the season, add groups of black-eyed Susan and asters in the same colors, and leave the spent flower heads to stand over winter. Plant in moisture-retentive but free-draining soil for the best results.

Plant list

1 *Salvia nemorosa* 'East Friesland'
2 *Allium caeruleum*
3 *Achillea*—yellow variety

Recipes for color, texture, and scent

STEM INTEREST IN A SPRING BORDER

Few plants surpass the Himalayan birch for year-round stem interest. Set the tree's startling white trunks against a dark backdrop to produce the most eye-catching effect and choose a multistemmed form to increase the impact. Underplant the tree with shade-tolerant alliums, cranesbills, lady's mantle, and ferns to provide color and texture through spring and summer. These plants also cope with the well-drained soil conditions beneath a tree. In early spring, apply a mulch of well-rotted organic matter, such as shredded leaves.

Plant list

1 *Alchemilla mollis*
2 *Geranium himalayense* 'Gravetye'
3 *Galega* hybrid
4 *Allium* 'Purple Sensation'
5 *Geranium clarkei* 'Kashmir White'
6 *Betula utilis* var. *jacquemontii*

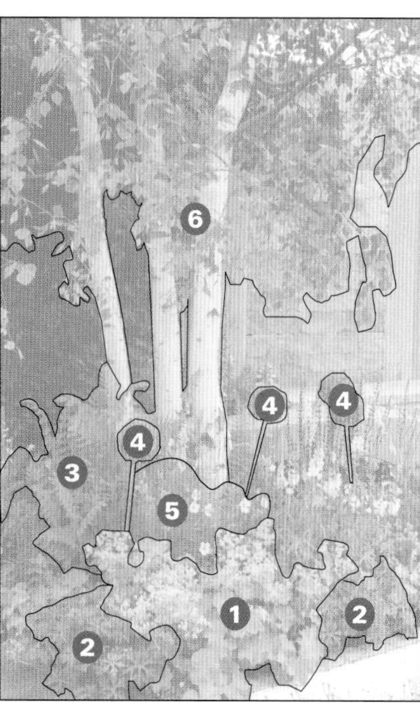

COLORFUL FOLIAGE EFFECTS

Create a medley of colorful foliage with this collection of trees, shrubs, and perennials. Position the Japanese maple in a prominent spot where it will provide the main focal point in the border. Its canopy of finely cut red foliage will fire up further in fall. The Japanese fatsia adds a large-leaved, green contrast, while low-growing coral bell and knotweed lend foliage color at ground level. These plants enjoy moist but free-draining soil. Ensure the knotweed is mulched and kept well watered in summer.

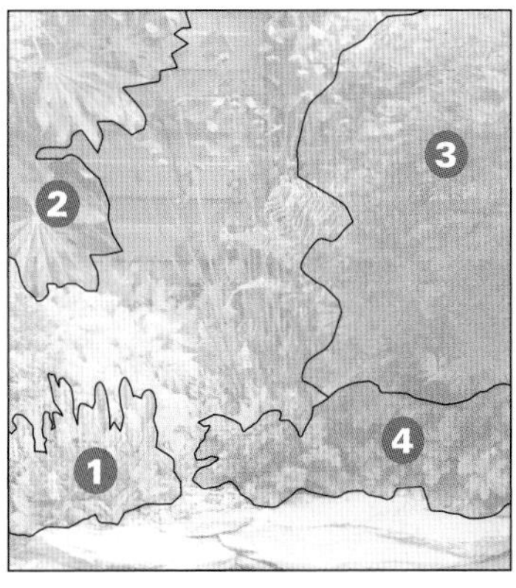

Plant list
1 *Persicaria affinis* 'Superba'
2 *Fatsia japonica*
3 *Acer palmatum* 'Atropurpureum'
4 *Heuchera micrantha* var. *diversifolia* 'Palace Purple'

FRAGRANT BORDER

Choose scented plants, such as lavender, to edge a seating area or path where they will emit their scent when brushed against. There is a wealth of fragrant shrub roses to choose from, so select those that suit your color scheme and also consider climbing forms to create a scented wall behind the border. Or, you could weave in regal lily at the back of the scheme, and use garden pinks to edge the front. Provide plants with a sunny site and free-draining soil.

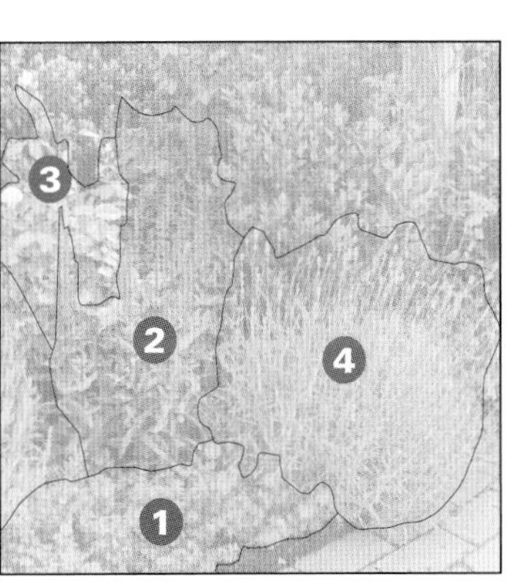

Plant list
1 *Geranium sanguineum*
2 *Salvia nemorosa*
3 Fragrant shrub rose, e.g. *Rosa* 'Claire Austin'
4 *Lavandula angustifolia* 'Munstead'

Recipes for seasonal effects

COLORFUL SUMMER BORDER

For midsummer color, combine this group of perennials and grasses for a contemporary border. The hot orange and yellow yarrow and euphorbia are tempered by the grass, pheasant's tail grass, and blue sea holly, which also introduce different shapes and forms. Repeat these plants throughout your border to produce a cohesive design, and also include some alliums, masterwort, and irises to create interest earlier in the season. Plant this collection in a sunny site in free-draining soil.

Plant list

1 *Eryngium* x *zabelii*
2 *Anemanthele lessoniana*
3 *Achillea* 'Walther Funcke'
4 *Euphorbia* species
5 *Trifolium* species
6 *Achillea* 'Terracotta'

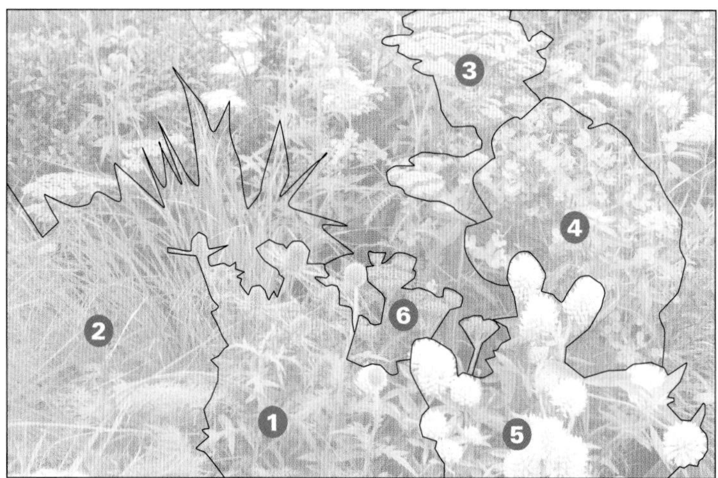

LATE SPRING BORDER

Ideal for a bog garden or moisture-retentive clay, this border of leafy ferns and perennials, interspersed with colorful flowers, will perform well in part-shade. The ostrich fern and giant rhubarb are large plants, so ensure you allow them sufficient space and do not let them swamp the dainty primroses and irises in front. To extend the color into summer, also include astilbe and meadowsweet. Mulch in spring and add organic matter.

Plant list

1 *Primula* species
2 *Dicentra formosa*
3 *Iris sibirica*
4 *Gunnera manicata*
5 *Matteuccia struthiopteris*
6 *Hosta* species

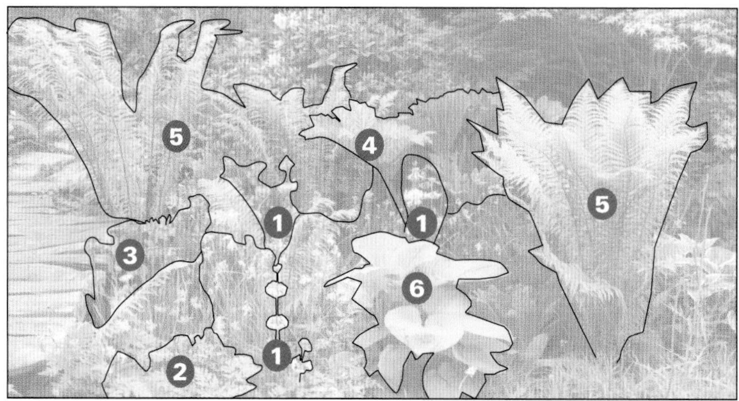

WINTER COLOR AND INTEREST

Bolster winter interest with a border filled with evergreen conifers. Choose a variety of shapes, colors, and textures for maximum impact. Even slow-growing types can eventually form large plants, so check plant labels for heights and spreads carefully before buying. All of these conifers prefer a sunny site and moist but free-draining soil.

Plant list

1 *Picea glauca*
2 *Juniper communis*
3 *Picea pungens*
4 *Thuja plicata* 'Collyer's Gold'
5 *Cryptomeria japonica* 'Elegans Compacta'
6 *Cupressus arizonica* var. *glabra*
7 *Chamaecyparis obtusa* 'Nana Aurea'

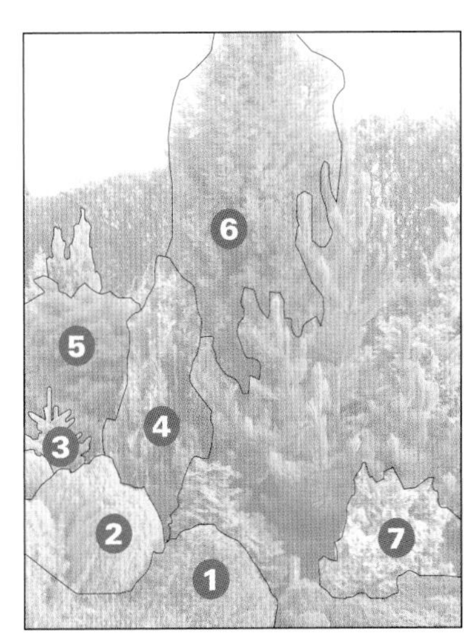

Recipes for problem areas

SLUG-PROOF BORDER

All plants can be attacked by slugs and snails but, in a mixed border, the pests are more likely to take the easy option and target those with soft succulent leaves. A selection of the most slug- and snail-resistant plants are illustrated on pp.386–389, and others include plants with tough foliage, such as evergreen boxwood and many aromatic herbs—slugs find their pungent flavors and downy leaves unpalatable. Oregano, thyme, and lavender cotton are all resistant to attack. You can also try growing sacrificial plants, such as the pot marigolds in this scheme, which tempt slugs and snails and draw them away from your prized flowers or crops.

Plant list

1 *Buxus sempervirens*
2 *Thymus vulgaris*
3 *Origanum vulgare* 'Aureum'
4 *Phlomis russeliana*
5 *Calendula officinale*
6 *Santolina pinnata*

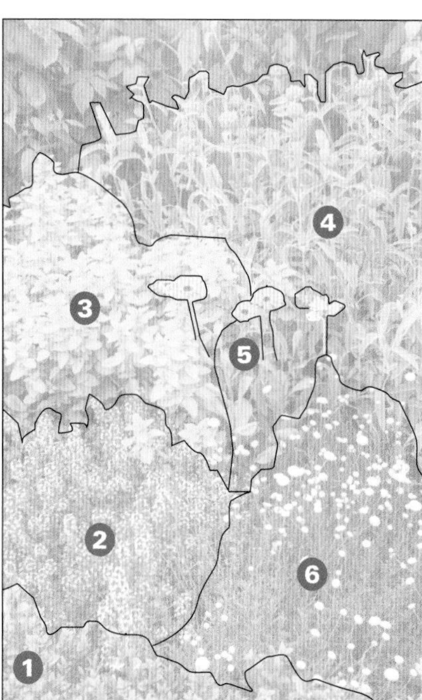

GROUND COVER IN SUN

The range of plants suitable for ground cover in a sunny site is large and in addition to those illustrated on pp.380–383, consider those shown here. Ideal for sandy soil, sage and thyme are both aromatic herbs, and if trimmed regularly by pinching off their tips, they will form dense, bushy clumps. For further color, plant green- or yellow-leaved thyme varieties and variegated sage. The euphorbia is a tender plant, which is useful for adding summer color while also suppressing weeds.

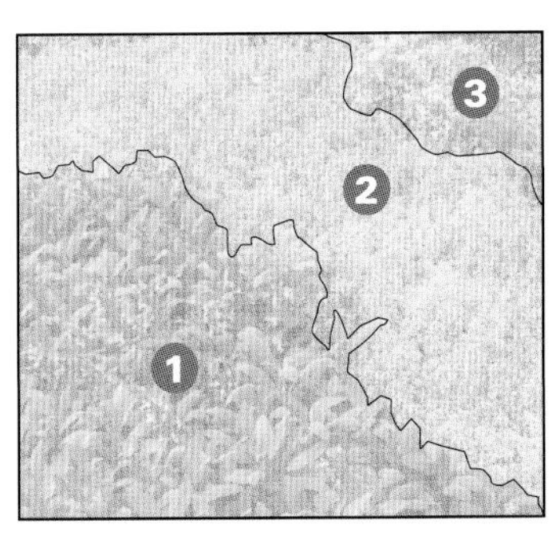

Plant list

1 *Salvia officinalis* 'Purpurascens' (purple sage)
2 *Thymus pulegioides* 'Aureus' (golden thyme)
3 *Euphorbia hypericifolia* DIAMOND FROST

HOT, DRY BORDER

Sunny dusty sites can produce beautiful flowering displays if you choose your plants carefully. Corn poppies and larkspur, which are sown annually in spring, together with marguerite daisies, will produce a long show of color in summer, while the perennial yellow-eyed grass adds color and structure in between. The poppies and larkspur may self-seed if you turn the soil over with a fork each year to encourage germination. Any unwanted seedlings can easily be removed.

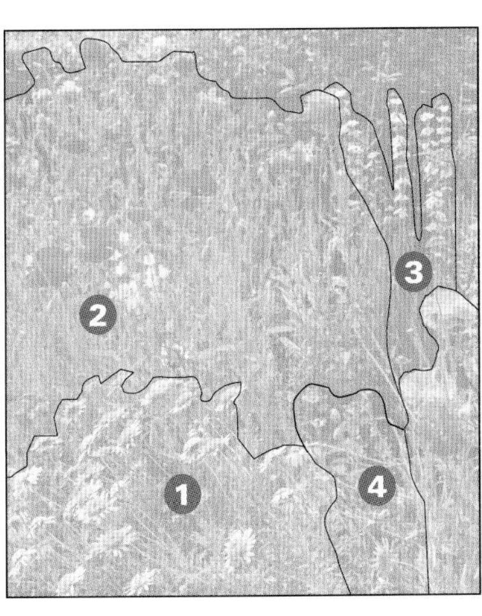

Plant list

1 *Argyranthemum* cultivar
2 *Papaver rhoeas*
3 *Sisyrinchium striatum*
4 *Consolida ajacis*

PLANTS for GARDEN STYLES

Whatever your taste or garden size, there's a style to suit you, from the clean lines of a formal garden to the relaxed informality of a cottage scheme. You may also find it easier to create a unified planting plan by focusing on a theme. Consider, too, how much work you want to do in the garden, and choose a style that matches your needs. For example, contemporary perennials and wildlife gardens use tough plants that need little attention, while lush tropical plantings and Asian-style gardens demand more time.

Plants for contemporary perennial designs

Contemporary perennial designs focus on tough, hardy perennials and grasses that are combined to form waves of color and texture.

When creating your own scheme, use a limited palette of species and knit together large swaths of contrasting heights and shapes to produce beautiful patterns. Although this planting style tends to suit big gardens, it can work in smaller spaces if you reduce the number of species but still plant in large groups. Try "see-through" plants like purpletop vervain toward the front of your scheme, and include key plant shapes, such as flat-topped yarrow, spiky salvia, and daisy-like coneflower, together with a few grasses for foliage interest. Leave the seedheads and stems to stand over winter, then cut them down in early spring.

PERENNIAL LARGE

Achillea filipendulina

YARROW An upright perennial with deeply divided pale green leaves and dense domed flower heads of tightly packed yellow, daisy-like summer flowers. The blooms can be left to dry for fall color; also good for cutting or drying indoors.

↕4½ft (1.4m) ↔24in (60cm)

Z3–8

PERENNIAL LARGE

Actaea racemosa

BLACK COHOSH This upright perennial has deeply divided leaves, above which branched bottlebrush spikes of white flowers form in midsummer. The dried brown seedheads are also attractive. Grow it at the rear of a bed.

↕5ft (1.5m) ↔24in (60cm)

Z3–8 Ⓝ

PERENNIAL LARGE

Actaea simplex

BUGBANE This upright perennial has divided foliage and white-tinged purple bottlebrush flowers in fall. Plant with contrasting green-leaved perennials in shade or behind sun-lovers. Purple-leaved 'Brunette' (above) is popular.

↕4ft (1.2m) ↔24in (60cm)

Z4–8

PERENNIAL LARGE

Agastache foeniculum

ANISE HYSSOP This upright perennial has leaves that smell and taste of licorice. Plant it in swaths toward the front of a bed to show off its spikes of fluffy lavender-blue summer flowers, which are attractive to bees and butterflies.

↕4ft (1.2m) ↔12in (30cm)

Z4–9 Ⓝ

BULB LARGE

Allium 'Purple Sensation'

FLOWERING ONION This perennial bulb produces sturdy stems topped with spherical heads of purple flowers in early summer. Plant the bulbs in groups in fall between perennials that will disguise the leaves, which fade as the flowers appear.

↕32in (80cm)

Z3–8

ANNUAL/BIENNIAL LARGE

Angelica archangelica

ANGELICA A tall biennial with an upright, branching habit and large deeply cut, decorative green leaves. It forms a clump of foliage in the first year and flowers the next, bearing domed heads of tiny green blooms during summer. It self-seeds freely.

↕6ft (2m) ↔3ft (1m)

Z4–8

PERENNIAL LARGE

Aster cordifolius

Renamed *Symphyotrichum cordifolium* This blue wood aster produces small leaves and, from late summer to fall, sprays of blue-tinted white daisy-like flowers that add color and texture toward the rear of a bed.

↕4ft (1.2m) ↔18in (45cm)

Z3–8 Ⓝ

PERENNIAL MEDIUM

Astilbe x *ardensii* 'Fanal'

ASTILBE This perennial has broad green leaves divided into smaller leaflets and upright, tapering feathery heads of tiny, crimson summer flowers, which turn brown and keep their shape in winter. It is ideal for boggy areas and pond margins.

↕24in (60cm) ↔18in (45cm)

Z3–8

PERENNIAL LARGE

Calamagrostis brachytricha

KOREAN FEATHER REED GRASS An upright deciduous grass with arching gray-green leaves that turn straw-colored in winter and tall feather-shaped pink-tinted silver flower heads. Use it as a backdrop to colorful blooms from summer to fall.

↕4½ft (1.4m) ↔20in (50cm)

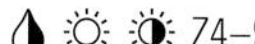

Z4–9

PERENNIAL MEDIUM

Centranthus ruber

RED VALERIAN This perennial has gray-green foliage and, from late spring to early fall, rounded clusters of small reddish pink flowers. It self-seeds freely, creating naturalistic groups in a bed, but can become invasive.

↕3ft (1m) ↔24in (60cm) or more

 Z5–8

PERENNIAL LARGE

Crambe cordifolia

COLEWORT This tall perennial produces mounds of dark green foliage below clouds of tiny white fragrant blooms that appear on sturdy stems in summer. Its see-through flowers mean it can be used toward the front of a bed.

↕6ft (2m) ↔4ft (1.2m)

Z5–9

PERENNIAL LARGE

Cynara cardunculus

CARDOON This upright perennial, also grown as an annual, has spiny, silver-gray foliage and large, thistlelike purple blooms. Mix with other sun-lovers; use at the back of a bed from summer to fall. Considered invasive in some West Coast areas.

↕6ft (2m) ↔3ft (1m)

Z7–9

PERENNIAL MEDIUM

Echinacea purpurea 'Rubinstern'

CONEFLOWER A perennial with oval dark green leaves and, from summer to mid-fall, large, daisy-like dark pink blooms. Remove the spent flower heads to encourage further flowering. Sold as 'Ruby Star'.

↕32in (80cm) ↔18in (45cm)

Z3–8 Ⓝ

PERENNIAL MEDIUM

Echinacea purpurea 'White Swan'

CONEFLOWER This upright perennial has dark green leaves and large white flowers with spiky centers from late summer to fall. Plant it near the front of a bed, and use to contrast with darker-flowered plants.

↕24in (60cm) ↔18in (45cm)

 Z3–8 Ⓝ

PERENNIAL LARGE

Echinops ritro

SMALL GLOBE THISTLE This upright perennial has prickly, divided green leaves and globe-shaped, spiky metallic blue flower heads in late summer. Use it to plug the gaps left by tall alliums as they begin to fade. Varieties include 'Veitch's Blue'.

↕4ft (1.2m) ↔30in (75cm)

Z3–9

PERENNIAL LARGE

Eryngium giganteum

SEA HOLLY A short-lived upright perennial with marbled heart-shaped gray-green foliage and tall stems topped with silvery gray conelike summer blooms surrounded by spiny bracts. It self-seeds in free-draining soil to create natural swaths.

↕3ft (1m) ↔12in (30cm)

Z4–8

PERENNIAL LARGE

Eutrochium purpureum

JOE PYE WEED This bold upright perennial has coarse green leaves on tall purple-flushed stems and, from late summer to early fall, fluffy domed purple-pink flower heads. Plant it at the rear of a bed for screening or to create a backdrop.

↕7ft (2.2m) ↔3ft (1m)

 Z4–9 Ⓝ

PERENNIAL LARGE

Gaura lindheimeri

WAND FLOWER This upright perennial produces green spoon-shaped leaves and pink-tinged buds that open to reveal small white flowers throughout summer. Weave it in groups between flat-headed flowers, such as stonecrop and yarrow.

↕5ft (1.5m) ↔3ft (1m)

Z5–9 Ⓝ

PERENNIAL MEDIUM

Geranium sylvaticum

WOOD CRANESBILL This perennial produces clumps of lobed midgreen leaves and, from late spring to early summer, round white-centered blue-purple flowers. Grow it in groups in moist soil at the front of a bed.

↕30in (75cm) ↔24in (60cm)

Z3–8

PERENNIAL MEDIUM

Geum rivale

WATER AVENS This perennial forms neat rosettes of rounded green leaves and, from late spring to summer, pink or dark orange bell-shaped flowers on slender stems. Plant it at the front of a bed in moist soil; it may self-seed.

↕↔24in (60cm)

Z3–8

PERENNIAL LARGE

Gillenia trifoliata

syn. *Porteranthus trifoliatus* Bowman's root is a spreading perennial with lobed, prominently veined dark green leaves and, from late spring to late summer, airy sprays of red-budded starry, white flowers. Use it mid-bed with groups of colorful flowers.

↕4ft (1.2m) ↔24in (60cm)

Z4–8 Ⓝ

PERENNIAL MEDIUM

Helenium 'Moerheim Beauty'

SNEEZEWEED This upright perennial has daisy-like, dark-centered coppery red blooms. Plant it in swaths in the middle of a sunny bed, where it will lend an eye-catching focal point to a summer scheme.

↕3ft (1m) ↔24in (60cm)

Z4–8

PERENNIAL MEDIUM

Hemerocallis 'All American Chief'

DAYLILY This upright clump-forming perennial has arching straplike leaves and trumpet-shaped yellow-throated red blooms. Flowers last a day, but are borne over many weeks.

↕32in (80cm) ↔9in (23cm)

Z3–9

PERENNIAL MEDIUM

Knautia macedonica

KNAUTIA This upright perennial has lobed, green basal leaves and produces a succession of buttonlike crimson flowers on wiry stems in summer. Weave small groups of this plant through the front of a sunny bed.

↕30in (75cm) ↔24in (60cm)

Z5–9

PERENNIAL SMALL

Nepeta racemosa

CATMINT A spreading perennial with aromatic foliage and masses of violet-blue summer flower spikes. A good front-of-border plant, combine it with contrasting red- and yellow-flowered plants. 'Walker's Low' (above) is a popular variety.

↕12in (30cm) ↔18in (45cm)

Z4–8

PERENNIAL MEDIUM

Osmunda cinnamomea

CINNAMON FERN This deciduous fern bears tall upright midgreen fronds that emerge from a central base, giving it a shuttlecock-like appearance. Reproductive fronds appear in summer. Will eventually form a small colony.

↕3ft (1m) ↔18in (45cm)

pH Z3–9 Ⓝ

PERENNIAL LARGE

Ligularia przewalskii

LEOPARD PLANT This upright perennial has large, round, deeply cut dark green leaves with an architectural appeal. From mid- to late summer, it bears tall narrow spires of spidery, daisy-like yellow flowers. Provide support and deadhead spent flower stems.

↕6ft (2m) ↔3ft (1m)

Z4–8

PERENNIAL MEDIUM

Penstemon digitalis 'Husker Red'

BEARDTONGUE An upright, bushy perennial with lance-shaped dark red young stems and leaves. Contrasting, tubular white blooms appear on branching stems from late spring to midsummer. Plant near the front of a bed.

↕30in (75cm) ↔12in (30cm)

Z3–8 Ⓝ

PERENNIAL MEDIUM

Monarda 'Cambridge Scarlet'

BEEBALM A clump-forming perennial with dark green aromatic leaves and trumpet-shaped rich red summer blooms arranged in whorls. Use it as a foil for paler-colored plants or to attract bees and hummingbirds.

↕3ft (1m) ↔18in (45cm)

Z3–9 Ⓝ

PERENNIAL LARGE

Persicaria amplexicaulis

RED BISTORT This vigorous perennial has oval green leaves and slender spikes of white or pink flowers from summer to early fall. It is ideal for a large garden with moist soil. Varieties include 'Firetail' (above), with bright red blooms.

↕↔4ft (1.2m)

Z4–8

PERENNIAL LARGE

Phlox paniculata

GARDEN PHLOX An upright perennial, with lance-shaped green leaves and large clusters of white, pink, or lilac flowers, which create a sea of color from summer to fall in a sunny border. 'Blue Paradise' (above) has violet-blue flowers.

↕4ft (1.2m) ↔3ft (1m)

 Z4–8 Ⓝ

PERENNIAL MEDIUM

Typha minima

DWARF CATTAIL A deciduous perennial marginal water plant with grasslike leaves. Spikes of rust-brown flowers in late summer are followed by decorative brown rounded seedheads. Confine the plant in a basket to keep it under control.

↕24in (60cm) ↔12in (30cm)

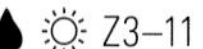 Z3–11

PERENNIAL MEDIUM

Rudbeckia hirta

BLACK-EYED SUSAN A short-lived upright, branching perennial, usually grown as an annual, with lance-shaped, midgreen foliage and large daisy-like, brown-centered golden flowers from summer to fall. 'Becky Mixed' (above) has dwarf yellow to orange flowers.

↕up to 3ft (1m) ↔18in (45cm)

Z3–7 Ⓝ

PERENNIAL MEDIUM

Sedum AUTUMN JOY

STONECROP This clump-forming perennial has oval, fleshy gray-green leaves and flat, star-shaped brick-red flowerheads in late summer, followed by brown seedheads that persist through winter. Combine with contrasting flower spires, such as salvias.

↕24in (60cm) ↔20in (50cm)

Z3–10

PERENNIAL LARGE

Verbena bonariensis

PURPLETOP VERVAIN A tall perennial with small dark green leaves and domed clusters of scented purple flowers from midsummer to fall. Plant in groups at the front or back of a bed. Considered invasive in many parts of Southeast and some areas of West Coast.

↕5ft (1.5m) ↔24in (60cm)

Z7–11

PERENNIAL MEDIUM

Salvia nemorosa

SAGE A compact upright perennial with lance-shaped wrinkled green leaves and spikes of violet-blue flowers. Weave long swaths of this plant through a bed, where it will inject color from summer to early fall.

↕up to 30in (75cm) ↔24in (60cm)

Z4–8

PERENNIAL MEDIUM

Sedum telephium Atropurpureum Group

STONECROP This perennial has domed pinkish white flower clusters from late summer to fall, and dark purple stems and leaves, which contrast with green-leaved perennials at the front of a bed.

↕24in (60cm) ↔12in (30cm)

Z4–9

PERENNIAL LARGE

Veronicastrum virginicum

CULVER'S ROOT An upright perennial with tall stems of dark green lance-shaped leaves topped with slender spikes of purple-blue, white, or pink flowers in late summer. Use it as a backdrop to rounded flowers in a sunny or part-shaded bed.

↕6ft (2m) ↔18in (45cm)

Z3–8 Ⓝ

PERENNIAL LARGE

Sanguisorba officinalis

GREATER BURNET This clump-forming perennial has green leaves, divided into oval leaflets, and slim stems that carry oval clusters of tiny dark red flowers from summer to early fall. Grow it toward the front of a bed.

↕4ft (1.2m) ↔24in (60cm)

Z4–8 Ⓝ

PERENNIAL LARGE

Stipa gigantea

syn. *Celtica gigantea* Golden oats is a clump-forming perennial grass with green arching leaves. Tall, purple-tinted oatlike flower spikes shoot up in summer and ripen to gold in fall. The see-through flowering stems work well toward the front of a bed.

↕8ft (2.5m) ↔3ft (1m)

Z5–10

OTHER SUGGESTIONS

Perennials

Achillea 'Moonshine' • *Achillea* 'Terracotta' • *Artemisia schmidtiana* 'Nana' • *Aster tataricus* • *Astilbe chinensis* var. *pumila* • *Astrantia major* 'Claret' • *Calamagrostis* 'Karl Foerster' • *Calamintha nepeta* 'White Cloud' • *Chamerion angustifolium* Ⓝ • *Cosmos atrosanguineus* Ⓝ • *Echinacea pallida* Ⓝ • *Echinacea purpurea* 'Fatal Attraction' Ⓝ • *Echinops sphaerocephalus* 'Artic Glow' • *Eutrochium purpureum* subsp. *maculatum* 'Gateway' Ⓝ • *Helenium* 'Rubinzwerg' • *Hemerocallis* 'Stella De Oro' • *Heuchera villosa* 'Autumn Bride' • *Molinia caerulea* 'Variegata' • *Monarda didyma* Ⓝ • *Monarda fistulosa* Ⓝ • *Panicum virgatum* RUBY RIBBONS Ⓝ • *Salvia nemorosa* 'East Friesland' • *Sedum telephium* 'Matrona'

Plants for formal and modern designs

Formal gardens conform to a symmetrical plan, while modern designs follow an asymmetrical format, but both can employ similar plants.

Closely clipped hedging is a common feature in formal designs and is used to carve out screens, parterres, and knot gardens. Boxwood and yew are traditional choices, but you can also try boxleaf honeysuckle to update the look. Modern designs often include blocks of leafy plants, such as bamboo, grasses, or hebe, to produce graphic slabs of color and texture. Also popular are pleached trees, where the stems are left bare and the branches trained horizontally to produce a slim hedge on stilts—the littleleaf linden can be used to create this effect. Use flowers sparingly to add splashes of seasonal color.

SHRUB SMALL

***Buxus sempervirens* 'Suffruticosa'**

COMMON BOXWOOD A slow-growing evergreen shrub with small, oval green leaves that are ideal for clipping into topiary and architectural shapes. Grow in a large pot or use as a low hedge or bed edging.

↕3ft (1m) ↔5ft (1.5m)

   Z6–8

TREE MEDIUM

Laurus nobilis

BAY LAUREL This evergreen tree has stems of dark green aromatic leaves that can be clipped into shapes to form topiary. Grow in a sheltered area, and plant in large containers of soil-based potting mix or as a centerpiece in a parterre.

↕40ft (12m) ↔30ft (10m)

 Z8–10

SHRUB SMALL

Hebe topiaria

HEBE A rounded evergreen shrub with dense stems of small gray-green leaves that are ideal for clipping, and clusters of small white summer flowers. Use it to edge a formal geometric bed or as a small topiary specimen. Best in West Coast gardens.

↕24in (60cm) ↔3ft (1m)

Z8–10

SHRUB MEDIUM

Lonicera nitida

BOXLEAF HONEYSUCKLE This bushy evergreen shrub, with arching stems of tiny dark green leaves, is used as a compact knee- or waist-high hedge. It can also be trimmed into topiary shapes. 'Baggesen's Gold' (above) has golden foliage.

↕6ft (2m) ↔10ft (3m)

Z7–9

SHRUB MEDIUM

Hydrangea macrophylla

BIGLEAF HYDRANGEA This compact deciduous shrub has broad oval leaves and clusters of small fertile and larger sterile blooms in pink, blue, or white. It makes an elegant mid-bed plant or edging for a path.

↕↔5ft (1.5m)

Z6–9

PERENNIAL SMALL

***Pelargonium* 'Lady Plymouth'**

SCENTED GERANIUM Grown as an annual, this spreading perennial has eucalyptus-scented silver-margined green leaves. In summer, lavender-pink flower clusters appear. Grow in an urn in a parterre.

↕16in (40cm) ↔8in (20cm)

Z10–11

SHRUB SMALL

***Rosa* GRAHAM THOMAS**

ENGLISH SHRUB ROSE A shrub rose or short climber with disease-resistant green leaves and cup-shaped, highly fragrant, yellow fully double blooms from summer to fall. Grow in a rose bed underplanted with geraniums or on an arch.

↕4ft (1.2m) ↔5ft (1.5m)

Z5–9

SHRUB SMALL

Rosa KENT

GROUNDCOVER ROSE A spreading ground-cover rose with disease-resistant, glossy midgreen leaves and clusters of flat, white semidouble flowers from summer to fall. Plant it in a large container of soil-based potting mix, or in a mixed bed.

↕32in (80cm) ↔3ft (1m)

 Z5–9

SHRUB SMALL

Rosa 'Penelope'

HYBRID MUSK ROSE A hybrid musk shrub rose with long arching stems, glossy dark green foliage and large clusters of fragrant, cream and pale pink semidouble flowers from summer to fall. Plant in a formal rose bed or formal bed.

↕↔3ft (1m) more if lightly pruned

Z6–9

SHRUB SMALL

Rosa SUNSET CELEBRATION

HYBRID TEA ROSE A hybrid tea rose with disease-resistant midgreen leaves and, from summer to fall, pointed, scented, orange-pink fully double flowers that age to rose-pink. Plant in groups to fill parterres or use as a specimen plant in formal designs.

↕3ft (1m) ↔32in (80cm)

Z7–10

PERENNIAL SMALL

Salvia splendens

SCARLET SAGE An upright tender perennial, grown as an annual, with spear-shaped dark green leaves and compact spikes of tubular, pink, red, and purple summer blooms. Plant at the front of a bed for a bold splash of color. Deadhead spent spikes.

↕10in (25cm) ↔14in (35cm)

Z10–11

PERENNIAL MEDIUM

Salvia x *sylvestris*

WOOD SAGE This compact perennial has small aromatic dark green leaves and branched spikes of violet blooms in summer. 'May Night' has indigo-blue flowers. It is an excellent front-of-bed plant or filler for a parterre.

↕28in (80cm) ↔12in (30cm)

Z4–9

TREE LARGE

Taxus baccata

ENGLISH YEW An evergreen tree with needlelike dark green leaves and red berries in fall. Clip it in spring and summer; tolerates hard pruning, if necessary. Use for dividing up a garden or to create a hedge for boundaries. All parts are highly toxic.

↕50ft (15m) ↔30ft (10m)

(!) Z6–7

TREE SMALL

Taxus x *media*

YEW An evergreen conifer with needlelike dark green leaves, lighter green below, and red fall berries. Faster growing than *T. baccata*, it makes a beautiful formal hedge. Trim the plant in early spring. All parts are highly toxic.

↕20ft (6m) ↔12ft (4m)

(!) Z5–7

TREE LARGE

Tilia cordata

LITTLELEAF LINDEN This deciduous tree has heart-shaped, glossy dark green leaves that turn yellow in fall, and small yellowish white summer flowers. Ideal for pleaching or as formal hedges; trim in summer. Makes a good shade or street tree.

↕100ft (30m) ↔40ft (12m)

 Z3–7

BULB MEDIUM

Tulipa 'Queen of Night'

TULIP This late-spring-flowering tulip produces gray-green leaves and cup-shaped, dark purple single flowers. Plant the bulbs in groups in beds or parterres in fall or in containers of soil-based potting mix with added grit.

↕24in (60cm)

(!) Z3–8

OTHER SUGGESTIONS

Perennials

Muhlenbergia rigens (N) • *Ophiopogon japonicas* 'Nanus' • *Pelargonium* Maverick Series • *Salvia splendens* Vista Series • Yucca rostrata 'Sapphire Skies' (N)

Bulbs

Allium 'Globemaster' • *Tulipa* 'Angélique' • *Tulipa* 'Greenland'

Shrubs

Buxus sempervirens 'Suffruticosa' • *Hydrangea paniculata* LIMELIGHT • *Ilex glabra* 'Compacta' (N) • *Ilex verticillata* 'Afterglow' (N) • *Itea virginica* 'Henry's Garnet' (N) • *Myrica pensylvanica* (N) • *Rosa* MARGARET MERRIL

Trees

Carpinus caroliniana (N) • *Ilex opaca* (N) • *Tilia cordata* 'Greenspire'

Plants for tropical gardens

Brightly-colored flowers and lush foliage create a tropical theme. While some plants hail from hot countries, many hardy types also create the look.

Choose plants with very large leaves that lend a sculptural quality to your designs. In cool climates, plant a backdrop of hardier foliage plants, such as hosta, bamboo, and ferns, and inject color in summer with a range of exotic-looking flowers. Dahlia, ginger lily, honeybush, and canna will survive mild winters if covered with a deep mulch of shredded bark or leaves—or simply bring the plants indoors if your climate is too cold. Likewise, many species of pineapple lily will survive outside in a pot, if turned on side to keep the soil dry and placed in a sheltered area.

SHRUB MEDIUM

Abutilon 'Kentish Belle'

FLOWERING-MAPLE This shrub, semievergreen in warm areas, bears small triangular leaves and orange and red, bell-shaped summer blooms. Plant it close to a sunny wall or use it as a screen to lend a tropical flavor to a sheltered garden.

↕↔ 8ft (2.5m)

Z9–11

PERENNIAL SMALL

Adiantum venustum

HIMALAYAN MAIDENHAIR FERN This deciduous fern, evergreen in mild areas, has triangular fronds, rusty brown in fall and winter, divided into fan-shaped segments. Plant in a shady area with contrasting foliage plants, such as coleus.

↕ 9in (23cm) ↔ 12in (30cm)

pH Z5–8

PERENNIAL LARGE

Agapanthus Headbourne hybrids

AFRICAN LILY A perennial with arching, straplike leaves and blue funnel-shaped flowers from late summer to early fall. Plant near the front of a bed. In cold areas, mulch with organic matter; remove spent blooms.

↕ 4ft (1.2m) ↔ 24in (60cm)

Z6–9

PERENNIAL LARGE

Agave americana

CENTURY PLANT An evergreen perennial with sharply pointed, lance-shaped, cream-edged gray-green leaves. In hot summers, cream flowers appear atop tall stems. Grow in a container in cold areas and overwinter the plant indoors.

↕↔ up to 5ft (1.5m)

Z9–11 Ⓝ

PERENNIAL MEDIUM

Aloe vera

ALOE An evergreen perennial with fleshy, spine-edged gray-green leaves. It is often grown as a house plant in cold areas, but makes an exotic contribution to sunny summer gardens when grown in a pot; overwinter it indoors.

↕ 24in (60cm) ↔ indefinite

Z10–11

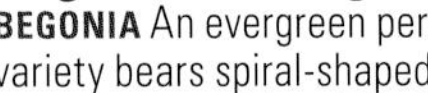

PERENNIAL SMALL

Begonia 'Escargot'

BEGONIA An evergreen perennial, this variety bears spiral-shaped, purple-tinted green leaves with swirly silver markings and small pink flowers in fall. Grow as a houseplant in winter and bring outdoors in a pot during summer.

↕ 10in (25cm) ↔ 20in (50cm)

Z10–11

SHRUB LARGE

Brugmansia x *candida*

ANGELS' TRUMPETS An evergreen shrub or small tree with oval green leaves and, from summer to fall, large exotic-looking trumpet-shaped night-scented blooms. 'Grand Marnier' (above) has apricot blooms. Protect it from frost.

↕ 15ft (5m) ↔ 8ft (2.5m)

(!) Z11

PERENNIAL LARGE

Canna 'Wyoming'

CANNA This perennial has paddle-shaped purple-bronze leaves and, from midsummer to early fall, pale orange gladioluslike flowers. Yellow, orange, or red blooms with colorful foliage are also available. Lift the rhizomes and overwinter indoors.

↕ 6ft (1.8m) ↔ 20in (50cm)

Z8–11

SHRUB LARGE

Chamaerops humilis

EUROPEAN FAN PALM This compact evergreen palm has fan-shaped, divided green leaves. Mature plants bear clusters of small yellow summer flowers. Relatively hardy, it lends an exotic look to sheltered tropical-style gardens.

↕ 10ft (3m) ↔ 6ft (2m)

Z8–11

ANNUAL/BIENNIAL LARGE

Cleome hassleriana

SPIDER FLOWER This tall annual bears spiny stems of divided foliage and rounded clusters of small, spidery white, pink, or purple flowers with a light fragrance in summer. Use it to add a tropical touch to beds.

↕4ft (1.2m) ↔18in (45cm)

CLIMBER LARGE

Cobaea scandens

CUP-AND-SAUCER VINE A Mexican native evergreen perennial climber, grown as an annual, with dark green leaves and scented, cup-shaped creamy green, aging to purple, blooms. It bears a wall of color from summer to fall when grown on trellis or wires.

↕15ft (5m)

Z9–11 Ⓝ

PERENNIAL LARGE

Colocasia esculenta

ELEPHANT'S EAR A marginal perennial with large spear-shaped leaves. Grow in a bog garden or large pot. In cold areas, lift before hard freeze and store clean corm in cool frost-free location. Considered invasive in Gulf Coast areas.

↕5ft (1.5m) ↔24in (60cm)

PERENNIAL MEDIUM

Crocosmia 'Lucifer'

MONTBRETIA This clump-forming perennial has narrow, sword-shaped midgreen foliage. In summer, it produces bright red flowers. Yellow-, red-, and orange-flowered varieties are also available. Can be weedy.

↕3ft (1m) ↔10in (25cm)

SHRUB MEDIUM

Cycas revoluta

JAPANESE SAGO PALM An elegant evergreen palm with a rough-textured trunk and arching, oval, glossy green leaves divided into needlelike leaflets. It is hardy to 12°F (-8°C) and will survive winters outside in a sheltered area.

↕↔6ft (2m)

Z8–10

BULB MEDIUM

Dahlia 'Yellow Hammer'

DWARF BEDDER SINGLE DAHLIA Grown from a tuber, this dahlia bears dark bronze foliage and orange-streaked bright yellow blooms. Plant in containers of soil-based potting mix or in groups at the front of a bed. Lift and overwinter indoors in cold areas.

↕24in (60cm)

Z9–11

PERENNIAL LARGE

Ensete ventricosum

ABYSSINIAN BANANA This palmlike evergreen perennial has paddle-shaped foliage with cream midribs, red beneath. Grow in a container of gritty soil-based potting mix; overwinter indoors. 'Maurelii' has red-splashed leaves with red midribs.

↕6ft (2m) ↔3ft (1m)

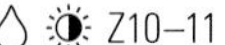

BULB MEDIUM

Eucomis bicolor

PINEAPPLE LILY This summer-flowering perennial bulb has wavy-edged basal leaves and clusters of greenish white flowers with purple-edged petals on spotted stems. The flowers, with their leaflike bracts, resemble pineapples.

↕20in (50cm)

PERENNIAL LARGE

Hedychium densiflorum

GINGER LILY This perennial forms large, lance-shaped green leaves. In summer, torchlike clusters of orange flowers appear. Grow it in groups in moist but well-drained soil to create a spectacular summer bed. Protect from cold with thick mulch.

↕6ft (2m) ↔24in (60cm)

Z8–11

SHRUB SMALL

Helichrysum petiolare

LICORICE PLANT This shrub, used as an annual bedding plant, is grown for its trailing stems of downy gray-green leaves. Perfect for edging pots or beds. 'Limelight' (above) has lime-green foliage, and makes a good partner for red-flowered plants.

↕6in (15cm) ↔12in (30cm)

Z9–11

PERENNIAL MEDIUM

Hemerocallis 'Chicago Apache'

DAYLILY This perennial has strap-shaped foliage and trumpetlike deep scarlet flowers throughout summer, with each bloom lasting just one day. Plant it in groups of three in a tropical-style scheme.
↕26in (65cm) ↔20in (50cm)

SHRUB LARGE

Hibiscus syriacus

ROSE OF SHARON An upright deciduous shrub with lobed dark green foliage and blue, violet, or white single flowers with dark centers from late summer to early fall. Considered invasive in some areas. 'Blue Bird' (above) is a blue-flowered variety.
↕10ft (3m) ↔6ft (2m)

Z5–9

PERENNIAL SMALL

Hosta 'Lakeside Cha Cha'

PLANTAIN LILY A perennial with large rounded cream-edged midgreen leaves, textured with veins. Pendent, tubular lilac flower spikes appear briefly in summer; remove after fading. Provides a lush leafy understory to tall plants. Protect from slugs.
↕↔18in (45cm)

Z3–8

CLIMBER MEDIUM

Ipomoea coccinea

RED MORNING GLORY This tender annual has heart-shaped green leaves and small, fragrant, tubular scarlet flowers with yellow throats. Grow this twining climber up a tripod where it will produce color throughout summer and early fall.
↕10ft (3m)

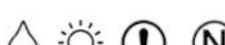

PERENNIAL MEDIUM

Lobelia cardinalis

CARDINAL FLOWER A deciduous perennial with narrow lance-shaped, glossy green leaves and spires of scarlet summer blooms. Ideal for a pond margin or bog garden. It is attractive to butterflies and hummingbirds. All parts of the plant are toxic.
↕30in (75cm) ↔9in (23in)

Z3–9

PERENNIAL SMALL

Lotus berthelotii

CORAL GEM The ferny gray-green foliage and clusters of orange-red beak-shaped summer flowers of this small trailing perennial, often grown as annual bedding plant, offer a decorative edge to a container display.
↕8in (20cm) ↔ indefinite

Z10–12

SHRUB LARGE

Melianthus major

HONEYBUSH This evergreen subshrub has blue-gray leaves divided into toothed-edged leaflets and small brownish red flowers in late spring. Shelter from cold winds; provide a dry mulch in winter. Plants in pots can be overwintered inside.
↕↔ up to 10ft (3m)

Z8–11

CLIMBER LARGE

Passiflora caerulea

BLUE PASSION FLOWER This evergreen or semievergreen climber has lobed glossy dark green leaves. From summer to fall, orange egg-shaped fruits follow the white flowers with purple filaments. Protect from cold or grow indoors in cooler areas.
↕30ft (10m) or more

Z8–11

PERENNIAL LARGE

Phormium tenax

NEW ZEALAND FLAX A clump-forming evergreen perennial that produces arching, sword-shaped, gray-green leaves and, during hot summers, tall stems of dark red flowers. It lends a tropical note to a bed or pot.
↕10ft (3m) ↔6ft (2m)

Z9–11

BAMBOO LARGE

Phyllostachys vivax f. *aureocaulis*

CHINESE TIMBER BAMBOO A tall upright, clump-forming bamboo with yellow canes, sometimes striped green, and lance-shaped midgreen leaves. Combine it with green foliage plants and colorful flowers.
↕20ft (6m) ↔10ft (3m) or more

Z7–10

SHRUB LARGE

Pittosporum tobira

JAPANESE PITTOSPORUM This evergreen shrub has a neat bushy-headed shape and long, oval dark green leaves. From late spring to early summer, small, scented, starry white flowers form, aging to creamy yellow. Also has decorative capsules.

↕30ft (10m) ↔10ft (3m)

 Z8–10

SHRUB SMALL

Plectranthus argentatus

SILVER SPURFLOWER This spreading evergreen subshrub, grown as an annual, has silver stems, gray-green leaves, and small spikes of bluish white summer flowers. Use as decorative edging in a large pot or a bed of contrasting colorful blooms.

↕↔3ft (1m)

Z10–11

BAMBOO MEDIUM

Sasa palmata

BROADLEAF BAMBOO A small vigorous bamboo with broad lance-shaped dark green leaves, the tips and margins of which turn brown in winter, creating a two-tone effect. It lends a tropical look to a garden; can be invasive.

↕6ft (2m) ↔indefinite

Z7–10

ANNUAL/BIENNIAL SMALL

Tropaeolum majus

NASTURTIUM This spreading annual has round green leaves and red, yellow, or orange trumpet-shaped flowers from summer to fall. Use it to provide color beneath taller plants. Alaska Series (above) has cream-splashed foliage.

↕12in (30cm) ↔18in (45cm)

PERENNIAL SMALL

Solenostemon scutellarioides

COLEUS A bushy perennial, grown as an annual, with spear-shaped foliage in a variety of colors including pink, red, green, and yellow. It creates a leafy edge to paths and beds or in containers. Cuttings can be overwintered in water.

↕18in (45cm) ↔12in (30cm) or more

Z11–12

ANNUAL/BIENNIAL LARGE

Tithonia rotundifolia

MEXICAN SUNFLOWER A tall, branching annual with coarse spear-shaped leaves and yellow centered bright orange daisy-like blooms from late summer to fall. Plant near the back of a bed, provide support, and deadhead regularly to prolong the display.

↕4ft (1.2m) ↔24in (60cm)

Ⓝ

TREE SMALL

Trachycarpus fortunei

WINDMILL PALM This evergreen palm has an unbranched stem and head of large, deeply divided, fanlike midgreen leaves. Sprays of fragrant creamy yellow flowers appear in early summer. Plant it in a sheltered area away from drying winds.

↕up to 6ft (2m) ↔8ft (2.5m)

Z8–10

SHRUB SMALL

Zamia pumila

FLORIDA ARROWROOT This slow-growing, frost tender shrub resembles a palm and has robust, green frondlike foliage and bears brown flower cones when mature. Grow in a large pot. Overwinter under cover; move outside once the risk of frost has passed.

↕4ft (1.2m) ↔6ft (2m)

 Z9–11 Ⓝ

ANNUAL/BIENNIAL SMALL

Zinnia elegans Dreamland Series

ZINNIA This bushy annual, native to Mexico, has oval dark green leaves, and red, yellow, purple, pink, or green daisy-like flowers from summer to early fall. It offers masses of color; grow in a pot or flowerbed.

↕↔12in (30cm)

Ⓝ

OTHER SUGGESTIONS

Annuals

Amaranthus caudatus • *Ipomoea batatas* • *Zinnia* 'Orange King'

Perennials, bulbs, and climbers

Adiantum pedatum Ⓝ • *Agapanthus africanus* 'Albus' • *Alstroemeria aurea* • *Begonia rex-cultorum* • *Canna* 'Firebird' • *Dahlia* 'Vancouver' • *Dryopteris filix-mas* Ⓝ • *Eucomis comosa* • *Gunnera manicata* • *Hemerocallis* 'Alabama Jubilee' • *Hibiscus coccineus* Ⓝ • *Hosta* 'Sum and Substance' • *Matteuccia struthiopteris* Ⓝ • *Musa basjoo* • *Passiflora incarnata* Ⓝ

Shrubs and trees

Abutilon megapotamicum • *Asimina triloba* Ⓝ • *Magnolia grandiflora* Ⓝ • *Rhapidophyllum hystrix* Ⓝ • *Washingtonia robusta* Ⓝ

Plants for Asian-style gardens

Reflecting Buddhist philosophies, Japanese gravel, stroll, and tea gardens are admired for their beauty and tranquility.

Japanese gravel gardens comprise large boulders and minimal planting—traditional dry gardens include only moss—with miniature pines and clipped Japanese holly used to decorate these spare schemes. The more exuberant stroll and tea gardens allow a greater planting range, including cloud-pruned topiary, colorful maples, bamboos, irises, and seasonal flowering shrubs, such as rhododendron and peony. Combine these plants to create a miniaturized woodland or water landscape and include winding paths and open spaces to achieve an authentic look.

TREE SMALL

Acer palmatum 'Bloodgood'

JAPANESE MAPLE A small tree with maplelike reddish purple leaves that turn bright red in fall. Winged red fruits follow the small purple spring flowers. Grow it as a feature in a Japanese stroll-style garden. May be invasive in some areas.
↕↔15ft (5m)

 Z5–8

SHRUB LARGE

Callicarpa bodinieri var. *giraldii*

BEAUTYBERRY This shrub has lance-shaped foliage and pink summer blooms. 'Profusion' (above) has purple-tinged young leaves that turn rosy pink in fall, and violet berries. Provide a sheltered site in zone 5 gardens.
↕10ft (3m) ↔8ft (2.5m)

  Z5–8

SHRUB SMALL

Cryptomeria japonica 'Globosa Nana'

JAPANESE CEDAR This dwarf evergreen domed conifer has scaly green foliage and green turning brown cones. Use to create a rounded shape between rocks in a gravel garden, or grow in a pot as a focal plant.
↕↔3ft (1m)

Z6–9

SHRUB LARGE

Eriobotrya japonica

LOQUAT This architectural shrub produces large, glossy dark green leaves, felted beneath, at the end of branched stems. It makes a dramatic focal point, but needs a sheltered site to produce its scented white flowers from fall to winter.
↕↔25ft (8m)

 Z8–11

SHRUB LARGE

Fatsia japonica

JAPANESE FATSIA An evergreen shrub with hand-shaped, glossy dark green leaves. Black fruits follow the spherical white fall flowers. Makes an attractive backdrop against a wall or fence; overwinter indoors or grow as a houseplant in cool areas.
↕↔12ft (4m)

Z8–10

TREE LARGE

Ginkgo biloba

MAIDENHAIR TREE This deciduous tree has fan-shaped green leaves, butter-yellow in fall. Grow as a focal point in Japanese- and Chinese-style gardens. Dwarf cultivars are ideal for small spaces. Plant male trees to avoid the messy and smelly fruits of females.
↕100ft (30m) ↔25ft (8m)

Z4–9

PERENNIAL SMALL

Hakonechloa macra 'Aureola'

JAPANESE FOREST GRASS This slow-growing grass has green-striped yellow leaves that age to reddish brown. Reddish brown flower spikes appear in early fall and last into winter. Grow in a pot or gravel garden.
↕16in (40cm) ↔24in (60cm)

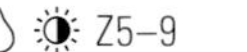 Z5–9

SHRUB MEDIUM

Hydrangea macrophylla

LACECAP HYDRANGEA This rounded shrub produces large, oval light green leaves and, from midsummer to early fall, lacecap flower heads formed of tiny blue flowers, and larger pale blue (in acidic soil), or pink petal-like florets.
↕6ft (2m) ↔8ft (2.5m)

Z6–9

SHRUB MEDIUM

Hydrangea quercifolia

OAKLEAF HYDRANGEA This mound-forming shrub has lobed midgreen leaves that turn red and purple in fall. From midsummer to fall, cone-shaped cream flower heads appear, which age to pink-tinged white. Requires neutral to acidic soil.
↕6ft (2m) ↔8ft (2.5m)

Z5–9 (N)

PERENNIAL MEDIUM

Iris laevigata

JAPANESE WATER IRIS This clump-forming perennial marginal has sword-shaped midgreen leaves and dark purple early summer flowers with gold marks on the lower petals. Plant it in aquatic baskets at the edge of a pond or pool.
↕3ft (1m) or more ↔indefinite

 Z4–9

PERENNIAL MEDIUM

Paeonia 'Bowl of Beauty'

PEONY This erect clump-forming perennial has divided green leaves and large bowl-shaped double flowers with rose-pink outer petals and cream centers. Use it to contribute summer color to a Japanese-style stroll garden.

↕↔ 3ft (1m)

 Z3–8

SHRUB MEDIUM

Paeonia suffruticosa

TREE PEONY An upright deciduous shrub with deeply lobed dark green leaves and, in late spring, white, pink, red, or purple bowl-shaped flowers that are sometimes scented. Use it to add height to a bed in a Japanese-style gravel or stroll garden.

↕↔ 6ft (2m)

 Z5–8

BAMBOO LARGE

Phyllostachys bambusoides

JAPANESE TIMBER BAMBOO This large bamboo, with its green or yellow canes and lush foliage, lends height to a scheme, and is a perfect plant to add an Asian note to a gravel garden. Alternatively, grow it as a screen.

↕ 25ft (8m) ↔ indefinite

Z7–10

BAMBOO LARGE

Phyllostachys nigra

BLACK BAMBOO A clump-forming evergreen bamboo with greenish brown grooved stems that turn black when mature, and long narrow leaves. Grow it as a screen or as a focal point in a stroll or tea garden.

↕ 25ft (8m) ↔ indefinite

Z7–11

SHRUB LARGE

Pieris japonica

LILY OF THE VALLEY BUSH This compact evergreen shrub has leathery dark green leaves, bright red when young, and pendent chains of white, red, or pink urn-shaped spring flowers. Dark red buds of 'Flamingo' (above) open to a deep pink.

↕ 12ft (4m) ↔ 10ft (3m)

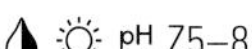 Z5–8

SHRUB SMALL

Pinus mugo

MUGO PINE This compact evergreen conifer will create a mound of needlelike dark green leaves. Pines are prized in Japan for their scaly bark and elegant forms. Set this plant among boulders in a gravel garden.

↕ 3ft (1m) ↔ 6ft (2m)

Z2–7

TREE LARGE

Prunus x *yedoensis*

YOSHINO CHERRY This spreading deciduous tree often takes center stage in Japanese gardens, and is revered for its abundance of almond-scented blush white spring blossom. It also has dark red fruits in summer and yellow fall leaf color.

↕ 50ft (15m) ↔ 30ft (10m)

Z5–8

SHRUB SMALL

Sarcococca humilis

SWEET BOX A clump-forming evergreen shrub with tiny white fragrant winter flowers and glossy dark green foliage, which can be clipped into a sphere and used in a gravel garden. Black berries appear after the blooms.

↕ 24in (60cm) ↔ 3ft (1m)

 Z6–9

BAMBOO LARGE

Semiarundinaria fastuosa

NARIHIRA BAMBOO This large, vigorous bamboo produces clumps of dark green canes and dark green lance-shaped leaves, which are gray-green beneath. Plant it in a gravel garden in groves or in a line as a screen.

↕ 20ft (6m) ↔ indefinite

Z6–9

SHRUB MEDIUM

Viburnum davidii

DAVID VIBURNUM This dome-shaped evergreen shrub has deeply veined green foliage and small white spring flowers. Female plants bear metallic blue fruits if both sexes are grown. Use it for shady ground cover in a stroll or tea garden.

↕↔ 5ft (1.5m)

Z7–9

OTHER SUGGESTIONS

Perennials

Asarum splendens 'Quicksilver' • *Paeonia lactiflora*

Climbers

Wisteria frutescens 'Amethyst Falls' Ⓝ

Shrubs

Abelia grandiflora • *Buxus microphylla* • *Chamaecyparis obtusa* 'Nana Lutea' • *Camellia sinensis* • *Ilex crenata* 'Soft Touch' • *Loropetalum chinense* 'Zhuhou Fuchsia' • *Mahonia aquifolium* Ⓝ • *Rhododendron catawbiense* Ⓝ • *Rhododendron* 'Rosy Lights'

Trees

Acer griseum • *Acer palmatum* 'Sango-kaku' • *Acer palmatum* var. *dissectum* 'Crimson Queen' • *Quercus dentata* 'Pinnatifida' • *Zelkova serrata*

Plants for cottage gardens

Fads and fashions come and go, yet the cottage garden endures as one of the most popular styles, loved for its nostalgic themes and romantic planting.

A feast for the eyes and stomach, traditional cottage gardens included herbs and vegetables (see pages 98, 106, 186). To create a cottage design, include wooden trellises and arbors laced with roses, vines, and honeysuckle, and underplanted with cushions of lavender. Pack your beds with as many bulbs and perennials as you can squeeze in, planting in groups of three or more, and select a range that will flower consistently from spring until fall. Use pots of annuals to fill any gaps as they appear. You may also want to showcase a few roses, compact shrubs, and topiary balls or pyramids to add some structure to the mix.

PERENNIAL MEDIUM

Achillea ptarmica The Pearl Group

SNEEZEWORT An upright, spreading perennial with linear dark green leaves. In summer, it is covered with small white pompomlike flowers that resemble pearls. Use it to edge a path.
↕↔24in (60cm)
Z3–8

PERENNIAL SMALL

Alchemilla mollis

LADY'S MANTLE This clump-forming perennial is ideal for the front of a border or shady corners. It has rounded pale green leaves and sprays of tiny greenish yellow flowers that last several weeks in summer. Trim back untidy leaves and spent blooms.
↕↔20in (50cm)
Z4–7

PERENNIAL LARGE

Anemone x *hybrida*

JAPANESE ANEMONE A slow spreading perennial with divided dark green leaves. From late summer to fall, it bears, pink or white saucer-shaped flowers on upright stems. 'Honorine Jobert' (above) has golden-eyed white flowers.
↕4ft (1.2m) ↔24in (60cm)
Z4–8

PERENNIAL SMALL

Anthemis punctata subsp. *cupaniana*

SICILIAN CHAMOMILE This drought-tolerant evergreen perennial makes a dome of silver foliage. In summer, it is covered with yellow-eyed white daisies. Use at the front of a sunny bed or plant in gravel.
↕↔12in (30cm)
Z6–9

PERENNIAL MEDIUM

Aquilegia vulgaris

COLUMBINE This clump-forming perennial has fernlike foliage. Nodding, bell-shaped blooms with spurred petals appear on upright stems from late spring to early summer. Flowers can be violet, blue, pink, or white.
↕3ft (1m) ↔18in (45cm)
Z3–8

PERENNIAL MEDIUM

Aquilegia vulgaris var. *stellata*

COLUMBINE This upright perennial has round divided leaves and, from late spring to early summer, pompomlike flowers on tall stems. 'Nora Barlow' (above) has greenish pink blooms, which become pink tipped with white as they age.
↕30in (75cm) ↔20in (50cm)
Z3–8

PERENNIAL MEDIUM

Argyranthemum frutescens

MARGUERITE A woody-based, tender evergreen perennial, often grown as an annual, with divided green or gray-green leaves and white, yellow, or pink daisy-like blooms, depending on the variety, from late spring to fall. Plant in pots or raised beds.
↕↔28in (70cm)
Z10–11

PERENNIAL MEDIUM

Aster ericoides

Renamed *Symphyotrichum ericoides*
This clump-forming heath aster has small, lance-shaped midgreen leaves and, from late summer to late fall, yellow-centered white daisy-like flower heads, sometimes shaded pink or blue.
↕3ft (1m) ↔12in (30cm)
Z4–8 Ⓝ

PERENNIAL LARGE

Aster novae-angliae

Renamed *Symphyotrichum novae-angliae* This New England aster has slim, green hairy leaves and, from late summer to fall, purple, pink, red, or white daisy-like flowers, depending on the variety. Taller forms may require staking.
↕up to 5ft (1.5m) ↔24in (60cm)

  Z4–8 Ⓝ

PERENNIAL SMALL

Astilbe x *arendsii*

ASTILBE A clump-forming perennial with deeply divided fernlike dark green foliage. In summer, it bears cone-shaped, dark pink feathery flower heads on slim stems. It also grows well in full shade.
↕18in (45cm) ↔12in (30cm)

 Z4–8

SHRUB MEDIUM

Ceanothus 'Dark Star'

CALIFORNIA LILAC This wall shrub produces arching branches covered with small, oval evergreen leaves and clusters of dark blue-purple flowers in late spring. Shelter the plants from cold winds. Can be trained.
↕6ft (2m) ↔10ft (3m)

Z9–11 Ⓝ

PERENNIAL MEDIUM

Centaurea pulcherrima

CENTAUREA This upright drought-tolerant perennial is a favorite of butterflies and has divided gray-green to silver foliage and large cornflowerlike, rose-pink midsummer blooms with pale yellow centers. Try it with *Salvia* x *sylvestris* 'May Night'.
↕30in (75cm) ↔24in (60cm)

 Z4–8

TREE SMALL

Cercis canadensis 'Forest Pansy'

EASTERN REDBUD This deciduous, spreading tree bears pale pink pealike blooms in spring, before the heart-shaped, rich purple leaves emerge. Use it as a specimen tree at the back of a cottage bed.
↕↔15ft (5m)

Z4–9 Ⓝ

ANNUAL/BIENNIAL SMALL

Cerinthe major

HONEYWORT This upright annual produces oval gray-green leaves and, in summer, tubular purple and yellow flowers on erect stems, which may need some support; plants may self-seed in gravel.
↕↔24in (60cm)

PERENNIAL SMALL

Chrysanthemum 'Grandchild'

DECORATIVE GARDEN MUM This compact perennial produces green lobed leaves and dense sprays of mauve-pink fully double blooms, which are perfect for cutting. Plant it at the front of a fall bed.
↕18in (45cm) ↔16in (40cm)

 Z5–9

CLIMBER MEDIUM

Clematis 'Jackmanii'

CLEMATIS This late-flowering clematis blooms from midsummer to early fall. The large, velvety violet-purple flowers with greenish cream stamens look beautiful trained up a wall or fence as a bed backdrop, or on a rustic trellis.
↕10ft (3m)

Z4–9

CLIMBER MEDIUM

Clematis 'Madame Julia Correvon'

CLEMATIS One of the Viticella Group of clematis, this vigorous climber bears abundant wine-red blooms with a central tuft of cream stamens from mid- to late summer. Try growing it through a tree.
↕11ft (3.5m)

Z4–9

CLIMBER LARGE

Clematis montana

HIMALAYAN CLEMATIS This vigorous deciduous climber bears masses of small yellow-centered, white or pink blooms from late spring to early summer. It provides a wonderful habitat and welcome source of nectar for bees and other beneficial insects.
↕40ft (12m)

Z6–9

Plants for cottage gardens

ANNUAL/BIENNIAL LARGE

Cosmos bipinnatus

COSMOS This upright annual has feathery foliage and saucer-shaped blooms. It is easily grown from seeds and looks at home among perennial border flowers. Varieties include 'Sensation Mixed', with white, red, and pink flowers from summer to early fall.

↕ up to 4ft (1.2m) ↔ 18in (45cm)

PERENNIAL LARGE

Crocosmia x *crocosmiiflora*

MONTBRETIA This clump-forming bulbous perennial has long narrow leaves and yellow to red mid- to late summer blooms. Darker flower buds provide an attractive highlight. Grow it front- to mid-bed with purple-flowered plants. Can be invasive.

↕↔ 4ft (1.2m)

Z6–9

BULB LARGE

Dahlia Bishop Series

DAHLIA This large bulb has divided, toothed-edged, purple-black flushed leaves and orange-, red-, yellow- or lavender-centered red blooms from midsummer to early fall. Mix with hot-hued late-flowering perennials. Stake the stems.

↕↔ up to 3ft (1m)

Z9–11

BULB LARGE

Dahlia 'Franz Kafka'

POMPON DAHLIA A pompom dahlia with divided green leaves and, from midsummer to fall, mauve-pink blooms, which are excellent for cutting. It is an ideal partner for pastel-shaded perennials, such as phlox and *Sidalcia.* Stems may need staking.

↕ 32in (80cm)

Z9–11

PERENNIAL LARGE

Delphinium elatum

LARKSPUR This bushy perennial has deeply cut dark green basal leaves. In summer, it produces tall spires of showy flowers in shades of blue and purple. Grow it at the back of a cottage bed. Stems need to be supported.

↕ 6ft (2m) ↔ 3ft (1m)

Z3–7

PERENNIAL SMALL

Dianthus 'Dad's Favourite'

GARDEN PINK This compact evergreen perennial forms a low mound of gray-green grasslike foliage. Throughout summer, it bears clove-scented, white semidouble flowers with maroon markings and is ideal for the front edge of a bed.

↕ up to 18in (45cm) ↔ 12in (30cm)

Z4–9

PERENNIAL LARGE

Echinops ritro

SMALL GLOBE THISTLE This upright branching perennial has prickly, divided dark green leaves and distinctive round, spiky steel-blue flower heads in late summer. Plant it mid-bed and support the stems. 'Veitch's Blue' is popular.

↕ 4ft (1.2m) ↔ 30in (75cm)

Z3–9

PERENNIAL SMALL

Erigeron hybrids

FLEABANE This clump-forming perennial, ideal for coastal sites, is grown for its yellow-centered flowers in white, pink, blue, purple, or, occasionally, yellow or orange, which appear over several weeks in summer. Plant it at the front of a bed.

↕↔ 20in (50cm)

Z5–8

PERENNIAL SMALL

Eryngium bourgatii

MEDITERRANEAN SEA HOLLY This drought-tolerant perennial has cut silver-veined leaves and, from mid- to late summer, dark silvery blue conelike flower heads, encircled by a spiny "ruff" on upright metallic blue stems. Grow with yarrow or beardtongue.

↕ 18in (45cm) ↔ 12in (30cm)

Z5–9

BULB LARGE

Fritillaria imperialis

CROWN IMPERIAL These tall perennial bulbs form a crown of blue-green leaves in spring, and bear large, pendent, orange or yellow bell-shaped flowers held on upright spikes in late spring. Plants go dormant after flowering.

↕5ft (1.5m)

Z5–8

SHRUB MEDIUM

Fuchsia magellanica var. *molinae*

HARDY FUCHSIA A deciduous shrub with green lance-shaped leaves and, from summer to early fall, pendent, pale pink blooms. Use at the back of a bed or for screening. Best in West Coast gardens.

↕↔6ft (2m)

Z7–9

SHRUB SMALL

Fuchsia 'Mrs Popple'

FUCHSIA A small bushy deciduous shrub with dark green leaves that are speckled with small, pendent, bell-shaped red and purple flowers in summer. Plant it in the middle of a bed or use to create an informal screen.

↕↔3½ft (1.1m)

Z9–11

BULB LARGE

Galtonia candicans

SUMMER HYACINTH This perennial bulb makes a clump of long lance-shaped leaves. In late summer, fragrant, white bell-shaped blooms appear on tall stems. A statuesque mid-bed plant, it also thrives in gravel beds.

↕4ft (1.2m)

Z6–10

PERENNIAL MEDIUM

Geranium pratense

MEADOW CRANESBILL A compact clump-forming perennial with lobed green leaves. In summer, it produces sprays of pale violet-blue flowers with white veining. Plant it in groups in moist soil toward the front of a bed.

↕↔24in (60cm)

 Z4–8

PERENNIAL MEDIUM

Geranium sylvaticum

WOOD CRANESBILL This clump-forming perennial has lobed midgreen leaves and round white-centered blue-purple flowers from late spring to early summer. Grow it in groups in a shady flower bed. 'Album' (above) has white blooms.

↕30in (75cm) ↔24in (60cm)

Z4–8

ANNUAL/BIENNIAL LARGE

Helianthus annuus

SUNFLOWER An iconic cottage plant, this annual has large heart-shaped leaves and erect stems bearing yellow, orange, mahogany, or cream blooms with a large yellow or brown central disk. Varieties range from dwarfs to giants.

↕up to 10ft (3m) ↔18in (45cm)

PERENNIAL MEDIUM

Helleborus orientalis

LENTEN ROSE This medium-sized evergreen woodland perennial has leathery dark green leaves divided into slim leaflets. From midwinter to spring, it produces saucer-shaped, white or greenish cream flowers, which age to dark pink.

↕24in (60cm) ↔18in (45cm)

PERENNIAL MEDIUM

Hemerocallis 'Beauty to Behold'

DAYLILY A clump-forming perennial with arching strap-shaped leaves. Through summer, multiple buds open in succession to reveal trumpet-shaped, lemon-yellow double blooms, each lasting a day.

↕24in (60cm) ↔30in (75cm)

Z4–10

PERENNIAL MEDIUM

Hyssopus officinalis

HYSSOP A shrubby, aromatic semievergreen herb with narrow leaves and spikes of small violet-blue blooms from summer to early fall. A front-of-bed plant, combine it with sage and pinks. 'Roseus' is a pink variety.

↕24in (60cm) ↔3ft (1m)

Z4–9

SHRUB LARGE

Kalmia latifolia

MOUNTAIN LAUREL This bushy, dense evergreen shrub. In early summer, large clusters of pink saucer-shaped flowers open from distinctively crimped buds amid glossy rich green foliage. Prefers acidic soil and cool microclimates.

↕↔ 10ft (3m)

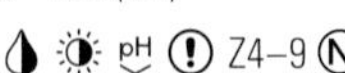 Z4–9

PERENNIAL LARGE

Kniphofia uvaria

RED-HOT POKER This perennial's strap-shaped evergreen leaves and tall spikes of red and yellow cone-shaped flower heads create an eye-catching feature in late summer when planted in swaths through the center of a bed.

↕ 4ft (1.2m) ↔ 24in (60cm)

Z5–9

CLIMBER MEDIUM

Lathyrus odoratus

SWEET PEA This annual climbs by tendrils, and has divided scented midgreen leaves and pink, blue, purple, or white flowers from summer to early fall. Plant in large pots or in a bed with a tripod support.

↕ 10ft (3m)

SHRUB SMALL

Lavandula angustifolia

ENGLISH LAVENDER An evergreen subshrub with narrow, aromatic silver-gray leaves and dense spikes of fragrant, deep purple flowers held on wiry stems from mid- to late summer. Other varieties have flowers in shades of white, pink, and mauve.

↕ 24in (60cm) ↔ 30in (75cm)

Z5–8

PERENNIAL MEDIUM

Leucanthemum x *superbum*

SHASTA DAISY Grow this upright perennial mid-bed for its lance-shaped leaves and large white, or sometimes yellow, daisies that appear from midsummer to fall. 'Wirral Pride' (above) has striking yellow-centered white double flowers.

↕ 3ft (1m) ↔ 24in (60cm)

Z5–9

BULB LARGE

Lilium longiflorum

EASTER LILY An upright perennial bulb with long, shiny lance-shaped leaves. This classic lily bears sprays of fragrant, large, outward-facing, funnel-shaped pure white summer flowers with slightly reflexed petals. Flowers are excellent for cutting.

↕ up to 3ft (1m)

Z7–9

BULB LARGE

Lilium regale

REGAL LILY This perennial bulb has tall unbranched stems topped with large, fragrant trumpet-shaped white flowers, yellow at the throat and pinkish purple on the outside. Plant it in pots or among tall delphiniums and shrub roses.

↕ 6ft (2m)

Z4–8

PERENNIAL LARGE

Lupinus 'The Chatelaine'

LUPINE This upright perennial has round leaves divided into lance-shaped leaflets. Tall spikes of dark pink and white flowers appear in summer, adding color to the middle of a border. Plants may need staking. The seeds are toxic.

↕ 4ft (1.2m) ↔ 18in (45cm)

Z4–8

ANNUAL/BIENNIAL MEDIUM

Malope trifida

ANNUAL MALLOW This fast-growing upright annual, with lobed leaves, is a magnet for bees and a good partner for soft fruits and vegetables. Trumpet-shaped purple-pink blooms with darker nectar guides open from summer to fall.

↕ 3ft (1m) ↔ 12in (30cm)

ANNUAL/BIENNIAL SMALL

Nemophila menziesii

BABY BLUE-EYES This summer-flowering, low-growing spreading annual has finely divided leaves and saucer-shaped sky-blue blooms with pale blue to white centers. Plant it in masses to edge a bed in a sunny or lightly shaded spot.

↕8in (20cm) ↔6in (15cm)

PERENNIAL MEDIUM

Nepeta 'Six Hills Giant'

CATMINT A vigorous clump-forming perennial with narrow, oval, toothed, aromatic gray-green leaves. In summer, it is covered with spikes of tubular lavender-blue flowers. Use it as bed edging or in front of a hedge or wall.

↕3ft (1m) ↔4ft (1.2m)

Z3–8

ANNUAL/BIENNIAL SMALL

Nigella damascena

LOVE-IN-A-MIST Sow this ferny-leaved annual in gaps in borders, where it will produce light blue flowers with delicate leafy ruffs in summer. Ornamental pods follow the blooms. Persian Jewel Group has pastel flowers in various shades.

↕18in (45cm) ↔8in (20cm)

PERENNIAL MEDIUM

Paeonia 'Bowl of Beauty'

PEONY This erect clump-forming perennial has divided green leaves and large bowl-shaped double flowers with rose-pink outer petals and cream centers. Great plant for summer color. Heavy blooms may require staking.

↕↔3ft (1m)

Z3–8

PERENNIAL MEDIUM

Paeonia mlokosewitschii

CAUCASIAN PEONY This clump-forming perennial produces pinkish shoots and bluish green leaves and lemon bowl-shaped late spring to early summer blooms. Grow it at the front of a bed with *Geranium* 'Johnson's Blue'.

↕↔30in (75cm)

Z5–8

PERENNIAL MEDIUM

Papaver orientale

ORIENTAL POPPY This medium-sized perennial has divided hairy foliage. It bears bowl-shaped, ruffled black-centered orange, pink, or white blooms in early summer. Purple-red blooms of 'Patty's Plum' (above) are effective with silvers.

↕3ft (1m) ↔24in (60cm)

Z3–9

ANNUAL/BIENNIAL MEDIUM

Papaver rhoeas

CORN POPPY Bred originally from the field poppy, this annual has bowl-shaped blooms, with tissue-paper-like petals, in shades of white, pink, and red. All the colored forms have white centers. Sow seeds directly in borders to fill gaps.

↕24in (60cm) ↔12in (30cm)

PERENNIAL MEDIUM

Penstemon 'Sour Grapes'

BEARDTONGUE This upright semievergreen perennial has light green lance-shaped leaves and, from midsummer to fall, tubular, bell-shaped purple-blue flowers suffused with violet and white inside. Plant it mid-bed in a sheltered garden.

↕24in (60cm) ↔18in (45cm)

 Z7–10

PERENNIAL MEDIUM

Penstemon 'Stapleford Gem'

BEARDTONGUE This bushy semievergreen perennial has narrow spires of tubular blue-flushed light purple flowers with whitish throats from late summer to fall. Grow it mid-bed against darker purples and magentas.

↕24in (60cm) ↔18in (45cm)

Z6–9

SHRUB SMALL

Potentilla fruticosa

CINQUEFOIL A bushy shrub with circular flowers in shades of white, pink, yellow, orange, or red from summer to early fall. Grow between perennials to brighten up borders. Tolerates part shade. Varieties include the yellow 'Goldfinger' (above).

↕3ft (1m) ↔5ft (1.5m)

Z2–7 Ⓝ

PERENNIAL SMALL

Primula japonica

JAPANESE PRIMROSE This perennial candelabra primula bears clusters of red, purple, orange, pink, or yellow flowers on upright stems in early summer. Grow at the front of a damp bed or pool side. 'Miller's Crimson' (above) has rich pink blooms.

↕↔18in (45cm)

 Z4–8

CLIMBER LARGE

Rosa 'Albertine'
CLIMBING ROSE A vigorous rose with arching, thorny reddish stems and glossy dark green foliage. In summer, it bears clusters of scented, salmon-pink fully double flowers in one flush. Grow it through a tree or on a large pergola.
↕15ft (5m)
Z5–9

SHRUB MEDIUM

Rosa 'Ballerina'
POLYANTHA ROSE This shrub rose bears clusters of small, white-centered pale pink single flowers in repeated flushes from midsummer to early fall. Deadhead or pick regularly to prolong the display. Mulch annually in spring.
↕5ft (1.5m) ↔4ft (1.2m)
Z5–9

CLIMBER LARGE

Rosa banksiae 'Lutea'
YELLOW BANKSIAN ROSE This vigorous semievergreen rambling rose bears abundant clusters of unscented, soft yellow double flowers in late spring. The thornless stems clamber over fences and trees, draping them in early color.
↕30ft (10m)
Z8–9

SHRUB SMALL

Rosa 'Buff Beauty'
HYBRID MUSK ROSE This mid-bed shrub has long arching stems, glossy leaves, and large clusters of fragrant double blooms over a long period from summer to fall. The apricot shading of the flowers lend an old-fashioned look to the garden.
↕↔4ft (1.2m)
Z5–9

SHRUB MEDIUM

Rosa 'Complicata'
GALLICA ROSE This shrub has open, mildly scented, white-centered midpink single blooms in a one flush during midsummer. Grow it mid-bed with later-flowering plants to give continued color. Deadhead regularly, and mulch with compost in spring.
↕7ft (2.2m) ↔8ft (2.5m)
Z4–9

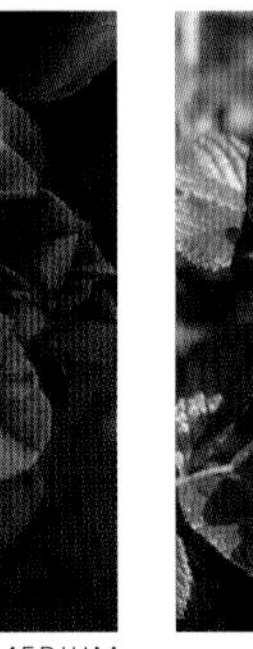

SHRUB MEDIUM

Rosa GERTRUDE JEKYLL
ENGLISH SHRUB ROSE A shrub or a small climber with large, richly scented, pink fully double flowers from summer to early fall. Plant at the back of a bed or train against a low fence. Deadhead regularly and mulch with compost during spring.
↕6ft (2m) ↔4ft (1.2m)
Z5–9

SHRUB MEDIUM

Rosa 'Roseraie de l'Hay'
RUGOSA ROSE This shrub produces prickly upright stems clothed in glossy green wrinkled foliage that provides a foil for the fragrant, purple-crimson double flowers from summer to fall. Tomatolike hips appear in fall.
↕7ft (2.2m) ↔6ft (2m)
Z4–9

CLIMBER MEDIUM

Rosa SUMMER WINE
CLIMBING ROSE This climbing rose has disease-resistant dark green leaves and small clusters of fragrant, flat-faced, coral-pink semidouble flowers from summer to fall. It is ideal for growing on a wall, fence, arch, or pillar.
↕10ft (3m)
Z5–9

SHRUB MEDIUM

Rosa 'Zéphirine Drouhin'
THORNLESS ROSE Grow this rose as a shrub, or train it as a small climber. It bears bright pink double flowers from summer to fall. An ideal back-of-bed plant, it tolerates shade. Deadhead often and mulch with organic matter in spring.
↕8ft (2.5m) ↔6ft (2m)
Z5–9

SHRUB SMALL

Salvia officinalis
SAGE An evergreen perennial with oval, aromatic gray-green leaves that are used to flavor meat dishes and to make stuffing. It bears spikes of lilac-pink summer flowers. Can be grown as an annual. 'Icterina' (above) has yellow and green variegated leaves.
↕32in (80cm) ↔3ft (1m)
Z5–8

PERENNIAL MEDIUM

Salvia pratensis

MEADOW SAGE A cottage garden favorite, this perennial bears a clump of large toothed leaves and, in early summer, upright stems of purple two-lipped flowers that are irresistible to bees and butterflies. Makes a great cut flower.

↕3ft (1m) ↔12in (30cm)

 Z3–9

SHRUB SMALL

Santolina pinnata

LAVENDER COTTON A mound-forming evergreen subshrub with finely toothed silver foliage that gives year-round color and pale lemon pompomlike summer blooms. This drought-tolerant plant will thrive in well-drained soils with minimal water.

↕30in (75cm) ↔3ft (1m)

Z9–11

PERENNIAL MEDIUM

Sidalcea malviflora

CHECKERBLOOM This upright branching perennial has lobed green leaves and, in summer, funnel-shaped, lilac or pale pink flowers on tall stems. Plant it in drifts in the middle of a bed; stake taller plants as required.

↕3ft (1m) ↔18in (45cm)

pH Z5–7 Ⓝ

SHRUB MEDIUM

Spiraea nipponica

SPIREA Use this shrub at the back of a bed, or as an informal hedge. Small oval leaves cover the wiry stems and rounded clusters of tiny white blooms clothe the sideshoots in summer. 'Snowmound' (above) is a vigorous variety.

↕↔8ft (2.5m)

 Z4–8

PERENNIAL SMALL

Stokesia laevis

STOKES' ASTER This evergreen perennial has narrow midgreen leaves, and bears large, cornflower-like lavender- or purple-blue flowers on short stems from midsummer to mid-fall. 'Purple Parasols' (above) has violet-purple blooms.

↕↔18in (45cm)

pH Z5–9 Ⓝ

SHRUB MEDIUM

Symphoricarpos x *doorenbosii*

SNOWBERRY This vigorous deciduous shrub has small, round dark green leaves and tiny greenish white summer flowers followed by showy clusters of round white fruits that provide winter interest. Useful as a hedging plant or bed backdrop.

↕6ft (2m) ↔indefinite

Z4–7

BULB MEDIUM

Tulipa 'China Pink'

TULIP This tall late-spring-flowering bulb has grayish green leaves and slender, waisted pure rose-pink flowers, with outward-curving pointed petals. It looks good teamed with cream wallflowers or lime euphorbia.

↕22in (55cm)

Z3–8

BULB MEDIUM

Tulipa 'Spring Green'

TULIP This Viridiflora Group tulip bears lance-shaped dark green leaves and cup-shaped creamy white flowers with green markings in late spring. For a cool combination, try it with forget-me-nots and double bellis daisies.

↕15in (38cm)

 Z3–8

PERENNIAL MEDIUM

Verbascum chaixii

NETTLE-LEAVED MULLEIN This perennial, ideal for creating focal points in a border, makes a rosette of coarse leaves. Pale yellow blooms form throughout summer on upright stems. 'Album' (above) has purple-eyed white flowers.

↕3ft (1m) ↔18in (45cm)

Z5–9

OTHER SUGGESTIONS

Annuals

Clarkia amoena Ⓝ

Perennials and bulbs

Asclepias incarnata 'Cinderella' Ⓝ • *Allium* 'Mount Everest' • *Anemone* x *hybrida* 'September Charm' • *Aquilegia vulgaris* 'Black Barlow' • *Astilbe* x *crispa* 'Perkeo' • *Camassia quamash* Ⓝ • *Chrysanthemum* 'Ruby Mound' • *Dahlia* 'Lismore Moonlight' • *Delphinium* 'Royal Aspirations' • *Dianthus* 'Cranberry Ice' • *Dianthus* 'Spangled Star' • *Eupatorium perfoliatum* Ⓝ • *Fritillaria persica* • *Ornithogalum magnum* • *Penstemon* 'Dark Towers' • *Symphyotrichum novae-angliae* 'Andenken an Alma Potschke' Ⓝ • *Tulipa* 'Menton' • *Veronica gentianoides*

Shrubs and trees

Ceanothus thyrsiflorus var. *repens* Ⓝ • *Cercis canadensis* 'Lavender Twist' Ⓝ • *Rosa filipes* 'Kiftsgate'

Plants for play

Children love to explore! Transform your garden into a jungle of secret hideouts and tunnels and add interesting plants to ensure they are never bored.

Weave narrow paths between tough shrubs, such as spotted laurel and or tall bamboo that tolerate wear and tear. Also consider a living plant feature, such as a tunnel or teepee made from willow—you can buy the "withies" (young stems) in early spring from specialist suppliers who will provide you with weaving instructions too. Plants that resemble animal features, such as hare's-tail grass and the cute mouse plant, will keep children entertained, while easy-to-grow annuals help stimulate their interest in gardening and nature—sunflowers and marigolds are good choices.

ANNUAL/BIENNIAL LARGE

Amaranthus caudatus

LOVE-LIES-BLEEDING This tall bushy annual is fun to grow from seed and produces tall sturdy stems from which hang long, pendulous, tassel-like red flowers from summer to fall. Children can also cut them for indoor displays.

↕4ft (1.2m) ↔18in (45cm)

ANNUAL/BIENNIAL SMALL

Antirrhinum majus

SNAPDRAGON Lending color to summer pots and flowerbeds, this upright annual bears spikes of two-lipped crimson, red, pink, burgundy, white, and yellow flowers. When pressed at the base, the blooms open up to reveal a dragonlike mouth.

↕↔18in (45cm)

PERENNIAL SMALL

Arisarum proboscideum

MOUSE PLANT This clump-forming perennial bears strange blooms that intrigue children. The maroon flowers have a white base and consist of a "hood," which is drawn out into a mouselike trap and conceals tiny flowers.

↕6in (15cm) ↔12in (30cm)

Z7–9

SHRUB MEDIUM

Aucuba japonica

SPOTTED LAUREL This evergreen shrub has large, glossy green leaves decorated with small yellow spots. A tough resilient plant, it can be used to provide shelter and privacy near a play area. Plant males; berries of females cause stomach upset if ingested.

↕↔6ft (2m)

Z7–10

ANNUAL/BIENNIAL MEDIUM

Calendula officinalis

POT MARIGOLD Children will enjoy growing this bushy annual from seed. Its aromatic pale green leaves are joined by edible, daisy-like single or double flowers in shades of yellow and orange from late spring to fall.

↕↔24in (60cm)

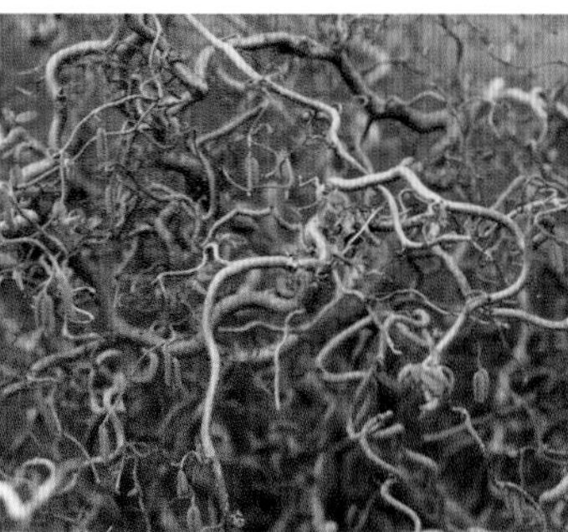

SHRUB LARGE

Corylus avellana 'Contorta'

HARRY LAUDER'S WALKING STICK The twisted shoots of this deciduous shrub fascinate children, and give the garden a spooky look, when the green leaves fall in fall. Considered invasive in the Northwest and some parts of the Northeast.

↕15ft (5m) ↔15ft (5m)

Z4–8

PERENNIAL SMALL

Fragaria vesca

ALPINE STRAWBERRY This type of strawberry produces small sweet berries all summer, which children love. Plant in pots or directly in the soil. It is easy to look after and is ideal for teaching children how to care for plants themselves.

↕12in (30cm) ↔indefinite

Z5–9 N

ANNUAL/BIENNIAL MEDIUM

Helianthus annuus

SUNFLOWER The edible seeds of this robust annual are easy for children to handle and sow. It bears classic daisy-like orange or yellow flowers throughout summer. Dwarf varieties include 'Teddy Bear' (above), with fluffy double blooms.

↕up to 3ft (1m) ↔24in (60cm)

N

ANNUAL/BIENNIAL SMALL

Lagurus ovatus

HARE'S-TAIL GRASS This clump-forming annual grass has green leaves and, in early summer, oval, furry white flower heads, which resemble soft rabbits' tails and last into fall. They also make beautiful indoor displays.

↕18in (45cm) ↔6in (15cm)

CLIMBER LARGE

Luffa cylindrica

SMOOTH LOOFAH Grow your own loofah sponge from seed with this climbing annual. It has maplelike leaves and yellow flowers followed by elongated fruits that produce loofahs when dried. It needs a sheltered, sunny site to thrive.

↕15ft (5m)

TREE SMALL

Malus domestica

APPLE TREE Plant a dessert apple tree for its delicious sweet fruits and pretty spring blossom. Opt for one on a dwarfing rootstock, such as M9, for a small garden. Varieties include 'Cox's Orange Pippin' (above), with sweet red apples.

↕↔25ft (8m)

 Z4–8

BAMBOO LARGE

Phyllostachys aureosulcata f. *spectabilis*

YELLOW GROOVE BAMBOO This bamboo has tall upright canes clothed in soft green leaves. It lends the garden a junglelike appearance, and can be used to provide shelter and privacy to an outdoor play area.

↕20ft (6m) ↔indefinite

Z5–11

PERENNIAL MEDIUM

Platycodon grandiflorus

BALLOON FLOWER The purple-blue flowers of this perennial open from balloonlike buds throughout early fall, creating beautiful displays in containers filled with soil-based potting mix. Add a frill of violas around the edge to inject more color.

↕24in (60cm) ↔18in (45cm)

Z3–8

TREE SMALL

Prunus x *subhirtella* 'Pendula'

HIGAN CHERRY This weeping cherry has pink buds that open into scented white spring flowers. The spreading branches create a private play space for children. Its fall color also adds to its decorative value.

↕↔25ft (8m)

Z6–8

TREE SMALL

Pyrus salicifolia 'Pendula'

WILLOWLEAF PEAR This small tree creates a skirt of weeping stems studded with narrow silvery green leaves, beneath which children can hide. Creamy white spring flowers are followed by inedible brown fruits.

↕25ft (8m) ↔20ft (6m)

Z4–7

TREE SMALL

Salix caprea 'Pendula'

PUSSY WILLOW This large deciduous shrub or small tree produces arching stems that develop soft furry catkins in late winter, which are loved by children. The dark green leaves follow in spring. Considered invasive in some areas.

↕↔6ft (2m)

Z6–8

PERENNIAL SMALL

Sempervivum arachnoideum

COBWEB HOUSELEEK This low-growing evergreen perennial has rosettes of fleshy green leaves covered with fine white hairs that resemble cobwebs. Children can easily grow it in containers and raised beds, where it will form neat mounded clumps.

↕5in (12cm) ↔4in (10cm) or more

Z5–8

ANNUAL/BIENNIAL SMALL

Solanum lycopersicum

BUSH TOMATO Tomato plants help to teach children how to care for plants, and reward even basic care with tasty summer fruits. Bush varieties that grow outside are the best choices, particularly dwarf types for patio containers.

↕↔18in (45cm)

PERENNIAL SMALL

Stachys byzantina

LAMB'S EARS This perennial produces downy silver-gray foliage and spikes of small mauve-pink flowers in summer. A tough plant with soft tactile leaves, it is perfect for edging a bed in a sunny family garden.

↕15in (38cm) ↔24in (60cm)

Z4–8

ANNUAL/BIENNIAL SMALL

Tropaeolum majus Alaska Series

NASTURTIUM A bushy annual with round cream-splashed dark green leaves and red and yellow trumpet-shaped summer to early fall blooms. Grow it in tall pots for children to pick the edible leaves and flowers.

↕12in (30cm) ↔18in (45cm)

SHRUB MEDIUM

Vaccinium corymbosum

HIGHBUSH BLUEBERRY This easy-to-grow soft fruit bush bears delicious sweet-tasting blue-black fruits in summer. Plant in a large pot of acidic soil mix in a sunny spot. Children will love the berries, which are packed with healthy vitamins.

↕↔5ft (1.5m)

pH Z3–7 Ⓝ

OTHER SUGGESTIONS

Annuals

Antirrhinum Bells Series • *Cucurbita pepo* 'Jack Be Little' • *Helianthus annuus* 'American Giant' Ⓝ

Perennials and climbers

Alocasia 'Borneo Giant' • *Acmella oleracea* • *Cosmos atrosanguineus* Ⓝ • *Geranium* 'Johnson's Blue' • *Ipomoea lobata* Ⓝ • *Muhlenbergia capillaris* Ⓝ • *Selaginella kraussiana* • *Sedum spectabile*

Shrubs and bamboos

Choisya 'Aztec Pearl' • *Choisya ternata* Ⓝ • *Fargesia murielae* • *Lavandula angustifolia*

Shrubs and bamboos

Cercidiphyllum japonicum f. *pendulum* • *Sassafras albidum* Ⓝ • *Sequoiadendron giganteum* 'Pendulum' Ⓝ

Plants for wildlife gardens

Whatever your design style, bring your garden to life with a collection of berries, seeds, and nectar-rich plants to attract birds and beneficial insects.

A wildlife garden can be formal or informal, although the scope is limited in a tightly controlled design. You can create habitats for nesting birds with prickly hedging and trees to protect them from predators. Include shrubs that bear nuts and berries, such as hawthorn and viburnum, to feed your feathered friends over winter. Plants rich in pollen and nectar will attract beneficial insects, including butterflies and bees, as well as those whose larvae help control pest populations. A naturalistic pool surrounded by moisture-loving plants will also draw in birds and beasts to drink and bathe.

TREE LARGE

Acer rubrum

RED MAPLE This large tree has green leaves that turn yellow and orange in fall. The red spring flowers provide pollen for bees, and winged fruits are food for birds and squirrels. 'Bowhall' has a columnar habit.

↕70ft (20m) ↔30ft (10m)

Z3–9 Ⓝ

PERENNIAL LARGE

Ageratina altissima

WHITE SNAKEROOT This clump-forming perennial has pointed, oval, toothed-edged leaves. From summer to early fall, upright stems are topped with clusters of tiny white blooms that are a rich source of nectar for butterflies.

↕4ft (1.2m) ↔18in (45cm)

Z4–8 Ⓝ

PERENNIAL LARGE

Alcea rosea

HOLLYHOCK A tall, short-lived perennial or biennial with rounded lobed leaves. From mid- to late summer, it bears purple, red, pink, white, or yellow cup-shaped blooms that attract butterflies and bees. Considered invasive in many areas; may self-seed.

↕6ft (2m) ↔24in (60cm)

Z3–9

BULB LARGE

Allium cernuum

NODDING ONION This upright perennial bulb produces strap-shaped gray-green leaves that fade before clusters of nectar-rich, drooping purplish pink flowers appear on slim stems in early summer. Use it to naturalize in meadows.

↕28in (70cm)

Z3–9 Ⓝ

PERENNIAL MEDIUM

Asclepias tuberosa

BUTTERFLY WEED This tap-rooted perennial bears flat heads of vivid orange or yellow flowers from late summer to fall. Great nectar source for pollinators and host plant for monarch butterflies. The milky sap is an irritant.

↕30in (75cm) ↔18in (45cm)

Z4–9 Ⓝ

PERENNIAL MEDIUM

Aster x frikartii

FRIKART'S ASTER An upright perennial with yellow-centered lavender-blue, daisy-like flowers that bloom over a long period from midsummer to fall, and provide nectar for butterflies. Plant in bold swaths in a flower border or naturalistic schemes.

↕28in (70cm) ↔16in (40cm)

Z5–8

SHRUB LARGE

Berberis darwinii

DARWIN'S BARBERRY An evergreen shrub, with tiny hollylike leaves, that is smothered with pendent clusters of dark orange flowers in spring that attract bees. Birds devour the blue-black berries that follow. Use as a specimen plant or hedge.

↕↔10ft (3m)

Z7–9

PERENNIAL SMALL

Bergenia SILVERLIGHT

PIGSQUEAK This neat clump-forming evergreen perennial has leathery rounded leaves. In spring, reddish stems carry clusters of white bell-shaped flowers that open from deep red buds, making an attractive contrast.

↕18in (45cm) ↔20in (50cm)

Z3–8

ANNUAL/BIENNIAL MEDIUM

Calendula officinalis

POT MARIGOLD The orange or yellow daisy-like flowers of this fast-growing bushy annual attract a wide range of insects. Choose single-flowered varieties for wildlife gardens, and sow seeds directly in flowerbeds or patio pots.

↕↔24in (60cm)

SHRUB SMALL

Calluna vulgaris

SCOTCH HEATHER This ground-cover evergreen shrub has upright stems covered with green, gold, or silver scalelike leaves that often color up in fall and winter. White, pink, red, or purple late summer to fall flowers offer nectar.

↕24in (60cm) ↔18in (45cm)

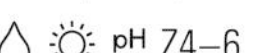 Z4–6

PERENNIAL SMALL

Campanula rotundifolia

HAREBELL A perennial meadow plant with small rounded basal leaves and, in summer, bell-shaped light blue flowers on slender upright stems. Grow this dainty bee plant in grassy patches or rock gardens; avoid using fertilizer.

↕↔12in (30cm)

Z5–7 Ⓝ

PERENNIAL SMALL

Cardamine pratensis

LADY'S SMOCK A neat clump-forming perennial with midgreen leaves, divided into leaflets. In spring, it bears spikes of lilac single flowers, although double forms (above) are also available. It is ideal for boggy areas or pond perimeters.

↕18in (45cm) ↔12in (30cm)

 Z4–8 Ⓝ

PERENNIAL SMALL

Centaurea montana

PERENNIAL CORNFLOWER Plant this perennial in informal schemes and allow it to self-seed. Branched stems bear green leaves and, in early summer, thistlelike, red-purple-centered blue blooms that bees adore. Cut back for a second flowering.

↕20in (50cm) ↔24in (60cm)

 Z3–8

PERENNIAL LARGE

Cephalaria gigantea

GIANT SCABIOUS Place this clump-forming perennial at the back of a large bed or naturalize in rough grass. In summer, pale yellow blooms that are attractive to butterflies appear above green divided leaves on towering branched stems.

↕8ft (2.5m) ↔24in (60cm)

Z3–7

PERENNIAL SMALL

Chamaemelum nobile

CHAMOMILE An evergreen perennial that forms a carpet of feathery aromatic leaves. From late spring to summer, it bears simple white daisy-like blooms. Plant it alongside wildflowers to create a naturalistic meadow effect.

↕4in (10cm) ↔18in (45cm)

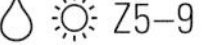 Z5–9

CLIMBER LARGE

Clematis montana

HIMALAYAN CLEMATIS A vigorous deciduous climber that flowers from late spring to early summer, bearing numerous small white blooms with yellow centers. It provides nectar as well as shelter for early-emerging insects.

↕40ft (12m)

 Z6–9

SHRUB LARGE

Cornus alba

TATARIAN DOGWOOD An upright deciduous shrub with bright scarlet shoots in winter. The creamy white early summer flowers are followed by bluish white fruits. Plant to provide cover around wildlife pools. Prune in late winter for more colorful stems.

↕↔10ft (3m)

Ⓘ Z2–7

SHRUB LARGE

Cornus mas

CORNELIAN CHERRY This useful deciduous shrub or small tree has reddish purple fall leaves and edible red fruits loved by birds. In late winter, it produces rounded clusters of nectar- and pollen-rich tiny yellow blooms on bare stems.

↕↔15ft (5m)

Z4–8

SHRUB LARGE

Corylus avellana

EUROPEAN FILBERT A spreading deciduous shrub or small tree, this plant bears round dark green leaves, yellow in fall, and dangling yellow early spring catkins, sometimes followed by filbert nuts. Use it to create a small woodland garden.

↕↔15ft (5m)

 Z4–8

SHRUB SMALL

Cotoneaster horizontalis

ROCKSPRAY This deciduous shrub has small, glossy dark green leaves and branches arranged in a distinctive "herringbone" pattern. It bears small, white summer blooms that are followed by vivid red berries, enjoyed by birds during fall and early winter.

↕3ft (1m) ↔5ft (1.5m)

Z4–7

BULB SMALL

Crocus vernus

DUTCH CROCUS This dwarf perennial bulb, with its small cup-shaped lilac or purple flowers from spring to early summer, provides nectar for early pollinating insects and can be naturalized in lawns. Plant the corms during fall in groups or drifts.

↕5in (12cm)

Z3–8

BULB LARGE

Dahlia 'Bishop of Llandaff'

DAHLIA This perennial, grown from spring-planted tubers, has divided, glossy black-purple leaves and dark-eyed bright red semidouble blooms. Single and semidouble dahlias like these are great nectar sources for butterflies and bees.

↕3ft (1m)

Z9–11

PERENNIAL LARGE

Deschampsia cespitosa

TUFTED HAIR GRASS A tuft-forming deciduous perennial grass with clouds of golden-yellow summer flowers. Ideal for providing habitat for insects and nesting material and food for birds; offers naturalistic setting to planting schemes.

↕6ft (2m) ↔20in (50cm)

Z4–9 Ⓝ

BULB SMALL

Eranthis hyemalis

WINTER ACONITE This clump-forming tuber has lobed green leaves and cup-shaped, yellow stalkless flowers with leaflike ruffs, from late winter to early spring. Grow it in pockets between rocks and combine with spring bulbs.

↕4in (10cm)

Z4–7

SHRUB SMALL

Erica carnea

WINTER HEATH This evergreen shrub, with needlelike leaves, makes a good front-of-bed or rock garden plant. The tiny pink, red, or white flowers from early winter to late spring are good for insects emerging from hibernation.

↕12in (30cm) ↔18in (45cm) or more

pH Z5-7

PERENNIAL SMALL

Erythronium 'Pagoda'

DOG'S-TOOTH VIOLET This tuberous-rooted perennial makes mounds of veined mottled leaves. With its nodding, nectar-rich pale yellow spring flowers with swept-back petals, it is perfect for woodland-style plantings.

↕14in (35cm) ↔8in (20cm)

Z4–8

PERENNIAL LARGE

Filipendula rubra

QUEEN OF THE PRAIRIE An upright moisture-loving perennial with large, deeply cut green leaves. From early to midsummer, it produces heads of fluffy pink flowers on tall slender stems. The blooms provide a source of pollen for bees.

↕up to 8ft (2.5m) ↔4ft (1.2m)

 Z3–8 Ⓝ

BULB MEDIUM

Fritillaria meleagris

SNAKE'S-HEAD FRITILLARY A bulbous perennial with narrow leaves and nodding, rich purple or white bell-shaped spring flowers with a checkered pattern. Ideal for naturalizing in wildflower meadows, it also works well in cottage beds.

↕12in (30cm)

Z4–8

PERENNIAL SMALL

Galium odoratum

SWEET WOODRUFF Though steadily spreading, this carpeting perennial with emerald-green leaves charms its way into any semiwild or woodland planting with its froth of starry white blooms that appear from late spring to midsummer.

↕6in (15cm) ↔12in (30cm) or more

Z4–8

PERENNIAL MEDIUM

Geranium maculatum

SPOTTED GERANIUM This bushy upright perennial has deeply divided leaves and, in late spring, clusters of pale to dark pink or lilac blooms with white centers. Given sufficient soil moisture, this woodlander will naturalize. Attractive to butterflies.

↕30in (75cm) ↔18in (45cm)

Z3–8 Ⓝ

PERENNIAL MEDIUM

Geranium pratense

MEADOW CRANESBILL A clump-forming perennial with lobed, deeply divided midgreen leaves that turn bronze in fall. Saucer-shaped, violet-blue veined flowers appear in summer. Plant it in meadows in heavy soils.

↕↔24in (60cm)

Z4–8

ANNUAL/BIENNIAL LARGE

Helianthus annuus

SUNFLOWER This classic cottage garden plant bears giant daisy-like yellow, orange, mahogany, or cream blooms throughout summer. Flowers attract bees while the seedheads serve as shelter for hibernating insects or food for birds.

↕up to 10ft (3m) ↔18in (45cm)

Ⓝ

BULB MEDIUM

Hyacinthoides non-scripta

ENGLISH BLUEBELL This perennial bulb has narrow strap-shaped leaves and blue, or occasionally white, bell-shaped fragrant spring blooms that hang from arching stems. Gives nectar for bees and butterflies. Plant in masses in open woodland.

↕16in (40cm)

(!) Z5-7

TREE LARGE

Ilex aquifolium

ENGLISH HOLLY A slow-growing evergreen tree with dark green spiny leaves. Females bear bright red winter berries if grown near a male. Grow in wildlife borders as it offers habitat and food for insects and birds. Can be invasive so consider using *I. opaca*.

↕70ft (20m) ↔20ft (6m)

(!) Z7–9

SHRUB LARGE

Ilex 'Sparkleberry'

WINTERBERRY This bushy deciduous shrub has pointed oval leaves that develop bold fall color before dropping. If a male plant is grown nearby, female plants bear small bright red berries that last well into winter, or until eaten by birds.

↕15ft (5m) ↔12ft (4m)

Z5–9

PERENNIAL LARGE

Inula magnifica

SHOWY ELECAMPAGNE This imposing perennial makes a clump of large leaves and, in late summer, bears branched stems topped with daisy-like yellow blooms with threadlike petals. Grow it in damp meadows or next to a wildlife pond.

↕6ft (1.8m) ↔3ft (1m)

Z5–8

ANNUAL/BIENNIAL SMALL

Limnanthes douglasii

POACHED-EGG FLOWER This low-growing spreading annual has ferny foliage and, from summer to fall, rounded yellow-centered white blooms. An insect magnet, plant it at the front of cottage beds, along path edges, and in gravel beds.

↕6in (15cm) ↔4in (10cm)

SHRUB MEDIUM

Mahonia x *media*

MAHONIA This winter-flowering evergreen shrub provides valuable nectar to early emerging insects when few other plants are in bloom. Chains of blue-black edible berries, which are loved by birds follow the flowers. Consider using native *M. aquifolium.*

↕15ft (5m) ↔12ft (4m)

Z7–9

PERENNIAL MEDIUM

Knautia macedonica

KNAUTIA This upright perennial has lobed basal leaves and, in summer, a succession of buttonlike crimson flowers on wiry stems. Combine this bee and butterfly attractor with ornamental grasses for a meadow effect.

↕30in (75cm) ↔24in (60cm)

Z5–9

PERENNIAL SMALL

Linaria alpina

ALPINE TOADFLAX This short-lived perennial bee attractor bears trailing stems with a succession of snap-dragon-like, orange-centered purple-violet flowers in summer. Allow it to trail over walls and raised beds, or spread through a gravel bed.

↕↔6in (15cm)

Z4–9

PERENNIAL MEDIUM

Maianthemum racemosum

FALSE SPIKENARD This upright perennial has prominently veined, oval green leaves and, from mid to late spring, scented, fluffy cream plumes, sometimes followed by red berries. Plant it to provide a wildlife habitat; shelter from strong winds.

↕3ft (1m) ↔24in (60cm)

Z3–8 Ⓝ

SHRUB SMALL

Lavandula angustifolia

ENGLISH LAVENDER An evergreen subshrub with linear, aromatic silvery gray leaves. In midsummer, it produces a profusion of small, fragrant violet-blue flower heads that are irresistible to bees. Try it with self-seeded California poppies.

↕32in (80cm) ↔24in (60cm)

Z5–8

TREE MEDIUM

Malus x *moerlandsii* 'Profusion'

FLOWERING CRABAPPLE A deciduous tree with pink spring blooms, which provide nectar for insects, followed by crab apples that ripen to deep purple in fall and are loved by birds. Provides habitat and nesting sites.

↕↔30ft (10m)

Z4–8

SHRUB MEDIUM

Leycesteria formosa

HIMALAYAN HONEYSUCKLE This deciduous shrub has large heart-shaped leaves and pendent chains of white summer blooms that attract bees and insects. Black berries in fall provide food for birds. Plant it at the back of a border; it may self-seed.

↕↔6ft (2m)

Z7–9

CLIMBER LARGE

Lonicera periclymenum

WOODBINE This climber has fragrant, nectar-rich red and white summer flowers that attract pollinating butterflies and insects. Glossy red berries appear from late summer to fall. Mature woody plants offer habitat. Considered invasive in some areas.

↕22ft (7m)

Z5–9

PERENNIAL SMALL

Meconopsis cambrica

WELSH POPPY This perennial has light green divided leaves and lemon-yellow or orange poppy-like blooms that are borne in succession on slim stems from late spring to early summer. Plants colonize beside shaded walls and in gravel.

↕18in (45cm) ↔12in (30cm)

Z5–9

PERENNIAL MEDIUM

Monarda 'Cambridge Scarlet'

BEEBALM This upright clump-forming perennial has aromatic dark green leaves and trumpet-shaped whorls of red summer blooms that attract bees and pollinating insects. Leave the spent stems standing for insect habitats and fall interest.

↕3ft (1m) ↔18in (45cm)

PERENNIAL LARGE

Monarda fistulosa

WILD BERGAMOT This clump-forming perennial bears whorled heads of small, two-lipped pale lilac blooms on tall stems in midsummer. The flowers attract bees and butterflies. Grow at the edge of a woodland garden or in a prairie-style setting.

↕4ft (1.2m) ↔18in (45cm)

Z3–9 Ⓝ

BULB MEDIUM

Muscari armeniacum

GRAPE HYACINTH A spring-flowering perennial bulb with narrow grassy leaves and cone-shaped clusters of small, fragrant, bell-shaped deep blue flowers, which attract early emerging butterflies and bees. Allow it to naturalize in wild gardens.

↕8in (20cm)

Z4–8

BULB LARGE

Nectaroscordum siculum

MEDITERRANEAN BELLS An upright bulb with narrow leaves that fade as fountain-shaped clusters of pendent, bell-shaped cream and purple flowers emerge in early summer. Attractive seedheads follow the blooms. Try naturalizing it in meadows.

↕4ft (1.2m)

PERENNIAL SMALL

Nepeta x *faassenii*

CATMINT This bushy perennial has small, grayish green aromatic leaves and spikes of lilac-purple flowers, irresistible to bees, from summer to fall. Cut back between flushes for repeat flowering. Plant at the front of cottage beds or as path edging.

↕↔18in (45cm)

Z4–8

TREE LARGE

Nyssa sylvatica

BLACK GUM This broadly conical graceful tree has insignificant greenish yellow late spring flowers, visited by honeybees. Deep blue fruits on female plants attract birds in fall when the oval leaves develop rich red or yellow shades.

↕70ft (20m) ↔30ft (10m)

pH Z4–9 Ⓝ

PERENNIAL MEDIUM

Panicum virgatum

SWITCH GRASS A clump-forming deciduous grass with blue-green leaves and clouds of pink-tinged green flower heads in summer. Gives a naturalistic appeal to gardens, and offers habitat, food, and nesting material to birds, mammals, and insects.

↕3ft (1m) ↔30in (75cm)

Z5-9 Ⓝ

ANNUAL/BIENNIAL MEDIUM

Papaver rhoeas

CORN POPPY This annual wildflower produces divided leaves and bowl-shaped, black-centered scarlet blooms in summer. Sow seeds in spring or fall, and turn over the soil annually to ensure repeat germination.

↕24in (60cm) ↔6in (15cm)

PERENNIAL SMALL

Primula veris

COWSLIP This evergreen or semievergreen perennial forms rosettes of corrugated, oval to lance-shaped leaves. Tight clusters of fragrant, nodding, butter-yellow tubular flowers appear on stout stems in spring. It is attractive to bees and butterflies.

↕↔10in (25cm)

SHRUB LARGE

Rhododendron luteum

PONTIC AZALEA A spring-flowering deciduous shrub with oblong- to lance-shaped leaves, which develop bold autumn shades and fragrant, funnel-shaped yellow flowers. Plant in a cool site and fertile soil.

↕↔12ft (4m)

Z7–9

PERENNIAL MEDIUM

Scabiosa atropurpurea

PINCUSHION FLOWER This short-lived, clump-forming perennial, grown as an annual, has narrow toothed leaves and domed heads of purple summer flowers with creamy anthers. Attracts bees and butterflies. Considered invasive.

↕up to 3ft (1m) ↔12in (30cm)

Z8–11

TREE MEDIUM

Prunus virginiana

CHOKECHERRY This suckering tree or shrub for wild gardens has short spikes of white flowers in spring, that are followed by red fruits, ripening to black. It attracts birds and other wildlife. Varieties include 'Schubert' (above), with dark purple oval leaves.

↕30ft (10m) ↔25ft (8m)

Z2–7 Ⓝ

PERENNIAL SMALL

Scabiosa lucida

GLOSSY SCABIOUS Plant this small, neat scabious with its basal clump of divided gray-green leaves and pale-lilac pincushion blooms from spring to fall to attract bees and butterflies. Group plants at the front of a border or gravel bed.

↕8in (20cm) ↔6in (15cm)

Z5–9

PERENNIAL SMALL

Pulmonaria angustifolia

BLUE LUNGWORT Forming a low clump of matte midgreen leaves, this spreading perennial bears blue trumpet-shaped blooms in spring. It gives nectar for early emerging insects. The leaves die back in summer; remove spent growth to keep tidy.

↕9in (23cm) ↔12in (30cm) or more

Z3–7

SHRUB LARGE

Rubus species

BRAMBLE There are many species of blackberries, brambles, and raspberries. Some are grown for their edible fruits and others for their attractive foliage, winter shoots, or flowers in shades of white, pink, red, or purple.

↕↔10ft (3m)

Z5–9

BULB MEDIUM

Scilla siberica

SIBERIAN SQUILL This perennial bulb with strap-shaped leaves and nodding, vivid blue bell-shaped flowers, attracts bees in spring. Plant the bulbs in drifts in fall, with spring-blooming perennials like primrose, bugle, and wood anemone.

↕8in (20cm)

Z4–8

TREE LARGE

Quercus rubra

RED OAK This large forest tree with a spreading crown has leaves with pointed lobes that turn rich reddish brown in fall, when the acorns ripen. Oaks feed native insects, including moths, and acorns are eaten by birds and mammals.

↕80ft (25m) ↔70ft (20m)

Z4–8 Ⓝ

SHRUB LARGE

Sambucus nigra

BLACK ELDER This large bushy shrub or small tree has divided leaves and, in early summer, flat rounded heads of creamy white flowers, which develop into bunches of black berries, much sought after by birds.

↕↔20ft (6m)

Z5–8

PERENNIAL SMALL

Sedum spectabile

SHOWY STONECROP This fleshy perennial blooms in late summer and produces large, flattened pink flower heads, attracting bees, pollinating insects, and butterflies. After flowering, leave the spent heads standing to provide interest during winter.

↕↔18in (45cm)

Z3–9

PERENNIAL LARGE

Selinum wallichianum

WALLICH MILK PARSLEY An upright architectural perennial with fernlike leaves and long-lasting umbrella-shaped heads of starry white flowers borne in summer. The blooms attract insects; plant it for a meadow effect.

↕4ft (1.2m) ↔16in (40cm)

Z7–10

PERENNIAL MEDIUM

Silene dioica

RED CAMPION A clump-forming semievergreen perennial with clusters of small vivid rose-pink flowers that appear from late spring to midsummer. Ideal for growing along hedgerows and in woodland areas. It attracts moths and butterflies.

↕32in (80cm) ↔18in (45cm)

Z6–9

ANNUAL/BIENNIAL SMALL

Tagetes patula

FRENCH MARIGOLD This Mexican native annual has cut, aromatic dark green leaves and yellow, orange, red, or mahogany flowers, which appear from summer to early fall. For butterflies and other insects, choose single or semidouble varieties.

↕↔12in (30cm)

PERENNIAL MEDIUM

Tellima grandiflora

FRINGE CUPS A semievergreen perennial with heart-shaped, purple-tinged bright green leaves and, from late spring to midsummer, long spikes of small, bell-shaped cream flowers that provide nectar for insects. Grow in dry areas under trees.

↕↔24in (60cm)

Z4–7

PERENNIAL LARGE

Thalictrum aquilegiifolium

MEADOW RUE This perennial has clusters of fluffy lilac-purple summer flowers and attractive seedheads, which appear above finely divided gray-green leaves. Grow it in wild areas or cottage-style borders to attract beneficial insects.

↕4ft (1.2m) ↔18in (45cm)

Z5–8

PERENNIAL LARGE

Verbena bonariensis

PURPLETOP VERVAIN This versatile border perennial has "see-through" stems and, from midsummer to fall, domed clusters of violet-purple scented blooms that attract bees and butterflies. Considered invasive in some areas of the West Coast and in Southeast.

↕5ft (1.5m) ↔24in (60cm)

Z7–11

PERENNIAL LARGE

Verbena hastata

AMERICAN BLUE VERVAIN This bushy upright perennial spreads by self-seeding. It has narrow toothed leaves and candelabra-like heads of violet-blue flowers that attract butterflies from midsummer to fall. 'Rosea' (above) has lilac-pink flowers.

↕5ft (1.5m) ↔24in (60cm)

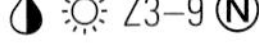

Z3–9

SHRUB LARGE

Viburnum prunifolium

BLACKHAW VIBURNUM A deciduous shrub, ideal for hedging, with oval glossy leaves that turn red and purple-bronze in fall. From late spring to early summer, it forms lacy white flowers, attractive to butterflies. Birds love the blue-black fruits that follow.

↕15ft (5m) ↔12ft (4m)

Z3–9

OTHER SUGGESTIONS

Perennials

Actaea pachypoda 'Misty Blue' (N) • *Aquilegia canadensis* 'Little Lanterns' (N) • *Aruncus dioicus* (N) • *Asclepias tuberosa* (N) • *Baptisia australis* • *Carex appalachica* (N) • *Chelone glabra* (N) • *Coreopsis verticillata* (N) • *Echinacea paradoxa* (N) • *Echinacea purpurea* (N) • *Eupatorium perfoliatum* (N) • *Liatris spicata* (N) • *Lobelia cardinalis* (N) • *Mertensia virginica* (N) • *Phlox paniculata* (N) • *Pycnanthemum muticum* (N) • *Rudbeckia triloba* (N) • *Schizachyrium scoparium* (N) • *Silphium perfoliatum* (N)

Shrubs and trees

Acer saccharum (N) • *Amelanchier canadensis* (N) • *Aronia arbutifolia* (N) • *Asimina triloba* (N) • *Cercis canadensis* (N) • *Clethra alnifolia* (N) • *Cornus florida* (N) • *Cornus racemosa* (N) • *Fothergilla major* (N) • *Lindera benzoin* (N) • *Myrica pensylvanica* (N) • *Juniperus virginiana* (N) • *Magnolia virginiana* (N) • *Pinus strobus* (N)

PLANTS for SEASONAL INTEREST

By selecting plants that perform at different times of the year, you can ensure there is never a dull moment in your garden, even in the depths of winter. The key is to plan ahead and plant a few stars for each season, such as bulbs and blossoming trees in spring, flowering perennials for early and late summer color, and berried shrubs and blazing foliage plants that perform in fall. Also include evergreens and plants that bloom during the darkest days of the year to brighten up winter scenes.

Plants for spring beds

As the cold, dark days of winter fade, the new season bursts into life with a blaze of colorful flowers and fresh green growth.

Hellebores are among the first to bloom in early spring, and look great together with bold groups of early daffodils and a sprinkling of anemones in front. As spring unfolds, more flowers join the party. Choose tulips, bergenias, and primroses in a range of bright or pastel shades to decorate beds, backed by shrubs and trees decked with blossoms. Also include a few fragrant plants in your design. Many viburnums have a delicious scent, as do daphnes and deciduous azaleas. However, large-flowered fritillaries have an unpleasant smell, so site them carefully with this in mind.

BULB MEDIUM

Allium neapolitanum

WHITE GARLIC This upright perennial bulb has strap-shaped gray-green leaves and loose spherical clusters of star-shaped white flowers in spring. Plant the bulbs in fall in groups toward the front of a spring border.

↕20in (50cm)

Z6–9

PERENNIAL MEDIUM

Amsonia tabernaemontana

WILLOW BLUE-STAR This upright deciduous perennial bears slim tapering leaves that turn yellow in fall. Clusters of star-shaped blue flowers appear from late spring to summer, offering a long season of color.

↕3ft (1m) ↔12in (30cm)

Z3–9 Ⓝ

PERENNIAL SMALL

Anemone blanda

GRECIAN WINDFLOWER Grow this tiny perennial corm, with its daisy-like blue, pink, or white early spring flowers, where it can be seen at the front of a bed or along a pathway. Plant the tubers in fall.

↕4in (10cm) ↔6in (15cm)

Z5–8

PERENNIAL SMALL

Anemone coronaria De Caen Group

POPPY ANEMONE This perennial has cut green leaves and shallow bowl-shaped red, blue-violet, and white early spring blooms that inject borders with vibrant seasonal color. Plant the tubers in fall.

↕12in (30cm) ↔6in (15cm)

Z8–10

PERENNIAL MEDIUM

Aquilegia vulgaris

COLUMBINE An upright perennial with green leaves divided into rounded lobed leaflets. From late spring to early summer, it produces pendent, single or double flowers in shades of violet, blue, pink, and white.

↕3ft (1m) ↔18in (45cm)

Z3–8

PERENNIAL SMALL

Bergenia purpurascens

PURPLE BERGENIA Grow this evergreen perennial toward the front of a bed, where its rounded dark green leaves and spikes of dark pink spring flowers will contrast well with bulbs, such as daffodils and grape hyacinth.

↕16in (40cm) ↔24in (60cm) or more

Z3–8

CLIMBER LARGE

Clematis montana

HIMALAYAN CLEMATIS This vigorous deciduous climber has cut midgreen foliage and, from late spring to early summer, numerous white or pink single flowers with yellow centers. Plant the roots in shade, and stems in sun. It needs a large support.

↕40ft (12m)

Z6–9

SHRUB SMALL

Cytisus x *praecox*

SCOTCH BROOM This bushy deciduous shrub has green stems, small leaves, and a profusion of pale creamy yellow pealike blooms, which lend an informal note to spring borders. Varieties include 'Allgold' (above) with golden-yellow blooms.

↕4ft (1.2m) ↔5ft (1.5m)

Z6–9

SHRUB MEDIUM

Daphne x *burkwoodii*

BURKWOOD DAPHNE Upright and semievergreen, this shrub has small green leaves and highly fragrant pink flowers, which complement tulips and columbine in a mixed late spring border. 'Somerset' (above) has purple-pink blooms.

↕5ft (1.5m) ↔3ft (1m)

Z4–8

PERENNIAL SMALL

Dicentra formosa

WESTERN BLEEDING HEART A spreading perennial with finely divided gray-green leaves and pendent, dark pink heart-shaped flowers from late spring to early summer. Grow toward the front of a bed. 'Bacchanal' (above) has dark red blooms.
↕18in (45cm) ↔12in (30cm)
Z3–9 Ⓝ

PERENNIAL SMALL

Epimedium grandiflorum

BISHOP'S HAT Grow this perennial with its heart-shaped green leaves, tinged bronze when young, in a shady border, where the nodding white, yellow, pink, or purple flowers will lend color in spring. 'Rose Queen' (above) has pink-flowers.
↕↔12in (30cm)
Z5–8

BULB MEDIUM

Erythronium californicum

FAWN LILY This clump-forming bulb has mottled dark green leaves and faintly scented, nodding creamy white spring flowers, with reflexed petals. Plant it at the front of a partly shaded border with dwarf daffodils and barrenwort.
↕14in (35cm)
Z3–9 Ⓝ

PERENNIAL LARGE

Euphorbia characias subsp. *wulfenii*

MEDITERRANEAN SPURGE This upright evergreen perennial, ideal for the back of a sunny spring border, bears linear gray-green leaves on tall stems and rounded clusters of yellow-green flowers.
↕↔4ft (1.2m)
Z7–10

SHRUB LARGE

Forsythia x *intermedia*

BORDER FORSYTHIA One of the first shrubs to bloom, it bears a bold display of bright yellow flowers on bare stems from late winter to early spring, before the leaves emerge. Plant it at the back of a bed or as a screen, and prune after flowering.
↕↔10ft (3m)
Z5–8

BULB MEDIUM

Fritillaria camschatcensis

BLACK SARANA An upright perennial bulb with dark green leaves and bell-shaped dark purple flowers opening up along upright slim stems in spring. It is ideal for a partly shaded border. Plant the bulbs in groups in fall.
↕24in (60cm)
 Z4–8 Ⓝ

BULB LARGE

Fritillaria imperialis

CROWN IMPERIAL Grow this tall perennial bulb in a bed, not too close to seating, as they emit an unpleasant musk scent. The bright orange-red bell-shaped blooms, topped with a tuft of leaves, appear in late spring.
↕5ft (1.5m)
Z5–8

PERENNIAL MEDIUM

Geranium maculatum

SPOTTED GERANIUM Forming a low carpet of cut green leaves, this perennial has pale pink to mauve flowers on short branching stems from spring to early summer. Ideal for cool shady corners. Deadhead after flowering to prevent self-seeding.
↕30in (75cm) ↔18in (45cm)
  Z3–8 Ⓝ

BULB MEDIUM

Muscari latifolium

GRAPE HYACINTH This dwarf bulb has strap-shaped gray-green leaves and oval clusters of tiny two-tone spring flowers, dark blue at the base and pale blue on top. Plant the bulbs in fall in gritty soil to decorate the front of a spring bed.

↕10in (25cm)

Z4–8

BULB MEDIUM

Narcissus cyclamineus

CYCLAMEN-FLOWERED DAFFODIL This tiny perennial bulb, best planted at the front of a bed, has narrow green leaves and dainty, pendent yellow flowers with long slim trumpets and swept-back petals. The flowers appear in early spring.

↕8in (20cm)

Z3–9

PERENNIAL SMALL

Helleborus x sternii

HELLEBORE This evergreen perennial bears upright branching heads of cup-shaped, purple-flushed green spring flowers with prominent stamens, lasting several weeks. Its mottled green foliage gives year-round interest. Deadhead to prevent self-seeding.

↕↔18in (45cm)

Z5–9

PERENNIAL MEDIUM

Mertensia virginica

VIRGINIA BLUEBELLS A compact perennial with soft blue-green leaves and clusters of nodding, blue funnel-shaped flowers in spring. The plant dies down in summer, so grow it in a bed with later-flowering perennials in front.

↕24in (60cm) ↔18in (45cm)

Z3–8 Ⓝ

PERENNIAL SMALL

Phlox divaricata subsp. laphamii

LAPHAM'S PHLOX This semievergreen perennial has small, lance-shaped green leaves and, in late spring, small pale to deep lilac blue blooms with narrow petal lobes. Use it under taller plants.

↕12in (30cm) ↔8in (20cm)

Z4–8 Ⓝ

PERENNIAL LARGE

Polygonatum x hybridum

SOLOMON'S SEAL An arching perennial with oval green leaves and, in late spring, clusters of small, tubular green-tipped white flowers that hang like beads from the stems. Site in dappled shade in a mixed spring bed. Often incorrectly listed as *P. multiflorum.*

↕up to 4ft (1.2m) ↔3ft (1m)

Z6–9

PERENNIAL SMALL

Primula Gold-laced Group

POLYANTHUS PRIMROSE Add drama to the front of a bed with a group of these evergreen perennials. In spring, gold-centered mahogany flowers with silver edges appear on upright stems and complement dwarf daffodils.

↕10in (25cm) ↔12in (30cm)

Z5–8

PERENNIAL SMALL

Primula japonica

JAPANESE PRIMROSE A perennial with basal rosettes of wrinkled green leaves and, in late spring, clusters of white, pink, crimson, or red flowers held on upright stems. 'Postford White' (above) has white flowers. Plant it in groups in moist soil.

↕↔18in (45cm)

Z4–8

SHRUB MEDIUM

Ribes sanguineum

FLOWERING CURRANT Plant this deciduous shrub at the back of a bed, where its pendent clusters of crimson flowers add a splash of color in spring. After the flowers fade the lobed green leaves lend a green backdrop in summer.

↕6ft (2m) ↔8ft (2.5m)

 Z6–8 Ⓝ

PERENNIAL SMALL

Primula vulgaris

ENGLISH PRIMROSE This perennial forms basal rosettes of oval pale green leaves and pale yellow flowers, often scented, in early spring. Plant it in groups with spring bulbs at the front of a bed in dappled shade.

↕8in (20cm) ↔14in (35cm)

 Z4–8

PERENNIAL SMALL

Pulmonaria saccharata

BETHLEHEM SAGE Edge the front of a spring bed with this clump-forming semievergreen perennial. Its white-spotted blue-green bristly leaves and clusters of funnel-shaped blue-purple flowers complement spring bulbs.

↕12in (30cm) ↔24in (60cm)

 Z3–8

SHRUB MEDIUM

Spiraea x *vanhouttei*

BRIDAL WREATH This deciduous shrub forms a mound of small green leaves and, from mid- to late spring, domed clusters of white flowers on arching stems. Good for cutting, plant it at the back of a border or use as an informal screen.

↕6ft (2m) ↔5ft (1.5m)

Z3–8

PERENNIAL SMALL

Trillium grandiflorum

WAKE-ROBIN Ideal for the front of a border in shade, this low-growing perennial has diamond-shaped green leaves and elegant, three-petaled white spring flowers. It looks best in groups beneath large shrubs or trees.

↕15in (38cm) ↔12in (30cm)

pH Z4–8 Ⓝ

BULB MEDIUM

Tulipa 'Prinses Irene'

syn. *Tulipa* 'Princess Irene' Blooming in mid-spring, this award-winning tulip has bowl-shaped orange flowers, with a purple flame on the outer petals, and gray-green leaves. Its sturdy stems hold up well in windy sites. Plant in groups in fall.

↕14in (35cm)

 Z3–8

SHRUB MEDIUM

Viburnum carlesii

KOREANSPICE VIBURNUM Plant this deciduous shrub at the back of a border, where its dark green leaves and clusters of fragrant, pink-budded white blooms will create a backdrop for spring bulbs. 'Aurora' (above) has red-budded pink blooms.

↕↔6ft (2m)

Z4–7

OTHER SUGGESTIONS

Perennials

Anemone blanda 'White Splendour' • *Bergenia* 'Baby Doll' • *Clematis fremontii* Ⓝ • *Helleborus* Brandywine Series • *Lamprocapnos spectabilis* 'Gold Heart' • *Phlox stolonifera* 'Pink Ridge' Ⓝ • *Primula* Belarina Series

Bulbs

Allium unifolium • *Erythronium californicum* 'White Beauty' Ⓝ • *Fritillaria pontica* • *Narcissus* 'Green Pearl' • *Narcissus poeticus* • *Tulipa* 'Little Beauty' • *Tulipa* 'Orange Princess'

Shrubs and climbers

Camellia japonica 'Adolphe Audusson' *Calycanthus floridus* 'Michael Lindsey' Ⓝ • *Clematis alpina* 'Pamela Jackman' • *Fothergilla gardeni* Ⓝ • *Rhododendron* 'March Madness'

Trees for blossom

Even small gardens can accommodate a deciduous tree and the breathtaking display of blossoms you will enjoy each spring is ample reward.

Trees also provide a structural counterpoint to low-growing bulbs, creating a canopy of flowers overhead followed by a carpet of petals as they fall. Before making a choice, consider the proportion as well as the decorative value of the tree. For tight spaces, choose upright or compact trees, such as a small flowering cherry, serviceberry, or flowering dogwood. Plant your tree at the back of a border in a sunny spot, or in the center of a lawn as a prominent feature, and underplant with spring bulbs, such as daffodils, grape hyacinths, and anemones, leaving a space of at least 24in (60cm) around the trunk.

TREE LARGE

Aesculus* x *carnea

RED HORSECHESTNUT This rounded deciduous tree produces large upright clusters of red flowers in late spring. It has dark green divided leaves and fall nuts. Varieties include 'Briotii' (above) with pink flowers.

↕70ft (20m) ↔50ft (15m)

Z5–8

TREE SMALL

Amelanchier canadensis

SHADBLOW SERVICEBERRY This upright deciduous tree or shrub has oval green leaves that develop fiery orange-red tones in fall. From mid- to late spring, it bears starry white flowers followed by edible berries that ripen to red in summer.

↕20ft (6m) ↔10ft (3m)

pH Z3–7 N

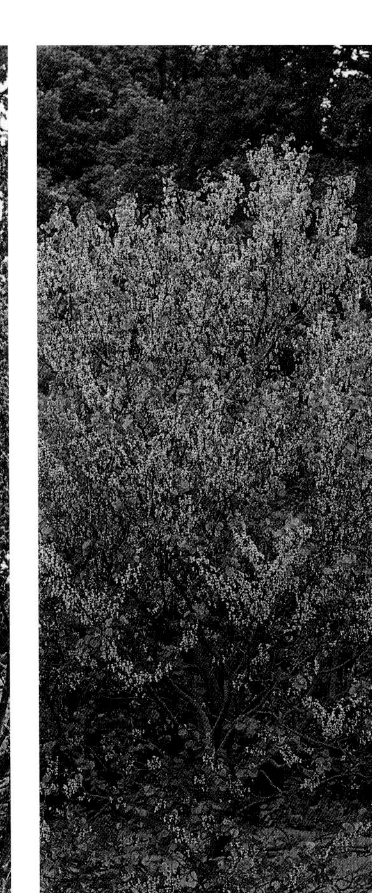

TREE SMALL

Cercis chinensis

CHINESE REDBUD The branches of this large shrub or small tree are covered with rosy pink pealike flowers in late spring, before the foliage emerges. Beanlike seedpods follow the blooms. Its large decorative green foliage is heart-shaped.

↕20ft (6m) ↔15ft (5m)

Z6–9

TREE MEDIUM

Cercis siliquastrum

JUDAS TREE This bushy deciduous tree, perfect for small gardens, is a picture in spring when its bare stems are clothed with pink blooms. Attractive heart-shaped green leaves appear in summer, and are followed by purplish seedpods.

↕↔30ft (10m)

Z6–9

TREE SMALL

Amelanchier laevis

ALLEGHENY SERVICEBERRY This small deciduous tree or large shrub produces sprays of white flowers in spring. Red fruits follow the blooms. Its young bronze leaves turn dark green in summer, then red and orange in fall.

↕↔25ft (8m)

pH Z4–8 N

TREE MEDIUM

Cercis canadensis

EASTERN REDBUD A spreading deciduous tree or shrub with pale pink pealike mid-spring flowers on bare stems. In fall, its heart-shaped leaves turn vivid yellow, giving late-season color. *C. canadensis* var. *alba* (above) has white flowers.

↕↔30ft (10m)

Z4–9 N

TREE SMALL

Cornus florida

FLOWERING DOGWOOD This conical deciduous tree or shrub produces a bold display in late spring when covered with tiny green flowers surrounded by showy white or pink bracts. The slightly twisted leaves turn red and purple in fall.

↕20ft (6m) ↔25ft (8m)

pH Z5–9 N

TREE MEDIUM

Halesia monticola

MOUNTAIN SILVERBELL This slow-growing tree has an elegant habit, and flowers freely in spring, bearing simple white bell-shaped blooms along its branches. It develops bright fall coloring, making it a useful specimen tree for larger gardens.
↕40ft (12m) ↔25ft (8m)

Z5–8 Ⓝ

TREE MEDIUM

Magnolia virginiana

SWEETBAY MAGNOLIA Grown as a large shrub or tree, it has large cup-shaped, vanilla-scented creamy white flowers set against dark green leaves from early summer to early fall. Generally deciduous, it retains some leaves in milder areas.
↕30ft (10m) ↔20ft (6m)

Z5–9 Ⓝ

TREE SMALL

Crataegus laevigata 'Paul's Scarlet'

ENGLISH HAWTHORN A deciduous tree with spiny stems of glossy green lobed leaves and, in late spring, numerous red double blooms. Grown as a small specimen tree or planted as part of a wildlife hedge.
↕↔25ft (8m)

Z4–7

TREE MEDIUM

Malus floribunda

JAPANESE FLOWERING CRABAPPLE This deciduous tree has showy pale pink flowers that emerge from crimson buds in spring after the oval leaves appear. Edible red and yellow fruits follow in fall. Plant it in a bed or lawn. Considered invasive.
↕↔30ft (10m)

Z4–8

TREE LARGE

Davidia involucrata

DOVE TREE Provide this deciduous tree with space to spread its large branches, which, in late spring, are covered with tiny flowers surrounded by white bracts that resemble handkerchiefs, alongside pointed, oval green foliage.
↕50ft (15m) ↔30ft (10m)

Z6–8

TREE MEDIUM

Magnolia 'Heaven Scent'

MAGNOLIA This tree produces goblet-shaped rosy pink flowers with a magenta stripe on each petal in mid-spring, creating a focal point in a lawn or bed. It has oval green leaves that appear at the same time as the flowers.
↕↔30ft (10m)

Z6–9

TREE MEDIUM

Magnolia stellata

STAR MAGNOLIA This rounded deciduous tree or shrub bears silky-haired buds on leafless stems that open to reveal fragrant, starry white flowers. The narrow green leaves appear just after the blooms. Protect the blooms from spring frosts.
↕↔30ft (10m)

Z4–8

TREE MEDIUM

Malus hupehensis

TEA CRABAPPLE This spreading deciduous tree is perfect for a lawn or bed focal point. In spring, it produces masses of fragrant white flowers, followed by cherrylike red fruits in fall. Oval dark green leaves appear before the blossom.
↕↔40ft (12m)

Z5–8

TREE MEDIUM

Malus x *moerlandsii* 'Profusion'

FLOWERING CRABAPPLE This deciduous tree bears masses of deep pink spring blooms set against purple-tinted leaves, which age to green and have bold fall tints. Purple fruits follow the flowers.

↕↔30ft (10m)

Z4–8

TREE SMALL

Mespilus germanica

MEDLAR Grown mainly for its edible fruits, this spreading deciduous tree also bears attractive, white single spring flowers, carried at the shoot tips. It is slow-growing and suitable for smaller gardens. Plant it in full sun in a sheltered position.

↕20ft (6m) ↔25ft (8m)

Z5–8

TREE SMALL

Prunus 'Accolade'

FLOWERING CHERRY Grow this compact deciduous tree in a small garden or a courtyard. It produces light pink semidouble spring flowers that open from dark pink buds before the oval leaves appear. The foliage has good fall color.

↕↔25ft (8m)

(!) Z4–9

TREE SMALL

Prunus pendula

WEEPING CHERRY Perfect as a focal point in a small garden, this deciduous tree has weeping branches that are covered with dark rose-pink blossom in early spring. The pointed oval leaves turn orange and red in fall.

↕↔20ft (6m)

(!) Z5–8

SHRUB LARGE

Prunus incisa

FUJI CHERRY Use this rounded deciduous shrub in a border or as hedging. Saucer-shaped white or pale pink flowers appear in early spring, followed by purple fruits. The leaves add value in fall when they turn orange-red.

↕↔25ft (8m)

(!) Z4–8

TREE MEDIUM

Prunus jamasakura

syn. *Prunus serrulata* var. *spontanea* This deciduous tree bursts into color in spring when clusters of pale pink buds open to reveal large white flowers. The bronze young foliage, which turns red and yellow in fall, adds to the effect.

↕↔40ft (12m)

(!) Z5–8

TREE MEDIUM

Prunus 'Kanzan'

syn. *Prunus serrulata* 'Kwanzan' This vase-shaped deciduous tree has pink double spring blooms that create a focal point in a lawn or bed. Bronze leaves, which follow the flowers, turn green in summer, then orange before falling. Makes a good street tree.

↕↔30ft (10m)

(!) Z5–8

TREE SMALL

Prunus 'Shirofugen'

JAPANESE FLOWERING CHERRY This compact deciduous tree is ideal for a small garden. In spring, masses of white double flowers, fading to pink, appear. The coppery brown young leaves mature to green and turn orange in fall.

↕25ft (8m) ↔30ft (10m)

(!) Z5–8

TREE SMALL

Prunus 'Shirotae'

JAPANESE FLOWERING CHERRY This deciduous tree has a spreading crown. It will decorate a paved urban garden or lawn with its fragrant, white semidouble spring flowers that appear with the green serrated foliage; the leaves also offer good fall color.

↕20ft (6m) ↔25ft (8m)

(!) Z5–8

TREE SMALL

Prunus 'Shogetsu'

JAPANESE FLOWERING CHERRY Grown for its pink double spring flowers, which fade to white, this small deciduous tree creates a focal point in a border or lawn. The bronze young foliage matures to green and turns orange and red in fall.

↕15ft (5m) ↔25ft (8m)

 Z5–8

TREE MEDIUM

Prunus 'Spire'

FLOWERING CHERRY This slim deciduous tree, perfect for growing in a small urban garden, is covered with pale pink blossom in spring. The leaves, which follow the flowers, are bronze when young, and turn red and orange in fall.

↕30ft (10m) ↔20ft (6m)

Z5–8

TREE SMALL

Prunus 'Ukon'

syn. *Prunus serrulata* 'Grandiflora' This spreading deciduous tree, ideal for a lawn or bed, has pink-budded, pink-tipped yellowish white double flowers, which open in spring. The green foliage, bronze when young, turns reddish brown in fall.

↕25ft (8m) ↔30ft (10m)

Z6–8

TREE LARGE

Prunus x *yedoensis*

YOSHINO CHERRY The stems of this spreading deciduous tree are covered with almond-scented blush-white blossom in spring, when it will lend seasonal color to a small garden. The dark green leaves turn yellow in fall.

↕50ft (15m) ↔30ft (10m)

Z5–8

TREE MEDIUM

Robinia x *slavinii* 'Hillieri'

LOCUST This deciduous tree bears pendent chains of slightly fragrant pale pink pealike late spring flowers, which lead to knobby, brown seedpods. Its lacy foliage produces only light shade, making it a good choice for small gardens.

↕↔30ft (10m)

Z4–8

TREE LARGE

Stewartia pseudocamellia

JAPANESE STEWARTIA Grow this deciduous tree, prized for its large, cup-shaped white flowers, as a feature plant in a summer garden. It also has attractive flaking bark and is good for providing fall leaf color.

↕70ft (20m) ↔25ft (8m)

 Z5–8

TREE MEDIUM

Styrax japonicus

JAPANESE SNOWBELL This spreading deciduous tree makes an elegant addition to a border or lawn. In early summer, it produces pendent clusters of fragrant, bell-shaped white or pink-tinged flowers. The leaves provide good fall color.

↕30ft (10m) ↔25ft (8m)

 Z5–8

OTHER SUGGESTIONS

Trees

Aesculus flava Ⓝ • *Aesculus glabra* Ⓝ • *Aleurites fordii* • *Amelanchier lamarckii* • *Cercis canadensis* 'Hearts of Gold' Ⓝ • *Cercis canadensis* var. *texensis* 'Oklahoma' Ⓝ • *Chionanthus retusus* • *Cornus mas* 'Golden Glory' • *Chionanthus virginicus* Ⓝ • *Cladrastis kentukea* Ⓝ • *Cornus kousa* • *Cornus* VENUS • *Crataegus coccinea* Ⓝ • *Crataegus flava* Ⓝ • *Franklinia alatamaha* Ⓝ • *Gymnocladus dioica* Ⓝ • *Halesia carolina* Ⓝ • *Laburnum* x *watereri* 'Vossii' • *Liriodendron tulipifera* Ⓝ *Magnolia* x *loebneri* 'Ballerina' • *Magnolia* x *brooklynensis* 'Yellow Bird' • *Magnolia denudata* • *Magnolia* x *soulangeana* • *Malus* CENTURIAN • *Malus* 'Jonagold' • *Malus* 'Indian Magic' • *Oxydendrum arboreum* Ⓝ • *Stewartia monadelpha* • *Styrax obassia* • *Syringa reticulata* 'Ivory Silk' • *Tetradium daniellii*

Spring flowers for containers

Plan ahead and plant up spring containers in fall. Many plants also provide a winter foliage display before the bulbs and bedding burst into life.

Plant bulbs from early- to late fall; allowing time for vernalization in frostproof containers. Snowdrops, an exception, are best potted up in leaf when in flower in spring. Small bulbs, such as crocus, grape hyacinth, and iris, are ideal for tiny pots, while tall daffodils and tulips look beautiful in large pots along with spring-flowering bedding plants, such as viola, wallflower, and primrose. Plant these over the bulbs to provide interest through winter and a dramatic display in spring. Use large, containerized shrubs, such as camellia and rhododendron, for their winter leaves, as well as spring blooms.

PERENNIAL SMALL

Aurinia saxatilis

BASKET OF GOLD Masses of long-lasting chrome-yellow flowers make this low-growing evergreen perennial a good choice for spring pots. The blooms sit above oval gray-green leaves. It will die back if exposed to high heat and humidity in summer.

↕9in (23cm) ↔12in (30cm)

Z4–7

PERENNIAL SMALL

Bellis perennis

ENGLISH DAISY This mound-forming perennial, grown as an annual, produces midgreen leaves and, in spring, pink, white, or red single or double pompomlike flowers. Plant in containers with potting soil with spring bulbs.

↕↔8in (20cm)

Z4–8

PERENNIAL SMALL

Bergenia SILVERLIGHT

PIGSQUEAK Grow this evergreen perennial with spring bulbs in containers of soil-based potting mix. It has large, oval dark green leaves, which create a foil for the clusters of white flowers that appear on its red-tinged stems.

↕18in (45cm) ↔20in (50cm)

Z3–8

SHRUB LARGE

Camellia japonica

JAPANESE CAMELLIA Grow this upright evergreen shrub in large containers of acidic soil mix in a sheltered site where cold winds and late frosts will not damage its large red, pink, or white early spring flowers.

↕10ft (3m) ↔6ft (2m)

pH Z7–9

SHRUB LARGE

Camellia x *williamsii*

CAMELLIA An evergreen shrub with oval, pointed, glossy green leaves and white, or red single or double pink blooms in spring. Varieties include 'Donation' (above) with pink, semidouble flowers. Plant in acidic soil mix. Water well in summer.

↕15ft (5m) ↔8ft (2.5m)

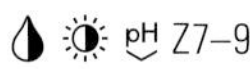

pH Z7–9

SHRUB SMALL

Cassiope 'Edinburgh'

CASSIOPE Plant this dwarf evergreen shrub in a container of gritty potting mix alongside short bulbs, such as species tulips. From spring to summer, tiny scalelike dark green leaves and nodding, white bell-shaped flowers appear.

↕↔8in (20cm)

pH Z2–6

CLIMBER MEDIUM

Clematis 'Frances Rivis'

CLEMATIS Add height to a patio display with this spring-flowering deciduous clematis. Plant in a container of soil-based potting mix, with a trellis or pyramid to support the twining stems of divided foliage and bell-shaped violet-blue flowers.

↕10ft (3m)

Z4–9

BULB SMALL

Crocus 'Snow Bunting'

CROCUS Plant this perennial corm in small pots in fall for an early spring display of fragrant white flowers with yellow centers and a purple blush on the outer petal surfaces. The grasslike leaves are green with white lines.

↕3in (7cm)

pH Z3–8

BULB SMALL

Cyclamen coum

HARDY CYCLAMEN This perennial bulb has silver leaves and, in early spring, bears dainty, downward-facing pink blooms with swept-back petals. Grow in containers of soil-based potting mix. Many varieties are available. Goes dormant in summer heat.
↕4in (10cm)

 Z5–9

ANNUAL/BIENNIAL SMALL

Erysimum cheiri

WALLFLOWER This biennial is planted in fall, its green leaves providing some interest through winter, in containers of potting mix. In mid-spring, it throws up spikes of bright yellow, orange, red, or pink scented flowers.
↕↔12in (30cm)

SHRUB SMALL

Erica x darleyensis

DARLEY HEATH This evergreen shrub has needlelike foliage, and flowers in late winter and early spring, becoming speckled with small, nodding urn-shaped white or pink flowers. Ideal for early color, plant it in containers in acidic soil mix.
↕10in (25cm) ↔20in (50cm)

pH Z6–8

BULB MEDIUM

Galanthus nivalis

SNOWDROP Either plant these perennial bulbs in containers of soil-based potting mix or with hellebores and heucheras in mixed displays, where their nodding white late winter to early spring flowers and grasslike foliage add a delicate touch.
↕6in (15cm)

Z3–8

PERENNIAL SMALL

Heuchera micrantha var. *diversifolia* 'Palace Purple'

CORAL BELLS This evergreen perennial has large, lobed, glossy purple foliage, offering year-round interest. In summer, small white flowers appear on wiry stems. Plant in containers of soil-based potting mix.
↕↔18in (45cm)

 Z3–8 Ⓝ

BULB MEDIUM

Hyacinthus orientalis

HYACINTH Introduce fragrance to a container collection with this early spring-flowering bulb. Its spikes of fragrant, bell-shaped flowers in many colors go well with evergreen perennials in containers of soil-based potting mix; plant in fall.
↕10in (25cm)

Z4–9

BULB SMALL

Iris reticulata

RETICULATED IRIS Plant this perennial bulb with dwarf irises of other colors in fall in small containers of gritty potting mix. The small reddish purple flowers with yellow and white marks on the lower petals appear in early spring.
↕6in (15cm)

Z5–9

SHRUB LARGE

Itea virginica

VIRGINIA SWEETSPIRE Best for permanent planting in a large pot, this evergreen shrub bears arching stems of spiny dark green leaves and flowers from midsummer to early fall producing trailing greenish white racemes. Grow in acidic soil mix.
↕10ft (3m) ↔5ft (1.5m)

pH Z5–9 Ⓝ

BULB MEDIUM

Muscari armeniacum

GRAPE HYACINTH Plant this spring bulb with daffodils and early tulips in fall in containers of soil-based potting mix. The small, deep blue fragrant flowers, held in cone-shaped clusters, are accompanied by grassy green leaves.
↕8in (20cm)

Z4–8

BULB MEDIUM

***Narcissus* 'Actaea'**

DAFFODIL This late-spring-flowering perennial bulb, with its scented white flowers and shallow red-rimmed yellow cups, combines well with red tulips in large pots or half barrels. Plant the bulbs in fall.
↕16in (40cm)

Z3–8

BULB MEDIUM

***Narcissus* 'Bridal Crown'**

DAFFODIL This perennial bulb bears sweetly scented, creamy white fully double blooms with yellow-speckled centers in spring. Plant in fall with spring bedding in containers filled with soil-based potting mix.
↕16in (40cm)

Z3–9

BULB MEDIUM

***Narcissus* 'Canaliculatus'**

DAFFODIL This bulb has slender green leaves and slim stems bearing clusters of small fragrant spring flowers, with reflexed white petals and yellow cups. Plant the bulbs in fall in containers of soil-based potting mix mixed with grit.
↕9in (23cm)

Z6–10

BULB MEDIUM

***Narcissus* 'Cheerfulness'**

DAFFODIL A perennial bulb that mixes well with single-flowered yellow daffodils. The fragrant, white double flowers with yellow centers appear in mid-spring. Plant the bulbs in fall in containers of soil-based potting mix.
↕16in (40cm)

Z3–9

BULB MEDIUM

***Narcissus* 'Jack Snipe'**

DAFFODIL Try combining this early- to mid-spring-flowering perennial bulb with grape hyacinth or primrose. It bears creamy white flowers with short bright yellow cups and narrow dark green leaves. Plant in fall in soil-based potting mix.
↕9in (23cm)

Z4–9

BULB MEDIUM

***Narcissus* 'Tahiti'**

DAFFODIL This double-flowered perennial bulb will brighten up mid-spring containers with its golden-yellow blooms and narrow green leaves. Plant the bulbs in fall in containers filled with soil-based potting mix.
↕18in (45cm)

Z3–9

PERENNIAL MEDIUM

Polygonatum odoratum

FRAGRANT SOLOMON'S SEAL This perennial has oval to lance-shaped, midgreen leaves and, from late spring to early summer, fragrant, hanging, green-tipped white bell-shaped flowers. Plant in containers in fall for spring color.
↕24in (60cm) ↔12in (30cm)

PERENNIAL SMALL

***Primula* Crescendo Series**

POLYANTHUS PRIMROSE These evergreen perennials, grown as annuals, are ideal for spring pots and windowboxes. Their corrugated dark green leaves and clusters of yellow-eyed multicolored flowers create a blaze of color.
↕↔8in (20cm)

Z5–7

PERENNIAL SMALL

Primula Gold-laced Group

POLYANTHUS PRIMROSE These evergreen perennials add a touch of class to patio containers. In spring, upright stems topped with gold-centered mahogany blooms with bright edging complement dwarf daffodils in containers of potting soil.

↕10in (25cm) ↔12in (30cm)

 Z5–8

PERENNIAL SMALL

Primula veris

COWSLIP This perennial forms a rosette of lance-shaped leaves. It bears clusters of nodding, almond-scented yellow blooms in spring. Deadhead to prolong the display. Plant in pots in fall or spring. Transplant to garden after flowering.

↕↔10in (25cm)

 Z3–8

BULB MEDIUM

Scilla siberica

SIBERIAN SQUILL This perennial bulb flowers in spring, producing upright stems of nodding, bell-shaped blue flowers. Plant groups of bulbs in small pots in fall, then plant out into larger mixed containers in spring.

↕8in (20cm)

Z4–8

BULB MEDIUM

Tulipa clusiana var. *chrysantha*

LADY TULIP This tulip blooms from early spring and makes a dainty feature in pots or troughs of gritty soil-based potting mix. It bears bowl-shaped yellow blooms, tinged red on the outside. Plant the bulbs in fall.

↕12in (30cm)

Z3–8

PERENNIAL SMALL

Tiarella wherryi

FOAM FLOWER This shade-tolerant leafy perennial, with deeply lobed, maroon-tinted green leaves, makes a great foil for spring bulbs such as daffodils. In late spring or early summer, frothy white or pink flower heads appear.

↕8in (20cm) ↔6in (15cm)

Z3–7 Ⓝ

BULB MEDIUM

Tulipa 'Purissima'

TULIP This bulb bears bowl-shaped creamy white flowers in mid-spring that are set against purple-marked gray-green leaves. Plant the bulbs in frostproof containers in fall. The tulips can then be transferred to mixed pot displays in spring.

↕16in (40cm)

 Z3–8

BULB MEDIUM

Tulipa 'Spring Green'

TULIP The late-spring cup-shaped blooms of this Viridiflora tulip are creamy white with green streaks and make elegant partners for hot-hued tulips and late-flowering daffodils. Plant the bulbs in frostproof containers in fall.

↕15in (38cm)

 Z3–8

PERENNIAL SMALL

Viola x *wittrockiana*

PANSY This valuable bedding plant produces oval leaves and flowers in almost every shade imaginable from late winter to spring, providing a colorful frill around containers of spring bulbs. Plant it in potting soil.

↕↔8in (20cm)

Z7–10

OTHER SUGGESTIONS

Biennials and perennials

Bellis perennis Pomponette Series • *Erysimum* 'Apricot Twist' • *Primula* Pacific Giants Series • *Tiarella* SUGAR AND SPICE

Bulbs

Crocus sieberi f. *tricolor* • *Crocus tommasinianus* • *Hyacinthus* 'Dark Dimension' • *Iris reticulata* 'Pixie' • *Muscari botryoides* 'Album' • *Muscari neglectum* • *Narcissus* 'Bridal Crown' *Narcissus* 'Mount Hood' • *Scilla siberica* 'Alba' • *Tulipa* 'Angélique' • *Tulipa* 'Candela' • *Tulipa* 'Esperanto'

Shrubs and trees

Camellia 'Brushfield's Yellow' • *Camellia* 'Water Lily' • *Clethra alnifolia* 'Ruby Spice' Ⓝ • *Erica x darleyensis* 'Furzey' • *Itea virginica* LITTLE HENRY Ⓝ • *Rhododendron* 'Dopey' • *Rhododendron* 'Percy Wiseman'

Plants for summer beds

With a vast choice of flowers for summer beds, making a selection for your garden will be easier if you first decide on the look you want to create.

Beds filled with an assortment of roses and perennials will produce a traditional cottage style, while bold groups of stiff-stemmed herbaceous plants convey a more contemporary design. Include perennials in groups of three or more to prevent a spotty, discordant appearance and choose a range of plants that flower consecutively to avoid a lull late in the season. Shasta daisy, beardtongue, and Russian sage will all help to link summer with fall to produce a continuous display, while fuchsia, hydrangea, and repeat-flowering roses provide great value, blooming for many months.

PERENNIAL MEDIUM

Achillea 'Fanal'

YARROW Plant this perennial with its flat heads of yellow-centered bright red flowers and ferny green foliage, in the middle of a bed for a splash of summer color. It contrasts well with blue flower spikes.

↕30in (75cm) ↔24in (60cm)

Z3–9

PERENNIAL LARGE

Anemone x *hybrida*

JAPANESE ANEMONE Ideal for the back of a shady bed, this upright perennial produces white or pink flowers on tall stems from late summer to fall above divided leaves. 'Queen Charlotte' (above) has pale pink semidouble blooms.

↕4ft (1.2m) ↔indefinite

Z4–8

PERENNIAL MEDIUM

Anthemis tinctoria

GOLDEN MARGUERITE Try this clump-forming perennial in a mixed bed with blue or pink perennials that contrast with its white or yellow daisy-like summer flowers and feathery aromatic leaves. 'E.C. Buxton' (above) has lemon-yellow flowers.

↕↔3ft (1m)

Z3–7

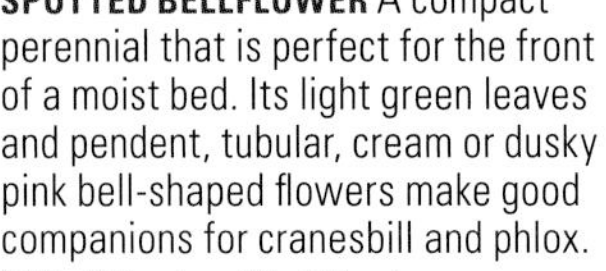

PERENNIAL SMALL

Campanula punctata

SPOTTED BELLFLOWER A compact perennial that is perfect for the front of a moist bed. Its light green leaves and pendent, tubular, cream or dusky pink bell-shaped flowers make good companions for cranesbill and phlox.

↕12in (30cm) ↔16in (40cm)

Z4–8

SHRUB MEDIUM

Ceanothus americanus

NEW JERSEY TEA This is a dense, rounded deciduous shrub that bears clusters of small, white scented flowers from late spring to midsummer. It is best planted at the back of a border with plants in front that provide color in summer.

↕↔6ft (2m)

Z4–8 Ⓝ

PERENNIAL SMALL

Calamintha nepeta

LESSER CALAMINT This perennial makes good edging for a wildlife summer bed. Its spikes of tiny lilac-pink flowers from late summer to early fall attract bees, and the small green leaves provide background color.

↕18in (45cm) ↔30in (75cm)

Z5–9

SHRUB SMALL

Cistus x *dansereaui*

ROCK ROSE Provide a sunny, sheltered site for this evergreen shrub with gray-green leaves and a succession of papery, white, pink, or purple bowl-shaped flowers in summer. 'Decumbens' (above) has white blooms with purple central blotches.

↕24in (60cm) ↔3ft (1m)

Z8–10

PERENNIAL LARGE

Campanula lactiflora

MILKY BELLFLOWER This upright branching perennial has tall back-of-bed varieties, and shorter forms, such as the violet-blue 'Prichard's Variety' (above) for the front. Blue, pink, or white, nodding bell-shaped flowers appear in summer.

↕up to 4ft (1.2m) ↔24in (60cm)

Z5–7

CLIMBER MEDIUM

Clematis 'Abundance'

CLEMATIS Use this deciduous clematis with its twining stems of midgreen leaves and creamy yellow-centered wine-red flowers from midsummer to late fall to cover a large shrub at the back of a bed.

↕10ft (3m)

Z4–9

CLIMBER MEDIUM

Clematis 'Fireworks'

CLEMATIS Flowering from late spring to early summer, and again in late summer, this large-flowered deciduous clematis, with its magenta-striped blue-mauve blooms, bears a colorful back-of-bed accent when threaded through trellis or a shrub.

↕12ft (4m)

 Z4–9

CLIMBER MEDIUM

Clematis 'Huldine'

CLEMATIS This deciduous climber, from mid- to late summer, bears abundant white flowers, mauve beneath. Climb it through large spring-flowering shrubs to prolong their color, or train it up freestanding obelisks. Keep the roots shaded.

↕12ft (4m)

💧 ☼ ◑ Z4–9

PERENNIAL SMALL

Coreopsis verticillata

THREADLEAF COREOPSIS This perennial is ideal for the front or middle of a bed, and to fills any gaps with its dense ferny foliage and slender stems topped with daisy-like yellow summer blooms. 'Moonbeam' (above) has lemon-yellow flowers.

↕20in (50cm) ↔18in (45cm)

💧 ☼ Z3–9 Ⓝ

PERENNIAL MEDIUM

Crocosmia 'Lucifer'

MONTBRETIA Ideal for late-summer color, this clump-forming perennial has upright sword-shaped leaves. Vibrant red tubular blooms appear on branched stems in late summer. Provide good support; deadhead after flowering. Can become weedy.

↕3ft (1m) ↔10in (25cm)

 Z6–9

PERENNIAL LARGE

Delphinium elatum

LARKSPUR An upright perennial, ideal for a mid-bed spot, with deeply cut green leaves and, in midsummer, tall spikes of bowl-shaped blooms in a wide range of colors. There are many tall and dwarf varieties to choose from; most forms require staking.

↕6ft (2m) ↔3ft (10m)

💧 ☼ Z3–7

PERENNIAL LARGE

Echinops ritro

SMALL GLOBE THISTLE This upright perennial has prickly, divided dark green leaves and globe-shaped, spiky metallic blue flower heads in late summer. Use it to plug the gaps left by tall alliums when they begin to fade earlier in the season.

↕4ft (1.2m) ↔30in (75cm)

💧 ☼ Z3–9

SHRUB MEDIUM

Escallonia 'Apple Blossom'

ESCALLONIA This compact evergreen shrub offers a green leafy backdrop to perennials and bulbs for most of the year, and injects color with its vase-shaped pink flowers into the planting scheme from early to midsummer. Best in West Coast gardens.

↕↔8ft (2.5m)

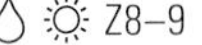 Z8–9

SHRUB SMALL

Fuchsia hybrids

FUSCHIA A compact deciduous shrub with dark green leaves and bell-shaped, red, pink, violet, white, and, sometimes bicolored, semidouble flowers. Can be grown as an annual in cooler areas. Ideal for the front of a summer bed.

↕24in (60cm) ↔18in (45cm)

💧 ◑ Z9–11

PERENNIAL MEDIUM

Gaillardia x *grandiflora*

BLANKET FLOWER Add this perennial to the front or middle of a border for a splash of color. It produces slim green leaves and rounded red summer blooms, with a yellow ring at the outer edges. Varieties include 'Kobold' (above).

↕3ft (10m) ↔18in (45cm)

💧 ☼ Z3–10 Ⓝ

PERENNIAL LARGE

Gaura lindheimeri

WAND FLOWER An upright perennial that bears masses of simple, star-shaped white flowers on wiry stems from midsummer to fall. It has an open habit and can be planted mid-bed with the plants behind remaining visible. Deadhead regularly.

↕5ft (1.5m) ↔3ft (1m)

💧 ☼ Z6–9 Ⓝ

PERENNIAL MEDIUM

Geranium pratense

MEADOW CRANESBILL Useful for sun or part-shade, this clump-forming perennial has divided leaves and violet-blue saucer-shaped summer flowers. Ideal to use as a front-of-bed plant. Varieties include the pinky gray 'Mrs Kendall Clark' (above).

↕↔24in (60cm)

 Z4–8

PERENNIAL MEDIUM

Geranium sylvaticum

WOOD CRANESBILL Ideal for the front of a shady bed alongside pastel or hot-hued partners, this perennial produces clumps of lobed midgreen leaves and blue-purple flowers from late spring to early summer. 'Album' (above) has white blooms.

↕30in (75cm) ↔24in (60cm)

 Z4–8

SHRUB SMALL

Hebe 'Great Orme'

HEBE This evergreen shrub bears slender pink flower spikes from midsummer to mid-fall that fade with age. Use at the back of a bed where its deep purple shoots and glossy dark green foliage will offer a foil for other plants. Best in West Coast gardens.

↕↔4ft (1.2m)

Z9–11

PERENNIAL MEDIUM

Hemerocallis 'Chicago Sunrise'

DAYLILY A clump-forming perennial with slender arching leaves and large, golden-yellow trumpet-shaped summer flowers. Each flower lasts a day, but are borne over several weeks. Water well in summer.

↕28in (70cm) ↔34in (85cm)

Z3–10

SHRUB LARGE

Hibiscus syriacus

ROSE OF SHARON Plant this deciduous shrub for color in late summer and early fall, when large, blue, violet, or white saucer-shaped single or double flowers appear. Grow at the back of a bed. 'Blue Bird' (above) has blue flowers. Considered invasive in some areas.

↕10ft (3m) ↔6ft (2m)

Z5–9

SHRUB LARGE

Hydrangea aspera Villosa Group

ROUGH-LEAVED HYDRANGEA Ideal for providing shelter, or for the back of a bed, this deciduous shrub has velvety leaves and flattened heads of tiny mauve late summer florets surrounded by larger white blooms.

↕↔10ft (3m)

Z7–9

SHRUB SMALL

Hydrangea macrophylla 'Lilacina'

LACECAP HYDRANGEA This deciduous, compact shrub has broad oval leaves and flattened clusters of tiny mauve-pink or blue flowers surrounded by pink blooms. Use it in the middle of a mixed bed.

↕↔4ft (1.2m)

Z6–9

SHRUB MEDIUM

Hydrangea quercifolia

OAKLEAF HYDRANGEA This mound-forming, deciduous shrub adds bulk to a shady bed. From midsummer to fall, its cone-shaped, cream flower heads, which age to pink-tinged white, shine out from the gloom. Plants require neutral to acidic soil.

↕6ft (2m) ↔8ft (2.5m)

Z5–9

PERENNIAL MEDIUM

Iris domestica

BLACKBERRY LILY This iris is grown for its orange and yellow star-shaped flowers and blackberrylike seeds from mid- to late summer. It is a rhizome- and clump-forming perennial, with blue-green swordlike foliage; and is ideal for summer beds.

↕3ft (1m) ↔24in (60cm)

Z5–10

SHRUB SMALL

Kalmia angustifolia

SHEEP LAUREL This mound-forming, evergreen shrub provides year-round interest in a shady border, but peaks in early summer when it becomes covered with small, pink bowl-shaped flowers. Use in a naturalized planting.

↕24in (60cm) ↔5ft (1.5m)

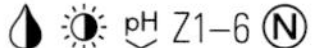 Z1–6

PERENNIAL LARGE

Kniphofia uvaria

RED-HOT POKER With its strap-shaped evergreen leaves, this perennial offers year-round interest, but it peaks in late summer, when tall spikes of cone-shaped, red and yellow flower heads create a bold feature among either hot or cool colors.

↕4ft (1.2m) ↔24in (60cm)

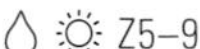

Z5–9

PERENNIAL SMALL

Lychnis flos-jovis

FLOWER OF JOVE A dainty perennial, ideal for the front of a bed. Its mat of gray hairy leaves on erect stems makes a good edging, while the clusters of small round flowers in red, pink, or white lend color throughout summer.

↕↔18in (45cm)

Z4–8

PERENNIAL MEDIUM

Knautia macedonica

KNAUTIA The dainty crimson summer flowers of this upright perennial add buttons of color between larger blooms from the front to middle of a sunny bed. The green leaves are lobed; stems may need to be supported.

↕30in (75cm) ↔24in (60cm)

Z5–9

PERENNIAL MEDIUM

Leucanthemum x *superbum*

SHASTA DAISY This perennial's tall stems of golden-eyed white daisies create impact in a summer bed. Plant it in swaths for the best effect, and use the blooms for cutting. Varieties include 'Beauté Nivelloise' (above).

↕up to 3ft (1m) ↔24in (60cm)

Z5–9

PERENNIAL MEDIUM

Monarda 'Cambridge Scarlet'

BEEBALM Plant this upright bushy perennial in soil that does not dry out during summer. Its bears aromatic, bronze-tinged leaves and two-lipped scarlet flower heads, which provide color and texture in summer.

↕3ft (1m) ↔18in (45cm)

Z3–9 Ⓝ

PERENNIAL MEDIUM

Kniphofia 'Alcazar'

RED-HOT POKER This evergreen perennial offers a dramatic display in late summer when its spikes of bright orange tubular flowers emerge from, and tower above, the straplike leaves. Use it to give a vertical accent to mixed herbaceous sunny borders.

↕3ft (1m) ↔18in (45cm)

Z6–9

PERENNIAL MEDIUM

Libertia grandiflora

NEW ZEALAND SATIN FLOWER Grown mainly for its fountains of grassy leaves, this evergreen perennial also produces slim stems of dainty, white daisy-like flowers in summer. Try planting it at the front of a sunny bed.

↕30in (75cm) ↔24in (60cm)

Z8–11

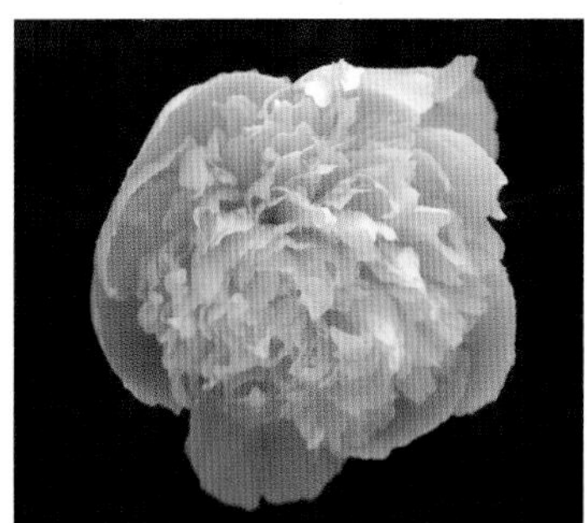

PERENNIAL MEDIUM

Paeonia lactiflora

PEONY This perennial has divided green leaves and large, bowl-shaped, white, pink, red, or mauve single or double blooms in early summer. Try it with early-flowering geraniums. Varieties include 'Laura Dessert' (above).

↕↔30in (75cm)

Z3–8

PERENNIAL LARGE

Lupinus x *hybrid*

LUPINE This perennial produces cone-shaped spikes of pink and white, bicolored flowers in shades of white, blue, pink, mauve, or yellow, and is best grown in summer beds with roses, delphiniums, and cranesbill. The seeds are toxic.

↕4ft (1.2m) ↔18in (45cm)

(!) Z4–8

PERENNIAL MEDIUM

Papaver orientale

ORIENTAL POPPY Grow this early-summer-flowering vibrant perennial for its large bright red flowers with black marks and dark eyes and decorative seedheads. Combine it with late-summer-flowering plants to plug the gaps left after it fades.

↕↔3ft (1m)

Z3–9

Plants for summer beds

PERENNIAL MEDIUM

Penstemon 'Osprey'

BEARDTONGUE This perennial's spikes of tubular, pink-edged white summer to early fall flowers and simple green leaves blend perfectly with Russian sage and pastel-colored dahlias in a sheltered, sunny bed. Deadheading prolongs the display.

↕3½ft (1.1m) ↔24in (60cm)

Z7–9

SHRUB SMALL

Perovskia 'Blue Spire'

RUSSIAN SAGE An upright deciduous subshrub with small blue-purple flowers held above silver-gray foliage from late summer to fall. Plant it in a mixed sunny bed to provide late season color. The spent flower stems will persist into winter.

↕4ft (1.2m) ↔3ft (1m)

Z5–9

PERENNIAL SMALL

Persicaria affinis 'Superba'

KNOTWEED This vigorous perennial forms a dense mat of oval green leaves that turn rich brown in fall. From early- to late summer, it bears upright spikes of soft pink blooms that darken with age. Plant it at the front of a bed and deadhead regularly.

↕10in (25cm) ↔24in (60cm)

Z3–8

PERENNIAL LARGE

Phlox paniculata

GARDEN PHLOX Producing large clusters of white, lilac, or pink flowers from summer to fall, this perennial forms dense blocks of color mid-bed. Many colorful varieties are available, such as 'Blue Paradise' (above). Keep plants well watered in summer.

↕4ft (1.2m) ↔3ft (1m)

Z4–8 Ⓝ

SHRUB SMALL

Phygelius aequalis

CAPE FUCHSIA Best in a sheltered site, this shrubby perennial produces tall, upright stems that carry clusters of pendent tubular dusky pink or yellow blooms all summer. Plant it mid-bed. 'Yellow Trumpet' (above) has creamy yellow flowers.

↕↔3ft (1m)

Z7–9

SHRUB SMALL

Potentilla fruticosa

CINQUEFOIL Grow this bushy, deciduous shrub with orange, red, yellow, white, or pink circular blooms that appear from summer to early fall, mid-bed between perennials. 'Abbotswood' (above) has white flowers.

↕3ft (1m) ↔5ft (1.5m)

Z3–7 Ⓝ

PERENNIAL SMALL

Potentilla megalantha

STRAWBERRY CINQUEFOIL This compact bushy perennial makes a neat edging in borders filled with hot-hued plants. Its divided midgreen leaves and saucer-shaped, orange-centered yellow summer flowers provide a long season of interest.

↕8in (20cm) ↔6in (15cm)

Z4–8

PERENNIAL LARGE

Romneya coulteri

TREE POPPY This back-of-bed perennial is grown for its large, fragrant, papery, golden-centered white late summer flowers. Combine it with repeat-flowering shrub roses and mulleins in a sheltered spot. Common to West Coast areas.

↕↔6ft (2m)

Z8–10 Ⓝ

SHRUB MEDIUM

Rosa 'Ballerina'

POLYANTHA ROSE This repeat-flowering shrub rose produces clusters of small, white-centered pale pink single flowers from midsummer to early fall, and creates a focal point in a bed among dark pink-, white-, and purple-flowered perennials.

↕5ft (1.5m) ↔4ft (1.2m)

Z5–9

SHRUB SMALL

Rosa Flower Carpet Series

GROUNDCOVER ROSE Ideal for adding color to large areas, this shrub forms a dense mound of disease-resistant foliage and bears cupped, pink, red, yellow, or white semidouble flowers all summer. Deadhead regularly and mulch with compost in spring.

↕↔24in (60cm)

Z5–10

SHRUB MEDIUM

Rosa GERTRUDE JEKYLL

ENGLISH SHRUB ROSE This shrub or short climber is perfect for the back of a mixed bed with its scrolled buds and large, scented, pink fully double flowers that provide colorful highlights from summer to early fall. Mulch annually in spring.

↕6ft (2m) ↔4ft (1.2m)

Z5–9

SHRUB MEDIUM

Rosa 'Madame Hardy'

DAMASK ROSE This erect strong-growing rose, which makes a medium-sized, prickly shrub with midgreen foliage, offers a single flush of fragrant, white fully double flowers that add an elegant note to mixed beds in early summer.

↕5ft (1.5m) ↔4ft (1.2m)

Z4–9

SHRUB MEDIUM

Rosa 'William Lobb'

MOSS ROSE Grow this moss rose on a trellis or pillar at the back of a bed. Its arching prickly stems that hold cupped, scented, crimson-purple fully double flowers and green leaves, create a colorful backdrop for pastel blooms in summer.

↕↔6ft (2m)

Z4–9

PERENNIAL MEDIUM

Rudbeckia fulgida var. *sullivantii*

BLACK-EYED SUSAN This compact perennial, with its mass of daisy-like, golden flowers, injects bright color into the front of a bed from late summer to fall. Leave faded flower heads to stand over winter.

↕30in (75cm) ↔12in (30cm) or more

Z4–9 Ⓝ

PERENNIAL MEDIUM

Sisyrinchium striatum

YELLOW-EYED GRASS A good choice for the front of a dry sunny bed, this evergreen perennial's gray-green sword-shaped leaves and spikes of small pale yellow summer flowers combine well with bearded irises, which enjoy similar conditions.

↕24in (60cm) ↔12in (30cm)

Z7–8

PERENNIAL MEDIUM

Salvia x *sylvestris*

WOOD SAGE Grow this clump-forming perennial, with its lance-shaped, wrinkled, green leaves and spikes of blue summer flowers, to provide a vertical accent at the front of a border. 'Blue Hill' (above) has violet-blue flowers.

↕32in (80cm) ↔12in (30cm)

Z4–9

PERENNIAL SMALL

Scabiosa 'Butterfly Blue'

PINCUSHION FLOWER Grow this small summer-flowering perennial, with its dark green leaves and wiry stems topped with small, rounded lavender-blue flowers, between daisies and other flower spikes that bloom at the same time.

↕↔16in (40cm)

Z3–9

PERENNIAL MEDIUM

Thermopsis villosa

CAROLINA LUPINE The spikes of small pale yellow summer flowers, which appear above this perennial's divided gray-green foliage, create a vertical accent behind cranesbill and yarrow in a sunny border.

↕3ft (1m) or more ↔24in (60cm)

Z4–9 Ⓝ

PERENNIAL MEDIUM

Verbascum chaixii

NETTLE-LEAVED MULLEIN Use this perennial as a vertical accent toward the back of a sunny bed. Spikes of pale yellow or white flowers appear on tall stems in summer above coarse leaves. 'Album' (above) has purple-eyed white blooms.

↕3ft (1m) ↔18in (45cm)

Z5–9

PERENNIAL SMALL

Veronica spicata 'Red Fox'

SPIKE SPEEDWELL Try combining this upright clump-forming perennial's spikes of dark pink summer flowers and lance-shaped green leaves with flat-headed yarrow, poppies, and golden marguerite toward the front of a sunny bed.

↕↔20in (50cm)

Z3–8

OTHER SUGGESTIONS

Perennials

Achillea millefolium 'Appleblossom' Ⓝ • *Achillea millefolium* 'Summerwine' Ⓝ • *Anemone* x *hybrida* 'Serenade' • *Campanula punctata* 'Cherry Bells' • *Callirhoe involucrata* Ⓝ • *Echinacea purpurea* 'Magnus' Ⓝ • *Eutrochium fistulosum* Ⓝ • *Gaillardia* 'Oranges and Lemons' Ⓝ • *Helianthus divaricatus* Ⓝ • *Helianthus maximiliani* Ⓝ • *Hosta* 'Guacamole' • *Lobelia siphilitica* Ⓝ • *Paeonia mlokosewitschii* • *Phlox paniculata* 'Bright Eyes' Ⓝ • *Physostegia virginiana* 'Miss Manners' Ⓝ • *Pycnanthemum muticum* Ⓝ • *Rudbeckia subtomentosa* Ⓝ

Bulbs

Agapanthus 'Peter Pan' • *Gladiolus* 'Princess Margaret Rose'

Shrubs

Hydrangea arborescens INCREDIBALL

Summer flowers for containers

While relaxing on patios in summer, you observe containers more, so ensure that plants are in peak condition and provide season-long interest.

Annual bedding plants, such as geranium, petunia, and nemesia, are invaluable in pots, providing continuous color from early- to late summer. Maintain plants by keeping them well watered and removing faded blooms regularly, which stimulates plants to produce more flowers. As part of your summer display, include a few leafy specimens, such as hebe and hosta, to balance the flowery forms. If you include slow-release fertilizer granules when planting, you will not need to feed your plants again until late in the season, when they can be topped up with a liquid fertilizer.

SHRUB LARGE

Abutilon 'Nabob'

FLOWERING MAPLE A tall evergreen shrub, grown as an annual, with maplelike foliage and bowl-shaped crimson summer flowers. Grow on a warm patio in soil-based potting mix; support with canes. To overwinter, take tip cuttings in late summer, or bring indoors.

↕↔ 10ft (3m)

Z9–10

ANNUAL/BIENNIAL SMALL

Ageratum houstonianum

FLOSS FLOWER This compact annual has abundant fluffy pink, white, and blue flowers in summer, set against coarse dark green leaves. Grow in containers, hanging baskets, and windowboxes in potting soil. Deadhead regularly; water well.

↕↔ 12in (30cm)

PERENNIAL SMALL

Anthemis punctata subsp. *cupaniana*

SICILIAN CHAMOMILE This spreading evergreen perennial has silvery leaves and masses of daisy-like summer blooms. Plant in soil-based potting mix with annuals in mixed planters. Deadhead regularly.

↕↔ 12in (30cm)

Z6–9

PERENNIAL SMALL

Antirrhinum majus Luminaire Series

SNAPDRAGON Grown as an annual, this perennial has short spikes of lightly scented flowers in many colors. Let it weep over the sides of containers and baskets. Place pots away from strong winds; deadhead often.

↕↔ 20in (50cm)

Z9–11

PERENNIAL SMALL

Bidens ferulifolia

APACHE BEGGARTICKS Grown as an annual, this perennial has trailing stems of ferny green foliage and yellow star-shaped blooms that are perfect for edging tall pots or baskets from summer to fall. Plant with geranium or dwarf zinnias in potting soil.

↕ 12in (30cm) ↔ indefinite

Z8–11 Ⓝ

ANNUAL/BIENNIAL SMALL

Brachyscome iberidifolia

SWAN RIVER DAISY Adding a decorative edge to pots and baskets, this bushy annual has feathery green leaves and blue, pink, purple, or white daisy-like flowers from summer to early fall. Plant it in potting soil.

↕ 10in (25cm) ↔ 18in (45cm)

SHRUB LARGE

Brugmansia x *candida*

ANGELS' TRUMPETS Usually grown as a houseplant, this shrub has huge, trumpet-shaped, scented white, yellow, or pink blooms. Keep on a warm patio over summer in a container of soil-based potting mix. 'Grand Marnier' (above) has apricot blooms.

↕ 15ft (5m) ↔ 8ft (2.5m)

(!) Z11

PERENNIAL SMALL

Calibrachoa Million Bells Series

MILLION BELLS This perennial, grown as an annual, bears pink, yellow, red, white, or blue trumpet-shaped flowers from summer to early fall. Use it for decorating containers. 'Cherry Pink' (above) is popular.

↕ 12in (30cm) ↔ 3ft (1m)

Z9–11

CLIMBER SMALL

Clematis SHIMMER

CLEMATIS This compact deciduous climber makes a beautiful patio feature, and bears large deep lilac blooms with a paler central bar on each petal throughout summer. Plant it in a large container of soil-based potting mix with a tripod support.

↕ 6ft (1.8m)

Z4–11

PERENNIAL SMALL

Convolvulus sabatius

GROUND MORNING GLORY This perennial, sold as summer annual, produces trailing leafy stems studded with purplish blue funnel-shaped flowers that soften the edges of pots and windowboxes. Plant it in potting soil or soil-based potting mix.
↕8in (20cm) ↔12in (30cm)

Z8–10

ANNUAL/BIENNIAL LARGE

Cosmos bipinnatus

COSMOS Large daisy-like flowers in pink, red, and white make this annual a favorite for summer patio pots. The blooms are set off by feathery green foliage. Plant it in containers of potting soil, and deadhead to prolong flowering. Can be weedy.
↕up to 4ft (1.2m) ↔18in (45cm)

Ⓝ

SHRUB SMALL

Cuphea ignea

CIGAR FLOWER A subshrub, grown as an annual, with lance-shaped leaves and tubular, black-tipped scarlet flowers. It makes a decorative feature in containers of potting soil, together with upright plants, such as fuchsias and geranium.
↕30in (75cm) ↔3ft (1m)

Z10–11 Ⓝ

BULB MEDIUM

Dahlia 'Gallery Art Deco'

DECORATIVE DAHLIA With double flowers comprising burgundy-edged pale orange petals, this bulb offers a splash of color from midsummer to fall. Grow in potting soil and protect bulb from cold. Lift tubers in zones 8 and above to overwinter.
↕18in (45cm)

Z9–11

PERENNIAL SMALL

Diascia barberae

TWINSPUR A mat-forming perennial, often sold as annual, with wiry stems of apricot-pink blooms from summer to fall. Use it to trail over the sides of pots and baskets. There are many varieties available. Feed and water well; deadhead regularly.
↕10in (25cm) ↔20in (50cm)

Z8–9

SHRUB SMALL

Fuchsia 'Thalia'

FUCHSIA This unusual fuchsia, with its pendent, tubular red flowers that appear from summer to fall and dark green leaves, maroon beneath, makes a beautiful centerpiece in a mixed display. Plant it in containers of soil-based potting mix.
↕↔24in (60cm)

Z9–11

SHRUB SMALL

Fuchsia 'Tom Thumb'

FUCHSIA A good choice for windowboxes and baskets, this dwarf, upright shrub produces pinky red and mauve-purple bell-shaped flowers throughout summer. Combine it with trailing lobelia and petunias, and plant it in potting soil.
↕↔20in (50cm)

Z9–11

PERENNIAL SMALL

Gazania Talent Series

TREASURE FLOWER A colorful addition to patio pots, this dwarf perennial, usually grown as an annual, bears yellow, orange, pink, or maroon daisy-like summer flowers. Plant it in containers or windowboxes with other annuals in potting mix.
↕↔10in (25cm)

Z8–10

PERENNIAL SMALL

Impatiens New Guinea Group

NEW GUINEA IMPATIENS Add a frill of flowers to containers with this short-lived colorful perennial. The rounded pink, red, and white flowers provide interest on their own or in mixed displays in containers of all-purpose potting soil.

↕14in (35cm) ↔12in (30cm)

Z10–12

PERENNIAL SMALL

Isotoma axillaris

LAURENTIA The feathery green foliage and lilac or blue star-shaped flowers make this perennial, grown as an annual, a good choice for summer pots. Grow it singly or with fuchsias and dahlias in large containers of all-purpose potting soil.

↕↔12in (30cm)

Z10–11

PERENNIAL SMALL

Gerbera hybrids

TRANSVAAL DAISY This pretty perennial, usually grown as an annual, has lobed green leaves and tall stems of daisy-like, summer flowers in a broad range of colors. Grow in all-purpose potting soil and use to decorate patios.

↕↔16in (40cm)

Z8–11

ANNUAL/BIENNIAL MEDIUM

Helianthus annuus

SUNFLOWER A summer-flowering annual, it is renowned for its large yellow flowers. Dwarf forms, such as 'Teddy Bear' (above) are ideal for pots. Pinch out the stem tips for several small heads, or leave to form a larger single bloom.

↕up to 10ft (3m) ↔24in (60cm)

SHRUB SMALL

Lavandula 'Willow Vale'

SPANISH LAVENDER A classic plant to grow in terracotta pots, this compact evergreen shrub has aromatic gray-green foliage and deep purple blooms that are topped with wavy reddish purple flower bracts from early- to midsummer.

↕↔28in (70cm)

Z8–9

PERENNIAL SMALL

Lobelia erinus

TRAILING LOBELIA This tender perennial, grown as an annual, has trailing stems of dark green leaves and tiny blue-purple blooms that appear from summer to fall if kept moist at all times. Plant in baskets and windowboxes in all-purpose potting soil.

↕8in (20cm) ↔6in (15cm)

Z10–11

ANNUAL/BIENNIAL SMALL

Nemesia 'KLM'

NEMESIA This annual forms a spreading mat of green leaves and wiry stems of small, blue and white scented flowers all summer. Ideal for windowboxes, containers, and baskets. A number of additional varieties are available.

↕12in (30cm) ↔6in (15cm)

PERENNIAL SMALL

Nicotiana Domino Series

FLOWERING TOBACCO This upright annual or tender perennial with oval leaves and scented, purple, pink, red, and white rounded summer blooms. It combines well with trailing lobelia or swan river daisies in containers of all-purpose potting soil.

↕18in (45cm) ↔16in (40cm)

Z10–11

PERENNIAL SMALL

Osteospermum hybrids

AFRICAN DAISY Long-flowering, white, pink, or yellow daisy-like blooms, which appear above this evergreen perennial's gray-green foliage from summer to early fall, are perfect for summer containers of soil-based potting mix. Often grown as an annual.

↕↔ 12in (30cm)

Z9–11

PERENNIAL SMALL

Pelargonium 'Lord Bute'

REGAL GERANIUM An herbaceous perennial, best grown as an annual, with deep purple-red blooms all summer and rounded hairy leaves. All varieties are ideal for windowboxes and containers; plant in all-purpose potting soil.

↕ 18in (45cm) ↔ 12in (30cm)

Z10–11

ANNUAL/BIENNIAL SMALL

Petunia PHANTOM

PETUNIA Dress up summer pots and baskets with this eye-catching bedding plant. It bears a mound of trumpet-shaped, almost black flowers, with a golden central star. It combines well with black-eyed Susan in containers of potting soil.

↕↔ 12in (30cm)

CLIMBER MEDIUM

Rhodochiton atrosanguineus

PURPLE BELL VINE Add height to patio displays by planting this native Mexican annual climber in a container of potting soil. It has heart-shaped leaves and dangling summer flowers with pinky red "hats" and maroon tubes. Stems need a tripod support.

↕ 10ft (3m)

Z10–11 Ⓝ

PERENNIAL MEDIUM

Rudbeckia hirta

BLACK-EYED SUSAN This perennial, usually grown as an annual, bears large, brown-centered golden daisy-like flowers from summer to fall. Varieties include 'Becky Mixed' (above). Ideal for pots; water well and deadhead regularly.

↕ 3ft (1m) ↔ 18in (45cm)

Z3–7 Ⓝ

PERENNIAL SMALL

Salvia splendens Cleopatra Series

SCARLET SAGE This perennial, grown as an annual, has short upright spikes of tubular red or purple flowers. Grow in containers of all-purpose potting soil, water and feed well, and deadhead often.

↕↔ 12in (30cm)

Z10–11

PERENNIAL SMALL

Sutera cordata

BACOPA This spreading perennial, grown as an annual, is used to trail over the sides of containers, baskets, and windowboxes, and forms a curtain of small white or pale pink blooms and green leaves. It flowers all summer if watered and fed well.

↕ 4in (10cm) ↔ indefinite

Z9–11

CLIMBER MEDIUM

Thunbergia alata

BLACK-EYED SUSAN VINE Grow this climber as an annual. It is ideal for large pots in a sunny spot up a trellis, which it will clothe with heart-shaped leaves and bright orange or yellow, dark-eyed flowers. Water and feed well; remove spent blooms.

↕ 10ft (3m)

Z11–15

PERENNIAL SMALL

Verbena Novalis Series

VERBENA A tender perennial, grown as an annual, it is a popular container plant. It has gray-green leaves and orange, purple, pink, red, or white rounded flower heads, which appear all summer. Use to fill gaps between larger flowers in containers of potting mix.

↕↔ 10in (25cm)

Z9–10

ANNUAL/BIENNIAL SMALL

Zinnia Thumbelina Series

ZINNIA Perfect for pots, this dwarf annual, has dark green leaves and semidouble flowers in shades of red, yellow, maroon, and pink blooms from summer to early fall. Grow it in containers, baskets, and windowboxes in all-purpose potting soil.

↕ 6in (15cm) ↔ 8in (21cm)

OTHER SUGGESTIONS

Annuals and perennials

Acalypha hispida • *Begonia* Illumination Series • *Bidens* 'Peter's Gold Carpet' • *Convolvulus tricolor* 'Royal Ensign' • *Diascia* Flirtation Series • *Euphorbia* DIAMOND FROST • *Eustoma grandiflorum* Ⓝ • *Isotoma* 'Avant Garde Blue' • *Osteospermum* Sunny Series • *Petunia* Mambo Series • *Rudbeckia hirta* Toto Series Ⓝ • *Sutera* 'Snowflake' • *Verbena* Aztec Series • *Verbena* 'Homestead Purple'

Shrubs

Argyranthemum Butterfly Series • *Fuchsia* 'Firecracker' • *Hibiscus rosa-sinensis* • *Lavandula* Ruffles Series

Climbers

Clematis JOSEPHINE • *Mandevilla* 'Alice du Pont'

Plants for fall beds

Often forgotten when planting in early summer, these late performers inject a new lease of life into tired beds, just when they need it most.

Boost color and interest at this time of year with a range of key plants, including asters and black-eyed Susan, which are available in a rainbow of colors to suit your style, from hot reds and yellows, to pastels and whites. Flowers are not the only features to consider—ornamental grasses produce decorative seedheads at this time of the year and make perfect partners for many fall blooms. The leaves of some deciduous shrubs also fire up now, while others are studded with decorative fruits. Combine a variety of plant forms to create a scene of contrasting colors, shapes, and textures.

TREE SMALL

Acer palmatum 'Sango-kaku'

CORAL-BARK MAPLE Perfect for a lightly shaded border in fall, this tree puts on a spectacular display of coral-red stems and lobed yellow leaves, which are pinkish yellow in spring and green in summer.

↕25ft (8m) ↔12ft (4m)

Z6–8

TREE LARGE

Acer rubrum

RED MAPLE Ideal to grow as a focal point at the back of a large bed, the rounded lobed foliage of this sizeable tree is dark green in summer and turns bright yellow or red in fall. It requires neutral to acidic soil.

↕70ft (20m) ↔30ft (10m)

pH Z3–9 Ⓝ

PERENNIAL LARGE

Actaea simplex

BUGBANE This upright perennial forms a clump of attractive divided foliage, above which rise tall wiry spikes of small fluffy off-white flowers from early- to mid-fall. Plant it at the back of a bed or as a backdrop to a pond or water feature.

↕5ft (1.5m) ↔24in (60cm)

Z4–8

PERENNIAL MEDIUM

Amsonia tabernaemontana

WILLOW BLUE-STAR An upright perennial with star-shaped blue flower clusters from late spring to summer. Its fall interest comes from its foliage, which develops rich seasonal shades before falling. Grow it mid-bed with fall blooms.

↕3ft (1m) ↔12in (30cm)

Z3–9 Ⓝ

PERENNIAL LARGE

Anemone hupehensis

CHINESE ANEMONE This perennial has large simple white, pink, red, or mauve fall flowers, which are held on upright stems above the dark green divided leaves. 'Hadspen Abundance' (above) has pale pink blooms. Provide support for tall varieties.

↕up to 5ft (1.5m) ↔24in (60cm)

Z5–7

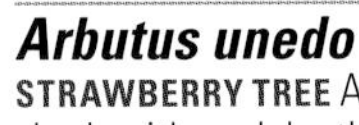

SHRUB LARGE

Arbutus unedo

STRAWBERRY TREE A large evergreen shrub with oval, leathery dark green leaves. In fall, clusters of white urn-shaped flowers appear at the same time as clusters of round green and amber strawberry-like fruits ripen to red.

↕↔25ft (8m)

pH Z7–9

PERENNIAL SMALL

Aster amellus

ITALIAN ASTER Use this clump-forming perennial at the front of a sunny bed, where its yellow-eyed lilac-blue flowers will gleam in early fall against the green lance-shaped leaves. 'King George' (above) has violet-blue blooms.

↕↔20in (50cm)

Z5–8

PERENNIAL MEDIUM

Aster 'Coombe Fishacre'

Renamed *Symphyotrichum* 'Coombe Fishacre' A fall-flowering perennial, calico aster has small pale lilac-pink flowers set against dark foliage. Use it as a contrast to the bright yellow and red blooms adding interest to the middle of a border.

↕3ft (1m) ↔14in (35cm)

Z5–8

PERENNIAL LARGE

Aster cordifolius

Renamed *Symphyotrichum cordifolium* Blue wood aster is a bushy upright perennial with oval, toothed dark green leaves and small, pale blue daisy-like flowers on arching stems from late summer to fall. Plant it near the back of a bed; provide additional support.

↕4ft (1.2m) ↔3ft (1m)

Z3–8 Ⓝ

PERENNIAL MEDIUM

Aster x *frikartii*

FRIKART'S ASTER Use this perennial to cool hot colors or blend with pastels. From late summer to early fall, it bears orange-centered, violet-blue daisy-like flowers on top of slim stems. Varieties include the lavender-blue 'Wonder of Staff' (above).

↕28in (70cm) ↔16in (40cm)

 Z5–8

PERENNIAL SMALL

Aster novae-angliae

Renamed *Symphyotrichum novae-angliae* This New England aster has green leaves and purple, pink, red, or white daisy-like late summer to fall blooms. It is more resistant to mildew disease than *A. novi-belgii.* 'Purple Dome' (above) has purple flowers.

↕up to 5ft (1.5m) ↔24in (60cm)

 Z4–8 Ⓝ

SHRUB SMALL

Caryopteris x *clandonensis*

BLUEBEARD This bushy deciduous shrub forms an upright compact mass of lance-shaped gray-green leaves and dense clusters of blue to purplish blue tubular flowers from late summer to fall. 'Worcester Gold' (above) has contrasting golden leaves.

↕3ft (1m) ↔5ft (1.5m)

Z6–9

SHRUB SMALL

Ceratostigma willmottianum

CHINESE PLUMBAGO This deciduous shrub is prized for its small green leaves that turn bright red in fall. Slender stems produce small sky-blue flowers from late summer to fall. The plant dies back in winter and re-shoots in spring.

↕3ft (1m) ↔5ft (1.5m)

Z6–8

PERENNIAL MEDIUM

Chelone obliqua

TURTLEHEAD On reliably moist soil, this upright perennial will produce spikes of dark pink or purple two-lipped flowers from late summer to early fall above toothed green leaves. Try combining it with the foamy white flowers of boneset.

↕3ft (1m) ↔20in (50cm)

 Z3–9 Ⓝ

PERENNIAL SMALL

Chrysanthemum hybrids

GARDEN MUM This perennial offers color to the fall garden with its sprays of rounded, red, pink, white, or orange single or double blooms, which appear above lobed foliage. It is good for cutting; deadhead regularly to prolong the display.

↕18in (45cm) ↔16in (40cm)

Z5–9

PERENNIAL LARGE

Eupatorium perfoliatum

BONESET Forming a dense clump of upright stems and coarse dark green leaves, this perennial bears branching heads of small, white pincushion-shaped flowers from midsummer to early fall. It needs moist soil and is ideal for bog gardens.

↕6ft (2m) ↔4ft (1.2m)

 Z3–8 Ⓝ

PERENNIAL LARGE

Eutrochium purpureum

JOE PYE WEED An upright perennial, it forms a dense clump of tough stems and large, dark green coarse leaves. From late summer to early fall, fluffy purple-pink blooms appear. Best for large, naturalistic gardens with moist soil.

↕7ft (2.2m) ↔3ft (1m)

 Z4–9 Ⓝ

PERENNIAL LARGE

Gaura lindheimeri

WAND FLOWER From summer to fall, this upright perennial bears white or pink starry flowers on long wiry stems that move freely in the wind. Plant it mid-bed as a see-through plant. 'Karalee White' (above) is a popular modern variety.

↕5ft (1.5m) ↔3ft (1m)

Z5–9 Ⓝ

PERENNIAL MEDIUM

Helenium 'Moerheim Beauty'

SNEEZEWEED This free-flowering perennial bears copper-red daisy-like flowers from midsummer to late summer. As the blooms fade, the centers remain, providing interest into fall. Plant it mid-bed.

↕3ft (1m) ↔24in (60cm)

 Z4–8

PERENNIAL LARGE

Helianthus 'Lemon Queen'

PERENNIAL SUNFLOWER Add a splash of color to the back of a fall border with this upright perennial, which produces dark green leaves and large, daisy-like pale yellow flowers on branched stems. The tall stems may need staking.

↕5ft (1.5m) ↔24in (60cm) or more

Z4–9 Ⓝ

PERENNIAL LARGE

Leucanthemella serotina

GIANTDAISY Ideal for a naturalistic or wild garden, this tall perennial produces yellow-eyed white daisies on top of leafy stems in fall. Use it along with asters and Joe Pye weed to brighten up the back of a bed.

↕5ft (1.5m) ↔3ft (1m)

Z4–9

PERENNIAL SMALL

Liriope muscari

LILYTURF An evergreen perennial with grasslike, glossy dark green leaves and spikes of tiny lavender or purple-blue fall flowers, followed by black berries. Use as edging for a shady border. Considered invasive in some areas of the Southeast.

↕12in (30cm) ↔18in (45cm)

pH Z6–10

PERENNIAL MEDIUM

Lysimachia clethroides

GOOSENECK LOOSESTRIFE This spreading perennial has gray-green foliage and, from late summer to fall, long, pointed, white flower heads. Can be aggressive; ideal for large or naturalistic gardens. Support the stems; remove unwanted growth in fall.

↕↔3ft (1m)

Z3–8

BULB MEDIUM

Nerine bowdenii

SPIDER LILY This spring-planted perennial bulb sleeps in summer, but bursts to life in fall when spidery pink flowers emerge on upright stems. Strap-shaped leaves unfurl later. Grow it at the front of a sunny bed.

↕24in (60cm)

(!) Z8–10

PERENNIAL MEDIUM

Panicum virgatum

SWITCH GRASS Use this upright deciduous grass as a leafy companion for fall-flowering-plants. It bears blue-green foliage, which turns yellow in fall, and clouds of pink-tinged green summer flower heads, which fade to beige.

↕3ft (1m) ↔30in (75cm)

Z5–9 Ⓝ

PERENNIAL MEDIUM

Pennisetum alopecuroides

FOUNTAIN GRASS This deciduous grass produces arching green leaves that turn bronze and spikes of bristly purple-tinged flower heads in late summer, followed by fall seedheads. Try it with dahlias, black-eyed Susan, and stonecrop.

↕3ft (1m) ↔18in (45cm)

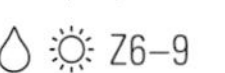

Z6–9

PERENNIAL MEDIUM

Rudbeckia fulgida

BLACK-EYED SUSAN This upright perennial has narrow midgreen leaves. From late summer to fall, it is awash with daisy-like golden flowers with brown centers, which give winter interest when the blooms fade. Plant it mid-bed in a sunny site.

↕3ft (1m) ↔18in (45cm)

Z4–9 Ⓝ

PERENNIAL LARGE

Rudbeckia laciniata

CUTLEAF CONEFLOWER A towering perennial that adds interest to the back of an early fall bed. The daisy-like bright yellow flowers that grow atop tall stems, combine well with asters. It performs best in soil that does not dry out.

↕6ft (2m) ↔30in (75cm)

Z3–9 Ⓝ

PERENNIAL LARGE

Salvia guaranitica

ANISE-SCENTED SAGE This tall perennial is at its best in fall when the tall stems are dotted with deep blue two-lipped flowers above midgreen leaves. Varieties include the rich blue 'Black and Blue' (above). Apply a thick mulch in winter.

↕5ft (1.5m) ↔24in (60cm)

Z7–10

PERENNIAL LARGE

Salvia involucrata

ROSYLEAF SAGE This tall perennial has heart-shaped leaves and is best combined with grasses and anemones at the back of a border, where its spikes of small, tubular pink flowers will bloom until mid-fall. Protect it from hard frosts.

↕5ft (1.5m) ↔3ft (1m)

Z8–11 Ⓝ

PERENNIAL MEDIUM

Salvia nemorosa

SAGE A compact upright perennial that blooms until early fall, when spikes of violet-blue flowers with pink bracts accompany midgreen lance-shaped leaves. Try planting it with stonecrop, grasses, and coneflower.

↕up to 30in (75cm) ↔24in (60cm)

Z4–8

PERENNIAL MEDIUM

Salvia patens

GENTIAN SAGE A perennial, sometimes grown as an annual, that bears upright stems of vivid blue two-lipped flowers, held above hairy green leaves from midsummer to fall. Plant it at the front of a sunny bed; deadhead regularly.

↕24in (60cm) ↔18in (45cm)

Z8–10 Ⓝ

PERENNIAL MEDIUM

Schizostylis coccinea

CRIMSON FLAG The sword-shaped leaves of this perennial are joined by spikes of salmon-pink starry flowers throughout fall. Try it with blue asters and stonecrop in moist but well-drained soil, and apply a thick mulch in winter.

↕24in (60cm) ↔12in (30cm)

Z7–9

PERENNIAL MEDIUM

Solidago GOLDEN BABY

GOLDENROD A reliable perennial for the back of a bed, it has flattened clusters of tiny golden flowers held on tall leafy stems in fall, and dark green lance-shaped foliage. A good choice for dry soils, try combining it with grasses.

↕24in (60cm) ↔18in (45cm)

Z4–8

PERENNIAL LARGE

Thalictrum delavayi

YUNNAN MEADOW RUE This clump-forming perennial has ferny green leaves and, from late summer to fall, large airy panicles of tiny lavender blooms. Varieties include 'Hewitt's Double' (above) with dainty double flowers. Grow on moist soil.

↕5ft (1.5m) ↔24in (60cm) or more

Z4–7

PERENNIAL SMALL

Sedum erythrostictum 'Mediovariegatum'

STONECROP Allow this small perennial's stems of oval, fleshy cream- and green-variegated leaves and tiny, star-shaped greenish white flowers in early fall to spread across the front of a sunny bed.

↕12in (30cm) ↔24in (60cm)

Z3–9

PERENNIAL LARGE

Veronicastrum virginicum

CULVER'S ROOT Tall spires of white, blue, or pink star-shaped flowers, on top of stems bearing dark green lance-shaped foliage, make this an ideal back-of-bed plant for late summer and early fall interest. 'Album' (above) has white flowers.

↕4ft (1.2m) ↔18in (45cm)

Z4–8 Ⓝ

PERENNIAL SMALL

Sedum spectabile

SHOWY STONECROP Ideal for the front of a sunny fall bed, this clump-forming perennial produces flat heads of rose-pink flowers followed by brown seedheads that persist over winter. The oval fleshy leaves are gray-green.

↕↔18in (45cm)

(!) Z4–9

OTHER SUGGESTIONS

Perennials and bulbs

Amsonia hubrechtii Ⓝ • *Chrysanthemum* 'Sea Urchin' • *Chelone lyonii* 'Hot Lips' Ⓝ • *Dahlia* 'Arabian Night' • *Echinacea paradoxa* Ⓝ • *Echinacea purpurea* 'Ruby Star' Ⓝ • *Echinacea purpurea* 'White Swan' Ⓝ • *Eutrochium purpureum* subsp. *maculatum* 'Gateway' Ⓝ • *Helianthus maximilianii* Ⓝ • *Rudbeckia* 'Gold Drop' • *Rudbeckia maxima* Ⓝ • *Rudbeckia triloba* Ⓝ • *Salvia nemorosa* 'Amethyst' • *Senna marilandica* Ⓝ • *Solidago rugosa* 'Fireworks' Ⓝ • *Symphyotrichum oblongifolium* 'October Skies' Ⓝ • *Tulbaghia violacea* • *Veronia noveboracensis* Ⓝ

Shrubs and trees

Acer palmatum 'Osakazuki' • *Viburnum trilobum* 'Wentworth' Ⓝ

Plants for fall leaves

While bulbs lift the spirits in spring, vibrant foliage color provides the perfect finale to the drama in the garden come fall.

The stars of the fall show are maples, which sport sculptural leaves that turn startling shades of crimson and orange before falling. Place them in a focal point in a lawn or bed to create a seasonal focal point. House walls and garden fences can also be set ablaze with the scarlet foliage of Boston ivy and crimson glory vine, which make a beautiful backdrop to container displays on a patio or seasonal beds. Contrast these bright reds with the warm, buttery tones of birch and hydrangea leaves and burnished bronze hornbeam and beech.

TREE SMALL

Acer henryi

HENRY'S MAPLE This small, often multi-stemmed, tree has dark green leaves, with three elliptical leaflets that develop glowing red and orange tints in early fall. Plant it in fertile soil in sun or light, dappled shade in a bed or lawn sheltered from strong winds.

↕25ft (8m) ↔30ft (10m)

Z5–7

TREE MEDIUM

Acer japonicum 'Vitifolium'

FULL MOON MAPLE A bushy deciduous shrub or tree ideal for the back of a bed, it produces large maple-shaped leaves and drooping red flower clusters in spring. In fall, the leaves turn purple, crimson-red, and orange.

↕↔30ft (10m)

Z5–7

TREE SMALL

Acer palmatum 'Atropurpureum'

JAPANESE MAPLE A dainty tree, with lobed, purple-red tinged summer foliage. Shelter, dappled shade, and moisture-retentive soil encourage the fiery red fall display and prevent leaf scorch.

↕↔25ft (8m)

Z6–8

TREE SMALL

Acer palmatum 'Nicholsonii'

JAPANESE MAPLE This is an elegant, arching tree with long, finely pointed, deeply lobed leaves. The foliage is purple-red in spring and turns green in summer. In fall, it makes a dazzling show of yellow, orange, and red.

↕↔25ft (8m)

Z6–8

TREE SMALL

Acer palmatum 'Osakazuki'

JAPANESE MAPLE This rounded tree, with its deeply lobed green leaves, drooping, red flower clusters, and winged seeds, makes a fine specimen toward the back of a sheltered bed. Given adequate moisture, the orange and scarlet-red fall foliage is striking.

↕↔20ft (6m)

Z6–8

TREE SMALL

Acer palmatum 'Shinobuga-oka'

JAPANESE MAPLE This small sparsely branched upright tree has cascading leaves with long, very narrow bright green leaflets. In fall, the leaf color transforms to a translucent yellow and gold.

↕↔25ft (8m)

Z6–8

TREE LARGE

Carya ovata

SHAGBARK HICKORY This walnut relative forms a large tree with leaves divided into pairs, and bears edible nuts in fall. As it matures, the bark peels away, hanging in rough strips. In fall, the foliage turns yellow and golden-brown.

↕80ft (25m) ↔50ft (15m)

 Z4–8 Ⓝ

TREE LARGE

Acer rubrum 'October Glory'

RED MAPLE This fine specimen tree has glossy, dark green lobed leaves and red spring-flower clusters on bare branches. Given neutral to acidic soil, the fall leaves glow bright crimson. Plant in open areas as the shallow roots can crack or lift sideways.

↕70ft (20m) ↔30ft (10m)

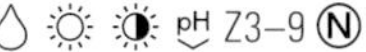 Z3–9 Ⓝ

TREE LARGE

Cercidiphyllum japonicum

KATSURA TREE This large tree, ideal for a sheltered woodland setting, is grown for its paired heart-shaped leaves, bronze-tinted when young. In fall, the leaves develop beautiful orange, pink, and yellow tints, and a toffee fragrance.

↕70ft (20m) ↔50ft (15m)

 Z4–8

TREE MEDIUM

Betula alleghaniensis

YELLOW BIRCH This medium-sized upright tree is ideal for a woodland grove with smooth light bronze bark, peeling in horizontal slivers. It has toothed-edged, oval, pointed leaves that turn butter-yellow in fall before dropping.

↕40ft (12m) or more ↔10ft (3m)

Z4–7 Ⓝ

SHRUB LARGE

Cornus alba 'Sibirica'

TATARIAN DOGWOOD This deciduous shrub displays bright red bare stems in winter and bears flattened heads of white early summer flowers followed by bluish white fruits. In fall, the leaves flush with rich shades of yellow, orange, and red before dropping.

↕↔10ft (3m)

Z2–7

TREE LARGE

Betula lenta

CHERRY BIRCH This large tree has glossy browny gray bark with prominent horizontal markings, often developing black vertical fissures as the tree matures. The broad oval leaves develop beautiful golden-yellow tints in fall.

↕50ft (15m) ↔40ft (12m)

Z3–7 Ⓝ

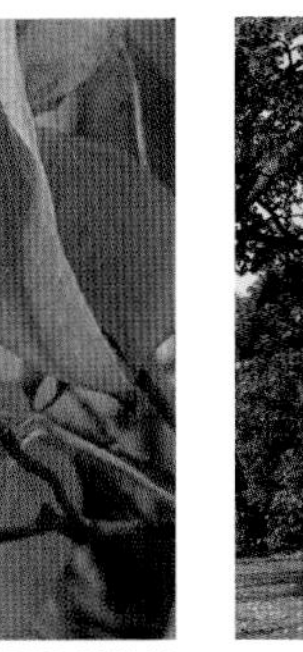

TREE SMALL

Cornus florida

FLOWERING DOGWOOD This deciduous tree has slightly curled green leaves. It becomes covered with white or pink, flowerlike bracts in late spring. In fall, its leaves develop bold orange and red shades before dropping.

↕20ft (6m) ↔25ft (8m)

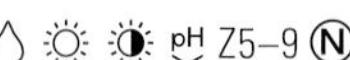 Z5–9 Ⓝ

TREE SMALL

Cornus kousa var. *chinensis*

CHINESE DOGWOOD Although this large shrub or small tree is grown for its tiny late spring flowers surrounded by cream-colored petal-like bracts, its fall display is equally fine. The oval leaves, which hang in tiers, color rich red and orange.

↕22ft (7m) ↔15ft (5m)

Z5–8

SHRUB LARGE

Cotinus 'Grace'

SMOKE TREE The broadly oval leaves of this shrub gradually turn from purple to scarlet-red and flame-orange in fall. Whether purple- or green-leaved, all smoke bush varieties offer an eye-catching fall display.

↕20ft (6m) ↔15ft (5m)

Z5–8

Plants for fall leaves

SHRUB LARGE

Disanthus cercidifolius

REDBUD HAZEL This bushy shrub, which thrives in moist soil and shade, has large, rounded to heart-shaped green leaves that color crimson, purple, and orange in fall, and are borne alongside small, scattered, starry maroon blooms.

↕↔10ft (3m)

Z5–8

SHRUB SMALL

Fothergilla gardenii

DWARF FOTHERGILLA Suitable for the middle of a bed, this dwarf shrub produces fragrant fluffy spring flowers followed by deep blue-green oval leaves. In fall, the foliage lights up with fiery red, orange, and yellow tints.

↕↔3ft (1m)

Z4–8 (N)

SHRUB MEDIUM

Fothergilla major

LARGE FOTHERGILLA The large rounded leaves of this medium-sized spring-flowering shrub with a dense bushy habit, light up with a brilliant scarlet display in fall, making a striking contrast when placed among dark evergreen plants.

↕8ft (2.5m) ↔6ft (2m)

Z5–8 (N)

PERENNIAL SMALL

Geranium x magnificum

SHOWY GERANIUM Although this ground-cover perennial is mainly grown for its violet-blue early summer blooms, its deeply cut leaves take on pale yellow, pink, or, sometimes, deep crimson tones, in fall as they age.

↕18in (45cm) ↔24in (60cm)

Z4–8

SHRUB MEDIUM

Hydrangea quercifolia

OAKLEAF HYDRANGEA The lobed leaves of this shrub make a fine backdrop for the cream cone-shaped clusters of midsummer to fall blooms. In fall, after developing maroon tints, the leaves take on striking red and purple hues.

↕6ft (2m) ↔8ft (2.5m)

(!) Z5–9 (N)

TREE LARGE

Liquidambar styraciflua

SWEETGUM Only suitable for large gardens, this deciduous tree is magnificent in fall when its lobed dark green leaves turn orange, red, and purple. Select one of the compact cultivars, such as 'Gum Ball', for a smaller garden.

↕80ft (25m) ↔40ft (12m)

Z5–9 (N)

TREE MEDIUM

Nyssa sinensis

CHINESE TUPELO This medium-sized spreading tree or large shrub is grown for its spectacular fall color, when the narrow oval leaves take on magnificent amber-scarlet hues. It performs best in moist soil in a sheltered site.

↕↔30ft (10m)

Z7–9

TREE SMALL

Parrotia persica

PERSIAN IRONWOOD This wide-spreading specimen tree or large shrub, sometimes multistemmed, has peeling bark. It is transformed in fall when the broad oval leaves turn red, purple, and amber, highlighting the veins.

↕25ft (8m) ↔30ft (10m)

Z4–8

CLIMBER LARGE

Parthenocissus tricuspidata

BOSTON IVY This large, vigorous, self-clinging deciduous climber has lobed, glossy green leaves that display spectacular crimson and red colors in fall. Grow on a large house wall or fence behind a fall bed. Considered invasive in some areas.

↕70ft (20m)

 Z4–8

TREE LARGE

Quercus alba

WHITE OAK This large tree has a broad, spreading crown at maturity. In fall, the dark green leaves with 7–9 lobes turn a spectacular wine red, with some brown and yellow tints, the brown persisting into winter.

↕↔100ft (30m)

Z4–9 Ⓝ

TREE LARGE

Quercus palustris

PIN OAK This tall pyramid-shaped tree has deeply lobed leaves that are green in summer, but turn vibrant reddish brown or crimson red in fall, making a magnificent focal point in a large garden. Good as a street tree.

↕70ft (20m) ↔40ft (12m)

Z4–8 Ⓝ

CLIMBER LARGE

Vitis coignetiae

CRIMSON GLORY VINE The impressively large heart-shaped leaves of this tendril climbing vine are green in summer and, given a warm sheltered aspect, develop spectacular purple, red, orange, and yellow shades through fall.

↕50ft (15m)

Z5–9

TREE LARGE

Prunus sargentii

SARGENT CHERRY Like many flowering cherries, this large tree has smoldering red and amber fall leaf color. 'Rancho' (above) is columnar with foliage that emerges red-brown after a showy display of large, pink single flowers in spring.

↕70ft (20m) ↔50ft (15m)

Z4–7

TREE LARGE

Quercus rubra

RED OAK This large tree, with a spreading to rounded crown, tolerates urban pollution and, in fall, provides a treat when its leaves with pointed lobes turn a rich reddish brown or crimson. It is an excellent shade tree for lawns.

↕80ft (25m) ↔70ft (20m)

Z4–8 Ⓝ

TREE LARGE

Zelkova serrata

JAPANESE ZELKOVA This large tree with a spreading to vase-shaped crown has alternately arranged long pointed leaves with prominent veins and serrated margins. The fall foliage is rich yellow-orange to red-brown. Best in large gardens.

↕100ft (30m) ↔80ft (25m)

Z5–8

TREE SMALL

Rhus typhina

STAGHORN SUMAC This deciduous tree or suckering shrub has large, dissected bright green leaves that turn yellow, orange, and red in fall and cone-shaped maroon fruits. 'Dissecta' (above) has finely cut leaves. Give enough room for suckers to naturalize.

↕↔10ft (3m)

Z3–8 Ⓝ

OTHER SUGGESTIONS

Shrubs and climbers

Aronia arbutifolia 'Brilliantissima' Ⓝ • *Cotinus obovatus* Ⓝ • *Hamamelis vernalis* Ⓝ • *Itea virginica* 'Merlot' Ⓝ • *Lindera benzoin* Ⓝ • *Parthenocissus henryana* • *Parthenocissus quinquefolia* Ⓝ • *Rhus aromatica* 'Gro-Low' Ⓝ • *Rhus copallinum* var. *latifolia* PRAIRIE FLAME Ⓝ • *Vaccinium corymbosum* Ⓝ • *Vaccinium parvifolium* Ⓝ • *Viburnum dentatum* AUTUMN JAZZ Ⓝ • *Viburnum prunifolium* Ⓝ • *Viburnum rufidulum* Ⓝ

Trees

Acer palmatum 'Beni Maiko' • *Acer palmatum* 'Orange Dream' • *Acer pensylvanicum* Ⓝ • *Acer saccharum* FALL FIESTA Ⓝ • *Asimina triloba* Ⓝ • *Carpinus caroliniana* Ⓝ • *Fagus grandiflora* Ⓝ • *Nyssa aquatica* Ⓝ • *Nyssa sylvatica* 'Wildfire' Ⓝ • *Oxydendrum arboreum* Ⓝ • *Quercus coccinea* Ⓝ • *Rhus glabra* Ⓝ • *Sassafras albidum* Ⓝ • *Taxodium distichum* Ⓝ

Plants for ornamental fruits

While flower choices are more limited in fall, there are fruits aplenty, adding color and texture to designs, as well as food for wildlife.

Decorate your garden with ornamental and edible fruits, such as apples and pears, for both taste and color. The classic red fruits of crabapple, cotoneaster, and roses introduce bright beads of color and combine well with berries in other shades. Try the violet berries of a beautyberry, the blue-black fruits of blackhaw viburnum, and the purple and pink, flowerlike berries of glory bower. Although many fruits are borne on large trees and shrubs, skimmia is ideal for a small garden, and climbers, such as climbing blueberry, will scale fences and trellises while taking up very little ground space.

PERENNIAL MEDIUM

Actaea pachypoda

WHITE BANEBERRY This clump-forming perennial has divided bright green leaves. In midsummer, it produces upright spikes of fluffy white flowers followed by oval, black-tipped white berries on stiff bright red stalks in fall.

↕3ft (1m) ↔20in (50cm)

Z3–8 (N)

SHRUB LARGE

Arbutus unedo

STRAWBERRY TREE This large evergreen shrub has dark green leathery leaves and white urn-shaped flowers, which appear at the same time as the strawberry-like fruits, which turn red in fall. Use it for seasonal interest at the back of a bed.

↕↔25ft (8m)

pH Z7–9

CLIMBER MEDIUM

Billardiera longiflora

CLIMBING BLUEBERRY This twining evergreen climber has narrow green leaves and small, bell-shaped greenish yellow flowers. In fall, unusual purple-blue edible fruits with a metallic sheen develop. Plant on warm sheltered walls.

↕6ft (2m)

Z8–9

SHRUB LARGE

Aronia x *prunifolia*

PURPLE CHOKEBERRY An upright shrub with dark green oval leaves, this natural hybrid has white spring flowers, which are followed by purple-black berries that make a stunning contrast to the glowing red fall foliage.

↕10ft (3m) ↔8ft (2.5m)

Z4–8 (N)

SHRUB LARGE

Callicarpa bodinieri var. *giraldii*

BEAUTYBERRY A bushy deciduous shrub, with oval purple-tinted leaves and tiny lilac flowers. Dense clusters of small, spherical violet berries, set at intervals along the stems, follow the blooms in fall.

↕10ft (3m) ↔8ft (2.5m)

Z5–8

SHRUB SMALL

Callicarpa dichotoma

PURPLE BEAUTYBERRY This small rounded shrub has arching stems bearing clusters of lilac summer flowers in the leaf axils. By early fall, these develop into clusters of violet berries, which persist as the oval green leaves turn yellow.

↕↔4ft (1.2m)

Z5–8

SHRUB LARGE

Clerodendrum trichotomum var. *fargesii*

GLORY BOWER This small tree or large upright shrub has broad heart-shaped leaves and fragrant white late summer to mid-fall flowers that lead to kingfisher-blue berries surmounted by maroon bracts.

↕↔20ft (6m)

Z7–9

TREE MEDIUM

Cornus capitata

EVERGREEN DOGWOOD This evergreen tree or large shrub favors a warm sheltered site. In early summer, the branches are smothered with flowers that have showy creamy petal-like bracts. These are followed by edible strawberry-like fruits, ripening in fall.

↕↔40ft (12m)

pH Z8–9

TREE SMALL

Cornus kousa

KOUSA DOGWOOD This early summer-flowering, slow-growing tree or large shrub has glossy oval leaves and showy petal-like cream-colored bracts that develop pink tints. Hanging clusters of knobby, pinkish red, spherical fruits follow in fall.

↕22ft (7m) ↔15ft (5m)

pH Z5–8

SHRUB SMALL

Cotoneaster horizontalis

ROCKSPRAY Best trained against a wall at the back of a narrow bed, this spreading, deciduous shrub produces stems in a "herringbone" pattern. These are dotted in fall and early winter with red berries, which later fall or are eaten by birds.

↕3ft (1m) ↔5ft (1.5m)

(!) Z4–7

TREE SMALL

Crataegus coccinea

HAWTHORN This small, spreading deciduous tree has broad leaves with jagged, toothed edges. In spring, white flowers appear, which are followed in fall by gleaming scarlet fruits that are attractive to wildlife.

↕↔20ft (6m)

(!) Z4–7 (N)

SHRUB LARGE

Decaisnea fargesii

BLUE BEAN SHRUB An upright deciduous shrub with large divided leaves and hanging clusters of clematis like yellow-green early summer flowers that lead to fall-ripening, pendulous metallic-blue bean pods. Protect from severe frosts.

↕↔20ft (6m)

Z7–9

SHRUB LARGE

Euonymus hamiltonianus

HAMILTON'S SPINDLE TREE A large, deciduous shrub, with lance-shaped leaves that have fiery fall colors. In fall, it produces unusual ornamental fruits, which are flesh-pink and split to reveal glossy orange-red seeds.

↕↔25ft (8m)

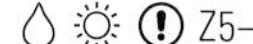

(!) Z5–8

SHRUB SMALL

Gaultheria mucronata

CHILEAN PERNETTYA This evergreen shrub, with dark prickly leaves and tiny white spring blooms, is chiefly grown for its spherical berries in shades of white, pink, or crimson. Females fruit if a male is planted close by. Best in West Coast gardens.

↕↔ 4ft (1.2m)

Z7–9

SHRUB LARGE

Ilex 'Sparkleberry'

WINTERBERRY This bushy deciduous shrub has oval pointed leaves that develop bold fall colors before dropping. If pollinated by a male plant, the bare stems become laden with small red berries that last well into winter, or until they are eaten by birds.

↕ 15ft (5m) ↔ 12ft (4m)

 Z5–9

PERENNIAL MEDIUM

Iris foetidissima

STINKING IRIS This shade- and drought-tolerant evergreen perennial has sword-shaped leaves and yellow-tinged purple blooms from early- to midsummer. In fall, its long seedpods split to reveal orange-red berries. Leaves may fade in colder areas.

↕ 3ft (1m) ↔ indefinite

 Z6–9

TREE MEDIUM

Malus floribunda

JAPANESE FLOWERING CRABAPPLE Plant this deciduous tree in a border or lawn. Its showy pale pink spring flowers emerge from crimson buds, after the oval leaves appear. Edible red and yellow fruits follow in fall. Considered invasive.

↕↔ 30ft (10m)

Z4–8

TREE MEDIUM

Malus 'Red Sentinel'

CRABAPPLE This deciduous tree is smothered in white single flowers in spring. In fall, bunches of glossy deep red cherrylike fruits form. The fruits last beyond leaf fall, decorating the bare winter branches.

↕ 40ft (12m) ↔ 30ft (10m)

Z5–8

PERENNIAL MEDIUM

Physalis alkekengi

CHINESE LANTERN This spreading perennial has upright stems and small cream flowers in midsummer followed by highly ornamental, orange "Chinese lanterns", concealing berrylike fruits. Cut early for indoor decoration.

↕ 30in (75cm) ↔ 3ft (1m)

 Z3–9

SHRUB LARGE

Pyracantha 'Mohave'

FIRETHORN This scab-resistant evergreen shrub has prickly stems and white summer-flower clusters followed by orange-red berries. Other varieties are available, with fruits that ripen in shades of orange, red, and yellow; all are ideal for wall-training.

↕↔ 12ft (4m)

Z6–9

SHRUB SMALL

Rosa 'Fru Dagmar Hastrup'

HYBRID RUGOSA ROSE This shrub rose has healthy crinkled foliage and bears fragrant, soft pink single blooms in flushes from summer to early fall, and large, deep red tomato-like hips alongside later flowers. The hips are attractive to birds.

↕ 3ft (1m) ↔ 4ft (1.2m)

Z3–9

SHRUB LARGE

Rosa moyesii

MOYES ROSE This large arching shrub rose produces orange-red single summer flowers, each with a central tuft of golden stamens. It is noted for its hanging clusters of glossy red flask-shaped fruits.

↕12ft (4m) ↔10ft (3m)

Z6–8

SHRUB MEDIUM

Skimmia japonica

JAPANESE SKIMMIA This evergreen shrub has glossy dark green leaves and dense heads of tiny, fragrant, pink- or red-budded, white spring flowers. Females develop red berries, which persist into winter, if a male plant is nearby. Best in West Coast gardens.

↕↔5ft (1.5m)

Z6–8

SHRUB SMALL

Skimmia japonica 'Fructo Albo'

JAPANESE SKIMMIA This dwarf evergreen shrub has neat dark green foliage and crops of white berries that develop from white spring flower clusters. To help fruiting, plant with a male. Best in West Coast gardens.

↕24in (60cm) ↔3ft (1m)

SHRUB LARGE

Viburnum prunifolium

BLACKHAW VIBURNUM A deciduous shrub, ideal for hedging, with glossy oval leaves that turn red and purple-bronze in fall. From late spring to early summer, it forms lacy white flowers, attractive to butterflies. Birds love the blue-black fruits that follow.

↕15ft (5m) ↔12ft (4m)

SHRUB LARGE

Zanthoxylum simulans

PRICKLY ASH A large shrub with glossy, divided aromatic leaves, long thorns and, in late spring, small greenish yellow flowers. Reddish brown fruits, splitting to reveal black seeds, form in fall if both sexes are planted together.

↕20ft (6m) ↔15ft (5m)

Z6–9

SHRUB MEDIUM

Symphoricarpos x *doorenbosii*

SNOWBERRY Use this vigorous deciduous shrub as an informal hedge. The small, round dark green leaves and tiny greenish white summer flowers create a useful backdrop, and showy round white fruit clusters provide winter interest.

↕6ft (2m) ↔indefinite

Z4–7

OTHER SUGGESTIONS

Climbers

Actinidia deliciosa

Shrubs

Aronia arbutifolia Ⓝ • *Callicarpa americana* Ⓝ • *Cotoneaster salicifolius* 'Scarlet Leader' • *Euonymus atropurpureus* Ⓝ • *Ilex verticillata* 'Red Sprite' Ⓝ • *Pyracantha* SILVER LINING • *Rosa palustris* Ⓝ • *Sambucus canadensis* Ⓝ • *Symphoricarpos orbiculatus* • *Viburnum dentatum* BLUE MUFFIN Ⓝ • *Viburnum lentago* Ⓝ

Trees

Cornus florida Ⓝ • *Crataegus viridis* 'Winter King' Ⓝ • *Diospyros kaki* • *Diospyros virginiana* Ⓝ • *Gymnocladus dioica* Ⓝ • *Ilex opaca* Ⓝ • *Malus* 'Prairifire' • *Maclura pomifera* Ⓝ • *Sorbus americana* Ⓝ • *Zanthoxylum americanum* Ⓝ

Fall and winter flowers for containers

As summer annuals begin to fade, rejuvenate tired container displays with a range of fall- and winter-flowering plants.

The choice of fall and winter flowers is not huge, but the color range equals that of summer schemes, with hot-hued chrysanthemums, primrose, and dahlias, or cool-colored Chinese aster, dainty cyclamen, and spider lily. When buying bedding plants in early fall, check the labels for hardiness if the plant will soldier on after the first frost. Also remember that winter-flowering pansies do not actually bloom that well during very cold weather—small-headed violas are more reliable. The best displays can be achieved by sheltering pots on windowsills or close to house walls.

PERENNIAL SMALL

Aster novi-belgii 'Professor Anton Kippenberg'

Renamed *Symphyotrichum novi-belgii* 'Professor Anton Kippenburg' This perennial's pastel-colored, daisy-like blooms are perfect for fall pots of soil-based potting mix. Water well to prevent powdery mildew.
↕14in (35cm) ↔18in (45cm)
Z4–8

PERENNIAL SMALL

Bellis perennis

ENGLISH DAISY This dwarf perennial, grown as an annual, bears pink, white, or red double or single blooms above green foliage starting from late winter in sheltered sites. Plant it in groups in potting soil with evergreen shrubs and violas.
↕↔8in (20cm)
Z4–8

ANNUAL/BIENNIAL MEDIUM

Callistephus chinensis

CHINA ASTER This bushy annual bedding plant has oval, lobed green leaves and fall flowers in shades of pink, purple, white, and yellow that add color to containers of soil-based potting mix. Deadhead to prolong the flowering display.
↕24in (60cm) ↔18in (45cm)

PERENNIAL SMALL

Ceratostigma plumbaginoides

PLUMBAGO Plant this small bushy perennial in a windowbox or container filled with soil-based potting mix. Small blue late season flowers appear annually. Its green oval leaves take on spectacular red color in fall.
↕18in (45cm) ↔8in (20cm)
Z5–9

PERENNIAL SMALL

Chrysanthemum hybrids

GARDEN MUM Plant this small-sized perennial in soil-based potting mix in a container or windowbox. Sprays of rounded, pink double blooms appear above lobed green foliage. Many variety in a large array of colors are available.
↕18in (45cm) ↔16in (40cm)
Z5–9

BULB MEDIUM

Colchicum byzantinum

AUTUMN CROCUS Use this dainty perennial corm in small pots or windowboxes for a fall display of open funnel-shaped soft lilac flowers. The leaves appear later. Plant the corms in summer in soil-based potting mix.
↕8in (20cm)
Z4–8

BULB MEDIUM

Colchicum 'Waterlily'

AUTUMN CROCUS This perennial bulb, grown from corms, blooms in fall when pinkish lilac fully double flowers develop, followed by strap-shaped leaves soon after. Plant the corms in summer in small containers of soil-based potting mix.
↕6in (15cm)
Z4–8

PERENNIAL MEDIUM

Cosmos atrosanguineus

CHOCOLATE COSMOS This perennial's bowl-shaped, chocolate-scented dark maroon flowers are held on tall slim stems, from late summer to early fall above divided green leaves. Plant it in large containers of gritty soil-based potting mix.
↕24in (60cm) or more ↔18in (45cm)
Z7–10 Ⓝ

BULB SMALL

Cyclamen coum

HARDY CYCLAMEN With its silver-marbled leaves and deep pink flowers, with twisted, swept-back petals, this dwarf perennial bulb offers late winter color. Plant in small containers or windowboxes in gritty soil-based potting mix. Goes dormant in summer.
↕4in (10cm)
Z5–9

BULB SMALL

Cyclamen hederifolium

IVY-LEAVED CYCLAMEN Add fall color to small containers filled with gritty soil-based potting mix with this dwarf perennial bulb. Its pink blooms bear swept-back petals and are followed by patterned silvery-green leaves. Goes dormant in summer.
↕4in (10cm)
Z5–8

BULB MEDIUM

Dahlia 'Yellow Hammer'

DWARF BEDDER SINGLE DAHLIA This dahlia blooms up to the first frost in fall with bright yellow single flowers above dark bronze foliage. Grow it in pots of gritty soil-based potting mix. In cold areas, dig tubers in fall and overwinter indoors.

↕24in (60cm)

Z9–11

BULB MEDIUM

Galanthus nivalis

SNOWDROP In late winter, this perennial bulb produces small, nodding white flowers, with green markings on some varieties, among clumps of gray-green, grassy leaves. Plant it in flower in containers of soil-based potting mix.

↕6in (15cm)

Z3–8

PERENNIAL MEDIUM

Helleborus orientalis

LENTEN ROSE This evergreen perennial is among the first to flower each year, and bears saucer-shaped flowers in shades of white or greenish cream, aging to dark pink, in midwinter on sturdy stems. Plant in containers of soil-based potting mix.

↕24in (60cm) ↔18in (45cm)

Z4–9

SHRUB SMALL

Juniperus communis 'Compressa'

COMMON JUNIPER Forming a slim cone of blue-gray foliage, this dwarf, slow-growing evergreen conifer partners well with small shrubs, flowers, and bulbs in fall and winter in containers of soil-based potting mix.

↕32in (80cm) ↔18in (45cm)

Z2–6 (N)

BULB MEDIUM

Nerine bowdenii

SPIDER LILY This perennial bulb with its spidery pink flowers followed by strap-shaped leaves decorates fall borders and brightens up late-season containers. Plant the bulbs in spring in gritty soil-based potting mix.

↕24in (60cm)

(!) Z8–10

PERENNIAL MEDIUM

Platycodon grandiflorus

BALLOON FLOWER The purple-blue flowers of this perennial open from balloonlike buds throughout early fall, creating beautiful displays in containers filled with soil-based potting mix. It has beautiful golden-yellow fall foliage.

↕24in (60cm) ↔18in (45cm)

Z3–8

PERENNIAL SMALL

Primula Crescendo Series

POLYANTHUS PRIMROSE This evergreen perennial, grown as an annual, is ideal for late winter pots and windowboxes. It features dark green corrugated leaves and clusters of yellow-eyed flowers in shades of red, yellow, white, and purple.

↕↔8in (20cm)

Z5–7

PERENNIAL SMALL

Sedum erythrostictum 'Frosty Morn'

STONECROP This perennial's variegated white and gray-green fleshy foliage and flat-headed clusters of pale pink flowers in early fall add color to container displays. Plant it in gritty soil-based potting mix.

↕12in (30cm) ↔18in (45cm)

Z4–9

PERENNIAL SMALL

Sedum 'Ruby Glow'

STONECROP With spreading dark red stems topped with oval purplish green leaves and ruby-red star-shaped flowers from late summer to early fall, it makes a decorative edging to containers of gritty soil-based potting.

↕8in (20cm) ↔16in (40cm)

Z5–9

PERENNIAL SMALL

Senecio cineraria

DUSTY MILLER This evergreen perennial, grown as an annual, has decorative, deeply cut silver leaves and will survive through early frosts. Plant in containers of soil-based potting mix. In cold areas, overwinter the cuttings or repurchase in spring.

↕↔12in (30cm)

Z8–11

PERENNIAL SMALL

Viola x *wittrockiana*

PANSY This mainstay of cold-season containers is treated as an annual. Plant the colorful rounded flowers in fall and winter containers and baskets in all-purpose potting soil. It flowers best in winter in sheltered sites.

↕9in (23cm) ↔12in (30cm)

Z7–10

OTHER SUGGESTIONS

Annuals

Callistephus chinensis 'Milady Series' • *Chrysanthemum carinatum*

Perennials

Chrysanthemum 'Clara Curtis' • *Chrysanthemum* 'Yellow Quill' • *Farfugium japonicum* var. *giganteum* • *Helleborus foetidus* • *Helleborus niger* • *Sedum* AUTUMN JOY • *Viola* 'Antique Shades' • *Viola cornuta*

Bulbs

Cyclamen persicum • *Dahlia* 'Art Nouveau' • *Dahlia* 'Pablo' • *Nerine sarniensis*

Shrubs

Camellia sasanqua 'Kanjiro' • *Skimmia japonica*

Plants for winter beds

Days may be cold and dark, but with a selection of winter flowers, berries, stems, and leaves, gardens can continue to look stunning.

Evergreens are the mainstay of the winter garden, but the colorful stems of birch, bamboo, and twig dogwoods can upstage even the most dramatic conifer. Flowers are at a premium at this time of year, but this makes those that do face the cold all the more charismatic. Some plants, including Oregon grapeholly, sweet box, and witch hazel also offer scent into the bargain. Combine these beauties with the seedheads of summer flowers and grasses, and plants with dangling catkins, such as silk-tassel bush.

SHRUB MEDIUM

Abeliophyllum distichum

WHITE FORSYTHIA Plant this deciduous shrub in a sheltered spot where hard frosts will not damage the fragrant, star-shaped, pink-tinged white flowers, which appear on bare stems in late winter. The dark green leaves appear later in spring.
↕↔ 5ft (1.5m)

Z5–8

PERENNIAL SMALL

Ajuga reptans

BUGLEWEED The purple-leaved form of this aggressive evergreen ground-cover perennial forms mats of foliage interest in winter beds. It has blue spring-flower spikes. 'Atropurpurea' (above) has bronze-tinted leaves. Considered invasive in some areas.
↕ 6in (15cm) ↔ 3ft (1m)

Z3–9

PERENNIAL SMALL

Arum italicum

ITALIAN ARUM The dark green arrow-shaped fall leaves of this perennial persist in winter in mild areas and are joined by white or yellow petal-like spring spathes. 'Marmoratum' has cream-patterned leaves. May be invasive.
↕ 12in (30cm) ↔ 6in (15cm)

Z5–9

TREE LARGE

Betula utilis var. *jacquemontii*

HIMALAYAN BIRCH Brightening up winter beds with its white trunk and stems, this deciduous tree can be used to create small woodlands. The diamond-shaped, dark green leaves, which turn yellow in fall, unfurl in spring after yellow catkins appear.
↕ 60ft (18m) ↔ 30ft (10m)

Z4–7

PERENNIAL MEDIUM

Carex flagellifera

WEEPING BROWN SEDGE This evergreen sedge has tufts of reddish brown leaves and late summer spikes of light brown flowers, followed by red-brown seedheads. Plant it at the front of a border in free-draining soil in areas of hard frosts.
↕ 32in (80cm) ↔ 24in (60cm) or more

Z7–10

PERENNIAL MEDIUM

Carex 'Ice Dance'

SEDGE Plant this decorative evergreen, perennial sedge at the front of a sunny or part-shaded bed. It produces mounds of grasslike, creamy edged green leaves and small white flowers in spring. Plant in mass or in woodland garden.
↕ 24in (60cm) ↔ 30in (75cm)

Z5–9

SHRUB LARGE

Chimonanthus praecox

WINTERSWEET This large deciduous shrub produces simple, lance-shaped midgreen leaves. In winter, bowl-shaped, fragrant, many-petalled sulfur-yellow flowers appear. These are followed by cylindrical or urn-shaped seed capsules.
↕ 12ft (4m) ↔ 10ft (3m)

Z7–9

CLIMBER MEDIUM

Clematis cirrhosa

EARLY VIRGIN'S-BOWER Plant this evergreen climber with toothed, green leaves on a sheltered surface to protect its bell-shaped, red-spotted cream late winter to early spring flowers. Shade the roots. 'Freckles' has speckled, creamy pink flowers.
↕ 10ft (3m)

Z7–11

CLIMBER LARGE

Clematis tangutica

GOLDEN CLEMATIS The lantern-shaped yellow flowers of this vigorous deciduous clematis are followed by fluffy silvery seedheads that provide winter interest at the back of a bed. Cut stems to the ground in late winter; plant with the roots in shade.
↕ 20ft (6m)

Z4–9

SHRUB LARGE

Cornus alba

TATARIAN DOGWOOD Grow this deciduous shrub in a bed where its colorful display of bright red young shoots will be most effective. For the best color, cut down old stems in late winter to spur new growth, and plant in moist soil.
↕↔ 10ft (3m)

Z2–7

SHRUB LARGE

Cornus mas

CORNELIAN CHERRY Grow this deciduous shrub or small tree at the back of a bed, with its rounded clusters of tiny yellow blooms, where it will transform a drab late winter scene. Oval green leaves and edible red fruits follow.

↕↔15ft (5m)

Z4–8

SHRUB LARGE

Cornus sanguinea

BLOODTWIG DOGWOOD The foliage of this deciduous shrub, grown for its reddish green stems, shows good fall color. 'Midwinter Fire' has bright orange-yellow and red winter shoots. Prune old stems to the ground in late winter.

↕10ft (3m) ↔8ft (2.5m)

Z4–7

SHRUB MEDIUM

Cornus sericea

TWIG DOGWOOD This deciduous shrub is grown for its colorful red winter stems, yellow-green in varieties such as 'Flaviramea' (above). Cut old stems to the ground in late winter to encourage colorful new growth. It also has fiery fall leaves.

↕6ft (2m) ↔12ft (4m)

Z2–8 (N)

SHRUB SMALL

Cotoneaster horizontalis

ROCKSPRAY Best trained against a wall at the back of a narrow bed, this spreading, deciduous shrub produces stems in a "herringbone" pattern, which are dotted with red berries from fall to early winter, before they fall or are eaten by birds.

↕3ft (1m) ↔5ft (1.5m)

Z4–7

SHRUB LARGE

Daphne bholua

PAPER DAPHNE Ideal for the back of a bed, this evergreen shrub has oval, leathery green leaves and fragrant white late winter flowers, flushed purple-pink, followed by black berries. Best in West Coast gardens. 'Jacqueline Postill' (above) has pink flowers.

↕10ft (3m) ↔5ft (1.5m)

Z7–9

PERENNIAL MEDIUM

Dryopteris affinis

GOLDEN MALE FERN This evergreen fern's "shuttlecock" of tall, lance-shaped, divided, pale green fronds, which mature to dark green, make a decorative addition to winter beds beneath trees and shrubs. Cut off old growth in early spring.

↕↔3ft (1m)

Z5–8

SHRUB MEDIUM

Edgeworthia chrysantha

PAPER BUSH Given a sheltered site, this deciduous shrub will produce a beautiful display of fragrant, tubular yellow flowers covered in silky white hairs from late winter to early spring. The dark green oval leaves follow in spring.

↕↔5ft (1.5m)

Z8–10

SHRUB SMALL

Erica carnea

WINTER HEATH Plant this small evergreen shrub at the front of a bed or in a pot of acidic soil mix on a patio where it will add color from winter to spring with its needlelike dark green leaves and spikes of tiny pink, red, or white flowers.

↕12in (30cm) ↔18in (45cm) or more

pH Z5–7

BULB MEDIUM

Galanthus nivalis

SNOWDROP Allow this perennial bulb to spread through beds where its small, nodding white flowers, with green markings on some varieties, will appear among grassy gray-green leaves in late winter. Plant it in groups after flowering in spring.

↕6in (15cm)

Z3–8

SHRUB LARGE

Garrya elliptica

SILK-TASSEL BUSH This dense evergreen shrub has leathery, wavy-edged gray-green foliage and gray-green midwinter to early spring catkins. Plant it in a sheltered area against a wall or fence; prune when the catkins fade. Best in West Coast gardens.

↕↔12ft (4m)

Z8–11 (N)

SHRUB LARGE

Hamamelis x *intermedia*

WITCH HAZEL This vase-shaped shrub is grown for its lightly scented spidery flowers, which appear on bare stems from early- to midwinter. The broadly oval leaves appear later in spring. 'Jelena' (above) has large coppery orange flowers.

↕↔ 12ft (4m)

 Z5–8

PERENNIAL MEDIUM

Helleborus foetidus

STINKING HELLEBORE This evergreen perennial brightens up late winter beds with its cup-shaped, nodding pale green flowers with red margins held on red stems. The dark green leaves are comprised of narrow toothed leaflets.

↕↔ 24in (60cm)

Z6–9

PERENNIAL SMALL

Helleborus niger

CHRISTMAS ROSE This clump-forming semievergreen perennial has leathery leaflets and, from winter to early spring, cup-shaped, nodding white or pink-flushed flowers with a touch of green at the base of the tuft of stamens.

↕↔ 12in (30cm)

Z3–8

PERENNIAL SMALL

x *Heucherella* 'Tapestry'

FOAMY BELLS In sheltered areas, this evergreen perennial retains its deeply lobed green foliage with purple centers and veins. Ideal for edging beds or in containers, it forms sprays of small pink flowers in early summer.

↕↔ 12in (30cm)

Z4–9

SHRUB LARGE

Hydrangea paniculata

PANICLE HYDRANGEA The faded conical clusters of white or pink flower heads form dried bronze sculptural features on skeletal stems and provide winter interest after the dark green leaves have fallen. Considered invasive in some areas of the Northeast.

↕↔ 10ft (3m)

Z3–8

TREE LARGE

Ilex aquifolium

ENGLISH HOLLY An iconic winter evergreen shrub, or tree, with wavy-edged, spiny dark green leaves and, on pollinated female plants, scarlet berries. Variegated cultivars provide additional cold-season color. Plant at the back of a bed. Considered invasive.

↕ up to 70ft (20m) ↔ 20ft (6m)

Z7–9

SHRUB LARGE

Jasminum nudiflorum

WINTER JASMINE This arching deciduous shrub has oval, dark green leaves followed by starry bright yellow flowers on bare green shoots from winter to early spring. Use as a backdrop to a bed by training the stems against a wall or fence.

↕↔ 10ft (3m)

Z6–10

SHRUB MEDIUM

Leucothoe fontanesiana

DROOPING LEUCOTHOE Decorate a winter garden with this mid- to back-of-bed evergreen shrub with arching red-tinged stems, green leaves, and cream bell-shaped spring flowers. 'Scarletta' (above) has bronze-tinted winter leaves.

↕ up to 5ft (1.5m) ↔ 6ft (2m)

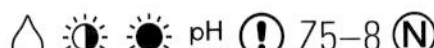 Z5–8 N

SHRUB SMALL

Mahonia aquifolium

OREGON GRAPEHOLLY An evergreen shrub with leathery, spine-edged dark green leaves that turn purplish in winter and provide interest before dense yellow flower clusters appear in spring. Round black berries follow. It will thrive in a shady bed.

↕ 3ft (1m) ↔ 5ft (1.5m)

Z5–8 N

SHRUB MEDIUM

Mahonia japonica

JAPANESE MAHONIA The leathery, spine-edged dark green leaves of this evergreen shrub add color to winter borders when they become tinted with purple. Dense clusters of fragrant yellow flowers open through winter followed by black berries.

↕ 6ft (2m) ↔ 10ft (3m)

Z6–9

PERENNIAL MEDIUM

Ophiopogon jaburan

WHITE TURFLILY Use this evergreen perennial in a sheltered winter bed to create an edge of grasslike dark green leaves. Violet-blue fruits follow white bell-shaped flowers summer flowers. 'Vittatus' (above) is cream- and green-striped.

↕ 24in (60cm) ↔ 12in (30cm)

Z7–10

PERENNIAL MEDIUM

Panicum virgatum

SWITCH GRASS An upright deciduous grass that forms clumps of blue-green leaves, which turn yellow in fall. Clouds of pink-tinged green summer flower heads, held on tall stems, fade to beige in fall and persist through winter.

↕3ft (1m) ↔30in (75cm)

Z5–9 Ⓝ

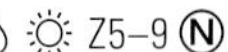

BAMBOO LARGE

Phyllostachys aureosulcata f. *aureocaulis*

GOLDEN GROOVE BAMBOO Use this clump-forming stately bamboo with tall yellow canes, sometimes crooked at the base, as a screen or focal point in a winter bed. Consider using root barriers in small areas.

↕20ft (6m) ↔indefinite

Z5–10

SHRUB LARGE

Pittosporum tenuifolium

KOHUHU This large evergreen shrub produces wavy-edged gray-green leaves that are held on dark stems. Plant it at the back of a sheltered bed to inject winter color. Varieties include 'Marjorie Channon', which is a variegated form.

↕30ft (10m) ↔15ft (5m)

Z8–11

SHRUB LARGE

Pyracantha 'Mohave'

FIRETHORN Train this scab-resistant evergreen shrub against a wall or fence at the back of a winter bed, where its prickly stems of glossy dark green foliage provide a foil for plants in front, and the orange-red berries lend color early in the season.

↕↔12ft (4m)

Z6–9

SHRUB MEDIUM

Rubus cockburnianus

GHOST BRAMBLE The arching prickly shoots of this dense deciduous shrub color brilliant white in winter, creating a ghostly effect in cold-season borders. Dark green diamond-shaped foliage appears in spring. Inedible black fruits follow purple summer blooms.

↕↔8ft (2.5m)

Z5–8

SHRUB MEDIUM

Sarcococca hookeriana var. *digyna*

SWEET BOX Grow this evergreen shrub in a winter bed to enjoy the fragrance of its tiny white flowers, which appear among narrow, lance-shaped green leaves. Spherical black fruits follow the blooms.

↕5ft (1.5m) ↔6ft (2m)

Z6–9

SHRUB LARGE

Stachyurus praecox

STACHYURUS Clusters of pale greenish yellow bell-shaped flowers of this deciduous shrub hang from bare stems from late winter to early spring, creating a focal point at the back of a bed filled with winter foliage. Dark green leaves unfurl later in spring.

↕12ft (4m) ↔10ft (3m)

pH Z6–8

PERENNIAL MEDIUM

Stipa calamagrostis

syn. *Achnatherum calamagrostis*
Feather grass forms semievergreen or deciduous tufts of long blue-green leaves in summer, which turn vibrant yellow in fall. It bears tall feathery flower heads in summer, which provide interest well into winter.

↕↔32in (80cm)

Z6–9

SHRUB LARGE

Viburnum x *bodnantense*

BODNANT VIBURNUM This deciduous shrub has richly fragrant pink or white late fall to early spring-flower clusters on bare stems. A good back-of-bed plant, grow it with evergreens in a winter border. 'Dawn' (above) has deep pink buds and pink flowers.

↕10ft (3m) ↔6ft (2m)

Z5–8

SHRUB LARGE

Viburnum farreri

FRAGRANT VIBURNUM Plant this deciduous shrub at the back of a bed close to a south-facing wall and it will reward you with fragrant white or pale pink flowers on bare stems throughout winter. The dark green foliage is bronze when it appears in spring.

↕10ft (3m) ↔8ft (2.5m)

Z5–8

OTHER SUGGESTIONS

Perennials

Ajuga reptans 'Burgundy Glow' • *Sedum* AUTUMN JOY • *Schizachyrium scoparium* Ⓝ • *Senna marilandica* Ⓝ • *Sorghastrum nutans* Ⓝ

Bamboo

Phyllostachys nigra

Shrubs

Cornus mas 'Golden Glory' • *Cornus stolonifera* ARCTIC FIRE Ⓝ • *Erica carnea* 'Ann Sparkes' • *Erica erigena* 'Irish Dusk' • *Fallugia paradoxa* Ⓝ • *Hamamelis* x *intermedia* 'Barmstedt Gold' • *Hamamelis vernalis* Ⓝ • *Ilex verticillata* 'Afterglow' Ⓝ • *Juniperus horizontalis* 'Mother Lode' Ⓝ • *Mitchella repens* Ⓝ

Trees

Ilex opaca Ⓝ • *Betula nigra* HERITAGE Ⓝ

Plants for evergreen effects

Providing a permanent stage for seasonal stars, evergreens have special value in small gardens, and help create continuity during lulls.

Although many are quiet and unassuming, in combination, evergreens with contrasting textures, shapes, and colors can make beautiful displays of their own. For example, large, handlike fatsia leaves, variegated holly foliage, and feathery ferns make an elegant combination for a shady garden. When creating a new planting scheme, place your evergreens first to provide a permanent framework for your design. Also check heights and spreads to ensure that they do not block seasonal plants and flowers or, if they are small and compact like hebe, that adjacent perennials won't swamp them in summer.

TREE SMALL

Abies nordmanniana 'Golden Spreader'

NORDMANN FIR Brighten up borders with this slow-growing conifer that has spreading branches of golden-yellow needlelike leaves. For year-round color, combine it with dark green- and blue-green-leaved evergreens.

↕3ft (1m) ↔5ft (1.5m)

pH Z4–6

SHRUB LARGE

Arbutus unedo

STRAWBERRY TREE Plant this evergreen shrub in a sheltered garden in fertile soil for the best foliage effects through the year. It has dark green leathery leaves and white urn-shaped flowers that appear in fall alongside red, strawberry-like fruits.

↕↔25ft (8m)

pH Z7–9

SHRUB SMALL

Arctostaphylos uva-ursi

BEARBERRY Grow this small low-growing evergreen shrub at the front of a bed in acidic soil. The oval dark green leaves, pink-tinted white summer flowers, and round scarlet fall fruits provide year-round interest.

↕4in (10cm) ↔20in (50cm)

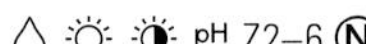

pH Z2–6 Ⓝ

PERENNIAL SMALL

Bergenia purpurascens

PURPLE BERGENIA This clump-forming, evergreen perennial has large, rounded, glossy green leaves and, in spring, spikes of dark pink blooms. Plant near the front of a bed, and remove tired or damaged leaves to keep it tidy.

↕16in (40cm) ↔24in (60cm) or more

Z3–8

PERENNIAL MEDIUM

Blechnum spicant

DEER FERN Perfect for evergreen color and texture, this fern forms low arching hummocks of divided, stiff leathery leaves, with narrow leaflets, and thrives in deep shade. The upright spore-bearing fronds resemble fish bones.

↕30in (75cm) ↔18in (45cm)

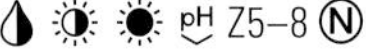

pH Z5–8 Ⓝ

SHRUB MEDIUM

Buxus sempervirens 'Elegantissima'

COMMON BOXWOOD A compact evergreen shrub with oval white-margined green leaves ideal for low hedges, topiary shapes, or dots of color in a bed. Clip topiary and hedges in early- and late summer.

↕↔5ft (1.5m)

! Z6–8

SHRUB SMALL

Calluna vulgaris

SCOTCH HEATHER The tiny gray, yellow, or bright green leaves of this bushy evergreen shrub liven up bed edges given acidic soil and full sun. From midsummer to late fall, pink, white, and purple bell-shaped flowers appear. Survives cold with protection.

↕12in (30cm) ↔14in (35cm)

pH Z4–6

TREE MEDIUM

Chamaecyparis pisifera 'Filifera Aurea'

SAWARA CYPRESS Use this slow-growing evergreen conifer as a colorful textured specimen with blue-leaved conifers in a mixed display. It makes a mound of weeping stems with golden-yellow scaly leaves.

↕40ft (12m) ↔15ft (5m)

Z4–8

SHRUB SMALL

Cryptomeria japonica 'Globosa Nana'

JAPANESE CEDAR Thriving in a sheltered spot, this rounded evergreen conifer's rich green foliage gives year-round interest in a border or gravel bed. Short, cordlike arching stems carry the scalelike leaves.
↕↔3ft (1m)

 Z6–9

SHRUB LARGE

Erica arborea

TREE HEATH This upright evergreen shrub has dark green needlelike leaves that lend year-round color. In spring, it bears pyramid-shaped clusters of bell-shaped, honey-scented grayish white flowers.
↕20ft (6m) ↔10ft 3m)

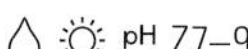 Z7–9

BAMBOO LARGE

Fargesia murielae

UMBRELLA BAMBOO This large clump-forming evergreen bamboo bears arching yellow-green canes and lance-shaped, bright green leaves. It makes a decorative year-round screen or accent plant in a border or gravel bed. Best in fertile soil.
↕12ft (4m) ↔indefinite

 Z5–9

SHRUB MEDIUM

Daphne odora

FRAGRANT DAPHNE A rounded evergreen shrub, grown for its glossy dark green leaves and clusters of richly scented, carmine-edged white winter to early spring flowers. 'Aureomarginata' (above) has yellow-edged foliage.
↕↔5ft (1.5m)

Z7–9

PERENNIAL MEDIUM

Dryopteris affinis

GOLDEN MALE FERN Evergreen in sheltered sites, this fern produces a "shuttlecock" of tall, divided, pale green lance-shaped fronds, which mature to dark green, with scaly, golden-brown midribs. Use it to decorate partly shaded beds.
↕↔3ft (1m)

Z5–8

SHRUB LARGE

Fatsia japonica

JAPANESE FATSIA The large, deeply lobed evergreen leaves of this shrub inject color and texture into containers and beds, and the round clusters of tiny white fall flowers and black fruits add to the effect. 'Variegata' has white-edged leaves.
↕↔12ft (4m)

Z8–10

SHRUB SMALL

Gaultheria mucronata

CHILEAN PERNETTYA This evergreen shrub has dark green prickly leaves that create a year-round backdrop to flowers in a border. Its tiny white late spring flowers are followed by white to purple-red berries on female plants. Best in West Coast gardens.
↕↔4ft (1.2m)

Z7–9

SHRUB SMALL

Hebe 'Red Edge'

HEBE The blue-green red-edged leaves of this compact evergreen shrub lend year-round interest to a sunny sheltered site. Clusters of pale mauve to white flowers add a colorful note in summer. Trim lightly after flowering, if necessary.
↕18in (45cm) ↔24in (60cm)

 Z9–10

PERENNIAL MEDIUM

Helleborus argutifolius

CORSICAN HELLEBORE Grown for its large, spiny-edged dark green leaves, this evergreen architectural perennial has long-lasting clusters of nodding, pale green bowl-shaped blooms from late winter to spring. Remove old foliage in winter.
↕24in (60cm) ↔18in (45cm)

Z6–9

PERENNIAL SMALL

x *Heucherella* 'Tapestry'

FOAMY BELLS This perennial, evergreen in sheltered sites, produces a carpet of deeply lobed green foliage, with purple centers and veins. It is ideal for edging beds or in containers. In early summer, sprays of small pink flowers form on upright stems.
↕↔12in (30cm)

Z4–9

Plants for evergreen effects

SHRUB SMALL

Hypericum calycinum

AARON'S BEARD This vigorous evergreen shrub makes good ground cover. Its dark green foliage provides year-round color. Large, open bright yellow flowers with fluffy stamens in the center appear from midsummer to mid-fall.

↕24in (60cm) ↔indefinite

 Z5–9

SHRUB MEDIUM

Leucothoe fontanesiana

DROOPING LEUCOTHOE This evergreen shrub has arching red-tinged stems, lance-shaped green leaves, red-tinted or mottled in some varieties, and cream spring flowers. 'Rainbow' (above) has mottled cream- and pink-variegated leaves.

↕up to 5ft (1.5m) ↔6ft (2m)

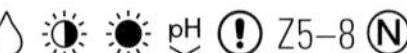 Z5–8 Ⓝ

PERENNIAL MEDIUM

Luzula nivea

SNOWY WOODRUSH This evergreen perennial forms loose clumps of dark green grasslike leaves, ideal for edging a bed. From early- to midsummer, tight clusters of tiny white flowers appear on slim stems. Try it in a shady spot in a wildlife garden.

↕↔24in (60cm)

Z4–9

TREE LARGE

Magnolia grandiflora

SOUTHERN MAGNOLIA This evergreen tree produces a rounded head of large, glossy dark green leaves and large, white fragrant midsummer to early fall flowers. It makes an eye-catching focal point in a sheltered garden or beside a south-facing wall.

↕60ft (18m) ↔50ft (15m)

 Z7–9 Ⓝ

SHRUB SMALL

Mitchella repens

PARTRIDGEBERRY This evergreen subshrub, with trailing stems of small, oval white-striped green leaves, is ideal for draping over the side of a raised bed. In early summer, tiny, white fragrant flowers appear, followed by red berries.

↕2in (5cm) ↔indefinite

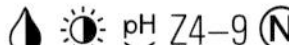 Z4–9 Ⓝ

SHRUB MEDIUM

Mahonia x *media*

MAHONIA An evergreen architectural shrub with long dark green leaves divided into paired spiny leaflets. Throughout winter, long clusters of scented yellow flowers appear. 'Buckland' has longer flower spikes and red-tinted winter leaves.

↕6ft (1.8m) ↔12ft (4m)

Z7–9

SHRUB SMALL

Microbiota decussata

RUSSIAN ARBORVITAE Use this low-growing evergreen coniferous shrub, with its sprays of tiny, scalelike bright green leaves, bronze-purple in winter, as a foil for shrubs with colorful foliage and flowers. The flowers and cones are inconspicuous.

↕3ft (1m) ↔indefinite

Z3–7

PERENNIAL SMALL

Ophiopogon planiscapus 'Nigrescens'

MONDO GRASS Perfect for bed edging or pots, this grasslike member of the lily family has shiny black foliage that contrasts well with bright gravel. Black fall berries follow the clusters of purple-pink summer blooms.

↕9in (23cm) ↔12in (30cm)

Z6–10

SHRUB LARGE

Osmanthus heterophyllus

FALSE HOLLY The glossy, bright green hollylike leaves of this evergreen shrub make a decorative feature or screen in sheltered gardens. It produces tiny, white fragrant flowers in fall. 'Aureomarginatus' (above) has gold-edged leaves.

↕↔15ft (5m)

Z7–9

PERENNIAL LARGE

Phormium tenax

NEW ZEALAND FLAX A clump-forming evergreen perennial with long, upright, then arching, sword-shaped gray-green leaves that create a dramatic effect at the back of a bed. Dark red or yellow flowers may form on tall stems during hot summers.

↕10ft (3m) ↔6ft (2m)

SHRUB LARGE

Pinus mugo

MUGO PINE This compact conifer forms a mound of needlelike evergreen foliage and makes a good foil for spring bulbs, perennials, and small shrubs. Select a dwarf form like 'Mops' (above) for pots and containers.

↕12ft (4m) ↔15ft (5m)

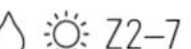 Z2–7

TREE LARGE

Picea breweriana

BREWER'S SPRUCE Make a year-round statement in a large garden with this cone-shaped evergreen conifer. Its drooping stems, covered with dark gray-green needles, create curtains of color. Grow in neutral to acidic soil in a sheltered site.

↕50ft (15m) ↔12ft (4m)

 Z5–6 Ⓝ

SHRUB LARGE

Pittosporum tenuifolium

KOHUHU The wavy-edged gray-green leaves of this evergreen shrub create a year-round textured effect in sheltered sites. Use as a backdrop to a sunny border. Select variegated forms, such as 'Marjorie Channon', for additional interest.

↕30ft (10m) ↔15ft (5m)

Z8–11

SHRUB LARGE

Pyracantha 'Mohave'

FIRETHORN Ideal for training against a wall or fence, the dark green leaves of this scab-resistant evergreen shrub provide a foil for plants growing in front. Its orange-red late summer berries persist into winter and are attractive to birds.

↕↔12ft (4m)

 Z6–9

SHRUB SMALL

Picea pungens 'Montgomery'

COLORADO SPRUCE This compact, mound-forming, slow-growing evergreen conifer, with needlelike gray-blue leaves, lends a splash of year-round color to a gravel bed or rock garden. Plant with contrasting green foliage plants. Needs neutral to acidic soil.

↕↔24in (60cm)

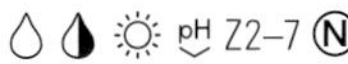 Z2–7 Ⓝ

SHRUB MEDIUM

Rosmarinus officinalis

ROSEMARY Given a sheltered site, this culinary, evergreen shrubby herb retains its aromatic, needlelike, dark green foliage year-round. Do not harvest the leaves in winter. Small blue flowers appear in spring. Cut back old growth in early summer.

↕↔5ft (1.5m)

Z8–10

SHRUB LARGE

Pieris japonica

LILY OF THE VALLEY BUSH This evergreen shrub has dark green leathery leaves, bright red when young, and clusters of urn-shaped white, pink, or red spring flowers. Grow it in a sunny site. 'Flamingo' (above) has dark red buds that open to a deep pink.

↕12ft (4m) ↔10ft (3m)

Z5–8

SHRUB LARGE

Pittosporum tobira

JAPANESE PITTOSPORUM Plant this evergreen shrub with decorative capsules in a sheltered site where it will produce a neat dome of long, oval, dark green leaves. Clusters of fragrant, starry, white flowers, aging to creamy yellow, add to the effect.

↕30ft (10m) ↔10ft (3m)

Z8–10

OTHER SUGGESTIONS

Perennials

Bergenia 'Bressingham Ruby' • *Bergenia* 'Winter Glow' • *Carex stricta* Ⓝ • *Dryopteris erythrosora* • *Helleborus argutifolius* 'Silver Lace' • *Opuntia compressa* Ⓝ • *Polystichum acrostichoides* Ⓝ • *Polystichum setiferum* Divisilobum Group

Shrubs and trees

Buxus CHICAGOLAND GREEN • *Chamaecyparis pisifera* 'Filifera Aurea' • *Choisya* x *dewitteana* 'Aztec Pearl' • *Erica vulgaris* 'Boeley Gold' • *Gardenia jasminoides* • *Juniperus virginiana* 'Grey Owl' Ⓝ • *Ilex opaca* 'Greenleaf' Ⓝ • *Illicium parviflorum* Ⓝ • *Mahonia aquifolium* 'Compacta' Ⓝ • *Morella cerifera* Ⓝ • *Podocarpus alpinus* 'Blue Gem' • *Pinus strobus* 'UConn' Ⓝ • *Sciadopitys verticillata* • *Skimmia japonica*

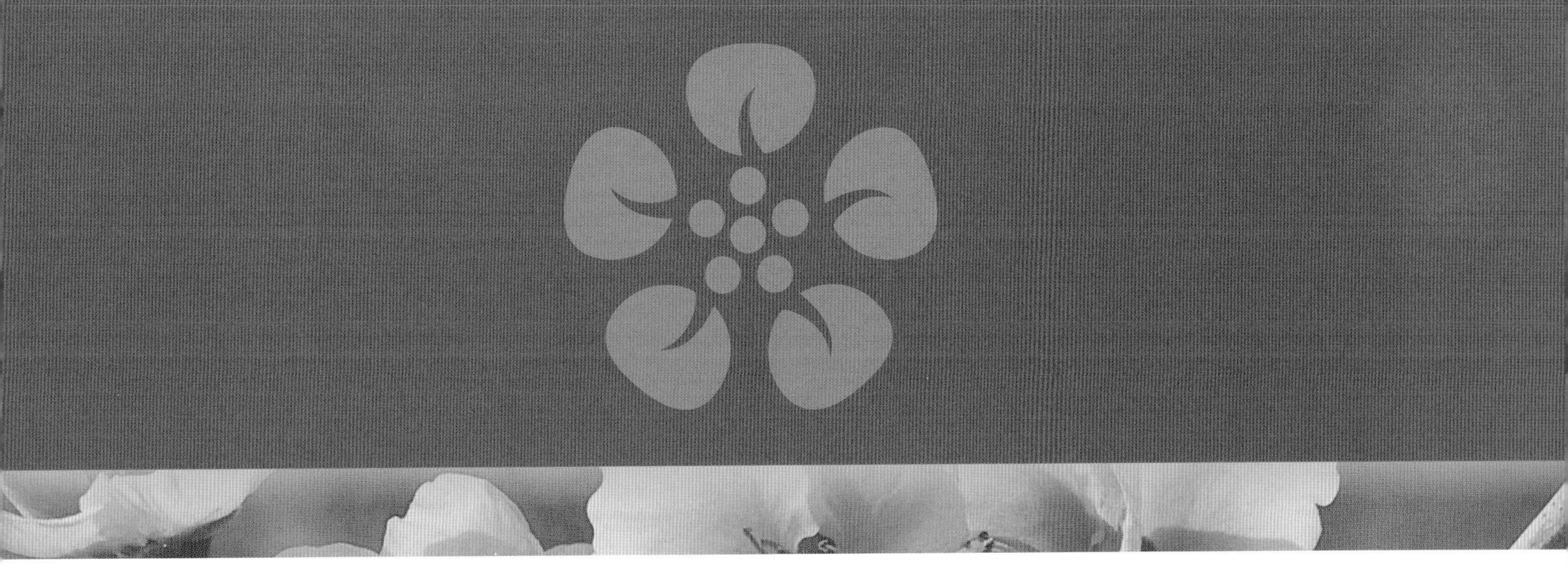

PLANTS for COLOR and SCENT

Scent and color affect our moods and perceptions and they can be used to great effect in the garden. Try planting lavenders close to seating, where the fragrance will help soothe frayed nerves, or use pastel colors, which produce a similar calming effect. Conversely, bright reds and oranges are stimulants, and help to energize planting schemes, as well as acting as focal points. You can also mimic wider landscapes, where colors pale as they extend toward the horizon, giving an illusion of distance.

Plants for cool colors

Ever since Vita Sackville West created her famous white garden in the 1930s, designers have raved about the beauty of monochrome planting schemes.

To achieve a similar effect, plant a succession of white flowers, starting in spring with hellebores and snowdrops, peaking in summer with peonies, roses, and shasta daisies, and concluding in fall with asters and Japanese anemones. If you find an all-white scheme too restrictive, include a few blues, which will blend well without jarring the overall effect. You can also create a cool, neutral backdrop for pastel or brightly colored flowers with blue and gray foliage, or use silver-leaved plants, such as wormwood, dusty miller, and lamb's ears, to reflect the sun and twinkle from beds like spotlights.

TREE LARGE

Abies concolor

WHITE FIR An evergreen conifer with an attractive "Christmas tree" shape. It makes a good lawn specimen and can be a feature in a mixed boundary scheme. The silver-gray needles are its main feature. Prune carefully, if required.

↕130ft (40m) ↔22ft (7m)

Z3–7 Ⓝ

PERENNIAL MEDIUM

Aconitum 'Stainless Steel'

MONKSHOOD This perennial makes a substantial clump of deeply divided leaves. Its mid- to late summer spires of unusual hooded silvery blue blooms create an elegant impression within a shaded bed. All parts are poisonous.

↕3ft (1m) ↔24in (60cm)

Z4–8

PERENNIAL MEDIUM

Agapanthus africanus

AFRICAN LILY This evergreen perennial has strap-shaped leaves and spherical heads of deep blue trumpet-shaped flowers on sturdy unbranched stems during summer. Suitable for mixed or single plantings. Provide protection from cold temperatures.

↕3ft (1m) ↔20in (50cm)

Z8–10

PERENNIAL LARGE

Anemone x *hybrida*

JAPANESE ANEMONE This upright, slowly spreading, clump-forming perennial has lobed leaves. With its spherical buds and pink or white, saucer-shaped single or semidouble blooms, it makes a lovely feature in late summer beds.

↕4ft (1.2m) ↔24in (60cm)

Z4–8

PERENNIAL SMALL

Anthemis punctata subsp. *cupaniana*

SICILIAN CHAMOMILE This carpeting evergreen perennial has filigree silver foliage that turns green in winter. It bears a mass of yellow-centered white daisies with a single bloom on each short stem in early summer.

↕↔12in (30cm)

Z6–9

PERENNIAL MEDIUM

Aquilegia vulgaris

COLUMBINE This upright clump-forming perennial has ferny foliage. From late spring to early summer, it bears nodding flowers with spurred petals in mainly pastel shades in violet, blue, and pink, as well as white.

↕3ft (1m) ↔18in (45cm)

Z3–8

PERENNIAL MEDIUM

Artemisia ludoviciana 'Silver Queen'

WESTERN MUGWORT Grown as a foil for flowers, this spreading perennial has narrow silver-gray leaves on upright stems. Remove the small yellow summer blooms to maintain the foliage effect. May spread aggressively.

↕↔30in (75cm)

Z4–9 Ⓝ

SHRUB SMALL

Artemisia 'Powis Castle'

WORMWOOD A semievergreen subshrub with fernlike silvery gray leaves that provide a foil for green-leaved plants, including roses and sun-loving border perennials. Snip off the yellow pompomlike flowers to enhance the effect.

↕↔3ft (1m)

Z7–9

PERENNIAL MEDIUM

Aster ericoides

Renamed *Symphyotrichum ericoides* Plant this clump-forming heath aster mid-bed with small-leaved fall-interest plants. Sprays of tiny white daisies are borne for weeks and make an excellent foil for larger, more solid blooms and leaves.

↕3ft (1m) ↔12in (30cm)

Z5–8 Ⓝ

PERENNIAL SMALL

Athyrium niponicum var. *pictum*

JAPANESE PAINTED FERN This deciduous fern produces deeply divided gray-green leaves with metallic purple and silver highlights. Use it between blocks of green foliage in shady beds.

↕12in (30cm) ↔indefinite

 Z4–8

SHRUB SMALL

Ballota pseudodictamnus

GRECIAN HOREHOUND This compact, low-growing evergreen shrub has vertical stems with evenly spaced pairs of small, round gray-green leaves that are covered with woolly white hairs. Trim over after the whorls of tiny pink blooms fade.

↕24in (60cm) ↔3ft (1m)

Z7–9

PERENNIAL SMALL

Bergenia SILVERLIGHT

PIGSQUEAK A compact, clump-forming evergreen perennial, with leathery round leaves and white bell-shaped spring flowers held on red-tinged stems. The blooms, which sometimes become pink tinged, have contrasting deep red bud cases.

↕18in (45cm) ↔20in (50cm)

Z3–8

PERENNIAL SMALL

Brunnera macrophylla

SIBERIAN BUGLOSS A ground-cover perennial, it is useful for adding sparkle under trees or in a shady urban setting. It has broad oval to heart-shaped leaves, often overlaid or edged with white. Sprays of blue flowers appear in spring.

↕18in (45cm) ↔24in (60cm)

Z3–8

PERENNIAL SMALL

Calamintha nepeta

LESSER CALAMINT Grown for its upright spikes of tiny lilac-pink flowers, which appear from late summer to early fall, this perennial also bears herbal-scented green leaves. Plant near a path where it can be brushed against to release the aroma.

↕18in (45cm) ↔30in (75cm)

Z5–9

PERENNIAL SMALL

Campanula carpatica

CARPATHIAN HAREBELL This low-growing perennial forms a dense mat of heart-shaped leaves. Throughout summer, it is smothered in violet-blue or white bell-shaped flowers. Use it as ground cover or to fill gaps in walls and paving.

↕4in (10cm) ↔12in (30cm)

Z4–7

BULB LARGE

Cardiocrinum giganteum

GIANT LILY This giant perennial bulb has heart-shaped leaves. In summer, fragrant, trumpet-shaped white blooms with purple throats open at the top of sturdy unbranched stems. Plant it in a sheltered site and rich soil.

↕↔10ft (3m)

 Z7–9

SHRUB SMALL

Caryopteris incana

COMMON BLUEBEARD This domed shrub has slender stems that bear gray-green, aromatic toothed-edged leaves. In early fall, tiny blue flowers form in dense clusters in the leaf axils. It is attractive to bees and butterflies.

↕4ft (1.2m) ↔5ft (1.5m)

Z6–9

SHRUB MEDIUM

Ceanothus americanus

NEW JERSEY TEA This is a dense, rounded deciduous shrub that can tolerate drought but needs a sheltered site. From late spring to midsummer, it produces thimble-shaped heads of tiny fragrant white flowers that attract butterflies.

↕↔up to 6ft (2m)

Z4–8 Ⓝ

SHRUB MEDIUM

Ceanothus x *delileanus* 'Gloire de Versailles'

CALIFORNIA LILAC A bushy deciduous shrub with oval leaves and clusters of tiny, fragrant powder-blue flowers in loose thimble-shaped heads from summer to fall. Makes a foil for roses. Best in West Coast gardens.

↕↔5ft (1.5m)

Z7–10 Ⓝ

SHRUB SMALL

Convolvulus cneorum

SILVERBUSH This low, spreading evergreen shrub, which can be grown as an annual, has narrow, oblong metallic silver leaves. In summer, funnel-shaped white flowers open from pink buds. Grow at the front of a sheltered bed or in gravel.

↕24in (60cm) ↔3ft (1m)

Z8–11

TREE LARGE

Cedrus atlantica Glauca Group

BLUE ATLAS CEDAR This evergreen conifer makes a conical-shaped tree when young, and a broad crown when mature. It bears striking silvery blue-green needles. Plant it as a lawn specimen in a large garden.

↕130ft (40m) ↔30ft (10m)

Z6–9

BULB LARGE

Crinum x *powellii* 'Album'

POWELL LILY This richly fragrant perennial bulb has broad, arching strap-shaped leaves. From late summer to fall, it produces large, funnel-shaped white blooms on sturdy stems. It needs protection in winter in cold regions.

↕3ft (1m)

Z7–10

PERENNIAL LARGE

Delphinium elatum

LARKSPUR This tall perennial has deeply divided green leaves and is famous for its striking columns of midsummer flowers. Pale blue or white varieties provide a cooling contrast for hot shades. The stems need sturdy stakes.

↕6ft (2m) ↔3ft (1m)

Z3–7

PERENNIAL SMALL

Centaurea montana

PERENNIAL CORNFLOWER This vigorous self-seeding perennial has tapered leaves with hairy undersides. In early summer, it produces open, thistlelike purple, white, blue, or pink flower heads with red-purple centers. Cut back to promote reflowering.

↕20in (50cm) ↔24in (60cm)

Z3–8

SHRUB MEDIUM

Deutzia x *magnifica*

TALL DEUTZIA This early summer-flowering deciduous shrub makes a lovely arching specimen or back-of-bed feature. Small oval leaves appear along slender branched stems and snowy double flowers open in profusion in spring.

↕8ft (2.5m) ↔6ft (2m)

Z5–8

PERENNIAL MEDIUM

Echinacea purpurea 'White Swan'

CONEFLOWER This perennial has a neat upright habit and oval leaves. From summer to fall, it produces large, daisy-like blooms with white drooping petals surrounding prominent gingery brown cones.

↕24in (60cm) ↔18in (45cm)

Z3–8 Ⓝ

PERENNIAL LARGE

Eryngium giganteum

SEA HOLLY This short-lived self-seeding perennial produces a basal clump of marbled, heart-shaped gray-green leaves. Tall upright stems hold the conelike silvery blue summer flowers, which are surrounded by silver leaflike bracts.

↕3ft (1m) ↔12in (30cm)

Z4–8

TREE LARGE

Eucalyptus gunnii

CIDER GUM This slender evergreen tree has rounded, aromatic blue-gray young foliage, which, as the tree matures, gives way to sickle-shaped leathery leaves. Cut it back periodically to produce more young growth and colorful foliage.

↕up to 80ft (25m) ↔50ft (15m)

Z8–10

TREE MEDIUM

Eucryphia glutinosa

NIRRHE This upright deciduous or semievergreen tree or shrub has green foliage divided into glossy toothed-edged leaflets. In summer, white, bowl-shaped single or double blooms with a central tuft of stamens appear.

↕30ft (10m) ↔20ft (6m)

 Z8–11

PERENNIAL LARGE

Euphorbia characias subsp. *wulfenii*

MEDITERRANEAN SPURGE This evergreen perennial has multiple upright stems with whorls of slender gray to blue-green leaves. Long-lasting yellow-green flower heads appear in second spring. Sap is an irritant.

↕↔4ft (1.2m)

Z7–10

PERENNIAL SMALL

Euphorbia myrsinites

MYRTLE SPURGE This ground-hugging evergreen perennial has woody stems clothed in scalelike, fleshy gray leaves. Stems are tipped with vivid yellow-green flower heads in spring. Remove the spent blooms. The sap can cause skin irritation.

↕3in (8cm) ↔8in (20cm)

Z5–9

SHRUB MEDIUM

Exochorda x *macrantha*

PEARLBUSH This deciduous shrub makes a mound of dense stems covered with small dark green leaves that develop bold fall tints. From late spring to early summer, small, saucer-shaped white blooms smother the arching branches.

↕6ft (2m) ↔10ft (3m)

Z5–8

PERENNIAL SMALL

Festuca glauca

BLUE FESCUE This evergreen grass is commonly grown for its arching tufts of fine steel-blue threadlike leaves. Short flower spikes appear in summer, but are best removed to maintain the plant's uniform shape and color.

↕↔20in (50cm)

Z4–8

BULB MEDIUM

Galanthus 'Sam Arnott'

SNOWDROP This perennial bulb produces gray-green grasslike leaves. In late winter, small, fragrant, nodding white flowers with green "V" marks on the inner segments appear. It looks effective when planted in natural drifts.

↕6in (15cm) ↔3in (8cm)

Z4–8

PERENNIAL MEDIUM

Geranium clarkei 'Kashmir White'

CRANESBILL This spreading perennial has elegantly divided leaves and saucer-shaped white late summer blooms with pink nectar guides on the petals. Use it to underplant roses or at the front of a bed.

↕↔24in (60cm)

Z5–8

PERENNIAL MEDIUM

Helictotrichon sempervirens

BLUE OAT GRASS This evergreen perennial grass produces long silvery blue leaves that form an airy mound. Light blue flowers with long-lasting straw-colored seedheads appear from early- to midsummer on arching stems.

↕3ft (1m) ↔24in (60cm)

Z4–8

PERENNIAL SMALL

Helleborus foetidus

STINKING HELLEBORE An evergreen perennial with handsome dark green leaves divided into toothed leaflets. From late winter to early spring, clusters of cup-shaped pale green flowers with red-edged petals appear.

↕↔24in (60cm)

Z6–9

PERENNIAL SMALL

Helleborus niger

CHRISTMAS ROSE Perfect for winter gardens, this semievergreen perennial forms clumps of lobed dark green leaves. Saucer-shaped white blooms that age to pink appear from winter to early spring. 'Potter's Wheel' (above) has pure white blooms.

↕↔12in (30cm)

Z3–8

SHRUB MEDIUM

Hydrangea arborescens

SMOOTH HYDRANGEA This rounded shrub bears oval midgreen leaves and, in midsummer, dome-shaped flattened clusters of long-lasting blooms that open from lime-green buds and age to creamy white, and produce papery winter skeletons.

↕↔5ft (1.5m)

Z4–9 Ⓝ

SHRUB MEDIUM

Hydrangea macrophylla

LACECAP HYDRANGEA This broad-leaved shrub bears flat heads of tiny blue flowers surrounded by petal-like florets from midsummer to early fall. Varieties within the species may bear white, purple, pink, or blue flowers depending on soil pH.

↕6ft (2m) ↔8ft (2.5m)

 Z6–9

PERENNIAL MEDIUM

Iris confusa

BAMBOO IRIS This spreading evergreen perennial produces tufts of strap-shaped leaves on upright stems. In mid-spring, white or pale blue flowers with yellow- or purple-speckled yellow crests appear on branched stems.

↕3ft (1m) ↔indefinite

Z7–10

PERENNIAL LARGE

Iris sibirica

SIBERIAN IRIS A vertical clump-forming perennial with broad grasslike leaves and blue, purple, or white blooms that open from tapered buds from early- to midsummer. The base of the lower petals is blotched and streaked.

↕up to 4ft (1.2m) ↔20in (50cm)

 Z3–8

SHRUB SMALL

Lavandula 'Willow Vale'

SPANISH LAVENDER A compact evergreen subshrub with narrow, aromatic gray-green leaves. From early- to midsummer, upright stems bear short spikes of dark flowers that are topped with tufts of showy, violet-purple wavy bracts.

↕↔28in (70cm)

Z8–9

SHRUB SMALL

Juniperus squamata 'Blue Star'

SINGLESEED JUNIPER This dense evergreen conifer forms a low mound of short, stiff, tightly packed blue-gray leaves. It spreads slowly, making an irregular and undulating carpet; ideal in gravel or among rocks.

↕16in (40cm) ↔3ft (1m)

 Z4–8

PERENNIAL MEDIUM

Lamprocapnos spectabilis 'Alba'

BLEEDING HEART A clump-forming perennial with deeply cut, light green fernlike leaves and heart-shaped white blooms from late spring to early summer. The plant dies back in late summer.

↕30in (75cm) ↔24in (60cm)

Z3–9

PERENNIAL MEDIUM

Leucanthemum x *superbum*

SHASTA DAISY An upright perennial with spreading clumps of dark green lance-shaped leaves. In summer, unbranched stems carry large, white single or double daisies. 'Beauté Nivelloise' (above) bears threadlike petals.

↕up to 3ft (1m) ↔24in (60cm)

Z5–9

BULB LARGE

Lilium longiflorum

EASTER LILY This perennial bulb, ideal for planting mid-bed, has shiny lance-shaped leaves. From mid-to late summer, large, highly fragrant, flared, outward-facing, funnel-shaped pure white blooms appear on tall stems.

↕3ft (1m)

 Z7–9

BULB LARGE

Lilium regale

REGAL LILY This bulbous perennial has upright stems clothed in narrow leaves and topped, in summer, by numerous large, fragrant, outward-facing white trumpets. The petals are yellow at the throat and pinkish purple outside.

↕6ft (2m)

Z4–8

TREE MEDIUM

Magnolia stellata

STAR MAGNOLIA The silk-budded, fragrant, white star-shaped flowers make this deciduous tree a favorite for early spring beds. Slim green leaves appear after the blooms. Plant it in a sheltered site to protect the blooms from frost.

↕↔ 30ft (10m)

 Z4–8

PERENNIAL LARGE

Meconopsis betonicifolia

BLUE POPPY A short-lived rosette-forming perennial with rusty haired heart-shaped leaves. Leafy stems bear poppylike yellow-centered blue blooms in late spring. Needs cool, moist conditions. Can be difficult to grow; best in Pacific Northwest gardens.

↕ 4ft (1.2m) ↔ 18in (45cm)

pH Z7–8

BULB MEDIUM

Narcissus 'Ice Follies'

DAFFODIL This mid-spring-flowering perennial bulb makes a great companion plant with blue hyacinth. Its creamy white flowers have frilled primrose cups that fade to white. Plant the bulbs in drifts in fall.

↕ 16in (40cm)

Z3–8

PERENNIAL SMALL

Nepeta x *faassenii*

CATMINT This bushy edging perennial has aromatic, small grayish green leaves. From summer to fall, masses of soft purple-blue flower spikes appear. Cut back after the first main flush to keep the plant tidy and compact.

↕↔ 18in (45cm)

Z4–8

SHRUB LARGE

Osmanthus x *burkwoodii*

OSMANTHUS This large, rounded, slow-growing evergreen shrub has small, oval dark green leaves and, in spring, clusters of tiny, highly fragrant, funnel-shaped white flowers. Black berries may follow. Grow in beds or as hedge plant.

↕↔ 10ft (3m)

Z7–9

SHRUB SMALL

Perovskia atriplicifolia

RUSSIAN SAGE A woody-based perennial with erect white stems clothed in deeply divided, gray-green aromatic leaves. Airy heads of lavender-blue flowers appear from late summer to fall. The bare white winter stems are a feature.

↕ 4ft (1.2m) ↔ 3ft (1m)

Z5–9

SHRUB MEDIUM

Philadelphus 'Belle Etoile'

MOCK ORANGE This deciduous shrub has slightly arching stems that bear deeply veined oval leaves. In early summer, highly fragrant, white single blooms with a maroon staining at the center open. Grow at the back of a bed.

↕ 6ft (2m) ↔ 4ft (1.2m)

Z5–8

SHRUB SMALL

Phlomis fruticosa

JERUSALEM SAGE A spreading evergreen shrub with round whorls of yellow trumpet-shaped summer flowers on upright stems and gray-green leaves, which release a musky herbal scent when brushed. The seedheads provide interest over winter.

↕ 3ft (1m) ↔ 5ft (1.5m)

Z8–10

PERENNIAL LARGE

Phlox paniculata 'Mount Fuji'

GARDEN PHLOX This clump-forming perennial produces tall stems of lance-shaped leaves that are topped with large domed heads of fragrant white blooms from midsummer to early fall, provided the soil is moist.

↕ 4ft (1.2m) ↔ 24in (60cm)

SHRUB MEDIUM

Phygelius x *rectus*

CAPE FUCHSIA This upright semievergreen shrub has green lance-shaped leaves and clusters of long, tubular flowers in summer. It may die back in winter when young. Varieties include 'Moonraker' (above) with custard-yellow blooms.

↕ 3ft (1m) ↔ 4ft (1.2m)

Z8–9

TREE LARGE

Picea pungens 'Koster'

COLORADO SPRUCE This cone-shaped evergreen conifer bears stiff, bright silvery blue needlelike foliage. Upright cones form toward the ends of the branches. Grow it in a specimen or screen in neutral to acidic soil. Copes with all but wet soils.

↕ 50ft (15m) ↔ 15ft (5m)

pH Z2–7 (N)

SHRUB SMALL

Potentilla fruticosa 'Abbotswood'
CINQUEFOIL This tough, reliable deciduous shrub has a bushy rounded or domed habit and round white blooms for many weeks from summer to fall. The foliage is divided into small leaflets.
↕3ft (1m) ↔5ft (1.5m)
Z3–7 Ⓝ

BULB MEDIUM

Puschkinia scilloides var. libanotica
STRIPED SQUILL A perennial bulb with strap-shaped leaves and clusters of bell-shaped white spring blooms with a blue stripe on each petal. Grow in drifts in lawns or with spring bulbs.
↕6in (15cm)
Z4–8

TREE SMALL

Pyrus salicifolia 'Pendula'
WILLOWLEAF PEAR A small tree with branches trailing to the ground and cream spring flowers that appear before the narrow silver-gray leaves are fully open. Its size and spread may be controlled by trimming into a bell-domed standard.
↕25ft (8m) ↔20ft (6m)
Z4–7

PERENNIAL LARGE

Romneya coulteri
TREE POPPY A late summer-flowering, back-of-bed shrubby perennial with elegant, deeply cut gray-green leaves and fragrant, white bowl-shaped flowers with a central dome of golden stamens. Common only to the West Coast, where it is native.
↕↔6ft (2m)
Z8–10 Ⓝ

CLIMBER LARGE

Rosa 'Félicité Perpétue'
RAMBLING HYBRID SEMPERVIRENS ROSE This vigorous rambling rose has glossy semievergreen leaves. Grow it up a large tree or over a wall, where the spectacular summer flush of blush pink to white, fragrant fully double blooms can be appreciated.
↕15ft (5m)
Z6–9

SHRUB SMALL

Ruta graveolens
COMMON RUE A rounded evergreen shrub with aromatic, blue-green ferny foliage divided into oval leaflets. Ideal for herb gardens. Remove the yellow flowers to promote a stronger leaf effect. Toxic, if ingested; sap may blister skin in sunlight.
↕3ft (1m) ↔30in (75cm)
Z4–8

SHRUB SMALL

Salvia officinalis 'Purpurascens'
PURPLE SAGE This woody-based evergreen subshrub, grown as an annual, has aromatic oval leaves, purple when young and dusty purple-green when mature, and lilac summer blooms. Use at the front of mixed beds.
↕up to 32in (80cm) ↔3ft (1m)
Z5–9

PERENNIAL MEDIUM

Salvia patens
GENTIAN SAGE This herbaceous perennial has oval to triangular, hairy leaves that clothe the upright stems. From midsummer to fall, the stems are topped with open heads of two-lipped vivid blue flowers. 'Cambridge Blue' has paler blooms.
↕24in (60cm) ↔18in (45cm)
Z8–10 Ⓝ

PERENNIAL MEDIUM

Santolina chamaecyparissus
LAVENDER COTTON A dwarf evergreen perennial, grown as an annual, with dense foliage made up of cut, narrow, aromatic silver-gray leaves. Remove the flowers before they open to maintain the silvery effect. Can be grown as low hedge.
↕30in (75cm) ↔3ft (1m)
Z6–9

PERENNIAL SMALL

Senecio cineraria
DUSTY MILLER A woody-based evergreen perennial, often grown as an annual in bedding schemes. In mild gardens and sheltered sites, the finely divided, felted silver leaves last well into fall. Cut back to prevent flowering.
↕↔12in (30cm)
Z8–11

SHRUB MEDIUM

Spiraea x vanhouttei
BRIDAL WREATH A deciduous shrub with a mound-forming habit. It has small leaves and arching stems of white flower heads from mid- to late spring. Grow as an informal flowering hedge, a back-of-bed plant, or as a specimen.
↕6ft (2m) ↔5ft (1.5m)
Z3–8

PERENNIAL SMALL

Stachys byzantina

LAMB'S EARS A mat-forming perennial with soft-to-the-touch, oval silvery gray leaves. In summer, spikes of mauve-pink, tiny flower clusters form on felted stems. It overwinters best in sunny, sheltered areas.

↕15in (38cm) ↔24in (60cm)

Z4–8

TREE MEDIUM

Styrax japonicus

JAPANESE SNOWBELL A deciduous tree with pointed oval leaves and a spreading habit, it makes a choice specimen for a bed or lawn. Clusters of white, fragrant bell-shaped blooms hang from the branches in early summer.

↕30ft (10m) ↔25ft (8m)

pH Z5–8

SHRUB LARGE

Syringa vulgaris 'Madame Lemoine'

COMMON LILAC A deciduous shrub or small tree with heart-shaped foliage and trusses of cone-shaped heads of strongly perfumed spring flowers that open from creamy buds. Considered invasive in some areas.

↕↔22ft (7m)

Z3–7

PERENNIAL SMALL

Trillium ovatum

COAST TRILLIUM This woodland perennial, slowly spreading by rhizomes, bears single stems, each with three, equally spaced heart-shaped leaves, above which sit three-petaled white flowers in early spring. Leave it undisturbed to slowly naturalize.

↕15in (38cm) ↔8in (20cm)

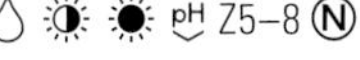

pH Z5–8 Ⓝ

ANNUAL/BIENNIAL LARGE

Verbascum olympicum

OLYMPIC MULLEIN This biennial forms a rosette of large, gray felted leaves in its first year, which may die back in winter. The next spring, it bears tall, upright silver stems and saucer-shaped golden flowers from mid- to late summer. May need staking.

↕6ft (2m) ↔3ft (1m)

Z5–9

PERENNIAL SMALL

Veronica gentianoides

GENTIAN SPEEDWELL A perennial with mats of oval, glossy evergreen leaves and slender spires of very pale blue blooms in early summer. It is ideal for bed edging or rock gardens. Remove spent flower spikes; water in dry spells.

↕↔18in (45cm)

Z4–7

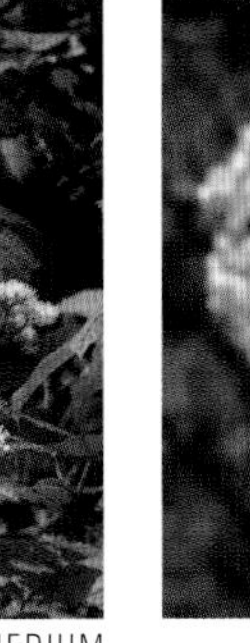

SHRUB MEDIUM

Viburnum acerifolium

MAPLELEAF VIBURNUM This upright deciduous shrub thrives in partially shaded beds, adding highlights with its green lobed leaves and early summer heads of fluffy creamy white flowers. Fall color and fruits are a bonus.

↕6ft (2m) ↔4ft (1.2m)

Z4–8 Ⓝ

SHRUB LARGE

Viburnum x *carlcephalum*

FRAGRANT SNOWBALL A bushy, rounded deciduous shrub with dense ball-shaped clusters of small, sweetly fragrant white blooms that open from pink buds from mid- to late spring. Red-turning-black summer fruits sometimes follow.

↕↔10ft (3m)

Z6–8

OTHER SUGGESTIONS

Perennials

Artemisia absinthium • *Brunnera* 'Jack Frost' • *Carex laxiculmis* BLUE BUNNY Ⓝ • *Delphinium* 'Blue Butterfly' • *Dianthus* *Hosta* 'Blue Mouse Ears' • *Symphyotrichum laeve* 'Bluebird' Ⓝ

Bulbs

Allium 'Mount Everest' • *Caladium* 'Aaron' • *Puschkinia scilloides* 'Alba'

Climbers

Wisteria frutescens 'Nivea' Ⓝ

Shrubs and trees

Camellia japonica 'Alba Plena' • *Caryopteris* x *clandonensis* 'Longwood Blue' • *Choisya* x *dewitteana* 'Aztec Pearl' • *Cornus kousa* 'Milky Way' • *Hydrangea arborescens* 'Annabelle' Ⓝ • *Osmanthus delavayi* • *Picea pungens* 'Hoopsii' Ⓝ • *Rhododendron* 'White Lights' • *Shepherdia argentea* Ⓝ

Plants for pastel colors

Romantic and feminine, a planting scheme of pinks, purples, peaches, and custard-yellows produces a calming effect in the garden.

These easy-on-the-eye shades are much sought-after and you will find a wide variety of plants to suit such a scheme. The only danger is that designs made up exclusively of soft shades can look rather bland, so to balance the pale hues add a few high- and lowlights, such as bright pinks and dark burgundy. A sprinkling of small white blooms will also lighten subdued pastel schemes. In addition, lift the focus to eye level and above by planting climbers, such as a pink climbing rose or an elegant purple clematis. Use foliage plants like coral bells, New Zealand flax , and stonecrop for long-lasting color.

SHRUB LARGE

Abutilon hybrids

FLOWERING MAPLE These upright deciduous shrubs have narrow, lobed, felted gray-green foliage. From late spring to early summer, they produce flowers in many soft tones. Suitable as an annual in colder areas.

↕12ft (4m) ↔8ft (2.5m)

Z9–10

TREE LARGE

Acer negundo

BOXELDER This tree has lobed reddish brown young leaves that turn midgreen in summer. Grow the variety 'Flamingo' (above) for its white- and pink-variegated foliage, but remember that the leaves of all forms turn bright yellow in fall.

↕50ft (15m) ↔30ft (10m)

Z3–8

PERENNIAL MEDIUM

Achillea 'Taygetea'

YARROW The combination of this perennial's feathery gray-green foliage and flat heads of pale yellow summer flowers give a subtle highlight in a pastel-themed bed or border. Plant it with purple and dark pink flower spikes in free-draining soil and full sun.

↕24in (60cm) ↔20in (50cm)

Z3–8

PERENNIAL MEDIUM

Agastache 'Black Adder'

HYSSOP Decorate sunny beds with this perennial's spikes of fluffy violet-purple flowers, which appear from late summer to mid-fall above slim green leaves. Use it with other pastels or to contrast with white or fiery shades.

↕24in (60cm) ↔18in (45cm)

Z6–9

BULB MEDIUM

Allium cristophii

STARS OF PERSIA Prized for its large spherical heads of star-shaped violet flowers in early summer, this bulb also forms decorative seedheads, providing a long season of interest. The narrow gray-green leaves fade as the flowers appear.

↕16in (40cm)

Z5–8

BULB LARGE

Allium 'Purple Sensation'

FLOWERING ONION This perennial bulb offers globes of small purple flowers held aloft on sturdy stems in early summer. They are followed by decorative buff-colored seedheads. Disguise the strap-shaped leaves, which fade as the flowers appear.

↕32in (80cm)

Z3–8

BULB MEDIUM

Allium senescens

GERMAN GARLIC This early-summer-flowering bulb has short stems topped with spherical purple-pink flower heads that bloom for many weeks, and blue-green foliage. Plant it in fall. *A. senescens* subsp. *glaucum* has pale lilac flowers.

↕24in (60cm)

Z4–9

PERENNIAL SMALL

Androsace lanuginosa

ROCK JASMINE This trailing evergreen perennial forms a low mat of oval, silky gray-green tapering leaves and makes a beautiful border edging or rock garden specimen. It bears clusters of small lilac-pink flowers in midsummer.

↕1½in (4cm) ↔7in (18cm)

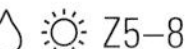

Z5–8

PERENNIAL MEDIUM

Aster x *frikartii*

FRIKART'S ASTER Add this long-flowering perennial to the middle of a sunny bed, where it will produce yellow-centered, lavender-blue or lilac daisy-like flowers from midsummer to early fall. Try it with coneflowers and Japanese anemone.

↕28in (70cm) ↔16in (40cm)

Z5–8

SHRUB LARGE

Camellia x *williamsii*

CAMELLIA The flowers of the williamsii camellias come in a range of pastel pinks, and appear on this evergreen shrub in spring among glossy dark green leaves. It tolerates full shade and prefers a sheltered north- or west-facing site.

↕15ft (5m) ↔8ft (2.5m)

pH Z7–9

PERENNIAL SMALL

Anemone coronaria De Caen Group

POPPY ANEMONE Plant this perennial corm in gravel beds and border edges. Comes in mixture of colors; avoid the red variant in pastel schemes. From early spring, bowl-shaped blooms are held above green leaves.

↕12in (30cm) ↔6in (15cm)

Z8–10

PERENNIAL LARGE

Campanula lactiflora

MILKY BELLFLOWER Both the tall varieties of this perennial and shorter forms, such as 'Prichard's Variety' (above), bear bell-shaped, nodding violet-blue, occasionally pink or white, flowers in summer. Plant in groups among other pastel-colored blooms.

↕4ft (1.2m) ↔24in (60cm)

Z5–7

PERENNIAL SMALL

Aster novi-belgii

Renamed *Symphyotrichum novi-belgii* With its pastel-colored daisy-like flowers, this michaelmas daisy is perfect for fall containers of soil-based potting mix, or in moist soil at the front of a bed. 'Professor Anton Kippenberg' has blue blooms.

↕14in (35cm) ↔18in (45cm)

Z4–8 Ⓝ

PERENNIAL SMALL

Campanula punctata

SPOTTED BELLFLOWER The pendent dusky pink blooms of this perennial lend an elegant touch to the front of a bed. Partner it with cool colors or purple blooms, such as cranesbill, but avoid bright, hot colors that may eclipse its delicate hue.

↕12in (30cm) ↔16in (40cm)

Z4–8

PERENNIAL MEDIUM

Aster 'Coombe Fishacre'

Renamed *Symphyotrichum* 'Coombe Fishacre' Use this fall-flowering calico aster as a contrast to the bright yellows and reds that abound at this time of the year. The pale lilac-pink flowers sprays set against dark foliage add interest to the middle of a bed.

↕3ft (1m) ↔14in (35cm)

Z5–8

CLIMBER MEDIUM

Billardiera longiflora

CLIMBING BLUEBERRY This twining evergreen climber works well as a backdrop to a sheltered bed. It produces slender, bell-shaped green-yellow summer flowers followed by purple-blue fall fruits. Provide winter protection in cold areas.

↕6ft (2m)

Z8–9

PERENNIAL MEDIUM

Catananche caerulea

CUPID'S DART Plant this hardy perennial in groups in a wild or naturalistic garden, where its dainty blue or white starlike blooms will wave in the breeze on tall, wiry stems above gray-green foliage. 'Bicolor' (above) is a white semidouble form.

↕24in (60cm) ↔12in (30cm)

Z4–8

SHRUB MEDIUM

Chaenomeles speciosa

FLOWERING QUINCE Choose a pink- or peach-flowered form of this vigorous, bushy deciduous shrub to dress up a pastel scheme in spring. The thorny stems are ideal for training up a sunny or part-shaded wall.

↕8ft (2.5m) ↔15ft (5m)

Z4–8

CLIMBER MEDIUM

Clematis alpina

ALPINE CLEMATIS This deciduous clematis, with divided midgreen leaves and lantern-shaped blue, pink, or white flowers, makes a beautiful feature when grown through a spring-flowering shrub or up an arch. Fluffy seedheads follow the flowers.

↕10ft (3m)

Z4–9

CLIMBER MEDIUM

Clematis 'Bees Jubilee'

CLEMATIS Grow this compact, large-flowered deciduous clematis in partial shade against a wall or fence, or up a rose arch to complement pastel plantings. The rose-pink early summer flowers feature a central, darker pink stripe on each petal.

↕8ft (2.5m)

Z4–9

TREE SMALL

Cornus florida

FLOWERING DOGWOOD White or pink flowerlike bracts cover this deciduous tree or shrub in late spring and make a focal point in a pastel-themed setting. The curled, red and purple fall leaves give a colorful backdrop to late-season beds.

↕20ft (6m) ↔25ft (8m)

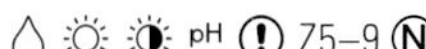
pH (!) Z5–9 (N)

CLIMBER MEDIUM

Clematis 'Guernsey Cream'

CLEMATIS The large cream flowers with a green bar down the center of each petal appear on this compact evergreen clematis in early summer and again in late summer. Use them to decorate an arch, or a wall or fence at the back of a border.

↕8ft (2.5m)

Z4–9

SHRUB MEDIUM

Clethra alnifolia

SUMMERSWEET This bushy shrub bears slender spires of small, fragrant, white bell-shaped blooms in late summer. It offers a complementary backdrop to pastel pinks and purples in a damp, shady spot. The foliage turns yellow in fall.

↕↔8ft (2.5m)

pH Z3–9 (N)

TREE SMALL

Cornus florida 'Welchii'

FLOWERING DOGWOOD This conical-shaped tree or large deciduous shrub has tiny green flowers surrounded by white petal-like bracts in late spring and variegated leaves, which feature pink fall leaf tints.

↕20ft (6m) ↔25ft (8m)

(!) Z5–9 (N)

SHRUB MEDIUM

Cornus mas 'Aurea'

CORNELIAN CHERRY Use this deciduous shrub as a backdrop to a bed of dark pinks and purples. Its pale golden-yellow spring leaves turn lime-green in summer and clusters of small bright yellow flowers appear on bare branches in early spring.

↕6ft (2m) ↔10ft (3m)

Z5–8

BULB SMALL

Crocus vernus

DUTCH CROCUS This dwarf, spring to early-summer-flowering bulb produces small, cup-shaped lilac or purple flowers and can be naturalized in lawns, or combined with other pastel flowers in tubs or pots filled with gritty soil-based potting mix.

↕5in (12cm)

Z3–8

BULB SMALL

Cyclamen coum Pewter Group

HARDY CYCLAMEN This perennial, grown from fall-planted tubers, has rounded, dark green leaves, often with silver patterning. The small pink flowers with swept-back petals appear in winter or early spring with the leaves.

↕3in (8cm)

Z5–9

BULB LARGE

Dahlia 'Franz Kafka'

POMPOM DAHLIA Grown from spring-planted tubers, this perennial bears pink pompon flowers with a honeycomb texture above the foliage from mid- to late summer and early fall. There are many pastel-colored dahlia varieties to grow.

↕32in (80cm)

Z9–11

PERENNIAL LARGE

Delphinium elatum

LARKSPUR Available in a range of pastel blues, pinks, and purples, this upright perennial adds spikes of color to a bed when its flowers appear in midsummer above deeply cut green leaves. Provide support to the stems.

↕6ft (2m) ↔3ft (1m)

Z3–7

PERENNIAL SMALL

Diascia barberae 'Apricot Queen'

TWINSPUR Perfect for growing in pots or the front of a sunny bed, this perennial, sold as annual bedding, produces spikes of apricot-salmon flowers above heart-shaped tapering leaves from summer to fall.

↕10in (25cm) ↔20in (50cm)

Z8–9

SHRUB SMALL

Deutzia x *elegantissima* 'Rosealind'

ELEGANT DEUTZIA Plant this rounded deciduous shrub where the fragrance of its blooms can be enjoyed. Pink-flushed white flowers lend scent and color to late spring and early summer beds.

↕4ft (1.2m) ↔5ft (1.5m)

Z6–8

BULB LARGE

Dierama pulcherrimum

ANGEL'S FISHING ROD The elegant arching stems of this summer-flowering corm bear dangling, funnel-shaped deep pink flowers, and emerge from a clump of narrow strap-shaped evergreen leaves. Use it to edge a bed with cream and purple blooms.

↕5ft (1.5m) ↔24in (60cm)

Z8–10

PERENNIAL MEDIUM

Dianthus caryophyllus

CARNATION This perennial, with gray-green leaves and tall slender stems of rounded flowers in a range of pastel shades, is suited to a cottage or rock garden. Dwarf forms, ideal for pots or the front of a border, are also available in pastel shades.

↕32in (80cm) ↔9in (23cm)

Z6–10

SHRUB LARGE

Dipelta floribunda

ROSY DIPELTA Unassuming for much of the year, this deciduous shrub, with lance-shaped green leaves, comes to life from late spring to early summer, when clusters of creamy white funnel-shaped flowers with orange and pink throats appear.

↕↔12ft (4m)

Z6–8

PERENNIAL LARGE

Eremurus robustus

FOXTAIL LILY This perennial produces tall slim spikes of pale pink blooms and looks most dramatic when planted in groups where the sun can bake the tubers in late summer. Add grit to the soil before planting tubers in spring; stems may need staking.

↕10ft (3m) ↔4ft (1.2m)

Z5–8

SHRUB SMALL

Erica x *darleyensis*

DARLEY HEATH Plant drifts of this dwarf evergreen shrub to form a carpet of urn-shaped white or pink flowers from late winter to early spring. The lance-shaped foliage is dark green. 'White Glow' (above) is compact with masses of white flowers.

↕10in (25cm) ↔20in (50cm)

Z6–8

PERENNIAL LARGE

Eryngium x *tripartitum*

SEA HOLLY This rosette-forming perennial has spiny gray-green leaves and tall, violet-blue branched stems, topped with conelike, small purple flower heads and surrounded by narrow, dark blue bracts. Grow in a bed with peach and white neighbors.

↕4ft (1.2m) ↔20in (50cm)

Z5–8

SHRUB MEDIUM

Escallonia 'Apple Blossom'

ESCALLONIA Use this bushy evergreen shrub as hedge or a backdrop to a bed. Its glossy, spine-edged green leaves are joined by pink and white tubular flowers from summer to early fall, which complement cool and pastel colors. Best in West Coast gardens.

↕↔8ft (2.5m)

Z8–9

SHRUB MEDIUM

Fuchsia magellanica var. *molinae*

HARDY FUCHSIA Suitable for the back of a partly shaded bed, this deciduous shrub has lance-shaped leaves and bell-shaped, pale pink pendent flowers from summer to early fall. Best in West Coast gardens.

↕↔6ft (2m)

Z7–9

PERENNIAL LARGE

Gaura lindheimeri

WAND FLOWER The wandlike stems of this upright perennial are dotted with butterfly-shaped, starry, pink-budded white flowers all summer and appear above the green lance-shaped leaves. Use its "see-through" stems at the front of a bed or beside a path.

↕5ft (1.5m) ↔3ft (1m)

Z6–9 Ⓝ

PERENNIAL MEDIUM

Geranium sylvaticum

WOOD CRANESBILL Producing a carpet of saucer-shaped blue-purple flowers with white centers over lobed leaves from late spring to early summer, this clump-forming perennial makes excellent ground cover for a pastel bed in sun or part shade.

↕30in (75cm) ↔24in (60cm)

Z3–8

BULB LARGE

Gladiolus 'Passos'

GLADIOLUS This bulb's deep purple- and red-centered pale purple flower spikes create a focal point in summer borders. The swordlike foliage also adds interest. Plant the bulbs at two-week intervals from early spring to summer to lengthen the flowering period.

↕4ft (1.2m) ↔6in (15cm)

Z8–10

PERENNIAL SMALL

Helleborus purpurascens

HELLEBORE Use this clump-forming perennial in shady beds with pale yellow or white daffodils that bloom in early spring, when its nodding, purple cup-shaped blooms with light purple or green interiors and cream stamens appear.

↕↔12in (30cm)

Z4–8

PERENNIAL SMALL

Hemerocallis 'Arctic Snow'

DAYLILY A deciduous perennial with arching, straplike green leaves that provide a foil for other flowers before sturdy stems of large cream blooms with pale yellow margins and throats appear from summer to early fall. Each bloom lasts a day.

↕22in (55cm) ↔20in (50cm)

Z3–9

SHRUB LARGE

Hydrangea aspera Villosa Group

ROUGH-LEAVED HYDRANGEA This upright deciduous shrub makes a good partner for pale-hued perennials. It has large hairy leaves and small mauve late summer flower clusters, surrounded by pale blooms.

↕↔10ft (3m)

Z7–9

PERENNIAL MEDIUM

Hyssopus officinalis

HYSSOP This upright perennial is a decorative herb that can also be used in mixed sunny beds. It has aromatic leaves that smell and taste of anise, and spikes of fluffy lavender-blue summer flowers that attract bees and butterflies.

↕24in (60cm) ↔3ft (1m)

Z4–9

PERENNIAL MEDIUM

Lamprocapnos spectabilis

BLEEDING HEART Use this perennial in a late spring bed, when its fernlike midgreen foliage is joined by arching stems that bear heart-shaped rose-red and white flowers. Try it in a bed with early-flowering cranesbills.

↕↔3ft (1m)

Z3–9

PERENNIAL MEDIUM

Hemerocallis 'Dan Mahony'

DAYLILY This perennial forms a clump of upright, arching straplike foliage. Large, trumpet-shaped pink flowers with darker centers appear over several weeks in summer. Each bloom lasts a day. It resents root disturbance.

↕26in (65cm) ↔4½in (11cm)

Z3–9

PERENNIAL MEDIUM

Iris 'Harriette Halloway'

BEARDED IRIS This bearded iris's large, scented pale blue summer flowers, with yellow centers, and swordlike foliage lend elegance to the front of a sunny bed or path edge. Plant the rhizomes just above the soil surface to allow them to bake in the sun.

↕28in (70cm) ↔12in (30cm)

Z3–9

CLIMBER MEDIUM

Lathyrus odoratus

SWEET PEA Add height to a pastel scheme by training this annual tendril climber on a tripod support. The pink, blue, purple, or white flowers bloom from summer to early fall when deadheaded regularly. Performs best in cool areas with good air circulation.

↕10ft (3m)

PERENNIAL SMALL

Heuchera 'Plum Pudding'

CORAL BELLS This leafy evergreen perennial is grown for its small white summer flowers and rounded, lobed and veined maroon-purple leaves, which make a great match for pink, cream, and pale yellow flowers. Remove spent blooms and old foliage.

↕20in (50cm) ↔12in (30cm)

Z4–9 Ⓝ

PERENNIAL LARGE

Liatris spicata

GAYFEATHER This upright perennial produces pokerlike spikes of fluffy pink-purple or white flowers from late summer to early fall above clumps of linear leaves. 'Kobold' (above) has vivid purple-pink blooms.

↕5ft (1.5m) ↔18in (45cm)

Z4-9 Ⓝ

Plants for pastel colors

PERENNIAL MEDIUM

Malva moschata

MUSK MALLOW This perennial bears heart-shaped basal leaves and a profusion of pale pink saucer-shaped flowers from summer to early fall. Its loose habit makes it ideal for a wildflower or naturalistic scheme.

↕3ft (1m) ↔24in (60cm)

Z3–8

BULB MEDIUM

Narcissus 'Canaliculatus'

DAFFODIL A good partner for pale lemon daffodils and purple hellebores, this bulb has clusters of small fragrant flowers, with reflexed white petals and yellow cups, that appear from early to mid-spring among linear green leaves. Plant the bulbs in fall.

↕9in (23cm)

Z6–10

ANNUAL/BIENNIAL SMALL

Nemophila menziesii

BABY BLUE-EYES Use this annual with its gray-green serrated leaves and white-centered, blue, saucer-shaped summer flowers to edge patio pots or sunny beds. Combine it with taller plants that have pastel or hot-hued blooms.

↕8in (20cm) ↔6in (15cm)

BULB MEDIUM

Nerine bowdenii

SPIDER LILY Decorate the front of fall beds with this spring-planted perennial bulb, which produces slim stems topped with spidery pink flowers before the strap-shaped leaves unfurl. Try it with the pastel-colored asters.

↕24in (60cm) ↔6in (15cm)

Z8–10

ANNUAL/BIENNIAL SMALL

Nigella damascena

LOVE-IN-A-MIST Sow this annual in a sunny bed for its feathery foliage effect and white, lavender, purple, rose, and blue saucer-shaped flowers. The unusual blooms sport a "ruff" of spidery leaves and are followed by large decorative seedpods.

↕18in (45cm) ↔8in (20cm)

PERENNIAL SMALL

Oenothera speciosa

PINK EVENING PRIMROSE Ideal for the front of a free-draining, sunny bed, this perennial has divided green leaves and, , pink-flushed white, fragrant cup-shaped flowers from late spring to early summer. Try intermingling with baby blue-eyes.

↕12in (30cm) ↔12in (30cm)

Z4–8 Ⓝ

PERENNIAL MEDIUM

Paeonia lactiflora

PEONY A reliable perennial for a pastel-color-themed bed, with red, mottled stems of dark green, divided leaves and, from early- to midsummer, single or double, bowl-shaped, fragrant white to pale pink flowers with yellow centers.

↕↔28in (70m)

Z3–8

SHRUB MEDIUM

Paeonia suffruticosa

TREE PEONY An upright deciduous shrub with deeply lobed dark green leaves and, in late spring, white, pink, red, or purple bowl-shaped flowers, sometimes scented. Use it to add height and substance to a perennial bed or mixed border.

↕↔6ft (2m)

Z5–8

PERENNIAL MEDIUM

Papaver orientale 'Patty's Plum'

ORIENTAL POPPY Use this perennial with its large, ruffled dusky purple summer flowers, which are followed by decorative seedheads, as a contrast to cream and pale yellow blooms.

↕3ft (1m) ↔24in (60cm)

Z3–9

PERENNIAL MEDIUM

Persicaria bistorta

BISTORT In sun or part-shade, this clump-forming perennial produces a mat of oval foliage below spikes of soft pink flowers, which bloom from early- to late summer. Plant it with purple, white, and dark pink partners in moist soil.

↕30in (75cm) ↔24in (60cm)

   Z4–8

PERENNIAL SMALL

Pelargonium 'Lady Plymouth'

SCENTED GERANIUM This is a small perennial, usually grown as an annual, that produces eucalyptus-scented, lobed, silver-margined green leaves. Clusters of lavender-pink flowers appear in summer.

↕16in (40cm) ↔8in (20cm)

Z10–11

PERENNIAL SMALL

Petunia 'Celebrity Series'

PETUNIA This perennial, grown as an annual, bears trumpet-shaped blooms from summer to early fall, and provides a rich source of pastels for color-themed containers and raised beds. Deadhead the flowers regularly to ensure a long display.

↕10in (25cm) ↔18in (45cm)

Z10–11

PERENNIAL MEDIUM

Phlomis russeliana

STICKY JERUSALEM SAGE Offering a long season of interest, this perennial has large, rough-textured heart-shaped leaves and unusual hooded, butter-yellow summer flowers, set at intervals up the tall stems. The seedheads provide winter interest.

↕3ft (1m) ↔24in (60cm) or more

Z4–9

PERENNIAL SMALL

Penstemon 'Evelyn'

BEARDTONGUE This compact, bushy semievergreen perennial makes a colorful addition to summer beds. It has narrow foliage and, from summer to early fall, slim panicles of rose-pink tubular flowers. Protect with a dry mulch in winter.

↕↔18in (45cm)

Z7–10

PERENNIAL MEDIUM

Phormium 'Evening Glow'

NEW ZEALAND FLAX With forms available in a range of pinks and purples, this leafy perennial forms fountains of evergreen foliage creating focal points in beds or containers filled with soil-based potting mix. It complements pastel-colored flowers.

↕↔30in (75cm)

Z9–11

SHRUB SMALL

Phygelius aequalis

CAPE FUCHSIA This shrub bears tall stems of pendent, tubular, dusky pink or yellow summer blooms in a sunny, sheltered site. If hit by winter frosts, cut stems to the ground in spring; it should reshoot. 'Yellow Trumpet' (above) has creamy yellow blooms.

↕↔3ft (1m)

 Z7–9

PERENNIAL SMALL

Primula denticulata

DRUMSTICK PRIMROSE This perennial forms a rosette of toothed green leaves and from mid-spring to summer, clusters of yellow-eyed purple or white flowers. Plant at pond edges in damp soil and do not allow to dry. *P. denticulata* var. *alba* has white blooms.

↕↔18in (45cm)

 Z3–8

PERENNIAL SMALL

Primula vialii

ORCHID PRIMROSE Perfect for areas with damp soil, this clump-forming perennial bears unusual tapering two-tone cones of bluish purple and dark red flowers on sturdy stems in late spring. The blooms appear above a rosette of oval leaves.

↕24in (60cm) ↔12in (30cm)

   Z5–8

PERENNIAL SMALL

Pulmonaria saccharata

BETHLEHEM SAGE Use this clump-forming semievergreen perennial with daffodils and Dutch irises in pastel-themed beds. Its white-spotted blue-green leaves make great edging and the funnel-shaped blue-purple spring-flower clusters attract bees.
↕12in (30cm) ↔24in (60cm)

Z3–8

CLIMBER LARGE

Rosa 'Albertine'

CLIMBING ROSE This rambler rose's stems of dark green leaves and scented, salmon-pink fully double flowers, which appear in a single flush in summer, make a beautiful backdrop to a bed when trained on a large wall or fence, or over a pergola.
↕15ft (5m)

Z5–9

SHRUB SMALL

Rosa 'Buff Beauty'

HYBRID MUSK ROSE A vigorous shrub with long, arching stems of glossy foliage and clusters of small, fragrant apricot-yellow and buff semidouble flowers from summer to fall, which contrast well with purples and dark pinks.
↕↔4ft (1.2m)

Z5–9

CLIMBER LARGE

Rosa 'Climbing Lady Hillingdon'

CLIMBING HYBRID TEA ROSE Train this vigorous rose on a wall behind a pastel-themed bed, where its green foliage, copper-mahogany when young, and apricot summer blooms will form a colorful backdrop.
↕15ft (5m)

Z6–9

PERENNIAL MEDIUM

Sidalcea malviflora

CHECKERBLOOM The informal style of this upright perennial lends itself to wildlife and cottage schemes. Tall stems of pink or lilac-pink funnel-shaped flowers appear above kidney-shaped basal leaves in summer. Combine it with cranesbill and yarrow.
↕3ft (1m) ↔18in (45cm)

pH Z5–7 Ⓝ

SHRUB MEDIUM

Rosa glauca

REDLEAF ROSE The rose-pink single summer flowers with pale centers and red stems of grayish purple leaves make this rose a perfect addition to pastel-themed plantings. Use it at the back of a bed or as an informal hedge; prune in late winter.
↕6ft (2m) ↔5ft (1.5m)

Z2–8

PERENNIAL MEDIUM

Salvia farinacea

MEALYCUP SAGE Use this upright perennial, grown as an annual, at the edge of a bed or in pots with lavender, pink, and cream blooms. Its spikes of small purple-blue flowers appear over a long period from summer to fall, if deadheaded often.
↕24in (60cm) ↔12in (30cm)

Z8–11 Ⓝ

PERENNIAL SMALL

Sedum erythrostictum

STONECROP This clump-forming perennial bears fleshy gray-green leaves and greenish white starry flowers in early fall. Varieties include 'Mediovariegatum' (above) with cream-splashed variegated leaves. Grow it in sun in gritty soil.
↕12in (30cm) ↔24in (60cm)

Z3–9

SHRUB LARGE

Stachyurus praecox

STACHYURUS From late winter to early spring, the pale greenish yellow bell-shaped flowers of this deciduous shrub hang in clusters from bare stems, creating an exciting feature. Slim, dark green tapering leaves unfurl in spring.
↕12ft (4m) ↔10ft (3m)

pH Z6–8

PERENNIAL SMALL

Stokesia laevis

STOKES' ASTER Ideal for cottage or informal beds, this evergreen perennial has midgreen leaves and lavender- or purple-blue cornflower-like blooms on short stems from midsummer to mid-fall. 'Purple Parasols' (above) has violet-purple blooms.
↕↔18in (45cm)

pH Z5–9 Ⓝ

PERENNIAL LARGE

Thalictrum aquilegiifolium

MEADOW RUE This useful perennial for shady beds and moist soil has clusters of fluffy, lilac-purple summer flowers that are ideal for pastel-colored plantings. Its finely cut gray-green leaves and attractive fall seedheads add to its appeal.

↕4ft (1.2m) ↔18in (45cm)

Z5–8

BULB MEDIUM

Tulipa 'Negrita'

TULIP Combine this dark purple-pink tulip with pale pink and cream varieties that flower at the same time in mid-spring and use it in a pastel bed or to fill a formal parterre. Plant the bulbs in groups in a sunny site in fall.

↕18in (45cm)

Z3–8

SHRUB MEDIUM

Syringa x *persica*

PERSIAN LILAC This compact bushy shrub, suited to the back of a bed in a small garden, infuses the air with the scent of its purple flowers, which appear in small dense clusters in late spring. The lance-shaped foliage is dark green.

↕↔6ft (2m)

Z3–7

PERENNIAL LARGE

Veronica spicata

SPIKE SPEEDWELL A mat of slim, lance-shaped green foliage sits beneath this perennial's upright spikes of blue, pink, white, or purple star-shaped summer flowers. For a pastel scheme, select a purple form such as 'Romily Purple' (above).

↕4ft (1.2m) ↔24in (60cm)

Z3–8

SHRUB LARGE

Syringa vulgaris

COMMON LILAC Grown in beds or as a boundary screen, this vigorous deciduous shrub offers scent and color when the pastel-colored conical-flower clusters form in late spring after the heart-shaped foliage unfurls. Has become invasive in some areas.

↕↔22ft (7m)

Z3–7

BULB MEDIUM

Tulipa 'China Pink'

TULIP This lily-flowered form bears rosy pink blooms in late spring and has broad gray-green foliage. Other varieties offer a spectrum of pastel-colored flowers from mid- to late spring. Plant the bulbs in groups in fall.

↕22in (55cm)

Z3–8

PERENNIAL LARGE

Veronicastrum virginicum

CULVER'S ROOT This upright perennial bears slender spikes of small, white, blue, or pink star-shaped flowers on tall leafy stems. Plant it at the back of a bed and provide support. 'Album' (above) has cool white flowers.

↕4ft (1.2m) ↔18in (45cm)

Z4–8 Ⓝ

OTHER SUGGESTIONS

Perennials and bulbs

Anthyrium niponicum var. *pictum* 'Burgundy Lace' • *Crocus sieberi* ssp. *sublimis* f. *tricolor* • *Coreopsis rosea* 'American Dream' Ⓝ • *Dahlia* 'Otto's Thrill' • *Delphinium* 'Summer Skies' • *Dianthus* 'Bath's Pink' • *Echinacea pallida* Ⓝ • *Gaura lindheimeri* 'Crimson Butterflies' Ⓝ • *Gentiana asclepiadea* • *Geranium maculatum* Ⓝ • *Hemerocallis* 'Summer Wine' • *Heuchera* 'Caramel' • *Lilium* 'Mona Lisa' • *Paeonia* 'Kopper Kettle' • *Phlox paniculata* 'Bright Eyes' Ⓝ • *Salvia patens* Ⓝ • *Sidalcea* 'Party Girl' • *Symphyotrichum oblongifolium* Ⓝ • *Tulipa* 'Menton' • *Veronicastrum virginicum* 'Fascination' Ⓝ

Shrubs and climbers

Clethra alnifolia 'Ruby Spice' Ⓝ • *Kolwitzia ambalis* 'Pink Cloud' • *Rhododendron* 'Purple Splendour' • *Rhododendron* 'Hoopla'

Plants for hot and dark colors

Hot-hued flowers create drama in the garden, especially when teamed with smoldering dark purple or blue-black foliage plants.

Brightly colored blooms also produce striking combinations with golden-leaved plants, such as Bowles' golden sedge and sunburst honeylocust, and look effective when cooled with a selection of neutral greens. Purple foliage complements almost any color, but take care when matching up golds with pastel shades of pink or peach to avoid unsightly clashes. Beds aglow with sizzling reds, oranges, and yellows catch the eye and add highlights to more subtle color schemes, while compact plants, such as bedding dahlias and varieties of scarlet sage, make arresting focal points in container displays.

SHRUB MEDIUM

Abutilon megapotamicum

TRAILING ABUTILON In a sheltered, sunny site, this evergreen shrub will brighten schemes with its bell-shaped yellow and red summer flowers, which contrast with its heart-shaped dark green leaves. Train the stems up a wall; protect against frost.
↕↔ 6ft (2m)

Z8–10

SHRUB MEDIUM

Acer palmatum var. *dissectum*

JAPANESE MAPLE This deciduous shrub's dark purple foliage complements bright, hot shades. It has a domed habit and lobed leaves with finely divided tapering "fingers." Plant under shelter. Considered invasive in some Mid-Atlantic and Northeastern areas.
↕ 5ft (1.5m) ↔ 3ft (1m)

Z5–8

TREE SMALL

Acer shirasawanum 'Aureum'

FULL MOON MAPLE This deciduous shrub or small tree with lobed bright yellow foliage complements a hot-hued border or gravel garden. It also features small crimson spring flowers and its palmate leaves turn scarlet in fall.
↕↔ 20ft (6m)

Z5–7

PERENNIAL MEDIUM

Achillea 'Moonshine'

YARROW This short-lived perennial is perfect for the front of a sunny hot color-themed bed. Flat-topped yellow flower heads, held on slim stems above the silvery ferny foliage, appear over a long period in summer. It is resistant to flopping.
↕ 24in (60cm) ↔ 20in (50cm)

(!) Z3–8

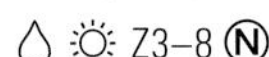

PERENNIAL MEDIUM

Achillea millefolium 'Paprika'

YARROW This semievergreen perennial's flat heads of tiny rosy red flowers with yellow centers, which fade to buff as they mature, combine well with scarlet blooms and contrasting golden-yellow plants. Its feathery leaves are silvery green.
↕ 18in (45cm) ↔ 16in (40cm)

Z3–8 (N)

PERENNIAL LARGE

Actaea simplex Brunette'

BUGBANE Use the divided dark purple foliage of this perennial as a foil for bright yellows and reds, or to complement moodier shades. From early- to mid-fall it bears off-white tinged purple bottlebrush blooms.
↕ 4ft (1.2m) ↔ 24in (60cm)

Z4–8

CLIMBER LARGE

Actinidia kolomikta

VARIEGATED KIWI VINE A vigorous deciduous climber grown for its large heart-shaped leaves, many of which are marked with bold silver or pink patches. Planted on a wall or fence, it makes a good backdrop to brightly colored plants. Best in shelter.
↕ 12ft (4m)

Z5–8

TREE SMALL

Aesculus pavia

RED BUCKEYE This small tree lights up in spring when upright panicles of orange-red tubular flowers appear. The large, divided dark green leaves create an architectural feature. The fall seeds are poisonous.
↕ 15ft (5m) ↔ 10ft (3m)

(!) Z4–8 (N)

BULB MEDIUM

Anemone coronaria

POPPY ANEMONE To create a dazzling early spring display in raised beds, combine this diminutive bulb, with its dark-eyed bright red, blue, or white flowers, with yellow daffodils and irises. The flowers sit above lobed dissected leaves.

↕10in (25cm)

 Z8–10

PERENNIAL MEDIUM

Aquilegia vulgaris

COLUMBINE A few forms of this perennial are in darker shades, including 'William Guinness' (above), which features intricate white-centered purple-black flowers from late spring to early summer above fernlike midgreen leaves.

↕3ft (1m) ↔18in (45cm)

Z3–8

PERENNIAL MEDIUM

Begonia sutherlandii

SUTHERLAND'S BEGONIA Plant this perennial, with trailing stems of lobed green leaves and small bright orange summer flower clusters, in a pot or basket for an eye-catching display. Grown from spring-planted tubers. Treat as an annual.

↕32in (80cm) ↔indefinite

Z9–11

ANNUAL/BIENNIAL SMALL

Brassica oleracea

ORNAMENTAL CABBAGE This annual offers decorative colorful leaves to brighten up fall and winter containers, and bedding displays. With loose rosettes of plain or frilly-edged, white, red, or pink leaves, it combines well with violas.

↕↔18in (45cm)

ANNUAL/BIENNIAL MEDIUM

Calendula officinalis

POT MARIGOLD The orange or yellow daisy-like flowers of this bushy annual inject punchy hot color into summer schemes. Sow seeds in flower beds or patio pots in spring, and use in an informal garden or formal parterres.

↕↔24in (60cm)

SHRUB SMALL

Calluna vulgaris 'Gold Haze'

SCOTCH HEATHER Use this small gold-leaved evergreen shrub to carpet the front of a bed with color, or plant it with dwarf conifers in a large pot of acidic soil mix. Small white flowers appear from late summer to fall.

↕18in (45cm) ↔24in (60cm)

pH Z4–7

SHRUB LARGE

Camellia japonica

JAPANESE CAMELLIA The glossy evergreen leaves of this shrub lend a neutral backdrop to hot-hued borders year-round, punctuated by early spring blooms. Choose a richly hued form, such as the salmon-red 'Blood of China' (above), for hot schemes.

↕10ft (3m) ↔6ft (2m)

pH Z7–9

PERENNIAL LARGE

Canna TROPICANNA

CANNA The large paddle-shaped foliage of this perennial creates a spectacular display of orange- and dark green-striped leaves from late spring, followed by ruffled orange flowers on tall stems in late summer, offering a complete hot-hued package.

↕5½ft (1.6m) ↔20in (50cm)

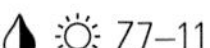 Z7–11

PERENNIAL SMALL

Carex comans

NEW ZEALAND HAIR SEDGE This perennial forms clumps of arching, hairlike green or bronze foliage. Inconspicuous flower heads appear on long stems in summer. Cascade it over the sides of pots or try it in a raised bed as a foil for orange and red flowers.

↕14in (35cm) ↔30in (75cm)

 Z7–9

PERENNIAL SMALL

Carex elata

BOWLES' GOLDEN SEDGE Ideal for lively bog garden schemes, this evergreen perennial forms tufts of long, arching golden-yellow leaves. Thin grasslike blackish brown flower spikes appear in summer. Try it with scarlet lobelias and golden marsh marigolds.

↕28in (70cm) ↔18in (45cm)

 Z5–9

TREE MEDIUM

Catalpa bignonioides 'Aurea'

INDIAN BEAN TREE This medium-sized deciduous tree, with its large golden-yellow leaves, makes a bright backdrop to a hot-hued border. The foliage turns light yellow-green in summer when showy white flowers appear.

↕↔30ft (10m)

Z5–9 Ⓝ

PERENNIAL SMALL

Celosia argentea 'Fairy Fountains'

COCKSCOMB This perennial, sold as annual bedding plant, brightens up beds with its large, plumelike, fluffy hot-colored summer flower heads that appear above pale green lance-shaped leaves.
↕↔12in (30cm)

💧 ☼

TREE SMALL

Cercis canadensis 'Forest Pansy'

EASTERN REDBUD This deciduous spreading small tree or shrub is grown for its heart-shaped purple leaves that turn yellow in fall and make a fiery feature in the garden. Pale pink pealike flowers appear in mid-spring.
↕↔15ft (5m)

💧 ☼ Z4–9 Ⓝ

SHRUB SMALL

Chaenomeles x *superba*

FLOWERING QUINCE Heat up the color of a late-spring garden with this spiny deciduous shrub. Its orange, white, pink, or red cup-shaped flowers clothe the stems before the leaves unfurl. For a burst of orange-red, choose 'Crimson and Gold' (above).
↕3ft (1m) ↔6ft (2m)

💧 ☼ ◐ Z5–8

TREE SMALL

Cordyline australis

CABBAGE PALM Use this palmlike evergreen tree, with sword-shaped green- or purple-shaded leaves, as an accent plant in a brightly colored flower scheme. Grow on a patio in a tall container to accommodate its taproot, and overwinter indoors.
↕10ft (3m) ↔3ft (1m)

💧 ☼ Z10–11

SHRUB LARGE

Cotinus 'Grace'

SMOKE TREE Plant this large deciduous shrub at the back of a bed where it will create a blaze of fiery red oval leaves in fall. This variety has rich purple leaves in summer; other forms produce green or pale yellow summer foliage.
↕20ft (6m) ↔15ft (5m)

💧 ☼ Z5–8

PERENNIAL MEDIUM

Crocosmia x *crocosmiiflora*

MONTBRETIA This perennial's arching, sword-shaped green leaves and trumpet-shaped summer to fall flowers are perfect for hot-hued borders. Try the golden 'Star of the East' (above) with orange-yellow blooms. Considered invasive in some coastal regions.
↕28in (70cm) ↔3in (8cm)

💧 ☼ Z6–9

PERENNIAL MEDIUM

Crocosmia 'Lucifer'

MONTBRETIA A clump-forming perennial with tubular red late summer flowers that inject fiery color into beds. Other varieties have flowers in bright oranges, yellows, or reds. The architectural sword-shaped leaves are a bonus. Can be weedy.
↕3ft (1m) ↔10in (25cm)

💧 ☼ Z6–9

SHRUB SMALL

Cuphea ignea

CIGAR FLOWER A subshrub, grown as an annual, with black-tipped red flowers that shine all summer from among the green lance-shaped leaves, making a decorative bed edging or feature in containers of potting mix. Thrives in sun and part shade.
↕30in (75cm) ↔3ft (1m)

💧 ☼ Z10–11 Ⓝ

BULB LARGE

Dahlia 'Bishop of Llandaff'

DAHLIA Few flowers can outshine the red semidouble flowers of this popular tuber. The smoldering dark foliage provides the perfect foil for the fiery blooms. Plant the tubers outside after threats of frosts; may need staking.
↕3ft (1m)

💧 ☼ Z9–11

BULB LARGE

Dahlia 'Fire pot'

WATERLILY DAHLIA The flowers of this bulb, grown from spring-planted tubers, sport a blend of sizzling pink and orange with a dash of yellow in the center. Use it to brighten up the back of a bed or in a large patio container of soil-based potting mix.
↕3ft (1m)

💧 ☼ Z9–11

BULB MEDIUM

Dahlia 'Yellow Hammer'

DWARF BEDDER SINGLE DAHLIA The single orange-streaked bright yellow flowers of this dahlia will draw the eye in hot-colored borders, while the dark bronze foliage provides a dramatic contrast. Dig in fall and overwinter indoors in colder areas.
↕24in (60cm)

 Z9–11

PERENNIAL SMALL

Dicentra formosa

WESTERN BLEEDING HEART In a brightly colored bed, this perennial's pendent, pink or red heart-shaped flowers will combine well with orange-tinted tulips from late spring to early summer. Its divided gray-green foliage provides a leafy foil.
↕18in (45cm) ↔12in (30cm)

 Z3–9 Ⓝ

ANNUAL/BIENNIAL SMALL

Eschscholzia californica

CALIFORNIA POPPY Sprinkle the seeds of this clump-forming annual in fall at the front of a well-drained sunny bed for masses of bowl-shaped orange, red, and yellow flowers in summer. It may self-seed after its first season. Can be weedy.
↕12in (30cm) ↔6in (15cm)

 Ⓝ

PERENNIAL MEDIUM

Euphorbia griffithii

GRIFFITH'S SPURGE Inject color into a partly shaded bed in early summer with this perennial's red stems of narrow copper-tinged dark green leaves topped with domed clusters of orange-red flowers. Best in moist fertile soil. Sap can irritate skin.
↕30in (75cm) ↔20in (50cm)

 Z4–9

SHRUB SMALL

Euryops acraeus

BUSH DAISY Brighten up a rock or gravel garden with this dome-shaped evergreen shrub's bright yellow daisy-like flowers from late spring to early summer and silvery blue leaves. Try planting it with purple aubretia and late-flowering tulips.
↕↔12in (30cm)

Z8–11

SHRUB LARGE

Forsythia x *intermedia* 'Lynwood Variety'

BORDER FORSYTHIA This upright vigorous deciduous shrub shines from late winter to spring when its long bare stems are clothed with bright yellow star-shaped flowers before the small bright green leaves appear.
↕↔10ft (3m)

Z5–8

BULB LARGE

Fritillaria imperialis

CROWN IMPERIAL Combine this perennial bulb with hot-hued tulips for a dazzling late spring display. It forms a crown of blue-green leaves above large, orange or yellow bell-shaped flowers held on sturdy stems. Plants go dormant after flowering.
↕5ft (1.5m)

Z5–8

SHRUB SMALL

Fuchsia 'Genii'

FUCHSIA Use this bushy deciduous shrub's fiery combination of gold-green young foliage, fading to lime-green in summer, and profusion of pendent, cerise and purple summer to fall blooms in borders or in a container of soil-based potting mix.
↕↔30in (75cm)

 Z8–10

PERENNIAL SMALL

Gazania Kiss Series

TREASURE FLOWER This perennial, treated as an annual, has contrasting-eyed bronze, pink, gold, or white, daisy-like summer to early fall blooms set against dark green leaves. Grow in a shallow container of potting mix or at the front of a sunny bed.
↕12in (30cm) ↔10in (25cm)

 Z8–10

PERENNIAL SMALL

Geum coccineum

AVENS This clump-forming perennial has cheerful red or orange flowers with prominent yellow stamens. It adds a vibrant highlight to the front of a sunny bed in summer. Best in damp soils. 'Cooky' (above) is a popular orange variety.
↕↔12in (30cm)

Z5–7

TREE MEDIUM

Gleditsia triacanthos 'Sunburst'

HONEYLOCUST This deciduous tree is prized for its large golden-yellow leaves divided into leaflets, which turn green in summer and bright yellow in fall. Long, pendent seedpods appear in fall.

↕40ft (12m) ↔30ft (10m)

Z3–8 Ⓝ

SHRUB LARGE

Hamamelis x *intermedia*

WITCH HAZEL This exceptional vase-shaped shrub blooms in the depths of winter, producing lightly scented spidery flowers on bare stems. The leaves appear in spring. 'Jelena' (above) has large coppery orange flowers.

↕↔12ft (4m)

pH Z5–8

PERENNIAL MEDIUM

Helenium 'Wyndley'

SNEEZEWEED Sprays of daisy-like orange-brown flowers with brown central disks top the sturdy stems of this perennial from midsummer to early fall. The foliage is lance-shaped and dark green. Plant it mid-bed with dahlias and grasses.

↕32in (80cm) ↔20in (50cm)

(!) Z4–8

PERENNIAL SMALL

Helianthemum 'Fire Dragon'

ROCK ROSE This small-sized evergreen perennial produces trailing stems of soft gray-green leaves. Vivid fiery orange-red rounded flowers appear in summer. Use it to add sparkle to the edge of a raised bed.

↕12in (30cm) ↔18in (45cm)

Z6–8

ANNUAL/BIENNIAL LARGE

Helianthus annuus

SUNFLOWER A classic cottage plant, this easy-to-grow annual includes dwarf and tall forms, with daisy-like yellow, orange, mahogany, or cream summer blooms. The seedheads that follow provide food for birds. Protect young plants against slugs.

↕up to 10ft (3m) ↔18in (45cm)

Ⓝ

PERENNIAL MEDIUM

Hemerocallis 'All American Chief'

DAYLILY This perennial forms an upright clump of arching straplike leaves and trumpet-shaped deep red summer blooms with yellow throats, each flower lasting just a day. Plant in a sunny bed.

↕32in (80cm) ↔30in (75cm)

Z3–9

PERENNIAL SMALL

Heuchera 'Amber Waves'

CORAL BELLS A clump-forming evergreen perennial with lobed, ruffled orange-yellow leaves, pale burgundy underneath, and sprays of small, bell-shaped pink summer flowers. Use it to edge pots or beds. It works well with dark-leaved forms.

↕12in (30cm) ↔20in (50cm)

Z4–9

PERENNIAL SMALL

Heuchera 'Plum Pudding'

CORAL BELLS The rounded, lobed dark maroon-purple leaves of this leafy evergreen perennial provide a contrasting foil for hot pink, yellow, or red flowers. Wiry stems of small insignificant white flowers appear in summer.

↕20in (50cm) ↔12in (30cm)

Z4–9 Ⓝ

PERENNIAL SMALL

Hosta 'Fire and Ice'

PLANTAIN LILY A clump-forming perennial with large, heart-shaped, ribbed green leaves, which are boldly marked with prominent white splashes. It contrasts well with brightly colored blooms and can be used to underplant larger shrubs.

↕16in (40cm) ↔indefinite

Z3–8

PERENNIAL SMALL

Ipomoea batatas 'Blackie'

SWEET POTATO VINE A trailing evergreen perennial, grown as an annual, with lobed, dramatic ivy-shaped, almost black, leaves that blend beautifully with hot-colored flowers. Use it to edge containers of all-purpose potting soil or a raised bed.

↕10in (25cm) ↔24in (60cm)

(!) Z9–11

CLIMBER MEDIUM

Ipomoea coccinea

RED MORNING GLORY An exotic twining annual climber with heart-shaped green leaves and small, fragrant, tubular yellow-throated, scarlet flowers. Grow it up a tripod to produce an accent of color in a bed or large pot from summer to early fall.

↕10ft (3m)

(!) Ⓝ

BULB LARGE

Lilium Golden Splendor Group

TRUMPET LILY Use this tall upright bulb with scented trumpet-shaped, golden summer flowers to create a dramatic highlight at the back of a bed. Plant the bulbs in spring; stake the stems.

↕6ft (2m)

 Z5–8

PERENNIAL MEDIUM

Monarda 'Cambridge Scarlet'

BEEBALM Plant this clump-forming upright perennial mid-bed in moist soil to enjoy the aromatic dark green leaves and spidery red blooms in summer. Try it with hot pink and orange flowers for a sizzling display. Stems may need staking.

↕3ft (1m) ↔18in (45cm)

 Z3–9 Ⓝ

SHRUB MEDIUM

Lonicera nitida 'Baggesen's Gold'

BOXLEAF HONEYSUCKLE Use this evergreen shrub as a backdrop to a fiery bed of red, yellow, and orange blooms. Its arching stems of yellow-green leaves make for a dense screen.

↕6ft (2m) ↔10ft (3m)

 Z7–9

BULB MEDIUM

Narcissus 'Pipit'

JONQUILLA DAFFODIL Plant this dwarf perennial bulb in masses in beds or large containers to create a sea of fragrant lemon-yellow flowers with creamy white cups from mid- to late spring. Plant bulbs in fall with tulips that flower at the same time.

↕10in (25cm)

Z4–8

PERENNIAL MEDIUM

Lychnis coronaria

ROSE CAMPION This perennial or biennial with its profusion of small, round, bright pink summer flowers is ideal for the front of a bed. The silver-gray slightly downy foliage adds to its charm. Allow it to self-seed to create a naturalistic effect.

↕24in (60cm) ↔18in (45cm)

Z4–8

SHRUB MEDIUM

Paeonia delavayi

TREE PEONY This upright deciduous shrub has tall stems with large, deeply lobed dark green leaves, blue-green beneath, and nodding cup-shaped, dark red late spring flowers. Plant it at the back of a hot color-themed bed or along a boundary.

↕↔6ft (2m)

Z4–8

BULB MEDIUM

Lilium lancifolium

TIGER LILY This upright perennial bulb has long, narrow lance-shaped leaves and, from summer to early fall, nodding turks-cap pink- to red-orange flowers. 'Splendens' (above) has larger black-spotted, bright red-orange blooms.

↕24in (60cm) or more

pH Z3–8

PERENNIAL SMALL

Meconopsis cambrica

WELSH POPPY This perennial is perfect for naturalistic gardens. Use its lemon-yellow or orange poppylike blooms to brighten beds and gravel beds from late spring to summer. The divided leaves are light green. It will self-seed readily in free-draining soil.

↕18in (45cm) ↔12in (30cm)

Z5–9

PERENNIAL MEDIUM

Paeonia mlokosewitschii

CAUCASIAN PEONY The showy bowl-shaped lemon-yellow flowers of this clump-forming perennial look dramatic from late spring to early summer in a sunny or partly shaded bed. Pinkish leaf buds unfurl to reveal bluish green oval foliage.

↕↔30in (75cm)

Z5–8

PERENNIAL MEDIUM

Papaver orientale

ORIENTAL POPPY Grow this early-summer-flowering perennial for its large bright red blooms, with black marks and dark eyes, and decorative seedheads. Combine it with peonies and late-summer-flowering plants to plug the gaps left after it fades.

↕↔3ft (1m)

Z3–9

SHRUB MEDIUM

Phygelius x *rectus*

CAPE FUCHSIA This upright semievergreen subshrub produces long stems dripping with pendent, yellow or red tubular flowers above lance-shaped green leaves. Varieties include 'African Queen' (above), with orange-red blooms.

↕3ft (1m) ↔4ft (1.2m)

Z8–10

PERENNIAL MEDIUM

Penstemon digitalis 'Husker Red'

BEARDTONGUE This bushy perennial's dark red lance-shaped leaves and stems create a smoldering foil for orange and red flowers at a bed front. From late spring to midsummer, white tubular flowers appear.

↕30in (75cm) ↔12in (30cm)

Z3–8 Ⓝ

SHRUB MEDIUM

Philadelphus coronarius 'Aureus'

MOCK ORANGE Use this upright deciduous shrub's package of bright yellow young leaves, which age to lime-green and scented creamy white early summer blooms as a backdrop to a hot-hued border.

↕8ft (2.5m) ↔5ft (1.5m)

Z4–8

SHRUB LARGE

Physocarpus opulifolius

NINEBARK This deciduous shrub has lobed green, yellow, or purple-red leaves, which can be used as a backdrop to hot-hued schemes. Domed clusters of pale pink summer blooms are followed by brown fruits. 'Diabolo' sports deep purple foliage.

↕10ft (3m) ↔15ft (1.5m)

Z3–7 Ⓝ

CLIMBER MEDIUM

Rosa FOURTH OF JULY

CLIMBING ROSE This rose has dark green glossy leaves and, from summer to fall, cupped, cherry-flecked cream semidouble flowers with ruffled edges and a light fruity perfume. The foliage is dark green and disease-resistant.

↕10ft (3m)

Z5–9

CLIMBER MEDIUM

Rosa SUMMER WINE

CLIMBING ROSE From summer to fall, this climber bears fragrant coral semidouble flowers that add vibrancy to a bed of red- or yellow-flowered plants. A disease-resistant variety, it has glossy dark green leaves. Deadhead regularly; mulch in spring.

↕10ft (3m)

Z5–9

PERENNIAL MEDIUM

Rudbeckia hirta

BLACK-EYED SUSAN Grown as an annual, this short-lived perennial adds a wealth of large, daisy-like purple-centered golden-yellow flowers to the front of a sunny bed from summer to early fall. The midgreen leaves offer a cool-colored foil.

↕up to 3ft (1m) ↔18in (45cm)

Z3–7 Ⓝ

PERENNIAL SMALL

Salvia splendens

SCARLET SAGE Grow this perennial as an annual at the front of a bed or in containers of all-purpose potting soil for its purple, red, pink tubular flower spikes that appear all summer above dark green spear-shaped leaves. Deadhead faded flower spikes.

↕10in (25cm) ↔14in (35cm)

Z10–11

SHRUB LARGE

Sambucus nigra BLACK LACE

BLACK ELDER The divided, blackish fernlike foliage of this deciduous shrub offers a dark foil for brightly colored flowers. It has pale pink late spring flowers and blackish red fall berries. May die back in colder areas.

↕↔20ft (6m)

 Z5–7

PERENNIAL SMALL

Solenostemon scutellarioides

COLEUS A small bushy perennial, grown as an annual, with spear-shaped pink, red, green, and yellow leaves, which add fiery hues to path and border edges and baskets and containers filled with potting mix. Cuttings can be overwintered in water.

↕18in (45cm) ↔12in (30cm) or more

Z11–12

ANNUAL/BIENNIAL SMALL

Tropaeolum Jewel Series

NASTURTIUM This fast-growing annual will quickly smother the front of a border with its combination of round green leaves and funnel-shaped flowers in bright shades of red, yellow, or orange from summer to early fall. Also use it to edge tall pots.

↕12in (30cm) ↔18in (45cm)

ANNUAL/BIENNIAL SMALL

Tagetes patula

FRENCH MARIGOLD With its divided, dark green aromatic leaves and yellow, orange, red, or mahogany flowers from summer to early fall, this Mexican native will brighten up the edges of fiery borders. Sow seeds indoors in early spring; protect from frost.

↕↔12in (30cm)

Ⓝ

CLIMBER MEDIUM

Tropaeolum speciosum

FLAME CREEPER Let the twining stems of this perennial climber scramble through a large shrub at the back of a bed where its scarlet flowers, set against lobed blue-green leaves, will offer a focal point. Bright blue fruits follow the blooms in fall.

↕10ft (3m)

pH Z8–11

SHRUB LARGE

Sambucus racemosa

EUROPEAN RED ELDER Prized for its bronze serrated leaves aging to golden-yellow in early summer, this upright deciduous shrub is ideal for the back of a hot-hued, partly shaded bed. The scarlet fruits that follow yellow spring flowers add to the effect.

↕↔10ft (3m)

Z3–7

BULB MEDIUM

Tulipa 'Prinses Irene'

syn. *Tulipa* 'Princess Irene' This mid-spring-flowering tulip bears bowl-shaped orange blooms with contrasting purple markings on the outer petals. Use to create hot fiery displays with other red or yellow varieties. Plant the bulbs in groups in fall.

↕14in (35cm)

! Z3–8

PERENNIAL MEDIUM

Sedum telephium Atropurpureum Group

STONECROP This perennial's dark purple stems, fleshy leaves, and pinkish white flower clusters from late summer to fall offer a dramatic contrast to hot-hued flowers and green-leaved perennials.

↕24in (60cm) ↔12in (30cm)

Z4–9

CLIMBER MEDIUM

Thunbergia alata

BLACK-EYED SUSAN VINE Grow this annual twining climber up a tripod in a bed to add a pyramid of toothed heart-shaped to oval leaves and rounded, flat-faced, dark-eyed orange, yellow or peach flowers from early summer to early fall.

↕10ft (3m)

Z10–11

OTHER SUGGESTIONS

Annuals

Celosia 'New Look' • *Salvia splendens* Vista Series • *Tagetes* 'Tangerine Gem'

Perennials and bulbs

Caladium 'Freida Hemple' • *Hemerocallis* 'Golden Chimes' • *Heuchera* 'Circus' • *Hibiscus coccineus* Ⓝ • *Lamprocapnos spectabilis* 'Gold Heart' • *Phormium* 'Platt's Black' • *Rudbeckia hirta* 'Prairie Sun' Ⓝ • *Tulipa* 'Black Hero'

Climber

Lonicera sempervirens 'Major Wheeler' Ⓝ

Shrubs and trees

Calluna vulgaris 'Golden Feather' • *Camellia japonica* 'Bob's Tinsie' • *Chamaecyparis pisifera* 'Golden Mop' • *Choisya ternata* SUNDANCE Ⓝ *Cuphea llavea* 'Flamenco Samba' Ⓝ • *Genista lydia* • *Loropetalum chinense* 'Zhuhou Fuchsia' • *Rosa* 'Golden Showers' • *Weigela florida* FRENCH LACE

Plants for colorful stems

As temperatures plummet and deciduous plants lose their leaves, a few species choose to put on their best performance of the year.

Twig dogwoods decorate winter gardens with spiky bouquets of scarlet, gold, and lime-green stems, while the stark white trunks of Himalayan birches make ghostly silhouettes in barren landscapes. Other plants produce intricately patterned bark to make your garden sparkle. The stems of snake bark maples resemble that reptile's skin, while the London plane tree's multicolored stems look like designer wallpaper—only select this large tree if you have plenty of space. Bamboos work well in modern, minimalist planting schemes—their graphic stems injecting a hint of gold, blue, or apple green.

TREE MEDIUM

Acer capillipes

SNAKE BARK MAPLE This stunning deciduous tree features decorative green- and gray-striped bark and has an elegant spreading habit. The three-lobed dark green leaves turn spectacular shades of orange and red in fall.
↕↔30ft (10m)

💧 ☼ ◑ Z5–7

TREE MEDIUM

Acer griseum

PAPER-BARK MAPLE This spreading deciduous tree is grown for its distinctive bronze flaking bark that can be seen most clearly in winter after the leaves have fallen. The lobed, dark green decorative foliage turns bright orange and red in fall.
↕↔30ft (10m)

💧 ☼ ◑ Z4–8

TREE SMALL

Acer palmatum 'Sango-kaku'

CORAL-BARK MAPLE The coral-red stems of this small deciduous tree look great when combined with its yellow leaves in fall. The lobed foliage unfurls pinkish yellow in spring and turns green in summer.
↕25ft (8m) ↔12ft (4m)

💧 ☼ ◑ Z6–8

TREE MEDIUM

Acer pensylvanicum

SNAKE BARK MAPLE An upright deciduous tree with green- and white-striped bark, which looks beautiful year-round, and rounded green leaves that turn yellow in fall. 'Erythrocladum' (above) has reddish brown and white-striped bark.
↕40ft (12m) ↔30ft (10m)

💧 ☼ ◑ Z3–7 Ⓝ

ANNUAL/BIENNIAL SMALL

Beta vulgaris

SWISS CHARD Grown as an edible crop, this annual has brightly colored stems in shades of red, orange, and yellow and can be treated as an ornamental. Sow seeds from spring to summer for color all year. Plant it at the front of a bed or in pots.
↕↔18in (45cm)

💧 ☼

TREE LARGE

Betula nigra

RIVER BIRCH The reddish brown peeling bark of this upright deciduous tree makes a focal point in winter gardens and looks good all year, especially when contrasted with the yellow spring catkins. Its diamond-shaped green leaves turn yellow in fall.
↕50ft (15m) ↔30ft (10m)

💧 ☼ ◑ Z4–9 Ⓝ

TREE LARGE

Betula utilis var. *jacquemontii*

HIMALAYAN BIRCH Grown for its white trunk and stems, this deciduous tree looks stunning from winter to spring when yellow catkins appear. The diamond-shaped leaves turn yellow in fall. Choose multistemmed forms for small gardens.
↕60ft (18m) ↔30ft (10m)

💧 ☼ ◑ Z4–7

BAMBOO LARGE

Chusquea culeou

CHILEAN BAMBOO Best on free-draining soils, this clump-forming bamboo produces glossy yellow-green to olive-green canes with long, papery-white leaf sheaths, giving young canes a striped appearance. It has midgreen linear leaves. Ideal for screening.
↕15ft (5m) ↔8ft (2.5m) or more

💧 ☼ Z8–11

SHRUB LARGE

Cornus alba

TATARIAN DOGWOOD Grown for its bright red winter stems, this deciduous shrub looks good year-round. It bears flattened heads of white flowers in early summer; the leaves turn yellow, orange, and red in fall. Cut the stems to the ground in late winter.
↕↔10ft (3m)

💧 ☼ 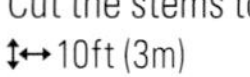 Z2–7

SHRUB LARGE

Cornus sanguinea

BLOODTWIG DOGWOOD The young stems of this deciduous shrub turn reddish green in winter, and the green spring foliage develops a fiery fall color. 'Midwinter Fire' has orange-yellow and red winter shoots. Prune old stems to the ground in late winter.

↕10ft (3m) ↔8ft (2.5m)

 Z4–7

SHRUB MEDIUM

Cornus sericea

TWIG DOGWOOD A deciduous shrub grown for its stunning red winter stems, or bright yellow-green in varieties such as 'Flaviramea' (above). The fiery fall leaves are an added attraction. Cut old stems to the ground in late winter.

↕6ft (2m) ↔12ft (4m)

Z2–8 Ⓝ

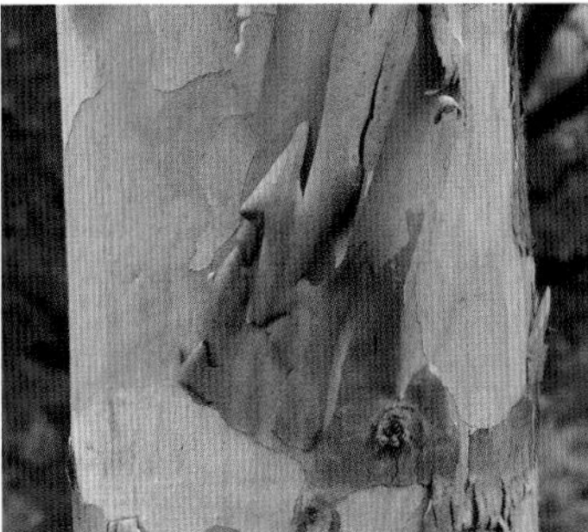

TREE LARGE

Eucalyptus gunnii

CIDER GUM This slender evergreen tree has smooth whitish green bark that peels in late summer to reveal pink-flushed grayish green young bark, creating a two-tone effect. The rounded, blue-gray young foliage leads to sickle-shaped green leaves.

↕80ft (25m) ↔50ft (15m)

Z8–10

BAMBOO LARGE

Fargesia murielae

UMBRELLA BAMBOO This large clump-forming bamboo produces arching yellow-green canes and bright green lance-shaped leaves, and makes a beautiful screen. A popular choice for gardens, because it is not very aggressive but is quite cold hardy.

↕12ft (4m) ↔indefinite

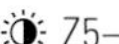 Z5–9

BAMBOO LARGE

Phyllostachys aureosulcata f. *aureocaulis*

GOLDEN GROOVE BAMBOO Use this upright clump-forming bamboo, with yellow canes striped at the base and lance-shaped midgreen leaves, as a screen. Remove the roots to limit its spread or use root barriers.

↕20ft (6m) ↔indefinite

Z5–10

BAMBOO LARGE

Phyllostachys nigra

BLACK BAMBOO This large clump-forming evergreen bamboo produces grooved greenish brown canes, which turn black in their second season and look stunning against a light-colored backdrop. The green foliage is lance-shaped.

↕25ft (8m) ↔indefinite

Z7–11

BAMBOO LARGE

Phyllostachys viridiglaucescens

GREENWAX GOLDEN BAMBOO Try this clump-forming evergreen bamboo with greenish brown canes, aging to yellow-green, and bright green leaves in blocks in a geometric bed in a modernist scheme.

↕25ft (8m) ↔indefinite

 Z7–11

TREE MEDIUM

Prunus serrula

PAPER-BARK CHERRY A deciduous tree, prized for its gleaming, coppery red peeling bark, which looks particularly effective on multistemmed specimens. Oval, tapering dark green leaves that turn yellow in fall, are joined by small white flowers in late spring.

↕↔30ft (10m)

Z5–6

SHRUB MEDIUM

Rubus cockburnianus

GHOST BRAMBLE The arching prickly shoots of this deciduous shrub are bright white in winter, creating a dramatic ghostly effect. Diamond-shaped dark green foliage follows in spring; inedible black fruits follow the purple summer flowers.

↕↔8ft (2.5m)

Z5–8

OTHER SUGGESTIONS

Perennials

Bergenia purpurascens • *Rheum* x *hybridum*

Bamboo

Phyllostachys violascens • *Semiarundinaria yashadake* f. *kimmei* • *Thamnocalamus crassinodus*

Shrubs

Cornus amomum Ⓝ • *Cornus stolonifera* Ⓝ

Trees

Acer davidii • *Betula albosinensis* • *Betula papyrifera* RENIASSANCE REFLECTION Ⓝ • *Betula* ROYAL FROST • *Cornus kousa* var. *chinensis* • *Luma apiculata* • *Pinus bungeana* • *Platanus* x *acerifolia* 'Bloodgood' • *Platanus occidentalis* Ⓝ • *Stewartia monadelpha* • *Stewartia pseudocamellia*

Plants for fragrant blooms

Guaranteed to lure visitors into the garden, scented plants are a welcome asset, and add a new dimension to any garden design.

Site fragrant flowers close to seating areas, doorways, and paths, and ensure that plants which require nudging to release their perfume, such as lavender, are brushed against to achieve this effect. Plants with a heady perfume like regal lily may be too overpowering for beds close to dining areas, so test them out before including any. To keep your spirits raised year-round, include roses that bloom in fall, Oregon grapeholly and witch hazel for winter gardens, and a selection of the vast legion of fragrant plants that flower in spring and summer.

SHRUB LARGE

Abelia x *grandiflora*

GLOSSY ABELIA This arching semievergreen shrub, with small dark green leaves, has pale pink to white bell-shaped blooms with a light fragrance that appear for weeks in midsummer. It is ideal for a sheltered spot next to a sunny patio.
↕10ft (3m) ↔12ft (4m)

Z6–9

PERENNIAL MEDIUM

Agastache 'Tangerine Dreams'

GIANT HYSSOP This tender perennial has gray-green, minty-anise-scented leaves and, from summer to fall, long-lasting spikes of small, pale orange-pink, nectar-rich tubular blooms. Overwinter as cuttings.
↕↔24in (60cm)

Z7–10

SHRUB SMALL

Arctostaphylos uva-ursi

BEARBERRY This creeping evergreen shrub has oval, glossy green leaves with a silver reverse and small, urn-shaped, pink or white fragrant flowers that bloom from spring to early summer. The flowers are followed by red berries.
↕4in (10cm) ↔20in (50cm)

pH Z2–6 Ⓝ

SHRUB LARGE

Brugmansia x *candida*

ANGELS' TRUMPETS This large shrub, usually overwintered in a conservatory, will enjoy summer on a warm patio. The huge hanging trumpets of night-scented blooms are white, yellow, or pink-apricot in 'Grand Marnier' (above). It is highly toxic.
↕15ft (5m) ↔8ft (2.5m)

(!) Z11

SHRUB LARGE

Chimonanthus praecox

WINTERSWEET This large deciduous shrub produces lance-shaped midgreen leaves. In winter, sulfur-yellow flowers with heady fragrance appear on bare stems followed by cylindrical or urn-shaped seed capsules.
↕12ft (4m) ↔10ft (3m)

Z7–9

SHRUB MEDIUM

Choisya ternata

MEXICAN ORANGE This rounded evergreen shrub has aromatic, glossy green leaves. It has sweetly perfumed late-spring-flower clusters, which repeat in fall. 'Aztec Pearl' is free-flowering. This Mexican native performs best in West Coast gardens.
↕↔8ft (2.5m)

Z8–10 Ⓝ

CLIMBER MEDIUM

Clematis recta

CLEMATIS This herbaceous perennial climber scrambles up over other shrubs. Large clusters of small, white fragrant blooms appear from summer to early fall, followed by fluffy seedheads. 'Purpurea' has coppery young foliage.
↕6ft (2m)

Z3–9

SHRUB MEDIUM

Clethra alnifolia

SUMMERSWEET This bushy shrub, with neat serrated leaves that turn yellow in fall, bears candlelike spires in late summer made up of tiny white bells with fluffy stamens and a rich floral perfume. Plant close to paths and entrances.

↕↔ 8ft (2.5m)

Z3–9 Ⓝ

PERENNIAL MEDIUM

Cosmos atrosanguineus

CHOCOLATE COSMOS The added pleasure of growing this slightly tender, maroon-flowered perennial is that its dish-shaped blooms, appearing from late summer to early fall on slender stems, are chocolate-scented. Grow in patio pots.

↕ 24in (60cm) or more ↔ 18in (45cm)

Z7–10 Ⓝ

BULB LARGE

Crinum x *powellii* 'Album'

POWELL LILY This bulb-forming evergreen perennial produces arching strap-shaped leaves and large, funnel-shaped, richly perfumed white flowers from late summer to fall on sturdy erect stems. Protect plants in cold regions.

↕ 3ft (1m) ↔ 2ft (60cm)

(!) Z7–10

SHRUB LARGE

Daphne bholua

PAPER DAPHNE This evergreen shrub, with oval dark green leaves, is grown for its late winter clusters of sweetly fragrant, pinkish purple-flushed white flowers, ideal near doorways. 'Jacqueline Postill' (above) is popular. Best in West Coast gardens.

↕ 10ft (3m) ↔ 5ft (1.5m)

(!) Z7–9

SHRUB MEDIUM

Daphne x *burkwoodii*

BURKWOOD DAPHNE This is a neat semievergreen shrub with small green leaves and highly fragrant pink late-spring-flower clusters, which are followed by red fruits. Varieties like 'Somerset' (above) are perfect for narrow patio borders.

↕ 5ft (1.5m) ↔ 3ft (1m)

(!) Z4–8

SHRUB SMALL

Deutzia gracilis

SLENDER DEUTZIA This upright to arching deciduous shrub, with small bright green leaves, is smothered in clusters of starry white blooms from late spring to early summer. The mass of blooms produces an attractive fragrance.

↕↔ 3ft (1m)

Z5–8

ANNUAL/BIENNIAL MEDIUM

Dianthus barbatus

SWEET WILLIAM This bushy upright biennial is a mainstay of cottage garden beds with its lance-shaped leaves and domed heads of sweet-scented pink, red, burgundy, white, or bicolored blooms in early summer.

↕ 28in (70cm) ↔ 12in (30cm)

PERENNIAL MEDIUM

Dianthus caryophyllus

CARNATION This traditional perennial, ideal for a cottage or cutting garden, has narrow gray-green leaves and tall slender stems of sweetly scented blooms in a range of pastel shades. Dwarf forms are also available.

↕ 32in (80cm) ↔ 9in (23cm)

Z6–10

PERENNIAL SMALL

Dianthus 'Dad's Favourite'

GARDEN PINK This dwarf evergreen perennial, ideal as bed edging, has short, gray-green grasslike leaves and a succession of semidouble white flowers with maroon markings all summer. The blooms have a rich clove scent.

↕ up to 18in (45cm) ↔ 12in (30cm)

Z4–9

SHRUB MEDIUM

Edgeworthia chrysantha

PAPER BUSH This late winter- to early-spring-flowering shrub thrives in sheltered beds. It has a spicy clove fragrance. The rounded clusters of yellow blooms are silky haired in bud, creating a frosted look.

↕↔ 5ft (1.5m)

Z8–10

ANNUAL/BIENNIAL SMALL

Erysimum cheiri

WALLFLOWER A cottage garden favorite, this powerfully fragrant biennial, planted in fall, produces heads of bright yellow, orange, red or pink blooms in mid-spring, attracting bees and butterflies. 'Blood Red' (above) bears deep red flowers.

↕↔ 12in (30cm)

Z3–7

SHRUB MEDIUM

Euphorbia mellifera

HONEY SPURGE This plant is a dome-shaped evergreen shrub that gives a Mediterranean effect planted in gravel. In late spring, rounded heads of honey-scented brownish flowers form at the ends of shoots.

↕ 6ft (2m) ↔ 8ft (2.5m)

Z9–10

SHRUB LARGE

Hamamelis x *intermedia*

WITCH HAZEL This spreading shrub is grown for its shredded citrus-peel-like yellow, copper, or mahogany flowers that emerge on bare stems from early- to midwinter 'Jelena' (above) bears copper-colored blooms.

↕↔ 12ft (4m)

pH Z5–8

BULB MEDIUM

Hyacinthus orientalis

HYACINTH This early-spring-flowering perennial bulb has broad spikes of heavily fragrant, bell-shaped waxy blooms in colors including blue, purple, pink, red, orange, yellow, and white. 'City of Haarlem' (above) has pale yellow blooms.

↕ 10in (25cm)

Z4–9

SHRUB LARGE

Hamamelis mollis

CHINESE WITCH HAZEL A large spreading shrub with broad leaves that turn yellow in fall, this late winter flowering shrub has spidery yellow blooms that sprout from the bare branches. Plant close to a path or drive to enjoy the scent.

↕↔ 12ft (4m) or more

pH Z5–8

SHRUB SMALL

Heliotropium arborescens

HELIOTROPE This bushy evergreen shrub, grown as an annual in pots and bedding displays, has oval, dark green crinkled leaves topped by clusters of purple or white, sweet and spicy vanilla-scented blooms throughout summer.

↕↔ 18in (45cm)

Z10–11

CLIMBER LARGE

Jasminum officinale

COMMON JASMINE This vigorous twining semievergreen climber with paired leaflets produces clusters of white flowers from summer to fall. Headily perfumed in the evening, it is a great choice for an arbor over a patio.

↕ 40ft (12m)

Z8–10

CLIMBER MEDIUM

Lathyrus odoratus

SWEET PEA An annual tendril climber with oval leaflets. Its richly perfumed flowers in shades of pink, blue, purple, or white bloom summer to early fall if regularly picked. Choose "old-fashioned" mixes for stronger scent.

↕ 10ft (3m)

SHRUB SMALL

Lavandula angustifolia

ENGLISH LAVENDER This evergreen subshrub with narrow, aromatic silver-gray leaves has short spikes of fragrant, blue-purple, pink or white flowers from mid- to late summer. Clip after blooming. 'Hidcote' (above) is a dwarf form.

↕ 24in (60cm) ↔ 30in (75cm)

Z5–8

BULB LARGE

Lilium 'Red Hot'

ORIENTAL LILY The exotic perfume of lilies is unmistakable. This large bulb produces arching stems that bear slender leaves that are topped with white-edged red blooms in summer. The blooms are particularly fragrant.
↕3ft (1m)

 Z5–8

CLIMBER LARGE

Lonicera periclymenum

WOODBINE A deciduous twining climber with clusters of flared tubular blooms that are a combination of creamy white yellow and pink during summer, depending on the variety. The perfume becomes stronger at twilight. Considered invasive in some areas.
↕22ft (7m)

Z5–9

SHRUB MEDIUM

Mahonia japonica

JAPANESE MAHONIA This evergreen architectural shrub with prickly-edged leathery leaflets becomes purple tinged in winter. From late fall to early spring, drooping pale yellow flower tassels fill the air with lily-of-the-valley scent.
↕6ft (2m) ↔10ft (3m)

Z6–9

TREE MEDIUM

Magnolia virginiana

SWEETBAY MAGNOLIA This moisture-loving deciduous or semievergreen shrub or tree has large glossy leaves, bluish white beneath, and lemon-vanilla scented, cream cup-shaped flowers in early summer and sporadically until fall.
↕30ft (10m) ↔20ft (6m)

Z5–9 Ⓝ

SHRUB MEDIUM

Mahonia x *media*

MAHONIA These hybrids add architectural interest in the winter garden with their large, divided glossy leaves and stems topped with clusters of fragrant yellow flower spikes. The blooms of 'Buckland' (above) are striking.
↕6ft (1.8m) ↔12ft (4m)

Z7–9

BULB LARGE

Lilium regale

REGAL LILY A cottage garden classic, this richly perfumed bulb in summer produces several large white trumpets at the top of upright stems. The throats are yellow and petal pinkish purple at the reverse. Loosely tie stalks to support blooms.
↕6ft (2m)

Z4–8

PERENNIAL SMALL

Matthiola incana

STOCK A short-lived perennial or annual with large pastel-shaded flower heads above the gray-green-leaved stocks that fill the cottage garden bed with their sweet clove fragrance and last from late spring into summer.
↕↔10in (25cm)

CLIMBER LARGE

Lonicera x *heckrottii*

GOLDFLAME HONEYSUCKLE This large deciduous or semievergreen twining climber has oval dark green leaves. Its summer flowers are a richly-perfumed pink with orange throats, the scent especially strong in the evenings and early mornings.
↕15ft (5m)

Z6–9

BULB MEDIUM

Narcissus 'February Gold'

DAFFODIL This variety is one of the first daffodils to bloom in spring, bearing rich yellow single flowers with a sweet peppery scent. Plant them in groups during fall in lawns and beds, and leave them to naturalize. Ideal for spring containers.
↕12in (30cm)

Z3–9

Plants for fragrant blooms

BULB MEDIUM

Narcissus 'Pipit'

JONQUILLA DAFFODIL Noted for their powerful perfume, these daffodils are perfect for pots and planters around doorways or for planting in mass in raised beds. The lemon-yellow, cream-cupped multiheaded flowers bloom in mid-spring.

↕10in (25cm)

Z4–8

ANNUAL/BIENNIAL MEDIUM

Nicotiana 'Lime Green'

FLOWERING TOBACCO An upright annual summer bedding plant with spoon-shaped leaves that are sticky to touch. In late summer and fall, it produces open, trumpet-shaped, twilight-scented greenish yellow flowers.

↕24in (60cm) ↔10in (25cm)

PERENNIAL LARGE

Nicotiana sylvestris

FLOWERING TOBACCO This perennial, grown as a summer annual, has very large sticky leaves and tall stems topped with heads of tubular white flowers that are flared at the ends. Plant in pots or patio beds to enjoy the evening scent.

↕5ft (1.5m) ↔30in (75cm)

Z10–11

ANNUAL/BIENNIAL LARGE

Oenothera biennis

EVENING PRIMROSE This erect biennial produces foliage in its first year, then flowers the following summer, bearing tall spike-like racemes. The bowl-shaped, lemon-scented blooms open during the evening and darken in color as they age.

↕5ft (1.5m) ↔24in (60cm)

Z4–8 Ⓝ

PERENNIAL SMALL

Petunia Prism Series

PETUNIA This compact large-flowered perennial, grown as an annual, has trumpet-shaped blooms all summer in a wide range of shades. Plant in baskets and windowboxes around doorways. The sweet scent is strongest in the evening.

↕14in (35cm) ↔20in (50cm)

Z10–11

SHRUB LARGE

Philadelphus 'Virginal'

MOCK ORANGE This vigorous upright shrub with dark green oval leaves is festooned with clusters of richly perfumed, white double or semidouble blooms that fill large areas of the garden with their scent from early- to midsummer.

↕10ft (3m) ↔8ft (2.5m)

Z5–8

SHRUB SMALL

Rosa 'Buff Beauty'

HYBRID MUSK ROSE This romantic-looking musk rose is a strong grower with long arching stems, glossy leaves, and clusters of small apricot-yellow and buff semidouble blooms, which add fragrance from summer to fall.

↕↔4ft (1.2m)

Z5–9

SHRUB MEDIUM

Rosa GERTRUDE JEKYLL

ENGLISH SHRUB ROSE This upright shrub rose or short climber has richly perfumed, midpink fully double blooms, which open flat from summer to early fall. Grow around an arbor or against the house wall near a doorway.

↕6ft (2m) ↔4ft (1.2m)

Z5–9

CLIMBER LARGE

Rosa 'New Dawn'

CLIMBING ROSE This vigorous disease-resistant climbing rose has dark glossy leaves and heads of lightly fragrant, pale pink double blooms with elegant buds. The flowers are produced through summer into fall. It is useful for a north wall.

↕1ft (5m)

Z5–9

SHRUB MEDIUM

Syringa meyeri 'Palibin'

MEYER LILAC This delightful dwarf lilac is slow-growing, bushy, and deciduous with upright heads of lilac-pink fragrant flowers in late spring and early summer. An ideal shrub for courtyard gardens and narrow patio beds.

↕↔ 5ft (1.5m)

Z3–7

SHRUB SMALL

Sarcococca confusa

SWEET BOX This bushy evergreen shrub with lance-shaped, glossy dark green leaves is grown for the sweet winter fragrance emanating from the tiny white flowers. A must for walkways through trees or shady city courtyards.

↕↔ 3ft (1m)

Z6–9

SHRUB MEDIUM

Sarcococca hookeriana var. *digyna*

SWEET BOX This clump-forming evergreen shrub has narrow lance-shaped leaves and tiny white fragrant flowers in winter. Plant it near a doorway or driveway. 'Purple Stem' has pink-flushed flowers.

↕ 5ft (1.5m) ↔ 6ft (2m)

Z6–9

SHRUB LARGE

Syringa vulgaris

COMMON LILAC This vigorous deciduous shrub has large cone-shaped clusters of fragrant late spring flowers in shades of purple, pink, yellow, and white. Choose compact varieties for smaller plots. Considered invasive in some areas.

↕↔ 22ft (7m)

Z3–7

CLIMBER LARGE

Trachelospermum jasminoides

STAR JASMINE This evergreen climber has twining stems and small oval leaves that turn bronze with colder nights. Clusters of small, pin-wheel-shaped white flowers form in midsummer, releasing a rich scent.

↕ 28ft (9m)

Z8–10

SHRUB LARGE

Viburnum x *bodnantense*

BODNANT VIBURNUM An upright deciduous shrub that produces sweet, almond-scented pink to white flowers in rounded clusters along bare branches from late fall to early spring. Varieties of this shrub include 'Dawn' (above).

↕ 10ft (3m) ↔ 6ft (2m)

Z5–8

SHRUB MEDIUM

Viburnum carlesii

KOREANSPICE VIBURNUM In late spring, this deciduous shrub bears domed heads of pink buds, opening to white, trumpet-shaped blooms with a sweet spiced fragrance, followed by red and black fall berries. Plant at the back of a sunny bed.

↕↔ 6ft (2m)

Z4–7

PERENNIAL SMALL

Viola odorata

SWEET VIOLET This creeping semievergreen perennial with heart-shaped leaves flowers from late winter to early spring, bearing violet or, sometimes, white flowers with a sweet but delicate scent. Plant beneath shrubs or in paving cracks.

↕ 8in (20cm) ↔ 12in (30cm)

Z6–8

PERENNIAL SMALL

Viola x *wittrockiana*

PANSY These cool weather bedding plants produce flat-faced flowers in a wide range of colors and shades, which have a sweet scent. They are most noticeable in bold groups and are suitable for edging or in containers as accents.

↕↔ 8in (20cm)

Z7–10

OTHER SUGGESTIONS

Annuals

Matthiola longipetala subsp. *bicornis* • *Tagetes erecta* Ⓝ

Perennials and bulbs

Hyacinthoides non-scripta • *Lilium* 'Tiger Woods' • *Lilium* 'Pink Perfection' • *Mirabilis jalapa* • *Petunia* 'Blue Daddy' • *Spiranthes odorata* Ⓝ

Shrubs and climbers

Brugmansia suaveolens • *Calycanthus floridus* Ⓝ • *Cladrastis kentukea* Ⓝ • *Clematis montana* 'Elizabeth' • *Clerodendrum trichotomum* • *Daphne odora* • *Gelsemium sempervirens* Ⓝ • *Illicium parviflorum* Ⓝ • *Jasminum humile* 'Revolutum' • *Lavandula stoechas* • *Magnolia denudata* • *Rhododendron arborescens* Ⓝ • *Rosa* 'Frau Dagmar Hastrup' • *Viburnum* x *burkwoodii* • *Wisteria frutescens* 'Amethyst Falls' Ⓝ

PLANTS for SHAPE and TEXTURE

While colorful flowers enjoy celebrity status in the garden, designers often focus on plants with striking shapes and textures before considering blooms because such features offer more enduring interest. Choose a selection of foliage plants and those with attractive stems to create a decorative backdrop to flowers, or use them as features to embolden your schemes. Trees with peeling bark, such as river birch, make a statement, while architectural leaves, including those of a Japanese fatsia or palms, produce a dramatic effect.

Stems for shape and texture

While bright colors shout "look at me," contrasting shapes and textures can be used as the *corps de ballet*, supporting and defining a planting design scheme.

Although most stem textures are quite subtle, creating intrigue as you get up close, a few also compete for center stage. The cinnamon-colored peeling trunks of paper-bark maple and shaggy orange and white stems of the river birch are hard to miss and make beautiful focal points. Twisted stems also provide impact, particularly in winter. If you have space, the wiggly stems of the dragon's-claw willow make a dramatic display. In small gardens, include a Harry Lauder's walking stick with its mop of curly stems and dangling catkins which appear in spring.

TREE MEDIUM

Acer griseum

PAPER-BARK MAPLE One of the best specimens for textural interest, this spreading deciduous tree has cinnamon flaking bark. Remove lower stems to show off the trunk. It also has lobed leaves that turn bright orange and red in fall.

↕↔30ft (10m)

Z4–8

BAMBOO LARGE

Chusquea culeou

CHILEAN BAMBOO A clump-forming bamboo with glossy yellow-green canes that have long, white papery leaf sheaths. The resulting striped effect is a feature. Remove weak canes and the bottom third of side branches to enhance the look.

↕15ft (5m) ↔8ft (2.5m) or more

Z8–11

TREE LARGE

Betula nigra

RIVER BIRCH The peeling bark of this upright deciduous tree creates eye-catching texture, and looks especially effective when contrasted with the yellow spring catkins. The diamond-shaped green leaves turn yellow in fall.

↕50ft (15m) ↔30ft (10m)

Z4–9 Ⓝ

TREE LARGE

Betula papyrifera

PAPER BIRCH This tall deciduous birch tree is narrow, and sparsely branched when young, with a smooth white bark that peels in broad scrolling pieces to reveal its pale orange reverse. Perfect as a multistemmed specimen.

↕70ft (20m) ↔30ft (10m)

Z2–7 Ⓝ

TREE LARGE

Cedrus atlantica Glauca Group

BLUE ATLAS CEDAR This evergreen conifer has a spreading tiered crown. The young loosely conical tree has slender dipping branches covered in silvery blue-green needles that create an attractive tracery.

↕130ft (40m) ↔30ft (10m)

Z6–9

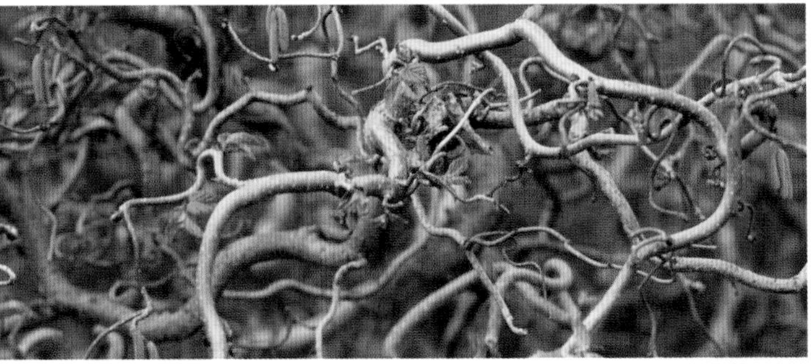

SHRUB LARGE

Corylus avellana 'Contorta'

HARRY LAUDER'S WALKING STICK This deciduous shrub has corkscrew stems and broad distorted oval leaves. In winter and early spring, its sculptural branches hang with catkins. Considered invasive in the Northwest and some areas of the Northeast.

↕↔15ft (5m)

Z4–8

PERENNIAL LARGE

Dicksonia antarctica

AUSTRALIAN TREE FERN An evergreen fern for a large pot, this perennial has a fibrous "trunk" made up of old leaf bases, creating a chevron pattern. On top is a "shuttlecock" of much-divided leaves and unfurling fronds. Overwinter indoors.

↕up to 20ft (6m) or more ↔12ft (4m)

Z9–11

TREE SMALL

Parrotia persica

PERSIAN IRONWOOD In winter, this wide-spreading tree or large shrub, shows a pattern of peeling bark on its multiple stems. Outer brown layers drop, revealing a patchwork of grays, greens, and whites. The fall leaf color is stunning.

↕25ft (8m) ↔30ft (10m)

pH Z4–8

BAMBOO LARGE

Phyllostachys aureosulcata f. *aureocaulis*

GOLDEN GROOVE BAMBOO This clump-forming bamboo has upright, occasionally zig-zagged, pale yellow canes that darken with age, and green vertical stripes at the base. Use root barriers in a small area.

↕20ft (6m) ↔indefinite

 Z5–10

BAMBOO LARGE

Phyllostachys nigra

BLACK BAMBOO A clump-forming bamboo with gently arching greenish brown canes, which turn glossy black when mature. Thin out weak stems and prune off lower-level side branches to show off the stems.

↕25ft (8m) ↔indefinite

Z7–11

TREE LARGE

Pinus nigra

AUSTRIAN PINE This exposure-tolerant pine forms a large domed-headed evergreen tree with long needles and yellow-brown cones. The ornamental bark, split by dark fissures, shows irregular patches of caramel and gray.

↕100ft (30m) ↔25ft (8m)

Z4–7

SHRUB MEDIUM

Rubus cockburnianus

GHOST BRAMBLE This deciduous shrub, in winter, forms strands of prickly arching shoots that have a ghostly white quality. In summer, its stems are concealed by dark green leaves and purple blooms. Inedible black fruits follow the flowers.

↕↔8ft (2.5m)

Z5–8

TREE LARGE

Pinus pinea

STONE PINE This pine has a characteristic parasol-shaped crown when grown as a single-stemmed tree. The bark is patterned, forming smooth, irregularly-shaped, rusty colored or chestnut plates, outlined by dark fissures.

↕70ft (20m) ↔40ft (12m)

Z9–11

TREE MEDIUM

Prunus serrula

PAPER-BARK CHERRY This deciduous tree is grown for its gleaming coppery red bark that peels as it matures, leaving trunks and stems looking like they have been bound in satin ribbon. Yellow fall leaf color adds to the effect.

↕↔30ft (10m)

Z5–6

TREE MEDIUM

Salix babylonica 'Tortuosa'

DRAGON'S-CLAW WILLOW This deciduous tree is grown for its corkscrewed shoots and narrow wavy leaves, which partially disguise the stems in summer. Its size may be controlled by pollarding. May become invasive.

↕↔40ft (12m)

 Z5–8

TREE SMALL

Salix caprea 'Pendula'

PUSSY WILLOW This is a small mushroom-headed weeping tree with long trailing branches. Silver-colored, soft furry catkins form in late winter. Prune to thin the head and maintain an airy framework. Considered invasive in some areas.

↕↔6ft (2m)

Z6–8

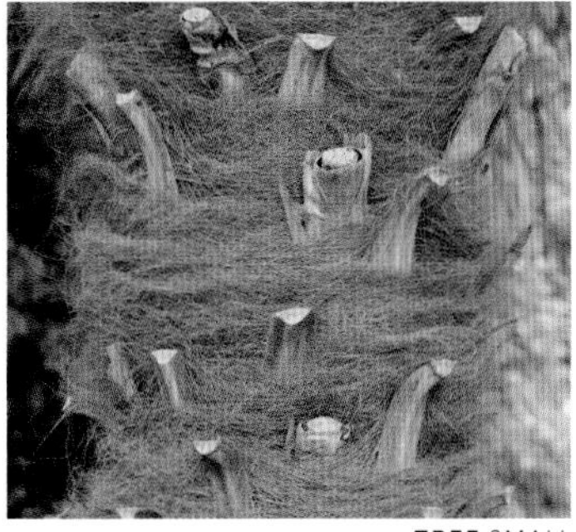

TREE SMALL

Trachycarpus fortunei

WINDMILL PALM This evergreen palm has large fanlike leaves held on long flexible stems that sprout from a central trunk. Young plants have a bushy habit and take several years to develop the woody trunk with its fibrous coating.

↕up to 6ft (2m) ↔8ft (2.5m)

Z8–10

OTHER SUGGESTIONS

Shrubs

Hydrangea aspera subsp. *sargentiana* • *Rosa sericea* subsp. *omeiensis* f. *pteracantha* • *Physocarpus opulifolius* 'Diabolo' Ⓝ

Trees

Acer capillipes • *Acer rufinerve* • *Betula ermanii* • *Carya ovata* Ⓝ • *Carpinus betulus* 'Fastigiata' • *Fagus grandifolia* Ⓝ • *Juglans nigra* Ⓝ • *Metasequoia glyptostroboides* • *Nyssa sylvatica* 'Zydeco Twist' Ⓝ • *Platanus occidentalis* Ⓝ • *Populus tremuloides* Ⓝ • *Quercus rubra* Ⓝ • *Quercus palustris* Ⓝ • *Stewartia pseudocamellia* • *Zanthoxylum americanum* Ⓝ

Plants for textured foliage

Plants with textured foliage make ideal specimens, creating impact when used on their own as focal points or as a contrast to their neighbors.

One of the main tools of a garden designer's trade, textured foliage offers year-round interest and looks most effective when teamed with contrasting smooth or shiny leaves. Conifers, such as pines and spruces, produce stems of evergreen, brushlike leaves that combine well with a boxwood topiary or an underskirt of heather for a year-round textural display. As part of a seasonal scheme at the front of a sunny bed, try the downy leaves of lamb's ears with the blue, spiky foliage of a Mediterranean sea holly. In a shady spot bring together a collection of ferns, hostas, and frilly, burgundy-leaved coral bells for a feast of textures.

TREE SMALL

Acer palmatum 'Sango-kaku'

CORAL-BARK MAPLE This deciduous tree's divided foliage, borne on coral-red stems, offers three seasons of interest, unfurling pinkish yellow in spring, turning green in summer, and then butter-yellow in fall.
↕25ft (8m) ↔12ft (4m)

Z6–8

PERENNIAL SMALL

Begonia 'Escargot'

BEGONIA This tender evergreen perennial offers large attractive spiral-shaped, purple-tinted green leaves with silver swirly markings and small pink flowers in fall. Grow it as a house plant in winter, and outdoors in a pot in summer.
↕10in (25cm) ↔20in (50cm)

Z10–11

TREE LARGE

Betula ermanii

ERMAN'S BIRCH This decorative deciduous tree, prized for its peeling cream bark on the trunk and papery brown bark on the branches, also features textured, distinctly veined, toothed oval foliage, which turns yellow in fall. Catkins appear in spring.
↕70ft (20m) ↔40ft (12m)

Z5–8

PERENNIAL SMALL

Adiantum aleuticum

WESTERN MAIDENHAIR FERN A deciduous or semievergreen fern with small pale green branching fronds, clothed with oblong leaflets that create an exciting textural effect. New fronds may be tinged pink. Try at the front of a bed with dwarf daffodils.
↕↔18in (45cm)

Z3–8 Ⓝ

TREE SMALL

Acacia baileyana

COOTAMUNDRA WATTLE An evergreen tree with finely cut, decorative silvery gray leaves, which contrast well with plants bearing smooth green foliage and, from late winter to spring, fingerlike clusters of fluffy yellow flowers. Grow in neutral to acidic soil.
↕↔20ft (6m)

pH Z9–11

PERENNIAL MEDIUM

Asplenium scolopendrium

HART'S TONGUE FERN This rosette-forming evergreen fern has leathery, bright green tongue-shaped fronds. The spores beneath the fronds create a striped effect on upper surfaces. Forms such as Crispum Group (above) have crinkled-edged leaves.
↕28in (70cm) ↔24in (60cm)

Z5–9

PERENNIAL SMALL

Brunnera macrophylla

SIBERIAN BUGLOSS This perennial is ideal for use as ground cover in partly-shaded gardens. Grown for its oval tapering leaves with soft hairs, often speckled or edged with silvery white (above), and sprays of small bright blue flowers appear in spring.
↕18in (45cm) ↔24in (60cm)

Z3–8

TREE SMALL

Carpinus japonica

JAPANESE HORNBEAM This deciduous tree produces serrated, textured prominently veined foliage, which contrasts well with plants bearing smooth leaves. Green catkins, which mature to brown, appear in spring.

↕↔25ft (8m)

Z4–9

PERENNIAL LARGE

Crocosmia masoniorum

MONTBRETIA Grown for its arching stems of orange-red flowers in late summer, this clump-forming perennial has sword-shaped dark green leaves, which are pleated lengthways, and offer dramatic shape and texture. Good for use on roof top gardens.

↕4½ft (1.4m) ↔18in (45cm)

Z6–9

PERENNIAL LARGE

Cynara cardunculus

CARDOON This upright perennial can be treated as an annual. Its spiny silver-gray ornamental foliage is ideal for use as a focal point in a sunny bed. Large, thistlelike purple flowers appear from summer to fall. Considered invasive in West Coast areas.

↕6ft (2m) ↔3ft (1m)

Z7–9

PERENNIAL LARGE

Ensete ventricosum

ABYSSINIAN BANANA This evergreen perennial has large, paddle-shaped green leaves, red beneath, with cream midribs, and marked horizontal veins that create a ridged effect. Grow it in a large pot in cold regions, and bring under cover in winter.

↕↔10ft (3m) in a pot

Z10–11

PERENNIAL SMALL

Eryngium bourgatii

MEDITERRANEAN SEA HOLLY This upright perennial has rich textures. Its silver-veined leaves have spiny edges, creating a prickly show, while the conelike summer flowers sport spiny ruffs. The seedheads retain this spiky look. Combines well with grasses.

↕18in (45cm) ↔12in (30cm)

Z5–9

TREE LARGE

Eucalyptus gunnii

CIDER GUM The smooth blue-gray young foliage of this tall evergreen tree makes a good contrast with the rough-textured leaves, which become gray-green and more leathery as they mature. Its colorful peeling bark also offers textural interest.

↕80ft (25m) ↔50ft (15m)

Z8–10

TREE LARGE

Fagus sylvatica

EUROPEAN BEECH This large deciduous tree, often clipped to create hedging, has prominently veined, textured, wavy-edged green leaves, which turn coppery brown in fall. It retains its fall foliage through winter when used as hedging.

↕80ft (25m) ↔50ft (15m)

Z4–7

PERENNIAL LARGE

Foeniculum vulgare

FENNEL A perennial herb with ferny leaves on slender upright stems and clusters of tiny yellow flower heads in summer. Use it in borders to contrast with plants that produce larger smooth-textured foliage. Considered invasive in some areas.

↕6ft (1.8m) ↔18in (45cm)

Z4–9

TREE LARGE

Ginkgo biloba

MAIDENHAIR TREE This deciduous conical tree has frilly-edged, pale green fan-shaped leaves that create a textural effect from spring to summer, and inject color in fall, when they turn yellow. Grow male cultivars to avoid messy and smelly fruits.

↕100ft (30m) ↔25ft (8m)

Z4–9

PERENNIAL SMALL

Heuchera micrantha var. *diversifolia* 'Palace Purple'

CORAL BELLS Combine this evergreen perennial with small-leaved plants, such as boxwood. It has rounded, lobed and veined, metallic bronze-purple leaves and small white summer flowers on wiry stems.

↕↔18in (45cm)

Z3–8 Ⓝ

PERENNIAL SMALL

Hosta 'Halcyon'

PLANTAIN LILY This compact perennial has slug-resistant, long, heart-shaped blue-gray leaves and a ribbed thick-textured appearance. It makes a good foil for dark green foliage plants, and provides both color and texture in shady borders.

↕16in (40cm) ↔28in (70cm)

Z3–8

SHRUB MEDIUM

Hydrangea quercifolia

OAKLEAF HYDRANGEA This mound-forming shrub has rough-textured lobed leaves, which develop maroon tints, and take on striking red and purple hues in fall. Cone-shaped flower clusters appear from midsummer to fall.

↕6ft (2m) ↔8ft (2.5m)

pH ! Z5–9 Ⓝ

PERENNIAL MEDIUM

Matteuccia struthiopteris

OSTRICH FERN Most ferns offer interesting textures, but this shuttlecock-shaped deciduous species is among the best. It produces tall pale green fronds divided into toothed segments, and is ideal for damp soils in a woodland setting.

↕3ft (1m) ↔18in (45cm)

Z2–8 Ⓝ

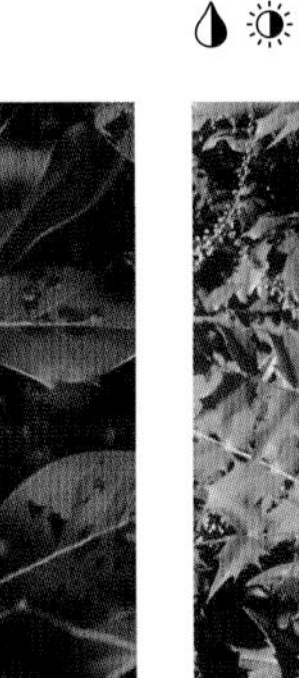

TREE LARGE

Ilex aquifolium

ENGLISH HOLLY A slow-growing evergreen tree known for its dark green spiny leaves. Offering a prickly year-round textural effect, it makes a good foil for smooth-leaved plants. Females bear red winter berries. Considered invasive in some areas.

↕up to 70ft (20m) ↔20ft (6m)

! Z7–9

SHRUB MEDIUM

Mahonia x *media*

MAHONIA This evergreen shrub creates a spiky texture in shady gardens. It has dark green leaves divided into paired spiny leaflets. Clusters of scented yellow flower spikes appear in winter. Varieties include 'Buckland' with red-tinted winter leaves.

↕6ft (1.8m) ↔12ft (4m)

Z7–9

SHRUB SMALL

Picea pungens 'Montgomery'

COLORADO SPRUCE The mound of gray-blue needlelike leaves produced by this compact, slow-growing evergreen conifer creates a bristly textured effect. Combine it with smooth green foliage plants in a sunny site. Requires neutral to acidic soil.

↕↔24in (60cm)

pH Z2–7 Ⓝ

TREE LARGE

Pinus radiata

MONTEREY PINE A vigorous evergreen conifer, suitable for large gardens with a broad crown of dense, dark green needlelike foliage, which will create a textured feature in a lawn. The tree also bears large conical to oval-shaped cones.

↕130ft (40m) ↔40ft (12m)

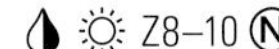

Z8–10 Ⓝ

SHRUB SMALL

Plectranthus argentatus

SILVER SPURFLOWER Grown as an annual, this evergreen subshrub has silver stems, gray-green foliage, and bluish white flower spikes in summer. Use to create textural contrasts with leathery- and glossy-leaved plants. Makes a decorative edging for pots.

↕↔ up to 3ft (1m)

Z10–11

PERENNIAL LARGE

Rheum palmatum

CHINESE RHUBARB The huge leaves of this perennial offer texture and drama. The foliage is dark green, purple-red beneath, jaggedly lobed, and features distinctive veining. Large plumes of cream to red fluffy flowers appear in early summer.

↕↔ 6ft (2m)

Z4–7

PERENNIAL LARGE

Rodgersia podophylla

RODGERSIA A perennial with large divided leaves made up of jagged-edged leaflets with a distinctive veined texture. The foliage is bronze-purple when young, maturing to green, and turning bronze-red in fall. Creamy flower panicles appear in summer.

↕ 5ft (1.5m) ↔ 6ft (1.8m)

Z5–8

PERENNIAL MEDIUM

Salvia argentea

SILVER SAGE This short-lived perennial forms a rosette of silvery leaves with a soft woolly texture that combine well with green foliage plants in sunny or lightly shaded beds. Spikes of blush white flowers appear in late summer.

↕ 3ft (1m) ↔ 24in (60cm)

Z5–8

PERENNIAL SMALL

Sempervivum giuseppii

HENS AND CHICKS This evergreen perennial injects textural interest into rock gardens, small pots, and cracks in walls. Its rosettes of spiky green leaves with pointed purple tips are joined by upright stems topped with star-shaped pink or red flowers in summer.

↕ in flower 4in (10cm) ↔ 4in (10cm)

Z7–9

PERENNIAL SMALL

Stachys byzantina

LAMB'S EARS A mat-forming perennial with oval silvery gray leaves that have a soft downy texture. In summer, spikes of clustered, tiny mauve-pink blooms form on felted stems. The foliage remains attractive in winter in mild areas.

↕ 15in (38cm) ↔ 24in (60cm)

Z4–8

PERENNIAL MEDIUM

Stipa tenuissima

MEXICAN FEATHER GRASS A deciduous perennial grass with fine green leaves, and silvery green summer flowers that turn beige as seeds form, creating a hazy hairlike texture. Use it as a front-of-bed plant with flowering perennials.

↕ 24in (60cm) ↔ 16in (40cm)

Z7–11 Ⓝ

TREE SMALL

Trachycarpus fortunei

WINDMILL PALM This evergreen palm adds texture to exotic-style schemes with its large, glossy green fan-shaped leaves, which are held on long flexible stems. Plant it in a sheltered spot or in a large container of soil-based potting mix when young.

↕ up to 6ft (2m) ↔ 8ft (2.5m)

Z8–10

ANNUAL/BIENNIAL LARGE

Verbascum olympicum

OLYMPIC MULLEIN This biennial forms a rosette of large gray leaves with a soft, tactile felted texture. These may die back in their first winter. Saucer-shaped bright golden flowers appear the next year from mid- to late summer. It may need staking.

↕ 6ft (2m) ↔ 3ft (1m)

Z5–9

OTHER SUGGESTIONS

Perennials

Aloe polyphylla • *Amsonia hubrechtii* Ⓝ • *Asplenium bulbiferum* • *Echeveria elegans* Ⓝ • *Helianthus salicifolius* Ⓝ • *Helleborus* x *sternii* • *Hosta* 'Krossa Regal' • *Muhlenbergia capillaris* Ⓝ • *Musa basjoo* • *Opuntia macrorhiza* Ⓝ • *Sempervivum arachnoideum* • *Sporobolus heterolepis* Ⓝ • *Thymus pseudolanuginosus* • *Veratrum nigrum* • *Verbascum bombyciferum*

Shrubs

Aesculus parviflora Ⓝ *Hamamelis virginiana* Ⓝ • *Rhus aromatica* 'Gro-Low' Ⓝ • *Viburnum dentatum* BLUE MUFFIN Ⓝ • *Viburnum* x *rhytidophylloides* 'Alleghany'

Trees

Abies procera 'Glauca' Ⓝ • *Carpinus betulus* • *Carpinus caroliniana* Ⓝ • *Ilex opaca* Ⓝ • *Pinus palustris* Ⓝ • *Pinus strobus* 'Contorta' Ⓝ

Plants for architectural foliage

The large, shapely leaves of a tree or shrub create features that can equal the dramatic impact of the brightest, most colorful flowers.

Use plants with sculptural foliage as a focal point at the end of a path or as gatekeepers to guard an entranceway. Many big-leaved species prefer shady locations, where a group with foliage of different sizes, shapes, and textures will produce an elegant scheme that sings out from the gloom. In sunny sites, spiked-plants and sword-shaped leaves to draw the eye—their dramatic outlines create an effective contrast to rounded and small, tear-shaped foliage. Some trees and shrubs, including Indian bean tree, should be pruned hard in late winter to encourage young stems that bear the largest leaves.

PERENNIAL LARGE

Acanthus mollis

COMMON BEAR'S BREECHES This upright semievergreen perennial, with its deeply cut, glossy dark green leaves, lends an architectural note to sunny and shaded gardens. Tall spikes of funnel-shaped, white and purple flower heads form in summer.

↕4ft (1.2m) ↔24in (60cm)

Z7–11

PERENNIAL LARGE

Actaea simplex

BUGBANE An upright perennial, grown for its divided, dark green sculptural foliage. From early- to mid-fall, it produces arching stems of bottlebrush, off-white-tinged purple flowers. 'Brunette' (above) is a dark purple-leaved variety.

↕4ft (2m) ↔24in (60cm)

Z4–8

PERENNIAL MEDIUM

Aeonium arboreum

TREE AEONIUM Grow this tender evergreen perennial in a pot and stand it outside in summer to enjoy its rosettes of fleshy, pale green spoon-shaped leaves, purple-black in some forms, which appear on branching stems. Overwinter under cover.

↕↔24in (60cm)

Z9–11

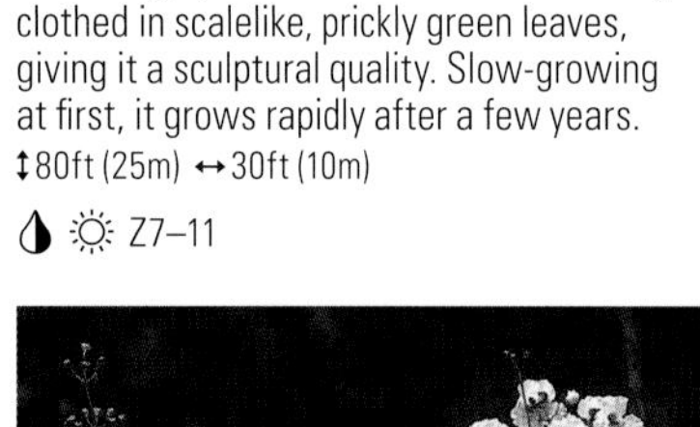

TREE LARGE

Araucaria araucana

MONKEY PUZZLE This evergreen conifer, suitable for large gardens, has an unusual branching, open habit. Its stems are densely clothed in scalelike, prickly green leaves, giving it a sculptural quality. Slow-growing at first, it grows rapidly after a few years.

↕80ft (25m) ↔30ft (10m)

Z7–11

PERENNIAL MEDIUM

Beschorneria yuccoides

MEXICAN LILY Ideal for a container of gritty soil-based potting mix, this evergreen perennial has pointed, fleshy gray-green strap-shaped leaves, creating a sculptural focal point. Yellow-green tubular flowers, with red bracts, may form in summer.

↕↔5ft (1.5m)

Z9–11 Ⓝ

PERENNIAL LARGE

Calamagrostis x *acutiflora*

FEATHER REED GRASS The fountain of long, arching green leaves produced by this clump-forming deciduous grass offers architectural interest for most of the year. The tall bronze summer flower heads fade to buff. Cut back in early spring.

↕6ft (1.8m) ↔4ft (1.2m)

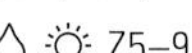

Z5–9

PERENNIAL LARGE

Canna TROPICANNA

CANNA Grown for its large paddle-shaped foliage, this perennial offers a spectacular display of orange and dark green, striped leaves, creating a sculptural focal point. In late summer, tall stems topped with ruffled orange flowers appear.

↕5½ft (1.6m) ↔20in (50cm)

Z7–11

TREE LARGE

Catalpa bignonioides

INDIAN BEAN TREE This spreading deciduous tree has distinctive large, broadly oval pale green leaves. Pollard to enhance the foliage. Beanlike seedpods follow the white summer flowers. Considered weedy outside of native range.

↕50ft (15m) ↔50ft (15m)

Z5–9 Ⓝ

SHRUB LARGE

Chamaerops humilis

EUROPEAN FAN PALM This evergreen palm has fan-shaped, divided green architectural leaves, ideal for foliage schemes. Mature plants bear clusters of small yellow summer flowers. It is more likely to survive winters if grown in free-draining soil.

↕10ft (3m) ↔6ft (2m)

Z8–11

TREE SMALL

Cordyline australis

CABBAGE PALM This palmlike evergreen tree forms a sculptural fountain of sword-shaped leaves in shades of green and purple. Ideal to use as an accent plant in a bed or patio display; overwinter indoors. Protect young specimens from frost.

↕10ft (3m) ↔3ft (1m)

 Z10–11

PERENNIAL LARGE

Cynara cardunculus

CARDOON Grown for its spiny, silver-gray ornamental foliage, this upright perennial, is ideal as a sculptural focal point in a sunny bed. Thistlelike purple flowers appear from summer to fall. Can be grown as an annual. Considered invasive in West Coast areas.

↕6ft (2m) ↔3ft (1m)

Z7–9

SHRUB LARGE

Daphniphyllum macropodum

YUZURI-HA The large, slender oval leaves of this exotic-looking evergreen shrub are borne in clusters on branching stems, creating an architectural effect in sheltered gardens. Small purple-pink male or green female flowers appear in early summer.

↕↔20ft (6m)

 Z7–9

PERENNIAL LARGE

Darmera peltata

UMBRELLA PLANT This perennial is prized for its large, round, deeply veined green leaves, which can grow larger than dinner plates and turn red in fall. In spring, it bears clusters of white or pale pink flowers on hairy stems before the foliage appears.

↕4ft (1.2m) ↔24in (60cm)

Z5–7 Ⓝ

PERENNIAL MEDIUM

Dryopteris affinis

GOLDEN MALE FERN This evergreen fern's "shuttlecock" of tall, divided lance-shaped fronds, which are pale green when young and mature to dark green, create a sculptural effect in shady gardens. Cut off old growth in early spring.

↕↔3ft (1m)

Z5–8

PERENNIAL LARGE

Ensete ventricosum

ABYSSINIAN BANANA This evergreen perennial is ideal for foliage displays. It has large, tropical-style, paddle-shaped green leaves, red beneath. 'Maurelii' has red-tinted leaves. Grow in a large pot in cold regions; bring under cover in winter.

↕6ft (2m) ↔3ft (1m)

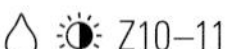 Z10–11

SHRUB LARGE

Eriobotrya japonica

LOQUAT This architectural shrub produces large, glossy dark green leaves, felted beneath, at the end of branched stems, and makes a dramatic focal point. Grow it in a sunny, sheltered spot to promote the scented white fall and winter flowers.

↕↔25ft (8m)

Z8–11

PERENNIAL MEDIUM

Farfugium japonica

LEOPARD PLANT The large, kidney-shaped green leaves of this evergreen perennial lend sculptural interest to shaded gardens. 'Argentea' (above) has variegated foliage. Bright yellow daisy-like flowers appear in late fall. Apply a deep mulch in winter.

↕↔24in (60cm)

Z7–10

SHRUB MEDIUM

x *Fatshedera lizei*

TREE IVY The dark green leaves of this upright evergreen shrub are deeply lobed and glossy. When trained as a climber up a pillar or against a wall, it creates tall columns of decorative foliage. Sprays of small white flowers appear in fall.

↕6ft (2m) ↔10ft (3m)

Z8–11

TREE SMALL

Ficus carica

FIG Although in warm climates, this tree or deciduous shrub is grown for its fruits, it lends sculptural interest to ornamental gardens in cooler climates with its gray-green foliage. Grow in a sheltered site. Considered invasive in some areas.

↕10ft (3m) ↔12ft (4m)

Z6–9

TREE LARGE

Gleditsia triacanthos

HONEYLOCUST A spreading deciduous tree, grown for its glossy dark green leaves divided into slim oval leaflets, creating a dramatic effect. Long, twisted seedpods in fall add to its charms. 'Rubylace' (above) has dark bronze-red young leaves.

↕50ft (15m) ↔15ft (5m)

Z3–8 Ⓝ

PERENNIAL MEDIUM

Helleborus argutifolius

CORSICAN HELLEBORE The dark green spiny-edged leaves of this architectural perennial provide interest year-round. From late winter to spring, clusters of nodding, pale green bowl-shaped flowers appear. Cut back before new blooms appear.

↕24in (60cm) ↔18in (45cm)

Z6–9

PERENNIAL MEDIUM

Hosta sieboldiana

PLANTAIN LILY The large rounded leaves of this perennial create a spectacular effect in a shady bed, where their rich blue-green color and puckered texture catch the eye. Spikes of lilac-tinged white flowers appear in early summer. Protect from slugs.

↕3ft (1m) ↔4ft (1.2m)

Z3–9

TREE LARGE

Liriodendron tulipifera 'Aureomarginatum'

TULIP TREE A deciduous tree, ideal for big gardens, it is notoriously slow to flower. Its unusual square, yellow-edged green foliage provides interest. Tuliplike pale green summer blooms form on old specimens.

↕100ft (30m) ↔50ft (15m)

pH Z4–9 Ⓝ

TREE LARGE

Magnolia grandiflora

SOUTHERN MAGNOLIA Although its large, fragrant white summer flowers are very attractive, this evergreen tree's rounded head of large, glossy dark green leaves also make an eye-catching feature in a sheltered site, or beside a south-facing wall.

↕60ft (18m) ↔50ft (15m)

Z7–9 Ⓝ

SHRUB MEDIUM

Mahonia x *media*

MAHONIA Grown for its large leaves, comprised of dark green hollylike leaflets, this evergreen shrub makes an exciting architectural feature in shady sites. The long fingerlike spikes of small, scented, yellow winter flowers attract bees.

↕6ft (1.8m) ↔12ft (4m)

Z7–9

SHRUB LARGE

Melianthus major

HONEYBUSH This evergreen subshrub, grown for its striking sculptural blue-gray leaves, divided into toothed leaflets, and brownish red flowers in late spring. Shelter from cold winds and provide a dry mulch in winter. Can overwinter indoors.

↕up to 10ft (3m)

Z8–11

PERENNIAL LARGE

Osmunda regalis

ROYAL FERN This clump-forming deciduous fern, with divided green fronds, pinkish when young and red-brown in fall, makes a focal point in pondside plantings. Mature plants bear tassel-like spikes of rust-brown spores at the ends of tall fronds.

↕6ft (2m) ↔3ft (1m)

Z3–10 Ⓝ

PERENNIAL LARGE

Rheum palmatum

CHINESE RHUBARB The huge leaves of this upright perennial provide texture and drama. The foliage is dark green, purple-red beneath, jaggedly lobed, and features distinctive veining. In early summer, large plumes of cream to red fluffy flowers form.
↕↔ 6ft (2m)

 Z4–7

TREE SMALL

Trachycarpus fortunei

WINDMILL PALM The deeply divided fanlike architectural leaves of this evergreen palm are held on an upright stem that becomes fibrous with age. It makes a dramatic focal point in a sheltered position, away from cold drying winds.
↕ up to 6ft (2m) ↔ 8ft (2.5m)

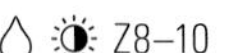 Z8–10

SHRUB MEDIUM

Paeonia delavayi var. *ludlowii*

TIBETAN PEONY Lobed green leaves, blue-green beneath, extend this shrub's appeal, giving interest even after the cup-shaped late spring flowers have faded. Grow at the back of a bed or beside a fence or wall.
↕↔ 8ft (2.5m)

Z6–9

TREE SMALL

Rhus typhina 'Dissecta'

STAGHORN SUMAC This small deciduous tree or suckering shrub produces large dramatic, finely cut bright green leaves that turn yellow, red, and orange in fall, when cone-shaped maroon fruits also appear. Give it room for the suckers to naturalize.
↕↔ 10ft (3m)

Z3–8 Ⓝ

TREE MEDIUM

Trochodendron aralioides

WHEEL TREE This broadly columnar tree or large shrub produces large, oval, tapering glossy leaves. From late spring to early summer, clusters of unusual, green spider-shaped flowers appear. Shelter from cold, drying winds. Suits tropical-style schemes.
↕ 30ft (10m) ↔ 25ft (8m)

 Z6–10

PERENNIAL SMALL

Podophyllum peltatum

MAYAPPLE The large glossy leaves of this perennial will lend a sculptural quality to the front of a shady border. Slightly scented white to pale pink single flowers appear beneath the leaves from spring to summer. Ripened fruits are edible.
↕ 18in (45cm) ↔ 12in (30cm)

Z3–8 Ⓝ

PERENNIAL LARGE

Rodgersia pinnata

RODGERSIA This clump-forming perennial is grown for its large, corrugated, divided dark green leaves. Conical spires of small pink, red, or yellow-white flowers appear in summer. 'Superba' (above) has bronze-tinged leaves and bright pink flowers.
↕ 4ft (1.2m) ↔ 30in (75cm)

Z4–7

SHRUB MEDIUM

Yucca filamentosa

ADAM'S NEEDLE The sword-shaped, spiky green leaves of this clump-forming evergreen shrub make it a useful accent plant in a sunny bed or large pot. Tuliplike pendulous flowers appear from mid- to late summer. 'Bright Edge' (above) is variegated.
↕ 6ft (2m) ↔ 5ft (1.5m)

Z4–11 Ⓝ

TREE LARGE

Sciadopitys verticillata

JAPANESE UMBRELLA PINE This slow-growing evergreen conifer bears long, linear dark green leaves, which produce an architectural effect. It has textured red-brown bark and oval cones. It makes a good focal feature in a large lawn.
↕ 70ft (20m) ↔ 25ft (8m)

Z5–8

OTHER SUGGESTIONS

Perennials

Alchemilla mollis 'Thriller' • *Actaea pachypoda* 'Misty Blue' Ⓝ • *Alocasia amazonica* • *Cynara scolymus* 'Green Globe Improved' • *Dryopteris filix-mas* Ⓝ • *Gunnera manicata* • *Gunnera tinctoria* • *Heuchera micrantha* var. *diversifolia* 'Palace Purple' Ⓝ • *Hibiscus acetosella* 'Haight Ashbury' • *Iris virginica* var. *shrevei* Ⓝ • *Polemonium reptans* 'Stairway to Heaven' Ⓝ • *Rheum palmatum* var. *tanguticum* • *Rodgersia aesculifolia* • *Syneilesis aconitifolia*

Shrubs

Cycas revoluta • *Rhus copallina* var. *latifolia* PRAIRIE FLAME Ⓝ

Trees

Asimina triloba Ⓝ • *Magnolia macrophylla* Ⓝ • *Tilia cordata* • *Trachycarpus wagnerianus*

Leaves for containers

Foliage is an essential ingredient of a well-balanced container display. Use leaves as foils for flowers and to add shape and form to a design.

Ferns, coral bells, and ivy leaves add rich texture to a fall or winter display of violas, while bronze sedges set against dwarf daffodils will liven up a spring pot. To create a tropical look in summer, pair dark-leaved coleus or the broody blackie sweet potato vine with scarlet and cerise dahlias, verbenas, and salvias. Some leafy plants need no flowery partners to make a statement. Striped and spiked agave is best planted solo; a single large-leaved hosta will produce a beautiful display of color and form; and Japanese fatsia's handsome glossy foliage sets off a glazed pot to perfection.

PERENNIAL SMALL

Acorus gramineus

GRASSY-LEAVED SWEET FLAG This semievergreen perennial is grown for its grassy arching foliage. Use as a specimen or in a mixed display in permanently wet soil-based potting mix. 'Ogon' (above) has creamy yellow-striped foliage.

↕10in (25cm) ↔6in (15cm)

Z5–9

PERENNIAL SMALL

Adiantum aleuticum

WESTERN MAIDENHAIR FERN Ideal for pots in shade, this semievergreen fern has small, pale green branching fronds clothed with tiny leaflets. Grow as a specimen or in a mixed display with other ferns. Water well and protect from dry winds.

↕↔18in (45cm)

Z3–8 Ⓝ

PERENNIAL MEDIUM

Aeonium 'Zwartkop'

PURPLE CREST AEONIUM This tender evergreen succulent has upright stems, clothed with glossy purple-black leaves. Grow it in containers of well-drained all-purpose potting soil in a sunny, sheltered site. Overwinter under cover.

↕24in (60cm) ↔3ft (1m)

Z9–11

PERENNIAL LARGE

Agave americana 'Variegata'

CENTURY PLANT A tender perennial succulent grown for its fleshy, pointed, cream-edged lance-shaped leaves. Plant in a large container of all-purpose potting soil in full sun, positioned where the spines won't cause injuries. Overwinter indoors.

↕↔5ft (1.5m)

Z9–11 Ⓝ

PERENNIAL MEDIUM

Asparagus densiflorus 'Myersii'

FOXTAIL FERN Grown for its fine lacy leaves, this tender perennial has a dense, plumelike appearance. Ideal for containers and windowboxes in light shade. Move it under cover for winter protection.

↕3ft (1m) ↔20in (50cm)

(!) Z10–11

PERENNIAL MEDIUM

Aspidistra elatior

CAST-IRON PLANT This slow-growing evergreen perennial has upright, glossy dark green leaves, and looks attractive in a large container. Plant in a sheltered site, away from cold winds. 'Variegata' (above) has cream-striped leaves.

↕24in (60cm) ↔18in (45cm)

Z7–10

PERENNIAL SMALL

Athyrium niponicum var. *pictum*

JAPANESE PAINTED FERN This small deciduous fern has deeply divided gray-green leaves with metallic purple and silver highlights. Grow in a large container. Water well in summer.

↕12in (30cm) ↔indefinite

Z4–8

PERENNIAL SMALL

Begonia 'Escargot'

BEGONIA This tender evergreen perennial is grown for its silver-edged, green-tinted purple heart-shaped leaves that have a distinctive coiled appearance. Place it outside in summer in a shady, sheltered spot, and move it under cover in winter.

↕10in (25cm) ↔20in (50cm)

Z10–11

PERENNIAL LARGE

Canna TROPICANNA

CANNA Ideal for large containers, this perennial is grown for its large paddle-shaped leaves with vivid orange veins. In late summer, it produces tall stems topped with orange blooms. Water well, remove spent flowers, and protect during winter.

↕ 5½ft (1.6m) ↔ 20in (50cm)

 Z7–11

PERENNIAL MEDIUM

Carex buchananii

LEATHERLEAF SEDGE This evergreen perennial has narrow, grasslike, upward, then arching, copper-colored leaves, red toward the base. Suitable for baskets and windowboxes for summer and winter displays; the leaves trail over the sides.

↕ 24in (60cm) ↔ 8in (20cm)

Z6–9

PERENNIAL SMALL

Carex comans

NEW ZEALAND HAIR SEDGE A grasslike evergreen perennial, grown for its arching, copper-brown hairlike leaves that form an airy tuft. Ideal for containers, it cascades over the sides; it is also suitable for winter interest. Remove dead growth in spring.

↕ 14in (35cm) ↔ 30in (75cm)

Z7–9

PERENNIAL SMALL

Dichondra argentea 'Silver Falls'

SILVER PONYFOOT This evergreen perennial has trailing silver stems with rounded, shiny silvery green leaves. Plant in baskets and windowboxes. Quick-growing, it may compete with neighboring plants.

↕ 20in (50cm) ↔ indefinite

Z10–12

PERENNIAL SMALL

Carex oshimensis

JAPANESE SEDGE Useful for summer and winter container displays, this perennial has arching, glossy dark green leaves with cream stripes. 'Evergold' (above) is yellow-striped and brightens up shady areas. Water well; shelter from cold winds.

↕↔ 8in (20cm)

 Z5–9

BULB MEDIUM

Dahlia 'Roxy'

SINGLE DAHLIA Perfect for pots dwarf dahlias are grown for their flowers and foliage. This variety has dark purple-green leaves that provide a useful backdrop to other flowering plants in mixed containers. Lift the tubers and overwinter indoors.

↕ 18in (45cm) ↔ 16in (40cm)

Z8–11

SHRUB LARGE

Dasylirion acrotrichum

GREEN SOTOL This slow-growing evergreen shrub has slender, stiff spearlike leaves, radiating out from a central crown, forming a leafy globe. Mature plants develop a trunk topped with leaves. Plant in container of all-purpose potting soil; protect in winter.

↕ 20ft (6m) ↔ 7ft (2.2m)

Z9-11 Ⓝ

SHRUB LARGE

Fatsia japonica

JAPANESE FATSIA Suited to large pots, this evergreen shrub has large hand-shaped, glossy dark green leaves. Use young plants for winter bedding in windowboxes in a sheltered site. Grow as a houseplant in cold areas in soil-based potting mix.

↕↔ 12ft (4m)

Z8–10

PERENNIAL MEDIUM

Geranium maculatum

SPOTTED GERANIUM This perennial bears pink flowers from spring to early summer, but is also grown for its cut green leaves, which form a low mound and provide contrast in a mixed planter. Ideal for cool, shady corners; remove the spent flowers.

↕ 30in (75cm) ↔ 18in (45cm)

 Z3–8 Ⓝ

PERENNIAL SMALL

Hakonechloa macra 'Aureola'

JAPANESE FOREST GRASS A slow-growing deciduous grass, it is grown for its vivid green and yellow-striped foliage and elegant trailing habit. Red-brown flower spikes appear in early fall and last into winter.

↕ 16in (40cm) ↔ 24in (60cm)

Z5–9

SHRUB SMALL

Helichrysum petiolare

LICORICE PLANT Grown as an annual, this shrub has downy gray-green leaves carried on trailing stems. Ideal for mixed containers and windowboxes, it can be overwintered under cover. 'Limelight' (above) has pale lime-green foliage.

↕ 6in (15cm) ↔ 12in (30cm)

Z9–11

PERENNIAL SMALL

Heuchera 'Amber Waves'

CORAL BELLS Suitable for containers, this clump-forming evergreen perennial has vivid orange-yellow lobed leaves providing color and texture. It bears sprays of tiny white blooms in summer. Other forms have green, silver, or purple foliage.
↕12in (30cm) ↔20in (50cm)

  Z4–9

PERENNIAL SMALL

Hosta 'So Sweet'

PLANTAIN LILY This clump-forming perennial has dark green textured leaves with irregular pale yellow edges. Grow as a specimen plant in a large container of soil-based potting mix; site in the shade of taller plants. Water well; protect from slugs.
↕14in (35cm) ↔22in (55cm)

 Z3–9

PERENNIAL LARGE

Leymus arenarius

SEA LYME GRASS An upright vigorous perennial grass with long, slender steel-blue leaves forming an airy clump in summer with tall flower stems that persist into fall. Plant in a container of gritty soil-based potting mix. Deadhead regularly.
↕5ft (1.5m) ↔indefinite

Z4–10

PERENNIAL SMALL

Ipomoea batatas 'Blackie'

SWEET POTATO VINE Grown as an annual, this tender perennial has trailing stems of deeply lobed, blackish ivy-shaped leaves. Ideal for containers, windowboxes, and baskets, it can used to provide contrast to brightly colored plants in mixed displays.
↕10in (25cm) ↔24in (60cm)

 Z9–11

PERENNIAL SMALL

Ophiopogon planiscapus 'Nigrescens'

MONDO GRASS A mound-forming evergreen perennial member of the lily family, it has black leaves and purple-pink summer-flower clusters. Ideal for long-term planting in pots, it lends contrast to bright plants.
↕9in (23cm) ↔12in (30cm)

 Z6–10

PERENNIAL SMALL

Hosta 'June'

PLANTAIN LILY Grown for its large blue-green leaves, marked with pale green flashes and form a dense crown, this perennial has short-lived summer flowers. Use as a foliage specimen in a container of soil-based potting mix. Protect from slugs.
↕15in (38cm) ↔28in (70cm)

Z3–9

PERENNIAL MEDIUM

Panicum virgatum

SWITCH GRASS An upright clump-forming deciduous grass, it gives a long season of interest in a container, with its green, grassy leaves, which turn yellow in fall, and clouds of pink-tinged summer flower heads. The dried flowers persist into winter.
↕3ft (1m) ↔30in (75cm)

Z5–9 Ⓝ

PERENNIAL SMALL

Hosta 'Revolution'

PLANTAIN LILY Grown as a foliage plant, this perennial has cream-splashed dark green leaves that add color in dappled shade. Plant in soil-based potting mix; remove the short-lived lavender flowers as soon as they fade. Protect from slugs.
↕20in (50cm) ↔3½ft (1.1m)

 Z3–9

PERENNIAL MEDIUM

Lamium galeobdolon

YELLOW ARCHANGEL This evergreen perennial has two-lipped, yellow summer flowers, but is grown for its nettlelike silver-variegated leaves. Use the popular 'Hermann's Pride' (above) to give color to summer and winter container displays.
↕24in (60cm) ↔indefinite

Z4–8

PERENNIAL SMALL

Pelargonium 'Lady Plymouth'

SCENTED GERANIUM This small bushy evergreen perennial, perfect for containers and windowboxes, produces scented, lobed, silver-margined green leaves and lavender-pink summer blooms. Overwinter the plant under cover.
↕16in (40cm) ↔8in (20cm)

  Z10–11

PERENNIAL SMALL

Pelargonium 'Royal Oak'

SCENTED GERANIUM A bushy evergreen perennial, often treated as an annual, it has lobed, crinkled dark green leaves that have crimson central flashes as they age. Pink flowers form sparingly in summer. Grow in pots and baskets as a foil for bright flowers.

↕15in (38cm) ↔12in (30cm)

 Z9–10

PERENNIAL MEDIUM

Persicaria microcephala 'Red Dragon'

KNOTWEED Ideal as a specimen plant in pots of moist compost, this spreading perennial has heart-shaped, reddish green leaves with bold silver and bronze markings, and tiny white flowers in midsummer.

↕28in (70cm) ↔3ft (1m)

Z5–9

PERENNIAL MEDIUM

Phormium 'Bronze Baby'

NEW ZEALAND FLAX This compact evergreen perennial forms an upright fountain of dark bronze leaves that give year-round interest. Use it as a specimen in a large container of soil-based potting mix. Overwinter indoors in colder areas.

↕↔24in (60cm)

Z9–11

SHRUB SMALL

Plectranthus madagascariensis

MINTLEAF Grown as an annual, this trailing evergreen shrub has lobed green leaves. Use the variegated form 'Variegated Mintleaf' (above) in mixed plantings in pots. Pinch out long stems for bushy growth.

↕12in (30cm) ↔ indefinite

Z10–11

CLIMBER MEDIUM

Senecio macroglossus 'Variegatus'

CAPE IVY A tender twining climber, grown for its angular, ivylike yellow-edged, dark green leaves. Train it up a wigwam in a pot, or let the stems trail. It flowers sparingly in summer. Overwinter under cover.

↕10ft (3m)

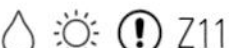 Z11

PERENNIAL SMALL

Solenostemon 'Black Prince'

COLEUS Grown as an annual, this bushy perennial has large, dark purple toothed leaves. Plant singly or in mixed summer containers; pinch out the tips regularly to encourage bushiness and to deter flowering. Overwinter cuttings in water.

↕↔20in (50cm)

Z11–12

PERENNIAL SMALL

Solenostemon scutellarioides

COLEUS A bushy perennial, grown as an annual, with pink, red, green, and yellow spear-shaped leaves. Best in large pots, it makes a bold specimen plant. Pinch out the tips to promote bushy growth and to deter flowering. Overwinter cuttings in water.

↕18in (45cm) ↔12in (30cm) or more

Z11–12

PERENNIAL MEDIUM

Stipa tenuissima

MEXICAN FEATHER GRASS This clump-forming perennial grass gives interest to pots from summer to fall, with its fine green leaves and airy summer flower heads that dry and persist until winter. Grow as a specimen plant in soil-based potting mix.

↕24in (60cm) ↔16in (40cm)

 Z7–11 Ⓝ

PERENNIAL SMALL

Tiarella wherryi

FOAMFLOWER This spreading evergreen perennial has lobed green leaves with veins that turn bronze-red in winter. In late spring, spikes of fluffy white flowers form. Use it to lend interest in winter and spring, then plant it out in a bed in summer.

↕8in (20cm) ↔6in (15cm) or more

 Z3–7 Ⓝ

PERENNIAL MEDIUM

Tolmiea menziesii

PIGGYBACK PLANT This semievergreen perennial has textured, green ivy-shaped leaves that provide contrast in mixed container displays and hanging baskets. 'Taff's Gold' (above) has cream- and green-variegated foliage.

↕24in (60cm) ↔6ft (2m)

Z6–9 Ⓝ

OTHER SUGGESTIONS

Perennials

Adiantum capillus-veneris Ⓝ • *Alocasia plumbea* 'Nigra' • *Athyrium* 'Lady in Red' • *Begonia boliviensis* Bonfire Series • *Begonia rex-cultorum* • *Carex comans* 'Frosted Curls' • *Chlorophytum comosum* 'Variegatum' • *Heuchera villosa* 'Bronze Wave' Ⓝ • *Heuchera* 'Chocolate Ruffles' • *Solenostemon* 'Fishnet Stockings' • *Solenostemon* 'Gay's Delight' • *Strobilanthes dyerianus*

Bulbs

Caladium 'Florida Sweetheart' • *Dahlia* 'David Howard'

Trees

Acer palmatum 'Beni-kawa' • *Cordyline* 'Red Star'

Trees for small gardens

Large plants can actually make small gardens look bigger by blurring the boundaries and creating the impression that the space extends further.

When selecting trees for a small garden, choose compact varieties that won't loom over the whole plot, and site taller specimens on the north and east sides of your property where they will create the least shade. Opt for slim or vase-shaped trees to fit into corners and a spreading species to create a shady feature in the center of your garden. Also consider seasonal interest when making your choices. Evergreens are tempting since they afford year-round color and privacy, but deciduous trees that produce spring blossoms, fruits, and fall tints offer great value as well.

TREE SMALL

Acer palmatum 'Atropurpureum'

JAPANESE MAPLE A small bushy-headed tree with purple-red summer foliage that turns fiery red in fall. Older specimens form a pleasing tracery of branches in winter. Plant in shelter to prevent scorch.
↕↔25ft (8m)

Z6–8

TREE SMALL

Amelanchier laevis

ALLEGHENY SERVICEBERRY An upright shrub or small spreading tree with bronze-tinted young leaves, maturing to green, and finally becoming orange-red in fall. White spring blossom is followed by red to purple, round edible fruits.
↕↔25ft (8m)

pH Z4–8 Ⓝ

TREE LARGE

Betula nigra

RIVER BIRCH The peeling bark of this upright deciduous tree creates an eye-catching texture, and looks especially effective when contrasted with the yellow spring catkins. Its diamond-shaped green leaves turn yellow in fall.
↕50ft (15m) ↔30ft (10m)

Z4–9 Ⓝ

TREE SMALL

Betula pendula 'Youngii'

YOUNG'S WEEPING BIRCH This weeping form of silver birch has gray-white bark and a wide spreading crown of cascading branches that reach the ground. Brownish yellow catkins appear in spring and the foliage turns yellow in fall.
↕25ft (8m) ↔30ft (10m)

Z2–6

TREE LARGE

Betula utilis var. *jacquemontii*

HIMALAYAN BIRCH Grow this eye-catching white-stemmed birch as a multistemmed tree to enhance its effect as a lawn or bed specimen. The yellow dangling catkins and yellow fall foliage color are added attractions.
↕60ft (18m) ↔30ft (10m)

Z4–7

TREE LARGE

Carpinus betulus 'Fastigiata'

EUROPEAN HORNBEAM This large tree, with its young, columnar form and flame-shaped mature crown, is perfect to be grown in limited spaces. The oval toothed leaves have a pleated look and turn yellow in fall.
↕80ft (25m) ↔70ft (20m)

Z4–8

TREE SMALL

Cercis chinensis

CHINESE REDBUD Grow this small multibranched tree in a sunny space to encourage good crops of the vivid pealike flowers. The flowers are unusual in that clusters sprout direct from the wood, before the heart-shaped leaves appear.
↕20ft (6m) ↔15ft (5m)

Z6–9

TREE SMALL

Cornus alternifolia 'Argentea'

PAGODA DOGWOOD This aptly named large spreading shrub or small deciduous tree produces beautiful horizontally tiered branches that are covered with oval white-edged green leaves. The foliage turns red in fall.

↕↔ 20ft (6m)

 Z3–7 Ⓝ

TREE MEDIUM

Cercis siliquastrum

JUDAS TREE A compact and bushy deciduous tree, this is suitable for a sunny courtyard. In mid-spring, clusters of rosy pink pealike blooms sprout from bare branches, followed by heart-shaped leaves and purplish seedpods.

↕↔ 30ft (10m)

Z6–9

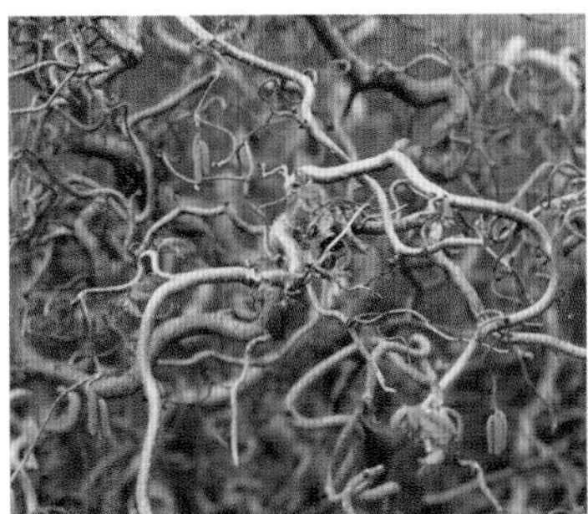

SHRUB LARGE

Corylus avellana 'Contorta'

HARRY LAUDER'S WALKING STICK The sculptural branches of this deciduous shrub, with corkscrew stems, are decked with catkins from winter to early spring. Use as a winter accent plant. Considered invasive in the Northwest and some Northeast areas.

↕↔ 15ft (5m)

Z4–8

TREE SMALL

Chionanthus virginicus

FRINGE TREE Perfect where space is at a premium, this unusual tree or large shrub bears a spreading crown decked with fragrant white summer flowers with long petals. Once the oval leaves fall, its peeling bark is revealed.

↕↔ 10ft (3m)

Z4–9 Ⓝ

TREE LARGE

Gleditsia triacanthos 'Rubylace'

HONEYLOCUST A spreading deciduous tree grown for its large glossy leaves divided into ferny leaflets. The deep red new leaves darken to bronze-green, making it a handsome tree for a small plot.

↕ 50ft (15m) ↔ 15ft (5m)

 Z3–8 Ⓝ

TREE MEDIUM

Gleditsia triacanthos 'Sunburst'

HONEYLOCUST This golden-yellow deciduous tree has an airy appearance, with the foliage divided into small, bright ferny leaflets, which darken through summer. Pendent seedpods appear in fall.

↕ 40ft (12m) ↔ 30ft (10m)

Z3–8 Ⓝ

TREE LARGE

Ilex aquifolium

ENGLISH HOLLY A slow-growing, columnar to conical evergreen tree that can be clipped to shape. It has glossy dark green spiny leaves and red winter berries on female plants. Choose a variegated variety to light up shade. Considered invasive.

↕ up to 70ft (20m) ↔ 20ft (6m)

Z7–9

TREE SMALL

Juniperus scopulorum

ROCKY MOUNTAIN JUNIPER The narrow forms of this evergreen conifer with scalelike leaves include 'Skyrocket' (above), with blue-gray foliage, and the steely blue 'Blue Arrow'. Both make bold columns, but don't eat up valuable space.

↕20ft (6m) ↔30in (75cm)

  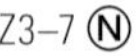 Z3–7 Ⓝ

TREE SMALL

Magnolia x *loebneri* 'Merrill'

LOEBNER MAGNOLIA This small bushy deciduous tree has an upright habit and oblong leaves that open after the flowers appear. The starry, goblet-shaped, many-petaled white blooms are produced in abundance in mid-spring.

↕25ft (8m) ↔22ft (7m)

 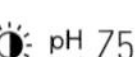 Z5–9

TREE SMALL

Magnolia x *soulangeana*

SAUCER MAGNOLIA A spreading deciduous tree, branching close to the ground, with white, pink, or purple goblet-shaped mid- to late spring flowers. It makes a lovely lawn or bed specimen with carpeting bulbs. Protect buds from late frost.

↕↔20ft (6m)

 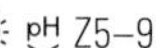 Z5–9

TREE MEDIUM

Malus floribunda

JAPANESE FLOWERING CRABAPPLE This small deciduous tree, perfect for a tight space, has a rounded head with pale pink flowers that open from crimson buds in spring. Bold fall foliage follow the red and yellow edible fruits. Considered invasive.

↕↔ up to 30ft (10m)

Z4–8

TREE MEDIUM

Malus x *moerlandsii* 'Profusion'

FLOWERING CRABAPPLE Ideal for limited space, this tree offers a long season of interest. Purple fruits and purple-tinted leaves follow the deep pink flowers in spring. It develops bold fall foliage color.

↕↔30ft (10m)

Z4–8

TREE SMALL

Malus 'Royalty'

FLOWERING CRABAPPLE With a spreading head, this tree has dark purple foliage that turns red in fall. It gives a spectacular show in spring, when purple-red blossom smothers the branches. Small dark purple fruits form in late summer.

↕↔25ft (8m)

 Z4–8

TREE SMALL

Mespilus germanica

MEDLAR Though this tree develops a wide-spreading crown and often has a multistemmed habit, it can be trimmed to a more formal shape. The large white spring flowers are ornamental and develop into edible fruits.

↕20ft (6m) ↔25ft (8m)

Z5–8

TREE MEDIUM

Prunus 'Kanzan'

syn. ***Prunus serrulata* 'Kwanzan'**
Sumptuous in bloom, this deciduous cherry has a vase-shaped head and pink double spring blossoms, opening just as the bronze-tinged foliage unfurls. The green leaves turn orange in fall. Makes a good street tree.

↕↔30ft (10m)

Z5–8

TREE MEDIUM

Prunus 'Okame'

FLOWERING CHERRY This large shrub or medium-sized bushy tree is an early-spring-flowering ornamental cherry with delicate, fragrant, pink single blooms that open from reddish buds. The leaves color in fall, with fiery oranges and reds.

↕30ft (10m) ↔25ft (8m)

Z6–8

TREE MEDIUM

Prunus 'Spire'

FLOWERING CHERRY This columnar cherry is ideal for adding height in a small plot. In spring, pale pink blossom covers the upright branches. The new leaves are bronze-tinted, turning green in summer and changing to orange and red in fall.

↕30ft (10m) ↔20ft (6m)

Z5–8

TREE SMALL

Ptelea trifoliata

HOP TREE Related to a citrus plant, this is a rounded shrub or small tree with three part aromatic leaves and small, greenish white fragrant flowers opening in early summer, which are followed by papery hanging fruit clusters.

↕↔22ft (7m)

Z4–9 Ⓝ

TREE SMALL

Sophora SUN KING

KOWHAI In cold areas, this bushy evergreen tree is best planted against a south-facing wall. Its narrow leaves are made up of small oval leaflets. In late winter, large clusters of golden-yellow bell-shaped flowers appear.

↕↔ up to 10ft (3m)

Z8–10

TREE SMALL

Rhus typhina

STAGHORN SUMAC This large suckering shrub or small spreading tree, with forked felted stems, has large, divided leaves that turn red, orange, and yellow in fall. Deep red cone-shaped fruiting heads form on female plants.

↕15ft (5m) ↔20ft (6m)

Z3–8 Ⓝ

TREE SMALL

Ulmus glabra 'Camperdownii'

WYCH ELM A wide-spreading weeping deciduous tree, this grafted form has reddish green spring flowers and, later, papery seed cases, which appear among the opening leaves. The lumpy layered texture of the tree in leaf is attractive.

↕↔25ft (8m)

Z4–7

TREE SMALL

Salix caprea 'Pendula'

PUSSY WILLOW This small mushroom-headed tree has long trailing branches. In late winter, silver-colored catkins appear. Thin out select stems and prune away dead wood to keep the head airy. Considered invasive in some areas.

↕↔6ft (2m)

Z6–8

OTHER SUGGESTIONS

Trees

Acer negundo Ⓝ • *Acer palmatum* 'Sango-kaku' • *Aesculus glabra* Ⓝ • *Amelanchier canadensis* RAINBOW PILLAR Ⓝ • *Asimina triloba* Ⓝ • *Betula papyrifera* Ⓝ • *Carpinus caroliniana* Ⓝ • *Cercis canadensis* 'Forest Pansy' Ⓝ • *Chamaecyparis pisifera* 'Boulevard' • *Cornus florida* 'Jean's Appalachian Snow' Ⓝ • *Cotinus obovatus* Ⓝ • *Crataegus crus-galli* var. *inermis* Ⓝ • *Crataegus viridis* 'Winter King' Ⓝ • *Franklinia alatamaha* Ⓝ • *Ginkgo biloba* 'Mariken' • *Halesia monticola* Ⓝ • *Halesia tetraptera* Ⓝ • *Ilex opaca* Ⓝ • *Magnolia tripetala* Ⓝ • *Ostrya virginiana* Ⓝ • *Populus tremuloides* Ⓝ • *Prunus americana* Ⓝ • *Ptelea trifoliata* Ⓝ • *Thuja occidentalis* Ⓝ • *Tilia mongolica* HARVEST GOLD • *Zanthoxylum americanum* Ⓝ

Plants for focal points and topiary

Some plants are natural-born stars, upstaging others with their radiant color, graphic shape, or detailed texture to produce striking features.

While evergreens provide focal points all year round, deciduous plants often put on a show for just a brief spell and should be planted where they can be seen most clearly at those key times. For example, a cherry tree is best placed where its blossoms will be bathed in spring sunshine, with an underskirt of bulbs to complement the flowery canopy. Unlike focal plants, topiary specimens generally have neither color nor form to set them apart. However, their small insignificant leaves are exactly what's needed to mold them into amazing features guaranteed to draw the crowds.

TREE SMALL

***Acer palmatum* 'Bloodgood'**
JAPANESE MAPLE A shapely tree with delicate lobed purple leaves that turn brilliant red in fall, it is especially eye-catching set against evergreens. The skeletal winter framework is also pleasing. Considered invasive in a few areas.
↕↔ 15ft (5m)
Z5–8

TREE LARGE

Araucaria araucana
MONKEY PUZZLE This large evergreen conifer has a striking branching habit and stems densely clothed in small, scalelike, prickly green leaves. It is slow at first but grows rapidly after a few years, so allow it plenty of space.
↕ 80ft (25m) ↔ 30ft (10m)
Z7–11

TREE LARGE

Betula utilis* var. *jacquemontii
HIMALAYAN BIRCH Planted singly as a multistemmed tree or grouped to form a small grove, this white-stemmed birch makes a striking statement. The yellow dangling catkins and yellow fall foliage color are an extra bonus.
↕ 60ft (18m) ↔ 30ft (10m)
Z4–7

SHRUB LARGE

Buxus sempervirens
COMMON BOXWOOD This traditional evergreen hedging and topiary shrub has small, oval glossy leaves. When close-clipped, it will form intricate shapes and green sculptures, such as spirals. Prune between early- and mid- to late summer.
↕↔ 15ft (5m)
Z6–8

TREE LARGE

Catalpa speciosa
NORTHERN CATALPA This exotic-looking flowering tree has heart-shaped leaves bearing clusters of white orchidlike late summer blooms with purple and yellow spots on the throats. Long, thin, green-turning-dark brown seedpods follow.
↕↔ 50ft (15m)
Z4–8 Ⓝ

TREE LARGE

Cedrus deodara
DEODAR CEDAR This magnificent cedar needs plenty of space to accommodate its broad spreading canopy of tiered branches covered with short blue-green needles. The shape begins as conical, changing as the tree reaches maturity.
↕ 130ft (40m) ↔ 30ft (10m)
 Z6–8

TREE SMALL

Cordyline australis
CABBAGE PALM This evergreen accent tree makes a sculptural fountain of sword-shaped leaves, varying from green, through bronze and purple, to variegated. It eventually becomes palmlike. Grow in a tall pot to accommodate taproot; overwinter indoors.
↕ 10ft (3m) ↔ 3ft (1m)
Z10–11

SHRUB LARGE

***Cornus alba* 'Sibirica'**
TATARIAN DOGWOOD This winter interest deciduous shrub is grown for its bright red, strongly upright winter stems, particularly showy when grown in a swath against an evergreen backdrop. Hard prune in late winter for brighter stems.
↕↔ 10ft (3m)
Z2–7

TREE SMALL

Cornus kousa

KOUSA DOGWOOD This early-summer-flowering tree draws attention with its cream, petal-like bracts and hanging clusters of knobby pinky red fruits. In fall, the oval leaves turn into a striking reddish purple color.

↕22ft (7m) ↔15ft (5m)

pH Z5–8

PERENNIAL LARGE

Cortaderia selloana 'Silver Comet'

PAMPAS GRASS Forming an arching tussock of evergreen white-edged leaves, this variegated grass looks splendid in summer when tall stems carry creamy white flower plumes. Invasive in Southern areas.

↕5ft (1.5m) ↔3ft (1m)

pH Z7–10

TREE LARGE

Cornus controversa

GIANT DOGWOOD A large deciduous tree with an elegant tiered habit and glossy elliptical leaves that hang down from the branches. In summer, flat heads of tiny white flowers appear. The green leaves turn purple in fall.

↕↔50ft (15m)

Z5–8

TREE SMALL

Cornus florida

FLOWERING DOGWOOD This deciduous tree or shrub is transformed by the showy white or pink flowerlike bracts that smother the branches in spring. In fall, the curled green leaves develop rich red and purple coloring.

↕20ft (6m) ↔25ft (8m)

pH Z5–9 Ⓝ

BULB MEDIUM

Eucomis bicolor

PINEAPPLE LILY In patio pots, this late-summer bulb draws attention when the large head, reminiscent of a pineapple, packed with greenish white flowers and topped with leafy bracts, rises from the rosette of bold leaves.

↕20in (50cm)

Z8–10

TREE MEDIUM

Eucryphia glutinosa

NIRRHE In flower, this upright semievergreen tree turns heads. The pure white bowl-shaped blooms with a tuft of central stamens appear in summer against the glossy dark green leaves, which later show rich fall tints.

↕30ft (10m) ↔20ft (6m)

pH Z8–11

PERENNIAL LARGE

Euphorbia characias subsp. *wulfenii*

MEDITERRANEAN SPURGE Plant this evergreen perennial in gravel to enhance its architectural form. In spring, the upright stems, covered with gray-green leaves, are topped with tiny yellow-green flower heads.

↕↔4ft (1.2m)

Z7–10

PERENNIAL SMALL

Hakonechloa macra 'Aureola'

JAPANESE FOREST GRASS Use this yellow-striped deciduous grass singly in a pot or grouped at the front of a bed, or alongside a path. The glowing color and arching form of its ribbonlike leaves will light up a shady spot.

↕16in (40cm) ↔24in (60cm)

Z5–9

TREE MEDIUM

Laurus nobilis

BAY LAUREL This evergreen tree, with sweetly aromatic dark green leaves, can be shaped into a number of topiary forms including cones and columns or ball-headed standards for patio pots, given winter protection in cold areas.

↕40ft (12m) ↔30ft (10m)

Z8–10

TREE MEDIUM

Malus x *moerlandsii* 'Profusion'

FLOWERING CRABAPPLE Spectacular when in full bloom and smothered in deep pink spring blossom, this tree offers a long season of interest with purple-tinged new growth, purple fruits, and rich fall color.

↕↔30ft (10m)

Z4–8

SHRUB SMALL

Hebe rakaiensis

HEBE This naturally dome-shaped evergreen shrub, with small olive-green leaves, can easily be trimmed into simple topiary forms or a low hedge; clip as necessary in early summer to remove the white flowers.

↕3ft (1m) ↔4ft (1.2m)

Z8–10

TREE MEDIUM

Nyssa sinensis

CHINESE TUPELO This medium-sized spreading deciduous tree makes a striking lawn specimen at maturity as the narrow oval leaves put on a spectacular show of amber and scarlet in fall, especially when provided neutral to acidic soil.

↕↔30ft (10m)

TREE SMALL

Juniperus scopulorum

ROCKY MOUNTAIN JUNIPER For an exclamation mark within a bed or gravel area, choose one of the upright varieties of this evergreen conifer, such as 'Blue Arrow' or 'Skyrocket', both of which have fine blue-gray foliage and are "pencil" thin.

↕20ft (6m) ↔30in (75cm)

Z3–7 Ⓝ

SHRUB MEDIUM

Lonicera nitida

BOXLEAF HONEYSUCKLE A quick-growing small-leaved evergreen, this is often used to shape topiary figures. It develops faster than traditional boxwood, but need more regular trimming. 'Baggesen's Gold' (above) has yellow leaves.

↕6ft (2m) ↔10ft (3m)

Z7–9

TREE SMALL

Parrotia persica

PERSIAN IRONWOOD As a specimen, this deciduous tree or large shrub with multiple stems has much to offer. In winter, the branches show patchwork patterns of peeling bark in grays, greens, and white. Its fall leaf color is striking.

↕25ft (8m) ↔30ft (10m)

pH Z4–8

PERENNIAL LARGE

Kniphofia caulescens

RED HOT POKER This perennial has a subtropical look and forms mounds of gray-green strap-shaped evergreen leaves topped with spikes of coral-red, opening to yellow, flowers on stout upright stems from late summer to fall.

↕4ft (1.2m) ↔24in (60cm)

Z6–11

TREE LARGE

Magnolia grandiflora

SOUTHERN MAGNOLIA The large, glossy green leaves of this evergreen tree, often grown in the shelter of a south-facing wall, give it a tropical look, a characteristic enhanced when the giant, scented white blooms open in midsummer.

↕60ft (18m) ↔50ft (15m)

Z7–9 Ⓝ

PERENNIAL LARGE

Phormium tenax

NEW ZEALAND FLAX This clump-forming evergreen perennial, with arching or upright sword-shaped leaves, creates a dramatic contrast set against less defined plants. During hot summers, tall stems of dark red flowers appear.

↕10ft (3m) ↔6ft (2m)

Z9–11

SHRUB LARGE

Photinia x *fraseri*

RED TIP This evergreen shrub is grown for the color of its new leaves, many cultivars have been selected for bright red emerging foliage. White flower clusters appear in spring, followed by red fruits that persist through winter into spring.

↕↔ 10ft (3m)

Z7–9

TREE LARGE

Picea pungens 'Koster'

COLORADO SPRUCE This bright silvery blue evergreen conifer makes a handsome lawn specimen with its relatively slow growth, symmetrical form, and stiff needlelike leaves. Upright cones form toward the ends of the branches. Adapts to all but wet soil.

↕50ft (15m) ↔15ft (5m)

Z2–7 Ⓝ

SHRUB LARGE

Pittosporum tobira

JAPANESE PITTOSPORUM Grow this evergreen shrub as a hedge or use to form a neat dome shape in a sheltered site. Its oval leaves form attractive whorls. Sweetly scented, creamy white late-spring-flower clusters are followed by decorative capsules.

↕30ft (10m) ↔10ft (3m)

Z8–10

TREE MEDIUM

Taxus baccata 'Fastigiata'

IRISH YEW This evergreen conifer has a naturally narrow upright form, and is used as an exclamation mark in a border or to create a formal avenue of columns on either side of a path. This female plant bears red fruits. All parts are toxic.

↕30ft (10m) ↔12ft (4m)

Z6–7

TREE SMALL

Trachycarpus fortunei

WINDMILL PALM With an upright stem that becomes fibrous with age, and large, deeply cut fanlike leaves, this evergreen palm makes a dramatic focal point in a border or large container of soil-based potting mix. Plant it in a sheltered site.

↕6ft (2m) ↔8ft (2.5m)

Z8–10

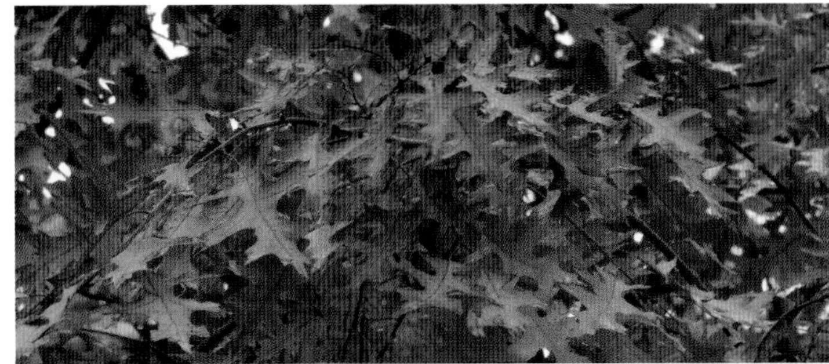

TREE LARGE

Quercus palustris

PIN OAK Planted at the end of a large lawn, this tall pyramid-shaped oak would make a striking focal point. Apart from the attractive shape, the lobed leaves turn brilliant crimson-red and reddish brown in fall, offering interest.

↕70ft (20m) ↔40ft (12m)

Z4–8 Ⓝ

SHRUB MEDIUM

Yucca filamentosa

ADAM'S NEEDLE The sword-shaped, spine-tipped leaves of this evergreen make a useful accent in gravel gardens or large pots. 'Bright Edge' (above) is particularly striking. From mid- to late summer, tall stems carry white blooms.

↕6ft (2m) ↔5ft (1.5m)

Z4–11 Ⓝ

OTHER SUGGESTIONS

Perennials

Euphorbia characias 'Tasmanian Tiger' • *Kniphofia uvaria* • *Phormium* 'Sundowner'

Shrubs

Buxus microphylla 'Justin Brouwers' • *Gardenia jasminoides* • *Hydrangea quercifolia* 'Ruby Slippers' Ⓝ • *Ilex glabra* Ⓝ • *Ilex verticillata* 'Maryland Beauty' Ⓝ • *Prunus lusitanica* • *Viburnum nudum* BRANDYWINE Ⓝ • *Yucca aloifolia* Ⓝ

Trees

Acer palmatum 'Katsura' • *Brahea armata* Ⓝ • *Calia secundiflora* Ⓝ • *Cercis canadensis* LAVENDER TWIST Ⓝ • *Cornus kousa* 'Milky Way' • *Cupressus sempervirens* • *Ilex vomitoria* Ⓝ • *Juniperus chinensis* • *Picea glauca* 'Conica' • *Taxus* x *media* 'Hicksii' • *Thuja occidentalis* Ⓝ • *Tsuga canadensis* Ⓝ

PLANTS for GARDEN PROBLEMS

Only the lucky few have gardens with rich fertile soil and smooth level beds that almost any plant will enjoy. And even those blessed with an ideal site and soil may still be plagued by rabbits or slugs determined to consume their prized plants. The good news is that most problems can be overcome by choosing plants that are adapted to your conditions. So, whether you need flowers for parched earth, foliage for soggy soils, or species that will cling to your hillside garden, there's something here for you.

Plants for sun-baked areas

Choices are limited for free-draining soils that retain few plant nutrients, yet some highly prized species have adapted to grow well in them.

Most sun-loving wildflowers abhor rich soil, and many cultivated plants, such as hollyhock and cosmos, will also thrive in free-draining, sun-baked conditions. As well as the plants listed here, others cope with poor soils once they are established, so take a look at the selection for sandy soils too (see pp.44–51), and provide water and some fertilizer for the first few seasons after planting. One benefit of well-drained soils is that plants that suffer in cold, wet soils over winter, such as perennial wallflower and fleshy-leaved succulents, are more likely to survive in dry conditions.

PERENNIAL LARGE

Achillea filipendulina

YARROW Perfect for dry soil and full sun, this clump-forming perennial has finely cut gray-green leaves and sturdy stems punctuated with flat-topped golden-yellow flower heads in summer. 'Gold Plate' (above) is a tall variety growing up to 5ft (1.6m).

↕4ft (1.2m) ↔24in (60cm)

Z3–8

PERENNIAL LARGE

Alcea rosea

HOLLYHOCK This upright perennial may self-seed in cracks and dry, dusty soils. Its rounded leaves are joined by white, yellow pink, or red cup-shaped flowers that attract bees and butterflies from mid- to late summer. Considered invasive in many areas.

↕6ft (2m) ↔24in (60cm)

Z3–9

SHRUB SMALL

Caryopteris x *clandonensis*

BLUEBEARD This bushy deciduous shrub thrives in free-draining soils. It forms clumps of gray-green lance-shaped leaves and dense clusters of small purplish blue flowers from late summer to fall. 'Worcester Gold' (above) has contrasting golden foliage.

↕3ft (1m) ↔5ft (1.5m)

Z6–9

ANNUAL/BIENNIAL SMALL

Cosmos sulphureus

SULPHUR COSMOS Hailing from scrublands, this upright bushy annual bears a wealth of bowl-shaped, yellow, orange, or scarlet semidouble flowers all summer. Its feathery green leaves are attractive, too. It is easy to grow from seed in spring. Can be weedy.

↕16in (40cm) ↔8in (20cm)

BULB SMALL

Crocus chrysanthus

CROCUS Plant this tiny perennial bulb in fall in a sunny spot in free-draining soil, where its cup-shaped blooms with dark green linear leaves appear in early spring. Varieties include 'Gypsy Girl' (above) with purple-striped yellow flowers.

↕3in (7cm)

Z3–8

PERENNIAL SMALL

Delosperma nubigenum

ICE PLANT This ground-hugging evergreen perennial, perfect for sun-baked soils, produces mats of triangular, succulent green leaves and lemon-yellow daisy-like flowers in summer. Use it to edge a bed; it may need frost protection in cold areas.

↕2in (5cm) ↔20in (50cm)

Z6–8

PERENNIAL SMALL

Dianthus alpinus

ALPINE PINK Plant this mat-forming evergreen perennial in raised beds or at the front of a dry bed. Its gray-green foliage is joined in summer by white or pink blooms held on short stems. 'Joan's Blood' (above) has deep crimson solitary blooms.

↕3in (8cm) ↔4in (10cm)

Z3–8

ANNUAL/BIENNIAL SMALL

Dorotheanthus bellidiformis

LIVINGSTON DAISY Grow this low-growing annual to edge the front of a sun-baked bed, where it will thrive. It produces small fleshy leaves and red, pink, orange, and white daisy-like summer flowers, which open in sun, closing again in the evenings.

↕6in (15cm) ↔12in (30cm)

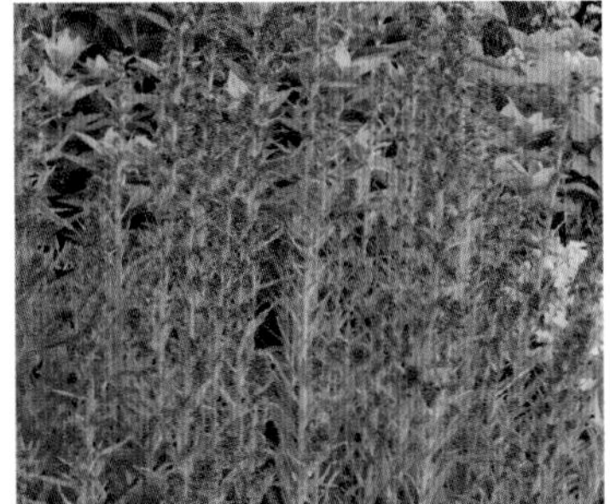

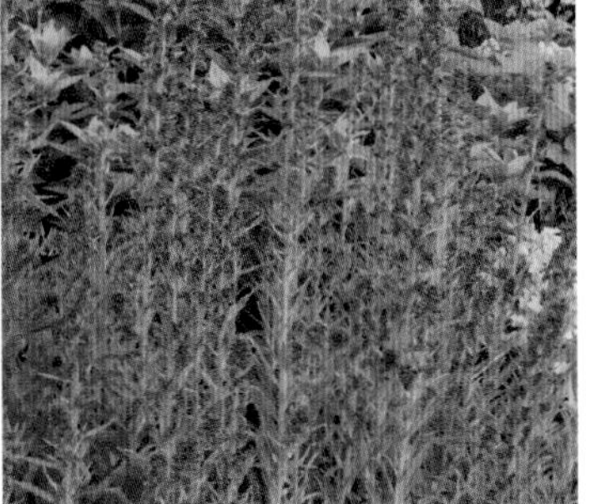

ANNUAL/BIENNIAL SMALL

Echium vulgare

VIPER'S BUGLOSS A bristly biennial with a basal rosette of lance-shaped leaves. In early summer, it produces slender spires of vivid violet-blue bell-shaped blooms. This drought-tolerant plant is ideal for wildlife gardens and sun-baked beds.

↕24in (60cm) ↔12in (30cm)

Z3–8

PERENNIAL SMALL

Eryngium maritimum

SEA HOLLY Found growing on exposed rocky coastal sites, this upright perennial has prickly, white-veined, blue-green basal leaves. Thimblelike metallic blue blooms with spiny collars appear on branched stems from early summer to early fall.

↕20in (50cm) ↔18in (45cm)

Z5–9

PERENNIAL MEDIUM

Erysimum 'Bowles's Mauve'

PERENNIAL WALLFLOWER Ideal for a sunny bed, this drought-tolerant evergreen perennial produces slim gray-green leaves and spikes of mauve flowers from late winter to summer. Deadhead regularly to prolong the display.

↕24in (60cm) ↔16in (40cm)

 Z6–10

ANNUAL/BIENNIAL SMALL

Eschscholzia californica

CALIFORNIA POPPY Easy to grow from seed in spring, this clump-forming annual bears masses of orange, red, and yellow, bowl-shaped summer flowers. Grow in sun-baked beds, where it will offer the best show. May self-seed after first season. Can be weedy.

↕12in (30cm) ↔6in (15cm)

PERENNIAL SMALL

Gypsophila repens

CREEPING BABY'S BREATH This spreading semievergreen perennial can cope with dry, stony slopes in the Mediterranean. It forms mat of narrow bluish green leaves, above which rise sprays of round pale pink summer flowers. Trim back after flowering.

↕8in (20cm) ↔12in (30cm) or more

Z4–8

PERENNIAL SMALL

Jovibarba hirta

JOVIBARBA This evergreen perennial, similar to a houseleek, produces rosettes of hairy-margined, triangular, spiny green leaves, often red-tinted, and yellow-brown bell-shaped flowers in summer. It tolerates very dry soils and thrives in full sun.

↕6in (15cm) ↔4in (10cm)

Z4–8

ANNUAL/BIENNIAL SMALL

Lobularia maritima

SWEET ALYSSUM Easy to grow from seed, this mat-forming annual bears green lance-shaped leaves and masses of white or pink, sweetly scented rounded blooms in summer. Thrives in dry soils. 'Easter Bonnet' (above) is popular. Considered invasive in some areas.

↕4in (10cm) ↔12in (30cm)

PERENNIAL MEDIUM

Malva moschata

MUSK MALLOW This bushy perennial, with woody stems, will grow happily in free-draining soils and full sun. It produces deeply lobed, dark green leaves and saucer-shaped, pale pink blooms from summer to fall. It may self-seed.

↕3ft (1m) ↔24in (60cm)

Z3–8

SHRUB SMALL

Phlomis fruticosa

JERUSALEM SAGE This evergreen Mediterranean shrub is adapted to rocky soils, and will thrive in full sun. It has gray-green leaves and hooded yellow flowers on upright stems in summer. The seedheads provide interest over winter.

↕3ft (1m) ↔5ft (1.5m)

Z8–10

PERENNIAL SMALL

Sedum erythrostictum 'Frosty Morn'

STONECROP Ideal for sandy soil, the fleshy white and gray-green variegated foliage of this perennial is joined by pale pink flower clusters from late summer to early fall. The brown seedheads persist through winter.

↕12in (30cm) ↔18in (45cm)

Z4–9

PERENNIAL SMALL

Sempervivum giuseppii

HENS AND CHICKS Perfect for sun-baked cracks in walls or gravel beds, this diminutive evergreen perennial forms rosettes of spiky green leaves with purple pointed tips and, in summer, pink or red star-shaped flowers on upright stems.

↕in flower 4in (10cm) ↔4in (10cm)

 Z7–9

PERENNIAL MEDIUM

Solidago GOLDEN BABY

GOLDENROD Tolerant of a wide range of sites and soils, this perennial thrives in sun-baked beds. It forms an upright clump of pointed, narrow green leaves. Small golden-yellow blooms appear from midsummer to early fall. Deadhead regularly.

↕24in (60cm) ↔18in (45cm)

Z4–8

SHRUB MEDIUM

Yucca filamentosa

ADAM'S NEEDLE Drought-tolerant and sun-loving, this evergreen shrub offers a striking display of sword-shaped, dark green spine-tipped leaves. From mid- to late summer, white tuliplike flowers appear. 'Bright Edge' (above) is a variegated form.

↕6ft (2m) ↔5ft (1.5m)

Z4–11 Ⓝ

OTHER SUGGESTIONS

Annuals

Papaver rhoeas

Perennials

Achillea millefolium Ⓝ • *Agave parryi* Ⓝ • *Alyssum montanum* • *Amorpha canescens* Ⓝ • *Aubrieta* Cascade Series • *Cerastium tomentosum* • *Delosperma cooperi* • *Dianthus deltoides* • *Echeveria elegans* Ⓝ • *Echinops bannaticus* 'Blue Glow' • *Erigeron karvinskianus* Ⓝ • *Eryngium agavifolium* • *Eryngium giganteum* • *Erysimum linifolium* 'Variegatum' • *Euphorbia characias* subsp. *wulfenii* • *Jovibarba heuffelii* • *Malva alcea* var. *fastigiata* • *Ruellia humilis* • *Sedum spathulifolium* Ⓝ • *Sedum spectabile* • *Sempervivum arachnoideum*

Shrubs

Rhus aromatica 'Gro-low'

Plants for waterlogged sites

Gardens prone to waterlogging provide conditions similar to those on the margins of a natural pond where bog plants thrive (*see p.54* and *p.164*).

While most plants dislike wet feet for long periods of time, there are some, such as *Acorus*, *Gunnera*, and *Taxodium*, that thrive happily in such conditions. If your soil is intermittently waterlogged, consider choosing plants such as hostas, sedges (*Acorus* and others), kerria, and *Leycesteria*, that will tolerate a wide range of conditions. If you seek to improve your soil structure and open up air and drainage channels, dig in plenty of well-rotted manure or compost, together with horticultural grit. Also cover the surface with an organic mulch annually.

PERENNIAL LARGE

Aconitum napellus

MONKSHOOD A beautiful upright perennial for wet soils, it has deeply cut dark green foliage and tall spires of indigo-blue blooms from mid- to late summer. The tall stems may need staking. All parts are toxic if ingested; wear gloves when handling it.

↕5ft (1.5m) ↔12in (30cm)

Z3–8

PERENNIAL LARGE

Actaea racemosa

BLACK COHOSH Useful for waterlogged soils, this perennial bears a combination of deeply cut leaves and bottlebrush-like spikes of white midsummer flowers. The dried brown seedheads extend the season of interest. Grow at the back of a bed.

↕up to 5ft (1.5m) ↔24in (60cm)

Z3–8 Ⓝ

PERENNIAL SMALL

Astilbe x *arendsii*

ASTILBE This bog plant is a clump-forming perennial that thrives in waterlogged conditions. It produces deeply divided, dark green fernlike foliage and feathery plumes of white, pink, lilac, or red flowers from early- to late summer.

↕18in (45cm) ↔12in (30cm)

Z4–8

SHRUB MEDIUM

Cornus sericea

TWIG DOGWOOD This shrub is grown for its stunning red winter stems, bright yellow-green in varieties such as 'Flaviramea' (above). The dark green lance-shaped foliage turns orange and red in fall. Cut old stems to the ground in late winter.

↕6ft (2m) ↔12ft (4m)

Z2–8 Ⓝ

PERENNIAL LARGE

Eutrochium purpureum

JOE PYE WEED A good choice for boggy soils in wildlife or informal gardens, this upright perennial has coarse green foliage on tall purple-flushed stems and large, domed, purple-pink fluffy flower heads from late summer to early fall.

↕7ft (2.2m) ↔3ft (1m)

Z4–9 Ⓝ

PERENNIAL MEDIUM

Filipendula ulmaria

MEADOWSWEET Tolerant of waterlogged soils, this perennial has blue-green leaves, bright red in fall, and fragrant white summer-flower clusters. 'Aurea' (above) has golden-yellow spring foliage. Considered invasive in some Northeast and Midwest areas.

↕3ft (1m) ↔24in (60cm)

Z4–9

PERENNIAL MEDIUM

Hosta sieboldiana

PLANTAIN LILY This medium-sized leafy perennial is tolerant of waterlogged soils and shade. It features large, rounded rich blue-green leaves with a puckered texture. Spikes of lilac-tinged white flowers appear in early summer. Protect from slugs.

↕3ft (1m) ↔4ft (1.2m)

Z3–9

SHRUB MEDIUM

Hydrangea macrophylla

LACECAP HYDRANGEA This broad-leaved shrub grows well on clay soils and tolerates occasional waterlogging. From midsummer to early fall, it bears tiny flowers with petal-like florets. Other forms have white, pink, purple, or, on acidic soils, blue blooms.

↕6ft (2m) ↔8ft (2.5m)

Z6–9

SHRUB LARGE

Hydrangea paniculata

PANICLE HYDRANGEA This shrub adds color to beds with waterlogged soils. It has strap-shaped foliage and beardless lilac-pink flowers with gold marks on the lower petals from early- to midsummer. Considered invasive in some Northeastern areas.

↕↔10ft (3m)

Z3–8

PERENNIAL MEDIUM

Iris ensata 'Rose Queen'

JAPANESE WATER IRIS This perennial adds color to beds with waterlogged soils. It has strap-shaped foliage and, from early- to midsummer, beardless, lilac-pink flowers with gold marks on the lower petals. Blue, purple, and white varieties are available.

↕up to 3ft (1m) ↔indefinite

 Z4–9

PERENNIAL MEDIUM

Iris sibirica

SIBERIAN IRIS This perennial thrives in wet soils. It has upright, swordlike blue-green leaves and large, beardless flowers in blue, pink, white or yellow from late spring to early summer. 'Butter and Sugar' (above) has yellow and white blooms.

↕3ft (1m) ↔indefinite

Z3–9

PERENNIAL LARGE

Ligularia przewalskii

LEOPARD PLANT This upright perennial thrives in boggy soils. It bears large, rounded, deeply cut dark green leaves and, from mid- to late summer, tall, narrow spires of spidery, yellow daisy-like flowers. Stems may need additional support.

↕6ft (2m) ↔3ft (1m)

Z4–8

TREE MEDIUM

Magnolia virginiana

SWEETBAY MAGNOLIA This tree performs best on moist soils and will tolerate occasional waterlogging. From early summer to early fall, its large, vanilla-scented, creamy white cup-shaped flowers are set against large dark green leaves.

↕30ft (10m) ↔20ft (6m)

Z5–9 Ⓝ

PERENNIAL MEDIUM

Mimulus cardinalis

SCARLET MONKEY FLOWER This spreading perennial, grown as an annual, thrives in boggy soils. It produces a mass of small, toothed, green downy leaves and small, tomato-red two-lipped flowers that cover the plant from summer to early fall.

↕3ft (1m) ↔24in (60cm)

Z6–9 Ⓝ

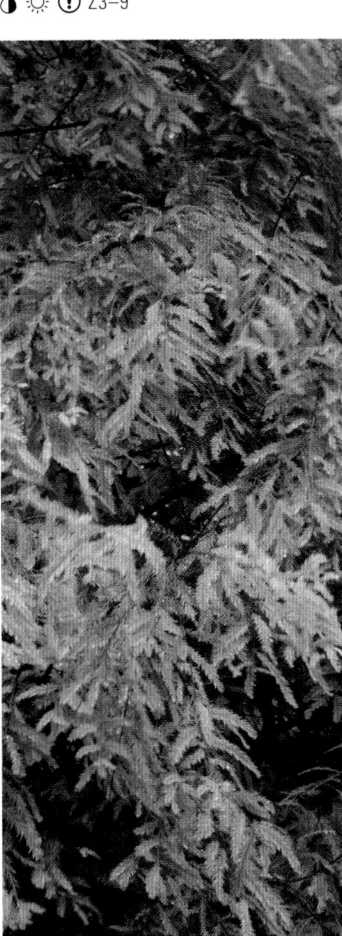

PERENNIAL LARGE

Monarda fistulosa

WILD BERGAMOT This clump-forming perennial thrives in moist soil and tolerates occasional waterlogging. In midsummer, it bears flower heads comprised of small, two-lipped, pale lilac blooms, which attract bees and butterflies.

↕4ft (1.2m) ↔18in (45cm)

Z3–9 Ⓝ

PERENNIAL LARGE

Persicaria virginiana

KNOTWEED This bog-loving perennial has oval midgreen leaves with dark green markings, and from late summer to early fall, spikes of red-turning cup-shaped flowers. 'Painter's Palette' (above) has variegated green, yellow, and pink leaves.

↕4ft (1.2m) ↔2ft (60cm)

Z4-8 Ⓝ

PERENNIAL MEDIUM

Primula beesiana

CANDELABRA PRIMROSE This primrose is a moisture-loving perennial, ideal for boggy soils. It bears basal rosettes of light green crinkly leaves and upright stems that are studded with rounded clusters of purple flowers from late spring to early summer.

↕24in (60cm) ↔12in (30cm)

TREE LARGE

Taxodium distichum

BALD CYPRESS This broadly conical deciduous conifer produces slim green foliage that turns yellow-brown in late fall before falling. Small oval cones appear in summer. Grow it in damp or waterlogged soils in a large garden.

↕130ft (40m) ↔28ft (9m)

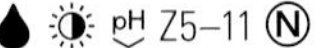 Z5–11 Ⓝ

PERENNIAL LARGE

Verbena hastata

AMERICAN BLUE VERVAIN Tolerant of waterlogged conditions, this upright moisture-loving perennial has narrow toothed leaves and candelabra-like violet-blue flower heads from midsummer to fall. 'Rosea' (above) has lilac-pink blooms.

↕5ft (1.5m) ↔24in (60cm)

Z3–9 Ⓝ

OTHER SUGGESTIONS

Perennials

Acorus gramineus • *Astilbe chinensis* var. *pumila* • *Actaea matsumurae* 'White Pearl' • *Eupatorium cannabinum* • *Gunnera manicata* • *Hosta* 'Francee' • *Hosta* 'Blue Angel' • *Ligularia dentata* 'Desdemona' • *Matteuccia struthiopteris* Ⓝ • *Mimulus rigens* Ⓝ • *Primula bulleyana* • *Rheum palmatum* • *Rodgersia pinnata* • *Spiranthes odorata* Ⓝ • *Zantedeschia aethiopica*

Shrubs

Cephalanthus occidentalis Ⓝ • *Cornus alba* • *Cornus stolonifera* Ⓝ • *Leycesteria formosa*

Trees

Cornus florida Ⓝ • *Persea borbonia* Ⓝ • *Nyssa sylvatica* Ⓝ • *Quercus bicolor* Ⓝ

Plants for banks and slopes

Slopes and banks add interest to designs, the layers of planting producing a three-dimensional effect. For best results, use tough, drought-tolerant plants.

Slopes offer a palette for color and texture, creating stunning features, but drought and erosion can present problems on steep hills. Plants with spreading root systems, such as cranesbills, junipers, heathers and heaths, bind the soil and protect it from erosion, while a leafy canopy minimizes rain damage. Choose drought-tolerant plants that can cope with dry soil; if the slope is exposed also consider their wind resistance. Most of these plants will cope with blustery conditions, but a few, including roses and hemlock, do best on slopes sheltered from prevailing winds.

SHRUB SMALL

Abies balsamea Hudsonia Group

BALSAM FIR A slow-growing evergreen conifer, it can cope with the well-drained conditions on a slope. It forms a spreading mound of needlelike, dark gray-green leaves. Plant it in neutral to acidic soil.

↕↔ 3ft (1m)

pH Z3–6 Ⓝ

PERENNIAL MEDIUM

Baptisia australis

FALSE INDIGO A clump-forming perennial with gray-green divided foliage, it thrives in well-drained soils and will decorate a slope with its spikes of small violet-blue summer flowers. Decorative dark gray seedpods form in fall.

↕ 30in (75cm) ↔ 24in (60cm)

Z3–9 Ⓝ

SHRUB LARGE

Berberis darwinii

DARWIN'S BARBERRY This tough and spiny evergreen shrub lends structure and height to a sloping site. Its tiny hollylike leaves are joined in spring by pendent clusters of dark orange flowers, which attract bees and are followed by blue-black berries.

↕↔ 10ft (3m)

Z7–9

SHRUB LARGE

Berberis x *stenophylla*

HEDGE BARBERRY Use this prickly evergreen shrub to decorate a bank or slope with its spine-tipped dark green leaves and small yellow spring flowers followed by blue-black fruits. Trim lightly in summer after the flowers have faded.

↕ 10ft (3m) ↔ 15ft (5m)

Z6–9

PERENNIAL SMALL

Bergenia purpurascens

PURPLE BERGENIA Tolerant of the free-draining conditions on a slope, this evergreen perennial forms clumps of large, fleshy rounded leaves that flush purple in cold weather, and clusters of dark pink spring blooms. Remove faded flower heads.

↕ 16in (40cm) ↔ 24in (60cm) or more

Z3–8

SHRUB LARGE

Buxus sempervirens

COMMON BOXWOOD This traditional topiary and hedging evergreen shrub tolerates a wide range of conditions and grows well on a slope. Clip its small, oval glossy leaves to form hedges and green sculptures. Prune between early- to late summer.

↕↔ 15ft (5m)

Z6–8

SHRUB SMALL

Calluna vulgaris 'Gold Haze'

SCOTCH HEATHER A ground-hugging shrub, it has evolved to cope with life on moors and hillsides. Carpet a slope with its scaly foliage and small white flowers, which appear from late summer to fall. Needs acidic soil.

↕ 18in (45cm) ↔ 24in (60cm)

pH Z4–7

BULB MEDIUM

Chionodoxa forbesii

GLORY OF THE SNOW Use this diminutive, early-spring-flowering perennial bulb on a sloping sunny site. It has linear midgreen foliage and small star-shaped, blue white-eyed flowers. Plant the bulbs in groups in fall.
↕6in (15cm) ↔2in (5cm)
Z3–8

SHRUB MEDIUM

Clethra alnifolia

SUMMERSWEET This deciduous shrub's late summer spires of small white fragrant blooms add appeal to a wooded sloping site. The green leaves turn bright yellow in fall. It performs best on moist acidic soil at the bottom of a slope.
↕↔8ft (2.5m)
pH Z3–9 (N)

SHRUB SMALL

Cotoneaster horizontalis

ROCKSPRAY The branches of this deciduous shrub are arranged in a distinctive "herringbone" pattern and hug the contours of a slope. In summer, it bears small white blooms followed by vivid red berries from fall to early winter, which are eaten by birds.
↕3ft (1m) ↔5ft (1.5m)
(!) Z4–7

SHRUB SMALL

Daboecia cantabrica

IRISH HEATH This low-growing drought-tolerant shrub, ideal for a slope or bank, forms a mat of dark green leaves. Purple, white, or mauve urn-shaped flowers appear from early summer to fall. 'Bicolor' (above) has mixed flower colors on a single raceme.
↕18in (45cm) ↔24in (60cm)
pH Z6–8

PERENNIAL SMALL

Epimedium x *youngianum* 'Niveum'

YOUNG'S BARRENWORT This ground-cover perennial has heart-shaped, bronze-tinted serrated leaves that turn green and make a decorative mat on a slope or bank. Small white flowers appear in late spring.
↕↔12in (30cm)
Z4–8

SHRUB SMALL

Erica carnea

WINTER HEATH This ground-hugging evergreen shrub produces a mat of dark green needlelike leaves on a sunny slope or bank. From winter to spring, it is covered with tiny pink, red, or white blooms held on short spikes.
↕12in (30cm) ↔18in (45cm) or more
pH Z5–7

SHRUB LARGE

Elaeagnus x *ebbingei*

OLEASTER This tough vigorous evergreen shrub can be used as a windbreak on a sloping site. It has broadly oval dark green leaves covered with a silvery dusting. Small, white fragrant flowers appear in fall. 'Gilt Edge' is a colorful variegated form.
↕↔15ft (5m)
Z7–9

SHRUB SMALL

Gaultheria mucronata

CHILEAN PERNETTYA This evergreen shrub creates a decorative addition to a slope or bank, with its prickly dark green leaves. White to purple-red berries follow the white late spring blooms on females. Best in West Coast gardens.
↕↔4ft (1.2m)
pH (!) Z7–9

PERENNIAL SMALL

Geranium endressii

ENDRES CRANESBILL This clump-forming semievergreen perennial will clothe a slope with its green lobed foliage from spring to fall. Light pink summer blooms with slightly notched petals add to the effect. Easy to grow, it thrives in sun or part shade.
↕18in (45cm) ↔24in (60cm)
Z4–8

PERENNIAL SMALL

Geranium macrorrhizum

BIGROOT GERANIUM This easy-to-grow perennial covers a slope or bank with a carpet of aromatic leaves. Magenta blooms appear in early summer. Second flush may follow. Grow in partial shade in areas with hot summers.

↕15in (38cm) ↔24in (60cm)

Z4–8

PERENNIAL SMALL

Hepatica nobilis

LIVERLEAF A low-growing semievergreen perennial, ideal for a shaded sloping garden, where it will form a neat dome of rounded, lobed, fleshy green leaves and, in early spring, cup-shaped white, pink, blue, or purple blooms.

↕3in (8cm) ↔5in (12cm)

Z5–8

SHRUB LARGE

Itea virginica

VIRGINIA SWEETSPIRE This spreading shrub thrives on sheltered slopes protected from prevailing winds. It bears arching stems of spiny dark green leaves and, from midsummer to early fall, decorative greenish white racemes.

↕10ft (3m) ↔5ft (1.5m)

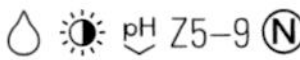

SHRUB SMALL

Juniperus procumbens

DWARF JAPANESE JUNIPER This compact evergreen conifer is often used as ground cover on banks and sloping sites, where its dense, prickly green leaves offer a mat of color. It bears small round brown or black fruits. Plant it in sun or light shade.

↕8in (20cm) ↔30in (75cm)

Z4–9

SHRUB SMALL

Lonicera pileata

PRIVET HONEYSUCKLE This spreading dense evergreen shrub is tolerant of the dry conditions on a sloping site. It covers the ground with stems of glossy dark green leaves. Violet-purple berries follow the white funnel-shaped late spring flowers.

↕24in (60cm) ↔8ft (2.5m)

Z5–9

PERENNIAL MEDIUM

Luzula sylvatica

GREATER WOODRUSH Use this clump-forming evergreen perennial as ground cover on a shady slope. 'Aurea' (above) has glossy green grassy leaves that become yellow-green from winter to spring, and tiny brown flowers from late spring to early summer.

↕16in (40cm) ↔18in (45cm)

SHRUB SMALL

Microbiota decussata

RUSSIAN ARBORVITAE Useful as ground cover on sunny sloping sites, this low-growing or prostrate evergreen coniferous shrub bears green, scalelike leaves, which turn bronze-purple in winter. Yellow-brown fruits appear in fall.

↕3ft (1m) ↔indefinite

Z3–7

BULB MEDIUM

Narcissus 'February Gold'

DAFFODIL This reliable daffodil copes well with free-draining sloping sites, while the short stems resist wind damage. It bears narrow midgreen leaves and scented yellow early spring flowers. Plant the bulbs in groups in fall, and let them naturalize.

↕12in (30cm)

Z3–9

SHRUB MEDIUM

Rhododendron yakushimanum

YAKUSHIMA RHODODENDRON Native to windswept mountainsides in Japan, this evergreen shrub, with leathery dark green leaves and bell-shaped, pink-budded white spring flowers, is ideal for sloping gardens.

↕↔6ft (2m)

pH Z5–8

SHRUB SMALL

Rosa Flower Carpet Series

GROUNDCOVER ROSE Plant this spreading rose on a sheltered slope to protect it from wind. Its cupped, white, pink, red, and yellow semidouble blooms appear from summer to fall above disease-resistant glossy green leaves.

↕18in (45cm) ↔4ft (1.2m)

Z5–9

SHRUB SMALL

Rosa KENT

GROUNDCOVER ROSE A spreading rose, ideal for sloping gardens, with disease-resistant, glossy midgreen leaves and clusters of flat, white semidouble flowers from summer to fall. Apply a mulch of organic matter annually in spring.

↕32in (80cm) ↔3ft (1m)

Z5–9

PERENNIAL MEDIUM

Stachys officinalis

BISHOP'S WORT Perfect for free-draining soils on hillside gardens, this upright perennial has oblong scalloped leaves, above which rise spikes of small reddish purple flowers from summer to early fall. Easy to grow, it thrives in sun or part shade.

↕24in (60cm) ↔12in (30cm)

Z4–8

SHRUB SMALL

Stephanandra incisa 'Crispa'

CUTLEAF STEPHANANDRA This deciduous shrub will cover a sloping bed with mounds of crinkled foliage that turns yellow and orange in fall. Clusters of tiny greenish white flowers appear in summer. Easy to grow, it tolerates most sites and soils.

↕24in (60cm) ↔10ft (3m)

Z4–7

SHRUB MEDIUM

Symphoricarpos albus

COMMON SNOWBERRY Vigorous and tolerant of most sites, this dense deciduous shrub bears small, round dark green leaves. Pink summer flowers are followed by round white fruits that stay on bare stems through winter. Trim to make a waist-high hedge.

↕↔6ft (2m)

Z3–7 Ⓝ

PERENNIAL SMALL

Trollius pumilus

GLOBEFLOWER This perennial can be seen growing wild on the foothills of the Himalayas. It brightens up late-spring beds with its yellow buttercup-like flowers that form above the glossy green leaves. Happy in sun or partial shade in moist soil.

↕12in (cm) ↔8in (20cm) or more

  Z4–8

SHRUB LARGE

Tsuga canadensis 'Pendula'

CANADIAN HEMLOCK A slow-growing evergreen conifer with a fountain of pendent stems of needlelike blue-green leaves, white beneath, and small brown cones. Ideal for weeping over a bank or growing on a gentle, sheltered slope.

↕↔15ft (5m)

 Z3–7

OTHER SUGGESTIONS

Perennials and bulbs

Amorpha canescens Ⓝ • *Andropogon gerardii* Ⓝ • *Anemone nemorosa* • *Chionodoxa forbesii* • *Festuca glauca* • *Galanthus nivalis* • *Panicum virgatum* 'Cloud Nine' Ⓝ • *Symphyotrichum oblongifolium* 'October Skies' Ⓝ

Shrubs, trees, and climbers

Acer rubrum Ⓝ • *Aronia melanocarpa* 'Autumn Magic' Ⓝ • *Betula nigra* HERITAGE Ⓝ • *Calluna vulgaris* 'Kerstin' • *Cotoneaster dammeri* • *Cornus amomum* Ⓝ • *Diervilla sessilifolia* COOL SPLASH Ⓝ • *Genista lydia* • *Hypericum prolificum* Ⓝ • *Juniperus chinensis* • *Juniperus virginiana* 'Grey Owl' Ⓝ • *Parthenocissus quinquefolia* Ⓝ • *Physocarpus opulifolius* SUMMER WINE Ⓝ • *Rhus aromatic* 'Gro-low' Ⓝ • *Rhus typhina* 'Laciniata' Ⓝ • *Ribes odoratum* Ⓝ • *Spiraea japonica* 'Anthony Waterer' • *Symphoricarpos orbiculatus* Ⓝ • *Taxus baccata* 'Repandens'

Plants for weed-suppressing ground cover

Spreading plants that cover the soil with mats of weed-proof stems and leaves can convert a labor-intensive garden into an easy-care, relaxing space.

Although these plants are tough, most have specific site requirements so check that your garden conditions suit your choices. Choose stonecrops and heathers for sunny areas and lady's mantle, gingers, and ferns for gloomy spots. As well as spreading leafy stems, many ground-cover plants also have beautiful flowers—a succession of wall rock cress and bunchberry followed by hardy geraniums and roses will provide months of colorful blooms. However, these vigorous plants may spread beyond their boundaries if not kept in check, so trim occasionally to prevent them from swamping more delicate specimens.

PERENNIAL SMALL

Ajuga reptans

BUGLEWEED This spreading evergreen perennial forms close-knit rosettes of glossy dark green leaves. Small blue flower spikes appear in late spring and early summer. 'Atropurpurea' (above) has bronze-tinted leaves. Considered invasive in some areas.

↕6in (15cm) ↔3ft (1m)

Z3–9

PERENNIAL SMALL

Alchemilla mollis

LADY'S MANTLE This perennial forms a mound of rounded pale green leaves that suppress surrounding annual weeds. In summer, it produces lax branching sprays of small lime-green blooms. Best planted in shade, it is ideal for the front of a bed.

↕↔20in (50cm)

Z4–7

PERENNIAL MEDIUM

Amsonia tabernaemontana

WILLOW BLUE-STAR This upright perennial forms a dense mound of weed-suppressing growth. It has blue star-shaped spring flowers and bold fall foliage. Plant it in groups or alongside other ground-cover plants for the best effect.

↕3ft (1m) ↔12in (30cm)

Z3–9 (N)

PERENNIAL LARGE

Anemone x *hybrida*

JAPANESE ANEMONE With its branching stems and white and pink flat-faced flowers that last into fall, this large perennial is ideal for late summer color. It has a spreading habit and forms a low canopy of foliage in summer.

↕5ft (1.5m) ↔indefinite

Z4–8

PERENNIAL SMALL

Arabis alpina subsp. *caucasica*

WALL ROCK CRESS This mat-forming evergreen perennial has hairy gray-green leaves and small white flowers from early spring to early summer. Plant it in groups at the front of a bed or in a rock garden.

↕↔6in (15cm)

Z4–7

PERENNIAL SMALL

Armeria maritima

THRIFT A clump-forming evergreen perennial with grassy mounds of slender green leaves. In summer, it bears rounded heads of small, white or pink papery blooms. Plant it at the front of a free-draining bed and allow it to naturalize.

↕4in (10cm) ↔6in (15cm)

Z4–8 (N)

PERENNIAL SMALL

Asarum canadense

WILD GINGER This ground-cover perennial produces rounded kidney-shaped ornamental leaves that form a green carpet. Small cup-shaped purple-brown flowers appear in summer, but are hidden. Plants are tolerant of deep shade.

↕6in (15cm) ↔12in (30cm)

Z3–7 (N)

PERENNIAL MEDIUM

Astrantia major

MASTERWORT An upright clump-forming perennial with divided green leaves and, from midsummer to early fall, sprays of small greenish white, pink, or red flowers. 'Sunningdale Variegated' (above) has cream-accented leaves.

↕3ft (1m) ↔18in (45cm)

Z4–7

SHRUB SMALL

Calluna vulgaris

SCOTCH HEATHER Grown for its pink, red, or white flowers that appear from midsummer to fall, this low-growing evergreen shrub has a spreading habit and makes excellent all-year ground cover. There are many varieties to grow, and all need acidic soil.

↕24in (60cm) ↔30in (75cm)

 Z4–6

PERENNIAL SMALL

Ceratostigma plumbaginoides

PLUMBAGO A bushy mound-forming perennial with oval green leaves, which develop bold fall color. From late summer to fall, it becomes speckled with small vivid blue flowers. Plant it at the front of a bed where it can spread.

↕18in (45cm) ↔8in (20cm)

Z5–9

PERENNIAL SMALL

Cornus canadensis

BUNCHBERRY This low-growing carpet-forming perennial bears white single flowers in late spring. The blooms appear in the center of the rounded clusters of green leaves. It is slow-growing but ideal for shady and woodland gardens.

↕6in (15cm) ↔12in (30cm) or more

Z2–7

SHRUB SMALL

Daboecia cantabrica

IRISH HEATH This spreading evergreen shrub has small dark green leaves, and flowers from early summer to fall, bearing urn-shaped, white, purple, or mauve single or double flowers. 'Bicolor' (above) has mixed flower colors on same raceme.

↕18in (45cm) ↔24in (60cm)

Z6–8

PERENNIAL LARGE

Dryopteris filix-mas

MALE FERN A deciduous or semievergreen fern with large midgreen fronds that arch outwards from a central crown, shading the surrounding soil and suppressing weeds. Ideal for shady and woodland gardens, plant it in groups or leave it to naturalize.

↕4ft (1.2m) ↔3ft (1m)

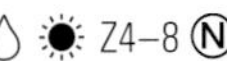 Z4–8

PERENNIAL SMALL

Epimedium grandiflorum

BISHOP'S HAT This clump-forming perennial forms a low canopy of heart-shaped, tough green leaves. In spring, pink, white, yellow, or purple nodding flowers appear. Cut back tired foliage. The popular 'Lilafee' (above) is sometimes sold as 'Lilac Fairy'.

↕10in (25cm) ↔12in (30cm)

Z5–8

PERENNIAL SMALL

Euphorbia polychroma

CUSHION SPURGE This perennial forms mounds of small green leaves on upright stems. In spring, it bears small yellow flowers surrounded by lime-yellow bracts. Ideal for the front of a bed, it is best planted in groups to cover the ground effectively.

↕↔20in (50cm)

Z5–8

SHRUB SMALL

Gaultheria procumbens

WINTERGREEN This evergreen shrub forms a dense mat of oval glossy green leaves. Small pink and white summer blooms lead to attractive scarlet fall berries. Ideal for planting beneath large shrubs. Needs moist soil and does best in cooler areas.

↕6in (15cm) ↔ indefinite

 Z3–8

PERENNIAL SMALL

Geranium 'Johnson's Blue'

CRANESBILL A clump-forming perennial with deeply lobed green leaves and saucer-shaped lavender-blue summer flowers. Plant in groups at the front of a bed and let it create a mat of colorful blooms. Cut back tired foliage in summer.

↕12in (30cm) ↔24in (60cm)

Z4–8

PERENNIAL SMALL

Geranium macrorrhizum

BIGROOT GERANIUM This resilient perennial forms a carpet of deeply lobed aromatic leaves. Small magenta blooms appear in early summer. Ideal for the front of a bed or beneath large shrubs. Best in partial shade in areas with hot summers.

↕15in (38cm) ↔24in (60cm)

Z4–8

PERENNIAL SMALL

Geranium x *oxonianum*

CRANESBILL This vigorous spreading evergreen perennial covers large areas with its divided, toothed green leaves and rounded pink flowers which appear from late spring to midsummer. 'Wargrave Pink' (above) is a popular variety.

↕18in (45cm) ↔24in (60cm)

PERENNIAL MEDIUM

Hosta sieboldiana

PLANTAIN LILY This perennial forms spreading clumps that shade the soil and suppress the surrounding weeds. It has large gray-blue leaves and flowers briefly in early summer, bearing spikes of pale lilac-gray bell-shaped blooms. Protect from slugs.

↕3ft (1m) ↔4ft (1.2m)

SHRUB SMALL

Hypericum calycinum

AARON'S BEARD This dwarf vigorous evergreen shrub forms a dense carpet of dark green leaves on arching stems and, from midsummer to mid-fall, bright yellow flowers. Ideal for sun or shade, use it to cover large areas.

↕24in (60cm) ↔indefinite

Z5–9

SHRUB SMALL

Juniperus horizontalis

CREEPING JUNIPER Providing year-round ground cover, this creeping evergreen conifer has scaly blue-green foliage that can suppress even perennial weeds. Ideal for covering large areas of ground. 'Bar Harbor' has purple-tinted winter foliage.

↕20in (50cm) ↔indefinite

Z3–9 (N)

PERENNIAL SMALL

Persicaria affinis 'Superba'

KNOTWEED This vigorous perennial forms a dense mat of oval green leaves and, from early- to late summer, upright spikes of soft pink blooms that darken with age. Useful for the front of a bed, it is quick-growing and may need restricting on smaller plots.

↕10in (25cm) ↔24in (60cm)

PERENNIAL SMALL

Lamium maculatum

SPOTTED DEADNETTLE This mat-forming ground-cover perennial has spikes of white flowers from late spring to summer. 'White Nancy' (above) has silver-variegated leaves. Considered invasive in some Northwest and Northeast areas. Grow beneath large shrubs.

↕6in (15cm) ↔3ft (1m)

Z4–8

PERENNIAL SMALL

Nepeta racemosa

CATMINT This spreading perennial forms a clump of lax stems covered with aromatic gray-green leaves and violet-blue flower spikes in summer. Use it at the front of a bed for colorful ground cover. 'Walker's Low' (above) is a popular variety.

↕12in (30cm) ↔18in (45cm)

Z4–8

PERENNIAL SMALL

Phlox subulata

CREEPING PHLOX This trailing evergreen perennial has needlelike green foliage and pink, white, or mauve star-shaped flowers in summer. Ideal for sunny sites where low-growing ground cover is needed. 'Emerald Pink' (above) has soft pink flowers.

↕6in (15cm) ↔20in (50cm)

Z3–9 (N)

SHRUB SMALL

Potentilla fruticosa

CINQUEFOIL A compact shrub with divided green leaves and small yellow, white, red, pink, or orange flowers, depending on the variety, from summer to fall. Plant in groups in part-shade and allow to merge. 'Goldfinger' (above) has yellow flowers.

↕3ft (1m) ↔5ft (1.5m)

Z2–7 (N)

PERENNIAL SMALL

Pulmonaria angustifolia

BLUE LUNGWORT This perennial forms a clump of matte green leaves and clusters of rich blue trumpet-shaped spring blooms. Useful for spring color, plant at the front of bed near other plants for later interest. New foliage appears in summer.

↕9in (23cm) ↔12in (30cm) or more

Z3–7

SHRUB SMALL

Rosa Flower Carpet Series

GROUNDCOVER ROSE This rose forms a spreading mass of disease-resistant, glossy green foliage and semidouble white, yellow, pink, and red flowers. Blooms continuously from spring through fall. The leafy stems are useful for covering large areas.

↕18in (45cm) ↔4ft (1.2m)

Z5–9

SHRUB SMALL

Rosa KENT

GROUNDCOVER ROSE This spreading shrub rose has disease-resistant, glossy midgreen leaves and clusters of flat, white semidouble flowers from summer to fall. Deadhead regularly to encourage new blooms; mulch with organic matter in spring.

↕32in (80cm) ↔3ft (1m)

Z5–9

PERENNIAL SMALL

Saxifraga stolonifera

MOTHER OF THOUSANDS Useful for covering shady corners, this spreading perennial forms rosettes of round, silver-veined dark green hairy leaves on spreading stems. In summer, it bears branching stems of small flaglike white blooms.

↕6in (15cm) or more ↔12in (30cm) or more

Z7–9

PERENNIAL MEDIUM

Tellima grandiflora

FRINGE CUPS Ideal for shady beds and woodland gardens, this semievergreen perennial forms a clump of textured, green heart-shaped leaves and, from late spring to midsummer, spikes of cream bell-shaped flowers. It spreads gradually.

↕↔24in (60cm)

Z4–7 Ⓝ

PERENNIAL SMALL

Sedum kamtschaticum

STONECROP Plant this spreading semievergreen perennial, with its orange-yellow late summer blooms, in groups or use to cover small areas. 'Variegatum' (above) has pink-tinted cream-edged leaves. Established plants are drought tolerant.

↕3in (8cm) ↔8in (20cm)

(!) Z3–8

PERENNIAL SMALL

Stachys byzantina

LAMB'S EARS Ideal for dry sunny areas, this spreading perennial forms a dense carpet of downy gray-green leaves and, in summer, spikes of small pink blooms. An attractive front-of-border plant, it offers contrast to brightly colored plants.

↕15in (38cm) ↔24in (60cm)

Z4–8

OTHER SUGGESTIONS

Perennials

Ajuga reptans 'Burgundy Glow' • *Athyrium* 'Lady in Red' • *Aurinia saxatilis* SUMMIT *Geranium endressii* 'Wargrave Pink' • *Geranium* 'Orion' • *Pachysandra procumbens* Ⓝ • *Packera aurea* Ⓝ • *Persicaria bistorta* 'Superba' • *Polygonatum biflorum* Ⓝ • *Pulmonaria officinalis* • *Salvia lyrata* 'Purple Knockout' Ⓝ • *Sedum spathulifolium* Ⓝ • *Solidago sphacelata* 'Golden Fleece' Ⓝ • *Stachys macrantha* • *Viola labradorica* Ⓝ

Shrubs

Erica vagans 'Mrs D.F. Maxwell' • *Helianthemum nummularium* • *Lithodora diffusa* 'Heavenly Blue' • *Mitchella repens* Ⓝ • *Rosa* HARLOW CARR • *Rubus pentalobus* • *Thymus* Coccineus Group

ANNUAL/BIENNIAL SMALL

Tropaeolum majus

NASTURTIUM Useful for summer-long ground cover, this annual forms a dense canopy of round blue-green leaves and orange or yellow flowers. Sow the seeds in a sunny site; self-seeds readily. Alaska Series (above) has variegated foliage.

↕12in (30cm) ↔18in (45cm)

PERENNIAL SMALL

Veronica gentianoides

GENTIAN SPEEDWELL This perennial forms a ground-hugging mat of tightly-knit glossy evergreen leaves, above which rise slender spires of pale blue early summer flowers. Grow with later-flowering plants for prolonged interest. Remove spent blooms.

↕↔18in (45cm)

Z4–7

PERENNIAL SMALL

Waldsteinia ternata

BARREN STRAWBERRY This semievergreen perennial forms spreading mats of scallop-edged dark green leaves and bright yellow saucer-shaped flowers from late spring to early summer. It offers good ground cover in deep shade; may be aggressive.

↕4in (10cm) ↔12in (30cm)

Z4–8

Plants for allergy sufferers

Gardens filled with pollen-rich plants are great for attracting bees and butterflies, but they can also promote allergy attacks.

If you have an allergy, choose plants with complex flower forms, such as fully double roses or pompom dahlias, whose intricate petals trap pollen inside the blooms. Weeds can produce large quantities of pollen, so remove them promptly before they flower, and do not plant ornamental grasses that, like their wild cousins, are responsible for the majority of allergic reactions. As well as planting low-allergen flowers, consider a boundary hedge, which may help reduce allergy attacks by trapping wind-borne pollen and preventing it from flying into your garden.

PERENNIAL LARGE

Agapanthus Headbourne hybrids

AFRICAN LILY This perennial has strap-shaped foliage and spherical clusters of blue late summer to early fall flowers that produce little pollen. Grow in a sheltered site in free-draining soil; mulch in winter.
↕4ft (1.2m) ↔24in (60cm)
Z6–9

PERENNIAL LARGE

Agave americana

CENTURY PLANT A low-allergen plant, this evergreen perennial has lance-shaped, sharply pointed gray-green leaves. Mature plants bear cream flowers. Grow in a pot; overwinter indoors. 'Variegata' (above) has cream-edged leaves.
↕↔5ft (1.5m)
Z9–11 Ⓝ

PERENNIAL SMALL

Ajuga reptans 'Atropurpurea'

BUGLEWEED A rhizome-forming evergreen perennial with rosettes of glossy bronze-purple leaves and short blue spring flower spikes, with a low pollen content. Spreading freely by runners, it forms good ground cover. Considered invasive in some areas.
↕6in (15cm) ↔3ft (1m)
Z3–9

BULB LARGE

Allium 'Purple Sensation'

FLOWERING ONION This perennial bulb has sturdy stems of spherical purple flower heads in early summer, which produce little pollen. Plant the bulbs in groups in fall between perennials that will disguise the leaves, which fade as the flowers form.
↕32in (80cm)
Z3–8

PERENNIAL MEDIUM

Campanula trachelium

NETTLE-LEAVED BELLFLOWER This tough perennial has nettle-like toothed leaves and tall leafy stems that hold clusters of bell-shaped blue to lilac flowers in summer. 'Bernice' has lilac-blue double flowers that are ideal for allergy sufferers.
↕3ft (1m)
Z4–8

BULB LARGE

Dahlia 'Franz Kafka'

POMPOM DAHLIA This tuber produces mauve-pink blooms that contain little pollen. The flowers appear on long stems above divided green leaves and look good in beds or large containers of gritty soil-based potting mix.
↕32in (80cm)
Z9–11

BAMBOO LARGE

Fargesia murielae

UMBRELLA BAMBOO This large clump-forming evergreen bamboo is perfect for allergy sufferers, since it rarely produces flowers. Use the arching yellow-green canes and lance-shaped, bright green leaves to create a screen or focal point.
↕12ft (4m) ↔indefinite
 Z5–9

PERENNIAL MEDIUM

Geranium psilostemon

ARMENIAN CRANESBILL A clump-forming perennial, ideal for a low-allergen garden. It produces lobed, toothed midgreen leaves that turn red in fall and saucer-shaped magenta flowers from early- to late summer with black centers and veins.
↕↔24in (60cm)
Z4–9

ANNUAL/BIENNIAL MEDIUM

Helianthus annuus

SUNFLOWER A robust annual with heart-shaped leaves and large daisy-like, orange or yellow flowers in summer, followed by edible seedheads. Double-flowered varieties, such as 'Teddy Bear' (above), are good choices for allergy sufferers.
↕up to 3ft (1m) ↔24in (60cm)

PERENNIAL SMALL

Hemerocallis 'Arctic Snow'

DAYLILY The straplike green leaves of this low-allergen deciduous perennial form a foil for the sturdy stems of cream blooms with yellow margins and throats. The flowers appear in succession from summer to early fall, each lasting a day.

↕22in (55cm) ↔20in (50cm)

Z3–9

PERENNIAL SMALL

Hosta 'Halcyon'

PLANTAIN LILY This compact leafy perennial provides both color and texture in low-allergen shady gardens. The long heart-shaped blue-gray leaves have a ribbed texture, and are joined briefly by tall stems of lavender-gray flowers in summer.

↕16in (40cm) ↔28in (70cm)

Z3–8

PERENNIAL LARGE

Iris sibirica

SIBERIAN IRIS Use this moisture-loving clump-forming perennial in a low-allergen garden, where it will decorate borders with its broad grasslike leaves and blue, purple, or white blooms which open from tapered buds from early- to midsummer.

↕3ft (1m) ↔24in (60cm)

   Z3–8

PERENNIAL SMALL

Petunia PHANTOM

PETUNIA Plant this eye-catching annual in windowboxes and baskets of potting mix to decorate a low-allergen patio garden. It produces a mound of trumpet-shaped, almost black flowers, with a golden central star, and oval midgreen leaves.

↕↔12in (30cm)

Z11

BAMBOO LARGE

Phyllostachys viridiglaucescens

GREENWAX GOLDEN BAMBOO A clump-forming evergreen bamboo that rarely blooms. It has bright green leaves and greenish brown canes that mature to yellow-green. Cut dead and weak canes in spring.

↕25ft (8m) ↔indefinite

Z7–11

PERENNIAL MEDIUM

Polemonium caeruleum

JACOB'S LADDER An upright clump-forming perennial with finely cut ferny foliage. Small lavender-blue flowers with orange-yellow stamens, which have a low pollen content, appear in early summer. It self-seeds freely.

↕↔24in (60cm)

Z4–8

CLIMBER MEDIUM

Rosa 'Aloha'

CLIMBING HYBRID TEA ROSE This rose has fragrant rose- and salmon-pink fully double flowers, which have little pollen, in summer and again in fall. The dark green foliage is disease resistant. Train the stems over an arch or on a wall.

↕8ft (2.5m)

 Z5–9

PERENNIAL LARGE

Veronica spicata

SPIKE SPEEDWELL This perennial bears spikes of star-shaped, blue, pink, white, or purple summer flowers that produce very little pollen, and appear above slim lance-shaped green foliage. 'Romily Purple' (above) is bushy with dark violet flowers.

↕4ft (1.2m) ↔24in (60cm)

Z3–8

PERENNIAL SMALL

Viola cornuta

HORNED VIOLET A dainty low-allergen evergreen perennial with toothed oval leaves and flat-faced, purplish blue, at times white, flowers from spring to late summer. Ideal for ground cover and for containers filled with soil-based potting mix.

↕8in (20cm) ↔8in (20cm) or more

Z6–9

OTHER SUGGESTIONS

Annuals

Nigella damascena

Perennials

Astilbe 'Fanal' • *Begonia semperflorens-cultorum* • *Cerastium tomentosum* • *Dryopteris filix-mas* Ⓝ • *Geranium himalayense* • *Geranium macrorrhizum* • *Hosta* 'Honeybells' • *Iris unguicularis* • *Pelargonium peltatum* • *Polemonium reptans* 'Stairway to Heaven' Ⓝ • *Sidalcea malviflora* Ⓝ

Bulbs

Dahlia 'Harvest Moonlight' • *Narcissus* species

Shrubs and climbers

Camellia japonica • *Clematis alpina* • *Clematis montana* • *Fuchsia magellanica* • *Juniperus conferta* 'Blue Pacific' • *Rhododendron decorum* • *Rosa* 'Compassion' • *Weigela florida*

Pest-proof plants: slugs

Slug-resistant plants include many beautiful species; there are ranges to suit a variety of different sites and soils.

Slugs attack a wide range of plants and cause severe damage to them as they nibble at the tender, succulent leaves and stems. They are, however, less keen on woody plants and aromatic foliage. While some plants, including cosmos and delphiniums, are never attacked by slugs, others are only consumed when young and tender, but become relatively slug-resistant once mature. To protect them during this vulnerable stage, use small quantities of slug pellets, encircle plants with copper collars—which give slugs a mild electric shock—or surround the stems with sand and grit.

PERENNIAL LARGE

Aconitum carmichaelii

MONKSHOOD Suitable for the back of a bed, this upright perennial has deeply divided green leaves and tall spikes of hooded lavender-blue flowers in fall. It requires support. 'Arendsii' (above) has rich blue flowers.

↕5ft (1.5m) ↔12in (30cm)

Z3–8

PERENNIAL SMALL

Alchemilla mollis

LADY'S MANTLE This clump-forming perennial has rounded, pale green leaves with crinkled edges and, in summer, sprays of small lime-green blooms. Best planted in shade, it is ideal for the front of a bed. Trim untidy leaves in summer.

↕↔20in (50cm)

Z4–7

BULB MEDIUM

Allium cristophii

STARS OF PERSIA This perennial bulb has gray-green leaves that wither in early summer, when its large, rounded heads of star-shaped violet flowers form. These dry in the garden, giving slug-proof interest into late summer. Ideal for beds and pots.

↕16in (40cm)

Z5–8

PERENNIAL MEDIUM

Aquilegia vulgaris var. *stellata*

COLUMBINE An upright perennial with tough divided leaves and tall stems of pompomlike double blooms from late spring to early summer. Deadhead often to prevent self-seeding. 'Nora Barlow' (above) has green-tipped pink blooms.

↕30in (75cm) ↔20in (50cm)

Z3–8

PERENNIAL MEDIUM

Astilbe 'Venus'

ASTILBE This perennial has coarse heavily divided leaves, unpalatable to slugs and, in midsummer, upright feathery plumes of tiny pale pink flowers, which dry and provide interest into winter. Prefers moist soil when planted in full sun.

↕↔3ft (1m)

Z3–8

PERENNIAL MEDIUM

Astrantia major

MASTERWORT A clump-forming perennial with divided midgreen leaves. It produces sprays of small greenish white, pink, or red flowers from midsummer to early fall. Deadhead regularly to prolong the display. It is best on moist but free-draining soil.

↕24in (60cm) ↔18in (45cm)

Z4–7

PERENNIAL SMALL

Bergenia purpurascens

PURPLE BERGENIA Perfect for the front of a bed, this evergreen perennial has large, fleshy rounded leaves that spread to form a clump and flush purple in cold weather. It bears dark pink spring-flower clusters. Cut damaged leaves in summer and fall.

↕16in (40cm) ↔24in (60cm) or more

Z3–8

PERENNIAL SMALL

Corydalis lutea

YELLOW CORYDALIS A mound-forming, evergreen perennial with delicate gray-green ferny leaves and, from late spring to summer, heads of small tubular yellow blooms. Suitable for shady and wild gardens but self-seeds freely.

↕↔12in (30cm)

Z5–7

PERENNIAL MEDIUM

Crocosmia x *crocosmiiflora*

MONTBRETIA This upright perennial forms clumps of arching, swordlike green leaves and, from summer to fall, flared, trumpet-shaped yellow, orange, and red flowers. Varieties include 'Star of the East' (above). Considered invasive in some coastal areas.

↕28in (70cm) ↔3in (8cm)

Z6–9

PERENNIAL SMALL

Dianthus 'Dad's Favourite'

GARDEN PINK Forming a low mound of resilient, gray-green grasslike leaves, this evergreen perennial also bears scented, white semidouble blooms with maroon markings all summer. All forms make good edging for a sunny bed.

↕up to 18in (45cm) ↔12in (30cm)

Z4–9

PERENNIAL LARGE

Echinops ritro

SMALL GLOBE THISTLE An upright perennial with coarse, prickly, divided, green leaves and spiky, metallic blue globe-shaped flower heads in late summer. Plant it at the back of a bed. Dried flower heads are short-lived, but may last into winter.

↕4ft (1.2m) ↔30in (75cm)

Z3–9

PERENNIAL SMALL

Epimedium perralderianum

BARRENWORT Ideal for ground cover in shady beds and woodland gardens, this semievergreen perennial has green heart-shaped foliage on branching stems. Prune in spring before new leaves and spikes of bright yellow pendent blooms appear.

↕12in (30cm) ↔18in (45cm)

Z5–8

ANNUAL/BIENNIAL SMALL

Eschscholzia californica

CALIFORNIA POPPY This quick-growing annual has finely cut gray-green leaves and large yellow, orange, and pink cup-shaped flowers that form all summer. Sow seeds directly in a sunny bed. Deadhead regularly. Can be weedy.

↕12in (30cm) ↔6in (15cm)

PERENNIAL MEDIUM

Euphorbia griffithii

GRIFFITH'S SPURGE A bushy perennial with copper-flushed green leaves and domed orange-red early summer-flower clusters. Suitable for sun or light shade, it spreads to form a large clump, and is best suited to larger gardens. The sap is a skin irritant.

↕30in (75cm) ↔20in (50cm)

Z4–9

PERENNIAL SMALL

Euphorbia myrsinites

MYRTLE SPURGE An evergreen perennial with creeping, woody stems and small, pointed, fleshy gray leaves and clusters of bright yellow-green flowers in spring. Let it spread along the front of a border in full sun. Remove spent flowers with gloves.

↕3in (8cm) ↔8in (20cm)

Z5–9

SHRUB SMALL

Fuchsia 'Swingtime'

FUCHSIA This shrub has dark green leaves and is grown for its pendent, frilly red and white flowers that are borne all summer. Tolerant of partial shade, it is suitable for beds and large containers. Bring plants indoor in winter in cold regions.

↕↔3ft (1m)

Z9–11

BULB MEDIUM

Galanthus nivalis

SNOWDROP This clump-forming perennial bulb has grassy gray-green leaves and nodding single late winter white flowers with green-tipped inner petals. It emerges before most slugs are active, so escapes damage. Plant in groups and let it naturalize.

↕6in (15cm)

Z3–8

PERENNIAL SMALL

Galium odoratum

SWEET WOODRUFF This perennial has rounded clusters of lance-shaped green leaves, which form a spreading carpet, and a mass of tiny white star-shaped blooms from late spring to midsummer. Ideal for naturalistic and woodland gardens.

↕6in (15cm) ↔12in (30cm) or more

Z4–8

PERENNIAL SMALL

Geranium macrorrhizum

BIGROOT GERANIUM Forming a spreading carpet, this perennial has aromatic deeply lobed leaves and abundant small magenta early summer blooms. Plant in partial shade in front of a bed or beneath large tree in areas with hot summers.

↕15in (38cm) ↔24in (60cm)

Z4–8

PERENNIAL MEDIUM

Geranium phaeum

MOURNING WIDOW An upright clump-forming perennial with lobed green leaves and nodding maroon or white flowers carried on lax stems from late spring to early summer. Plant it beneath shrubs or hedges, where it will slowly spread.
↕30in (75cm) ↔18in (45cm)

Z4–8

PERENNIAL SMALL

Helleborus x *hybridus*

LENTEN ROSE Ideal for early-season color, these clump-forming evergreen perennials have divided foliage and nodding purple, white, or pink cup-shaped flowers in winter or early spring. There are many varieties to grow. Deadhead to prevent self-seeding.
↕↔24in (60cm)

Z4–9

PERENNIAL SMALL

Hemerocallis 'Stella de Oro'

DAYLILY This perennial has narrow, upright, arching, glossy green foliage and, from mid- to late summer, large, yellow, trumpet blooms, each lasting a day. There are many varieties to grow, flowering in a wide range of colors.
↕12in (30cm) ↔18in (45cm)

Z3–10

SHRUB MEDIUM

Hydrangea macrophylla

BIGLEAF HYDRANGEA A medium-sized bushy shrub with broad green leaves. Varieties within the species may bear pink, white, purple, or blue flowers depending on soil pH. 'Lanarth White' (above) features pure white sterile flowers.
↕↔5ft (1.5m)

  Z6–9

SHRUB LARGE

Hydrangea paniculata

PANICLE HYDRANGEA An upright deciduous shrub with oval, deeply veined, pointed green leaves and frilly cones of pink or white late-summer flowers. Plant at the back of a bed. Considered invasive in some Northeast areas.
↕↔10ft (3m)

Z3–8

PERENNIAL MEDIUM

Knautia macedonica

KNAUTIA This perennial, grown for its crimson, pincushionlike blooms held on upright, wiry stems above deeply dissected foliage, suits naturalistic planting schemes. 'Melton Pastels' (above) has a mix of pink and dark red flowers.
↕30in (75cm) ↔24in (60cm)

Z5–9

SHRUB SMALL

Lavandula angustifolia

ENGLISH LAVENDER This subshrub is grown for its silver-green foliage and heads of small tubular summer blooms. Plant in full sun in free-draining soil. Also suitable for containers, it has a long season of interest. Slugs find the aromatic growth unpalatable.
↕32in (80cm) ↔24in (60cm)

Z5–8

BULB LARGE

Lilium henryi

TRUMPET LILY This upright perennial bulb has tall arching stems clothed with green pointed leaves and topped with bright orange turks-cap flowers with spotted faces. It is a good choice for a shady bed and can be left to slowly spread.
↕3ft (1m)

pH Z5–8

PERENNIAL MEDIUM

Papaver orientale

ORIENTAL POPPY This upright perennial has divided midgreen leaves and large pink, white, mauve, or red saucer-shaped blooms in summer. Its flowering season is short, but can be spectacular. 'Karine' (above) has salmon-pink flowers.
↕↔ up to 3ft (1m)

Z3–8

PERENNIAL SMALL

Pelargonium Multibloom Series

ZONAL GERANIUM Often used in annual bedding displays, this perennial has rounded green leaves with red markings and white, pink, or red flowers all summer. Water, feed, and deadhead regularly.
↕12in (30cm) ↔12in (30cm)

 Z10–11

PERENNIAL SMALL

Penstemon 'Evelyn'

BEARDTONGUE Suitable for summer borders and containers, this upright perennial has slender pointed foliage and bears spikes of rose-pink trumpet-shaped blooms from summer to early fall. Mulch in fall.

↕↔18in (45cm)

Z7–10

PERENNIAL MEDIUM

Potentilla fruticosa

CINQUEFOIL This deciduous perennial bears simple red, white, yellow, and orange rounded flowers set against small green divided leaves from summer to early fall. It is suitable for well-drained borders. Varieties include 'Red Ace' (above).

↕3ft (1m) ↔5ft (1.5cm)

Z3–7 Ⓝ

PERENNIAL MEDIUM

Rudbeckia hirta

BLACK-EYED SUSAN This short-lived upright perennial, often grown as an annual, has golden or red daisy-like flowers with brown centers from summer to fall. Plant it at the front of a sunny bed or in a summer pot. Varieties include 'Becky Mixed' (above).

↕3ft (1m) ↔18in (45cm)

Z3–7 Ⓝ

PERENNIAL MEDIUM

Polemonium caeruleum

JACOB'S LADDER This clump-forming perennial bears clusters of blue or white bell-shaped flowers in early summer above the divided lance-shaped leaves. Ideal for shady beds in naturalistic and woodland-style gardens.

↕↔24in (60cm)

Z4–8

PERENNIAL SMALL

Pulmonaria officinalis

LUNGWORT A semievergreen perennial with coarse, bristly green leaves, which are disliked by slugs. It bears pink, blue, or white, funnel-shaped spring blooms, depending on the variety. 'Sissinghurst White' (above) has white flowers.

↕12in (30cm) ↔24in (60cm)

Z4–8

PERENNIAL MEDIUM

Santolina chamaecyparissus

LAVENDER COTTON A mound-forming evergreen perennial, which can be grown as an annual, with finely cut, aromatic silvery gray foliage. It bears yellow pompomlike flowers in summer. Trim off the spent flowers to keep it tidy.

↕30in (75cm) ↔3ft (1m)

Z6–9

PERENNIAL LARGE

Polystichum setiferum

SOFT SHIELD FERN This clump-forming deciduous fern is grown for its large arching fronds consisting of tiny leaflets held on lateral stems that emerge from a central crown. Best in full or partial shade, it is ideal for woodland gardens.

↕4ft (1.2m) ↔3ft (1m)

Z6–9

PERENNIAL MEDIUM

Verbascum chaixii

NETTLE-LEAVED MULLEIN This perennial forms a rosette of large coarse green leaves. It is grown for its upright spikes of pale yellow flowers during summer. Grow it in a sunny bed. Varieties include 'Album' (above) with white purple-eyed blooms.

↕3ft (1m) ↔18in (45cm)

Z5–9

CLIMBER LARGE

Rosa banksiae 'Lutea'

YELLOW BANKSIAN ROSE Too vigorous to be affected by slugs, this climber bears masses of small, pale yellow double flowers that clothe the thornless stems during late spring in a single spectacular flush. Suited to large gardens, it needs a sturdy support.

↕30ft (10m)

Z8–9

OTHER SUGGESTIONS

Perennials

Anemone hupehensis 'September Charm' • *Aquilegia vulgaris* var. *stellata* 'Black Barlow' • *Bergenia cordifolia* • *Calamagrostis* x *acutiflora* 'Karl Foerster' • *Delphinium elatum* • *Dianthus* 'Coconut Punch' • *Euphorbia dulcis* 'Chameleon' • *Helleborus foetidus* • *Pelargonium tomentosum* • *Penstemon* 'Garnet' • *Phlox paniculata* Ⓝ • *Phlox subulata* Ⓝ • *Sedum spurium* 'Dragon's Blood'

Bulbs

Allium 'Purple Sensation' • *Galanthus nivalis* 'Flore Pleno' • *Tulipa* species

Shrubs and climbers

Cotinus coggygria • *Forsythia* x *intermedia* • *Juniperus horizontalis* ICEE BLUE Ⓝ • *Lavandula stoechas* • *Leycesteria formosa* • *Santolina rosmarinifolia*

Pest-proof plants: rabbits and deer

Deer and rabbits have an appetite for garden plants, crops, and trees and can be a menace in gardens in the countryside or close to parks and open spaces.

Both rabbits and deer tend to nibble on anything that we find tasty or ornamental. One way to keep them at bay is to install barriers. To keep out rabbits, you will need a chicken wire fence that is at least 3ft (1m) high and buried 3in (7cm) in the ground to prevent them from digging under it. Wire mesh fences 8ft (2.5m) tall are required to keep deer out, or plant a tall hedge around your garden using a pest-proof plant, such as boxleaf honeysuckle or forsythia. If it is not feasible to erect fences, opt for plants, such as Griffith's spurge and others described here, which these pests find unpalatable.

PERENNIAL LARGE

Achillea filipendulina

YARROW This perennial forms a clump of finely cut, aromatic gray-green leaves and large, flat-topped, bright yellow flower heads on sturdy stems in summer. The flowers can be cut and dried. 'Gold Plate' (above) is a tall variety.

↕4ft (1.2m) ↔24in (60cm)

Z3–8

PERENNIAL LARGE

Aconitum napellus

MONKSHOOD This upright perennial has deeply divided dark green foliage and tall spires of indigo-blue blooms from mid- to late summer. Best planted in a shady site; it needs additional support. All parts are toxic if ingested; handle it with gloves.

↕5ft (1.5m) ↔12in (30cm)

(!) Z3–8

SHRUB LARGE

Aesculus parviflora

BOTTLEBRUSH BUCKEYE Best suited to large gardens, this deciduous shrub has palm-shaped leaves and bears spires of fluffy white flowers from mid- to late summer. It has a suckering habit and spreads to form a large clump of stems.

↕10ft (3m) ↔15ft (5m)

(!) Z4–8 (N)

PERENNIAL MEDIUM

Artemisia ludoviciana 'Silver Queen'

WESTERN MUGWORT This clump-forming perennial is grown for its slender, aromatic silvery gray leaves on upright stems, and small yellow flowers in summer that are best removed. Can spread aggressively.

↕↔30in (75cm)

Z4–9 (N)

PERENNIAL MEDIUM

Asplenium scolopendrium

HART'S-TONGUE FERN This clump-forming evergreen fern has long, tapering, tough, glossy green fronds, which are replenished in late spring. Plant beneath trees and taller shrubs, or as ground cover in shady beds. Remove damaged leaves in spring.

↕30in (75cm) ↔18in (45cm)

Z5–9 (N)

SHRUB LARGE

Cotinus coggygria

SMOKE TREE Grown for its colorful leaves, this shrub develops fiery fall tints and plumes of smokelike summer flowers. 'Royal Purple' (above) has rich purple leaves and flower plumes. Plant it near a bed as a deer-deterrent screen.

↕↔15ft (5m)

Z5–8

PERENNIAL MEDIUM

Euphorbia griffithii

GRIFFITH'S SPURGE A bushy perennial with red stems of narrow, copper-tinged dark green leaves topped with clusters of orange-red flowers in early summer. Suited to larger beds, it spreads fast. Animals find the toxic milky sap unpalatable.

↕30in (75cm) ↔20in (50cm)

(!) Z4–9

SHRUB SMALL

Fuchsia 'Tom Thumb'

FUCHSIA Suitable for beds and containers, this dwarf variety has oval dark green leaves, and flowers from summer to fall, bearing red and mauve bell-shaped blooms. If attacked by deer or rabbits in spring or summer, the plant recovers soon.

↕↔20in (50cm)

Z9–11

PERENNIAL SMALL

Geranium sanguineum

BLOODY CRANESBILL This spreading perennial forms a neat mound of deeply dissected dark green leaves and bears magenta-pink single flowers in summer. Tolerant of sun or shade, it can be planted in many positions in the garden.

↕10in (25cm) ↔12in (30cm) or more

Z4–8

PERENNIAL SMALL

Helleborus x *hybridus*

LENTEN ROSE With dense divided foliage, this clump-forming evergreen perennial bears nodding, cup-shaped white, pink, or purple flowers from winter to early spring. Plants hybridize readily and are highly variable. Self-seeds if not deadheaded.

↕↔24in (60cm)

(!) Z4–9

SHRUB SMALL

Hypericum 'Hidcote'

ST. JOHN'S WORT This evergreen or semievergreen shrub forms a dense bush of narrow dark green leaves and has masses of large golden-yellow flowers from midsummer to early fall. Use it as a low barrier to deter deer and rabbits.

↕4ft (1.2m) ↔5ft (1.5m)

 Z6–9

PERENNIAL SMALL

Lamium maculatum

SPOTTED DEADNETTLE A low-growing semievergreen perennial with variegated foliage and hooded late-spring flower spikes. 'White Nancy' (above) has white blooms and silver foliage. Considered invasive in some areas of Northeast and Northwest.

↕6in (15cm) ↔3ft (1m)

 Z4–8

TREE LARGE

Liquidambar styraciflua

SWEETGUM This deciduous tree is grown for its lobed, aromatic, glossy green leaves that turn brilliant shades of orange, red, and purple in fall. Plant it near borders as a deer-resistant barrier. Choose compact varieties for small gardens.

↕80ft (25m) ↔40ft (12m)

 Z5–9 Ⓝ

PERENNIAL MEDIUM

Paeonia officinalis

PEONY A resilient bushy perennial, it has divided dark green leaves and tough, pink, red, or white bowl-shaped flowers from early to midsummer. Grow it mid-bed among later flowering plants. 'Rubra Plena' (above) has red double blooms.

↕↔30in (75cm)

Z3–8

PERENNIAL MEDIUM

Rudbeckia fulgida

BLACK-EYED SUSAN This perennial has narrow green leaves, and bears daisy-like golden flowers with brown centers from late summer to fall. The flowers fade but the centers remain, offering winter interest. Plant it mid-bed and stake the stems.

↕3ft (1m) ↔18in (45cm)

 Z4–9 Ⓝ

PERENNIAL MEDIUM

Physalis alkekengi

CHINESE LANTERN A spreading perennial that gives good fall color, it has upright stems and blooms in midsummer, producing cream flowers that lead to decorative orange "lanterns" containing a berrylike fruit. Best in a larger bed; provide support.

↕30in (75cm) ↔3ft (1m)

Z3–9

PERENNIAL MEDIUM

Sedum telephium Atropurpureum Group

STONECROP This perennial is grown for its fleshy purple stems and leaves, and domed heads of pink-white flowers, which appear from late summer to fall, then dry and persist into winter. Provide support.

↕24in (60cm) ↔12in (30cm)

Z4–9

PERENNIAL MEDIUM

Polystichum acrostichoides

CHRISTMAS FERN This evergreen fern has tough, lance-shaped dark green fronds divided into comblike segments. Slow-growing, it forms a clump over time and tolerates most soils. Ideal for woodland gardens, plant it beneath larger shrubs.

↕24in (60cm) ↔18in (45cm)

Z3–9 Ⓝ

PERENNIAL MEDIUM

Trollius x *cultorum*

GLOBEFLOWER An upright clump-forming perennial, ideal for wildlife gardens, with lobed, dark green toothed leaves and bowl-shaped buttercup-like flowers from late spring to early summer. 'Lemon Queen' (above) has pale yellow blooms.

↕24in (60cm) ↔18in (45cm)

Z3–7

SHRUB LARGE

Rhododendron luteum

PONTIC AZALEA This deciduous shrub is grown for its fragrant yellow spring flowers and vivid fall foliage. Ideal for large and woodland-style gardens, it recovers quickly if attacked by deer. It prefers a cool site with fertile acidic soil.

↕↔12ft (4m)

Z7–9

OTHER SUGGESTIONS

Annuals and biennials

Digitalis purpurea • *Tagetes patula* Ⓝ • *Zinnia elegans* Ⓝ

Perennials

Acanthus mollis • *Agapanthus* 'Blue Giant' • *Amsonia hubrechtii* Ⓝ • *Aquilegia vulgaris* • *Echinops ritro* • *Geranium maculatum* 'Espresso' Ⓝ • *Kniphofia uvaria* • *Lobelia cardinalis* Ⓝ • *Lysimachia clethroides* • *Perovskia atriplicifolia* 'Little Spire' • *Pulmonaria saccharata* • *Symphyotrichum ericoides* Ⓝ • *Symphyotrichum novi-belgii* Ⓝ • *Viola odorata*

Bulbs

Allium schoenoprasum • *Chionodoxa luciliae* • *Narcissus* 'Mount Hood'

Shrubs

Ceanothus species Ⓝ • *Fatsia japonica* • *Hydrangea* species • *Ruscus aculeatus* • *Picea pungens* 'Fat Albert' Ⓝ

Index

A

B

C

D

E

F

G

H

Q

R

S

T

Acknowledgments

Picture credits

The publisher would like to thank the following for their kind permission to reproduce their photographs:
(Key: a-above; b-below/bottom; c-center; f-far; l-left; r-right; t-top)

Every effort has been made to trace the copyright holders. Dorling Kindersley apologizes for any unintentional omissions and would be pleased, if any such case should arise, to add an appropriate acknowledgment in future editions.

4 Dorling Kindersley: Arnie Maynardrhs/Designer: RHS Chelsea Flower Show 2012 (br). **5 Dorling Kindersley:** Arnie Maynardrhs/Designer: RHS Chelsea Flower Show 2012 (bl). **11 Neil Fletcher:** (clb). **14 Dorling Kindersley:** Brian North (bl). **16 Dorling Kindersley:** Glazenwood, Essex (bl). **17 Lucy Claxton:** (tr). **24 Dorling Kindersley:** Thomas Hoblyn/Designer: RHS Chelsea Flower Show 2012 (c). **27 Dorling Kindersley:** Kari Beardsell/Designer: RHS Hampton Court 2008 (b). **33 Dorling Kindersley:** Andy Sturgeon/Designer: RHS Chelsea Flower Show 2012 (t). **44 Dorling Kindersley:** Waterperry Gardens (tr). **52 Dorling Kindersley:** Zia Allaway (bc). **63 Dorling Kindersley:** Claudia de Yong/Designer: RHS Hampton Court Flower Show 2008. **96 Dorling Kindersley:** Ayletts Nurseries, St Albans (br). **100 Alan Buckingham** (c). **Dorling Kindersley:** (tl). **101 Lucy Claxton:** (c). **Alan Buckingham** (c) **Dorling Kindersley:** (bc/Sour cherries). **102 Alan Buckingham** (c). **Dorling Kindersley:** (bl, tl, fcl, cl). **103 Alan Buckingham** (c) **Dorling Kindersley:** (bc). **119 Lucy Claxton:** (bc). **Dorling Kindersley:** Ness Botanic Gardens/Designer: RHS Tatton Park Flower Show 2008 (t). **126 Dorling Kindersley:** Waterperry Gardens (bc). **132 Dorling Kindersley:** Geoff Whiten/Designer: RHS Tatton Park Flower Show 2008 (cra). **133 Dorling Kindersley:** Dan Miller/Designer: RHS Tatton Park Flower Show 2008. **150 Dorling Kindersley:** Waterperry Gardens (tr). **157 Dorling Kindersley:** Noel Duffy/Designer: RHS Hampton Court Flower Show 2008 (crb). **183 Dorling Kindersley:** Waterperry Gardens (c). **188 Getty Images:** Photodisc/S. Solum/PhotoLink (tc/Peppermint). **190 Dorling Kindersley:** Linda Fairman of Oasthouse Nursery/Designer: Hampton Court 2012 (cr). **222 Lucy Claxton:** (bc). **223 Dorling Kindersley:** Jack Dunckley/Designer: RHS Hampton Court Flower Show 2012 (clb); Brian North (tr). **224 Dorling Kindersley:** OneAbode Ltd/Designer: RHS Hampton Court Flower Show 2012 (bl). **225 Dorling Kindersley:** Nillufer Danis/Designer: RHS Hampton Court Flower Show 2012 (l). **227 Dorling Kindersley:** Paul Dyer/Designer: RHS Tatton Park Flower Show 2008 (tl). **228–229 Dorling Kindersley:** Chris Beardshaw/Designer: RHS Chelsea Flower Show 2012 (b). **230 Dorling Kindersley:** Chris Beardshaw/Designer: RHS Chelsea Flower Show 2012 (cr). **231 Dorling Kindersley:** Fire and Iron and Castle Gardens/Designer: RHS Hampton Court Flower Show 2008 (tl). **232 Dorling Kindersley:** Arnie Maynardrhs/Designer: RHS Chelsea Flower Show 2012. **266 Dorling Kindersley:** Waterperry Gardens (c). **305 Justyn Willsmore:** (tc/*Pittosporum tenuifolium*). **310 Dorling Kindersley:** Arnie Maynardrhs/Designer: RHS Chelsea Flower Show 2012. **320 Lucy Claxton:** (bc). **350 Dorling Kindersley:** Waterperry Gardens (tr). **372 Dorling Kindersley:** Waterperry Gardens (bc).

Dorling Kindersley would like to thank the following:

DK photographers Peter Anderson, Brian North

Design assistance Elaine Hewson, Neha Wahi, Pooja Verma

US editors Kathy Fahey and Constance Novice

Editorial assistance Alexander Scammell, Arani Sinha, K Nungshithoibi Singha, Aditi Batra, Dorothy Kikon, Charis Bhagianathan, Manasvi Vohra

Indexing Jane Coulter

Jacket images: Front cover main image: Brian North (c) Dorling Kindersley

Front jacket: (left to right) *Helleborus* x *hybridus*: **Peter Anderson (c) Dorling Kindersley.** *Euphorbia characias* subsp. *wulfenii*: **Roger Smith (c) Dorling Kindersley.** *Dahlia* HS 'First love': **Mark Winwood (c) Dorling Kindersley.** *Geranium* 'Ann Folkard': **Andrew Lawson (c) Dorling Kindersley.**

Spine: *Helenium* 'Crimson Beauty': **Roger Smith (c) Dorling Kindersley.**

Back jacket: (left to right) *Hosta* 'El Capitan': **Mark Winwood (c) Dorling Kindersley.** *Rosa* 'Boscobel' (Auscousin): **Brian North (c) Dorling Kindersley.** Blueberries: **Peter Anderson (c) Dorling Kindersley.** *Hemerocallis* 'Serena Sunburst': **Mark Winwood (c) Dorling Kindersley.** *Deschampsia flexuosa* 'Tatra Gold': **Brian North (c) Dorling Kindersley.**

Seattle
OLYMPIA
Portland
Columbia
SALEM
HELENA
Missouri
BISMARCK
BOISE
PIERRE
SALT LAKE CITY
CARSON CITY
SACRAMENTO
San Francisco
CHEYENNE
DENVER
Las Vegas
Colorado
Los Angeles
SANTA FE
San Diego
PHOENIX
Tucson
Rio Grande
San Antonio
Hawaii
HONOLULU
0 25 50 100
Miles
Kilometers
0 45 90 180
Anchorage
JUNEAU
0 40 80 160
Miles
Kilometers
0 50 100 200
Alaska
0 75 150 300
Miles
Kilometers
0 100 200 400